Contemporary Chinese Civil and Commercial Law

Zhixun Cao

Civil Judgments at First Instance

Comparative Experience and Chinese Solution

Springer

Zhixun Cao
Peking University Law School
Beijing, China

ISSN 2524-6194 ISSN 2524-6208 (electronic)
Contemporary Chinese Civil and Commercial Law
ISBN 978-981-97-8661-9 ISBN 978-981-97-8662-6 (eBook)
https://doi.org/10.1007/978-981-97-8662-6

This Springer imprint is published by the registered company Springer Nature Singapore Pte Ltd.
The registered company address is: 152 Beach Road, #21-01/04 Gateway East, Singapore 189721, Singapore

For
my father CAO Peihua, my mother CHEN Yuling and my wife HUANG Ruowei

Foreword by Masahisa Deguchi

In modern societies, individuals are prohibited from resolving disputes themselves and the state provides the court system and ensures law and order. The Code of Civil Procedure, like all procedural laws, is part of public law. It therefore does not regulate between the equal parties, but between the court and the parties; Friedrich Stein once argued that civil procedure is a "technical law" that is determined by a constantly changing expediency and has no eternal value. Today, however, such a view is no longer appropriate. Procedural law regulates the relationship between the individual and the state. The task of procedural law is to limit the influence of the parties and the courts on the course of the proceedings. This limitation is strongly influenced not only by considerations of expediency but also by the principles of civil procedural law shaped by a particular worldview, which have changed at least since the promulgation of each country's civil procedural law.

Modern Chinese civil procedure law is a legacy of historical civil procedure jurisprudence like Japan which has modeled also on Western legal systems, especially German and Austrian civil procedure law, since the Meiji era. Since the reform and opening-up policy of His Excellency Deng Xiaoping, the technical aspects of civil procedure jurisprudence have been introduced in a very sophisticated form. The author of this book, Prof. Dr. (Hector) Zhixun Cao, Peking University Law School, was supervised by leading civil procedure lawyer Prof. Dr. Dr. h. c. Peter Gottwald, University of Regensburg (former President of the International Association of Procedural Law). The author does not only deal with the technical aspects of German civil procedure jurisprudence, but also with the question of how to idealize civil procedure law in China from the perspective of comparative civil procedure law. Since I met Prof. Dr. Zhixun Cao in Regensburg at the inauguration ceremony of the commemorative publication for the 70th birthday of Prof. Dr. Dr. h. c. Peter Gottwald, we have been working together academically through international comparative civil procedure law conferences in Kyoto and the Comparative Procedural Law and Justice (CPLJ) project of the former Max Planck Institute for Procedural Law in Luxembourg. I very much hope that this book, which was written in English, will be taken up as a topic for discussion on the stage of international comparative civil procedure law in the world.

Kyoto, Japan
August 2024

Prof. Dr. Masahisa Deguchi
Honorary Vice President
of International Association
of Procedural Law (IAPL)
Law Faculty of Ritsumeikan University

Foreword by C. H. van Rhee

This book, by Prof. Zhixun Cao, is an exemplary comparative study in English on central aspects of Chinese civil procedure at the first instance (or "at the trial level", as an American lawyer would have it). A comparative perspective is offered through the Japanese and German civil procedures—a natural choice since the early roots of Chinese civil procedure can be found, at least in part, in these preceding procedural civil law systems. The informed reader will note that later influences are also present, such as elements of the procedural models of the former Soviet Union and, more recently, Anglo-American procedures, in addition to several specific Chinese features. The author carefully introduced these features to an international audience that may not immediately be familiar with them. Herein, for example, we might mention the role of the Supreme People's Court and its guiding opinions on procedural matters concerning the new Chinese Civil Procedure Law and the so-called petitions via letters and visits. In addition, developments outside mainland China, such as those in Hong Kong, Macao and Taiwan, are mentioned and studied, demonstrating that the author is an all-round procedural lawyer with extensive knowledge of developments, including those outside mainland China.

The book discusses topics high on the international procedural agenda yet always within the specific Chinese procedural context. For instance, highly relevant topics are the role of the court and the parties in applying the law, fact-finding, the burden of proof, res judicata and alternative dispute resolution. Another relevant area is online dispute resolution (ODR), in which China is currently a global leader. The author is aware of the advantages of ODR and the problems posed by this new type of dispute resolution and discusses them in depth.

The layout of the chapters indicates that the author is familiar with global procedural developments, which may come as no surprise to those who know that he is a professor at Peking University Law School with its tradition in comparative civil procedure, has spent considerable time studying procedural law overseas (in Regensburg, Germany) and is an important member of the International Association of Procedural Law (albeit the small number of Chinese members). Moreover, his knowledge of foreign languages has certainly enhanced the quality of his comparative studies.

This volume will be welcomed by all those who are active in law reform because it discusses central issues with which all modern procedural systems agree, especially concerning one of the major and largest economic powerhouses of the world. One of these issues concerns the number of cases reaching the courts and the difficulties encountered in handling them. China has been able to deal with this issue satisfactorily given delay in justice administration which is not a problem in mainland China. The maxim "justice delayed is justice denied" seems not to be an issue since cases are handled expeditiously. Meanwhile, one should know that too much expedition may not always be a blessing, and this book offers valuable information regarding the same in the context of China.

I recommend this book to international readers because most information herein is available for the first time and is in English. This volume may be an eye-opener for the non-initiated and the initiated international readers. Professor Zhixun Cao has successfully written a book that is a "must" for comparative lawyers of civil procedure and anyone interested in litigation in civil matters before the Chinese courts—whether in a scholarly or professional context or both.

Maastricht, Netherlands
September 2024

Professor C. H. van Rhee

Preface

This monograph is on first-instance civil judgments in China from a Chinese proceduralist in global context. It is partially based on my previous publications in this area, especially my book on adjudicative techniques published in 2022 by the Law Press in Chinese, while several chapters are incorporated in this book from independent articles. During the editorial process, I try to update the chapters and adjust the content to make it more readable for English speakers. I hope it may contribute a little bit for foreigners to understand the Chinese civil justice and civil judgments.

Judgments, as the final judicial products which affect the legal relationship between both parties or even multiple parties, provide desirable objects to observe and can evaluate the service of judicial proceedings and the protection of parties' procedural rights. And since judgments are in most cases regarded as the default termination of any civil litigation, there is no need to argue for a comparative study on this topic which has already inspired Chinese doctrines and the newest reforms. One of the aims of such research is to modernize Chinese civil justice considering the experience of leading legal counterparts.

Next to the theoretical analysis, this book intends to introduce empirical data in China to the English literature, which could provide a vivid illustration for legal researchers to be better informed about the Chinese legal system and its version of rule of law. In other words, this monograph would like to describe the real judicial practice in China and summarize how Chinese lawyers understand and facilitate the production of civil judgments.

As discussed in numerous places through this contribution, it is believed that the more established legal research with Chinese characteristics should be based on the typical practice and common understanding in Chinese context. The expected research should go further to locate the functional difference between Chinese practice and comparative experience and inquire whether the procedural safeguards for realizing substantive rights in China have reached the extent consistent with the requirements according to principles of civil procedure. On the one hand, the proceduralists have to discover the real situation of the typical foreign legal experience. On the other hand, it is necessary to well prepare for a set of more systematic procedural rules with clearly identified elements and incorporate the discussion on procedural ideology into the interpretation of current legal institutions.

Special thanks are primarily to be presented to Prof. Yulin Fu who invites me to take part in the Contemporary Chinese Civil and Commercial Law Series, while she was also supervising my doctoral dissertation between 2010 and 2014 on the adjudicative methods in first-instance civil judgments. I intend to express my gratitude to Prof. Margaret Woo and Prof. Peter Chan, who are the co-editor-in-chief for the book series and have being guiding me to become a better proceduralist for many years. My academic supervisor in Germany, Prof. Dr. h. c. Peter Gottwald, shared with me his insights into the procedural legal science since we first met in the first week of October 2011. Prof. Dr. Masahisa Deguchi in Japan shows me how to get involved in international cooperation from the perspective of Eastern Asia. Peking University Law School provides me with outstanding workplace, scientific support and the tenureship, which encourage me to complete this project without much hesitation or worry. This monograph should be dedicated to its 120th anniversary, while I joined this law school as one of its undergraduate students admitted in 2004 exactly twenty years ago.

I may not have the confidence to apply for and accomplish this project without the help and assistance of my editing team. Mr. Yunbiao Guan works as the chief assistant for me in arranging the process of editing and proofreading, which means his efforts are invested in all pages of this book. As members of the editorial team, Mr. Yujian Jiang, Mr. Shihao Liu, Mr. Xuanren Qu, Ms. Yang Yang, Ms. Qiongjiao Zeng and Mr. Junhao Zhao help me correct minor errors, the citation style and the form of layout of this contribution. Mr. Shihao Liu and Ms. Ying Xie polish the literature part as well. For the proofreading, Mr. Fengquan Wang, Mr. Brendan Low, Ms. Xuran Zhang and Ms. Katie Zhang, together with Ms. Qihang He, Ms. Yang Yang and Ms. Meng Zhang, help me correct many errors I made either in writing or in translating. With no doubt, I owe my wife, Ms. Ruowei Huang, many thanks for her countless pieces of advice while she is always busy with her practice in law and is diligent in the field of European intellectual property law.

I hope this monograph puts at least one step forward to the expected procedural legal research in the shared future. "Über den Bergen, weit, weit drüben, Sagen die Leute, wohnt das Glück".

Beijing, China
May 2024, revised in Nov 2024

Zhixun Cao

Contents

Abbreviations

Abbreviations of the normative documents cited in this contribution are presented in the end.

ADR	Alternative Dispute Resolution
AI	Artificial Intelligence
BCI & BIMC	Benchmark Chambers International & Benchmark International Mediation Center
BGH	Federal Court of Justice (*Bundesgerichtshof*) of Germany
ChatGPT	Chat Generative Pre-trained Transformer
CIETAC	China International Economic and Trade Arbitration Commission
CPC	Communist Party of China
ECJ/EuGH	European Court of Justice (*Europäischer Gerichtshof*)
EU	European Union
NPC	National People's Congress of the P.R.C.
ODR	Online Dispute Resolution
P.R.C.	People's Republic of China
SAR	Special Administrative Region of the People's Republic of China
SCIA	Shenzhen Court of International Arbitration
SCMC	Shanghai Commercial Mediation Center
SPC	Supreme People's Court of the P.R.C.
U.S.	United States

Chapter 1
General Introduction

Generally speaking, there is no doubt about the undeniable importance and significance of judicial decisions in legal practice and judicial reform. Especially in China, in 1999, 2009 and 2015, the SPC has directly set the reform of judicial decisions as one of its objectives in three individual *Five-Year Outline of the Program for Reform of People's Courts*. In 2018, it released a comprehensive judicial interpretation under the title of the *Opinions Reasoning Judicial Decisions*, which completed its reform task for that period of years. In 2021, the *Opinions on Core Values* was published to restate the importance of making value judgments while handling judicial cases.

In recent years, the SPC has continued to actively develop its platform for publicizing final judicial decisions, which was reiterated in its fifth *Five-Year Outline of the Program for Reform of People's Courts* issued in 2019. As a vision for the future, this latest reform declaration requires "to increase the comprehensive disclosure of judicial decisions, to strictly implement the approval mechanism for cases which are not suitable to be uploaded into the platform and to eliminate the problem of selective uploading of cases". Such requirements suggest the need to further improve the quality of judicial decisions, which should not be rejected to be publicized solely due to insufficient reasoning or wording errors (Article 4 of the *Administrative Measures for the Proclamation of Judicial Decisions of the SPC*).

Among them, the crucial ones for the reform of judicial decisions are the final civil judgments, which directly impact the resolution of disputed cases and the allocation of substantive interests between the parties. The final judgments can be a window for outsiders to discover and evaluate the performance of civil proceedings in China and even the rule of law in civil matters. While sometimes the law-based approach is well recognized in national and even international contexts, these judgments themselves, which are by nature reflective and responsive, qualify for the purpose of this contribution.

Although this contribution aims primarily at the existing problems and difficulties in Chinese academic and practical context, the comparative experience has with no doubt been relied on or referred to by this contribution in countless places. Besides

Z. Cao, *Civil Judgments at First Instance*, Contemporary Chinese Civil and Commercial Law, https://doi.org/10.1007/978-981-97-8662-6_1

introducing the historical and current development of making civil judgments in China, the purpose of this contribution is to enhance the possibility of comparing the Chinese approach with foreign counterparts all over the world.

Moreover, this contribution tries to cover several jurisdictions to enhance the possibility of extracting comparative lessons that China could learn from, while Germany is taken as the primary counterpart to be elaborated. It is partially attributed to the fact that the German practice may supplement the toolbox of adjudicative techniques of Chinese civil procedure, whereas the German counterpart can also act as a solid basis for any further comparative discussion. Beginning from this starting point and along with continuous research, this contribution may be revised and improved via additional comparison with international observation in the future.

After a concise introduction, this contribution contains ten sequent chapters which intend to provide a comprehensive analysis. Chapter 2 shows multiple examples of Chinese civil judgments. To be presented are real judgments both on the merits and on procedural issues, judgments published in the SPC Gazette (最高人民法院公报) and guiding cases which enjoy more binding effects, as well as the significant first-instance judgment of the Pengyu case which stands unedited by any court. Moreover, an extracted specialized judicial interpretation in this field is attached as well to show what the judiciary in China considers as the most appropriate approach to preparing civil judgments.

The structure of civil judgments and functions of different parts of judgments deserve discussion in the overarching Chap. 3. This chapter provides a concise description of expected civil judgments. Based on the current situation and reform attempts of civil judgments in China, and learning from the counterparts of civil law systems, an independent part of alleged facts of the case should be introduced into the structure of civil judgments in China. This part ought to be composed of the original claim for relief of the plaintiff, the facts and reasons alleged by the parties, the cause of action of the case determined by the judge after court hearings, and the special procedural circumstances during proceedings, in order to highlight its function of recording and proving the disputed case. Meanwhile, the current factual part of the judgment, namely the part of "it is ascertained upon trial", and the part of "the court considers that" should be together regarded as the judgment's reasoning. Within such reasoning, there should be the determination of the evaluation of evidence, finding of facts and application of law in the current case. Thus, under the consensus that the factual issues should be reasoned as well, the necessity of combining the factual and legal issues shall be further strengthened. The judge ought to pay attention to the justification of the fact-finding results and the publicity of grounds for establishing the evidential evaluation. Meanwhile, in the part of application of law, in addition to the principles of citing legal norms, the judge shall also respond to the issues that the parties may have doubts about or the disputed legal issues, and it is necessary to improve the judgment's reasoning by enriching the materials which are accessible to the judge.

Chapter 4 concerns the application of law in civil judgments. During the reasoning of civil judgments, the citation of legal norms is of great importance. According to the current law, legal provisions may be completely and specifically cited in the parts of judgment reasoning or of judgment basis within civil judgments, and the scope of citation varies depending on these specific parts. The subsumption technique which is popular in continental Germany is qualified to be used as a reference for citation from a comparative perspective. The citation of legal norms in civil judgments should center on the grounds of substantive rights in the field of civil law, while citations of both substantive law and procedural law norms are affected by such grounds. The extent of completeness of cited norms and their quantity may not follow a unified standard. The concept of application of law is all-inclusive, and the whole normative system of substantive law as well as procedural law can be covered hereby. Due to the focus and the ability of this contribution, this chapter can merely try to embrace issues of methods of law application and the citation of norms therein concisely.

In Chap. 5, it is argued that the documentary evidence plays a crucial role in the civil judicial practice in China. Whether this kind of evidence is authentic needs to be discussed systematically. The special claim for the declaration of the truthfulness of the document is regular in the continental legal system and its existence shows an exception to the general principle of the declaratory claim. However, there is no need to stipulate this specific procedure in China. Instead, the truthfulness of the documentary evidence ought to be a disputed issue in any ordinary civil litigation. Considering the experience in different continental legal systems together with the legal practice in China, as a formal requirement, the Chinese law is supposed to request generally that the opposing party to the evidence provider has to declare first whether the authenticity of this evidence is to be challenged. It is also necessary to take notice of the possible exception in China. As a substantial requirement, instead of the specific proof status of to-be-proved factual allegations, the norm theory should be the standard for the allocation of burden of proof regarding the truthfulness of documents. It is necessary to stress the fact-finding effect of the identification of evidence as well as the other legal regulations and technologies, among which the judicial inspection is the most crucial one. The differences between proving force (*Beweiskraft*) of public and private documents and the distinction between the formal proving force and the substantial one should be taken into consideration seriously. In the system of documentary proving, it is to be confirmed that the formal proving effect of documents indicates the authenticity of documents. Besides, the presumption of formal proving force of public documents could be interpreted under the existing Chinese law.

The focus of Chap. 6 is how to give a civil judgment on the merits when unfortunately the individual judge with the duty to make judicial decisions cannot find the facts of the case. While the continental system admits the *non-liquet* status in fact-finding and emphasizes its process of legal application, the Anglo-American counterpart takes the other way. It is related to the legal methodology, the starting points of civil litigation, the attitude toward pragmatism as well as the jury system. The main academic perspective in China inclines to the conception of objective burden of proof, which however does not systematically appear in the legislative and judicial activities for many years. Actually, the application of burden of persuasion is more prevalent. This separation between theory and practice, which is very common in the process of legal transplantation in other nations and jurisdictions, is the partial result of an overdue legal reality approach, litigation aims giving priority to dispute resolution coupled with procedure institution represented by factual review standard in appellate proceedings.

Then, this contribution moves to two kinds of special effects of judgments in China. It is provided under Chinese law that facts found in the enacted judgment have the predetermined effect, which is the object of Chap. 7. Yet, from the perspective of legislation theory, this predetermined effect shall be rejected. The predetermined effect of facts cannot gain support from the traditional theory of *res judicata* effect. In order to expand *res judicata* effect, the intermediate declaratory claim shall be filed. Although the scope of *res judicata* effect is sometimes suggested to be expanded in comparative law, the predetermined effect is not suitable for China in that there are blurred criteria, lack of predictability and possible waste of litigation resources. The misunderstanding caused by the cases published on the SPC's Gazette shall be clarified. Additionally, the predetermined effect is different from the fact-exclusive force of *res judicata* effect and the rule of probative force of public documents.

In Chap. 8, this contribution tries to develop another effect of final judgments based on Chinese experience. Chinese judges are supposed to follow the mode of examining the validity of civil contracts in any civil process *sua sponte*. Ordinarily, the identification of this validity, which is not located in the operative part of the final judgment, also enjoys the *res judicata* effect of final judgments. In civil law traditions, since there is no need to review every related issue, the identification appearing only in the reasoning part of the judgment has no such effect. The *res judicata* effect of the identification of contract's validity in the reasoning part will be acknowledged by both Chinese law and civil law traditions, if any party explicitly claims for the determination of preliminary legal relationship in the case. The Chinese court should consider the validity of civil contracts as disputed issues of its court hearings. Accordingly, the rule of judicial review of the validity of civil contracts *sua sponte* could be substantially reformed, while it is procedurally necessary to demand the judge to give clear direction to the parties regarding the scope of *res judicata* effect. For the determination of *res judicata* effect of this rule of judicial review, there should be further explanation of the legal requirements for relitigation. The aforementioned understanding of *res judicata* effect is distinct from the theory of issue preclusion since this understanding could provide a much clearer solution for legal application.

It is additionally noticed in Chap. 9 that errors could exist in civil judgments all the time. While there are different kinds and degrees of errors, the formal errors should be first corrected through correction rulings. China should further improve the rules on correction rulings to avoid the abuse in practice. While considering the comparative legal experience, China should pay attention to the difference in correction procedures for obvious errors and errors in the part of alleged facts within final judgments. The obviousness of errors should be the criterion for correction, so as to the convenience of correction and judicial efficiency. Correction rulings should also be applied to errors in the record of the operation of proceedings. Formal errors and their corrections may seem insignificant, but the improvement of adjudicative techniques and the quality of judicial decisions begins with addressing even the least issue.

Chapter 10 looks outward to the surroundings of civil judgments in China. When it comes to the judicial system, court organization, judicial openness and lawsuit-related petitions via letters and visits are evaluated. For litigation mechanisms, judicial mediation and the interaction between the different stages of a civil process, and the ongoing judicial reform in China which is to separate the complicated cases from the simple ones are to be discussed.

The last chapter, Chap. 11, refers to the special situation in recent years which includes Internet-based technological issues. The outbreak of the COVID-19 pandemic shows another contextual element of civil judgments besides the ones covered in the last chapter. In the time of a global pandemic, it is hardly possible to insist on regular judicial activities in most cases. Rather, many jurisdictions have had to adjust to the usage of online dispute resolution, which has also been adopted by the Chinese court system. The development of these dispute resolution mechanisms could have a long-lasting impact even after the termination of the pandemic. In China, all dispute resolution mechanisms have introduced online dispute resolution system into their operations. China is running an ongoing reform experiment, which has a separate part on improving electronic litigation. Among others, the filing of civil lawsuits, submission of evidence and the proceedings of court hearings have special arrangements compared to the ordinary civil justice. Although the Internet justice in China has proved itself to be a very successful system which is still developing rapidly, it definitely encounters some difficulties and challenges as well. There may be specific fields in which online dispute resolution has been proved especially effective at resolving disputes, and, on the other hand, some types of cases that are not suitable for being tried online. The principle of due process requires the Internet-based judiciary to provide a suitable dispute resolution mechanism. The impact of technologies should be taken seriously. It is online dispute resolution which must be fit for circumstances in national context and not the other way around.

Chapter 2
Examples of Chinese Civil Judgments in Practice

2.1 Introduction

To introduce and research civil judgments in China, the most direct materials must be the real judgments given by courts at different levels. Since there are various types of judgments, it is not the objective of this contribution to present an all-inclusive list of all the styles of these judgments. For instance, as in other chapters, merely first-instance judicial decisions are the target of this chapter. Rather, after giving examples of real judgments on both the merits and procedural issues, this chapter intends to show examples of judgments published in the SPC Gazette and even those published as guiding cases which were modified by the SPC in the first place and then enjoy more binding effects in China. The Pengyu case, which was given in 2007 and sparked intense debate with the severely negative social impact, is reported additionally as a special illustration of the fact-finding difficulty in judge's real decisions. Lastly, a specialized judicial interpretation, given by the SPC directly and serving as a kind of legal source de facto, is supplemented to reflect the guiding opinions of the Chinese judiciary.

2.2 Ordinary Civil Decisions at First Instance

2.2.1 Civil Judgments on the Merits

First-instance civil judgments on the merits represent the most ordinary and formal results of civil proceedings. It has been challenged that the quality of civil judgments in China is relatively low. It is true that in civil cases before grass-rooted local courts the judgments may not be very long while the basic structure according to the law will still be respected. It can be correctly argued that a distinction between complicated cases and simple cases during preparing the written judgments should

Z. Cao, *Civil Judgments at First Instance*, Contemporary Chinese Civil and Commercial Law, https://doi.org/10.1007/978-981-97-8662-6_2

be made. In other cases, e.g. in areas of intellectual property law or commercial law, the preparation of judgments is generally better and more preferred to show how the procedural requirements of making judgments are followed in practice.

Hence, this contribution takes one judgment made by Beijing Internet Court, a local district primary court, to show what a well-prepared judgment on the merits could look like. This case, *Tencent Technology (Shenzhen) Co., Ltd. et al. v. Beijing Qingshu Network Technology Co., Ltd.* (腾讯科技(深圳)有限公司等诉北京青曙网络科技有限公司侵害作品信息网络传播权纠纷案), refers to a dispute over infringement of the right to disseminate work's information on the Internet.[1]

Beijing Internet Court

Civil Judgment

(2019) Jing 0491 Min Chu No. 16794

Plaintiff: Tencent Technology (Shenzhen) Co. Ltd., domiciled in 35/F, Tencent Building, Keji Middle 1st Road, SHIP, Nanshan District, Shenzhen, Guangdong.

Legal representative: Ma Huateng, Chairman and General Manager.

Attorney: Yan Chunde, lawyer of Unitalen Law Office Shanghai Branch.

Attorney: Zhou Dandan, lawyer of Unitalen Law Office.

Plaintiff: Shenzhen Tencent Computer Systems Co., Ltd., domiciled in 5–10/F, FIYTA High-tech Building, Gaoxin South 1st Road., SHIP, Nanshan District, Shenzhen, Guangdong.

Legal representative: Ma Huateng, General Manager.

Attorney: Yan Chunde, lawyer of Unitalen Law Office Shanghai Branch.

Attorney: Wang Jiayu, lawyer of Unitalen Law Office.

Defendant: Beijing Qingshu Network Technology Co. Ltd., domiciled in Room A-0812, 2/F, Building No. 3, Courtyard No. 30, Shixing Street, Shijingshan District, Beijing.

Legal representative: Xia Yan, Executive Director.

Attorney: Sun Yueheng, lawyer of Beijing Jinshi Law Office.

Basic Facts

In respect of the dispute over the infringement of the right to communicate works through an information network between the plaintiffs Tencent Technology (Shenzhen) Co. Ltd. (hereinafter referred to as "Tencent Technology") and Shenzhen Tencent Computer Systems Co., Ltd. (hereinafter referred to as "Tencent Computer") and the defendant Beijing Qingshu Network Technology Co. Ltd. (hereinafter

[1] The translation is provided by www.pkulaw.com and modified by the author: https://www.pkulaw.com/en_case/a6bdb3332ec0adc4405c3725ee1055b1ba9282b65e3ace57bdfb.html?way=listView.

referred to as "Qingshu"), after the case was accepted, the court applied ordinary procedures according to law and held the hearing in public. Yan Chunde and Zhou Dandan, the attorneys of the plaintiff Tencent Technology, Yan Chunde and Wang Jiayu, the attorneys of the plaintiff Tencent Computer, and Sun Yueheng, the attorney of the defendant Qingshu, participated in the court session online through the electronic litigation platform of the court. So far, the trial of this case has been concluded.

The two plaintiffs jointly claim as follows: to order the defendant to pay CNY 500,000 for economic losses and reasonable expenses, of which the reasonable expenses include the attorney fee CNY 10,000 and notarization fee CNY 544, a total of CNY 10,544. Facts and grounds: On 29 August 2016, Tencent Technology completed the fine art work "WeChat Emoticons Series 1.0", which includes 6 WeChat emoticons of fine art work involved (hereinafter referred to as "WeChat emoticons involved", see Annex 1), and registered it on 20 July 2018. On 10 January 2011, Tencent Technology authorized Tencent Computer to operate the WeChat app and its upgraded versions and granted Tencent Computer the exclusive right to use the corresponding fine art work. All the WeChat emoticons involved are used in the WeChat app. Since the WeChat app was put on the market, it has quickly accumulated hundreds of millions of users for the plaintiffs and has achieved a very high visibility and influence among the relevant public. Once the WeChat emoticons and other features provided in the WeChat app were launched, they gained widespread response and popularity. The plaintiffs found that the defendant developed and operated the app ChuiNiu and provided download and installation services on its official website (www.meetqs.com) and several mobile app download platforms. The chat emoticons provided in the ChuiNiu app (hereinafter referred to as "alleged infringing emoticons", see Annex 2) are identical with or substantially similar to the plaintiffs' prior WeChat emoticons involved. The defendant's act has infringed the plaintiffs' right to communicate works through an information network with respect to the WeChat emoticons involved.

The defendant's defense: First, the defendant recognizes that the WeChat emoticons involved are original and constitute fine art works. Second, the evidence on the record cannot prove that the plaintiffs hold the copyright of the WeChat emoticons involved. (1) Jin Zhaoping applied for registering the trademark on 21 November 2017, which was earlier than the registration date on Tencent Technology's work registration certificate. So the company cannot be confirmed as the copyright owner of the emoticon "facepalm". (2) The emoticon "smirk" is identical with or substantially similar to the prior emoticon "funny" designed by Baidu. Thus, Tencent Technology cannot be confirmed as the copyright holder of the emoticon "smirk". (3) Some of the WeChat emoticons involved come from the contribution of the WeChat emoticons open platform. Their copyright doesn't belong to the plaintiffs. (4) The prototype of the emoticon "heyha" comes from Lu Zhengyu's photos. So Tencent Technology cannot be confirmed as the copyright owner of the emoticon "heyha". (5) The plaintiffs are able to modify the signature information of the chat emoticons in the WeChat app. Third, even though Tencent Technology has the copyright of the WeChat emoticons involved, it has granted the copyright of the WeChat emoticons involved to Tencent Computer for its exclusive use. Hence, only Tencent Computer can initiate the litigation for right protection. Tencent Technology is not a qualified plaintiff. Fourth, the defendant used the alleged infringing emoticons which are identical with the WeChat emoticons involved in the ChuiNiu app without the permission of the right holder. However, the defendant has stopped the above use. Fifth, the economic losses and reasonable expenses claimed by the plaintiffs are too high and lack legal basis. (1) The plaintiffs did not suffer any losses due to the WeChat emoticons involved, nor did the defendant profit from them. The WeChat emoticons involved are free. So the plaintiffs neither make a profit nor suffer any economic losses. The defendant did not charge the public for the alleged infringing emoticons in the ChuiNiu app. Nor would the relevant public choose to download the ChuiNiu app because of the WeChat emoticons involved, thus bringing proceeds to the defendant. (2) Existing evidence cannot prove that the infringement claimed by the plaintiffs lasts long. The download number of the ChuiNiu app is cumulative and has nothing to do with the number and influence of the app that contains the alleged infringing emoticons downloaded by the relevant public. So the plaintiffs' evidence cannot be used as a reasonable basis for determining the amount of compensation. (3) The plaintiffs' claim for the compensation amount lacks evidential support. In summary, the defendant requests the court to dismiss all the plaintiffs' claims.

Finding of Facts

The parties submitted evidence based on their claims. The court organized evidence exchange and cross-examination among the parties, on which basis the following facts are ascertained.

I. Facts about the Ownership of the WeChat Emoticons Involved

(I) Facts about Tencent Technology's Alleged Claims in Respect of the WeChat Emoticons Involved

On 3 August and 29 August 2016, Tencent Technology successively applied for evidence preservation for the files "New Emoticons 0729.zip" and "Big Yellow Face.zip" to authenticate the two files at the UniTrust Time Stamp Authority (http://www.tsa.cn) and downloaded the corresponding trusted timestamping authentication certificates. The "Big Yellow Face.zip" contains the WeChat emoticons involved, and the "New Emoticons 0729.zip" contains the WeChat emoticons involved except the emoticon "frown". Both trusted timestamping authentication certificates specify that "this is to certify that the file (or electronic data) has already existed since the time of timestamping application, and the content remains intact without any alteration", and show their respective digital fingerprints. Through verification, it was found that the digital fingerprints on the above original files are the same as those on the respective trusted timestamping authentication certificates.

On 18 October 2016, Tencent Technology applied for evidence preservation for the file "WeChat Emoticon 20161018.zip", which contains the WeChat emoticons involved except the emoticon. On 28 November 2016, the file "The History of Yellow Face 1.jpg" was subject to evidence preservation. Both the two trusted timestamping authentication certificates specify that "this is to certify that the file (or electronic data) already exists at the time of timestamping application, and the content remains intact without any alteration", and show their respective digital fingerprints. Through verification, it was found that the digital fingerprints on the above original files are the same as those on the respective trusted timestamping authentication certificates.

The screenshot of the WeChat's emoticon management platform submitted by Tencent Technology shows that the "Big Yellow Face" emoticon was submitted to the WeChat emoticon management platform on 29 August 2016, and was put into use on 30 August 2016. With exception to the above information, some information on the screenshot was pixelated. The defendant raised objections to the authenticity of the screenshot. In this regard, the court believes that the screenshot did not obscure the key information such as the emoticon's name, the time of submission, and the time when it was put into use. Without evidence to the contrary, the authenticity of the evidence cannot be denied.

Tencent Technology registered the work "WeChat Emoticon Series 1.0" on 20 July 2018. The registration number is Guo-Zuo-Deng-Zi-2018-F-00584306. The author is Tencent Technology. The category of the work is fine art work. The completion time is 29 August 2016. The first publication time is 30 August 2016. The "WeChat Emoticon Series 1.0" contains the WeChat emoticons involved in the case.

Huang Ying issued a statement on 5 June 2019, stating that he is an employee of Tencent Technology and the designer of the fine art work "WeChat Emoticon Series 1.0" (registration number: Guo-Zuo-Deng-Zi-2018-F-00584306). "The ideas of the work are the results of my design team members' discussions. The work is based on the company's 'QQ emoticons', created by me according to the company's requirements, specifically designed and produced by myself through communication with team members, and finally confirmed and released by the company. The company enjoys the complete copyright of the work. So the corresponding liability relating to the work should be borne by the company, and has nothing to do with me". The statement is accompanied by a copy of Huang Ying's ID card and a copy of his work card, which are affixed with the official seal of Tencent Technology.

Liang Sikun issued a statement on 5 June 2019, stating that he is an employee of Tencent Technology Company, "On 29 August 2016, he uploaded the fine art work 'WeChat Emoticon Series 1.0' (registration number: Guo-Zuo-Deng-Zi-2018-F-00584306) created by the company's employee Huang Ying onto the company's intranet "timestamping for work protection" (http://time.oa.com)". The statement is accompanied by a copy of Liang Sikun's ID card and a copy of his work card, which are affixed with the official seal of Tencent Technology.

(II) Facts about Tencent Computer's Alleged Claims for the WeChat Emoticons Involved

On January 10, 2011, Tencent Technology issued a letter of authorization as the copyright holder of the WeChat app to authorize Tencent Computer to operate the above application and its upgraded versions, and meanwhile granted the copyright of the above application and its upgraded versions (including but not limited to the copyright of related elements and works used in the application) to Tencent Computer for exclusive use without excluding the use by Tencent Technology. Tencent Computer may, by itself or jointly with Tencent Technology, apply for remedies against the infringement of the aforementioned legal rights by litigation and non-litigation means. The authorization expires when the authorizer withdraws this authorization. So far, Tencent Technology has not withdrawn its authorization.

During the trial, the defendant raised objections to the authenticity of the above letter of authorization. In this regard, the court holds that first, the two parties involved in the authorization letter are the plaintiffs of this case, and they both recognize the authenticity of the authorization letter; second, based on the actual performance, the WeChat app and related elements and works are actually operated and used by Tencent Computer, which can prove that there is indeed a relationship between the two plaintiffs in respect of the licensed use of the works; finally, the defendant did not submit contrary evidence to deny the authenticity of the authorization letter. Therefore, the court admits the above authorization letter and confirms the relationship between the two plaintiffs in respect of the licensed use of the works.

(III) Facts about the Defendant's Defense in Respect of the WeChat Emoticons Involved

On 21 November 2017, Jin Zhaoping applied for registering as a trademark. The registration number is 27608754. It is designated for use on shirts, baby suits, scarves and other goods. The preliminary review announcement date was 13 August 2018. The trademark is currently in dispute.

The emoticon "funny" (Baidu Tieba emoticon) is designed by the Baidu team. On 9 April 2015, Baidu Experience published an article "Drawing a Super Funny Emoticon with PS", which showed the process of drawing the emoticon "funny". The defendant contends that the emoticon "smirk" claimed by the plaintiffs is identical with or substantially similar to the Baidu team's emoticon "funny", and that the emoticon "funny" was published in April 2015, and its copyright owner is not the plaintiffs. The plaintiffs believe that there are substantial differences between the above two emoticons.

On 29 July 2015, the WeChat emoticon team issued an announcement to invite artists to create chat emoticons and submit contributions. The announcement said that the copyright of the emoticon works uploaded to the WeChat emoticon open platform still belonged to the contributors or authorizers.

On 25 May 2019, the defendant took screenshots of relevant WeChat emoticons, which showed that the emoticon came from "Small Yellow Face Acting Cute (卖萌小黄脸)" authored by "Wang Peipei"; the emoticon "wronged" and the emoticon "squint eyed grim" came from "Non-official Small Yellow Face (非官小黄脸)" created by "Lin Xiaona"; the emoticon "facepalm" came from "Magic Big Yellow Face (魔性大黄脸)①". The plaintiffs contended that the above emoticons were submitted and put into use after the WeChat emoticons involved as claimed by the plaintiffs were completed, submitted and put into use, and submitted several screenshots of the WeChat emoticon management platform which show the "Non-official Little Yellow Face" emoticons were submitted on 13 November 2016 and put into use on 8 December 2016; the "Little Yellow Face Acting Cute" emoticons were submitted on 16 January 2017 and put into use on 13 February 2017; the "Magic Big Yellow Face ①" emoticons were submitted on 31 July 2018 and put into use on 18 August 2018; and part of the information in the above screenshots was pixelated. The defendant raised objections to the authenticity of the screenshots submitted by the plaintiffs. In this regard, the court holds that the defendant's evidence on the record cannot prove the completion and publication time of the relevant WeChat emoticons. Furthermore, the screenshots submitted by the plaintiffs did not obscure key information such as emoticon name, submission time and the time when the emoticon was put into use. In the absence of evidence to the contrary, the authenticity of the evidence cannot be denied. Hence, the plaintiffs' counter-evidence is admitted.

On 21 November 2016, Timedg.com published an article from its official website "Has the Big Yellow Face Emoticon 'heyha' Flooded Your Screen Recently? Never Thought that the Prototype Was Him!". The article stated that the prototype of the emoticon "heyha" was Lu Zhengyu, and attached a photo of Lu Zhengyu (see Annex 3). Hence, the defendant believes that the emoticon was not created by the plaintiffs, so the plaintiffs do not own its copyright. The illustrations of the article displayed the "Latest Sequel to the Classic Big Yellow Face Emoticon", but the information "WeChat Face" was not shown. The defendant alleged that it found the plaintiffs claimed the authorship of the big yellow face emoticon album when collecting evidence on 25 May 2019, thus believing that the plaintiffs were able to modify the information of relevant web pages.

The above facts can be supported by notarial certificates (2018) Y. G. G. Z. No. 178062, (2019) Y. G. N. Y. No. 12846, (2018) S. Q. Z. Z. No. 028505, and (2019) Y. G. N. Y. No. 12847, statements, trusted timestamping authentication certificates, web page screenshots and the authorization letter submitted by the plaintiffs, web page screenshots submitted by the defendant, as well as the parties' presentation and trial transcripts.

II. Facts about the Defendant's Alleged Infringement

The copyright owner of the ChuiNiu app is the defendant. The registration number is 2018SR010307, and the registration date is 4 January 2018. During the trial, the defendant stated that the ChuiNiu app was mainly used for social chatting and purchase of game equipment. On 23 October 2018, Tencent Technology found the ChuiNiu app (for iOS and Android) operated by the defendant used six chat emoticons exactly the same as the WeChat emoticons involved.

The above facts can be supported by the notarial certificates (2018) S. Q. Z. Z. No. 026015, No. 029770 and No. 029771 submitted by the plaintiffs, the parties' statement and trial transcripts.

III. Facts about the Damages and Reasonable Expenses Claimed by the Plaintiffs

(I) Facts about the Visibility and Usage of the WeChat Emoticons Involved

On 28 December 2016, Tech.qq.com published an article with the title of "Zha Wen: WeChat Users Like Cute Emoticons the Most More Than 50% of Users Use

Small Yellow Faces Every Day", which indicated that "Emoticons are popular with Chinese users because they can fully express feelings in exaggerated and humorous ways… The number of emoticons sent is huge and can be hundreds of millions. The exposure is much better than ordinary ads, …" On 15 February 2017, mobile.163.com published an article "99% of Netizens Like Using the Bitchy WeChat Emoticon 'Facepalm'" which contained the WeChat emoticon involved. On 24 February 2017, Baijiahao published the article "The Prototype of the WeChat Emoticon Is Him? Will You Still Use It After Reading This Article?" which specified "Do you know the average number of WeChat users who log in every day? 768 million! More than 50% of these users use the system-default small yellow faces". The article was illustrated with the WeChat emotions "facepalm" and "frown" involved.

(II) Facts about the Download Number of the ChuiNiu App

According to the data update on 11 October 2018, the ChuiNiu app had been downloaded for 320,000 times on Huawei application market, 189,000 times on Wandoujia, and 60,000 times on Baidu Mobile Assistant, a total of 569,000 downloads. As shown on the notarial certificate (2019) S. Q. Z. Z. No. 005152 and related screenshots, as of 22 January 2019, according to the statistics of Qimai Data, the total downloads of the ChuiNiu app had exceeded 7.18 million, and the average daily downloads in the past 30 days exceeded 100,000. The notarial certificate also showed the download data of the app on eight application markets including Baidu, myapp.com and 360.

(III) Facts about the Plaintiffs' Reasonable Expenses

The plaintiffs have paid attorney fees of CNY 10,000 and notary fees of CNY 544 for the lawsuit in this case.

The above facts can be supported by the notarial certificates (2019) S. Q. Z. Z. No. 005151 and (2018) S. Q. Z. Z. No. 026016 and invoices submitted by the plaintiffs, statement of the parties and transcripts.

Judgment Reasoning

The court holds that:

According to the contentions of the plaintiffs and the defendant, the issues of the dispute in this case are: I. Whether the plaintiffs own the copyright of the WeChat emoticons involved and whether Tencent Technology is a qualified plaintiff in this case; II. Whether the defendant has infringed the plaintiffs' right to communicate works through an information network (a so-called information dissemination right), and should bear the legal liability if an infringement is constituted.

I. Whether the Plaintiffs Own the Copyright of the WeChat Emoticons Involved and Whether Tencent Technology Is a Qualified Plaintiff in This Case

(I) Whether the WeChat Emoticons Involved Constitute a Work

Article 2 of the *Regulations for the Implementation of the Copyright Law* provides that "the term 'works' as referred to in the *Copyright Law* means intellectual creations with originality in the literary, artistic or scientific domain, insofar as they can be reproduced in a tangible form". The eighth paragraph of Article 4 of the *Regulations for the Implementation of the Copyright Law* stipulates that "'fine art work' means two-dimensional or three-dimensional works of the plastic arts created with lines, colors or other media which impart aesthetic effects, such as paintings, works of calligraphy and sculptures". In this case, all the WeChat emoticons involved are vivid and interesting cartoon images that adopt the "yellow face expressions" as a design concept, namely, representing the face by a yellow round and, on the basis of this basic shape, showing emotions by variation in the expressions of eyes, mouth, and gestures. They reflect certain personalized choices and original expressions in the use of lines and colors and are of aesthetic significance, thus constituting works of fine art and are protected by the *Copyright Law*.

The defendant asserts that the emoticon "smirk" is identical with or substantially similar to the prior emoticon "funny" designed by Baidu. In this regard, the court holds that by comparing the above two emoticons, we can see that both the two are cartoon images with "yellow face expressions" as the design concept, but there are obvious and objectively identifiable differences in the position, length and shape of eyebrows, the position, size and shape of eyes, and the shades of blush and so forth. The emotions and meanings conveyed by the two emoticons, namely the emoticons "funny" and "smirk", also differ significantly. This difference is also reflected in the naming of the two. Therefore, the emoticon "smirk" is original. This defensive claim of the defendant cannot be established.

(II) Whether Tencent Technology Owns the Copyright of the WeChat Emoticons Involved

According to Article 11 of *Copyright Law*, the copyright in a work shall belong to its author; the citizen, legal entity or other organization whose name is mentioned in connection with a work shall, in the absence of proof to the contrary, be deemed to be the author of the work; where a work is created under the auspices and according to the intention of a legal entity or other organization, which bears liability for the work, the said legal entity or organization shall be deemed to be the author of the work. In this case, the WeChat emoticons involved were registered by the copyright authority, and their author is Tencent Technology. Besides, Tencent Technology also submitted the statements of the creator and the uploader of the WeChat emoticons involved, the trusted timestamping authentication certificates and the application information of the "Big Yellow Face.zip" containing the WeChat emoticons involved and other files, and the screenshots of the WeChat emoticon management platform and other evidence, together forming a chain of evidence to *prima facie* prove that Tencent Technology is the author of the WeChat emoticons involved. Furthermore, the above evidence shows that the WeChat emoticons involved were completed on 29 August 2016. Thus Tencent Technology has been holding the copyright of the WeChat emoticons involved since that date.

The defendant alleges that the emoticon "facepalm" involved is the same as Jin Zhaoping's trademark, which was registered on 21 November 2017, earlier than the registration time of the WeChat emoticon involved, and thus Tencent Technology is not the author of the emoticon "facepalm" involved. The court holds that a copyright exists when a work is completed. Tencent Technology has *prima facie* proved that the WeChat emoticon involved was created on 29 August 2016, and was first published on 30 August 2016, both earlier than Jin Zhaoping's application for trademark registration. In addition, the defendant did not submit evidence to prove that the trademark was created by Jin Zhaoping, thus failing to prove Jin Zhaoping is the author of the "facepalm" emoticon involved. Therefore, the defendant's defense cannot be established.

As to the defendant's contention that the emoticon "smirk" involved is identical with or substantially similar to the prior emoticon "funny" designed by the Baidu team, and therefore Tencent Technology is not the copyright owner. Because the court has found that there are objectively identifiable differences between the two and that the emoticon "smirk" involved is the work of Tencent Technology, the defendant's argument that Tencent Technology is not the copyright owner cannot be established.

Regarding the defendant's claim that the prototype of the emoticon "heyha" involved comes from Lu Zhengyu's photos and thus Tencent Technology is not the copyright owner, the court believes that first, the evidence on the record cannot prove Lu Zhengyu's photos were created earlier than the emoticon "heyha"; second, even if the prototype of the emoticon indeed comes from Lu Zhengyu's photos, the forms of expression are not the same. People's facial expressions are only the natural facial expressions or facial performances that express feelings. They are not works. In order to create a chat emoticon from the expressions of a real person, the author has to select, judge and make choices on lines and colors and so forth, which is intellectual work with originality. Therefore, the defendant's argument that Tencent Technology is not the copyright owner cannot be established.

The defendant also asserted that Tencent Technology is not the copyright owner of some of the WeChat emoticons involved as they were derived from the emoticons "squint eyed grim", and "wronged" on the WeChat emoticons open platform. However, according to the work registration certificate submitted by Tencent Technology and the screenshots of the WeChat emoticon management platform, the WeChat emoticons involved were first published on 30 August 2016, earlier than the time when the three emoticons from the open platform were submitted and put into use. Hence, the defendant's claim that the copyright owner of the WeChat emoticons involved is not Tencent Technology is not sustained. The defendant believes that Tencent Technology has the ability to modify the WeChat emoticon's signature information, but the evidence on the record is insufficient to prove its claim, so the court does not support its grounds for defense.

To sum up, Tencent Technology is the author of the WeChat emoticon involved and enjoys the copyright by operation of law.

(III) Whether Tencent Technology Is a Qualified Plaintiff in This Case

Pursuant to Article 119 of the *CPL* (2017), the plaintiff must be a citizen, legal person or any other organization that has a direct interest in the case. This case is about a dispute over copyright infringement, so only the copyright owner or other interested persons have the right to institute the lawsuit. The defendant contends that as Tencent Technology has granted the copyright of the WeChat emoticons involved for the exclusive use by Tencent Computer, only Tencent Computer can sue for the right protection and Tencent Technology is not a qualified plaintiff in this case.

The court holds that as the author of the WeChat emoticons involved, Tencent Technology enjoys all personal and property rights of the WeChat emoticons involved. It clearly stated in the letter of authorization for Tencent Computer that "Tencent Technology grants Tencent Computer exclusive use right without excluding the use by Tencent Technology. Tencent Computer may remedy against the infringement of the aforementioned legal rights by itself or jointly with Tencent Technology by litigation and non-litigation means". Therefore, Tencent Technology only granted partial property rights to Tencent Computer and did not waive the copyright in the WeChat emoticons involved and the right to institute the lawsuit. As the copyright owner of the WeChat emoticons involved, it has direct interests in this case and has the right to file a lawsuit as a plaintiff. The defendant's defense that Tencent Technology is not the qualified plaintiff has no factual and legal basis and thus is not supported by the court.

Accordingly, both Tencent Technology, as the author of the WeChat emoticons involved, and Tencent Computer, based on the authorization of Tencent Technology, have legal rights in the WeChat emoticons involved and are protected by the *Copyright Law*.

II. Whether the Defendant Infringed the Plaintiffs' Right to Communication through an Information Network, and Should Bear the Legal Liability if an Infringement Is Constituted

According to the first paragraph of Article 48 of the *Copyright Law*, anyone who commits any of the following acts of infringement shall, depending on the circumstances, bear civil liability such as ceasing the infringement, eliminating the bad effects of the act, making an apology or paying compensation for damages. In this case, the defendant, who without permission used chat emoticons exactly the same as the WeChat emoticons involved in the ChuiNiu app operated by it so that the app users can access the WeChat emoticons involved at the time and place of their choice, infringed upon the plaintiffs' legal right to communicate works through an information network and should bear corresponding civil liability.

The plaintiffs' claim that the defendant should compensate them for economic losses and reasonable expenses has factual and legal basis and is thus upheld by the court.

Regarding the specific amount of compensation, Article 49 of the *Copyright Law* stipulates that the compensation shall include the reasonable expenses that the right owner has paid for putting a stop to the infringement; where the actual losses of the right owner or the unlawful gains of the infringer cannot be determined, the People's court shall, in light of the circumstances of the infringement, decide on a compensation amounting to not more than CNY 500,000. In regard to the application of this clause, the second paragraph of Article 25 of the Interpretation of the SPC on Several Issues Concerning the Application of Law in the Trial of Copyright Dispute Cases provides that the People's court should fully consider circumstances such as the work type, reasonable use fee, the nature and consequences of the infringement before making determinations. Furthermore, when determining the amount of compensation, it should also be noted that not only should the compensation system be made full use of to recover the right holder's actual losses, but also to punish and curb infringements.

In this case, the plaintiffs failed to present evidence to prove their actual economic losses or the defendant's illegal proceeds and contended to calculate the economic losses as per statutory compensation. The court believes that, given the above provisions, the factors that should be considered in applying the statutory compensation include: (1) the type, popularity and market value of the work, the visibility of the right holder, the originality of the work and so forth; (2) the defendant's subjective negligence, way, time, scope and consequences of the infringement and so forth; (3) other factors. For this case, the court will take the following factors into consideration to determine the compensation amount as appropriate in accordance with law: (1) Chat emoticons are an artistic form of human daily expressions in the network environment. Creative chat emoticons can increase the chat fun of network users, produce unexpected chat effects, and improve users' experience. (2) The WeChat app, a piece of instant messaging software, has hundreds of millions of users. As the relevant elements in the use of the WeChat app, the valid and interesting WeChat emoticons involved have a large usage volume and high popularity. Through their widespread use and dissemination, they have been widely recognized and loved by numerous users. (3) The WeChat emoticons involved appreciate in value due to widespread use and dissemination. From the perspective of business operations, if others want to be authorized for the WeChat emoticons involved, they need to pay higher consideration. (4) The defendant, the operator of the ChuiNiu app, which is also an instant messaging tool mainly used for commercial purposes, used chat emoticons exactly the same as the WeChat emoticons involved while knowing the prior use of the WeChat emoticons involved and their high visibility, showing obvious subjective negligence. In addition, both the download number and infringement scope of the ChuiNiu app are large. (5) The WeChat emoticons involved are creative to a certain degree. But the creation is neither costly nor very difficult. Moreover, the ChuiNiu app has stopped using the WeChat emoticons involved. In view of the above, the court believes that the economic losses claimed by the plaintiffs lack sufficient basis and the amount is relatively high, and determines the defendant should compensate the plaintiffs for CNY 300,000 for their economic losses.

In response to the defendant's assertion that neither did the plaintiffs suffer losses nor did the defendant make profits due to the defendant's use of the WeChat emoticons involved, so the plaintiffs should not be compensated. The court holds that first, according to the *Copyright Law*, obtaining permission and paying remuneration is the basic premise for using others' works; second, the network economy is an "attention economy". The free business mode does not mean no profit or less profit. The use of chat emoticons helps to expand the users' ways of expression. Their interestingness improves users' experience to a certain extent and increases the attraction of the app to the users, so that the defendant can make profits through other value-added services by taking advantage of netizens' attention. Therefore, it is not true that the defendant's use of the WeChat emoticons involved neither caused economic damage to the plaintiffs nor brought benefits to the defendant because of no charge. Such a claim is not upheld by the court.

With regard to the exact amount of reasonable expenses, the plaintiffs claimed CNY 10,000 for attorney fees and CNY 544 for notarization costs and submitted the corresponding receipts. This claim is fully supported by the court.

Judgment Conclusion

In view of the foregoing, according to the 12th sub-paragraph of the first paragraph of Article 10, Article 11, the first paragraph of Article 48 and Article 49 of the *Copyright Law*, it is ordered as follows:

1. The defendant Beijing Qingshu Network Technology Co. Ltd. shall compensate the plaintiffs Tencent Technology (Shenzhen) Co. Ltd. and Shenzhen Tencent Computer Systems Co., Ltd. for CNY 300,000 for their economic losses within ten days from the effectiveness of this judgment;
2. The defendant Beijing Qingshu Network Technology Co. Ltd. shall compensate the plaintiffs Tencent Technology (Shenzhen) Co. Ltd. and Shenzhen Tencent Computer Systems Co., Ltd. for CNY 10,544 for their reasonable expenses within ten days from the effectiveness of this judgment;
3. Other claims of the plaintiffs Tencent Technology (Shenzhen) Co. Ltd. and Shenzhen Tencent Computer Systems Co., Ltd. are dismissed.

If the defendant Beijing Qingshu Network Technology Co. Ltd. fails to fulfill its obligations with respect to pecuniary payment within the period specified by this judgment, it shall pay double interest on the debt for the belated payment in accordance with Article 253 of the *CPL* (2017).

The case acceptance fee is CNY 8,800, of which CNY 3,000 shall be borne by the plaintiffs Tencent Technology (Shenzhen) Co. Ltd. and Shenzhen Tencent Computer Systems Co., Ltd. (already paid) and CNY 5,800 shall be assumed by Beijing Qingshu Network Technology Co. Ltd. (it shall be paid within seven days from the effectiveness of this Judgment).

If unsatisfied with this Judgment, the unsatisfied party may file an appeal to Beijing Intellectual Property Court via the court within fifteen days from the service of this Judgment.

Presiding Judge Jiang Ying

Judge Lu Zhengxin

Judge Zhu Ge

19 July 2019

Judge Assistant Lu Ning

Clerk Li Minglei

Annexes:

1. The WeChat emoticons involved.
2. The Alleged infringing emoticons.
3. Lu Zhengyu's relevant photos.

2.2.2 Other Decisions on Procedural Issues

Other than civil judgments on the merits, the length of judicial decisions on procedural issues is normally shorter. After the introduction to parties and basic facts, there could be merely several paragraphs left. However, when it comes to crucial procedural issues, Chinese courts will still provide detailed reasoning. This contribution chooses a relatively comprehensive civil ruling as an example, an objection to jurisdiction raised by Shi Ruichao in a lawsuit over the bareboat charter filed by Good Vantage Shipping Co. Ltd. The case is named as *Good Vantage Shipping Co. Ltd. v. Shi Ruichao, Chen Fuxiang and Xie Cantang* (益利船务有限公司诉施瑞朝等光船租赁合同纠纷案).[2]

Xiamen Maritime Court

Civil Ruling

(2020) Min 72 Min Chu No. 239

Plaintiff: Good Vantage Shipping Co. Ltd.

Domicile: Room B, 4/F, Ngan House, 210 Des Voeux Road Central, Hong Kong.

Legal Representative: Pan Yang, director.

Attorney: Zhang Lihua, lawyer from Shanghai Yaojiang Law Firm.

Attorney: Yang Lihua, lawyer from Shanghai Yaojiang Law Firm.

Defendant: Shi Ruichao.

Defendant: Chen Fuxiang.

Defendant: Xie Cantang.

With respect to the case of dispute concerning a bareboat charter between the plaintiff Good Vantage Shipping Co. Ltd. (hereinafter referred to as "Good Vantage") and the defendants Shi Ruichao, Chen Fuxiang and Xie Cantang, the court accepted it on 20 April 2020.

Good Vantage claimed as follows: on 14 July 2010, Good Vantage signed a Bareboat Charter with an outsider Continental International Shipping Co. Ltd. (hereinafter referred to as "Continental Shipping"). Meanwhile, the defendants Shi Ruichao, Xie Cantang and Chen Fuxiang respectively signed a guarantee contract with Good Vantage as surety, promising to be jointly liable for the performance of any and all

[2] The translation is provided by www.pkulaw.com and modified by the author: https://www.pkulaw.com/en_case/c05aeed05a57db0a7c6f798667a9292f0fbc040d6ba3d420bdfb.html?way=listView.

liabilities and obligations of Continental Shipping under the Bareboat Charter. Since 11 June 2015, the Charterer Continental Shipping had never paid any hire. By 4 September 2015 when the Bareboat Charter was prematurely terminated, the total outstanding hire had reached USD 12,665,919.98, plus the disbursements paid by Good Vantage in the course of retrieving the ship in total amount of USD 696,737.81. After being retrieved, the ship was sold out at the price of USD 5.2 million. In Good Vantage's view, as the Charterer Continental Shipping failed to pay hire in due time, according to the Bareboat Charter, the Owner shall have the right to request for premature termination of the Bareboat Charter and the Charterer's compensation for its loss, while according to the guarantee contracts, Shi Ruichao, Xie Cantang and Chen Fuxiang shall be jointly liable for the performance of the Charterer's obligations to pay hire and compensate for damages under the Bareboat Charter.

During the time period for making defense, Shi Ruichao raised objection to jurisdiction on the following grounds: (1) Under the principal contract (i.e. the Bareboat Charter), it is agreed that any and all disputes should be resolved through mediation (arbitration plus mediation), so before both sides of the parties agree to refer to mediation or arbitration, any court shall not accept the filing of the disputes. Hence, the act of the Plaintiff directly filing the lawsuit before Xiamen Maritime Court is in violation of the Chinese law and regulations on foreign-related arbitration and the obligations of China as a state signatory to the United Nations Convention on International Settlement Agreements Resulting from Mediation (hereinafter referred to as "Singapore Convention on Mediation"); (2) It is also agreed under the principal contract that the courts of Hong Kong have exclusive jurisdiction to settle any dispute arising out of or in connection with the Bareboat Charter. Even if the guarantee contracts have a different jurisdiction clause, the jurisdiction should be subject to the provision of the principal contract. Therefore, Xiamen Maritime Court has no jurisdiction; (3) It is agreed under the guarantee contracts that the courts of Hong Kong shall have exclusive jurisdiction. Therefore, proceedings shall be taken first in the courts of Hong Kong and then concurrent proceedings may be taken in Xiamen Maritime Court; (4) It is not convenient to investigate into the case facts if this case is tried by Xiamen Maritime Court. The courts of Hong Kong have jurisdiction, and it will be more convenient for the courts of Hong Kong to try this case.

In response to Shi Ruichao's objection to jurisdiction, Good Vantage defended as follows: (1) Although it is agreed under the principal contract that the courts of Hong Kong have non-exclusive jurisdiction, mediation or arbitration is not agreed thereunder; (2) As the creditor only sues the sureties, the courts of the place where the guarantors are resident shall have jurisdiction; (3) The guarantee contracts grant Good Vantage the right to take proceedings in any jurisdiction and do not require Good Vantage to first take proceedings in the courts of Hong Kong before taking any proceedings in any other jurisdiction. Hence, Shi Ruichao's argument regarding concurrent proceedings and inconvenient court cannot stand and Xiamen Maritime Court has jurisdiction over this case.

Through investigation, the following facts are ascertained: on 14 July 2010, a Bareboat Charter was entered into by and between Good Vantage and the outsider Continental Shipping, under which it was agreed that Continental Shipping was to charter

M/V "Fortune East" owned by Good Vantage. The Bareboat Charter was reasonably amended from the BIMCO Standard Bareboat Charter Code Name: "BARECON 2001".Under the Bareboat Charter, dispute resolution is addressed in Clause 30, with Clause 30(a), Clause 30(b) and Clause 30(c) thereunder all about reference to arbitration, specifically, Clause 30(a) providing application of English law and reference to arbitration at London, Clause 30(b) providing application of the U.S. laws and reference to arbitration at New York and Clause 30(c) providing application of the laws of the place mutually agreed by the parties and reference to arbitration at a mutually agreed place. When the Bareboat Charter was finally signed by the two parties, Clause 30(a), Clause 30(b) and Clause 30(c) were all struck out. But Clause 30(d) was not struck out, which provides as follows: "Notwithstanding Clause 49 in the Additional Clauses, the parties may agree at any time to refer to mediation any difference and/or dispute arising out of or in connection with this Contract. In the case of a dispute in respect of which arbitration has been commenced under (a), (b) or (c) above, the following shall apply:

(i) Either Party may at any time and from time to time elect to refer the dispute or part of the dispute to mediation by serving on the other party of a written notice (the "Mediation Notice") calling on the other party to agree to mediation.
(ii) The other party shall thereupon within 14 calendar days of receipt of the Mediation Notice confirm that they agree to mediation, in which case the parties shall thereafter agree on a mediator within a further 14 calendar days, failing which on the application of either party a mediator will be appointed promptly by the Arbitration Tribunal ("the Tribunal") or such person as the Tribunal may designate for that purpose. The mediation shall be conducted in such place and in accordance with such procedure and on such terms as the parties may agree or, in the event of disagreement, as may be set by the mediator.
(iii) If the other party does not agree to mediate, that fact may be brought to the attention of the Tribunal and may be taken into account by the Tribunal when allocating the costs of the arbitration between the parties.
(iv) The mediation shall not affect the right of either party to seek such relief or take such steps as it considers necessary to protect its interests.
(v) Either party may advise the Tribunal that they have agreed to mediation. The arbitration procedure shall continue during the conduct of the mediation but the Tribunal may take the mediation timetable into account when setting the timetable for steps in the arbitration. …"

Clause 49 of the Bareboat Charter is concerning the applicable law and jurisdiction, under which Clause 49.2 provides "Subject to Clause 49.4 the courts of Hong Kong have exclusive jurisdiction to settle any dispute arising out of or in connection with this Charter", while Clause 49.4 provides "[T]his Clause 49 is for the benefit of the Owner only. As a result, the Owner shall not be prevented from taking proceedings relating to a Dispute in any other courts with jurisdiction. To the extent allowed by law, the Owner may take concurrent proceedings in any number of jurisdictions".

On the same day, 14 July 2010, Shi Ruichao and Chen Xiangfu, as guarantors, both signed a Personal Guarantee with Good Vantage. Provisions on jurisdiction are set out in Clause 9 of the Personal Guarantees, under which Clause 9.1 provides "For the benefit of the Owner, and subject to Clause 9.4 below, each and every Personal Guarantor hereby irrevocably agrees that the courts of Hong Kong shall have exclusive jurisdiction", while Clause 9.4 provides "Nothing in this Clause 9 limits the right of the Owner to bring proceedings, including third-party proceedings, against any Personal Guarantor, or to apply for interim remedies, in connection with this Guarantee in any other court and/or concurrently in more than one jurisdiction. The obtaining by the Owner of judgment in one jurisdiction shall not prevent the Owner from bringing or continuing proceedings in any other jurisdiction, whether or not these shall be founded on the same cause of action".

Through investigation, it is also ascertained that China signed the Singapore Mediation Convention on 7 August 2019, but has not yet ratified it so far.

After review, the Court holds the views as follows: the dispute in this case arose from guarantee contracts in connection with a bareboat charter. As the registered office of the Plaintiff Good Vantage was in the Hong Kong Special Administrative Region, this case is a case involving Hong Kong. In accordance with the provision of Article 551 of the *ICPL* (2020), the People's courts may refer to the special provisions on foreign-related civil procedures when trying civil lawsuits involving the Hong Kong Special Administrative Region. Further, Article 259 of the *CPL* (2017) provides "this Part shall apply to civil actions within the territory of the P.R.C. involving foreign parties. For matters not addressed in this Part, the other relevant provisions of the Law shall apply". It is a procedural issue to judge whether the jurisdiction clauses in this case can exclude the jurisdiction of the People's court in the Mainland of China and whether the Court has jurisdiction over this case, and thus the laws of the P.R.C. shall apply. The key issues over jurisdiction in this case lie in: 1. whether the Bareboat Charter has arbitration and mediation clauses and whether these clauses exclude the jurisdiction of the Court; 2. whether the jurisdiction clause under the Bareboat Charter excludes the jurisdiction of the Court; 3. whether the jurisdiction clause under the Personal Guarantees excludes the jurisdiction of the Court; and, 4. whether the Court will be an inconvenient court if this case is finally tried by the Court.

I. Whether the Bareboat Charter Has Arbitration and Mediation Clauses and Whether These Clauses Exclude the Jurisdiction of the Court

It is in reliance on Clause 30(d) under the Bareboat Charter that Shi Ruichao argued that the dispute should be referred to mediation. However, seen from the specific content of this clause, which mainly provides that the parties may agree to refer to mediation, gives guidance on how to apply for mediation in the arbitration procedure, how to elect a mediator, and how to deal when the other party does not agree to mediate and especially points out that the arbitration procedure shall continue during the conduct of the mediation, it is in fact unclear whether the parties may agree to refer to mediation in respect of which no arbitration has been commenced. Given this, the Court reviewed the Drafting Notes published by BIMCO for the BIMCO Standard Bareboat Charter Code Name: "BARECON 2001". As explained in the

Drafting Notes, mediation referred to in Clause 30(d) is only triggered once arbitration proceedings have commenced and then runs in parallel with those proceedings, if the parties so choose, and this has been done to ensure that one party cannot invoke mediation as a delaying tactic. In the opinion of the Court, as the standard bareboat charter based on which the Bareboat Charter was made was drafted by BIMCO, BIMCO's Drafting Notes may be deemed as a supplement to the matters not addressed in the Bareboat Charter and courts may refer to such notes to interpret the Bareboat Charter. Hence, the Court considers according to the provision of Clause 30(d), the precondition for the dispute to be referred to mediation is that arbitration has been commenced in respect of the dispute. In this case, as Clause 30(a), Clause 30(b) and Clause 30(c) were struck out when the Bareboat Charter was signed, no arbitration clause has been agreed under the Bareboat Charter, which means the parties have not agreed to refer to arbitration, and thus the precondition for mediation in the arbitration procedure is not satisfied. Accordingly, Shi Ruichao's argument that this case should be referred to arbitration or mediation and the jurisdiction of the Court is excluded cannot stand. This Court accepting this case is not in breach of the obligations of China as a state signatory to the Singapore Mediation Convention.

II. Whether the Jurisdiction Clause under the Bareboat Charter Excludes the Jurisdiction of the Court

In the view of the Court, Clause 49.2 and Clause 49.4 of the Bareboat Charter jointly constitute an asymmetrically exclusive jurisdiction clause, specifically, the courts of Hong Kong have exclusive jurisdiction only when the Owner has chosen to bring proceedings in courts of Hong Kong, in which case the Charterer shall be subject to the agreement on exclusive jurisdiction, but it does not limit the right of the Owner to take proceedings in any other jurisdiction. This clause does not violate *CPL*, and should be considered valid and effective. In this case, the Plaintiff did not choose to take proceedings in any court of Hong Kong, but filed a lawsuit before Xiamen Maritime Court, so the condition for exclusive jurisdiction of the courts of Hong Kong is not satisfied. Hence, Shi Ruichao's argument that the courts of Hong Kong have exclusive jurisdiction cannot stand and that the Court will not support it.

III. Whether the Jurisdiction Clause under the Personal Guarantees Excludes the Jurisdiction of the Court

The court also holds that Clause 9.1 and Clause 9.4 of the Personal Guarantees jointly constitute an asymmetrically exclusive jurisdiction clause, and specifically, the courts of Hong Kong have exclusive jurisdiction only when the Owner has chosen to bring proceedings in courts of Hong Kong, but it does not limit the right of the Owner to take proceedings in any other jurisdiction. In this case, the Plaintiff did not choose to bring proceedings in any court of Hong Kong, but filed a lawsuit before Xiamen Maritime Court, so it is in conformity with the contractual agreement and the relevant legal provisions in the Mainland of China. Hence, Shi Ruichao's argument that the courts of Hong Kong have exclusive jurisdiction cannot stand and the Court will not support it.

IV. Whether the Court Will Be Inconvenient If This Case Is Finally Tried by The Court and Whether Proceedings Should be Taken First Before the Courts of Hong Kong

Article 532 of the *ICPL* (2020) provides: "the People's court may dismiss the filing of a lawsuit by the plaintiff and inform the plaintiff to bring the lawsuit with a more convenient foreign court if the following situations have been satisfied at the same time: (1) The defendant raised the request that the case shall be handled by a more convenient foreign court, or proposed oppositions to the jurisdiction; (2) The parties concerned have no agreement on selecting a court of the P.R.C. as the competent court; (3) The case is subject to no exclusive jurisdiction of the courts in the P.R.C.; (4) The case involves no interests of the nation, citizens, legal entities or other organizations in the P.R.C.; (5) Main facts in dispute in the case has not occurred within the boundary of the P.R.C., and the case shall not be governed by laws of the P.R.C., due to which the People's court may confront substantial difficulties in terms of ascertaining facts and applying laws when trying the case; (6) A foreign court has jurisdiction upon the case and would be more convenient to try the case". In this case, Shi Ruichao, Xie Cantang and Chen Fuxiang are all residents in the Mainland of China, so this case involves the interest of the Mainland of China, and therefore the situations set out above are not satisfied. As regards whether proceedings should be taken first in the courts of Hong Kong, Clause 49.4 of the Bareboat Charter and Clause 9.4 of the Personal Guarantees both grant the Owner (the creditor) the right to take proceedings against the Personal Guarantors (the debtor) in more than one jurisdiction, but they contain no requirement that the Owner (the creditor) must take proceedings in the courts of Hong Kong before it takes proceedings in any other jurisdiction. Hence, Shi Ruichao's argument that the Court is an inconvenient court and that proceedings shall be taken first in the courts of Hong Kong cannot stand and the Court will not support it.

Based on the above, according to Article 129 of the *Judicial Interpretation of the SPC on Some Issues Regarding the Application of the Guarantee Law of the P.R.C.* which provides "when a dispute between the principal and the guarantee contract is brought to court, the jurisdiction of the case shall be determined on the basis of the principal contract. Where a dispute arises from the guarantee contract of joint liability guarantee and the creditor claims against the guarantee provider, such lawsuit shall be under the jurisdiction of the court at the locality where the guarantee provider has his domicile. Where the courts of jurisdiction selected in the principal and guarantee contracts are different, the jurisdiction shall be determined based on the principal contract", under the circumstance that it was both agreed under the principal contract and the guarantee contracts in this case that, if the creditor takes proceedings, the courts of Hong Kong shall have non-exclusive jurisdiction and the jurisdiction of the People's courts in the Mainland of China is not excluded, as the Plaintiff brought this lawsuit by reliance on the guarantee contracts, and the domiciles of the defendants Shi Ruichao, Xie Caotang and Chen Fuxiang are all in Fujian Province which is under the jurisdiction of the Court, the Court thus has jurisdiction over this case and the objection to jurisdiction raised by the defendant Shi Ruichao cannot stand

and shall be overruled according to law. In accordance with paragraph 1 of Article 127 of the *CPL* (2017) and Article 129 of the *Judicial Interpretation of the SPC on Some Issues Regarding the Application of the Guarantee Law of the P.R.C.*, the Court hereby renders down the ruling as follows:

The objection to jurisdiction raised by Shi Ruichao in this case shall be overruled.

The case acceptance fee in the amount of CNY 50.00 shall be borne by the defendant Shi Ruichao.

If dissatisfied with this Ruling, the Plaintiff Good Vantage Shipping Co. Ltd. may, within thirty (30) days, and the defendants Shi Ruichao, Chen Fuxiang and Xie Cantang may, within ten (10) days after receipt of this Ruling served by the Court, submit to the Court a statement of appeal as well as duplicates thereof in the number of the counterparties, to file appeal before the High People's Court of Fujian Province.

Presiding Judge: Tian Xingyu

People's Juror: Wei Wei

People's Juror: Zou Ling

8 July 2020

Judge Assistant: Zhang Zhuwei

Court Clerk: Lin Sanhong

2.3 Modified Judgments with More Binding Effects

2.3.1 Civil Judgments Modified and Published in the SPC Gazette

Other than raw judicial decisions, which remain unedited before release, there are also some judicial decisions which are to be further processed before being published in new forms. While these new judgments with essential changes are not similar with the precedents in other jurisdictions, they may enjoy stronger effects than the firsthand ones in China.

In this sense, the ones researching Chinese judgments must know that some judgments are published in the SPC Gazette monthly. Normally, the selecting judges in the SPC think the related cases are of importance in various aspects and then decide to suggest their publication in the official Gazette. It is said that the Gazette is an official dossier of the SPC which has been organized by the general office of the SPC and published monthly since 1985, also distributed overseas.[3] Important judicial

[3] A historical review, see Yang (2010).

information, such as judicial interpretations, judicial documents, and typical cases, is released through this platform.[4]

During the editorial work, the selecting judges may modify the collected real judgments to emphasize crucial issues or even change the main viewpoints of the responsible courts and the content of the written reasoning. In other words, the significant legal development provided by Gazette's cases may not exist in the original judgments. To provide a simple example of this kind of modified judgments, this contribution chooses an ordinary case, *Gao Zhiqing and Dai Yuqing v. Zhang Fengqing and Yuan Liping* (高志清、戴雨晴与张凤清、袁丽萍房屋买卖合同纠纷案), which handles a house purchase and sale contract.[5] Among others, the Gazette provides an official abstract of judgment at the very beginning of the published judgment.

Abstract of Judgment

A proprietor's condominium ownership includes the ownership of the exclusive area, the common ownership of the common area, and the joint management right. These aforementioned three kinds of rights are inseparable. When a proprietor transfers a house, the exclusive right to use the common area enjoyed by the proprietor according to the agreement on joint management shall be concurrently transferred. The existing agreement on joint management shall continue to be effective for the house transferee that obtains the proprietor's right through derivative acquisition and the house transferor shall provide assistance in the delivery of the common area he exclusively used to the transferee.

Plaintiff: Gao Zhiqing.

Plaintiff: Dai Yuqing.

Defendant: Zhang Fengqing.

Defendant: Yuan Liping.

Basic Facts

Plaintiffs Gao Zhiqing and Dai Yuqing filed a lawsuit with the Primary People's Court of Jiangning District, Nanjing City, Jiangsu Province against defendants Zhang Fengqing and Yuan Liping for a dispute over the purchase and sale of a house.

Plaintiffs Gao Zhiqing and Dai Yuqing alleged that: On 21 February 2016, the plaintiffs concluded a house purchase and sale contract with defendants Zhang Fengqing and Yuan Liping and they purchased the house (Room A in Building X of Shanshui Fangzhou Yayuan Community) from the defendants. In 2020, due to urban civilization construction, plaintiffs learned that the basement area in the unit to which their house belongs had been divided for all proprietors of the unit in August 2007 and the divided basement No. 7 was used by the proprietor of Room A.

---

4 SPC (2024).

5 The translation is provided by www.pkulaw.com and modified by the author: https://www.pkulaw.com/en_case/c05aeed05a57db0a7e27d3e82343c718a0fa5dbe9a9a3cfcbdfb.html?way=listView.

However, the defendants did not tell the plaintiffs the situation, nor did they deliver the basement No. 7 to the plaintiffs, and the defendants continued to occupy and use such basement. On 2 September 2020, the plaintiffs and the defendants had a dispute over the use of the basement No. 7 and mediation conducted by the People's mediation committee failed. The plaintiffs thus filed a lawsuit before the court and requested the court to confirm that the basement No. 7 should be used by the plaintiffs, and order the defendants to empty and deliver the basement No. 7 and pay the plaintiffs the fee for occupying and using the basement (calculated at the standard of CNY 400 per month from 1 August 2016 to the date when the basement No. 7 was actually delivered).

Defendants Zhang Fengqing and Yuan Liping contended that: (1) According to the commercial housing purchase and sale contract concluded between the defendants and the property developer, the basement for Room A was not included in the shared public area and was not within the common area of proprietors. (2) Half a year after the property developer delivered the house involved, the defendants received a notice of discussion on division of the unit basements. The proprietors claimed equal division at that time, but equal division could not be realized due to the structure of such unit basements. In the end, small basements with various areas were divided and the proprietors obtained the use rights by drawing lots. The defendants drew the basement No. 7 and paid the division fee of CNY 676. As a consequence, the basement No. 7 was not a subsidiary facility of a house, it had nothing to do with Room A, and the defendants may dispose of it on their own. (3) After the plaintiffs bought the house, the housing price soared and the housing premium obtained by them within half a year after they purchased the house exceeded that obtained by the defendants after they purchased the house ten years ago. The contract concluded by both parties stipulated that the liquidated damages were only CNY 20,000, but the defendants did not breach the contract and sold the house as agreed and they committed no breach of contract in the performance of the contract. In conclusion, since the house purchase and sale contract between the plaintiffs and the defendants did not stipulate that the basement No. 7 should be transferred to the plaintiffs, the defendants requested the court to dismiss claims of the plaintiffs.

In the trial of first instance, the Primary People's Court of Jiangning District, Nanjing City, Jiangsu Province found that: On 21 February 2016, defendants Zhang Fengqing and Yuan Liping (Party A) entered into an Existing Housing Trading Contract with plaintiff Gao Zhiqing (Party B) and a party not involved Nanjing Cunfang Real Estate Agency Co., Ltd. (Party C). They agreed that Party A sold the house (Room A in Building X of Shanshui Fangzhou Yayuan Community located in No. 2199 Hongyun Avenue, Dongshan Sub-district, Jiangning District, Nanjing City) to Party B; the building area was 125.05 square meters, the unit construction area was 111.14 square meters, and the shared public area was 13.91 square meters; and the housing price was CNY 1.98 million. After the conclusion of the contract, Gao Zhiqing paid the housing price and Zhang Fengqing and Yuan Liping assisted in undergoing the ownership transfer formalities. On 29 March and 1 April of the same year, the house ownership and the land use rights were separately altered and registered under the names of Gao Zhiqing and Dai Yuqing. On 11 May of the same year, Zhang Fengqing and Yuan Liping actually delivered the house involved to Gao Zhiqing and Dai Yuqing.

On 25 June 2006, defendants Zhang Fengqing and Yuan Liping concluded a Commercial Housing Purchase and Sale Contract with Nanjing Hongfa Real Estate Development Co., Ltd. and purchased the house (Room A in Building X of Shanshui Fangzhou Yayuan Community). In August 2007, all the proprietors of the unit to which Room A belongs jointly entrusted the property service provider of the Community with dividing the basements in the unit. There were 12 rooms in the unit and 12 small basements were divided and numbered in sequence. The users were determined by drawing lots. The basement No. 7 was for use by the proprietor of Room A and Zhang Fengqing and Yuan Liping paid the division fee of CNY 676. While selling the house involved, Zhang Fengqing and Yuan Liping failed to inform Gao Zhiqing and Dai Yuqing of the situation of the basement No. 7 in a timely manner.

On 24 August 2020, plaintiffs Dai Yuqing and Gao Zhiqing notified defendants Zhang Fengqing and Yuan Liping of emptying the basement No. 7 before the end of August. Since Zhang Fengqing and Yuan Liping failed to empty the basement within the prescribed time limit, Dai Yuqing and Gao Zhiqing changed the door lock of the basement No. 7 and both parties thus had a dispute. On 2 September 2020, upon mediation by the People's Mediation Committee of Dongshan Sub-district, Jiangning District, Nanjing City, Dai Yuqing and Gao Zhiqing delivered the key to the door lock of the basement involved to Zhang Fengqing and Yuan Liping and both parties agreed that the dispute over the use of the basement involved should be settled through litigation. At present, there is still stuff of Zhang Fengqing and Yuan Liping in the basement No. 7.

In the trial, to prove the loss arising from the occupation and use of the basement No. 7 by defendants Zhang Fengqing and Yuan Liping, plaintiffs Gao Zhiqing and Dai Yuqing provided basement lease advertisements downloaded from Beike App and 5i5j App, proving that the rental of a basement with similar area was about CNY 600 per month. In the cross-examination, Zhang Fengqing and Yuan Liping deemed that the authenticity of such advertisements could not be confirmed.

Judgment's Reasoning

In the trial of first instance, the Primary People's Court of Jiangning District, Nanjing City, Jiangsu Province held that: The Existing Housing Trading Contract concluded by plaintiffs Gao Zhiqing and Dai Yuqing and defendants Zhang Fengqing and Yuan Liping did not violate the compulsory provisions of laws and administrative regulations and was valid. The parties should fully perform their obligations as agreed. The parties should follow the principle of good faith and perform such obligations as notification, assistance, and confidentiality according to the nature and objectives of the Contract and the trading practice.

1. As to whether the basement involved was commonly owned by proprietors, the law prescribes that other public places and houses for common facilities and property management services in the building area shall be commonly owned by

proprietors. In this case, the unit basement for Room A was not an exclusive area of the proprietor in the condominium ownership and it was a common facility in the building area and commonly owned by proprietors. In addition, the unit to which Room A belongs is relatively independent in its structure and functions. The basements in this unit can be individually used and they have vital interests with proprietors of this unit in terms of use. Therefore, the basements in this unit were commonly owned by proprietors of this unit. The basement No. 7 was divided from the basements in the unit to which Room A belongs, it was a common area allocated to the proprietor of Room A for exclusive use, and in nature, it was commonly owned by proprietors. The contentions of Zhang Fengqing and Yuan Liping that the basement No. 7 was not commonly owned by proprietors and they may dispose of the basement on their own lacked factual and legal basis and the court does not admit such contentions.

2. As to whether defendants Zhang Fengqing and Yuan Liping should deliver the basement No. 7 to plaintiffs Gao Zhiqing and Dai Yuqing, the law prescribes that a proprietor enjoys the right to share and jointly manage the common area. Where a proprietor transfers a residential house or operational house in a building, the right to share and jointly manage the common area enjoyed by him/her shall be transferred concurrently. The court held that: From the perspective of maintaining the public order of the community and safeguarding the interests of proprietors, when a proprietor transfers the area he exclusively owns, he should concurrently transfer the right to share and jointly manage the common area and the exclusive right to own the common area he enjoys according to the agreement on joint management of proprietors. The existing agreement on joint management remains in force to the transferees of the house who obtain the proprietor's rights through acquisition and the house transferors should provide assistance in delivery of the common building area they exclusively used to the transferees. In this case, based on the mutual assent on common management, Zhang Fengqing and Yuan Liping exclusively use the basement No. 7. Zhang Fengqing and Yuan Liping transferred Room A to Gao Zhiqing and Dai Yuqing, the exclusive right to use the basement No. 7 should be concurrently transferred, and Zhang Fengqing and Yuan Liping should provide assistance in the delivery of the basement No. 7 to Gao Zhiqing and Dai Yuqing. As a consequence, the court upholds the claims of Gao Zhiqing and Dai Yuqing that the basement No. 7 should be confirmed to be used by Gao Zhiqing and Dai Yuqing and Zhang Fengqing and Yuan Liping should empty and deliver the basement No. 7. The contentions of Zhang Fengqing and Yuan Liping that the house purchase and sale contract did not stipulate delivery of the basement No. 7 and they should not deliver the basement to Gao Zhiqing and Dai Yuqing lack factual and legal basis and should not be admit.
3. As to how to recognize the occupation and use fee claimed by plaintiffs Gao Zhiqing and Dai Yuqing, the law prescribes that "if a party fails to perform its obligations under a contract, or its performance fails to satisfy the terms of the contract, he shall bear the liabilities for breach of contract to continue to perform its obligations, take remedial measures, or compensate for loss". In this case,

defendants Zhang Fengqing and Yuan Liping refused to deliver the basement No. 7 to Gao Zhiqing and Dai Yuqing, which constituted a breach of contract, and Gao Zhiqing and Dai Yuqing had the right to claim that Zhang Fengqing and Yuan Liping should compensate for their loss. Since both parties did not stipulate the time limit for the delivery of the basement No. 7, Gao Zhiqing and Dai Yuqing may require Zhang Fengqing and Yuan Liping's delivery at any time, but they should offer Zhang Fengqing and Yuan Liping some time to make preparations. On 24 August 2020, Gao Zhiqing and Dai Yuqing required that Zhang Fengqing and Yuan Liping empty and deliver the basement No. 7 before the end of August. Zhang Fengqing and Yuan Liping failed to perform the obligation in a timely manner. Therefore, the occupation and use fee should be calculated from 1 September 2020. By taking into full account such factors as the nature, area, and use purpose of the basement No. 7, it is decided with the court's discretion to calculate the occupation and use fee at the standard of CNY 180 per month. Considering that Zhang Fengqing and Yuan Liping paid the corresponding cost for obtaining the use right of the basement No. 7, for the purpose of reducing the litigation burdens of the parties, the court determines that the occupation and use fee up to 22 December 2020 was offset by the cost paid by Zhang Fengqing and Yuan Liping, and Zhang Fengqing and Yuan Liping should no longer pay the occupation and use fee during the aforementioned period.

Judgment

In conclusion, on 30 December 2020, the Primary People's Court of Jiangning District, Nanjing City, Jiangsu Province entered a judgment in accordance with the provisions of Articles 60 and 107 of the *Contract Law of the P.R.C.* and Articles 70, 72, and 73 of the *Property Law of the P.R.C.*: (1) The basement No. 7 for Room A in Building X of Shanshui Fangzhou Yayuan Community located in No. 2199 Hongyun Avenue, Dongshan Sub-district, Jiangning District, Nanjing City should be for use by plaintiffs Gao Zhiqing and Dai Yuqing. (2) Defendants Zhang Fengqing and Yuan Liping should, within ten days after the judgment came into force, empty and deliver the basement No. 7 for Room A in Building X of Shanshui Fangzhou Yayuan Community located in No. 2199 Hongyun Avenue, Dongshan Sub-district, Jiangning District, Nanjing City to plaintiffs Gao Zhiqing and Dai Yuqing. (3) Defendants Zhang Fengqing and Yuan Liping should, within ten days after the judgment took effect, pay plaintiffs Gao Zhiqing and Dai Yuqing the occupation and use fee (calculated at the standard of CNY 180 per month from 23 December 2020 to the date when defendants Zhang Fengqing and Yuan Liping delivered the basement No. 7 for Room A in Building X of Shanshui Fangzhou Yayuan Community located in No. 2199 Hongyun Avenue, Dongshan Sub-district, Jiangning District, Nanjing City to plaintiffs Gao Zhiqing and Dai Yuqing. (4) Other claims of plaintiffs Gao Zhiqing and Dai Yuqing should be dismissed.

After the judgment of first instance was pronounced, neither party appealed and the judgment of first instance took effect.

2.3.2 *Civil Judgments Modified and Published as Guiding Cases*

Compared to the judgments published in the SPC's Gazette, guiding cases hold a stronger position according to the judicial interpretations. To be named are the *Provisions on Case Guidance*[6] as the primary source, while other documents such as *Several Opinions on Promoting the High-quality Development of Case Guidance*[7] and *Detailed Rules on Case Guidance*,[8] are also worthy of attention. Even the SPC emphasizes that the Gazette's judgments do not have the special effect of guiding cases.[9] Partially due to this reason, the SPC selected and published seven Gazette's cases in public law areas and eight ones in private law areas to be the ninth and tenth patches of guiding cases.

Theoretically speaking, it can be argued that all ordinary civil judgments could be of convincing force in any subsequent civil dispute, and some of them could be binding in practice. In comparison, a guiding case in Chinese context could serve as a certain reference for any later legal process. This new system of guiding cases has an independent institutional effect, representing a remarkable Chinese innovation based on experience in comparative law. The scope of this effect is not limited by the essential points of a guiding case, which are outlined at the beginning of the case. The related statutes emphasized in a guiding case do not restrict the further influence of the case either. The difference between convicted facts and legal reasoning of published and original versions of the case could also matter and the published version should be preferred in principle. The strength of this effect is demonstrated by a special duty to reason when the guiding case is not to be followed. When this duty is violated, there could be errors of legal application, errors of factual identification, or improper acts in terms of judicial administration and management. In addition, a mandatory report on the deviation of guiding cases is not necessary.[10]

Until 15 December 2023, there are 224 guiding cases covering almost all areas of law and about 130 ones in private law areas. Among them, the Guiding Case No. 142 of the SPC refers to a dispute over the right to life, which is titled as *Liu Minglian, Guo Lili, and Guo Shuangshuang v. Sun Wei and Xinyang Branch of Henan Lanting Real Estate Management Co., Ltd.* (刘明莲、郭丽丽、郭双双诉孙伟、河南兰庭物业管理有限公司信阳分公司生命权纠纷案). This final judgment was deliberated and adopted by the Judicial Committee of the SPC on 9 October 2020.[11]

---

[6] No. 51 [2010] of the SPC. Its Article 7 says that when trying similar cases, People's courts at all levels shall use the guiding cases issued by the SPC as a reference. Hence, to explain what this effect to be reference means is one of the attractive points during the last 15 years.

[7] No. 294 [2021] of the SPC.

[8] No. 130 [2015] of the SPC.

[9] Civil Ruling of the SPC (2014) Zui Gao Fa Min Shen No. 441. Further discussion, see Li (2010, pp 86–96).

[10] In detail, see Cao (2016).

[11] The translation is provided by www.pkulaw.com and modified by the author: https://www.pkulaw.com/en_case/a6bdb3332ec0adc4f2deabca628d7b0d7bd680a67efd2770bdfb.html?way=listView.

Guiding Case no. 142

Keywords: civil; right to life; dissuasion; reasonable limits; one's diseases.

The Key Issue of Judgment

Where the actor dissuades the other party from leaving the scene of the collision to safeguard the lawful rights and interests of a victim due to the collision and the dissuasion does not exceed reasonable limits, it is a lawful act. Where the person dissuaded suffers sudden death due to his own disease and his close relative claims that the actor should bear the tortious liability, the People's court should not support such a claim.

Relevant Provisions: Article 6 of the *Tort Law of the P.R.C.*

Basic Facts

At around 19:40 on 23 September 2019, Guo rode a folding bicycle to the exit on the south gate of the Boshi Mingcheng Community from the road on the east of the square near the south gate of the Community and collided with Luo, a five-year-old child, in the square, resulting in Luo's injury and bleeding on the right jaw and fall to the ground. After seeing this situation, Sun Wei, who took his child playing there, helped Luo up and contacted Li A (here and below, part of name withheld, mother of Luo) through the voice calling of WeChat, but there was no response. Sun Wei then asked a neighbor nearby to notify Li A and asked Guo to wait for Luo's parents to deal with the matter. Guo said that Luo had run into him and that he had his own business and needed to leave. As a consequence, he had a verbal argument with Sun Wei. Sun Wei dissuaded Guo from leaving by standing in front of Guo's bicycle.

The first video of the incident showed that Guo moved forward the bicycle, Sun Wei stood in front of the bicycle, held the mobile phone in Sun's left hand, grasped the handlebar of the bicycle with Sun's right hand, and pushed the handlebar with Sun's right hand twice after eight seconds. The argument between Guo and Sun Wei was mainly as follows: Guo said to Sun Wei, "Are you reasonable?" Sun Wei said, "I am reasonable and I ask you to wait for a moment". Guo said, "You have nothing to do, but I have my own business". Sun Wei said, "Am I wrong? You ran into a child". Guo said, "I have my own business". Sun Wei said, "You ran into a child and I had a lengthy talk with you". Guo said, "Is it that I ran into the child or the child ran into me?" The second section of the video showed that Sun Wei, Guo, Li B (here and below, part of name withheld, a security guard of the Boshi Mingcheng Community), and Wu were all around the second stone seat counted from south to north in the eastern exit on the south gate of the Boshi Mingcheng Community. Sun Wei held a mobile phone in his left hand and put his right hand on the handlebar of Guo's bicycle for about five seconds. Li B and Wu persuaded Guo not to curse at Sun Wei and Guo said that he would call 110. At that time, Guo was heated with passion and he cursed at Sun Wei.

At around 19:46 on 23 September 2019, Sun Wei called 110. Guo parked the bicycle and sat on the first stone seat counted from south to north in the eastern exit on the south gate of the Boshi Mingcheng Community. In less than two minutes after he sat on the stone seat, Guo fell to the ground. The video of the incident with the duration of 14 s submitted by Sun Wei showed that after falling to the ground, Guo attempted to get up; and Sun Wei was operating his mobile phone and reporting the location.

At around 19:48 on 23 September 2019, Sun Wei called 120. Sun Wei sent his child home and returned to the scene. The medical care personnel arrived at the scene and implemented the rescue of Guo. Guo died of sudden cardiac arrest despite all rescue efforts.

It was also found that Guo was once admitted to the Central Hospital of Xinyang City, Henan Province by complaining of "unconsciousness accompanied by limb twitch for one hour" on 4 September 2019 and he was then diagnosed with "right cerebral infarction, secondary epilepsy, hypertensive disease of level 3 (extreme risk), Type 2 diabetes, cerebrovascular malformation, and paroxysmal atrial fibrillation". The Central Hospital of Xinyang City issued a critical condition notice to Guo based on his diseases and the notice showed that "after active treatment of the medical care personnel, the patient is still in a critical condition and there is possible further deterioration of the disease and the life of the patient may be endangered at any time". During the period of treatment in the Central Hospital of Xinyang City, possible risks and complications of Guo were stated in the records of communication, including: the symptoms of cerebral infarction may be worsened; cerebral hernia may form respiratory and cardiac arrest; and nausea and arrhythmia may cause sudden death. It was recorded in the progress note of Guo on 16 September 2019 that Guo and his family members requested discharge from the hospital and the request was approved by the chief physician.

Liu Minglian (Guo's wife) and Guo Lili and Guo Shuangshuang (Guo's daughters) filed a lawsuit and claimed that Sun Wei should bear the tortious liability of compensation and Xinyang Branch of Henan Lanting Real Estate Management Co., Ltd. should bear the compensatory liability for poor management.

Judgment

On 30 December 2019, the Primary People's Court of Pingqiao District, Xinyang City, Henan Province entered a civil judgment ((2019) Yu 1503 Min Chu 8878) that the claims of the plaintiffs Liu Minglian, Guo Lili, and Guo Shuangshuang should be dismissed. After the judgment was pronounced, no party appealed. The judgment of first instance took effect.

Reasons for Judgment

According to the effective judgment entered by the People's court, the issues of this case are whether the defendant Sun Wei has committed a tort, whether there was causation between Sun Wei's act of dissuading Guo from leaving and Guo's death; and whether Sun Wei was at negligence.

First, after Guo collided with young Luo by riding a bicycle, Luo got injured and bled on his right jaw and fell to the ground. As one party involved in the incident, Guo failed to actively and reasonably deal with the matter and was determined to leave. For any act detrimental to children's health and infringing on children's lawful rights and interests, any organization or individual has the right to dissuade such an act or file a complaint with the relevant department. As a minor, Luo has relatively weak self-protection ability and requires special protection from adults. After seeing that Guo collided with Luo, to protect Luo's interests, Sun Wei asked Guo to wait for Luo's mother to deal with the collision matter and the act of Sun Wei was in line with common sense. According to the time when the videos were sent in the chat records of the group of Boshi Mingcheng owners on the night of the incident, the telephone records of Sun Wei's calls to 110 and 120, and other evidence, it may be confirmed that Sun Wei's dissuasion of Guo lasted for about eight minutes. In the process of dissuasion, although Sun Wei and Guo had a verbal argument, the remarks of Sun Wei were not provocative. Sun Wei put his hand on the handlebar of Guo's bicycle, but there was no physical conflict between both parties. The manner and content of Sun Wei's dissuasion were all within normal limits. Therefore, Sun Wei's dissuasion was a lawful act, did not exceed reasonable limits, and was not illegal and it should be recognized and supported.

Second, Guo had several diseases including cerebral infarction, hypertensive disease, heart disease, diabetes, and secondary epilepsy. In the month when the incident occurred, he was once hospitalized and one week before the incident occurred, and he was discharged from the hospital at the request of himself and his family members. Sun Wei dissuaded Guo from leaving, Guo sat on a stone seat and died from sudden cardiac arrest. The death of Guo was regrettable. As close relatives of the deceased Guo, Liu Minglian, Guo Lili, and Guo Shuangshuang were sad and filed this lawsuit, which was understandable. Sun Wei's dissuasion did not result in Guo's death and the actual reason for Guo's death was sudden cardiac arrest. As a consequence, there was no legal causation between Sun Wei's dissuasion and Guo's death.

Third, although Sun Wei dissuaded Guo from leaving, which evoked Guo's rage, Sun Wei was not acquainted with Guo before the incident involved occurred and he did not know that Guo had several dangerous diseases. Sun Wei dissuaded Guo from safeguarding the interests of a child and he did not have the intention or negligence to harm Guo. After Guo fell to the ground, Sun Wei called 120 for treatment and rescue. It may be seen that Sun Wei did not foresee the death of Guo and he was not at negligence for Guo's death.

(Judges of the effective judgment: Yi Song, Peng Jie, and Zhou Chengyun)

2.4 Pengyu Case as a Special Illustration for Fact-Finding Difficulty

The Pengyu case, which is named after the name of the defendant of the case and was adjudicated by a first-instance court on the merits, has attracted much attention since 2007. This case, especially concerning its legal reasoning regarding the happening of the accident, must be one of the most well-known civil cases in China. Among others, this judgment provides a proper illustration of the judicial difficulty in fact-finding area. While it could contribute to the overview of Chinese civil judgments, e.g. showing the style of real Chinese judgments (this decision was given even over 15 years ago), it could also be used to explore other crucial issues discussed in this contribution, e.g. the use of *prima facie* evidence and the legal elements which may be significant for making judgments of good quality.[12]

Concretely speaking, it is argued by this contribution that there should be two modes of applying the *prima facie* evidence, namely the ordinary one and the reduced one. The first mode has already been taken into consideration, where the application of *prima facie* evidence is generally allowed when its possibility is sufficient enough. If not, the *prima facie* evidence is not *prima facie* enough and the parties and the judge have to come back to the ordinary proving system and use the means of evidence. Nevertheless, the judge should have a theoretical tool like the reduced mode of the *prima facie* evidence, which could help the judge fulfill the judicial duty to give reasons in civil cases. It is an exception to the ordinary mode. The judge shall search for any other possibility with some factual indication in the case which may overturn the presumed fact according to the *prima facie* evidence. If the judge is convinced that there is no possibility at all while the standard of proof could be reduced, the application of *prima facie* evidence is able to eventually settle the factual disputes. The party who bears the burden of proof is supposed to argue the non-existence of any other possibility, which means shouldering the burden of allegation at the same time, and convincing the judge with a preponderance of evidence.[13]

The major issue in this case pertains to the question of whether both parties collided with each other. Without solid evidence to prove this factual allegation, what should the judge do to ascertain the disputed facts of the case?

The Primary People's Court of Gulou District

Civil Judgment

(2007) Gu Min Yi Chu Zi No. 212

Plaintiff: Xu Shoulan, female, Han nationality, born on 9 August 1942, residing at No. X12, Nanjing City.

Attorney: Tang Ning, lawyer from Nanjing × Law Firm.

Defendant: Peng Yu, male, Han nationality, born on 2 July 1980, an employee of the Jiangsu × Co., Ltd., residing at No. × 2 × 3–1, Nanjing City.

Citizen Agent: Li Shu, female, Han nationality, born on 8 August 198X, residing at No. XX 19, Nanjing City.

Attorney: Gao Shidong, lawyer from Jiangsu × Law Firm.

As for the dispute of personal injury damages between the plaintiff Xu Shoulan and the defendant Peng Yu, after accepting the case, the court formed a collegial

[12] In detail, see Cao (2020); Cao (2019).

[13] Cao (2019).

bench in accordance with the law and held the hearing in public. The plaintiff Xu Shoulan and her attorney Tang Ning, the defendant Peng Yu and his attorneys Li Shu and Gao Shidong appeared in court. So far, the trial of this case has been concluded.

The plaintiff Xu Shoulan alleged that on the morning of 20 November 2006, she waited for Bus No. 83 at Shuiximen Bus Station. At about 9: 30 a.m., two No. 83 buses arrived at the station. The plaintiff was about to take the second No. 83 bus. When the plaintiff reached the back door of the first bus, she was knocked down by the defendant, who rushed out of the first bus. As a result, the plaintiff suffered a fracture of the left femoral neck and was hospitalized. Because the plaintiff and the defendant failed to reach a mediation agreement in the Chengzhong Police Station of Nanjing Public Security Bureau Public Traffic Security Sub-bureau, the plaintiff filed a lawsuit requiring for demanding the defendant to compensate the plaintiff for medical expense of CNY 40,460.7, nursing expense of CNY 4,497 (nursing expense of CNY 897 during hospitalization and nursing expense of CNY 3,600 after leaving hospital), nutrition expense of CNY 3,000, food subsidies of CNY 346, food subsidies for hospitalization of CNY 630, compensation for disability of CNY 71,985.6, compensation for mental damage of CNY 15,000 and appraisal fee of CNY 500, with a total amount of CNY 136,419.3, and to require the defendant to bear the litigation costs of this case.

The defendant, Peng Yu, argued that he was the first to get out of the bus. Before getting out of the bus, someone on the bus bumped into him from behind, but after getting out of the bus, there was no collision between the plaintiff and the defendant. When the defendant found that the plaintiff had fallen down, he did a good deed and helped the plaintiff to stand up instead of colliding with and hurting the plaintiff. The plaintiff did not have sufficient evidence to prove that the defendant had committed any tort, and the defendant did not infringe the plaintiff's personal rights objectively, so the defendant should not bear compensation liability in torts law. It was not conducive to the promotion of social justice to assume liability for doing good deeds. The plaintiff's claims lacked legal and factual basis, and the defendant required the court to dismiss the claims in accordance with law.

The court ascertained that on the morning of 20 November 2006, the plaintiff waited for bus No. 83 at Shuiximen Bus Station, and at about 9: 30 a.m., two No. 83 buses pulled into the station simultaneously. When (the plaintiff) arrived at the back door of the first bus, in order to catch the latter bus, coincidentally, the defendant also exited the bus through the same door. The plaintiff fell and got injured. The defendant noticed and helped the plaintiff to the side. After the relatives of the plaintiff arrived, the defendant and other relatives of the plaintiff took the plaintiff to the hospital. Later the plaintiff was diagnosed with left femoral neck fracture and was hospitalized for hip replacement surgery, which resulted in losses of medical, nursing and nutrition expenses and so forth.

After the accident, the Chengzhong Police Station of Nanjing Public Security Bureau Public Traffic Security Sub-bureau received the report, handled the accident according to the law and prepared interrogation transcripts. After the case was brought to the Court, the police officer who was responsible for the accident went to the court and made a statement about the main course of the accident and produced conversation records, the main contents of which included: There was a collision between the plaintiff and the defendant. The plaintiff did not object to the said records of conversation. The defendant thought that the conversation records of the responsible police were the restatement of interrogation transcripts of both the plaintiff and the defendant given on the day of the accident and the next day. The conversation records were not checked with the interrogation transcripts, and the authenticity of the conversation records could not be ascertained. Therefore, the conversation records could not be taken as the basis to ascertain the facts of the case.

During the trial of the case, Chengzhong Police Station of Nanjing Public Security Bureau Public Traffic Security Sub-bureau, which handled the case, submitted the electronic file and its transcribed materials of the interrogation transcripts of the defendant. The electronic file showed that it was made on 21 November 2006, the second day after the accident. The electronic file of the interrogation transcripts mainly included: Peng Yu said he did not bump into Xu Shoulan, but he was bumped into by Xu Shoulan. The plaintiff did not object to the electronic file and the transcribed materials of the interrogation transcripts and believed that the contents clarified the fact of the collision between the plaintiff and the defendant. The defendant did not admit the evidence on the ground that the electronic file and the transcribed materials of the interrogation transcripts were duplicates without the original to be verified. Then, the authenticity of the transcripts could not be ascertained and a lot of the contents were not what the defendant had said. The current case was a civil case and the Public Security Bureau had no power to collect evidence. Therefore, such electronic files and the transcribed materials could not be used as the basis to ascertain the facts of the case.

The defendant applied for Chen Erchun to attend the court as a witness. Chen Erchun testified as follows: On 20 November 2006, he was waiting for No. 21 bus at Shuiximen Bus Station, and the plaintiff was waiting next to him. Not long after, two buses came over and the plaintiff wanted to take the second bus and ran over in front of him. At that time, the plaintiff was holding a bag and a thermos bottle in her hands. Later when he saw the plaintiff fall down to the ground, the defendant as well as he went to help the plaintiff up. However, he did not see the moment when the plaintiff fell down to the ground, nor did he see the whole process of the plaintiff falling down. When he saw that, the plaintiff had already fallen down to the ground and the defendant was holding the plaintiff up. In the afternoon of that day, as notified by Chengzhong Police Station of Nanjing Public Security Bureau Public Traffic Security Sub-bureau, he went there to take the record. A policeman surnamed Shen received him. The plaintiff objected to the testimony of the witness and claimed that there was a third party on the scene at the time of the accident, but the third party was not the witness as applied by the defendant. The defendant affirmed the testimony of the witness and held that such testimony should be taken as the basis to ascertain the facts of the case.

It was also found out by the court that on the day of the accident, the defendant once paid more than CNY 200 to the plaintiff and did not ask the plaintiff to return afterward. With regard to the reason for the payment, the parties stated differently: the plaintiff thought it was an advance payment of the compensation while the defendant thought it was a loan.

During the trial hearing, the parties also had different opinions on the liability for the accident and whether there was collision between the plaintiff and the defendant. The plaintiff claimed that she fell down and was injured in the collision with the defendant who got off the bus first; the defendant claimed that he did not collide with the plaintiff and that it was a good deed for him to hold the plaintiff.

Due to the failure of the plaintiff and the defendant to reach an agreement on compensation, the plaintiff filed a lawsuit with the court requiring the defendant to compensate the plaintiff's losses including medical expenses, nursing expenses, nutrition expenses and food subsidies in the hospital and undertake the litigation costs of the case.

During the court proceedings, the plaintiff applied for a judicial authentication on the degree of her disability and the court authorized Nanjing Xindun Expert Institute to do the authentication according to the law. The authentication result showed that the injury of the appraised person, Xu Shoulan, constituted a degree of disability of eight.

Due to the disagreements of the parties, the mediation attempt failed.

The aforementioned facts could be supported by statements of the parties concerned; the hospitalization records and bills for medical expense provided by the plaintiff, the oral testimony of the witness Chen Erchun who was applied by the defendant, the plaintiff's inquiry records, the electronic files of the defendant's interrogation records and its transcription materials submitted by Chengzhong Police Station of Nanjing Public Security Bureau Public Traffic Security Sub-bureau; the authentication report entrusted by the court, the interview records of the court and the court hearing records and so forth.

The court held that the legitimate rights and interests of the parties shall be protected by law. The plaintiff and the defendant did not object to the basic fact of the case that the plaintiff fell to the ground and was injured when she was going to take the bus at Shuiximen Bus Station on the morning of 20 November 2006. However, the parties had different opinions on whether the plaintiff was knocked down and injured by the defendant. Based on the claims and defenses of both parties, the court summarized the disputed issues as follows: first, whether the plaintiff and the defendant collided with each other; second, the amount of the plaintiff's losses; third, whether the defendant should bear the losses of the plaintiff. The relevant evaluation of the court is as follows.

I. Whether the Plaintiff and the Defendant Collided with Each Other

The court held that the plaintiff was injured after the collision with the defendant for the following reasons.

(1) Based on the analysis of the daily experience, in addition to being knocked down by others' external force, the plaintiff also has other reasons attributable to herself, such as tripping and slipping. However, neither party stated the fact that the plaintiff tripped or slipped at the court hearing, and the defendant did

not provide counter-evidence with respect to the fact; therefore, based on the existing evidence of the case, the court should focus on the analysis of the external force that caused the plaintiff to be knocked down. After a person is knocked down by an external force, the first thing to do is to determine the source of the external force and to identify the person who has collided with the external force. If the person who has collided with the external force escapes, the first reaction of the person who has been knocked down is to call for help and ask someone to help stop the person who escapes. The accident occurred at a bus station with many people, which is a public place. The accident happened in the morning and it should be in relatively good view. The course of the accident was very short, so the person who knocked down the plaintiff could not have escaped easily. According to the defendant's admission, he was the first person to get off the bus, so it was more likely that he collided with the plaintiff.

If the defendant was doing a good deed, it would have been more practical to catch the person who knocked down the plaintiff rather than just helping the plaintiff stand up out of the kindness of heart; if the defendant was doing a good deed, according to social sense and kindness, he could have told the plaintiff's family what had happened and asked the plaintiff's family to take the plaintiff to the hospital, and then left. But the defendant did not make such a choice, and his conduct was clearly contrary to common sense.

Interrogation and inquiry by Chengzhong Police Station of Nanjing Public Security Bureau Public Traffic Security Sub-bureau of the parties concerned is the basic method to deal with public security disputes. The evidence submitted in this case can corroborate each other and form a chain of evidence and therefore should be admitted. Even though the defendant objected without providing any contrary evidence, his defense will not be taken by the court. According to the relevant evidence such as the interview transcripts of the plaintiff by Chengzhong Police Station of Nanjing Public Security Bureau Public Traffic Security Sub-bureau, the electronic files of the interview transcripts of the defendant and transcribed materials, the defendant did not deny that he had collided with the plaintiff, but merely assumed that it was the plaintiff who had bumped into the defendant. Based on the evidence and the above analysis, it can be concluded that the plaintiff was knocked down and injured after colliding with the defendant.

(2) The testimony of the witness Chen Erchun applied by the defendant could not prove the cause of the plaintiff falling to the ground, and the possibility of the defendant and the plaintiff colliding with each other cannot be ruled out. As the witness was unable to provide documents such as an ID card to prove his identity in court, and the court was unable to verify his true identity in court, which led the plaintiff to believe that the third party who was present at the scene was not a witness before court. The witness submitted his ID card on the second day after the court hearing to prove his identity, and the court confirmed the witness' identity, rejecting the plaintiff's claim that the third party who was present at the scene was not a witness before court. The witness Chen Erchun stated in court that he did not see the process of the plaintiff falling down, and

what he saw was only the condition of the plaintiff after the plaintiff had fallen to the ground. Therefore he could not prove the specific cause of the plaintiff's fall, and the possibility of the plaintiff and the defendant colliding with each other cannot be ruled out.

(3) Based on the evidence available, the defendant did not mention the circumstance of doing boldly what is righteous both before the court hearing and during the first hearing, but made the statement only in the second hearing. If he was really doing boldly what is righteous, it is impossible for him not to rely on it as a defense in the first place during the dispute, and the timing of the statement is not convincing. Therefore, his claim of doing boldly what is righteous is not accepted.

(4) The defendant paid more than CNY 200 to the plaintiff on the day of the accident and had not asked the plaintiff to return the sum. The plaintiff and the defendant unanimously admitted the fact of the above payment, but their statements on the reason of payment were different: the plaintiff thought it was the compensation payment in advance, while the defendant thought it was the loan. According to ordinary daily experience, the plaintiff and the defendant never knew each other, and usually they will not borrow money rashly. Even if it was the loan alleged by the defendant, when there is the possibility of bearing the responsibility for the accident, the defendant should ask another uninterested person on the bus station to testify, or explain the situation to the relative of the plaintiff and ask for written materials such as receipt for a loan (or explanation). However, in this case, the defendant has done nothing mentioned, and in the circumstance that the plaintiff was accompanied to the hospital by her relative, it is not very possible for the defendant to lend the loan to the plaintiff; and if the defendant gets someone else injured by collision, the most reasonable thing to do is to pay some money in advance. The witness of the defendant proved that both the plaintiff and the defendant went to Chengzhong Police Station of Nanjing Public Security Bureau Public Traffic Security Sub-bureau to handle this accident, and this fact can be presumed that the plaintiff thought she was knocked down by the defendant other than any other person at that time, in which case it is more impossible for the defendant to offer the loan. Based on the above facts and analysis, it can be determined that the monetary payment is not a loan but money for compensation.

II. Scope and Specific Amount of the Plaintiff's Losses

(1) Medical expense. According to the evidence provided by the plaintiff, such as the hospitalization records and the disability appraisal report, the medical expense claimed by the plaintiff is necessary for the relevant diseases caused by accident, and there are corresponding medical instruments to prove it. Therefore, the medical expense of CNY 40,460.7 claimed by the plaintiff complies with law and is affirmed by the Court.

(2) Nursing expense. The nursing expense claimed by the plaintiff is CNY 4,497, including nursing expense of CNY 897 during hospitalization and CNY 3,600 afterward. As the plaintiff is an elder in her sixties, and her left femoral neck

fracture was caused by the accident which constitutes a grade eight disability, she indeed needs nursing care since the injury until her rehabilitation. Therefore, the nursing expense of CNY 4,497 claimed by the plaintiff complies with law and is affirmed by the Court.

(3) Food subsidies for hospitalization. The plaintiff was hospitalized for a total of 35 days, and the food subsidies claimed by the plaintiff are CNY 630. This claim complies with law and is affirmed by the Court.

Additionally, the plaintiff claimed for CNY 346 also for food subsidies and provided the hospitalization records and vouchers to prove it. Since such expense is within the scope of food subsidies for hospitalization mentioned, and the claim of CNY 346 and the aforementioned CNY 630 are repeated, the court did not support the plaintiff's claim.

(4) Appraisal fee. The plaintiff claimed for CNY 500 for disability appraisal fee, which can be proved by invoice, and is affirmed by the Court.
(5) Compensation for disability. The disability compensation claimed by the plaintiff is CNY 71,985.6. However, according to the plaintiff's medical history and disability appraisal report, the plaintiff is disabled at grade eight. Therefore, according to relevant regulations, the compensation should be confirmed as CNY 67,603.2 (14,084 * (20–4) * 30%).
(6) Nutrition expense. Considering the degree of injury of the plaintiff, the court set the compensation amount of CNY 1,000 at its discretion.

In conclusion, each of the plaintiff's losses amounts to CNY 114,690.9.

III. Whether the Defendant Shall Bear the Plaintiff's Losses

According to the previous analysis, the plaintiff was injured after the collision with the defendant and suffered losses. Whether the plaintiff and the defendant shall be accountable for the losses shall be determined by applying relevant principles in the *Tort Law of the P.R.C.*

In this case, when the plaintiff, who was chasing the second bus arrived at the back door of the front bus, she collided with the defendant suddenly, who was the first one getting off the front bus. When chasing the bus, the plaintiff could not foresee that she would collide with the defendant; meanwhile, when getting off the bus, the defendant's vision was restricted and he could not accurately judge the situation about the back door. Therefore, the plaintiff and the defendant were not at negligence in the accident. Considering this, in this case, the losses suffered by the plaintiff ought to be properly distributed between the parties based on the principle of fair liability. Fair liability means that when both parties are not at negligence and the liability without negligence is not applicable according to law, the court, based on the concept of fairness, taking into consideration the losses of the victim, the property status of the parties and other relevant circumstances, orders the injuring party to partially compensate for the property losses of the victim, and the parties shall distribute the losses properly. According to the facts of this case, it is appropriate for the Court to use its discretion to require the defendant to compensate 40% of the plaintiff's losses.

As to the issue on the compensation for mental damages claimed by the plaintiff. Although the accident caused considerable mental sufferings to the plaintiff, as neither party was at negligence, the plaintiff's claim for compensation of mental damages in the amount of CNY 15,000 has no legal basis and shall not be supported by the Court.

In summary, in order to safeguard the legitimate rights and interests of the parties, in accordance with Article 98 and Article 119 of the *General Principles of the Civil Law of the P.R.C.*, and Article 17 of the *Interpretation of the SPC on Some Issues Concerning the Application of Law in the Trial of Cases on Compensation for Personal Injury* (2003), the Court hereby renders the following verdict:

Within ten days from the date when this judgment takes effect, the defendant Peng Yu shall pay Xu Shoulan CNY 45,876.36 in one lump sum to the plaintiff.

If the defendant Peng Yu fails to perform the obligation of monetary payment within the period as specified in this judgment, he shall, in accordance with Article 232 of the *CPL* (1991), pay double debt interest for the period of delay in performance.

The filing fee of this case is CNY 890 and the other litigation costs are CNY 980, totaling CNY 1,870. The plaintiff Xu Shoulan should bear CNY 1,170 and Peng Yu should bear CNY 700, which has been paid by the plaintiff in advance. Therefore, the defendant shall pay the same to the plaintiff when performing its obligation.

If the parties do not accept the judgment, an appeal may be filed in Nanjing Intermediate People's Court of Jiangsu Province by submitting an appeal to the Court with copies according to the number of the other party within 15 days after service of this judgment.

Chief Judge Wang Hao

Acting Judge ×××

Acting Judge ××

3 September 2007

Trainee Clerk ××

2.5 Guiding Opinions of the Chinese Judiciary

On 1 June 2018, the SPC published concise guidance to the courts at all levels regarding the adjudicative techniques in preparing the reasoning of civil judgments, i.e. *Opinions Reasoning Judicial Decisions*. Based on the translation of PKULAW,[14] this contribution presents an extracted and modified version of the translation to show how the Chinese judiciary would expect civil judgments of good quality.

[14] The translation is provided by www.pkulaw.com and modified by the author. https://www.pkulaw.com/en_law/b3783fd833eff3a1bdfb.html?flag=list.

Article 1

The purpose of the analysis and reasoning in judicial decisions is, by elucidating the process of making the decision's conclusion and the justifications therefor, to improve the acceptability of decisions and achieve the organic unity of legal effect and social effect; and its main value is to enhance equity and transparency of adjudicative conducts, regulate the exercise of adjudicative power, improve judicial credibility and judicial authority, exert the role of adjudication in settling disputes and guiding values, promote core socialist values, strive to enable the people to feel impartiality and justice in every judicial case, practically safeguard the lawful rights and interests of litigants, and promote social harmony and stability.

Article 2

The analysis and reasoning in judicial decisions shall elucidate factual grounds, explain the facts of the case convicted by the decisions and the bases and reasons therefor and demonstrate the objectivity, equity, and accuracy of the factual conviction of the case; explain legal principles, and state the law on which the decision is based and the reasons for the application of the law; clarify the common sense, and to reflect the coordination of the statutory rules, natural laws, and common sense and comply with the mainstream social values; as well as pay attention to the literary form, and use standard language and accurate expressions, apply clear logic, and rationally exploit reasoning skills, so as to enhance the effect of reasoning.

Article 3

The analysis and reasoning in judicial decisions shall be with correct position, legal content, and due procedure and comply with the spirit and requirements of the core socialist values; reasoning should be done by centering on the examination and determination of evidence, finding of facts, and application of law, reflect the reasoning process, and achieve clear logic; reasoning should aim at claims and disputes issues and consider the situation of court hearings, and have clear objects in discussion; and the judge should provide the reasoning in adequate length according to the social impact of cases, trial proceedings applied, stages of civil proceedings, and other conditions, namely reasoning briefly for simple cases and delicately for complicated cases, and strive to serve the purpose precisely.

Article 4

The determination of evidence in the judicial decisions shall consider the production of evidence and cross-examination by all parties to legal proceedings, the investigation and verification of evidence by the court, and other information, comply with the evidential rules as well as apply logical reasoning and *prima facie* evidence, and if necessary use means such as presumption and judicial notice, conduct comprehensive, objective, and equitable examination and determination with a focus on the relevance, legality and authenticity of evidence and elucidate the reasons for the admissibility and probative value of the evidential means.

…

Article 6

Judicial decisions shall make an analysis and reasoning based on production of evidence, cross-examination, court hearings, court's investigation and verification of evidence, and other information and focus on the facts found by decisions or disputed facts. When the facts are established on the basis of indirect evidence, the reasoning shall center on whether there is a corroborative relationship between indirect evidence and whether a complete proof system can be formed, and so forth. When the facts are established by presumption, the reasons for the initiation of presumption, the facts and reasons for rebuttal shall be stated, and the process of adjudication shall be explained.

Article 7

Where no party to legal proceedings has disputes over the application of law, and it is unnecessary to elucidate the meaning of laws, the judicial decisions shall focus the analysis and reasoning on the content and standard of adjudication. Otherwise, the judge shall respond to the focus of the legal disputes item by item and explain the reasons. Where there is a concurrence or conflict of laws during the application of law, the judicial decisions shall state the reasons for the selection. For a civil case where no legal rule can be taken as the direct basis for making judgments, the judge shall first seek the most similar rules for making a judgment; and if there are no similar rules, the judge may make the judgment based on custom, legal principles, and legislative purposes and so forth, while the judge should sufficiently justify and reason the judgment's basis via reasonably using legal interpretative methods. When a judge makes the decision by exercising the discretion, the judge shall adhere to the principles of lawfulness, reasonableness, equity, and prudence, fully justify the basis for the exercise of discretion and clarify the relevant factors considered for the discretion.

Article 8

For the following cases, judicial decisions shall strengthen analysis and reasoning: difficult and complex cases; cases involving major disputes between parties to legal proceedings; cases attracting extensive publicity in society and having a major impact; … cases of new type, or which may become model cases; cases whose final judgments are challenged by the state prosecutor which lead to the commencement of trial supervision proceedings; cases whose results are reversed by the court of appeal, or which are remanded for a new trial; cases for a new trial; cases for retrial; and cases otherwise requiring strengthened reasoning.

Article 9

For the following cases, judicial decisions may simplify analysis and reasoning: cases heard using simplified proceedings or small claims proceedings; cases heard using special proceedings, summary procedure for debt collection, or the procedure for publicizing a public notice for urging and asserting claims in case that a negotiable instrument is stolen, lost or extinguished; …cases to which ordinary proceedings do apply while little disputes exist between the parties to the legal proceedings; and cases otherwise suitable for simplified reasoning.

Article 10

Judicial decisions made by courts of appeal or courts of retrial shall strengthen analysis and reasoning with a focus on the claims and grounds with respect to the appeals of the parties, challenges for trial supervision proceedings initiated by the state prosecutor, or petitions for retrial. If judicial decisions made by a court of appeal or court of retrial found facts different from those by the court of first instance or court of prior trial, or if it is held that the court of first instance or court of prior trial establishes facts ambiguously, and applies the law erroneously, reasoning specifically shall be made on the basis of facts ascertained and corrected application of law; and for the matter for which the court of first instance or court of prior trial has stated the reason thoroughly, and each party to the legal proceedings has no dispute, or for the matter for which there is no new evidence or new grounds, analysis and reasoning may be simplified.

Article 11

Judicial decisions shall be prepared according to the technical specifications and standards as provided by *Specifications for Decisions, Style of Litigation Documents for Civil Petition for Retrial, Specifications for Preparing Judicial Decisions in Foreign-related Commercial and Maritime Cases, Model Legal Instruments of People's Courts for Bankruptcy Procedure (for Trial Implementation), Style of Litigation Documents for Civil Simplified Proceedings (for Trial Implementation)*, …, and other documents, provided that the style and structure of the parts of convicted facts and reasoning may be adjusted adequately according to the circumstances of the case.

Article 12

Where a judicial decision cites normative legal documents for analysis and reasoning, the citation shall be governed by the relevant provisions such as *Provisions on Citation in Judicial Decisions*, and the title of the normative legal documents and the number of sub-paragraph, paragraph, or article shall be specified accurately and completely; and if it is necessary to use quotation marks to cite provisions, the expressions shall be accurate and complete.

Article 13

Besides the provisions of laws, regulations, and judicial interpretations, judges may justify the reasoning of their judgments using the following means, in order to improve the legitimacy and acceptability of the judgment's conclusions: guiding cases issued by the SPC; normative documents for adjudicative business issued by the SPC which are not judicial interpretations; self-evident truth, common sense, *prima facie* evidence, trading practices, custom, and professional ethics; legislative statements and other legislative materials; materials used for historical, systematic, comparative, and other legal construing methods; legal principles and generally accepted academic viewpoints; and other means not in conflict with normative legal documents such as laws and judicial interpretations.

Article 14

In order to facilitate analysis and reasoning, judicial decisions may adopt any of the following means of expression if adequate: if the case is complicated, key points of adjudication may be listed; if the facts of the case or the computation of amounts is complicated, forms or tables may be attached; if it is easier to describe clearly the content of the adjudication by appending diagrams, diagrams may be attached; if there is too much evidence, the evidence or evidence list for the whole case constituting the evidence chain may be presented by appendixes; and other kinds of annex may be adopted.

Article 15

Judicial decisions shall contain normalized, accurate, clear, simple, solemn, and condensed expressions and generally refrain from dialects, slangs, idioms, rare words, ancient words, and foreign words; if they must be used for special circumstances, their actual meanings shall be given. The analysis and reasoning in judicial decisions shall avoid subjective and arbitrary expression, inappropriate rhetorical methods, and academic writing styles, abstain from terms derogating from dignity, of strong emotion, or obviously contrary to common sense, and refrain from the direct use, without analysis and justification, of expressions such as "there is no factual and legal basis and hence, this court does not grant the claim" to be the conclusive determination of the decisions.

...

Article 21

These Guiding Opinions shall come into force on 13 June 2018.

References

Cao Z (2016) On the effect of guiding cases in China and their application in the legal process. Journal of Comparative Law 6:111–134 (in Chinese)

Cao Z (2019) Two modes of applying the *prima facie* evidence: reconsidering the 'Pengyu' decision. The Jurist 5:31–44+192 (in Chinese)

Cao Z (2020) Reconsidering the fact-finding reasoning in the 'Pengyu' decision. Northern Legal Science 3:89–98 (in Chinese)

Li Y (2010) Why guiding cases are not binding. Law and Social Development 4:86–96 (in Chinese)

SPC (2024) Introduction to the SPC Gazette. http://gongbao.court.gov.cn/SinglePage.html?result=introduction. Accessed 2 May 2024 (in Chinese)

Yang J (2010) Change of civil cases reported in the "SPC Gazette." Modern Law Science 4:182–193 (in Chinese)

Chapter 3
Civil Judgments in China: Structure, Reasoning and Reform

3.1 Introduction

It is crucial to focus on the structure and reasoning process of judicial decisions, while their diversified functions at different levels are recognized among jurists.[1] Among others, the SPC released in 2018 a comprehensive judicial interpretation under the title of the *Opinions Reasoning Judicial Decisions* (Chap. 2).[2] Although there are various calls for reforming judicial decisions at different levels, it is difficult to break the path dependence established since the SPC began to experiment with its model style of judicial decisions in 1992. In terms of their structure, the Chinese style of judicial decisions arbitrarily separates the ascertainment of facts ("it is ascertained upon trial") from the evaluation of evidence and application of law ("the court considers that"), dividing them into two distinct parts. The "it is ascertained upon trial" part typically only presents the fact-finding conclusion, while the reasons to justify the judgment, namely the evaluation of evidence and the process of factual determination, are usually taken as the "reasoning of judicial decisions" and placed in the part of "the court considers that".

In the 2016 version of *Style Litigation Documents*, the "it is ascertained upon trial" part has been replaced by "the court ascertains that", and the judge must state whether the evidence submitted by the parties is admissible (including the opinions and reasons for examining the disputed evidence), and clarify their opinions and reasons for the ascertainment of facts.[3] The original structure of judicial decisions and the newly revised requirements reflect the good intention to distinguish between factual and legal issues. Moreover, the *Style of Litigation Documents* further clarifies the necessity and placement of the reasoning of fact-finding.

---

[1] For example, Hu (2009, pp. 48–49); Fu (2000).

[2] For the provisions on reasoning in previous judicial documents and the drafting process of the *Opinions Reasoning Judicial Decisions*, see Liu (2020, pp. 6–11, 383–425).

[3] Shen (2016, pp. 248, 251–252).

Z. Cao, *Civil Judgments at First Instance*, Contemporary Chinese Civil and Commercial Law, https://doi.org/10.1007/978-981-97-8662-6_3

In practice, the aforementioned structure of judicial decisions may lead to issues such as judges and their judgments not giving adequate attention to parties' statements and submissions in the judicial decision-making process, the uncertain status of evidence submissions, examination, and certification, repetition of fact-finding in the "the court considers that" part, separation of fact-finding from the reasoning within the judgment,[4] and insufficient notice of the reasoning for fact-finding. At the same time, the structure of a judicial decision not only involves the division of different parts within it, but also covers the fulfillment of reasoning by the judicial decisions. Such duty of judicial reasoning is also clearly stipulated by Article 155 paragraph 1 of the *CPL* and Article 105 of the *ICPL*. Since judicial reasoning has its roots in written judgments themselves, all parts of a written judgment are equally closely related to the function of reasoning, which not only determines the place of reasoning, but also affects the fundamental rules regarding the methods and forms of reasoning.

Observers usually challenge the reasoning of judicial decisions based on empirical research. For example, as one of the honorable Justice of the SPC, Hu Yunteng once pointed out that there are some drawbacks in judicial reasoning. To be named are the formalization, unwillingness, fear of judicial reasoning, and improper reasoning by the judges. Then, according to Hu Yunteng, it is necessary to emphasize the nature of the case, legal principles, theoretical understanding of the laws, the circumstances of the case, and literary rules within the reasoning.[5] Some judges also think that the insufficient reasoning of judicial decisions can be categorized into four types: overly abstract and general type, reading by the book type, logically confusing type, and simplistic and rough type.[6] Ultimately, although the realization of detailed reasoning still has to encounter various existing obstacles encountered in practice,[7] most scholars explicitly advocate for the strengthening of the sufficiency and specificity of judicial reasoning.[8]

From a comparative law perspective, it is worth noting that both continental and common law legal systems value judicial reasoning[9] and appear to reach similar

---

[4] Zhang (2005, p. 71).

[5] For example, Hu (2009, pp. 49–51). Similar viewpoints, see He B (2009, pp. 40–43); Liu (2005, pp. 10–11); Wang (2005, pp. 85–86). In this regard, Article 2 of the *Opinions Reasoning Judicial Decisions* states this requirement explicitly (chapter 2). For further explanation, see Hu and Liu (2018, pp. 7–9).

[6] Zhuang (2015, pp. 83–84).

[7] For example, Zhuang (2015, pp. 85–92); Li and Fan (2015, pp. 97–98); Luo (2015); Wang (2011, pp. 94–95); Xu (2003, pp. 31–32). For early discussion, see Tang W (2000, pp. 147–156).

[8] For example, the *Notice Improving Civil Decisions*.

[9] In addition to the tradition of the civil law system, the research in common law systems, which has long been conservative regarding a general duty of reasoning, is also abundant. Andrews (2019); Zuckerman (2013); Ho (2000, p. 42). Meanwhile, the duty of reasoning has also become an international standard to a large extent: Article 6 paragraph 1, European Convention on Human Rights; ALI/UNIDROIT Principles of Transnational Civil Procedure 23.2.

objectives merely through different means.[10] However, due to the prevailing legal tradition and the choice of the substantive law in China, this contribution mainly refers to the adjudicative techniques and the structure of judicial decisions in the civil law systems of Germany and Japan. The part of facts of the current case in the written judgment of civil law systems, known as *Tatbestand*, corresponds to several parts of a Chinese counterpart. These include recording the special circumstances in the case trial proceedings and the claims as well as allegations of both plaintiff and defendant. Such part of facts of the current case overlaps with the undisputed facts in the "it is ascertained upon trial" part and the introduction to the overview of evidence investigation in "the court considers that" part. The judicial reasoning in civil law systems includes the finding of facts in the "it is ascertained upon trial" part and the evaluation of evidence and the application of law in the "the court considers that" part. The different modes of the continental and common law traditions extend beyond merely stylistic differences in form, but also to the theoretical divergences with regard to legal methodology, litigation ideology, adjudicative techniques and other related factors. In order to mirror the Chinese situation, this contribution is to briefly discuss these issues if necessary.

This chapter aims to address two questions by examining the relevant concerns raised by scholars in China and comparing the structure of judgments in China with those of Germany and Japan. On one hand, regarding the reasoning in judicial decisions, this chapter will explore the function of the part of facts in Chinese judgments and determine which items should be covered here. On the other hand, this chapter will examine the scope of the part of judicial reasoning and evaluate whether it should incorporate the specific reasons with regard to factual and legal issues simultaneously. In addition, it is important to note that the deficiencies in the structure and reasoning of civil judgments are the result of multiple factors, including political, judicial, social, and other forces mutually. Simply adjusting the structure of judgments is unlikely to solve all problems, not to mention that such adjustment is not able to change the fact that in practice, the published reasoning of some judgments is sometimes distinct from the real considerations behind it. This chapter focuses on the room in which reforming the laws and adjudicative techniques could give rise to some improvement in the current practice. In this way, the solution to legal issues could be transformed into a more technical discussion that can be progressively refined and specified.

[10] For example, Wei (2012, pp. 53–54); Cai and Cheng (2006); Su (2001, pp. 5–12) (judicial system, political system and social institutional environment); Zhang (1998, pp. 28–31).

3.2 Current Legal Situation in China and Comparative Law Experience

3.2.1 Current Structure of Judgments in China

In addition to the introductory part containing information regarding the parties concerned and the concluding part, in accordance with Article 155 paragraph 1 of the *CPL*, Article 32 of the *Provisions on Simplified Proceedings* in 2003, No. 41 of the *Style of Courts' Litigation Documents* in 1992 and No. 13–16 of the *Style of Litigation Documents for Civil Simplified Proceedings (for Trial Implementation)* in 2003, a civil judgment shall also encompass the following items. A civil judgment should begin by recording the cause of action and any special circumstances in the case trial proceedings,[11] then provide a detailed account of the plaintiff's claim for relief and the respective facts and reasons, as well as the defense put forth by the defendant, and finally summarize the disputed factual allegations and respective reasons of both parties. Subsequently, the civil judgment should state the facts and evidence ascertained by the court which is led by the expression of "it is ascertained upon trial" or "the court ascertains that" (which is revised by the *CPL* statute of 2012, whereas there is between these two slightly changed sentences no substantial difference at all), and the reasons and legal basis for the judgment in the introduction of "the court considers that". At the end of the judgment, the judgment should indicate the results of judgment and the allocation of litigation costs, as well as the deadline for appeal and the competent appellate court.

In addition, according to the defendant's different attitudes toward the plaintiff's claim for relief and factual allegations, there are four circumstances in which simplified proceedings are applicable: the parties have relatively serious disputes over the facts of the case, the defendant disagrees with the plaintiff merely over parts of the facts or the claim for relief, the parties have no disputes over the facts of the case, and the defendant admits all the claims of the plaintiff. In the last circumstance (including the partial admission), or upon the consent of both parties, or when trade secrets or personal privacy are involved, the judge may simplify the facts or the reasoning of the judgment (Article 270 items 2–4 of the *ICPL*). Similarly, due to the limited judicial resources and the consideration of litigation efficiency, the parts of facts and reasoning can also be simplified in small claims proceedings (Article 280 of the *ICPL*). It is important to note that the separation of complicated and simple judgments is certainly a significant issue, in terms of the structure and reasoning of judgments. This has been identified as a reform goal by Article 6 of the *2nd Five-Year Outline of the Program for Reform of People's Courts* (2005), Article 34 of the *4th*

[11] This is also the common happening in practice. For example, the SPC adheres to the aforementioned viewpoint in its judge-training textbooks, see Xi et al. (2013, p. 160). The Beijing High People's Court issued the *Format and Explanation of the Beijing High People's Court for the Judgment of First Instance of Commercial Cases Applying Ordinary Procedure* in 2008, and subsequently still holds such viewpoints. Wu et al. (2013, p. 195). Similar viewpoints, see He B (2009, p. 37); Wu (2002, p. 55); Gong (2000, p. 18).

Five-Year Outline of the Program for Reform of People's Courts (2015) and Article 41 of the *5th Five-Year Outline of the Program for Reform of People's Courts* (2019). The issue of separating complicated and simple judgments has also been addressed in the experimental work of Article 14 of the *2020 Pilot Program*. However, as the focus of this contribution is on the fundamental model of judgments, further development of this issue regarding the separation of judgments is beyond the scope of this discussion.

As a further refinement to the aforementioned fundamental rules, in practice, a court will generally record the parties' attitude toward the evidence, their cross-examination of the evidence, and the contents of the court's certification. These details are then incorporated into the judgment primarily in the space between "the factual grounds and their reasons" (of the parties) and the court's findings of facts.[12] In the training materials compiled by the Beijing High People's Court earlier, such practice is further specified into different models as follows: first describing the facts and then producing evidence, analyzing the evidence at the very beginning, determining the facts according to the parties' allegations, examining disputed facts, and deciding the evidence comprehensively.[13] Moreover, scholars have also discussed the function of judicial decisions to report the trial process,[14] whereas an overly long recording of these details may obscure the main body of the judgment and make it difficult for readers to understand the essential parts of the decision.[15]

In response to the practical problems regarding the structure and reasoning of judgments, some researchers have pointed out that such problems stem from the current structure of judgments and therefore, some structural changes in the sense of legal techniques are necessary. For example, commentators argue that the operative part of the judgment should be placed before the parts of facts and reasoning,[16] and the claims for relief together with factual allegations of the parties and the judicial reasoning should be introduced together in a unified reasoning part,[17] or that the part for adducing evidence and the cross-examination of evidence should be combined with the factual allegations of the parties as one part within the judgment, while the judge's certification of the evidence should be combined with the judgment's reasoning.[18]

---

[12] Since this refers to the usual practice of written judgments, this contribution merely takes the aforementioned *Format and Explanation of the Beijing High People's Court for the Judgment of First Instance of Commercial Cases Applying Ordinary Procedure* as an illustration.

[13] Wu et al. (2013, p. 202).

[14] Fu (2000, pp. 127–131); Zhou (2014, pp. 73–74).

[15] He B (2009, pp. 40–41); Zhang (2005, p. 70). For similar viewpoints, see Wu (2002, p. 55).

[16] He and Wang (2005, p. 6); Fu (2000, p. 125); Zhong and Fan (2002). Since this contribution focuses on the structure and reasoning of judgments, this issue will not be discussed.

[17] Xiao (2008, pp. 280–289).

[18] Zhang (2000, pp. 50–51).

3.2.2 Overall Framework of German and Japanese Judgments

As mentioned previously, although civil law systems cover the same objects to be judged, they have adopted different adjudicative techniques and judgment structures from those used in China. In order to observe the procedural arrangement of these systems in detail precisely, this contribution will focus on the classical modes of Germany and Japan as the primary counterparts. Specifically, this contribution will examine and discuss not only the overall structure of the judgment, but also its two main parts, namely the facts of the case and the reasoning of the judgment. It is worth noting that this contribution does not intend to draw lessons from the experience of France, which represents another typical civil law jurisdiction that is still affecting many jurisdictions nowadays. Besides the reason of the Chinese legal tradition, this contribution realizes that the French judgments are often written in a relatively concise manner, and an overemphasis on the deductive method can often lead readers to feel that the reasoning is not sufficiently supported.[19] The French experience is therefore not suitable for China, as it needs to further improve the level of legal techniques and specialization, as well as the degree of elaboration of judicial reasoning.

At the same time, this contribution also observes that Japan has tried to make visible adjustments and efforts to the classical tradition in Germany. Since the end of the last century, in order to avoid repeating the part of facts in the part of the reasoning, to reduce the burden of judges in writing judgments, and to improve the acceptability of judgments by the parties, the Japanese Supreme Court has advocated a new approach to combining the parts of facts and of reasoning into one part which has its focus on the disputed issues. Accordingly, besides other procedural matters which need to be recorded, the part of facts and reasoning within the judgment are then developed into three parts, namely the claim for relief, a summary of the case, and the court's decisions on the disputed issues.[20] Under the influence of the aforementioned recent development, China Taiwan has also inherited this approach in theory and practice. Although this contribution acknowledges the potential positive effects of structuring judgments around disputed issues,[21] it still argues in favor of the classical mode for China's current stage of transplanting civil law adjudicative techniques. Partially the success of this issues-centering model relies on the handling of disputed issues, which is still an underdeveloped area of procedural law.

---

[19] Steiner (2010, pp. 181–187); Goutal (1976, pp. 43, 45, 59–61).

[20] Shindo (2019, pp. 670–672) (previous Chinese translation: Shindo (2008, pp. 461–462)); Ito (2016, pp. 502–507) (Chinese translation: Ito (2019, pp. 341–344)); Matsumoto and Ueno (2015, pp. 594–596). For a detailed introduction and discussion, see Wang (2010, pp. 216–230).

[21] Judge Zou Bihua also argued that a special paragraph should be designated in the judgment to list the issues in dispute. Zou (2010, pp. 49–50). For the discussion by Chinese Taiwanese scholars on the concentrated court hearing regarding disputed issues based on China Taiwan's legislation and legal interpretations in recent years, see Zhang et al. (2006, pp. 175–176, 180–181, 189, 199–200). Arguing for writing in the "the court considers that" part and concentrating on the disputed issues, see Huang (2021, pp. 237–256).

After Chinese adjudicative techniques are established, we may first conduct a comprehensive evaluation of the advantages and disadvantages of the comparative modes according to China's current real situation, then advocate the Chinese characteristics of the judgment structure.[22] The difference between the comparative classical modes and the present Chinese structure lies in the understanding of the functions of the individual parts, while a prospective renovation of the current structure is unlikely to have a significant impact on the judges' daily working habits. On the contrary, the mode with a focus on disputed issues raises higher demands upon Chinese judges in general. Although some judges have successfully implemented the mode that focuses on disputed issues in practice, additional training and preparation may be necessary to ensure that the disputed issues are properly emphasized within civil judgments.

From another perspective, the main difference between the classical mode and the mode focusing on disputed issues is twofold: whether the facts of the case have an independent part in the structure of civil judgments or not and the approach to reasoning within the individual judgments. For the latter approach, as to be introduced in later parts, responding to the disputed issues raised by the parties in the reasoning of judgments is necessary, even in the classical mode the disputed issues could be emphasized more sufficiently. First-instance judgments in China Taiwan[23] indicate that its practice adopts a compromise approach. That is, after recording the claims of the parties concerned, the judgments on whether the legal reasons could be upheld are to be given according to the disputed points of the case. As for the independent part of judgments with the function of recording, this contribution suggests that a more pressing issue in China's current practice is exactly the accurate recording and reorganization of the parties' statements based on essential facts and the burden of producing factual allegations (*Behauptungslast*), which obviously differs significantly from the background of Japan's judicial reform.[24]

In general, a civil judgment under the classical mode is mainly divided into five parts.[25] The first part is the introductory part, which includes information about the parties themselves and their litigation representatives, the court handling the case, the name of the judge(s), and the date of the last oral hearing (Article 313 paragraph 1 item 1–3 of the *German Code of Civil Procedure*). The second part is the operative part of the judgment (Article 313 paragraph 1 item 4 of the *German Code of Civil Procedure*), that is, the substantive results of the subject matter of claims of the case, including the main claim and the accessory claims dependent on the main claim

[22] For a similar attitude in Japanese practice, see Wang (2010, p. 304).

[23] Civil judgments were collected by using "contract" as the search term on 1 December 2014 and found that the parts of facts and reasoning in the judgment first distinguish between procedural and substantive issues, then further introduce the parties' claims and allegations, undisputed facts and disputed issues item by item, and finally analyze the reasons for obtaining the evaluation of evidence. For example, 102 Litigation No. 2211 (Taipei Local Court), 103 Litigation No. 330 (Kaohsiung Local Court), 102 Litigation No. 3500 (Taichung Local Court).

[24] Grounds for the Japanese Reform: Shindo (2019, pp. 670–671); Ito (2016, pp. 504–505) (Chinese translation: Ito (2019, pp. 342–343)).

[25] For an overall introduction, see Gottwald (2011, pp. 127 et seq.) (For Chinese translation, see Gottwald (2015)).

(Article 4 of the *German Code of Civil Procedure*). The third part is the facts of the case part (*Tatbestand*) (Article 313 paragraph 1 item 5 of the *German Code of Civil Procedure*), which includes the facts presented by the parties and not yet evaluated by the judge. The fourth part is the reasons for the judgment (Article 313 paragraph 1 item 6 of the *German Code of Civil Procedure*), which sets out the judge's reasoning in relation to the operative part of the judgment. The facts contained in this part represent the judge's evaluation of the litigation materials and the corresponding evaluation results of the evidence. The fifth and final part is the judge's signature, which serves as a sign of the end of the judgment (Article 315 paragraph 1 of the *German Code of Civil Procedure*).

In Japan, traditionally, a civil judgment shall also record the operative part, facts, reasons, the date of the last oral hearing, the parties and their legal representatives, and the trial court (Article 253 paragraph 1 of the *Civil Procedure Law of Japan*). The relevant facts are similar to those facts of the case in the German counterpart and serve similar functions. In the facts part, it is unnecessary to quote all the factual allegations submitted by the parties. Rather, the judge only needs to select the necessary facts that can justify the operative part of the judgment (Article 253 paragraph 2 of the *Civil Procedure Law of Japan*).

Among them, the most crucial parts of the judgment are the operative part of the judgment, the facts of the case, and the reasoning of the judgment. Regarding the structure of civil judgments, German law has since 1976 no longer expressly required a significant distinction between the operative part and the other two parts. However, in practice, the operative part is still placed at the beginning of the judgment alone in order to clarify its contents and to facilitate the preparation of an execution order on the basis of a final judgment for performance (Article 317 paragraph 2 sentence 2 of the *German Code of Civil Procedure*).[26] To distinguish the finding of facts and legal evaluation of the case, it is necessary to separately write the part of facts of the case and the part of the judgment's reasoning (the so-called principle of separation).[27] However, when it comes to the constitution of these parts, the facts confirmed in the reasoning part of judgment also substantially belong to the facts of the case and have probative force, as described later in detail.[28] In addition, although the aforementioned three parts are essential elements of German civil judgments, the absence of any of them does not make the relevant judgments void. Instead, remedies are provided in different ways depending on the needs of individual cases.[29] Finally, it is important to observe that the German criminal judgments do not distinguish between the facts of the case and the judgment's reasoning (Article 267, 268 and 275 of the *German Criminal Procedure Law*), whereas such judgments subdivide their conviction part into three parts: the narrative of the case, the evaluation of proof,

---

[26] Althammer (2018, § 313 Rn 20); Musielak (2020, § 313 Rn 10); Hunke (2020, § 313 Rn 11); Wach (1896, pp. 124–125). For similar viewpoints in China, see Zhang (2015, p. 85).

[27] Rosenberg et al. (2018, § 60 Rn 26); Althammer (2018, § 313 Rn 58); Musielak (2020, § 313 Rn 20 Fn 83); Hunke (2020, § 313 Rn 17).

[28] BGHZ 154, 171 = NJW 2003, 2158, 2159; Huber (2003, Rn 374 et seq.).

[29] Althammer (2018, § 313 Rn 7); Musielak (2020, § 313 Rn 1, 18 et seq.).

and the legal analysis. Similar to the part of "it is ascertained upon trial" in Chinese civil judgments, the facts of the case in German criminal judgments must meet the requirements of constitutive elements of a crime and establish a confirmed version of natural facts based on the evidence from the perspective of an eyewitness.[30]

3.3 Facts Alleged in the Case Instead of Ascertained Facts in the Part of Facts

Through comparing the aforementioned different structures of civil judgments, it is noticeable that the traditional "it is ascertained upon trial" part in Chinese judgments is aimed at the results of the judge's finding of the facts of the case, while the "facts of the case" part in German civil judgments is related to the facts that have not yet been evaluated by the court. The function of the former is to determine and confirm, while the latter is to record and prove. Therefore, although both target the issue of facts, they are obviously not the same. Considering both modes, this contribution is in support of the latter approach, which is mainly based on the division of labor between the factual part and other parts ("the factual grounds and their reasons" of the parties and the part of judgment's reasoning) of the same judgment. Meanwhile, the current fact-finding function should be undertaken by the reasoning part of the judgment, to better facilitate the judge's reasoning on the application of law.

3.3.1 Part of Alleged Facts in the Case in the Structure of German Judgments

3.3.1.1 Specific Contents of Facts Alleged in the Case

Since the facts of the case are known to the parties either at the pre-action stage or during the course of litigation (and they even know better than the judge),[31] the part of facts of the case should record the procedural claims asserted by the parties in a concise and clearly structured manner, the relevant means of attacks and defense as well as the claim for relief (Article 313 paragraph 2 sentence 1 of the *German Code of Civil Procedure*). With the part of facts of the case in this sense, a lawyer should be able to conduct their own reasoning and obtain the judgment results, even without prior knowledge of the case.[32] This part should include the statements of

[30] Huber (2004, Rn 38, 62 et seq.); Huber (2004, Rn 332). Due to the limitation of topics, this contribution will not discuss the structure and reasoning of Chinese criminal judgments.

[31] BT-Drucks 7/2729, p. 131 (ultimately adopted by the legal committee: BT-Drucks 7/5250, p. 10 Zu Nr. 29); Musielak (2020, § 313 Rn 4).

[32] Some scholars consider that it is not necessary to make the judgment fully understandable by any third party: Hunke (2020, § 313 Rn 14); Balzer and Walther (2018, Rn 253, 261).

the parties, the findings of evidentiary investigations as well as the interlocutory decisions and other procedural histories of the case, whereas there should be no judge's own evaluation and determination ("substantial neutrality"[33]). Specifically speaking, regardless of whether the claim for relief raised by the plaintiff is erroneous or the defendant's denial is not specific enough to enjoy the relevant procedural effects, the judge should record the statements of the parties truthfully in the part of facts of the case. In general, the facts of the case should state the results of the evidence investigation directly, while the specific process of such investigation shall be indicated with reference to the court hearing transcript. However, the judge should not further determine whether relevant factual allegations are to be confirmed based on the relevant investigation results.[34]

For the purpose of brevity and clarity, when it comes to specific matters upon which both parties have reached an agreement or have disputes, the part of facts of the case should[35] refer to the pleadings, trial transcripts or other materials (Article 313 paragraph 2 sentence 2 of the *German Code of Civil Procedure*) in order to be as concise as possible without compromising the coherence of the provided information. In addition to other materials stored in the case dossier, judgments on other cases involving the same parties concerned or related to the oral hearing of the current case may also be referred to in the judgment.[36] By contrast, no reference may be made in the sentencing of criminal convictions in principle (Article 267 paragraph 1 sentence 3 of the *German Criminal Procedure Law*).[37] The aforementioned provisions of German law do not imply a reduction in the substantial requirements for the judge to find the facts of the case, but merely a reduction in the amount of paperwork (*Schreibarbeit*).[38] Because the aims of civil litigation are to realize substantive rights or to resolve disputes via the results of the judgment, the quality of judgment cannot be improved solely with the formal integrity of the judgment.[39] As for the specific approach to making reference within the judgment, the leading opinion demands that

[33] Höhne (2005, p. 294).

[34] Musielak (2020, § 313 Rn 12 et seq.); Knöringer (2018, Rn 5.01–5.02); Balzer (1995, p. 2450).

[35] This is obviously different from the usage of "may" before the legislative amendment, and at least this requirement becomes a procedural duty. Balzer (1995, p. 2449). However, this rule is still different from the preceding sentence of the same paragraph (the contents of the facts alleged in the case) regarding the effect of the rule. For example, some scholars interpret the preceding sentence of this paragraph as a "must" clause in essence, which refers to stronger compulsory force than a "shall" clause. Fischer (2005, p. 905).

[36] BGHZ 39, 333 = NJW 1963, 2272, 2275; BGH NJW-RR 1991, 830.

[37] Huber (2004, Rn 39).

[38] BT-Drucks 7/2729, p. 131; Seiler (2019, § 313 Rn 12, 25).

[39] Höhne (2005, p. 290).

the pleadings referred to should be specified,[40] while the minor opinion holds that it is sufficient to generally refer to all pleadings together.[41]

Regarding how to distinguish the fundamental and specific contents of the parties' statements is a matter of opinion. For example, when the German law was amended in 1976, the German Senate (*Bundesrat*) provided a simplistic mode of the facts of the case, which merely mentioned that the parties had a traffic accident, had presented different cases regarding the accident, and had different viewpoints on the decision on fault and the amount of damage. However, there was no summary of the disputed matters between the parties.[42] On the contrary, the federal government expressed its reservations on the basis of the concerns that the consideration of the judges could not be understood by the parties when the facts of the case and the judicial reasoning were too short. Then, it would be difficult to restore the disturbed status of legal peace (*Rechtsfrieden*) and even disadvantageous to the self-examination of the judges.[43] Taking the detailed discussions in a majority of guiding books for writing judicial decisions into account, the current practice tends to not treat such a writing paradigm, which is so simple that hinders the understanding of the parties and the appellate court regarding the disputed case, as a fundamental principle of writing. Rather, it is required at least to provide the outline of the accident and the major disputed issues.[44]

3.3.1.2 Proving Effects of Alleged Facts in the Case

The main function of the part of facts of the case is to prove the statements of the parties in a written form.[45] As there are few systematic interpretations regarding this function in China, a brief introduction is necessary hereby. Both the facts directly recorded in the part of facts of the case and the summary of the statements of the parties in the part of judgment's reasoning have the probative force of a public document. The part of facts of the case could merely ascertain the statements of the

[40] Althammer (2018, § 313 Rn 52); Feskorn (2020, § 313 Rn 18); Hunke (2020, § 313 Rn 16) (Due to the replacement of author since this edition, the new author switches to support the idea of specific reference while keeping the original wording of the previous author to the greatest extent untouched. However, there are inaccurate citations in the current wording of this edition because the new author made as few revisions as possible). Long-term viewpoints in previous editions: Hartmann (2019, § 313 Rn 16); Zimmermann (2019, Rn 385); Pielke, (2006, p. 204); Fischer (2005, p. 906).

[41] Knöringer (2018, Rn 5.13) (Knöringer (2014, Rn 5.07 (deleted))); the previous edition states that specific reference shall be made regarding the litigation submissions); Huber (2003, Rn 347); Balzer and Walther (2018, Rn 303 et seq.); Siegburg (2002, pp. 639–640). (Claims and allegations in cases involving construction works can be cited in general, but in many cases specific citations are more appropriate); Balzer (1995, p. 2452).

[42] BT-Drucks 7/2729, p. 131; Hartmann (2019, § 313 Rn 29 (as model)) (this part has been deleted due to the replacement of the author: Hunke (2020)); Balzer (1995, p. 2450).

[43] BT-Drucks 7/2729, p. 143.

[44] Althammer (2018, § 313 Rn 33); Bischof (1980, Rn 308 et seq.).

[45] Rosenberg et al. (2018, § 60 Rn 22); Althammer (2018, § 313 Rn 30); Fischer (2005, p. 904).

parties, and not the facts themselves or the facts found by the court.[46] Specifically speaking, in addition to the statements of the parties in the part of facts of the case, all written statements lawfully submitted by the parties are deemed to have been submitted in fact (Article 137 paragraph 3 sentence 1 of the *German Code of Civil Procedure*) and shall also have the same effect as the statements within the facts of the case. However, as the parties are entitled to change their statements in the pleadings during the later hearings,[47] the records in the part of facts of the case shall prevail in case of any conflict.[48] Oral statements which are not recorded are deemed not to have been submitted. By contrast, the witness testimony, expert opinions or statements of the parties, which are means of evidence, are not included.[49]

From the perspective of adjudicative techniques, the aforementioned understanding is related to the dual probative effect of the records in the part of facts of the case. In general, the statements of the parties recorded in the part of facts of the case are deemed to have been submitted (positive probative force), and those not recorded are deemed not to have been submitted (negative probative force).[50] The exception is that the pleadings which are referred to in the judgments are not subject to the aforementioned negative probative force, and accordingly, the parties are not required to submit an application for supplementing the facts of the case through an order of rectification (Article 320 of the *German Code of Civil Procedure*).[51] There are three main reasons for these rules. Germany has long-relaxed the restriction on the oral reference of pleadings; it no longer requires the part of facts of the case to fully and precisely reflect the statements of the parties, and the proceedings at second instance are regarded as the ones having merely a limited fact-finding function within the judicial hierarchy.[52] In other words, German law no longer recognizes the negative probative force of the part of facts of the case. Even if a statement is not contained in such part, it is incorrect to conclude that the parties did not submit such a statement in their written submissions.

The aforementioned force of proof will only be denied if it is shown to the contrary by the transcript of the hearing (Article 314 sentence 2 of the *German Code of Civil Procedure*) or if the parties' statements recorded in the part of facts of the case are contradictory.[53] Since the records in the part of judicial reasoning have equal probative value, if they conflict with the records in the part of facts of the case (e.g. due to the direct reference to the party's pleadings or to oral statements

---

[46] Althammer (2018, § 313 Rn 58 Fn 118).

[47] BGHZ 144, 370 = NJW 2000, 3133, 3135.

[48] BGHZ 140, 335 = NJW 1999, 1339.

[49] BGH NJW 1983, 2030, 2032; Rosenberg et al. (2018, § 60 Rn 22).

[50] BGH NJW 1983, 885, 886.

[51] On the judical order of rectification and a special type of such orders regarding alleged facts of the case, see Cao (2017).

[52] BGHZ 158, 295 = NJW 2004, 2152, 2155; Rosenberg et al. (2018, § 60 Rn 22); Althammer (2018, § 314 Rn 9–10); Feskorn (2020, § 314 Rn 5).

[53] BGHZ 144, 370 = NJW 2000, 3133, 3135.

on the same issue), neither of them is of probative value.[54] The facts found may play a role in determining whether statements made by the parties concerned in the appellate hearings were within the scope of newly submitted means of attack or defense (Article 531 paragraph 2, Article 533 and Article 97 paragraph 2 of the *German Code of Civil Procedure*) and the adjudication objects of the third instance revision (Article 559 paragraph 1 of the *German Code of Civil Procedure*). The omitted oral statements must be remedied within the statutory time limit through the correction and rectification of the facts of the case or, in the case of the set-off defense, be remedied with the permission of the appellate court *sua sponte* (Article 533 paragraph 1 of the *German Code of Civil Procedure*).[55] Therefore, the more emphasis is placed on the limited fact-finding function and error correction function of the second instance, the greater significance is to strengthen the requirements on the facts of the Case.[56]

3.3.1.3 Internal Structure of Alleged Facts of the Case

After determining the primary role of the part of facts of the case, the next step is to outline its general contents. In German practice, a relatively fixed pattern has been established for the part of facts of the case. The judge may normally make an exception to adjust the order of items merely when it may affect the understanding of the case.[57] From a historical perspective, the German and Japanese approaches which divide the litigation materials into substantive claim and defense, re-defense and counter-defense, as well as means of attack and defense, represent the legacy of the system of the right of action under Roman law.[58] These approaches have even become a leading case-processing technique in Germany, namely the *Relationstechnik*[59] and have widely forged the judicial practice in Japan through the emphasis on the theory of essential facts by the Japanese Judicial Research Institute.[60] In order to clarify the specific contents of the part of facts of the case and provide a reference to the reform of civil judgments in China, this contribution aims to briefly introduce the German counterpart.

---

[54] BGH NJW 2011, 1513, 1514, Tz 12; NJW 1999, 641, 642; Musielak (2020, § 314 Rn 3 et seq.); Feskorn (2020, § 314 Rn 6).

[55] Knöringer (2018, Rn.5.03 et seq.).

[56] Huber (2003, Rn 333).

[57] Althammer (2018, § 313 Rn 33 et seq.); Seiler (2019, § 313 Rn 12 et seq.); Knöringer (2018, Rn 5.08 et seq.); Becht and Beck (2010, Rn 681 et seq.); Huber (2003, Rn 350 et seq.). For detailed analysis and deduction of this solution in China, see Duan (2012, pp. 100–110); Xu (2009, pp. 133–152).

[58] Bernhardt (1949, p. 15).

[59] Zimmermann (2019, Rn 10 et seq.); Fischer (2007, pp. 347 et seq.). For domestic introduction, see Wu (2020, pp. 96–102); National Judges College and German Agency for International Cooperation (2014, pp. 42–62, 227–352); Li and Yin (2009).

[60] For detailed introduction in China, see Xu (2009, pp. 133–152).

The part of facts of the case in a civil judgment should first briefly summarize the substance of the legal dispute between the parties (in a nutshell, e.g. whether the defendant architect should be liable for the defects of the premises or the plaintiff claims for damages against the defendant based on a traffic accident[61]). However, such a summary does not cover the relevant theoretical disputes and legal issues.[62] This summary serves a similar function as the cause of action in Chinese civil judgments, which is to make it easier for the reader to focus on the relevant issues.

Second, the undisputed facts of the case, i.e. the course of events and the facts which are admitted or presumed to be admitted by the relevant party (Article 138 paragraph 3 and Article 288 paragraph 1 of the *German Code of Civil Procedure*) should be introduced. Since there are different opportunities for remedies corresponding respectively to the withdrawal of an admission (Article 290 of the *German Code of Civil Procedure*) and the allegation of no legal preclusion of the procedural rights (Article 296 and 531 of the *German Code of Civil Procedure*), both cases of the factual admission should also be clearly distinguished. In order to not break up the internal relationship among the alleged facts, in relatively complicated cases, facts that are not in dispute may be introduced part by part in accordance with the disputed issues. Distinguishing whether the factual allegations are in dispute or not is a prerequisite for finding the facts,[63] as well as the basis for applying adjudicative techniques.

Third, the disputed facts raised by the plaintiff in its initial statement and its counter-defense shall be introduced. The criteria to determine whether the factual allegations are in dispute or not are formal ones. Therefore, the relevant factual allegation will be considered as disputed[64] irrespective of whether the defendant's denial or lack of knowledge (Article 138 paragraph 4 of the *German Code of Civil Procedure*) follows the legal requirements.[65] When necessary, the judge may also write down the relevant legal opinions of the parties.[66] A majority of doctrines hold that the judge shall, in principle, explain why an application for evidence has not been granted.[67] However, the other would say that there is no need to waste time on this while writing civil judgments. To be considered are the facts that the parties

[61] Fischer (2005, p. 905). On the contrary, arguing that since the writing of civil judgments mainly aims at the parties, it is unnecessary to summarize their disputes: Balzer and Walther (2018, Rn 261).

[62] Höhne (2005, p. 292).

[63] Becht and Beck (2010, Rn 687).

[64] However, due to the grammatical differences between Chinese and German, in German different tenses can be used (past tense + present tense + subjunctive mood of indirect speech) to show the existence of disputes, while in Chinese there is no similar grammatical option. Such difference highlights the importance of the distinction in form/structure of civil judgments.

[65] Knöringer (2018, Rn 5.09); Huber (2003, Rn 353). Dissenting viewpoints arguing that the legality of such attitudes of the defendant should be assessed: Seiler (2019, § 313 Rn 18).

[66] Althammer (2018, § 313 Rn 38).

[67] BVerfG NJW 2001, 2009 (the application for producing evidence inscribed in the transcripts needs not to be repeated in the part of facts of the case); Rosenberg et al. (2018, § 60 Rn 23); Althammer (2018, § 313 Rn 37); Feskorn (2020, § 313 Rn 14).

usually make a large number of applications and that it is possible to obtain the relevant information from evidentiary orders and transcripts of court hearings.[68] Also, the litigation history related to the claim for relief could be added in this part, such as the various judgments made by the judge, changes of the parties, changes of subject matters of claims and so forth.[69] Moreover, the judge is able to list the final version of the claim for relief and the application of the defendant to dismiss the claim in a clear manner. On the contrary, it is unnecessary for the judge to record the procedural issues which are up to its decision on its own initiative, such as litigation costs (Article 308 paragraph 2 of the *German Code of Civil Procedure*) and the *sua sponte* declaration of enforcement in advance (Article 708 and 709 of the *German Code of Civil Procedure*).

Fourth, it is necessary to address the defense presented by the defendant, which shall be listed according to the order of the facts for which the burden of proof is borne by the plaintiff and the defendant respectively, i.e. the defendant's denial or conditional denial of the plaintiff's factual allegations and the new factual defense of the defendant (facts obstructing the substantive rights of the plaintiff, facts extinguishing such rights and facts preventing such rights). When the defendant makes an incidental claim of set-off, the judge shall also record it. What is more flexible are the factual allegations in the plaintiff's re-answer (*Replik*) and the defendant's reply to it (*Duplik*). Although the specific positions of these two kinds of allegations should be after the original defense considering the time and logical sequence,[70] in order to keep an integrated oral hearing, they should in principle be incorporated into the statements of the plaintiff and the defendant respectively. It means that the re-defense of the plaintiff could be placed within the judgment prior to the original defense of the defendant. Of course, if before taking notice of the original defense based on the specific circumstances of the case, it is difficult for the reader to understand such factual allegations, these allegations may also be located after the original defense.[71]

Finally, some places in the part of facts of the case are reserved for procedural matters which could affect the final judgment and need to be cited in the judgment's reasoning, such as the summary of the evidentiary investigation in the case, the statements of the parties that may be related to the preclusion of procedural rights, the composition of the trial bench, the time for the service of the complaint, and the beginning and ending dates of adjournment of the proceedings. However, as mentioned previously, the relevant part here needs merely to specify the materials to be referred to in the case dossier rather than include the evaluation of evidence. And nor does such part need to include procedural matters irrelevant to making

---

[68] Huber (2003, Rn 354).

[69] Arguing that the relevant contents should be placed in the to-be-discussed consolidated litigation history part: Althammer (2018, § 313 Rn 44). Arguing that the relevant contents should be placed in the part for the claim for relief when the change of subject matters of claims or the partial withdrawal of the case may still make a difference at the time of making a judgment: Seiler (2019, § 313 Rn 19); Becht and Beck (2010, Rn 692); Huber (2003, Rn 355).

[70] Althammer (2018, § 313 Rn 42); Seiler (2019, § 313 Rn 21); Hartmann (2019, § 313 Rn 24) (this part has been deleted due to the replacement of the author: Hunke (2020); Huber (2003, Rn 357).

[71] Feskorn (2020, § 313 Rn 16); Knöringer (2018, Rn 5.09).

the judgment, such as petitions for the refusal of a judge, settlements withdrawn, the determination of the date of the court hearing for preparation, or the time of arrival of the pleadings. When it comes to a counterclaim, depending on whether the claim and the counterclaim involve the same facts, the counterclaim may be written structurally together or separately.[72] Even the parties' legal opinions that do not affect the judgment of the case should be briefly introduced in the part of facts of the case or the part of the judgment's reasoning to indicate that such opinions have been heard.[73] In particular, when the parties only have disputes over issues relating to law or their need to identify the dispute of the case via their legal opinions, it is more essential to grasp the viewpoints of the parties.[74] For instance, in a claim suing for attorney's liability, since the focus of the dispute is the possible judgment of the court in the event of the attorney's due diligence,[75] a brief of the parties' arguments should be required. Certainly, such legal opinions are not binding on the judge's judgment, and the judge should still make a judgment at its own discretion by analyzing the relevant litigation materials.[76] Since this contribution suggests that it is more appropriate to place the parties' legal opinions in the part of the judgment's reasoning, further discussion will be continued later.

3.3.2 *Functional Transformation of the Part of Facts in Chinese Judgments*

3.3.2.1 Significance of Introducing an Independent Part of Alleged Facts in the Case

The purpose of introducing the independent part of facts of the case is not to modify the form or structure of a civil judgment, but rather to reconsider the purpose and function of the part of facts of the case, which is to record the statements of the parties. Such reconsideration coordinates with the function of the part of the judgment's reasoning which is to explain the facts, legal approaches and value judgments on which the court makes the civil judgment.[77] The emphasis on recording and proofing leads to the attention of the judge to the factual basis of the case, then to the clarification of the parties' procedural intentions under the principles of the parties' disposition and of the parties' presentation.

Considering such functional orientation, the matters related to the collection of evidence also obtain a clear position in the civil judgment. Meanwhile, the attempt

---

[72] Musielak (2020, § 313 Rn 13); Knöringer (2018, Rn 5.11–5.12).

[73] Hunke (2020, § 313 Rn 26); Becht and Beck (2010, Rn 686).

[74] Balzer and Walther (2018, Rn 275 et seq.).

[75] For example: BGHZ 97, 372 = NJW 1986, 2043.

[76] Huber (2003, Rn 372).

[77] For a similar viewpoint which calls it as "the particulars of the case", see Yuan and Shao (2017, pp. 114–119).

to move the finding of facts to the part of judgment's reasoning also makes the issue of fact with no doubt become the object to be reasoned. This approach allows for a more objective and thorough collection of evidence in legal proceedings, while also granting the parties access to know that the judge has attentively considered their statements in a verifiable manner. Of course, the division of the parts of facts and reasoning within the judgment is not exclusive, and the nature of specific matters needs to be taken into account as well. Considering the aforementioned analysis of the proving effect of the facts in the part of facts of the case under German law, it is noticeable that the information contained in the part of judgment's reasoning may also constitute the facts of the case substantially. It means that such information also has the function of recording and proving.

In order to improve the judicial service in general, we have to realize that among others, the traditional part of "it is ascertained upon trial" gives rise to insufficient reasoning within civil judgments. Such part emphasizes that the judgment should show the fact-finding results determined by the judge exercising its judicial power and pay attention to the objectivity of the facts provided. Then, along with this approach, since the facts exist objectively and are not subject to the will of anyone, the civil judgment naturally does not have to provide reasons in detail.[78] No matter whether China has adopted the theory of objective facts or the theory of legal facts which is long disputed, or whether the current litigation mode in China still overemphasizes an enhanced version of the inquisitorial legal tradition, as far as the judgment itself is concerned, the aforementioned emphasis on fact-finding results may lead the judge to pay less attention to the statements of the parties and the recording of their arguments. Moreover, Chinese researchers generally deem that the evidence can be listed in the form of narrating and commenting at the same time, or in the form of narrating first and listing the evidence in forthcoming paragraphs.[79]

Yet, because the part of "it is ascertained upon trial" requires an objective description of the facts, the aforementioned two approaches may violate such a requirement and overlap with the reasons for the judgment. Thus, this challenging situation for the judge in drafting the judgment also partly gives rise to insufficient reasoning in the fact-finding part of the judgment.[80] On the contrary, as mentioned previously, although the objectivity of the facts of the case is also required by the adjudicative techniques of civil law systems, such objectivity refers to a completely different thing.

On the positive side, objectivity in civil judgments entails the objective and accurate recording of the litigation process and the statements of the parties. However, on the negative side, strict objectivity shows the rejection of the judge's recording of the results of its factual findings and the evaluation of the evidence in the part of facts of the case, i.e. the judge's subjective understanding. Starting from the literal meaning

[78] Zhang Z (2009, pp. 80–82). Some researchers, while emphasizing that the findings of facts should be reasoned, emphasize the accuracy of the factual ascertainment, and assign the task of reasoning to the parts of evidence and proof. For example, Tang X (2000, pp. 123–124).

[79] Liu (2005, p. 9); Gong (2000, pp. 19).

[80] Zhang (2000, p. 50).

of Article 155 paragraph 1 of the *CPL*, the recent reform regarding civil judgments emphasizes that the findings of the facts ought to be directly reasoned in the part of facts. From a normative perspective, such emphasis can resolve the problem of insufficient reasoning of the facts. As to be discussed later, this contribution is of the opinion that we should pay more attention to the dependence of the issue of facts on the solution of the issue of law. Theoretically speaking, it may be preferable to introduce an independent part of facts of the case and then enable the part of "the court considers that" to realize the function of reasoning at one time.

3.3.2.2 Specific Solutions for Improving the Part of Facts

In fact, the aforementioned functional transformation will not necessarily change the current judgment habits established by the current generation of Chinese judges. On the contrary, such transformation will clarify and strengthen a better approach to making judgments. The part of facts of the case primarily presents the statements of the parties and the facts alleged by them, which should be recorded and summarized by the neutral judge. Comparing the part of facts of the case in Chinese judgments with the factual part of the German counterpart, it becomes evident that the issues involved in both situations are quite similar. In Chinese practice, the judges are trying their best to repeat the facts alleged by the parties, and considering the trend of using electronic litigation materials, the workload which is led by such repeating could not be a big problem at all. Based on these litigation materials, the judges, the parties and other readers of the relevant judgment should be able to summarize the disputed issues of facts by themselves, so as to discover the crucial contents of the court hearing and the judgment.[81]

This contribution takes hereby the well-known judgment of the Pengyu case at first instance as an example (Chap. 2), in which the presiding judge made use of the *prima facie* evidence to (unsuccessfully) uncover the fact of collision between the parties. The judge first recorded the undisputed facts of the case, that is, "[w]hen (the plaintiff) arrived at the back door of the first bus, in order to catch the latter bus, coincidentally, the defendant also exited the bus through the same door. The plaintiff fell and got injured. The defendant noticed and helped the plaintiff to the side". Subsequently, the judge introduced the evidence and different factual allegations of the parties in detail, which reflected the requirements of the part of facts of the case properly. Moreover, because the part of facts of the case deals with the facts alleged by the parties rather than with a comprehensive restatement of the evidence collected, an introduction of an independent part of facts of the case does not indicate a mixture of the final judgment and the trial transcript.

---

[81] For similar viewpoints, see He (2004). For an example of the judgment which is in accordance with the suggestions made in this contribution regarding alleged facts of the case, see Civil Judgment of the Beijing First Intermediate People's Court (2014) Yi Zhong Min Zai Zhong Zi No. 07940 (Judge Wang Maogang of this court is to be thanked for his incidental reminder of this judgment on the platform of Weibo).

Under German law, the dispute of the part of facts of the case mainly lies in its degree of specificity and the methods to refer to pleadings. As for the former issue of degree, the preparation of the part of facts of the case is, of course, influenced by the individual cases and the personal habits of the judge, so it is difficult to discuss its degree of specificity in general. Especially in complex commercial and other kinds of civil cases, it is clearly impossible to summarize the facts in such a simple way as in the example of the German legislation mentioned previously. Even in ordinary simple disputes of sales contracts or traffic accidents, it is necessary to highlight the fundamental facts of the case and the disputed issues. In this sense, there is no need to omit the introduction to unessential facts.[82] As for the controversial issue of how to refer to pleadings under German law, this contribution deems that the specific indicating case by case is more appropriate than referring to all pleadings in general. This is helpful to enhance the understanding of the judgment and is widely accepted in China's judicial practice.

Especially in the process of recording the evidence submitted by the parties, then checking and ascertaining the relevant facts, Chinese courts often explain the individual object to be proven (such as all kinds of documentary evidence, witness testimonies, expert opinions, various kinds of transcripts and so forth) one by one in all types of proceedings, which can specify the contents of the considered pleadings.[83] Even if the judge chooses to introduce the ascertained facts at first, and then indicates that "the aforementioned facts are supported by… (documentary evidence), statements of the parties and so forth",[84] it is also in compliance with the requirement of specification as long as how each item of the documentary evidence affects the judge's evaluation of evidence is explained in the process of finding the facts, or the facts of the case are particularly simple.[85] Otherwise, we could imagine that when the case file involves dozens of pleadings (especially in commercial and intellectual property cases), even if it is the first-instance judge and the parties along with their lawyers that are reading the judgment, they will find it difficult to immediately discover which pleadings the contents found in the judgment came from.

Of course, the difficulties this situation gives rise to for the second-instance judge and other researchers of the judgment are even more significant.[86] However, this is

[82] An opposing viewpoint: Balzer and Walther (2018, Rn 273).

[83] For example, Civil Judgment of the People's Court of Lushi County of Henan Province (2014) Lu Min Er Chu Zi No. 229; Civil Judgment of the People's Court of Longhui County of Hunan Province (2014) Long Min Er Chu Zi No. 298; Civil Judgment of the People's Court of Ziliujing District of Zigong City of Sichuan Province (2014) Ziliu Min Chu Zi No. 2718; and Civil Judgment of the People's Court of Qiyang County of Hunan Province (2014) Qi Min Chong Chu Zi No. 1074.

[84] For example, Civil Judgment of the People's Court of Weiyang District of Xi'an City of Shaanxi Province (2014) Wei Min Chu Zi No. 04852.

[85] For example, in a long-term transaction, it is not necessary to specify the details of each transaction. If the case involves only one promissory note accepted by both parties, not stating the facts to be proved will not affect understanding. For example, Civil Judgment of the People's Court of Yu County of Hebei Province (2015) Wei Min Chu Zi No. 8.

[86] For the necessity of specification due to the large number of citations in some areas and examples thereof, see Civil Judgment of the High People's Court of Guangdong Province (2011) Yue Gao Fa Min San Chu Zi No. 2.

actually more of a working requirement and suggestion within the judiciary, and we must seek a balance between reducing the judge's writing pressure and the adequacy of supplying judicial information. Therefore, this contribution suggests that, although the practice of specific reference to parties' pleadings is generally to be agreed on, the way in which materials are referred to should not impact the parties' statements' effectiveness. Even if no specific pleadings are indicated in the judgment, all pleadings submitted by the parties are still considered to be orally produced and should become litigation materials in the current civil proceedings.[87]

Although this contribution emphasizes that the function of the part of facts of the case needs to be altered primarily, it is equally essential to reform and improve the overall quality of civil judgments. For instance, the procedural issues during the whole proceedings should also be recorded and reasoned in Chinese final judgments.[88] The SPC has also pointed out in the *Notice Improving Civil Decisions* that "the crucial procedural matters and litigation activities during the proceedings should be clearly reported, including the dates when the plaintiff sues and the appellant appeals, the submission and transfer of crucial litigation materials and evidence, the procedural facts that result in the extension of the deadline of concluding the case due to jurisdictional objections, the suspension of litigation, organizing expert identification and so forth, and taking pre-action or in-litigation measures to preserve property and so forth".

In China's practice, because the court needs to refer to expert opinions designated by the court itself during its fact-finding process, these opinions are typically presented in the part of "it is ascertained upon trial",[89] while the specific date the opinions were given may also be able to be found considering statements of the parties.[90] Other procedural matters may appear at the beginning of the judgment,[91] be recorded in the part of "it is ascertained upon trial",[92] and may be even not clearly

[87] In German practice, citation as a whole is not prohibited. For example, BGH NJW 2004, 3777, 3778.

[88] Hu (2014, pp. 82–83); He B (2009, pp. 37–39); Liao (2003); Fu (2000, p. 131); Gong (2000, p. 18). For the opposing viewpoint, see Zhang (2005, p. 70).

[89] For instance, Civil Judgment of the People's Court of Weishi County of Henan Province (2014) Wei Min Chu Zi No. 422; Civil Judgment of the People's Court of Xishan District of Kunming City of Yunnan Province (2014) Xi Fa Min Chu Zi No. 3252. Some judgments are directly recorded in the part of judgment's reasoning, for instance, see Civil Judgment of the Intermediate People's Court of Wuhu City of Anhui Province (2013) Wu Zhong Min Yi Zhong Zi No. 00848 (presumed based on the judgment of second instance).

[90] For instance, Civil Judgment of the People's Court of Taobei District of Baicheng City of Jilin Province (2014) Bai Tao Min Yi Chu Zi No. 588.

[91] For instance, Civil Judgment of the People's Court of Baodi District of Tianjin (2014) Bao Min Chu Zi No. 1205; Civil Judgment of the Beijing Fourth Intermediate People's Court (2014) Jing Tie Zhong Min Chu Zi No. 29.

[92] For instance, Civil Judgment of the People's Court of Dong'e County of Shandong Province (2013) Dong Min Chu Zi No. 1535; Civil Judgment of the People's Court of Pingyang County of Zhejiang Province (2014) Wen Ping Shang Chu Zi No. 820; Civil Judgment of the Intermediate People's Court of Taizhou of Jiangsu Province (2013) Tai Zhong Min Chu Zi No. 0104.

recorded in the judgment in spite of their actual occurrence.[93] As for the crucial dates during the process of putting the proceedings forward, such as the date of case filing and the formal court hearing, different courts and judges will make their preference on whether to specify them or not.

As mentioned previously, most researchers deem that the judgment-related procedural matters should appear at the beginning of the judgment. However, such requirement is based on the premise that the structure of the Chinese civil judgments remains untouched, because it is obviously more inappropriate to put these procedural matters in the part of "it is ascertained upon trial" which has the function of fact-finding. On the contrary, if the function and contents of the factual part of the judgment are to be adjusted according to the suggestions of this contribution, it is more reasonable to record the procedural matters in this part of "it is ascertained upon trial".

At the same time, considering the nature of procedural issues during civil proceedings, the judge would merely have the duty of giving detailed reasoning when the relevant legal provisions are unclear or there are some difficult or new types of issues. For example, because the third sentence of Article 68 paragraph 2 of the *CPL* and Article 102 paragraphs 1 and 2 of the *ICPL* narrow the application of evidential preclusion, the judge shall explain the fault of the parties, the relationship between the evidence and the essential facts, and the factors considered by the judge in exercising its discretion, in order to justify the legal consequences (especially when the evidence is rejected) to the evidence provided by the party concerned after the due time.[94] Of course, taking the function of the part of facts of the case into account, the aforementioned reasoning shall be placed in the reasoning part of civil judgments.

Finally, the cause of action that could be categorized as procedural matters should appear in the factual part of the judgment, regardless of whether such understanding is attributed to the function of proving procedural identification or some direct transplantation of foreign counterparts. The cause of action is a summary of legal reasons made by the parties concerned and the court, which is not equivalent to the theoretical concept of the subject matter of claims. Even if the cause of action of a case needs to be changed during the ongoing proceedings, it is enough to indicate such change in the part of facts of the case.[95]

---

[93] This is especially true for taking measures of property preservation. Sometimes, judgments only reflect the result that the defendant shall bear the property preservation costs. For instance, Civil Judgment of the People's Court of Kuiwen District of Weifang City of Shandong Province (2014) Kui Shang Chu Zi No. 1582.

[94] In practice, it is not uncommon to find cases which cannot explain accordingly. For instance, Civil Judgment of the People's Court of Yiwu City of Zhejiang Province (2013) Jin Yi Min Chu Zi No. 1175; Civil Judgment of the People's Court of Cixi City of Zhejiang Province (2014) Yong Ci Min Chu Zi No. 1697. Of course, this contribution merely intends to raise this issue and does not expect that judges should/can fully give reasons on the issue of preclusion of evidential rights at present. The reason is that scholars have neither provided a set of sufficiently detailed and systematic reasoning methods and nor has the SPC given clear guidance. Considering this, it is too much to request the judge of first instance of a case to do as above. The specific elements of various preclusion of procedural rights, such as the preclusion of the defendant's answer, should be considered in the reasoning part of civil judgments. For suggestions under Chinese law, see Cao (2014, pp. 501–504).

[95] Cao (2020c, pp. 294–295).

3.4 Combining Findings of Facts and Application of Law in the Part of Reasoning

3.4.1 Reasoning in the Structure of German Judgments

3.4.1.1 Fundamental Rules on Judgment's Reasoning

In Germany, whose legal system is regarded as a classical mode of civil law jurisdictions, the judge's duty to provide reasons for the court's judgment is derived from the constitutional statutory right to be heard (Article 103 paragraph 1 of *German Basic Law*). The parties are entitled to request the court to provide the facts of the case, the evaluation of the evidence, and their opinions on legal issues (Article 313 paragraph 3 of the *German Code of Civil Procedure*), and the court must also accept and consider the litigation materials provided by the parties.[96] Due to the obvious difference between judging a case in the end and hearing the same case during the proceedings, regarding the writing style, the judge may first state the final conclusion, then indicate the reasons for such a conclusion.[97]

Specifically speaking, after the simplification law reform (*Vereinfachungsnovelle*) of 1976, Germany has reduced the requirement for judgment's reasoning. If the judge has already explained the relevant issues in detail at court hearings (Article 139 paragraphs 1 and 2, Article 278 paragraph 2 sentence 2 of the *German Code of Civil Procedure*; Article 278 paragraph 2 sentence 2 and paragraph 3 of the old version of the *German Code of Civil Procedure*) and truthfully recorded it in the clerk's transcript, the compulsory duty to give reasons is then not violated based on the legal construction of constitutionality.[98] Regarding the issues of facts, although the judge does not need to give opinions on all factual allegations of the parties,[99] it must analyze those allegations which are related to the focus of the case. Otherwise, the statutory right to be heard would be violated.[100]

The judge's personal conviction about the evidence is also an important part of the judgment's reasoning (Article 286 paragraph 1 sentence 2 of the *German Code of Civil Procedure*). The judge should examine specific items of the evidence and other relevant circumstances. If necessary, the judge should clarify the grounds for not considering relevant litigation materials.[101] As for the issues of law, the judge's judgments should be remarkably different from academic contributions which focus on academic trajectory and debating with other scholarly opinions.[102] Opinions that

---

[96] BVerfGE 83, 24 = NJW 1991, 1283, 1285.

[97] Seiler (2019, § 313 Rn 27); Knöringer (2018, Rn 6.01).

[98] Lücke (1987, pp. 161 et seq.).

[99] BGH GRUR 2008, 731, 732; Musielak (2020, § 313 Rn 17).

[100] BVerfGE 86, 133 = DtZ 1992, 327, 328; BGH NJW-RR 2011, 98, 99 (defense of prescription); NJW 2009, 2139, 2139–2140; Knöringer (2018, Rn 6.09–6.10) (echo principle).

[101] Thole (2018, § 286 Rn 17).

[102] Rosenberg et al. (2018, § 60 Rn 25).

are different from the usual understanding should be demonstrated in the judgments' reasoning,[103] but it is unnecessary to analyze erroneous legal opinions that are not directly relevant to the current case.[104]

Although the independent judicial power of judges contains their discretion to decide the scale of cited academic contributions,[105] it is to be emphasized that even judgments of the Federal Court of Justice (*Bundesgerichtshof*) of Germany, which refer to crucial legal issues, the development of laws or the unified law application (Article 543 paragraph 2 sentence 1 of the *German Code of Civil Procedure*), should not cite other materials excessively.[106] Whereas there are in practice occasionally some judgments citing dozens of precedents or hundreds of references, or even spending too much space to discuss undisputed issues, the practical significance of these judgments is doubtful.[107]

In addition, a final judgment that occurred between the parties and has been served, or a final judgment that did not occur between the parties but became the object of their oral court hearing may be referred to in the reasoning part of the judgment.[108] Also, the reasoning part of the judgment may refer to the pleadings submitted by the parties in the current case.[109] In general, similar to the part of facts of the case, the reasoning part is merely required to justify the current judgment. Regarding the preparation of civil judgments, to be sought is the balance between conciseness and completeness.[110]

3.4.1.2 Two Types of Elements of Judgment's Reasoning

Next, the focus shifts to the specific sequence for organizing the part of reasoning within civil judgments. This reasoning part should first discuss the admissibility of the claim (*Zulässigkeit der Klage*)/requirements of the proceedings (*Prozessvoraus-setzung*) in dispute, then focus on the issues of substantive law, so as to clarify the

[103] BVerfGE 81, 97 = NJW 1990, 566, 567; BVerfG NJW 2011, 1497.

[104] Hunke (2020, § 313 Rn 44–45).

[105] BVerfG NJW 1987, 2499. By contrast, under French law (similar as many decisions of the ECJ), the reference to which the decision takes into account is not explicitly indicated. Schack (2017, Rn 95).

[106] Büdenbender (2013, p. 163). In common law systems, although citing precedents represents the main approach to discovering law, it is also possible to have too many citations. Zuckerman (2013, para 22.22–22.31).

[107] Hunke (2020, § 313 Rn 44 et seq.) (this commentary does not change the viewpoint in its previous version which contains more thorough discussion: Hartmann (2019, § 313 Rn 45–46). In the United Kingdom, judges and academics have also expressed their dissatisfaction, directly or indirectly, with the lengthy judgments. Arden (2012, p. 515); Andrews (2019, para 27.45–27.48).

[108] BGHZ 39, 333 = NJW 1963, 2272, 2275; BGH NJW-RR 1991, 830.

[109] BGH NJW-RR 1991, 1406; Seiler (2019, § 313 Rn 28).

[110] Hunke (2020, § 313 Rn.32 et seq.) (specifically emphasizing that an individual decision need not be fully understood by outsiders of a case and need not set tests or establish rules for similar cases) On the contrary, emphasizing that such judgments should be understood by third parties: Becht and Beck (2010, Rn 698).

scope of *res judicata* effect of the judgment. If the requirements of the proceedings are undisputed, the judgment may simply state that the claim is admissible without any doubt. Only when the current case meets the requirements of the proceedings, the judge may make a judgment on the merits. Nevertheless, even when the parties have disputes in such requirements, the clarification of the admissibility of the claim is relatively simple. Since the aforementioned requirements of the proceedings respectively involve various dogmatic interpretations of laws, this contribution is not to develop in detail in this aspect.[111]

Furthermore, the substantive elements on the merits of the case should be examined. The judge should first clarify the substantive legal norms and results to be discussed. Then, focusing on grounds of substantive rights (*Anspruchsgrundlagen*), the facts of the case are to find their positions under the applicable legal norms.[112] The judge also needs to briefly explain why the means of attack and defense, such as factual allegations and evidence, are precluded.[113] When the evidential investigation and the process of proof are to be reasoned, it is necessary to first clarify the applicable special standard of proof (such as *prima facie* proof or the discretionary determination of damages).[114]

Later, it is to be explained why some means of evidence lead to a certain degree of personal conviction of the judge. For instance, why one should believe some particular statement of a witness or one party in case of conflicting statements,[115] or how to understand some objective evidence such as a physical examination or the written opinion of a traffic policeman in case of a traffic accident (Chap. 5).[116]

In the process of proof, the so-called indirect evidence and the *prima facie* evidence, which are related to the rule of evaluation of evidence, play a crucial role. To rely on the *prima facie* evidence, the reasoning mainly refers to the (in-) applicability of the relevant principle derived from experience (*Erfahrungssatz*). If the essential facts of the case are still *non-liquet* after all means of evidence have been exhausted, the court will have no choice but to make its final judgment based on the rule of burden of proof.[117]

In addition, attention ought to be paid to the boundary between the judgment's reasoning part and the operative part of the judgment. For instance, if the plaintiff does not claim for confirming the contract's validity in a lawsuit for performance, such confirmation can merely appear in the reasoning part rather than the operative part of the judgment. On such occasions, the determination of the contract's validity

---

[111] For example, Shao (2018, pp. 79–176); Zhang (2004).

[112] Cao (2021).

[113] Seiler (2019, § 313 Rn 30 et seq.); Feskorn (2020, § 313 Rn 20 et seq.); Becht and Beck (2010, Rn 700 et seq.); Huber (2003, Rn 394 et seq.).

[114] Although it is generally accepted that the standard of proof is a high degree of probability, in practice it is usually the judge's internal ascertainment that is decisive. Rosenberg et al. (2018, § 114 Rn 13 et seq.).

[115] Cao (2020b, pp. 94–97).

[116] Cao (2020d).

[117] Cao (2013); Huber (2003, Rn 415 et seq.).

should not enjoy *res judicata* effect. The relevant ascertainment of facts of the case could merely have a relative *res judicata* effect within the subject matter of claims (Chap. 7).[118]

3.4.2 Expansion of the Reasoning Part in Chinese Judgments

3.4.2.1 Necessity of Combining Issues of Facts and Law

According to the amendments of the *CPL* (2012), the findings of facts and the application of law shall both be components of the reasoning part of civil judgments. In China, it has been widely accepted that the part of "the court considers that" must cover the application of law, then there is no need to further continue its discussion here. What has been changed is the nature of the findings of facts and the relationship between the judgment's structure and the assignments which a civil trial must accomplish. With no doubt, the factual issues need to be ascertained and reasoned by the court at the same time. Yet, the crucial question to consider is in which part of a civil judgment the finding and the reasoning can be better suited for the requirements of adjudicative techniques.

Previously, some scholars considered that the findings of facts were the natural contents of the part of "it is ascertained upon trial". Since the part of "the court considers that" was understood as the (single) place for the judgment's reasoning, the fact-finding was different from the judgment's reasoning.[119] Considering the further examples within the new *Style Litigation Documents*, the current leading doctrine regards the findings of facts and the application of law as the components of the judgment's reasoning.[120] Under this consensus, there can be different suggestions as to the position where the reasoning of the findings of facts should appear. If we speak for a functional change of the factual part of the judgment, as this contribution suggests, then the factual reasoning should belong to the part of "the court considers that". However, if "the factual grounds and their reasons" and "the applicable law and reasons", which literally appear in the provision of the *CPL* statute, could only correspond to two independent parts of the judgment, then it is correct to say that the former should be placed in the part of "the court ascertains that" and the latter to the part of "the court considers that".

This contribution deems that the current discussion refers not merely to a "word game" regarding how to explain the concept of judgment's reasoning, i.e. legal reasons in a broad sense or a narrow sense, but also reflects whether and how the

[118] In this regard, for the viewpoints opposing the pre-determinant effect of civil decisions (regardless of whether it is reasonable to distinguish between "refute" and "reverse" in the current judicial interpretations in terms of effect) both *de lege ferenda* and from the comparative legal experience, see Cao (2020d, pp. 146–147); Cao (2015).

[119] For example, Yun (2012, p. 63); Liu (2005, pp. 9–11); Xu (2003, p. 30).

[120] For example, Jiang and Fu (2015, p. 112) (written by Fu Yulin); Xi (2012, pp. 310–312); He and Wang (2005, p. 6); Zhang (2005, p. 73).

reasoning of fact-finding is emphasized in China. In fact, the traditional structure of civil judgments, which excluded the reasoning of fact-finding from its part of "the court considers that", could have led to the insufficiency of the reasoning of the judgment.[121] Rather, this contribution agrees that, by comparing Article 155 paragraph 1 item 2 of the *CPL* with Article 138 paragraph 1 item 2 of the old version of the *CPL* before 2012, it is obvious that the current law takes both fact-finding and law application as the contents of judgment's reasoning. Such construction corresponds to the aforementioned functional transformation of the factual part of the judgment, which is exactly the same as the practice under German law (Article 313 paragraph 3 of the *German Code of Civil Procedure*). Also, such legal construction provides us with a legal basis to learn from the adjudicative techniques of civil law systems.

In practice, such understanding is not in lack of supporters. Besides the aforementioned minority opinion that considers the fact-finding as a part of the judgment's reasoning, even after the adoption of the original judgment styles and prior to the new revision of the *CPL*, there are in fact already judgments that integrate the evidential evaluation, the ascertainment of facts, and legal reasons as its one part all together.[122] Meanwhile, the judges in individual courts have also adopted the form of "judged as follows" to integrate the finding of facts and legal reasons within civil judgments.[123] Theoretically, although the free evaluation of evidence is emphasized in civil law systems, it is still noticeable that the reasoning of the judgment is clearly one of the crucial institutional guarantees for the free evaluation of evidence (Article 286 paragraph 1 sentence 2 of the *German Code of Civil Procedure*).[124] The factual issues must be included in the judgment's reasoning, and the reasons and results for determining the probative value of the evidence must be made public (Article 105 of the *ICPL*, and Article 14 of the *4th Five-Year Outline of the Program for Reform of People's Courts*). In addition, if the ascertainment of facts becomes a part of the judgment's reasoning, the analysis of evidence will also naturally enter such a part. Otherwise, the judge will not be able to justify its fact-finding conclusion. Thus, the viewpoint that the evidence must be analyzed in the part of facts of the case, as exemplified by the *Style Litigation Documents*,[125] is not in conflict with the core idea of factual reasoning suggested by this contribution.

However, this contribution's view is that the factual issues and legal issues should be reasoned in the part of reasoning, which, under the consensus that factual issues should be reasoned, emphasizes the necessity to further strengthen the combination of factual and legal issues. From the perspective of the legal application, the essential facts abstractly provided by grounds of substantive rights in, e.g., the *Civil Code of the P.R.C.* determine the facts to be proved in specific cases. Such facts, as the objects of proof, in turn, need to rely on direct or indirect evidence[126] to complete the

[121] For similar viewpoints, see Liu and Sun (2002, p. 19).

[122] Gong (2000, pp. 17–18).

[123] Zhang Y (2009, pp. 102–112).

[124] Rosenberg et al. (2018, § 114 Rn 1 et seq.).

[125] Zhong and Fan (2002).

[126] Cao (2020a).

reasoning process which connects such facts with the concrete facts of ordinary life (*Lebenssachverhalt*). It means that the cross-examination and evaluation of evidence depend on the facts to be proved, while the determination of such facts is premised on the clarification of legal issues. In this sense, the practice of reasoning which first goes on the fact-finding in the part of "the court ascertains that", and then on the application of law in the part of "the court considers that", seems to inherit the structural gene of the original judgment format. It is less likely to have an ordinary approach to dealing with factual and legal issues. Therefore, while writing civil judgments, the judge needs to first in the part of "the court considers that" assume that certain essential facts are necessary for making a judgment and then provide in the part of "the court considers that" detailed reasons on how to determine the aforementioned essential facts as the facts to be proved in the current case. Such understanding may not merely lead to the repetition and inconsistency in arguments, but also may cause errors made by the judge in the process of ascertaining facts or applying laws.

From another point of view, the distinction between factual issues and legal issues in the process of adjudication does not necessarily lead to the same distinction in the structure of the judgment. The former refers to the substantial judgment, while the structure of the judgment shows the formal meaning of the judgment. Both do not have the same focus. Although the finding of facts and the application of law can be distinguished from the perspective of the legal syllogism or, more precisely, from the perspective of subsumption, this does not mean that there should be independent parts of the same judgment. On the contrary, the structure of the judgment itself does not have to reflect the legal syllogism, nor do they have to correspond directly to each other.[127] In fact, the legal methodology represents the methods to think like a lawyer and is the internal logic supporting the judgment's reasoning. The emphasis on the formal distinction between facts and the laws will only bring about the rigidity, repetition, and fragmentation of the judgment.

Moreover, experience in comparative law does not provide support for this understanding. Partially due to the different adjudicators, it is possible in the Anglo-American structure of civil judgments to make a relatively strict distinction between the issue of facts and law. The jury, with its strong authority to ascertain facts, does not have to provide reasons for the found facts. In this regard, it can indeed be said that the issues of evaluating proof and finding facts do not belong to the judgment's reasoning.[128] However, for the trial mode led by professional judges, which China also adopts, the aforementioned practice is not only unimaginable but also difficult to learn from. In the context of U.S. law alone, it is noteworthy that in the vast majority of U.S. federal judicial cases in which the judge should find the facts, the judge is required to clarify its finding of facts and conclusion of law respectively (*U.S. Federal Rules of Civil Procedure*, Rule 52 (a)). In other words, the evaluation

---

[127] Some commentator deems that the approach to thinking these two issues together leads to the fragmentation of the current situation. Zhang Z (2009, p. 80) (but the usage of the term subsumption here is different from the usage in this contribution).

[128] Tong and Zhang (2002, p. 26).

of evidence and its process of establishment in individual cases are both required.[129] For instance, the trial judge must make a choice between conflicting testimonies and, if necessary, a further evidential investigation is to be taken. On the contrary, merely stating that a party has failed to meet the burden of proof on that fact is not acceptable.[130] Meanwhile, the factual reasoning of civil judgments should not be limited to the essential facts of the case. Rather, relevant indirect facts are to be covered by the judgment.[131]

3.4.2.2 Specific Solutions for Improving the Reasoning Part

As far as the finding of facts is concerned, there are three major defects existing in Chinese civil judgments, namely errors or omissions in the fact-finding itself, the lack of specific grounds to support the conclusion of the fact-finding via the evidence or other proofing means (or on the contrary, wasting time on producing evidence for undisputed facts), and the inconsistency between the fact-finding and the application of law.[132] The proper resolution of these issues requires a systematic analysis of the entire solution as well as specific rules in the evidence law and the legal methodology, which is beyond the scope of this contribution that focuses on the structure of civil judgments.

Specifically speaking, we have to further adopt the method of grounds of substantive rights and make use of the legal subsumption and the legal interpretation. When it comes to the justification of the factual ascertainment of disputed facts and the publication of the reasons for establishing the evidential evaluation, we should continue to distinguish between direct evidence and indirect evidence (circumstantial evidence) and their supporting systems under the law of evidence (even when uncertain legal concepts are involved).[133] Moreover, we have to respect the principles and rules within adjudicative techniques in terms of the admissibility of evidence, the object of proof, the burden of producing factual allegations and the burden of proof, the presumption of facts, the deadline for producing evidence, and the evaluation of proof.[134] Especially, we need to correctly understand the rules on the allocation of the burden of proof (Article 91 of the *ICPL*) and its specific application in various types of cases.

---

[129] 9C Wright and Miller, Fed. Prac. & Proc. Civ., §§ 2574, 2579 (westlaw).

[130] Khan v. Fatima, 680 F.3d 781, 785–786 (7th Cir. 2012). In contrast, the viewpoint based on English case law that judges do not have to reason about the evaluation of the testimony of such witnesses: Ho (2000, pp. 58–59).

[131] Kelley v. Everglades Drainage Dist., 319 U.S. 415, 422 (1943); Sabinsa Corp. v. Creative Compounds, LLC, 609 F.3d 175, 182 (3d Cir.2010), cert. denied, 131 S.Ct. 960, 178 L.Ed.2d 757 (2011); Zack v. CIR, 291 F.3d 407, 412 (6th Cir.2002).

[132] Lei and Huang (2009, pp. 96–97); He B (2009, p. 38); Wang (2006, p. 59).

[133] Cao (2020a, pp. 124–136). Similar viewpoints, see Hu and Liu (2018, pp. 19–20). For a dissenting view, see Ji (2012).

[134] For a discussion based on practical experience, see Yang and Shao (2020).

It is also necessary to realize that Article 108 of the *ICPL* emphasizes the necessity of identifying the "*non-liquet*" status of a certain factual allegation and the standard of proof of "high probability" as a general rule, which clarifies the differences among observers on the interpretation of Article 2 paragraph 2 and Article 73 of the *2001 Evidence Provisions* previously (Chap. 6).[135] When other standards of proof are involved, the judge should provide a specific indication which is similar to the German counterpart and explain the evaluation of evidence when there are conflicting means of evidence to be taken. Meanwhile, as mentioned previously, the evaluation of evidence is a part of the judgment's reasoning, and the writing order of such reasoning differs from the order of court hearings. Since the fundamental approach to reasoning within civil judgments is to state the conclusion first and then the reasons supporting it, the facts which the judge has established via the evidential evaluation should be presented first. The factual conclusion should then be justified through the evidence and rules of proof.[136]

Furthermore, the judgment's reasoning inevitably requires the correspondence between facts and the evidence, and the application of law. Similar to different judge's trial habits during court hearings,[137] the judge should provide reasons for the finding results of facts considering different situations of evidence collection in individual cases. Whether the evidence is grouped first[138] or the reasons for finding the facts are stated together, it is necessary to maintain the connection between the facts and the evidence, rather than separately record the individual means of evidence.[139] For example, in the first-instance judgment of the Pengyu case (Chap. 2), the judge evaluated the relevant evidence in the part of "the court considers that", introduced the relevant *prima facie* evidence to justify its fact-finding, and "determined that the plaintiff was injured due to the collision with the defendant". Although the *prima facie* evidence introduced by the judge itself does not meet the legal requirement sufficiently, its approach to justifying the factual conclusion has reflected the aforementioned suggestions of this contribution.

While applying the laws, the judge should pay attention to the requirements of citing legal provisions (Chap. 4) and respond to the matters that the parties may have doubts about or their legal arguments,[140] even if the judge is of the opinion that these matters or issues have nothing to do with the results of the case. What is

---

[135] Cao (2013).

[136] Dissenting viewpoints are that when discussing the specific evaluation of evidence (in the "it is ascertained upon trial" part), it is the evidence that should be discussed first, and logically follows the ascertainment of facts in the case. For example, Zhao (2010, pp. 163–165); Li (2002, p. 76); Gong (2000, p. 19).

[137] Zou (2010, pp. 130–133).

[138] For this approach in the "it is ascertained upon trial" part, see, for example, Civil Judgment of the People's Court of Xishan District of Kunming City of Yunnan Province (2014) Xi Fa Min Chu Zi No. 3252.

[139] Ying (2013, pp. 82, 84).

[140] For similar viewpoints, see Li and Fan (2015, p. 95); Zhou (2014, pp. 27–28); Hu (2009, p. 52); Li (2002, p. 76). For an example of this practice of the SPC, see Civil Ruling of the SPC (2013) Min Ti Zi No. 67. Common law jurisdictions also require reasoning that focuses on the disputed issues.

involved here is not only the so-called principle of *jura novit curia* and the summary of disputed issues during the court hearings (Article 226 and 228 of the *ICPL*), but also, from the perspective of persuading the parties to accept the outcome of the judgment, the judge's response to the parties should be the fundamental requirement of the judgment's reasoning. In other words, the judge is restricted by the parties' opinions on the issues in a limited manner, that is, the judge must respond, but the judge can choose his own legal viewpoints. Moreover, in practice, when both sides of the parties are assisted by legal professionals, the factual allegations and legal arguments of either side often sound plausible.

However, since the plaintiff's and defendant's cases are generally in conflict, the judge must find the right answer by itself.[141] The difference may exist either in facts or be caused by various interpretations of the laws and by their application. In either case, the judge must provide reasons why the judge is in support of a particular viewpoint, or even why the judge chooses a third possible factual finding or legal interpretation. If proofing factual allegations requests generally the judge's evaluation of the means of evidence, legal reasons provide the "means of evidence" (viewpoints) that "prove" the correctness of the judgment's results (supportive grounds).[142] In other words, even if the judge thinks that a legal issue is not crucial for the current case, the judge should consider the German and American law experiences and make it clear in the reasoning part of the judgment that such an issue should be dealt with within a more appropriate case in the future.[143] In this way, we may promote the Chinese system of guiding cases and even precedents which is better off in recent years.

Finally, with regard to referring to materials in the reasoning part of civil judgments, we have to take the various possibilities of such materials into account. Since there could be ancient cultural classics (such as the Book of Filial Piety (孝经)), Chinese political literature, scientific viewpoints of law (of course including the opinions of judges who also contribute to the academic research),[144] guiding cases, or other prior judgments and information on foreign laws and so forth, the situation may be complicated (Chap. 4). This contribution preliminarily deems that the reference in civil judgments should not be limited to the sources of law. Rather, non-binding materials can also play a persuasive role in judgments. As far as the citation of academic theories is concerned, the leading opinion and practice in China would say no.

Coleman v. Dunlop Ltd [1998] P.I.Q.R. 398, 403; Landbridge Transport Pty Limited v. Buckley [2014] NSWSC 1379 at [30]–[36]; see Arden (2012, pp. 515–516).

141 Christensen and Sokolowski (2005, p. 106).

142 Gast (2006, Rn 265).

143 For a similar suggestion on the judgment of the Supreme Court of China Taiwan, see Zhang T et al. (2006, p. 181) (statement by Huang Kuo-chang).

144 For instance, Civil Judgment of the People's Court of Xuanwu District of Nanjing City of Jiangsu Province (2013) Xuan Shang Chu Zi No. 580, which directly quoted the opinions expressed by scholars at the relevant academic symposium. For relevant information and the full-text judgment, see Yang (2014).

It also means that even if one party quotes the leading legal opinion or the viewpoints of famous jurists in its pleadings or other litigation documents,[145] the court will not explicitly give a response in the part of "the court considers that". Among the civil judgments which have been rendered in other proceedings, merely the officially published guiding cases have the legal effect of "should be referred to" (Article 7 of the *Provisions of the SPC on Case Guidance*). Apart from these cases, even the judgments published in the Gazette of the SPC are not capable of having legal effects like this.[146] However, if the judge chooses to explain the understanding of legal issues in more detail[147] and point out how the evaluation of evidence is established, it will also help improve the judgment's reasoning in China.[148] Moreover, even if the judge does not clarify what has influenced the viewpoints in the specific case, the judge's understanding of the laws cannot be derived from nowhere. Therefore, regardless of whether the legal sources of the judgment are directly quoted or not, they will have nothing to do with the viewpoints of the judge and its trial arrangement.[149]

Then it comes to other legal norms which are not provided by the statutes themselves but also have some normative effects in Chinese current law and practice. Rules of judicial interpretations have long been regarded as legal norms to be cited directly by the judge, while rules in other normative documents can also be directly cited in judgments (Article 4 sentence 1 and Article 6 of the *Provisions on Citation in Judicial Decisions*. Among them, these normative documents cover not only the ones made by other state authorities or the SPC, but adopt an extensive interpretation, also the business guidance of provincial higher People's Courts (compare Articles 8 and 9 of the *Several Opinions of the SPC on Regulating the Trial Work Relations between the People's Courts at Different Levels*, in order to enrich the materials available for judgment's reasoning).

In reality, such practice is still a minority.[150] In many cases, even if the parties explicitly refer to relevant normative documents, the individual courts will remain silent in the reasoning of their judgments. If we turn to the academic dispute on the source of laws, such a source is to solve the problem of "what is the law", which is not directly linked to the form and contents of judgment's reasoning. In this sense,

---

[145] For instance, Civil Judgment of the People's Court of Funing County of Hebei Province (2014) Fu Min Yi Chu Zi No. 1868; and Civil Judgment of the People's Court of Luolong District of Luoyang City of Henan Province (2014) Luo Long Min Chu Zi No. 2098.

[146] Civil Ruling of the SPC (2014) Min Shen Zi No. 441.

[147] For instance, Peng (2020); Li (2018).

[148] For instance, Civil Judgment of the People's Court of Putuo District of Shanghai (2013) Pu Min Er (Shang) Chu Zi No. 642 (including 54 footnotes and citing academic viewpoints). Judge He Fan of the SPC previously supported the idea of adding footnotes to judgments. He F (2009). From the perspective of judges' knowledge production, see Hou (2021, pp. 140–142).

[149] In the confrontation of viewpoints organized by the Procuratorate Daily (newspaper), neither the pros nor the cons denied the actual impact of experts' and scholars' opinions on judicial reasoning. Su and Wu (2015); Zhou and Wei (2015); also Wang (2020).

[150] For instance, Civil Judgment of the People's Court of Sanmen County of Zhejiang Province (2014) Tai San Jian Shang Chu Zi No. 195; Civil Judgment of the People's Court of Xindu District of Chengdu City of Sichuan Province (2015) Xin Du Min Chu Zi No. 109.

the social backgrounds, statistical data, life experiences and so on cited by judges in their reasoning are not "the law" in the sense of the source of laws. However, they could be part of the judgment's reasoning which may be supplement information for such reasoning. In fact, behind the formal difference in whether some materials are to be referred to, what makes a real difference is the inherent persuasiveness of the relevant viewpoints. As long as the viewpoints are to be understood as legal interpretation, they can be transformed into the answer of individual judges to legal issues of individual cases in any civil judgment, so as to meet the requirement of adjudicating according to law.

Therefore, considering the specificity and guiding effect of the aforementioned business guidance of provincial high People's Courts, this contribution speaks for expanding the scope of to-be-cited materials in the judgments' reasoning which is already recognized by Chinese practice. Such a solution could lead to more responses from the judge to disputed issues and strengthen the judgment's reasoning. Of course, since whether to indicate the academic reference in civil judgments is related merely to the form of judicial reasoning, the discretion of whether and how to do so should be in the hands of the individual judge. This understanding applies also to previous final judgments and the guiding cases. It is up to the judge of the case to determine whether to refer to them according to the specific circumstances (the technique of distinguishing facts). Nevertheless, simply referring to the judgment's conclusion in other cases does not satisfy the obligation of providing judicial reasoning.[151]

References

Althammer C (2018) In: Stein F, Jonas M, ZPO, Band 4, 23. Aufl. Mohr Siebeck, Tübingen

Andrews N (2019) Andrews on civil procedure. Intersentia, Cambridge

Arden DM (2012) Judgment writing, are shorter judgments achievable? Law Quarterly Review 128:515–535

Balzer C (1995) Schlanke Entscheidungen im Zivilprozeß. Neue Juristische Wochenschrift 48:2448–2457

Balzer C, Walther B (2018) Das Urteil im Zivilprozess. Erich Schmidt Verlag GmbH & Co, Berlin

Becht E, Beck SM (2010) Zivilprozessrecht im Assessorexamen. C. H. Beck, München

Bernhardt W (1949) Die Aufklärung des Sachverhalts im Zivilprozeß. In: Beiträge zum Zivilprozeßrecht, Festgabe zum siebzigsten Geburtstag von Leo Rosenberg, München und Berlin, pp 9–50

Bischof HH (1980) Der Zivilprozeß nach der Vereinfachungsnovelle. Kohlhammer, Stuttgart

Büdenbender U (2013) Die Analyse höchstrichterlicher Entscheidungen. Juristische Arbeitsblätter 45:161–165

Cai J, Cheng J (2006) Close and open: an analysis of argumentation style of judgment reasoning. Legal Forum 2:128–132 (in Chinese)

Cao Z (2013) Does *non liquet* status exist in civil system of proof in China? The Jurist 2:95–105+178–179 (in Chinese)

Cao Z (2014) The preclusion of the defendant's answer in ordinary proceedings. Peking University Law Journal 2:483–508 (in Chinese)

[151] Cao (2016, pp. 115–116).

Cao Z (2015) Reflection on the pre-determinant force of facts. Modern Law Science 1:130–138 (in Chinese)
Cao Z (2016) On the effect of the guiding cases in China and their application in the legal process. Journal of Comparative Law 6:111–134 (in Chinese)
Cao Z (2017) On the rectification of clerical mistakes in a civil judgment. Wuhan University Journal (Philosophy & Social Science) 4:70–79 (in Chinese)
Cao Z (2020a) Models of proof of factual allegations in civil process. Journal of Soochow University (Law Edition) 4:124–136 (in Chinese)
Cao Z (2020b) Reconsidering the fact-finding reasoning in the 'Pengyu' decision. Northern Legal Science 3:89–98 (in Chinese)
Cao Z (2020c) Reflection on the examination of the subject matter of claims in the civil case-filing proceedings. China Legal Science 1:283–303 (in Chinese)
Cao Z (2020d) The restriction of the presumption rule of the substantial proving effects of public document. Journal of National Prosecutors College 2:137–154 (in Chinese)
Cao Z (2021) On the citation of legal norms in civil litigation. Law and Modernization 3:150–161 (in Chinese)
Christensen R, Sokolowski M (2005) Die Krise der Kommunikation und die Möglichkeit juristischen Argumentierens. In: Lerch KD (ed) Die Sprache des Rechts, Band 2: Recht verhandeln: Argumentieren, Begründen und Entscheiden im Diskurs des Rechts. De Gruyter, Berlin
Duan W (2012) Reflection on the structure of norm-based civil judgments. Law Press, Beijing (in Chinese)
Feskorn C (2020) In: Zöller R, ZPO, 33. Aufl. Otto Schmidt, Köln
Fischer F (2005) Der Tatbestand im Zivilurteil unter besonderer Berücksichtigung der Bezugnahmen. Juristische Schulung 45:904–908
Fischer C (2007) Topoi verdeckter Rechtsfortbildungen im Zivilrecht. Mohr Siebeck, Tübingen
Fu Y (2000) The functions and styles of civil judicial decisions. Social Sciences in China 4:123–133 (in Chinese)
Gast W (2006) Juristische Rhetorik. C. F. Müller, Heidelberg
Gong C (2000) Thoughts on the reform of the mode of making civil judgments. Journal of Law Application 2:17–20 (in Chinese)
Gottwald P (2011) Die Begründung von Gerichtsentscheidungen in Deutschland: aus Sicht der Praxis und der Wissenschaft. In: Tichý L, Holländer P, Bruns A (eds) Centrum právní komparatistiky, Právnická fakulta Univerzity Karlovy, Praha.
Gottwald P (2015) Reasoning in German judicial judgments: practice and doctrine (trans: Cao Z). Journal of Soochow University (Law Edition) 4:83–92 (in Chinese)
Goutal JL (1976) Characteristics of judicial style in France, Britain and the U.S.A. The American Journal of Comparative Law 24:43–72
Hartmann P (2019) In: Baumbach A, Lauterbach W, Albers J, Hartmann P, ZPO. C. H. Beck, München
He X (2004) The standardization of civil judgments and the direction of reform. People's Court Daily, 7 January 2004 (in Chinese)
He B (2009) The making and reasoning of civil and commercial judicial decisions. People's Judicature 3:37–43 (in Chinese)
He F (2009) Is it superfluous to add footnotes to judgments? Southern Weekend, 4 June 2009 (in Chinese)
He X, Wang S (2005) Analysis of several issues concerning making civil judgments. People's Judicature 12:4–7 (in Chinese)
Ho HL (2000) The judicial duty to give reasons. Legal Studies 20:42–65
Höhne N (2005) Vom Sandwichdiagramm zur Struktur einer selektiven Dokumentation – Die Tatbestandsfassung im Zivilurteil. Juristische Arbeitsblätter 37:290–294
Hou M (2021) The operative process of justice: based on the observation of the SPC. China Legal Publishing House, Beijing (in Chinese)
Hu Y (2009) On the reasoning of judicial decisions. Journal of Law Application 3:48–52 (in Chinese)

Hu S (2014) Research on civil adjudication. Social Science Academic Press, Beijing (in Chinese)
Hu S, Liu S (2018) Construction of the system and normative interpretation of the reasoning within judicial decisions in the new era (I): understanding and application of the guiding opinions on strengthening and standardizing the interpretation and reasoning of judicial decisions. Journal of Law Application (Judicial Case) 16:3–20 (in Chinese)
Huang Y (2021) Induction of disputed issues in civil trial: technical analysis and comprehensive application. Law Press, Beijing (in Chinese)
Huber M (2003) Das Zivilurteil. C. H. Beck, München
Huber M (2004) Das Strafurteil. C. H. Beck, München
Hunke M (2020) In: Baumbach A, Lauterbach W, Hartmann P, Anders M, Gehle B, ZPO. C. H. Beck, München
Ito M (2016) Civil procedure law. Yuhikaku Publishing, Tokyo (in Japanese)
Ito M (2019) Civil procedure law (trans: Cao Y), 4th edn. Peking University Press, Beijing (in Chinese)
Ji G (2012) Does direct evidence really exist? Peking University Law Journal 3:594–606 (in Chinese)
Jiang W, Fu Y (eds) (2015) Civil procedure law. Peking University Press, Beijing (in Chinese)
Knöringer D (2014) Die Assessorklausur im Zivilprozess. C. H. Beck, München
Knöringer D (2018) Die Assessorklausur im Zivilprozess. C. H. Beck, München
Lei X, Huang W (2009) Analysis of current problems in courts' judgments and their reasons. Journal of Law Application 12:95–98 (in Chinese)
Li C (2002) On the writing technique of civil judgments. Journal of Law Application 4:75–77 (in Chinese)
Li M (2018) Legal theory and theories as the source of civil law. Law Science 6:99–115 (in Chinese)
Li D, Fan H (2015) A new exploration of the reasoning model of judicial decisions in China under the division of rigid and weak needs. Law and Social Development 3:93–108 (in Chinese)
Li W, Yin J (2009) The way of adjudication with disputed facts: a brief introduction to German court report method. Journal of Law Application 4:88–91 (in Chinese)
Liao Y (2003) Several mistakes should be avoided in the reform of civil judicial decisions. People's Court Daily, 16 September 2003 (in Chinese)
Liu X (2005) The reform and making of civil judicial decisions. People's Judicature 12:8–11 (in Chinese)
Liu S (2020) No reasoning is not 'book': 23 lectures on the reasoning of judicial decisions. China Procuratorate Press, Beijing (in Chinese)
Liu L, Sun J (2002) Comparison and reference of the reasoning of the judgments within two legal systems. Journal of Law Application 3:18–19 (in Chinese)
Lücke J (1987) Begründungszwang und Verfassung. Mohr Siebeck, Tübingen
Luo C (2015) Five misunderstandings to be avoided in promoting the reasoning reform of judicial decisions. People's Court Daily, 6 February 2015 (in Chinese)
Matsumoto H, Ueno Y (2015) Civil procedure law. Koubundou Publishers, Tokyo (in Japanese)
Musielak HJ (2020) In: Krüger W, Rauscher T, Münchener Kommentar ZPO, Band 1, 6. Aufl. C. H. Beck, München
National Judges College and German Agency for International Cooperation (2014) Methods of application of law and methods of case analysis of contract law. China Legal Publishing House, Beijing (in Chinese)
Peng Z (2020) On the judicial application of legal theory. Social Sciences in China 4:90–113+206 (in Chinese)
Pielke W (2006) Verweisungen im Tatbestand eines zivilgerichtlichen Urteils. Juristische Arbeitsblätter 38:202–205
Rosenberg L, Schwab KH, Gottwald P (2018) Zivilprozessrecht. C. H. Beck, München
Schack H (2017) Internationales Zivilverfahrensrecht. C. H. Beck, München
Seiler C (2019) In: Thomas H, Putzo H, ZPO, 40. Aufl. C. H. Beck, München
Shao M (2018) Jurisprudence of modern civil litigation and dispute procedure. Renmin University of China Press, Beijing (in Chinese)

Shen D (ed) (2016) The style of civil litigation documents. People's Court Press, Beijing (in Chinese)
Shindo K (2008) New civil procedure law (trans: Lin J). Law Press, Beijing (in Chinese)
Shindo K (2019) Civil procedure law. Koubundou Publishers, Tokyo (in Japanese)
Siegburg P (2002) Zum Tatbestand des erstinstanzlichen Urteils im Bauprozess. Zeitschrift für Deutsches und Internationales Bau- und Vergaberecht 25:635–640
Steiner E (2010) French law: a comparative approach. Oxford University Press, Oxford
Su L (2001) Behind the judgments. Chinese Journal of Law 3:3–18 (in Chinese)
Su Q, Wu X (2015) Pros: To enhance reasoning can scholars' opinions be directly cited. Procuratorate Daily, 1 April 2015 (in Chinese)
Tang W (2000) How judges reason cases: research and application of reasoning in judicial decisions. People's Court Press, Beijing (in Chinese)
Tang X (2000) Writing 'reasonable' judgment documents. Law Review 4:123–126 (in Chinese)
Thole C (2018) In: Stein F, Jonas M, ZPO, Band 4, 23. Aufl. Mohr Siebeck, Tübingen
Tong Z, Zhang H (2002) On the reform of reasoning of judgments. Journal of Zhejiang University (Humanities and Social Sciences) 2:26–33 (in Chinese)
Wach A (1896) Vorträge über die Reichs-Civilprocessordnung, 2. Aufl. De Gruyter, Berlin
Wang Z (2005) Research on the reasoning of judicial decisions. Shandong Social Sciences 8:84–86+156 (in Chinese)
Wang S (2006) Complicated civil judgments should be different from the simple ones. Journal of Law Application 12:58–60 (in Chinese)
Wang Y (2010) Adversary and adjudication: basic structures of civil procedure in Japan. Tsinghua University Press, Beijing (in Chinese)
Wang S (2011) Judge's rationality and reasoned judgments. Political Science and Law 12:86–96 (in Chinese)
Wang L (2020) Reconsidering the direct citations of scholars' opinions in judicial decisions. Legal Forum 4:93–100 (in Chinese)
Wei S (2012) Face-to-face reasoning, strengthening rhetoric and focusing on major issues: some thoughts over how to improve court decisions in China. Science of Law 5:48–60 (in Chinese)
Wu Q (2002) On the reform of judicial decisions and the exercise of judges' discretion. People's Judicature 12:54–57 (in Chinese)
Wu X (2020) Claim basis thinking and its opponents. Nanjing University (Philosophy, Human Sciences and Social Sciences) 2:90–106+159 (in Chinese)
Wu Z, Liu Y, Ma J (eds) (2013) Civil trial skills. China Democratic Legal Publishing House, Beijing (in Chinese)
Xi X (ed) (2012) Understanding and application of amendments to the civil procedure law of the P.R.C. People's Court Press, Beijing (in Chinese)
Xi X, Nan Y, Ying Y, Liu X (eds) (2013) Courses on the writing of judgments by the People's Courts. China Legal Publishing House, Beijing (in Chinese)
Xiao H (2008) Tradition and modern transformation of reasoning in Chinese judgments. Law Press, Beijing (in Chinese)
Xu R (2003) Some issues in the reform of civil and commercial judgments. Journal of Law Application 1–2:30–33 (in Chinese)
Xu K (2009) Civil trial methods: introduction to essential facts. Law Press, Beijing (in Chinese)
Yang L (2014) Nanjing court's judgment cites scholars' viewpoints, experts say that it is the first one countrywide and can enhance the degree of reasoning. http://www.thepaper.cn/newsDetail_forward_1287931. Accessed 2 May 2024 (in Chinese)
Yang H, Shao X (2020) Empirical analysis and regulation refining of evidential reasoning in judgment. Journal of Law Application 6:16–32 (in Chinese)
Ying X (2013) How judges identify the evidence during civil trials. Journal of Law Application 6:81–86 (in Chinese)
Yuan L, Shao X (2017) An analysis of the relevance of the structure and reasoning of civil judgments in Germany. Journal of Law Application 1:113–120 (in Chinese)
Yun L (2012) How to strengthen the reasoning of judgments. China Trial 2:61–63 (in Chinese)

Zhang Z (1998) The structure and style of judicial judgments. Law Science 10:26–32 (in Chinese)
Zhang G (2000) Improvement of the basic structure of civil judgments. Law Science Magazine 5:49–51 (in Chinese)
Zhang W (2004) Conditions of case registration and elements of judgments on the merits. Chinese Journal of Law 6:58–68 (in Chinese)
Zhang X (2005) Some jurisprudential considerations on the reform of judicial decisions. Journal of Law Application 2:70–73 (in Chinese)
Zhang Y (2009) Replacing 'it is ascertained upon trial' with 'the judgments are given as followed'. In: Wang L (ed) New exploration on making judgments. Shanghai Academy of Social Sciences Press, Shanghai (in Chinese)
Zhang Z (2009) Misunderstandings in making judicial decisions. Journal of the National Prosecutors College 2:77–84 (in Chinese)
Zhang W (2015) The principle of privity of *res judicata*: grounds, exceptions and institutionalization. Chinese Journal of Law 1:68–86 (in Chinese)
Zhang T et al. (2006) The third discussion on how to write a civil judgment. In: The Civil Procedure Law Research Foundation (ed) Discussion on civil procedure law (XIII). Sanmin Book Co., Taipei (in Chinese)
Zhao C (2010) The realistic expression of judicial adjudication. Law Press, Beijing (in Chinese)
Zhong M, Fan Y (2002) Civil and commercial judgments need to be improved. People's Court Daily, 18 June 2002 (in Chinese)
Zhou X (2014) Research on reasoning of civil judgments. Law Press, Beijing (in Chinese)
Zhou Z, Wei Z (2015) Cons: direct citation violates the requirement of taking the laws as the criterion. Procuratorate Daily, 1 April 2015 (in Chinese)
Zhuang X (2015) The realistic context and institutional rationality of judicial decisions. Journal of Law Application 11:83–92 (in Chinese)
Zimmermann W (2019) Klage, Gutachten und Urteil. C. F. Müller, Heidelberg
Zou B (2010) Nine-step method on elements of the civil trial. Law Press, Beijing (in Chinese)
Zuckerman AAS (2013) Zuckerman on civil procedure: principles of practice. Sweet & Maxwell, London

Chapter 4
Application of Law: Grounds of Substantive Rights, Citations of Legal Norms and Methodological Issues

4.1 Introduction

Similar to the judgment's reasoning in the fact-finding field which shows the focus of this contribution, the application of law plays a significant role in adjudicative techniques as well. Traditionally, the issue of legal application methods belongs to the research of jurisprudence. Nevertheless, such an issue is also crucial for understanding civil proceedings since it may reveal how the grounds for making judgments are established and then matched with the facts in individual cases. Therefore, it is necessary to understand the process of legal interpretation from the perspective of procedural law. Among others, the technique of subsumption (*Subsumtion*) is a very useful tool which attracts much attention in legal scholarship and practice. The process of subsumption is capable of clarifying the logical relationship among varied items or expressions within the judgment through a certain degree of abstract construction, then trying to expose possible omissions or errors. These techniques are suitable not only for simple cases, but also for difficult cases involving complex legal issues.

Other than jurisprudential scholars, substantive law scholars, who follow the tradition of legal dogmatics/hermeneutics in continental law systems, can also adopt the subsumption technique. By applying substantive law norms, they are able to improve the system of grounds of substantive rights (*Anspruchsgrundlage*) in civil law or the theory of constructive elements (*Tatbestand*) in criminal law. Meanwhile, the application of law is also reflected in the citation of legal provisions. There are some problems in China's practice in this regard.[1] Some scholars are of the opinion that it is often hard for the court to cite legal basis accurately in hard cases.[2] Some expert

[1] He and Zhong (2006).

[2] For example, Xia and Xu (2012).

Z. Cao, *Civil Judgments at First Instance*, Contemporary Chinese Civil and Commercial Law, https://doi.org/10.1007/978-981-97-8662-6_4

even mentions that the requirements of legal elements are merely used for endorsement in adjudicative activities, which provides a tool for judges to hide the real reasons for making their judgments and get rid of their own judicial responsibility.[3]

Hence, the SPC issued a judicial interpretation called *Opinions Reasoning Judicial Decisions* in 2018, which partially achieves the objectives of reforming judicial decisions set out in the *3rd Five-Year Outline of the Program for Reform of People's Courts* in 2015. Among others, this judicial interpretation emphasizes that "the purpose of analysis and reasoning in judicial decisions is to improve the acceptability of adjudication and achieve the organic unity of legal effect and social effect by clarifying the process of making judgments and providing justification for the conclusion of adjudication". Furthermore, it considers that "it is necessary to clarify legal reasons and explain legal provisions on which judicial decisions are based and the reasons for the application of legal norms".

And, when it comes to a more practical level, it matters not merely how to quote legal norms in the judgments' reasoning, but also whether the plaintiff should indicate the specific legal provisions in the claim form, rather than use the abstract expression "in accordance with the provisions of the Constitution and the laws". The relevant requirement can become a disputed issue in the discussion of the court's case-filing examination because it may be indirectly related to the choice of the theory of the subject matter of claims and affect the interpretation of the "specific procedural entitlement (诉讼请求)" required for the claim form in Article 122 item 3 of the *CPL*.[4]

In fact, the issues to be discussed hereby cover not merely the fundamental approaches of law at macro-level, but also the specific rules at meso-level, and the usage of specialized terms and concepts at micro-level. It is worth noting that the judgment's reasoning includes the reasoning of both judgments and other kinds of decisions made by judges. Concentrating on the main aim of this contribution, this

[3] Fang (2007, p. 29).

[4] This contribution uses deliberately the "specific procedural entitlement" for the translation of the expression in Article 122 item 3 of the *CPL* to reserve room for further elaboration of this provision. It is argued that in accordance with the continental legal tradition and Chinese legal practice, the fundamental meaning of the requirement for a concrete procedural entitlement refers to the specific relief sought (*Antrag*) by the claimant. Although this required condition of "procedural entitlement" could point to the subject matter of a civil process itself, during the case-filing phase this approach to interpretation is not desirable. Ideally, the legal reasoning part of the complaint and the cause of action of the claimant should not be regarded as preconditions for bringing a lawsuit and therefore have no connection to the subject matter issue. The exception is that the specific grounds for substantive rights (*Anspruch*) in the traditional substantive law theory, which could also be classified as legal reasons, relate to the subject matter of a civil claim. Nevertheless, considering the new case-filing registration system, the subject matter of the lawsuit should not be considered as an element of bringing a lawsuit. Rather, the court should bring the subject matter of the lawsuit into the scope of the requirements of the proceedings after accepting the case, as a procedural condition to be determined after the case-filing system and an issue to be resolved later. In practice, based on the modification of the traditional substantive law theory of the subject matter, there should at least be multiple possibilities of consolidating claims, among which the elective accumulation of claims (*alternative Klagenhäufung*) is one reasonable illustration. Cao (2020b, pp. 292–294).

chapter is limited to the reasoning of first-instance civil judgments. As for other judgments such as civil rulings on major procedural matters or the second instance or retrial decisions which additionally reflect the evaluation of court's decisions at prior stages in the judicial hierarchy (Article 10 of the *Opinions Reasoning Judicial Decisions*), the shared elements could also be addressed, while their special arrangement has to be left in the future.

4.2 Application of Law Centering on Grounds of Substantive Rights

4.2.1 Significance of the Method of Grounds of Substantive Rights in the Field of Civil Law

Corresponding to the subsumption technique in legal methodology, the method of grounds of substantive rights[5] originally in German civil law also provides a significant guide for the citation of legal norms. Taking the claim for performance (*Leistungsklage*) as a typical scenario, China's civil law academic circle broadly adopts the method of grounds of substantive rights to analyze substantive law issues. Even if in legal practice, adopting the method of grounds of substantive rights is still not standardized,[6] it nevertheless can be foreseen that the forthcoming civil law study is to focus more on re-interpreting the *Civil Code of the P.R.C.* which is expected since long ago.[7] The reason for this trend is simple and it is to provide reliable sources for judges to cite legal provisions in their judgments accurately. Then, both ordinary citizens and lawyers could expect forseenable adjudicative results with legal certainty. By doing it, the method of grounds of substantive rights can also gradually prevail in making judgments and citing legal norms.

For this purpose, first, it is necessary to locate the provisions in existing statutes that are related to grounds of substantive rights and the legal development accomplished through guiding cases selected and published by the SPC. Second, besides complete provisions which can solely represent a ground of substantive rights and lead to some certain legal consequences, there are interpretative provisions, restrictive provisions, provisions which merely refer to other provisions, and provisions having the function of legal fiction. Third, it is to be clarified whether some provisions are concurring and how to apply the law on such occasions. Then, by combining such results with the comparative experience as well as theories in Chinese civil law, it is possible to finally establish a grossly coherent theoretical system of grounds of substantive

[5] It is worth noting that Wang Yong's recent book attempts to explore the possible framework of private rights in civil law on the basis of Hohfeld's analysis of rights rather than relying on the now popular grounds of substantive rights. Wang (2020, pp. 67–202, 344–368).

[6] Jin (2021, pp. 89–90).

[7] For example, Wu (2019); Hu (2016).

rights.[8] This approach is also capable of winning supports by the case study method under the name of *Gutachten* (evaluation in English) or similar case study modes[9] which are now vigorously promoted within the domestic legal education circle. It is worth adding that, although the legal citation itself represents the major premise of the judicial syllogism within the application of law, on most occasions the legal provisions themselves cannot replace the argumentation for judgments' results and the reasoning of judicial decisions. The reason is that, when it comes to individual cases, there would be gaps between the major premise and the minor premise of the judicial syllogism and substantial reasons are then besides legal citations needed as well.

Since this contribution is unable to provide a comprehensive system of grounds of substantive rights in Chinese civil law, merely an illustration is to be presented hereby. Even as a proceduralist, in my course of Case Study on Civil Procedure (民事诉讼案例研习) offered by Peking University Law School, a system of grounds of substantive rights, which is provided by the course of Case Study on Civil Law (民法案例研习) organized by my colleagues in civil law completely, is accepted and utilized. Their answers are then regarded as the premise for discussion of procedural issues. For example, in the repeatedly mentioned first-instance judgment of the Pengyu case (Chap. 2), setting the issues of the subject matter of claims aside,[10] the judge "determined at his discretion that the defendant compensate 40% of the plaintiff's losses" on the basis of equality principle. Yet, the judge did not refer to Article 132 of the previous *General Principles of the Civil Law of the P.R.C.* (corresponding to Article 1186 of the *Civil Code of the P.R.C.* and Article 24 of the *Tort Law of the P.R.C.*) accordingly. Then it is to be considered that there is an error regarding the logic of legal application.[11] On such an occasion, Article 98 of the *General Principles of the Civil Law of the P.R.C.* cannot be understood merely as a legal principle. Rather, this provision stipulates the victim's rights and, together with Article 106 paragraph 2 of the *General Principles of the Civil Law of the P.R.C.*, constitutes the grounds of substantive rights of this case. Accordingly, Article 119 of the *General Principles of the Civil Law of the P.R.C.* only refers to the scope of damage (or the scope of liability).[12]

Conversely, as long as the private law is still unable to provide a system of grounds of substantive rights that is widely accepted by both the academic circle and the practice to a large extent, it is difficult for proceduralists to obtain relatively certain answers for crucial procedural issues. To be named are both the issue of subject

---

[8] For an introduction to grounds of substantive rights in Germany: Medicus and Peterson (2019); Kaiser, Kaiser and Kaiser (2018); also Medicus (2012). For a similar summary in China Taiwan, see Wang (2019, pp. 39–101, 147–585). This seems to be the leading theory in China's civil law academic community. For example, Ge (2014, pp. 307–312); Xu (2013, pp. 951–962) (also involving a discussion of procedural law norms); Duan (2012, pp. 27–29). For the positive evaluation from the practice, see Liu L (2020); Hu and Liu (2018, pp. 4–5); Zou (2010).

[9] Wang (2019, pp. 125–132); Ge (2015); Zhang (2011).

[10] Cao (2020a, p. 92).

[11] For similar views, see Zhang (2008, p. 105).

[12] For a different view, see Zhang (2008, p. 105).

matter of claims, in which the standard of identification is to be fixed, and of legal citation which is discussed hereby. The *Civil Code of the P.R.C.*, which took effect in 2020, cannot "cure all diseases overnight". Whether by its nature the procedural law is understood as a tool for realizing the goals of substantive law or that it has its independent institutional value, it is more acceptable to conclude that, as commonly seen in the field of comparative civil procedure, scholars of private law need to master both the substantive law and the procedural law simultaneously. Accordingly, private law research should also be based on both of them to provide comprehensive solutions for practical problems. In this regard, we should at least realize the significance of civil subjects (in principle two parties), legal basis and the content of the claim in the civil law, all of which are covered in the concept of grounds of substantive rights. Meanwhile, it is to be noticed that there is a corresponding relationship between constitutive elements of substantive rights (civil law)/essential facts (procedural law), on one side, and the plaintiff/defendant, the cited legal regulations and the claims for relief on the other hand.[13]

4.2.2 Citation of Substantive Law Norms Under the Method of Grounds of Substantive Rights

Considering that China's civil law system has its roots in continental law systems (especially Germany and Japan), Germany is taken as an example to introduce the potential approaches to improving the quality of legal citation in China. In German civil judgments, the application of law to the ascertained facts is carried out exactly based on grounds of substantive rights. It is attributed to its civil law system which is built up as a system of substantive rights and claims.[14] Different from China's tradition, German judges will not list all grounds of substantive rights and relevant legal norms involved in the case literally before the operative part of their judgments. Rather, they will merely indicate them while analyzing specific legal issues if necessary. Certainly, when it comes to German judgments published e.g. in the official Gazette or law journals, there are usually a number of legal provisions cited instantly under the titles, the form of which is similar to judgments in China. However, such citations in German judgments only function as guidance and reference for the legal research and are not an intrinsic and organic part of the judgments. Naturally, they are not capable of indicating the legal basis for making judgments. Once again, this function of indication is fulfilled by the reasoning part of German judgments.

Under normal circumstances, a civil judgment analyzes the legal issues involved in different parts separately, following the order of giving the interim conclusions first, discovering the legal basis second and giving the final conclusion based on the factual allegations of the parties and the results of evidential investigation of the judge last. During analyzing the legal basis hereby, the judge should accurately indicate

[13] Wang (2019, pp. 41–42).

[14] Schapp (1992, p. 537).

the legal conditions and the relevant articles, paragraphs, sentences, sub-sentences or even the different alternatives in a sentence of applying the grounds of substantive rights.[15] And all legal norms on which the judgment relied should be cited explicitly as well.[16]

As a simple illustration in German context, when the plaintiff claims for liability resulting from a negligent act tort, the scope of damage is to be determined considering both statutory provisions regarding the tort substantive right claiming for damages (Article 823 paragraph 1 of the *German Civil Code*) and general rules on damages (Article 249 of the *German Civil Code*). A more complex example would be if the plaintiff claims for the return of his painting based on his substantive right on return because of ownership (Article 985 of the *German Civil Code*). Since the relationship between owner and possessor is concerned, the statutory provisions on the acquisition and loss of ownership (Article 873, 925, 929 et seq. of the *German Civil Code*) and possession (Article 854 et seq. of the *German Civil Code*) may be applied. Even, regarding the interpretation of contractual consensus, the norms of legal transactions (Article 104 et seq. of the *German Civil Code*) and contracts (Article 145 et seq. of the *German Civil Code*) in the General Part of Civil Law are concerned as well. From the perspective of potential defenses of the defendant, it is necessary to consider whether the defendant is entitled to possession (Article 986 et seq. of the *German Civil Code*), which involves a real right of lien (Article 1204 et seq., Article 562 and Article 647 of the *German Civil Code*) or a contract in which possession is the content of the stipulated performance (Article 535 and Article 581 of the *German Civil Code*).

Among them, the norm on return of an item due to ownership is called the norm of substantive rights (*Anspruchsnorm*), while the other norms can be regarded separately as primary or secondary auxiliary norms (*Hilfnormen*) depending on their relationship with the norms of substantive rights.[17] Consolidating multiple norms together can establish a ground of substantive rights.[18] Hence, the same norm may be classified in varied cases as different types of norms because it is always to be inquired which relationship exists between a specific norm and the substantive right on which the plaintiff relies. When it comes to the concurrence of grounds of substantive rights, we need to further consider the essential elements of each ground of substantive rights. Lastly, it is worth noting that, under Chinese law, there is an academic dispute over the nature of the substantive right on such occasions. When private legal scholars are still debating whether it is the return of an item because of

[15] Wang (2019, pp. 42, 46–47 and 134). Article 53 item 1 of the *Code of Conduct for Judges* in 2010 also makes the same regulations.

[16] Musielak (2020, Rn 17); Becht and Beck (2010, Rn 702). Dissenting opinion (but the difference in practice is limited): Feskorn (2020, Rn 19a).

[17] Medicus and Peterson (2019, Rn 16–17). For overall analysis, see Larenz (1991, pp. 264 et seq.).

[18] Wang (2019, pp. 40–41 and 54–57).

ownership or the tort liability, the judges may cite different legal norms for the same type of cases in practice. Unified law application cannot be realized in this way.[19]

Hence, it can be observed that the number of legal provisions to be referred to may be very large, when it comes to relatively complicated judgments. And such provisions may be distributed among different parts of the *German Civil Code* or even other separate statute. For this reason, it is necessary to give clear indications of the legal basis of the claims throughout the judgment (Article 53 item 2 of the *Code of Conduct for Judges*). Otherwise, it will be impossible to clarify the provisions discussed, relevant essential preconditions or provide supporting information when there is any doubt. Then, indicating legal provisions would be merely of formal meaning rather than substantial contribution. In addition, when a legal provision explicitly refers to another one, both provisions should be cited together. For instance, provisions on sale contracts apply to exchange contracts (Article 480 of the *German Civil Code*).[20] Article 45 paragraph 2 of the *Interpretation of the SPC on Issues Concerning the Application of Law for the Trial of Cases of Disputes over Sales Contracts* of 2012 also requires the judges, when hearing non-gratuitous contracts which need reference to the relevant provisions on sales contracts, to first cite Article 174 of the previous *Contract Law of the P.R.C.* (currently Article 646 of the *Civil Code of the P.R.C.*), and then refer to the relevant provisions on sales contracts.

It deserves special discussion when the provisions involved both in parts of general part as well as typical contracts of the *Civil Code of the P.R.C.* are discussed. We may take sale contracts as an illustration. The German approach is that the judge ought to directly cite the principal contractual obligations within the part of sales contracts (Article 433 of the *German Civil Code*) as the ground of substantive rights. There is no need to come back to general rules within the general part of the *German Civil Code*. At least considering the ordinary principle that special rules are superior to general rules, such a way of citation may be more advisable.[21]

4.2.3 Citation of Procedural Law Norms Under the Method of Grounds of Substantive Rights

Besides the norms of substantive law, civil judgments also need to cite norms of procedural law. As the substantive law explicitly regards the grounds of substantive rights as the starting point for discussion, the citation of procedural legal norms should return to the fundamental concepts like the requirements of the proceedings (*Prozessvoraussetzungen*) and elements for judgments on the merits. While the German civil judgment can only be made after oral hearings, the civil judgment under Chinese law is to be made on the premise that the lawsuit meets the requirements of

[19] For relevant disputes, see, for example, Wang (2014, pp. 91–101); Wei (2011); Wang (2009); Cui (2007).

[20] BGH NJW 2006, 988, 989, Tz 9.

[21] For the same view, for example, Yao (2020, p. 41).

bringing a lawsuit and requirements of the proceedings. Otherwise, the lawsuit will be rejected to be registered or being dismissed on procedural grounds (Article 127 of the *CPL* and Article 208 paragraph 3 of the *ICPL*).[22] In other words, the procedural requirements represent in China the crucial issues which the judge ought to examine when applying the procedural law. And the requirements of bringing a lawsuit and requirements of the proceedings are in fact the same set of preconditions which are examined by the court at different stages of civil proceedings, i.e. case-filing stage vs. the forthcoming stages. They can be divided into three groups, namely the ones concerning the court, the parties and the subject matter of claims, all of which are aimed to examine whether the claims of the case meet the preconditions of making judgments on the merits. These elements provide by their nature formal standards, which may be proven in a simplified manner and should even be presumed true in principle, if the content of formal requirements examined overlaps with the substantive elements on the merits (so-called double-relevant facts[23]). As for the substantive elements on the merits, except for the evaluation of some procedural legal transactions (*Rechtsgeschäfte*) in the case, the court can moreover perform its examination with the grounds of substantive rights in substantive law.

First, this issue handles the understanding of the subject matter of claims. In China's practice, the so-called traditional substantive law theories are usually acknowledged as the leading opinion regarding the standard of identifying the subject matter of claims in civil proceedings.[24] Thus, grounds of substantive rights are believed to be able to determine the quantity and the content of the subject matter of claims of the case. Following the principle of disposition, it is the party, normally the plaintiff of the relevant claim, which can choose the grounds of substantive rights in the case and then determine the object of trial of the case. This party's fundamental procedural right may occur when multiple claims for relief aim for different objects of performance (e.g. Article 583 of the *Civil Code of the P.R.C.*), and but also when the same claim for relief, e.g. the return of a specific item, is supported by different grounds of substantive rights such as real rights, obligational rights and other kinds of statutory debts (e.g. Article 186 of the *Civil Code of the P.R.C.*). And besides the grounds of substantive rights, the court also needs to apply procedural legal norms such as Article 247 paragraph 1 of the *ICPL*, which directly stipulates the standard of

---

[22] Cao (2020b, pp. 292–294); Zhang (2015b).

[23] Cao (2021). It is then argued that factual allegations, which are simultaneously essential for the substantive success and procedural requirements of a civil case, are of specialty in a civil process. Currently, the Chinese law demands for a test of preliminary evidence during the procedural phase for jurisdicational objection. It happens practically not only in ordinary civil proceedings, but also in proceedings for intellectual property cases. The procedural requirement for the evidence, which differs from the preliminary evidence in sense of substantive law, has to handle its ambiguity. Instead, the German law tends to adopt a theory of double relevant facts (*doppelrelevante Tatsachen*). This theory rather presumes these facts to be true during the review of procedural preconditions of the civil litigation. Comparatively speaking, there are similar approaches in other jurisdictions which could also simplify the procedural examination. The protection of the defendant's interests, the emphasis on procedural preconditions and the comparison of procedural effects of different tests call for a shift from the preliminary evidence to the presumption of truth under Chinese law.

[24] For example, Zhao (2018, p. 30); and Zhang (2015a, pp. 55–56).

identifying relitigation. In this regard, the court may rely on this provision to demonstrate that the subject matter of claims in the current case differs from that of another case. Therefore, the court can now make a new judgment on the merits. As for the grounds of substantive rights such as cessation of infringement, removal of obstacles and elimination of danger (Article 179 paragraph 1 items 1–3 of the *Civil Code of the P.R.C.*), the application of Article 248 of the *ICPL* shall also be considered since repeated infringements could be prepared and realized.

Second, the grounds of substantive rights themselves predetermine the facts to be proved in individual cases. Generally speaking, the constitutive elements in legal provisions from the perspective of legal methodology, which are stipulated directly by grounds of substantive rights, mean essential facts to be proven from the perspective of civil procedure. When it comes to the process of resolving individual cases, the aforementioned (abstract[25]) essential facts will transform into the (concrete) major facts in the individual case.[26] Hence, it is widely accepted that the doctrine of applying substantive law norms (*Normentheorie*) represents the leading opinion on the allocation of burden of proof in China.[27] According to this doctrine, the substantive legal norms, which stipulate the grounds of substantive rights, also (implicitly) determine that which party shall bear the disadvantageous consequences when the factual allegation to be proved remains unclear (*non liquet*) (Chap. 6). Such results will furthermore be reflected in the allocation of the burden of allegation (*Behauptungslast*) and the necessity of adducing evidence in individual cases. In cases where the facts alleged by the plaintiff are insufficient to satisfy the specified major facts in the case, or the plaintiff even fails to mention the required major facts at all,[28] the judge has to dismiss the claim on the merits, when his relevant suggestions fail to correct the situation. In other words, all specialized issues, which are considered to belong to the field of procedural law and related to finding facts and evaluating evidence within the judgment's reasoning, also indirectly depend on the grounds of substantive rights and essential facts determined by it.[29] This relationship will not be affected no matter whether we adopt the principle of party presentation or of court's investigation, i.e. whether the facts to be found are determined by the parties or the court.[30]

Third, more special are procedural legal transactions taken by parties during civil proceedings. Legal transactions in procedural law seem to be in a "private plot" of civil procedure and thus should have nothing to do with the grounds of substantive rights which are concepts in civil law. However, this is not the case from a more substantial perspective. On the one hand, those procedural legal transactions

[25] In this regard, "abstract" means the relevant concept applies to all situations while "concrete" means the relevant concept is used merely in individual cases.

[26] For relevant discussion, see Cao (2020a, pp. 91–92).

[27] For example, Zhang (2019, pp. 251–253).

[28] In both situation, judge's dismissing can be attributed to a failure of consistency of the claim (*Schlüssigkeit der Klage*).

[29] Wu (2020).

[30] For relevant discussions, see, for example, Duan (2020, pp. 106–116); Zhang (2001).

concerning the aforementioned principles of disposition as well as party presentation cannot be separated from the grounds of substantive rights which are related to these principles directly. These transactions are e.g. modification and withdrawal of the claim, confession of adverse factual allegations, application for adducing evidence, investigation, and collection of evidence *ex officio*, deadline for producing evidence and specific investigation procedures corresponding to different means of evidence. On the other hand, transactions such as jurisdiction agreements (Article 35 of the *CPL*), agreements to opt for simplified proceedings (Article 160 paragraph 2 of the *CPL*) or small claims proceedings (Article 165 paragraph 2 of the *CPL*), the agreement to determine the deadline for producing evidence (Article 266 paragraph 1 and Article 275 paragraph 1 of the *ICPL*), and the consent of the addressee regarding litigation documents to be served by electronic means (Article 90 of the *CPL*) are also closely related to the interpretation of elements of the grounds of substantive rights under the contract law. The reason is that in these illustrations, there are always declarations of intention involved in procedural matters, either by one of the parties or via the agreement of both parties. It is difficult to imagine that the discussion of declaration of intention and its defects[31] can be operated without applying substantive laws. This conclusion applies even for procedural legal transactions which are attached with certain preconditions.[32] The well-known examples of these transactions are the elective consolidation of claims and the consolidation of the claim in chief and the subordinate claim (in the sense of *eventuelle Klagehäufung*) whose difference refers to whether the order of hearings has been determined by the plaintiff in advance. The discussion of procedural legal transactions has still much room for further development, while to achieve this objective, we have to trace back to the theory of attached preconditions of legal transactions in the field of civil law.

In contrast, only those procedural legal transactions that are purely related to procedural matters have the possibility of "keeping a distance" from the grounds of substantive rights. For example, as far as whether the court has violated its statutory obligations in exercising its discretion, attention should be paid to the control of conditions and processes in civil proceedings. Hence, to be developed are the substantial elements and the procedure of making civil judgments in individual cases. Just as we will still have to face up to the issue of judges' discretion on substantive law issues in the era of the "Civil Code", the dispute over judicial discretion on procedural law issues, namely its exercise, scope, and extent, will exist and then be reflected to the evaluation of procedural legal transactions. These procedural issues are crucial for the operation of civil justice, while they rely on a new set of knowledge and expertise other than the civil law. Another illustration in this regard refers to the internal structure of legal norms. There is a difference in the mandatory effect implied between a "must" clause and a "shall" clause in the context of the *CPL* which will also affect our understanding of relevant procedural legal transactions. For example, the "shall" clause stipulated in Article 67 paragraph 2 of the *CPL* providing that "the People's court shall investigate and collect evidence" embodies formal obligations

[31] For example, Yang (2018, pp. 235–276); Liu (1999).

[32] For example, Civil Ruling of the SPC (2019) Zui Gao Fa Min Shen No. 1016.

of the judge of the case, which sometimes has corresponding legal consequences.[33] In contrast, if the wording of the statutory clause is "must", the failure to satisfy the statutory requirements will lead to the voidness of relevant procedural legal transactions. Moreover, a distinction ought to be made between the "may" clause for the parties and the judge. The parties can decide to take it or leave it on their discretionary power, just like the similar rules in the field of civil law. When the law says the parties can sign a contract, it is up to the parties to make their choice. Yet, when a legal provision regulating the judge uses "may" in its text literally, the case may not be the same. We may argue that, when the relevant procedural rules do not expressly grant the judge any discretional power but merely use the "may" word, the judge is obliged to take action as the rules suggest. In other words, the "may" clause in statutes for the judge does not give the judge any freedom as to whether to act as the "may" clause states.

Lastly, when drafting civil judgments, it may be necessary to deal with the situations where procedural rules and substantive law norms overlap with each other. In such cases, the judge should refer to both norms with different natures, and the judge is even able to directly search for answers from substantive law when dealing with procedural matters. Regarding the former situation, for instance, in a dispute over whether the jurisdictional agreement in a standard contract is permissible and whether one party has "taken reasonable measures to draw the attention of consumers", the judges shall refer to Article 496 and 497 of the *Civil Code of the P.R.C.* (Article 39 and Article 40 of the previous *Contract Law of the P.R.C.*), Article 26 of the *Law on the Protection of Consumer Rights and Interests*, Article 6 and Article 10 of the *Interpretation of the Contract Law II* and Article 31 of the *ICPL*. In such a case, since the legal sources for the rule of standard contract are the *Civil Code of the P.R.C.* and the *Law on the Protection of Consumer Rights and Interests*, even if the *ICPL* has provided complete adjudicative norms, the *Civil Code of the P.R.C.* shall also be cited as the basis for making judgments. As a detailed elaboration of the rules of providing hints to consumers, the standard in Article 6 of the *Interpretation of the Contract Law II* that "at the time of concluding the contract, the party providing the standard clauses adopted special characters, symbols, fonts and other signs sufficient to arouse the other party's attention" shall also be included when the judge prepares the judgment's reasoning. The rule of the *ICPL* is interpretative regarding the aforementioned general rules in private law and is unable to support the judge's application of law. Whether, from the perspective of legislative policy, the mentioned formal obligation of giving hints fulfills the important task of protecting consumers, goes beyond the scope of this contribution. However, along with the current approach, it is not impossible to come back to the basic line provided by Article 496 and 497 of the *Civil Code of the P.R.C.* That is, on the basis of substantive law, to directly examine the validity of a procedural agreement.

---

[33] At least as far as the procedural legal transactions of the parties in civil law traditions are concerned, when the "shall" clause does not stipulate additional consequences, the failure to satisfy such a "shall" clause will not result in the invalidity of the relevant procedural legal transaction.

In the latter situation, a judge may believe that in a certain case, the authenticity of the signature on the contract should be entrusted for judicial identification (a court-designated expert with specialized knowledge) as a (major) factual issue to be proven (Article 92 paragraph 1 and Article 31 paragraph 2 of the *2019 Evidence Provisions*). And subsequently, the judge may determine whether there is a real contractual relationship based on the result of expert's evaluation. Then, the judge will determine what is the primary obligation of performance and whether the party sued is liable for breach of duty. Alternatively, if a judge deems it unnecessary to check the authenticity of the signature because the rule of apparent agency is applicable, the judge shall directly refer to the rule of apparent agency. In this way, it would be clear for everyone which ground of substantive rights is alleged and even disputed in the current case. In addition, considering that Article 13 paragraph 1 of the *CPL* stipulates explicitly that "in civil proceedings, the principle of good faith shall be adhered to", there is no need to cite Article 7 of the *Civil Code of the P.R.C.* stating that "[t]he parties to civil legal relationships shall conduct civil activities under the principle of good faith, adhere to honesty, and fulfill their promises". In contrast, under German law, there is no other choice but to directly cite Article 242 of the *German Civil Code* while applying the principle of good faith in procedural issues. And such procedural issues are classified as one of the main types of applying the rule of good faith in civil law.[34] Comparatively speaking, this is different from the rules on allocation of the burden of proof, which also needs to be found in substantive law norms, because the latter rules by themselves are a part of substantive law rules, while the application of the principle of good faith here refers to a purely procedural matter.

4.3 Requirements for Citing Legal Norms During Legal Application

4.3.1 General Rules on Citing Legal Norms

Within civil judgments, legal provisions can appear somewhere in the part of "the court considers that", and some crucial ones among them should also be cited before the operative part of the judgment as the basis for making judgments (*Style of Courts' Litigation Documents* in 1992). *Style Litigation Documents* in 2016 points out in its guidance of first-instance judgments that: "After the reasoning part and before providing the judgment conclusion, the legal basis should be cited. After reasoning item by item, a new paragraph can be started to summarize the general evaluation on whether the party's claims are upheld or not. Hence, it comes to the legal basis relevant in this case and then the operative part of the judgment. If the reasoning has already been completed, and there is no need to prepare the aforementioned summary,

[34] For detailed introduction in Chinese, see Ren (2014).

the judgment should directly refer to the legal basis and write the operative part of the judgment in a new paragraph".[35]

Before discussing specific issues, it is necessary to collect the current laws regarding the citation of legal provisions. From an interpretative perspective, Chinese law has made relatively clear provisions. Following the *Reply of the SPC on How the People's Court Makes Legal Documents and How to Quote Legal Normative Documents* in 1986, the *Several Provisions of the SPC on the Judicial Interpretation Work* in 1997 and 2007, the *Provisions on Citation in Judicial Decisions* in 2009 provides out clearer thoughts on this issue.

Specifically speaking, judicial decisions should cite relevant laws, regulations, and other normative legal documents as the basis for making judgments. Such citations ought to follow both the hierarchy of legal effectiveness and the order that substantive laws are superior to procedural laws, i.e. laws (fundamental laws are of even more priority) and statutory interpretations, administrative regulations, local regulations, autonomy regulations or special regulations, and judicial interpretations (Article 2 of the *Provisions on Citation in Judicial Decisions*). A possible exception is that, considering the reasoning of the case and the judge's habit of reasoning, the judge may also place a judicial interpretation in the field of substantive law instantly after the substantive law provisions to be interpreted.[36]

While citing related legal provisions, the name of the normative legal documents and sequential number of provisions shall be accurately and completely indicated, and if it is necessary to cite a specific provision, the whole provision ought to be cited directly. (Article 1 of the *Provisions on Citation in Judicial Decisions*). Article 3 paragraph 7 item 5 of the *Specifications for Decisions* in 2016 supplements that when any judicial interpretation of the SPC is cited, it shall be referred to in the format as published in the official announcement. Article 12 of the *Opinions Reasoning Judicial Decisions* also points out that when the aforementioned normative legal documents are referred to merely as the reasons for making judgments, the aforementioned specifications are also to be followed. And it is also said that if it is necessary to use quotation marks to cite some provisions, the expressions should be accurate and complete. In particular, Article 7 of the *Specifications for Decisions* provides in detail that "[t]he full name of a cited law, regulation, or judicial interpretation shall be indicated with the punctuation marks used to enclose the title of a book. If the full name of a law is too long, its abbreviation may be used and, in this case, the aforementioned punctuation marks are not to be used. After the full name appears for the first time, the abbreviation may be given in the following places. Where the provisions of a cited law, regulation, or judicial interpretation have serial numbers, writing these serial numbers shall be consistent with those as specified in the official version of the law, regulation, or judicial interpretation. When an official instrument is to be cited, the headline of the instrument shall be given in aforementioned punctuation marks and then the issuance number of the instrument

[35] Shen (2016, p. 252).

[36] Shen (2016, p. 252).

shall be presented in round brackets; while citing a text in a foreign language, the Chinese translation shall be attached".

4.3.2 Determining the Scope of Citing Legal Norms

The difficulty in citing legal provisions within civil judgments lies in the determination of the scope of the citation. A judicial decision ought to cite laws, statutory interpretations, or judicial interpretations, and may directly refer to applicable administrative regulations, local regulations, or autonomy regulations and special regulations (Article 4 of the *Provisions on Citation in Judicial Decisions*). Other normative documents that are examined and confirmed as legal and effective by the judge may also be taken as the basis for reasoning (Article 6 of the *Provisions on Citation in Judicial Decisions*). In other words, the argument of these documents can be used in individual cases and exercise their persuasive power substantially.[37]

Shifting to the exclusive provisions from a negative perspective, Article 3 paragraph 7 item 4 of the *Specifications for Decisions* requires that "the Constitution, the guiding documents on the adjudicative business of the courts at all levels and minutes of meetings within the court system, the reply opinions of all divisions of courts as well as the documents jointly issued by the courts and the relevant departments of the government may not be cited as the basis for making judgments. However, the principles and spirits embodied in the aforementioned documents may be elaborated in the reasoning part". It does attract much attention that the "laws" to be cited may, theoretically speaking, include the Constitution as it is the fundamental law in China, while the applicable rule given by the SPC addresses a negative answer. On the whole, citations of the Constitution can merely appear in the part of reasoning of civil judgments rather than the part of judgment's basis.[38] Empirical studies also show that when constitutional norms appear in judicial decisions, they usually play the function of supplementing the reasoning while applying general legal rules. And the citation of them is often not logical and coherent.[39]

Article 13 of the *Opinions Reasoning Judicial Decisions* further explains the possible components of judgment's reasoning, which include "guiding cases issued by the SPC; normative documents for adjudicative business issued by the SPC which are not judicial interpretations; self-evident truth, common sense, experiential rules, trading practices, custom, and professional ethics; legislative statements and other legislative materials; materials used for historical, systematic, comparative, and other

[37] For a similar view, see Luo (2006, p. 217).

[38] Zhang (2021).

[39] For relevant analysis, see Lin (2015, pp. 186–190). For relevant empirical studies, see also Xing (2015) (the journal also publishes an annual "Observation Report" for further development which is updated by the same author).

legal construing methods; legal principles and generally accepted academic viewpoints; and other arguments not in conflict with normative legal documents such as laws and judicial interpretations".[40]

In fact, these supplementary sources of reasoning cover several different situations. First, there are self-evident truth, experiential rules, and trading practices (including custom) that are expressly stipulated in current law and can be regarded as components of major premises within the legal methodology. Factual allegations, which fall into the former two, need not to be proved in civil proceedings (Article 10 of the *2019 Evidence Provisions*). And in accordance with Article 10 of the *Civil Code of the P.R.C.*, the last one may constitute an official legal source of a case when there is no express provision in the law.

Second, the guiding cases show a special type of legal source de facto with Chinese characteristics. After Article 7 of the *Provisions of the SPC on Case Guidance* in 2010 stipulates that guiding cases shall be used "as a reference" in all kinds of proceedings, Article 10 of the *Detailed Rules on Case Guidance* in 2015 further clarifies that "where courts at all levels refer to a guiding case during hearing similar cases, the relevant court shall quote the guiding case as judgment's reasoning rather than the basis for making judgment".

Third, there are materials needed for applying methods of legal interpretation, such as historical interpretation, teleological interpretation and theoretical interpretation. The restatement of Article 9 of the *Opinions on Core Values* in 2021 should also be noted. Article 5 of the *Opinions on Core Values* also stipulates that "where normative legal documents are taken as the legal basis for judicial decisions, the judge shall, consider the details of cases and clearly clarify relevant provisions of the normative legal documents at first. Then, in keeping with the original meaning of laws and applying socialist core values, the judge ought to further specify the content of laws, clarify the legislative intent and provide reasons for making judicial decisions".

Fourth, there are common sense and professional ethics, which will also be taken into account by the court in certain types of cases. Both types of materials are very common in various jurisdictions worldwide.

Lastly, there are normative documents for adjudicative business issued by the SPC which are not judicial interpretations issued by the SPC. These materials are not typical legal sources for civil cases in general while they do have great practical importance in China.[41] They could at least show the preference of the China's court system as a whole or even suggest the possible attitude of the individual court of appeal within the judicial hierarchy.

Regarding these supplementary materials, this contribution argues that behind the formal difference in whether to cite certain materials or not, the real key issue is the persuasive force of the relevant viewpoints. As long as some viewpoint is reasonable from an interpretative perspective, it can be absorbed by the judge in the answer to legal issues within the civil judgment. Although the aforementioned materials are

[40] For relevant explanations, see Hu and Liu (2018, pp. 15–17).

[41] Cao (2016, p. 113).

not the laws themselves, a judgment based on them can still meet the requirements of adjudicating according to the law.[42]

Besides, it comes to the situation where the to-be-cited legal provisions themselves are in doubt. On the one hand, when there is conflict of legal norms, the current law deems that a distinction should be made depending on whether the norms are able to be selected to apply. As stipulated in Article 7 sentence 3 of the *Opinions Reasoning Judicial Decisions*, where there is a concurrence or conflict of laws during the application of law, the judicial decisions shall state the reasons for the selection. Article 7 of the *Provisions on Citation in Judicial Decisions* states that "where the normative legal documents which need to be cited by the court during making judgments conflict with each other, and it is unable to make a choice in accordance with the *Legislation Law of the P.R.C.* and other relevant laws, the court shall request the competent authority to make a decision. The court shall not by itself examine and conclude the effectiveness of the relevant normative legal documents in its judgment".

On the other hand, Article 7 sentence 4 of the *Opinions Reasoning Judicial Decisions* considers the situation where there is no clear rule to be applied. It provides that "for a civil case where no legal rule can be taken as the direct basis for making judgments, the judge shall first seek the most similar rules for making a judgment; and if there are no similar rules, the judge may make the judgment based on custom, legal principles, and legislative purposes and so forth, while the judge should sufficiently justify and reason the judgment's basis via reasonably using legal interpretative methods". In this regard, judges' function of filling up the gaps in laws and even creating "new laws" through individual judgments has also been recognized to a certain extent.

Also, Article 6 of the *Opinions on Core Values* points out that: "where there are no normative legal document that can be taken as the direct legal basis for making judicial decisions in civil or commercial cases, the judge shall, besides the applicable customs, also under the guidance of socialist core values take the most similar legal provisions as the basis for making judicial decisions. When there are no similar legal provisions, the judge shall make judicial decisions in accordance with the spirit of legislation, the legislative intent, legal principles and so forth. The judge shall also make full use of socialist core values in stating the basis and reasons for making judicial decisions". Moreover, Article 7 of the *Opinions on Core Values* adds that "where the case encounters multiple possible orientations of values, the judge shall make judgments, exercise discretion, make choices and determine the orientation of values applicable in the case, in accordance with the spirit of legislation, legal principles, legal provisions and socialist core values. The judge ought to state in detail the basis and reasons within the judicial decision in the case".

42 Cao (2015, p. 245).

4.4 Extent of Citing Legal Norms During Legal Application

4.4.1 Extent of Completeness of Cited Norms

There should be a difference in the extent of citation of legal norms in civil judgments, which is mainly reflected in the extent of completeness of the citation and the quantity of the citation. As far as the completeness is concerned, this contribution does not agree with the approach chosen by Article 1 of the *Provisions on Citation in Judicial Decisions* that "if it is necessary to cite a specific legal provision, the whole provision shall be cited". Rather, in the part of "the court considers that", the extent of completeness of cited provisions should be different due to the relevant circumstances. In principle, a complete citation should be given if needed, but it is not advisable to require citing the whole provision at all times.

On the positive side, the currently dominating requirement of citing the whole provision avoids both the confusion to self-examination of the judge and the confusion to the appellate court, the parties and other readers from the incompleteness or even the lack of the provisions' content.[43] It can assist the parties to understand and finally accept the results of the judgment.[44] However, turning to the negative side, since the length of legal provisions in various statutes differs a lot, some overlong provisions may lead to redundancy of judgments and accordingly reduce their readability. Moreover, besides that the well-established principle of *jura novit curia* requires the judge's knowledge of full-text laws, it is also not difficult for the parties and other readers to find the content of laws if they have the serial numbers of the relevant provisions. It is just in this sense that the German doctrine holds that citing legal provisions is of necessity, while repeating full-text laws completely is not indispensable.[45]

In addition, because the judge can usually combine the laws with the facts of the case and analyze them accordingly, the "one-size-fits-all" requirement for quoting a whole provision often brings an unnecessary burden to the judge's writing. Therefore, the judge should have the discretion to decide the extent of the citation of legal provisions according to the circumstances of individual cases. Especially, depending on the content of relevant legal provisions, the judge should be allowed to mix the narrative writing and personal arguments regarding the same legal provision. Merely in very exceptional cases, for instance, when the judge has reasonable grounds to believe that the parties at stake cannot find the full text of relevant legal provisions (it cannot be denied that this kind of situation may still exist in remote areas in China), it is nevertheless necessary to attach the full-text laws.

---

[43] In addition, there are also suggestions for attaching the full text of all relevant legal provisions to the judgments, see Guo (2012, pp. 137, 139 and 140).

[44] He (2009, p. 43).

[45] Musielak (2020, Rn 17).

4.4.2 *Quantity of Cited Norms*

4.4.2.1 Judgment Reasoning and Judgment Basis

Now we come to the question how many provisions need to be cited. The answer should differ according to the places of inserting citation and the proceedings corresponding to the judgments.

On the one hand, the part of "the court considers that" of civil judgments and the part of legal basis just before the operative part of the judgment are obviously different in status and have varied functions within civil judgments.[46] Therefore, the citation of legal provisions should not be handled in the same manner. Legal rules cited before the operative part of the judgment should not merely be a list of legal provisions appearing in the reasoning part of the judgment. Rather, they should also indicate the major matters involved in the judgment, i.e. things which are directly related to the subject matter of claims together with controversial issues of parties in the case.[47] By contrast, legal rules that are neither disputed nor directly constitute any essential fact do not necessarily appear before the operative part of the judgment, although they may be mentioned in the reasoning part of the judgment.[48] In this regard, the legal basis should both be centered on the grounds of substantive rights and be kept as concise as possible. As for guiding cases, because they are not legal norms, they should only be cited in the part of reasoning of the judgment rather than used as a legal basis before the operative part of the judgment (Article 10 of the *Detailed Rules on Case Guidance* and Article 13 of the *Opinions Reasoning Judicial Decisions*).[49]

For matters of procedural law, the aforementioned requirements should be applied equally. In particular, for cases which concern the allocation of burden of proof or where it is to argue whether the evidence as litigation materials can prove the facts to be proved, the complete citation of Article 67 of the *CPL* and Article 90 of the *ICPL* is very common in practice. But, except for a few cases that do not require any proof, discussing the issue of evidence and proof seems to be common in almost all cases in the field of civil procedure. Citing these legal provisions specifically in the part of legal basis may have a strong declaratory effect in publicizing the concept of burden of proof. However, from a substantial perspective, it is better to say that such kind of citation is "chicken ribs" in Chinese old saying, namely things of limited value or interest. It could be argued that it is necessary to cite the legal provisions relating to the burden of proof only when the issue of proof does affect the results of the individual case. And when two parties merely have some disputes over legal issues rather than any factual issue, such way of citation is usually unnecessary.

[46] For example, Liu S (2020). It may also show the degree of standardization of the cited norms themselves. Hou (2021, pp. 116–119).

[47] For some similar opinion emphasizing that legal provisions to be cited here should be dependent on the disputed issues of the case, see Tang (2013, p. 52).

[48] For a similar viewpoint, see Lei and Huang (2009, p. 98).

[49] Cao (2016, p. 129 and Fn 73).

For example, this may occur in a case where a couple signs a service contract with a hospital for assisted human reproduction technology and whether the couple has the right to claim frozen embryos from the hospital is at issue. The outcome of these types of cases usually depends merely on how the individual judges of the cases understand relevant substantive rules.[50] At present, the dispute on this legal issue still appears from time to time in practice.[51] In this regard, Article 1009 of the *Civil Code of the P.R.C.* only generally provides that medical and scientific research activities concerning human genes and human embryos, among others, shall be carried out according to the laws and administrative regulations, and relevant provisions issued by the state. Such activities should never endanger human health, violate moral principles or damage public interests. Especially, there are still conflicting judgments as to whether the hospital is obligated to provide the plaintiff with the human assisted reproductive technology when the plaintiff's spouse passed away.[52]

If the application of a legal provision itself represents just the disputed issue between both parties, Article 7 sentence 2 of the *Opinions Reasoning Judicial Decisions* also indicates that "where parties to legal proceedings have disputes over the application of law or it is necessary to elucidate the meaning of laws, the judge shall respond to the focus of the legal disputes item by item and explain the reasons". In this regard, the judge has to respond to matters that the parties may have doubt about or related legal disputed issues, even if the judge deems that the viewpoints will not affect the results of the case. Alternatively, at the very least, the judge should not ignore the disputed issues entirely. Rather, the judge should in the reasoning part of the judgment clearly indicate that the issues will be dealt with in a more appropriate case in the future. Hence, the density of citation and reasoning should be increased even for those legal issues that are not the core of the case.

4.4.2.2 Judicial Reasoning in an Ordinary or Simplified Manner

On the other hand, the separation between reasoning in complex cases and simple ones is also an important factor to consider. As far as civil cases are concerned, Article 8 and Article 9 of the *Opinions Reasoning Judicial Decisions* respectively indicate typical types of cases in which the reasoning should be strengthened, and in which should be simplified with an unexhausted list. Among them, the former

---

[50] The different practice, see Civil Judgment of the Primary People's Court of Futian District of Shenzhen City of Guangdong Province, (2018) Yue 0304 Min Chu No. 40903.

[51] For example, Civil Judgment of Qingyuan Intermediate People's Court of Guangdong Province (2017) Yue 18 Min Zhong No. 2766; Civil Judgment of Shangrao County People's Court of Jiangxi Province (2018) Gan 1121 Min Chu No. 3180; The Beijing Second Intermediate People's Court (2019) Jing 02 Min Zhong No. 13918.

[52] Even in judgments rendered in the fourth quarter of 2019 by two different primary courts in Kunming City, Yunnan Province, there appeared to be opposing viewpoints. Civil Judgment of the Primary People's Court of Xishan District of Kunming City of Yunnan Province (2019) Yun 0112 Min Chu No. 9370; Civil Judgment of the Primary People's Court of Panlong District of Kunming City of Yunnan Province (2019) Yun 0103 Min Chu No. 6897.

include: difficult and complex cases; cases where disputes between parties to legal proceedings are severe; cases attracting extensive publicity in society and having a major impact; cases of new types, or which may become guiding cases with Chinese characteristics; cases whose final judgments are challenged by the state prosecutor which lead to the commencement of trial supervision proceedings; cases whose results are reversed by the court of appeal, or which are remanded for a new trial; cases for a new trial; cases of retrial in the trial supervision proceedings.

The latter type of cases whose reasoning should be simplified is provided as follows: cases heard using simplified proceedings or small claims proceedings; cases heard using special proceedings, summary procedure for debt collection, or the procedure for publicizing a public notice for urging and asserting claims in case that the commercial check was stolen; cases to which ordinary proceedings do apply while little disputes exist between the parties to the legal proceedings.

In addition, Article 4 of the *Opinions on Core Values* also presents an unexhausted list to preliminarily delineate the scope of judicial decisions which shall be of enhanced application of socialist core values during interpreting laws and reasoning within judgments: "cases involving state interests or major public interests, or arousing extensive public concerns; cases relating to epidemic prevention and control, settlement of emergencies or disaster relief, protection of heroes or martyrs, urgent aid to others for a just cause, justifiable defense, urgent danger prevention or acts of helping others, and cases that may trigger public moral evaluation; cases involving protection of senior citizen, women, children, disabled persons, other vulnerable groups or special groups of the population, and may give rise to extensive public concerns as a result of existence of relatively serious disputes between or among the parties concerned in legal proceedings; cases involving the public order and good customs, local traditions, equal protection of rights, ethnic groups and religions and so forth, which may give rise to extensive public concerns as a result of existence of relatively serious disputes between or among the parties concerned in legal proceedings; cases involving new circumstances or new issues requiring in-depth interpretation of legal provisions, judicial policies and so forth, which play a role in guiding social customs and establishing the orientation of values".

In particular, Article 14 of the *2020 Pilot Program* indicates the direction of the pilot reform of simplifying judicial decisions, at least from the perspective of court administration and case management of the judiciary: "if it is possible to extract and summarize some fixed elements of the case, the judgment may, in accordance with the elements of the case, state the plaintiff and defendant's opinions, evidence, reasons, legal bases and the results of the judgment; if a party expressly admits all the or major claims of the opposing party, and the parties have no dispute or have minor disputes over the facts of the case, the judicial decisions may contain merely the basic information of the parties, claims for relief, defense opinions, main facts, as well as brief reasons, legal bases and the operative part of the judgment".

In fact, this guidance of the SPC continues the practice of simplifying judgments stipulated by Article 32 of the *Provisions on Simplified Proceedings* in 2003.[53] Leaving the provisions regarding the mediation aside, the scope of application includes the following four types of cases: cases where a party expressly admits all or some of the claims of the opposite party during civil proceedings; cases where the parties have no or little dispute over the facts of the case; cases where both parties agree to simplify the judicial decisions; and the situation where in the case involves personal privacy or business secret, a party applies to simplify relevant sections in the judicial decisions and the court deems that the application has justified grounds.

In contrast, Article 270 of the *ICPL*, which was published for the first time in 2015 and later than the *Provisions on Simplified Proceedings* more than ten years, deletes the situation of cases where "the parties have no or little dispute over the facts of the case". Since the SPC explicitly emphasized that such a revision was "intentional", the part of facts and reasoning of judgments could not be simplified on such an occasion.[54] Nevertheless, when it comes to the judicial reform in 2020, this type of cases became once again the object of the pilot reform. Such transition can partly reflect the complexity of the SPC's understanding of the relevant issues. It is worth noting that the pilot program was not incorporated into the *CPL* statute while the relevant judicial interpretations stayed unchanged. Moreover, it seems to suggest that the recent judicial policy attaches great importance to the separation between complex and simple cases which is a long-lasting aim of civil justice system. The well-accepted background of "Too many cases but too few judges" may provide an appropriate footnote to this transition in SPC's attitude.

In this regard, while it is quite right that, every method of resolving disputes should find the disputes which are adequate for them,[55] such an observation should also be extended to the design and mode of simplified proceedings. Fu Yulin argued more than twenty years ago that we were supposed to "go beyond the narrow understanding of the relationship between 'justice and efficiency'. Rather, we should think about the procedural functions more from the position of the parties, and design rules of separating complex and simple cases that meet the needs of the diverse values of the society according to multiple and optional value orientations".[56]

[53] This judicial interpretation experiences a revision in 2020 due to the enhanced protection of personal information. Yet, the revision has nothing to do with the topic of this contribution.

[54] Shen (2015, p. 704).

[55] Pan (2000).

[56] Fu (2003, p. 63).

4.5 Subsumption Technique as a Method of Law Application

4.5.1 Significance of the Subsumption Technique

In the tradition of continental law systems, the fundamental approach regarding the citation of legal norms can be embodied in the so-called subsumption technique. While the concept of subsumption is still dominating in a period of more than a hundred years, the meaning of subsumption has changed greatly. People began to gradually recognize that there is always room for making value judgments, preconceptions or senses of the legal mind. Conceptually, it is argued that the judicial process of subsumption cannot be adequately called judicial syllogism,[57] and different scholars may have different viewpoints on the scope of the concept of subsumption. The main disagreement is how to define the part of legal evaluation outside the deductive reasoning while trying to fill up the gap between the major premise and the minor premise. Due to the topic, this contribution will not dwell on these jurisprudential divergences.[58]

In the concrete reasoning of civil judgments, the subsumption technique is mainly aimed at the process of bridging the gap between the statutory elements of the facts, which are stipulated directly by the grounds of substantive rights, and the facts of individual cases, which represent the historical events happened previously.[59] And within judgments themselves, this technique is expressed in the methods of applying the law and citing legal provisions to explain the reasons for making judgments. It is not only applicable in the logical reasoning in simple cases, but also for the solution of complex legal issues in difficult cases. Although the subsumption targets the legal application originally, it can also play its crucial role in applying the guiding cases with Chinese characteristics.[60]

In this regard, the structure and mode of legal reasoning become, following the tradition of continental law systems, the focus of the discussion of the theory of legal application.[61] And from the perspective of civil procedure, while we should always consider the claim for relief (requested performance in substantive law), the alleged substantive rights (no matter whether they have the procedural function to identify the subject matter of claims) and the essential elements of facts (directly stipulated by the grounds of substantive rights), the process of subsumption is embodied as a process of gradually specifying the element facts toward the historical facts of individual cases. Meanwhile, some more specific legal norms (*Fallnorm*) are established in the sense that the historical happening of the case would find the legal norm which is

---

[57] Kaufmann (2011, p. 129); Neumann (2011a, p. 299).

[58] Larenz (1991, pp. 283 et seq.); Kaufmann (1999, pp. 75–76); Zippelius (2012, p. 58); Engisch (1963, pp. 19–20, 26); also an integrated solution: Kramer (2010, p. 34, Fn 4).

[59] Koch and Rüßmann (1982, pp. 24 et seq.); Wang (2019, pp. 164–166).

[60] Huang and Zhang (2013, pp. 40–44).

[61] Alexy (2003, pp. 9, 16–17).

hypothetically merely prepared for it. This process of subsumption relies primarily on empirical judgments.[62] In addition, it is worth noting that, in the process of forming a conclusion, the judge should not only focus on resolving disputes within the individual case. Rather, the judge ought to pay great attention to the rules which may be applicable in other cases. That is, the judge should play the role in shaping general rules.[63]

Considering the development of private law at present, there is no doubt that the method of subsumption can be applied to the understanding and application of legal norms in China. Accordingly, this method will also have a direct impact on the factors that the judge should consider while citing legal provisions during making judgments. In the case of perhaps the simplest legal provision, "all citizens enjoy the right of life and health", even the ordinary citizen will not encounter any obstacles in applying this rule. To interpret the concept of "citizen" as an essential element of facts required is a pure legal fiction. In fact, such a basic concept[64] can already be understood directly literally. It is more or less a methodological presentation here to apply this basic concept to the simple legal provision and to conclude that person A should enjoy the aforementioned rights as natural person A belongs to the category of citizens.[65]

Moreover, there are obviously more possibilities of designing legal norms. The legal constructive elements (of facts) may need to be discovered from more than one legal provision (i.e. the so-called incomplete provision), such as provisions of description, limitation, citation and fiction, such a complicated situation exists especially when some provisions concur.[66] Also, a legal norm may also contain parallel optional elements of facts. As an example, Article 172 of the *Civil Code of the P.R.C.* says that "where an actor still performs an act of agency without a power of agency, beyond his or her power of attorney or after his or her power of attorney terminates, the act shall be valid if the opposing party has reason to believe that the actor has the power of attorney" which should be considered hereby. Leaving other requirements aside, only one of the three elements needs to be satisfied to make this provision applicable in this case. And hereby attention should also be paid to distinguish which situation is applied in the individual case so that the citation could be precise and correct.

Meanwhile, there may also be multiple legal consequences available, i.e. "anyone who damages the property of the state, a collective or another person shall restore

[62] Discovering empirical judgments and demonstrating their correctness are not the task of internal justification, but the object of external justification. Alexy (2006, pp. 278, 281); Koch and Rüßmann (1982, pp. 57–58, 117–118).

[63] Alexy (2006, p. 279); Larenz (1991, p. 314).

[64] A basic concept is a concept that no longer needs to be defined by other concepts, while its understanding may vary from scenario to scenario.

[65] Of course, we can not deny that there are such kind of relatively simple legal norms in fact, so that the basic model still has its practical significance. For a different viewpoint, see Zhang (2002, p. 127).

[66] Zippelius (2012, pp. 26 et seq.); Larenz (1991, pp. 257 et seq.); Wang (2019, pp. 51–54 and 95–101); Huang (2007, pp. 161–222).

the property to its original condition or reimburse its estimated price" (Article 117 paragraph 2 of the previous *General Principles of the Civil Law of the P.R.C.*). The scope of the legal consequence can also be uncertain, i.e. "the court shall determine the amount of compensation based on the actual situations" (the last sentence of Article 1182 of the *Civil Code of the P.R.C.*). Finally, when there are literally much room for interpretations of the expression of the legal provision itself, it is impossible to directly determine whether the provision can lead to a certain legal consequence, because there is already a controversy in whether the historical facts of the individual case can satisfy the constructive elements of the statutory grounds of substantive rights.[67]

4.5.2 *Traditional Judicial Syllogism*

As for how to establish concrete rules of law application, this contribution is of the opinion that the rules should rely on the further understanding of the subsumption technique as mentioned. In China, the most leading analytical framework is the so-called judicial syllogism, which has always been the object discussed by scholars in the field of legal logic. From the field of private law studied in this contribution, the relevant discussion can be traced back to the introduction of Chinese Taiwan prominent scholars Wang Tze-chien and Huang Mao-zong about 30 years ago.[68] With respect to the most basic complete legal provision,[69] the subsumption means as follows. First, specific legal norms (complete legal provisions) are composed of rules of conduct, which can be divided into several constitutive elements of grounds of substantive rights (*Tatbestand*, "T"), and the according legal consequences (*Rechtsfolge*, "R") serve as major premises. In this regard, the effect of R should occur to any case belonging to T ($T \rightarrow R$). Second, since specific historical facts of ordinary life (*Sachverhalt*, "S") are to be understood as an instance of T ($S = T$), S can be subsumed in constitutive elements to form minor premises. And finally, the aforementioned legal consequences are derived through logical inference ($S \rightarrow R$). As early as more than fifty years ago, these elaborations were widely spread by two German masters, Karl Engisch and Karl Larenz. And these viewpoints have had a wide influence.[70]

The aforementioned introduction has played an important role in the past and has become a cornerstone for subsequent judicial practice, legal education and academic research. However, from a critical point of view, there are obvious deficiencies in the previous discussions. Although both Engisch and Larenz emphasize that "looking

67 Alexy (2006, p. 276).

68 Wang (2019, pp. 164–166); Huang (2007, pp. 222–228).

69 Larenz (1991, p. 273); Engisch (1963, p. 15).

70 Larenz (1991, pp. 271 et seq.); Engisch (1963, pp. 3 et seq.).

back and forth between the major premise and the facts of ordinary life"[71] or "circulation in Hermeneutics"[72] during the process of subsumption, they do not reveal more accurately how specific facts of the case can meet the requirements of the essential elements of facts. Especially, it stays still unclear how to fill the gap between legal language and the facts of ordinary life.[73] Thus, a group of law scholars represented by Robert Alexy began to use the first-order predicate logic to better describe the subsumption technique.[74] Limited to the focus of this contribution, this chapter will not discuss it further in depth. And more crucially, related German research has not entered the leading judicial practice in China and partially because of this reason, it is less important for this contribution to develop this topic.

References

Alexy R (2003) Die logische Analyse juristischer Entscheidungen. In: Alexy R, Koch HJ, Kuhlen L, Rüßmann H, Elemente einer juristischen Begründungslehre. Nomos, Baden-Baden

Alexy R (2006) Theorie der juristischen Argumentation, 5. Aufl. Suhrkamp, Frankfurt am Main

Becht E, Beck SM (2010) Zivilprozessrecht im Assessorexamen. C. H. Beck, München

Cao Z (2015) Remodeling the structure and reasoning of civil judgments. China Legal Science 4:226–246 (in Chinese)

Cao Z (2016) On the effect of guiding cases in China and their application in the legal process. Journal of Comparative Law 6:111–134 (in Chinese)

Cao Z (2020a) Reconsidering the fact-finding reasoning in the 'Pengyu' decision. Northern Legal Science 3:89–98 (in Chinese)

Cao Z (2020b) Reflection on the examination of the subject matter of claims in the civil case-filing proceedings. China Legal Science 1:283–303 (in Chinese)

Cao Z (2021) On the double relevant facts in civil process. Global Law Review 1:117–131 (in Chinese)

Cui J (2007) Comments on choice and its foundation of the patterns of remedy for right in rem. Journal of Tsinghua University (Philosophy and Social Sciences) 3:111–116 (in Chinese)

Duan W (2012) Reflection on the structure of norm-based civil judgments. Law Press, Beijing (in Chinese)

[71] Engisch (1963, p. 15).

[72] Larenz (1991, pp. 279 et seq.) (Meanwhile, this book prepares examples to specifically explain how to extract the facts with legal significance from the facts of ordinary life).

[73] One of the reasons is that the situation discussed refers always to civil cases, so that in its context, the fact of the case is already fixed and is not far from the essential elements of facts. In particular, Wang Tze-chien discusses the idea of solving substantive issues in civil law examples and strengthening the system of grounds of substantive rights. However, the problems which are skipped by Wang's research are exactly the highlighted issues of civil litigation treated in this contribution. At the same time, in general theory of legal arguments, the issue of fact-finding is often not considered. Rather, the legal evaluation within individual cases are major targets hereby. Neumann (2011b, p. 334); as an exception, see Koch and Rüßmann (1982, pp. 271 et seq.). Finally, during their legal education, students are also not required to deal with (disputed) issues of facts. Wang (2019, p. 110).

[74] The aforementioned judicial syllogism is actually a part of first-order predicate logic. Neumann (2011a, p. 303); Klug (1982, pp. 48 et seq.). For an introduction, see e.g. Zhang (1998, pp. 26–27).

Duan W (2020) Non-binding nature of Chinese civil admission system and its revision. Chinese Journal of Law 1:100–116 (in Chinese)
Engisch K (1963) Logische Studien zur Gesetzesanwendung, 3. Aufl. C. Winter, Heidelburg
Fang L (2007) A cultural note on judicial behaviors and its selection. Science of Law 5:17–31 (in Chinese)
Feskorn C (2020) In: Zöller R, ZPO, 33. Aufl. Otto Schmidt, Köln
Fu Y (2003) The diversion of complicated and simple cases and the procedural safeguards. Chinese Journal of Law 1:50–63 (in Chinese)
Ge Y (2014) The ideal of legal education. Peking University Law Journal 2:285–318 (in Chinese)
Ge Y (2015) A case report based on the method of Anspruchsgrundlage: application of law on a car accident case. Peking University Law Review 2:272–311 (in Chinese)
Guo C (2012) Research on the citation of legal provisions in court's judgments. Law Science Magazine 7:136–140 (in Chinese)
He B (2009) The making and reasoning of civil and commercial judgment. People's Judicature 3:37–43 (in Chinese)
He L, Zhong H (2006) On publicity in application of law in judgments. Journal of Law Application 3:17–20 (in Chinese)
Hou M (2021) The operative process of justice: based on the observation of the SPC. China Legal Publishing House, Beijing (in Chinese)
Hu J (2016) Rules of grounds of substantive rights and codification of civil law. Journal of the East China University of Political Science & Law 6:38–48 (in Chinese)
Hu S, Liu S (2018) Construction of the system and normative interpretation of the reasoning within judicial decisions in the new era (II): understanding and application of the guiding opinions on strengthening and standardizing the interpretation and reasoning of judicial decisions. Journal of Law Application (Judicial Case) 18:3–19 (in Chinese)
Huang M (2007) Legal methods and modern civil law. Law Press, Beijing (in Chinese)
Huang Z, Zhang J (2013) Legal reasoning and its rules under the case guidance system. Chinese Journal of Law 2:38–59 (in Chinese)
Jin J (2021) Thinking based on grounds of substantive rights: the "engine" of legal dogmatics of case study. Political Science and Law 3:88–103 (in Chinese)
Kaiser T, Kaiser H, Kaiser J (2018) Materielles Zivilrecht im Assessorexamen, 9. Aufl. Vahlen, München
Kaufmann A (1999) Das Verfahren der Rechtsgewinnung. C. H. Beck, München
Kaufmann A (2011) Problemgeschichte der Rechtsphilosophie. In: Kaufmann A, Hassemer W, Neumann U, Einführung in Rechtsphilosophie und Rechtstheorie der Gegenwart, 8. Aufl. C. F. Müller, Heidelberg
Klug U (1982) Juristische Logik, 4. Aufl. Springer Berlin, Heidelberg
Koch HJ, Rüßmann H (1982) Juristische Begründungslehre. C. H. Beck, München
Kramer EA (2010) Juristische Methodenlehre, 3. Aufl. C. H. Beck, München
Larenz K (1991) Methodenlehre der Rechtswissenschaft, 6. Aufl. Springer Berlin, Heidelberg
Lei X, Huang W (2009) Analysis of current problems in courts' judgments and their reasons. Journal of Law Application 12:95–98 (in Chinese)
Lin X (2015) Empirical study on citation to constitutional norms in China's judgments. Science of Law 4:181–190 (in Chinese)
Liu R (1999) Defects in civil procedural legal transactions and its solution. China Legal Science 3:111–118 (in Chinese)
Liu L (2020) Reflection on the adjudication approaches in civil and commercial cases. Oriental Law 1:83–96 (in Chinese)
Liu S (2020) A jurisprudential differentiation between "judgment basis" and "judgment reasoning" and their practical forms: observation centering on the judgment's effect. Law and Modernization 3:123–138 (in Chinese)
Luo X (2006) Research on civil judgments: basis and countermeasures. People's Court Press, Beijing (in Chinese)

Medicus D (2012) Grundwissen zum Bürgerlichen Recht: ein Basisbuch zu den Anspruchsgrundlagen (trans: Chen W, Tian S, Wang H and Zhang S). Law Press, Beijing (in Chinese)
Medicus D, Peterson J (2019) Bürgerliches Recht, 27. Aufl. Vahlen, München
Musielak HJ (2020) In: Krüger W, Rauscher T, Münchener Kommentar ZPO, Band 1, 6. Aufl. C. H. Beck, München
Neumann U (2011a) Juristische Logik. In: Kaufmann A, Hassemer W, Neumann U, Einführung in Rechtsphilosophie und Rechtstheorie der Gegenwart, 8. Aufl. C. F. Müller, Heidelberg
Neumann U (2011b) Theorie der juristischen Argumentation. In: Kaufmann A, Hassemer W, Neumann U, Einführung in Rechtsphilosophie und Rechtstheorie der Gegenwart, 8. Aufl. C. F. Müller, Heidelberg
Pan J (2000) On the coherency between civil disputes and its solving methods. Modern Law Science 6:59–62 (in Chinese)
Ren Z (2014) On the enforcement of the principle of good faith in German civil procedure. The Jurist 4:166–175+180 (in Chinese)
Schapp J (1992) Das Zivilrecht als Anspruchssystem. Juristische Schulung 32:537–544
Shen D (ed) (2015) Understanding and application of the judicial interpretation of the civil procedure law of the SPC. People's Court Press, Beijing (in Chinese)
Shen D (ed) (2016) The styles of civil litigation documents. People's Court Press, Beijing (in Chinese)
Tang W (2013) Text editing of the guiding cases. Law and Social Development 2:47–56 (in Chinese)
Wang Y (2009) On methods of bearing tort liability. Journal of the Renmin University of China 3:15–21 (in Chinese)
Wang H (2014) Claim for return of original object: claim on property rights or form of tort liability. The Jurist 1:91–101+177 (in Chinese)
Wang T (2019) Legal thinking and case study: the system of grounds of substantive rights. China Taiwan (in Chinese)
Wang Y (2020) An analysis and reconstruction of private rights. Peking University Press, Beijing (in Chinese)
Wei Z (2011) On the claim for restitution. Peking University Law Journal 6:1171–1193 (in Chinese)
Wu X (2019) Systemization of grounds of substantive rights in the civil code codification. Social Sciences in Yunnan 5:95–105+187 (in Chinese)
Wu X (2020) Claim basis thinking and its opponents. Journal of Nanjing University (Philosophy, Humanities and Social Sciences) 2:90–106+159 (in Chinese)
Xia J, Xu Y (2012) The causes for the lack of explicit legal basis in civil judgments. Law Science 10:127–135 (in Chinese)
Xing B (2015) How the court cites the constitution—centering on the judicial practice after the nullification of the judicial reply in Qiyuling case. China Law Review 1:127–157 (in Chinese)
Xu D (2013) The application of doctrinal approach in legal reasoning. Peking University Law Journal 5:937–973 (in Chinese)
Yang H (2018) On procedural legal transactions of the parties. Law Press, Beijing, pp 235–276 (in Chinese)
Yao M (2020) Norms governing the liability for breach of contract in the civil code and grounds of substantive rights. Law and Modernization 5:39–45 (in Chinese)
Zhang Z (1998) The structure and style of judicial judgments. Law Science 10:26–32 (in Chinese)
Zhang W (2001) Investigation of facts: absoluteness tendency and its resolution. Chinese Journal of Law 4:70–79 (in Chinese)
Zhang J (2002) The rational construction of legal reasoning mode. Studies in Law and Business 4:122–129 (in Chinese)
Zhang J (2008) A small case, a great impact: a legal logical analysis of Nanjing's "Pengyu" first-instance judgment. Journal of CUPL 2:103–116+160 (in Chinese)
Zhang S (2011) Tort liability for damage by animals (Tierhaftung). In: Zhu Q, Wang H, Zhang S, Tian S (eds) Sino-German private law studies, Volume 7. Peking University Press, Beijing (in Chinese)

Zhang W (2015a) A study of repeated suits regulation with a discussion on non bis in idem. China Legal Science 2:43–65 (in Chinese)
Zhang W (2015b) Reflection and reconstruction on system of registrating civil cases. Studies in Law and Business 3:3–15 (in Chinese)
Zhang W (2019) Civil procedural law. Law Press, Beijing (in Chinese)
Zhang Z (2021) Cans and can-nots of judgments in citing the constitution—jurisprudential interpretation of the dichotomy between "judgment reasoning" and "judgment basis." Law Science 6:57–75 (in Chinese)
Zhao X (2018) Conflict and coordination between overlapped theories of grounds of substantive rights and of the subject matter of claims. SJTU Law Review 1:23–32 (in Chinese)
Zippelius R (2012) Juristische Methodenlehre 11. Aufl. C. H. Beck, München
Zou B (2010) Nine-step method on elements of the civil trial. Law Press, Beijing (in Chinese)

Chapter 5
Finding of Facts: Decisive Documentary Evidence in Civil Litigation and Its Proving Effects

5.1 Introduction

The core status of documentary evidence in civil litigation in China makes the authenticity of documents almost the most crucial issue during the trial of many civil cases. The strength of documentary evidence could often decide the final results of the disputed case before court. And if challenging the authenticity of decisive documentary evidence is successful, such a move is more likely to have a miraculous effect. Within the process of legal argument and fact-finding, a document may become the direct evidence of some legal elements or essential factual allegations, which leads to the determination of substantive results of the current case, and may also become the basis for determining the existence of a specific substantive legal relationship (such as a will or a contract).

When the issue of authenticity is in dispute and needs to be submitted to the court for determination, the related procedures are complex and diversified. In a broader sense, the authenticity of documentary evidence includes the authenticity of documentary evidence itself (whether the documentary evidence is real and not counterfeit) and its function of proving the facts (the probative force (*Beweiskraft*) of the documentary evidence). The main purpose of proving the authenticity of documentary evidence itself is to serve the purpose of proving the facts to be proved required by the judgments on the merits, while the necessary condition for proving these facts is to prove the authenticity. There are hereby obvious differences between the approaches of the common law and continental law, such as the handling of disputed issues on authenticity, the distinction between formal and substantial probative force of documents, and the rules for the presumption of the probative force of public and private documentary evidence.

The current law in China not merely generally stipulates that "the evidence must be verified before it can be regarded as the basis for finding facts" (Article 66 paragraph 2 of the *CPL*), but also particularly requires that the court shall verify the authenticity and determine the validity of the documentary evidence provided by relevant entities

Z. Cao, *Civil Judgments at First Instance*, Contemporary Chinese Civil and Commercial Law, https://doi.org/10.1007/978-981-97-8662-6_5

and individuals (Article 70 paragraph 2 of the *CPL*). And that "the main evidence on which the facts were ascertained in the original judgment or ruling was forged" is a statutory ground for the party to apply for retrial or challenge the correctness of the original judgment or ruling that has taken legal effect (Article 211 item 3 of the *CPL*). However, there is no special provision on the procedure for determining the authenticity of documentary evidence *de lege lata*. Rather, it is merely generally provided that the parties should have the chance to examine the authenticity of the evidence (Article 104 paragraph 1 of the *ICPL*) and Article 50 of the *2001 Evidence Provisions*), and judges may also examine and determine whether the content of the evidence is true item by item (Article 87 item 4 of the *2019 Evidence Provisions*, and Article 65 item 4 of the *2001 Evidence Provisions*),[1] while the court examination procedure for expert opinions is enhanced (Article 81 of the *CPL* and Article 79 to 84 of the *2019 Evidence Provisions*).

Nevertheless, the current law does endow public documentary evidence[2] with special weight of proof which is higher than that of ordinary evidence. For example, according to Article 114 of the *ICPL*, unless there is sufficient evidence to the contrary, the matters recorded in the documents prepared by state organs or other organizations with law-based social management functions within the scope of their authority should be presumed to be true. And Article 93 of the *ICPL* stipulates that the facts confirmed by effective court decisions do not need to be proved by the evidence produced by the party to whom the facts are beneficial. Rather, the opposing party shall bear the burden of proof and have to prove the non-existence of the relevant facts.

Also, the theoretical circle in China pays limited attention to the authenticity and probative force of documentary evidence. Hence, a series of theoretical issues need to be addressed. First, in terms of the relevant procedure, the German and Japanese counterparts among civil law jurisdictions allow the parties to bring a lawsuit to affirm the authenticity of documentary evidence, so that the authenticity issue can become an independent subject matter of claims (*Streitgegenstand*). There is no similar mechanism in China's legislation and practice, so it is to be asked whether it is necessary to transplant this systematic design. Second, it handles the allocation of responsibilities and risks between the parties, e.g. which party should file an application and then pay for the expert identification in advance when it is necessary to rely on such an expert to determine whether the document is authentic, and what the court should

---

[1] However, as discussed below, these rules refer to two different issues, i.e., the authenticity of documentary evidence itself (formal probative force) and whether the content of documentary evidence is consistent with objective truth (substantial probative force). Moreover, if the presiding judge neither investigates nor verifies a piece of documentary evidence nor invites the opposing party to examine it, this judge may be convicted of perverting the law in civil proceedings which refers to a crime. For example, Criminal Judgment by the Intermediate People's Court of Changzhi City of Shanxi Province (2016) Jin 04 Xing Zhong No. 321.

[2] The concept of public documents in China refers to the documents prepared by public servants within the scope of their function and authority, or by enterprises, public institutions and social organizations within the scope of their functions and authorities. Correspondingly, there are private documents prepared by other entities. Zhang (2017a, p. 29).

do to promote the ongoing proceedings where no application is filed or the objective conditions for expert identification are not met. Hence, the auxiliary facts (*Hilfstatsachen*) become a disputed issue now, and it should be determined which party has the subjective burden of proof or even the objective burden of proof. In this regard, Article 92 paragraph 1 of the *2019 Evidence Provisions* partly responds to this issue, while the related discussion is still open. Finally, it is well-known that public documents and private documents are to be distinguished in civil law jurisdictions and a theory of formal probative force (*formelle Beweiskraft*) is proposed in some civil law jurisdictions. Then, it has to be answered whether the aforementioned system of the authenticity of documentary evidence and the rule of presumption of public documents should learn from the comparative experience. This answer will directly affect the construction of the system of probative force of documentary evidence in China.

Therefore, following the basic judgment logic from the subject matter of claims to the facts and then to the proof with evidence, this chapter first focuses on the independent claim for declaration filed against the authenticity of documents under the laws of Germany, Japan and China Taiwan within civil law systems. Then, it turns to propose that China shall, on the basis of inheriting and developing such comparative experience, endeavor to consider the authenticity of relevant documents as a disputed issue of evidence in the ordinary civil proceedings, and construct its procedural mechanism from three aspects, namely the formal requirements, the allocation of burden of proof as well as the practical means to determine the authenticity. After discussing the meaning of the concept of formal probative force and the relationship between the concepts of the authenticity of documentary evidence and formal probative force, this chapter establishes the presumption rule of formal probative force of documentary evidence based on the interpretation of current Chinese law. Meanwhile, under the background that the civil evidence law shares some legal principles as well as evidential rules with the criminal evidence law,[3] this chapter also intends to deepen the Chinese approach regarding the authenticity of documents.[4]

In addition, although within the system of probative force of documentary evidence under civil law systems, the issue of authenticity of documentary evidence and the issue of substantial probative force of documentary evidence always appear simultaneously, this chapter is to focus on the authenticity of documentary evidence itself. As for most types of evidence, the issue of substantial probative force is decided by the decision-makers during their free evaluation. Similarly, the authenticity of electronic evidence,[5] which has attracted much attention recently, has its own particularity. Hence, this chapter is still to focus on the more traditional paperback documentary evidence.

[3] Yi (2017, pp. 435–440); Chen (2018, pp. 127–130, 146–148, 225–231, 250–273 and 307–309).

[4] For the independent value of researching the evidence in civil proceedings, see Zhang (2017a, pp. 1–5).

[5] For example, Chu (2018); Liu (2017).

5.2 Rejecting an Independent Declaratory Action for Authenticity of Documents

5.2.1 Factual Issues Cannot Be Subject Matters of a Declaratory Claim

Although the current law in China does not expressly permit the court to determine the authenticity of documents by an independent declaratory claim, such technical solution is praised by leading theories in the academic community[6] and supported by comparative legal experience. Hence, this chapter needs to evaluate this solution in Chinese context at first.

Generally speaking, it is unnecessary for the judge to decide factual issues by any independent judicial decision. Rather, the judge merely needs to respond to and make incidental determination in the final judgment on the merits. According to the theory of civil procedure in continental law systems, the factual issues cannot be subject matters of an independent declaratory claim or any interlocutory one normally. The reason is that a declaratory claim is a claim to directly confirm whether a legal relationship exists or not, and the requirements of "legal relationship" and "declaratory interests"[7] shall be satisfied when it comes to requirements of the proceedings. In other words, according to the judgment logic within the system of adjudicative techniques, composed of procedural claims for relief, grounds of substantive rights, essential facts and the alleged evidence, disputed issues of facts cannot be promoted to the level of grounds of substantive rights and therefore can be dealt with in the operative part of the final judgment. Accordingly, the determination made on the disputed points of facts cannot directly produce *res judicata* effect, while this determination can only serve as the reason for the judgment made.[8] If the traditional substantive law theories regarding the subject matter of claims are taken, just like the leading case in Chinese practice, the legal norms which lie between the claim for relief and essential facts in the following diagram (Fig. 5.1) are the ones which indicate the grounds of substantive rights, i.e. the subject matters of claims.

It also means, although the major purpose of civil proceedings is to settle disputes, the disagreement between two parties in respect of facts and the settlement thereof are merely a component of the settlement of the whole dispute rather than the subject matter of the judgment itself. From the perspective of realizing substantive rights, it is also difficult to recognize a special type of claim solely for ascertaining facts,[9] since the role of the judiciary should not be confused with that of the expert witness and the state prosecutor.[10]

---

6 For example, Zhang (2017a, pp. 42, 226).

7 Cao (2018, pp. 47–54). The general situation in Germany, see e.g. Rosenberg et al. (2018, § 91 Rn 7 et seq., 18 et seq.).

8 BGHZ 68, 331 = NJW 1977, 1288, 1290–1291.

9 Jacobs (2005, p. 302); Klass (1998, p. 291).

10 Bork (1988, pp. 102–103).

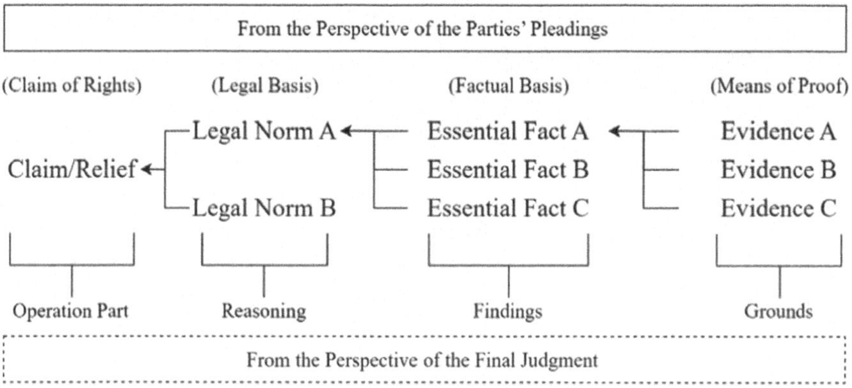

Fig. 5.1 Judgment logic within the system of adjudicative techniques .

However, there are some exceptions in this regard with local characteristics in different jurisdictions. Besides the forthcoming discussion on the declaratory claim for authenticity of documents, a special model claim for consumer confirmation is provided for in Article 2 paragraph 1 sentence 1 of the *German Capital Investor Model Proceedings Act* (*KapMuG*) and in Article 606 et seq. of the *German Code of Civil Procedure*, which came into force in November 2018. Moreover, within the amendment to the *Civil Procedure Law of China Taiwan* in 2000, the tradition of German law was broken and the original "claim for confirming the existence or non-existence of legal relationships" in Article 247 paragraph 1 sentence 1 of the *Civil Procedure Law of China Taiwan* was expanded to "claim for confirming legal relationships". It means that the subject matter to be declared is no longer subject to the restriction of "existence or non-existence" of legal relationships. Meanwhile, the exceptional subject matters of declaration provided for in Article 247 paragraph 1 sentence 2 of the *Civil Procedure Law of China Taiwan* include not merely the authenticity of documents, but also the fundamental facts of a legal relationship. This kind of expansion may give rise to new difficulties during legal interpretation.[11] However, after this amendment, China Taiwan's law still insists that the requirements of the proceedings of a declaratory claim include the special "declaration interests" (*Feststellungsinteresse*), which need to be determined according to the circumstances of individual cases.[12] Compared with the indirect approach established by the German law, in which the concept of "legal relationship" is interpreted extensively in some types of cases,[13] the China Taiwan's usage of "fundamental facts" in the legal provision explicitly, as the subject matter of a declaratory claim, provides a clearer and more predictable solution.

[11] For relevant discussion, see Chen and Lin (2014, pp. 279–282).

[12] Shyuu (2003, pp. 251–253); also Jiang (2016, pp. 404–405) (the difference among theories lies in the supplementary nature of the declaratory claim).

[13] Cao (2018, pp. 47–49).

5.2.2 *Authenticity of Documents May Be the Subject Matter of a Declaratory Claim*

5.2.2.1 Special Rules Regarding the Claim for Authenticity of Documents

Contrary to the aforementioned general principle, the authenticity of documents is generally recognized as one of the possible subject matters of claims in civil law systems. And accordingly, a special claim for authenticity of documents is technically established in respective statutes (Article 256 paragraph 1 of the *German Code of Civil Procedure*, Article 134 of the *Civil Procedure Law of Japan*, and Article 247 paragraph 1 sentence 2 of the *Civil Procedure Law of China Taiwan*). Considering its nature "as a preventive claim which helps to prevent the occurrence or expansion of disputes over rights and obligations",[14] the authenticity of documents has special value in theory and can be justified in theories of civil procedure in civil law systems. While China does not stipulate this special claim explicitly at present, it is argued in this contribution that it is not necessary to introduce this system in China. Yet, considering that this system spreads in various civil law systems, it still deserves to be addressed concisely.

Just as the name suggests, the claim for authenticity of documents is merely to confirm the authenticity, i.e. whether the document was indeed made by a relevant person or an organization,[15] rather than the effectiveness of a real document[16] or the truthfulness of its recorded content.[17] In substance, the plaintiff relies on a special claim to identify the formal probative force of the relevant documentary evidence. Moreover, this chapter also takes the German counterpart as the model to consider the possible legal regime *de lege ferrenda* in Chinese context. Within an independent declaratory claim for authenticity of documents, the party is also entitled to bring an interlocutory declaratory claim to confirm the existence of the legal relationship to which the document relates (Article 256 paragraph 2 of the *German Code of Civil Procedure*). After a judgment on the authenticity of documents takes effect, as the content of *res judicata* effect, the opposing party shall not raise any contrary allegation or opposing evidence against the producer of the document in subsequent proceedings. Since it has the form of an independent claim and a special *res judicata* effect, the declaratory claim for authenticity of documents is distinguished from the so-called independent evidentiary investigation procedure (Article 485 et seq. of the *German Code of Civil Procedure*).[18]

Despite that the party may file an interlocutory declaratory claim within an independent declaratory claim for authenticity of documents, as mentioned, no party may

---

[14] Zhang (2017a, p. 42).

[15] Roth (2016, § 256 Rn 41); Shindo (2019, p. 203).

[16] BayObLG NJW-RR 2003, 9, 11.

[17] Ito (2016, p. 180, Fn 27); Chen and Lin (2014, p. 282).

[18] Roth (2016, § 256 Rn 41–42); Althammer (2018, § 322 Rn 78).

confirm the authenticity of documents via an interlocutory declaratory claim in other ongoing proceedings, since the authenticity of an instrument constitutes a factual issue rather than an anticipated legal relationship. Instead, the party is merely able to have it confirmed through an interlocutory judgment (Article 303 of the *German Code of Civil Procedure*), or wait for the clarification of the judge within the reasoning part of the final judgment.[19]

5.2.2.2 Declaration Interests of the Declaratory Claim for Authenticity of Documents

The requirement of declaration interests is specifically designed for the declaratory claim to regulate the necessity of bringing a declaratory claim, which is not able to initiate the enforcement proceedings, rather than a claim for performance. During determining declaration interests in a declaratory claim for authenticity of documents, in principle, the content of the documentary evidence to be confirmed shall be able to prove some legal relationship and thus may play a significant role in determining the fundamental facts of the case. Merely on such occasions, the value of an independent declaratory claim can be justified.[20] Otherwise, just like the ordinary declaratory claim, the claim for authenticity of documents does not meet the requirements of the proceedings and then will be dismissed due to procedural reasons. As far as this is concerned, the Japanese law is more explicit than the German law and the legislation of China Taiwan. Under Japanese law, the scope of the instruments to be declared is literally limited to "the documentary evidence that proves the legal relationship" (Article 134 of the *Civil Procedure Law of Japan*). Hence, the declaration interests of significant documentary evidence in the field of factual reports such as a doctor's certificate of diagnosis are denied more explicitly.[21]

In this regard, Article 2 paragraph 1 of the *Private Lending Provisions* provides that "when filing a lawsuit on private lending with the People's court, the lender shall provide evidence of creditor's rights, such as receipts for the loan, receipts for payment and the bill signed in acknowledgment of debt, as well as other evidence that can prove the existence of the creditor-debtor relationship". In addition to emphasizing that the evidence must be submitted as long as the lawsuit is commenced, this special provision also, from the perspective of the object to be proven, expresses similar restrictions on the documentary evidence submitted.

[19] Roth (2016, § 256 Rn 103); Berger (2018, § 437 Rn 2); Ahrens (2014, § 437 Rn 9).

[20] OLG Karlsruhe, Beschluss vom 02. 07.2012—18UF 227/10 = BeckRS 2012, 18,789; Roth (2016, § 256 Rn 41); Jiang (2016, p. 409); Chen and Lin (2014, p. 282). Rejecting the declaration interests as a procedural precondition in theory, see Liu (2018).

[21] Matsumoto and Ueno (2015, p. 173).

5.2.3 *No Need to Introduce the Independent Claim for Authenticity of Documents in China*

Furthermore, this contribution is of the opinion that there is no need to introduce an independent claim for authenticity of documents in China. Indeed, it seems that the claim for authenticity of documents raises the theoretical level of factual issues in the framework of civil procedure knowledge, which responds to the crucial role that the authenticity of documents may play in some civil proceedings. If the authenticity could become the subject matter of an independent claim, the judge's determination of this issue will obtain *res judicata* effect, which is able to avoid the relitigation of the same issue in any subsequent lawsuit and can directly become the basis of the judgment of the relevant substantive rights in possible later lawsuits. However, as introduced, the disputes about the authenticity of documents only occur at the level of facts and do not refer to the realization of substantive rights or the actual resolution of disputes. To exceptionally promote its status, sufficient reasoning and justification must be produced. Especially to be considered is that there is no explicit provision on the possibility of raising this independent claim under Chinese law, and the judicial practice even takes a very cautious attitude toward the possibility of bringing ordinary declaratory claims. Hence, it is necessary to further examine the benefits and necessity of changing the adjudicative techniques accordingly, i.e. introducing the independent claim for authenticity of documents.

In fact, the influence of the authenticity of documents on litigation itself is rather indirect.[22] Even if a declaratory judgment confirms that the relevant document is true and real, its *res judicata* effect merely excludes the opportunity for the opposing party to submit evidence against the authenticity in any later lawsuit. Rather, the substantial evaluation of the judge in the later lawsuit is still necessary while the judge ought to consider other litigation materials as well. However, putting the solution of bringing an independent claim aside, we may consider what would happen if the authenticity of documents is merely taken as one disputed issue of the case. Then, it is true that the party concerned in a latter lawsuit can still make a factual allegation contrary to the determination of the authenticity of documents in the former lawsuit. Yet, since this disputed issue has been fully tried in the previous lawsuit, the judge in the latter lawsuit will normally not make any opposing determination in his free evaluation of evidence.

And from the perspective of litigation efficiency, it is difficult to finally resolve the substantial dispute merely by determining the authenticity of documents. For example, the determination of the authenticity of a will or a contract itself cannot completely decide the ownership of the relevant property, and the judge still needs to try issues such as legal inheritance or restitution of unjust enrichment in subsequent lawsuits. Even worse, once the former claim is limited to the authenticity of documents and needs to collect expert opinions, the hearing of substantial disputes will inevitably be suspended (Article 153 paragraph 1 item 5 of the *CPL*) or even

[22] Saenger (2019, § 256 Rn 8).

considered as inadmissible (which is illegal but could happen in practice). At least the court will not actively try other aspects of the case on the merits during the period of preparing the expert opinion since the first claim for authenticity of documents has nothing to do with the substantial dispute. This situation must damage the procedural interests of the parties concerned and misuse the scarce litigation resources.

When it comes to the comparative law experience, even in Germany, where the independent claim for authenticity of documents has been established, the *res judicata* effect of the related final judgment has not been paid so much attention. An example is that Germany has recognized the possibility of bringing an independent declaratory claim only for the authenticity issue, which clearly breaks the explicit principle stipulated in Article 256 paragraph 1 of the *German Code of Civil Procedure*. Then, the German law may have stepped forward and have regarded an interlocutory declaratory claim admissible to determine the authenticity issue if the *res judicata* effect of the declaratory judgment would be taken more seriously hereby. The direct effect of this interlocutory declaratory claim would be that the determination of authenticity of documents will also be covered in the *res judicata* effect of a judgment on performance when the party only brings this claim for performance.[23] On the contrary, as mentioned previously, the issue of authenticity of documents is still considered not to be fit for the requirement of the proceedings which is specifically required for an interlocutory declaratory claim in Article 256 paragraph 2 of the *German Code of Civil Procedure*, i.e. the anticipated nature of the legal relationship to be declared (*Vorgreiflichkeit des Rechtsverhältnisses*) in contrast to the primary claim.

Finally, the exceptional attribute of the claim for authenticity of documents has the consequence that fundamental principles of civil procedure have to establish corresponding exceptions. For example, in general, the object of *res judicata* effect refers to the legal consequences (rather than the findings of facts in case of the claim for authenticity), while the reasons for the judgment should not produce the *res judicata* effect.[24] Apart from the fact that there is no obvious need in China to create such exceptions at present, this new theoretical construction also needs special argumentation. Although the claim for authenticity of documents can play a certain role in foreign counterparts of legal rules, it does not necessarily have general and universal significance. Starting from the current situation in China, the burden of reasoning regarding introducing this exceptional independent claim into Chinese law should be on the scholars who advocate such legal transplantation.

---

[23] Roth (2016, § 256 Rn 22, 27 et seq.); Seiler (2019, § 256 Rn 26).

[24] Jacobs (2005, p. 302).

5.3 Approach to Determining the Authenticity of Private Documents as a Disputed Issue

Although the necessity of introducing the independent claim for authenticity of documents has been denied in terms of adjudicative techniques and procedures, this contribution has no intention to deny the importance of documentary evidence in practice. Rather, regarding the practical issue of which party shall provide further evidence, e.g. applying for witnesses or expert witnesses, when the authenticity of key documentary evidence is doubtful, the discussion on the claim for authenticity of documents and the objective burden of proof in ordinary proceedings of civil law jurisdictions should also be considered. Different from the claim for authenticity of documents with a very clear focus on the authenticity issue, in ordinary proceedings in which the individual subject matter of claims is not the authenticity of documents, the authenticity issue shall first become the object of the hearing and a disputed issue in individual cases. Then, this issue can have the chance to be determined in the proving process based primarily on the evidence collected.

When it comes to the specific litigation scenario, there is only one party presents some document which is simply questioned by the opposing party regarding its authenticity while the opposing party may further allege that the document is forged or signed fraudulently (which theoretically is still a denial rather than a positive defense with a new factual allegation).[25] The counterpart under German law, as one of the representatives of civil law systems, provides a possible solution that the opposing party should make a declaration as to the authenticity of the relevant document in the formal sense, which is subject to a broader obligation of clarifying the case of the parties (*Aufklärungspflicht der Parteien*),[26] and in the substantial sense, the judge should apply the norm theory (*Normentheorie*) of the burden of proof.

In theory, the former relates to the opposing party's obligation to participate in the proceedings (function of process control), while the latter corresponds to the allocation of tasks and the respective criteria between the parties (function of control with preconditions). In other words, the solution for the authenticity issue is twofold: on the one hand, the opposing party should make a clear declaration in form, while the criterion for determining who should do so is also a formal one, i.e. to consider which party presents the documentary evidence; on the other hand, the norm of burden of proof essentially determines the allocation of the risk of losing the case, while the criterion for determining it is the common objective rules for allocating the burden of proof, which has nothing to do with who formally presents the documentary evidence in individual cases. Moreover, this understanding is not just coherent with the German law but can also be accepted by the current Chinese law.

---

[25] BGH NJW 1995, 1683.

[26] For a more recent discussion, see Wu (2018, pp. 1360–1379).

5.3.1 Declaration of the Opposing Party as to the Authenticity of Documents

5.3.1.1 Requirements of German Law on the Authenticity of Private Documents

Under German law, since the rule of presumption of authenticity applies to public documents (Article 437 paragraph 1 of the *German Code of Civil Procedure*), it is primarily the case of private documents that needs to be discussed here. The opposing party has to make a declaration under its own perception as to whether the private document is true or false (Article 439 paragraph 1 of the *German Code of Civil Procedure*). And the subsequent proceedings are subject to that declaration. When the relevant document is denied by the opposing party as a genuine one, the burden of proving its truthfulness is generally on the party submitting the evidence (Article 440 paragraph 1 of the *German Code of Civil Procedure*). Nevertheless, if the opposing party accepts the document as genuine, no further proof is then required (Article 288 et seq. of the *German Code of Civil Procedure*). While keeping silence, the opposing party is to be regarded as having accepted the evidence (Article 138 paragraph 3, Article 439 paragraph 1 and 3 of the *German Code of Civil Procedure*). Additionally, the opposing party is not allowed to express ignorance except in the case where the document was not prepared by the opposing party (Article 138 paragraph 4, Article 439 paragraph 1 of the *German Code of Civil Procedure*).[27]

According to the different contents recorded in the instruments, the object of the declaration and the object of proof are also different. Considering the authenticity of a signed document should be concentrated on the authenticity of the signature itself (Article 439 paragraph 2 of the *German Code of Civil Procedure*). Once the truthfulness of the signature has been established, the legal presumption of facts that the document is presumed to be authentic applies (Article 440 paragraph 2 of the *German Code of Civil Procedure*). According to the general principle of procedural presumption, in order to overthrow the legal presumption of facts, the opposing party must either falsify the signature (factual basis) or falsify the document itself (presumed fact). Yet, when there is no signature involved, the authenticity of documents points rather to the content of the document directly.[28]

5.3.1.2 Chinese Law Should Establish the Requirement of Giving Declarations and Some Exceptions

It is then argued by this contribution that Chinese law should also emphasize that determining the authenticity of documents must be based on the precondition that the opposing party to the production of the document is to make a clear declaration as to

[27] Berger (2016, § 439 Rn 6 et seq.); Schreiber (2020, § 439 Rn 1 et seq.).

[28] Berger (2016, §§ 439 Rn 3 et seq., 440 Rn 2 et seq.); Schreiber (2020, § 440 Rn 3 et seq.).

the authenticity of documents. If the opposing party refuses to make such a statement, the document would be assumed to be true directly. Hence, there would be no need to consider the objective burden of proof regarding the authenticity of documents.[29] Only when the opposing party makes the declaration as required, the court is then necessary to decide whether to entrust a factual expert and push the proceedings forward. This is not merely the same as the aforementioned requirements under German or Japanese law,[30] but also the same as the common practice in Chinese judicial practice. In most cases, that the authenticity of documents becomes a disputed issue during hearings is just on the ground that the opposing party challenges it by relying on various reasons.

Yet, considering the reality of China's practice and the current judicial policy, the exception to the aforementioned requirement of giving a declaration is that the responsible judge believes that there may be false litigations. Hence, the authenticity of documents cannot be directly presumed because the opposing party has not made a declaration. This is particularly the case in private lending cases, where the court needs to comprehensively consider and determine whether the fundamental facts of the case have indeed occurred based on indirect facts such as the grounds of lending money, time, place, source of money, method of delivery, destination of money, the relationship between the lender and the borrower and the economic situation (Article 18 of the *Private Lending Provisions*).

In this case, there is a possibility that the party producing the document and the opposing party collude together to jeopardize the third party's interests, i.e. they may jointly produce false documents. Then, the opposing party cannot be expected to challenge the authenticity of the relevant documentary evidence in the ongoing pretended lawsuit. Therefore, the provisions of Article 67 paragraph 2 of the *CPL* and Article 96 paragraph 1 of the *ICPL*, which refer to the court's investigation and collection of the evidence *sua sponte* that the court deems necessary for hearing the case, should be applied analogically. It means that the court is to be authorized to examine the authenticity of documentary evidence on its own initiative. Once the documentary evidence cannot reflect the true facts of the case, there is no doubt that it should not be used as the basis for ascertaining the facts (Article 104 paragraph 2 of the *ICPL*).

5.3.2 Norm Theory of Allocating the Burden of Proof as the Solution

5.3.2.1 Norm Theory for Authenticity of Documents in Germany

In Germany, according to the leading norm theory (*Normentheorie*) on the allocation of burden of proof, this allocation is primarily derived from the provisions of

[29] For the same viewpoint, see Xiao (2010, p. 93).

[30] Shindo (2019, p. 653); Matsumoto and Ueno (2015, p. 504).

substantive law. It has nothing to do with the specific status of the parties during the individual lawsuit, i.e. whether they are plaintiffs or defendants or whether they occupy the relevant evidence. Nevertheless, this allocation does relate to the relationship between the relevant facts to be proven (which factual preconditions should be met) and the claim for relief (which consequences of the relevant substantive rights the plaintiff wants). This theory also applies to the declaratory claim in general.

Concisely speaking, allocating the burden of proof only needs to consider whether the facts involved can be classified as fundamental ones establishing substantive rights (*rechtsbegründende*), obstructing rights (*rechtsverhindernde*), extinguishing rights (*rechtsvernichtende*) or estopping rights (*rechtshemmende*).[31] The party has to take the burden of proof for the facts which are beneficial for its side. Hence, the party claiming for some substantive right is to take the burden of proof for the fundamental facts establishing the relevant right, and normally, when the plaintiff claims for certain substantive rights, it would be this party. Then, the opposing party is responsible for the rest three types of fundamental facts which are against the effectiveness of the substantive rights claimed by the first party. With no doubt, the burden of proof refers to a genuine issue only if it is of necessity for the court to consider these three defenses. Hence, the plaintiff has to justify its claim which in principle means that it has to prove the fundamental facts establishing the relevant right first.

As one of the declaratory claims, the claim for authenticity of documents follows the same principle.[32] Following these general principles, if the plaintiff claims to confirm the authenticity of the document recording the facts supporting the establishment of its substantive rights, the plaintiff should bear the objective burden of proof for the existence of such facts. Alternatively, the same applies to the situation where the plaintiff claims to confirm the authenticity of the document that is sufficient to prove the extinguishment of the defendant's rights (e.g. the plaintiff's debts have been performed and then liquidated), the plaintiff bears the objective burden of proof for such facts, even when in this case, it is the defendant who is claiming its substantive rights in this declaratory claim. In a claim for confirming that a certain document is false, if the facts proved by the document are that the rights of the defendant are established, the defendant shall also bear the burden of proving that the document is true. Similarly, in a lawsuit where the plaintiff asserting the existence of its rights confirms that the document used to allege the prescription of the rights is false, the fact proved by the document has the function of obstructing substantive rights. Hence, the defendant should bear the burden of proof regarding the truthfulness of the document. In other words, it does not matter whether the claim for relief is to confirm the authenticity of documents positively or not. Rather, as mentioned, the function of the relevant facts, i.e. establishing, obstructing, extinguishing or estopping, is of great significance.

[31] BGH NJW 1993, 1716, 1717; Rosenberg et al. (2018, § 116 Rn 9 et seq.); Thole (2018, § 286 Rn 105 et seq.); Prütting (2020, § 286 Rn 111 et seq., 123).

[32] Roth (2016, § 256 Rn 82 et seq.).

In ordinary civil proceedings, the same understanding should apply to the case where the authenticity of documents is merely a disputed issue rather a subject matter of claims. In such circumstances, due to the aforementioned declaration to be made by the opposing party, the party producing the evidence needs to prove the authenticity of the documentary evidence. Then, the plaintiff who claims for the substantive right should prove the truthfulness of the documents recording the facts establishing the right concerned, while the defendant who denies the right should prove the authenticity of documents for the facts obstructing, extinguishing or estopping the substantive right concerned.[33] In general, the burden of proof usually falls on the party producing the evidence, since both parties will exclusively apply for documents involving facts in their own favor.[34] However, in the exceptional cases where the evidence is obtained on the court's own initiative[35] and where the parties produce documents that are in fact beneficial to the opposing party, the burden of proof still needs to be determined according to the basic principle of the norm theory. In other words, the common happening in practice shows indeed that the party producing the evidence will usually bear the burden of proof. Yet, this happening only overlaps with the conclusion of the norm theory in the results.

5.3.2.2 Norm Theory is Fit for Determining the Necessity of Taking Expert Identification in China

In China, a puzzling and controversial issue in practice is that although expert identification (*Sachverständigung*) or inspection of physical evidence may be adopted to determine the authenticity of documents, the judge can only ascertain the necessity of expert identification of handwriting by itself in individual cases. Yet, the judge still has to decide which party shall apply for the expert identification of handwriting and then pay the expert identification fee in advance. Furthermore, the judge has to decide which party shall bear the disadvantageous consequences in the event of failure to prove the relevant facts when no party applies (e.g. both parties blame the other and are unwilling to prepay the fee) or the objective conditions for expert identification are not met (e.g. the expert identification matters are the time sequence of formation of different parts of the same document).

In practice, besides the viewpoints that the burden of proof is to be borne either by the party producing the evidence or the challenging opposing party, there are also opinions alleging that the burden of proof should be allocated according to the convenience of producing evidence.[36] It is *de lege lata* noted that Article 92 paragraph 1 of the *2019 Evidence Provisions* provides that the burden of proof for the authenticity of private documentary evidence shall be borne by the party who alleges to prove the facts of the case by such evidence. Still, theoretical discussion

[33] BGH NJW 2001, 448, 449; NJW 1995, 1683.

[34] For a similar view in Japanese law, see Yuan (2012, p. 129); also Zhang (2010, p. 155).

[35] Rosenberg et al. (2018, § 120 Rn 17, 45 et seq.).

[36] For example, Civil Judgment of the SPC (2018) Min Zai No. 13.

and debate will not cease merely because of the promulgation of this provision of a judicial interpretation.

It is argued in this contribution that if the opposing party denied the authenticity of documentary evidence, the party who bears the objective burden of proof shall also bear the subjective burden of proof accordingly, i.e. such a party has to produce the relevant evidence to satisfy the burden of proof. As the norm theory applies to the allocation of burden of proof for the fundamental facts in civil proceedings in China,[37] the norm theory also applies to the auxiliary facts such as the authenticity of documents. The reason for this understanding is not merely that the aforementioned German approach, which should be followed by the Chinese counterpart due to the tradition of civil law system or the path dependence of procedural rules. Moreover, a developed theory of burden of proof would definitely expect that allocating the burden of proof for fundamental facts and auxiliary facts would be harmonized and follow the same set of rules. In the whole process of proving and fact-finding in individual cases, proving the truth of the auxiliary facts is merely a means, while the purpose of doing so is still to prove the truth of the fundamental facts to be proved. Hence, it is reasonable that the party who needs to prove the facts to be proved corresponding to the legal elements according to substantive laws shall also prove that the documentary evidence for such facts can become the basis for deciding the case. Meanwhile, it is possible that whether the facts to be proved are consistent with the objective truth stays in the *non-liquet* status, the documentary evidence itself may be difficult to be certified or falsified as well. Like the case when the fundamental facts are *non-liquet*, the judge will also face the difficulties in the adjudicative methodology (Chap. 6). Therefore, the norm theory of burden of proof should still be our first choice in theory.

On such occasions, the allocation of burden of proof for specific documents is to be determined by whether the facts proved by the documentary evidence should be classified as the facts establishing, obstructing, extinguishing or estopping the substantive right concerned. This function of proving is usually realized by the expert identification of the relevant document. In addition to the forthcoming practical means of identifying the authenticity of documents, it is also necessary to consider the prepayment and allocation of the identification costs. Different from the general principle of allocating the burden of proof, since public documents are to be legally presumed to be authentic as well as of formal probative force, the burden of proof shifts to the opposing party. At the same time, even in the absence of the rule of legal presumption stipulated in the *German Code of Civil Procedure*, when the party submitting the document proves the authenticity of the signature on the document, this document can also be presumed to be true based on the factual presumption based on the *prima facie* evidence.[38] Furthermore, in the case of a seal on the document, because of the

[37] Li (2017); Ren (2017, p. 18 (abstract) and p. 27 Fn 54); Hu D (2017); Zhang (2017a, pp. 250–253); Wu (2017, p. 258 (abstract), p. 277 Fn 68); Hu X (2017); Chen (2000, pp. 261–272). For opinions alleging that in spite of the principle of the norm theory, the allocation of burden of proof in individual types of cases should be modified through the legal interpretation, see Yuan (2014). Criticizing the theory of allocating the burden of proof based on substantive legal rules and advocating procedural thinking and methods instead, see Wu (2020).

[38] Xiao (2010, p. 93).

possibility of being stamped without consent of the relevant person that the signature mechanism does not share, Japanese law provides an accessible solution. It is said that when the seal of the person who made the document is considered to be true, it is necessary to presume that the act of stamping is based on the intention of this person, and then to presume that the document itself is true.[39] This approach with the element of double presumption is also worth considering under Chinese law.

The aforementioned procedure of examining the authenticity of documents also provides new applicable examples for the norm theory, which is in China leading both *de lege lata* and *de lege ferrenda*. In determining whether a contract is a genuine one, the SPC once explicitly pointed out that the general rule on the allocation of burden of proof shall apply, i.e. "where the party represented by the private seal denies that such seal is its own and the act of stamping the seal is its own act, that is, this party denies the formation of any contractual relationship with the opposing party, the party claiming the formation of any contractual relationship shall bear the burden of proof and shall produce evidence to prove that such seal is owned by the other party and that the act of stamping the seal is done by the other party or by a third party entrusted by the other party".[40] Hence, after the other party who produces the evidence challenges the contract concerned and alleges that its seal on the contract is false, the party who claims the formation of the contract and the existence of substantive rights shall prove the seal is true. In such circumstances, the court shall not deem that the other party shall be a party to the relevant contract and bear civil liability on the ground that the other party has not provided evidence to prove the seal is false, especially when the first-instance court does not permit the expert identification of the seal.[41] Yet, if the opposing party recognizes the authenticity of the seal stamped to the document produced by the party having burden of proof and merely objects to the content of the documentary evidence, the aforementioned presumption of the stamping act and the authenticity of the document shall apply. Then, the opposing party needs to produce evidence to overturn the judge's evaluation of the presumed facts.[42]

For another example, in a testamentary inheritance dispute, the plaintiff provides a will stating that the relevant property is to be inherited by the plaintiff. If the defendant questions the authenticity of this will, it is to be deemed that the defendant completes its duty to give the declaration as to the authenticity of documents. If the materials provided by the party and obtained by the court *sua sponte* do not meet the conditions for expert identification, the authenticity of documents cannot be checked using means of forensic science. Then, the plaintiff who claims the substantive right shall bear the burden of proof. Regardless of following the general principle of allocation of burden of proof or the rule of Article 25 paragraph 2 of the *2001 Evidence Provisions* that "without justified reason … refuses to submit relevant materials, which leads to

---

[39] Shindo (2019, p. 654); Ito (2016, pp. 415–416); Takahashi (2007, pp. 107–108 and Fn 143).

[40] Civil Judgment of the SPC (2012) Min Kang Zi No. 55.

[41] Contrary practice, e.g., see Civil Judgment of the SPC (2015) Min Yi Zhong Zi No. 359.

[42] This situation, e.g., see Contract Dispute between Chen Chengyu and Inner Mongolia Changyu Stone Industry Co., Ltd., in the Gazette of the SPC, No. 3, 2016, pp. 38–39; Civil Ruling by the SPC (2016) Zui Gao Fa Min Shen No. 140.

the consequence that the disputed facts of the case cannot be ascertained by expert identification conclusions", the plaintiff shall bear the disadvantageous consequences due to the insufficient evidence. Specifically in terms of fact-finding technologies, because the will is accompanied by the signature of its maker, the plaintiff can prove the authenticity of the will through other indirect evidence, while the plaintiff can also change the issue of the authenticity of the will into that of the signature. Moreover, the court may also be requested to comprehensively consider the specific circumstances of the case, e.g. the contents of the testimony of the person writing the document for the plaintiff and the witness, whether there is any contradiction in the statements of the participants to the proceedings, whether there is any *prima facie* evidence with somewhat higher probability and so forth. Furthermore, the court may be able to determine substantially whether the plaintiff (which is also the party who submits the document in the case) has satisfied its objective burden of proof.

However, even if the doubts in the documentary evidence are fully verified and established after the expert identification, it does not necessarily mean that the documentary evidence must lose its substantial probative force. The reason is that, depending on the doubts, the document may be completely forged or merely partially supplemented or partially modified. What needs to be solved hereby is the issue of authenticity of documents, rather than whether the documentary evidence proved to be (partially) false can produce certain degree of probative force. For instance, after one party produces the receipts for the loan, the opposing party may argue that there is no private lending relationship, and it is proved by expert identification that the signing date of the receipts for the loan is modified and the stipulation of monthly interest is supplemented after the formation of the receipts. Yet, the court may still affirm the existence of the lending relationship relying on other accessible receipts. The court may even confirm the date of the revised receipt based on other evidence such as repayment guarantee with corresponding amount of money.[43]

5.3.3 *Practical Means to Determine Authenticity of Documents*

5.3.3.1 Needs for Additional Practical Means

In the ordinary litigation where the authenticity of documents refers to a disputed issue rather than the subject matter of claims, emphasizing the requirement of making the declaration and the application of the aforementioned norm theory are of great significance to handle the authenticity of documents in the theories of civil procedure. Yet, they cannot solve all problems. The role of the discussed theoretical proposal is to clarify, in the adjudicative methodology, who should tolerate the disadvantageous consequences when the authenticity of documents lies in the status of *non liquet*.

[43] Civil Judgment of the High People's Court of Ningxia Hui Autonomous Region (2014) Ning Min Wai Zhong Zi No. 1.

However, this proposal cannot achieve the justice in individual cases in the dimension of discovering the truth, nor can it reduce the uncertainty of fact-finding as a whole. The reason is that the allocation of burden of proof is merely allocating the final outcome of the case between the parties, which makes a judicial decision possible and perfects the adjudicative techniques.[44] It can never directly contribute to the ascertainment of objective facts. Thus, although the requirement of making the declaration and the norm of burden of proof make it possible to determine the authenticity of documents, the acceptability and the related judicial authority of the judgment may still be doubted by one party or even both parties. Moreover, there may be some parties maliciously misuse the litigation mechanisms and easily obtain unjust benefits through the abuse of the norm of burden of proof. And some judges may shirk their duty of finding facts by simply relying on the allocation of burden of proof rather than trying their best to dig into the objective facts.

Hence, it is no wonder that the judiciary in China has for a long time held a strong reserved attitude toward making judgments based on burden of proof, while these adjudicative techniques out of some civil law systems have been suggested by the academic circle and incorporated into Chinese legal regime (Chap. 6). Therefore, it is necessary to discuss feasible means of determining the authenticity of documents for the ascertainment of facts.

5.3.3.2 Possibility of Applying the Judicial Inspection

First of all, it may be considered that the judge can determine the authenticity of relevant documents directly through the inspection (*Augenschein*) of the documents. When it comes to the German counterpart, besides ordinary methods of proof, German judges are suggested to use handwriting comparison (Article 441 et seq. of the *German Code of Civil Procedure*), and they do sometimes use this method in practice. Handwriting comparison also belongs to the judicial inspection, while it also applies the rules for producing documentary evidence due to special legal provisions (Article 441 paragraphs 2, 3 and 4 of the *German Code of Civil Procedure*). Moreover, as a part of the evidentiary investigation of the court, it should be a part of the oral hearing and made accessible to the parties concerned (Article 357 of the *German Code of Civil Procedure*). It should be a routine practice for German judges, after receiving the evidence submitted by the parties, to first examine against the light the evidence for formal defects, such as for signs of deletion, erasure, addition or alteration (Article 419 of the *German Code of Civil Procedure*).[45]

In China, judges usually do not have sufficient knowledge and ability of doing expert identification by themselves, and handwriting comparison is not emphasized

---

[44] Yet, we must not exclude that because of the guiding function of allocating burden of proof, the party who is afraid of the disadvantageous consequences in this sense will in many cases try even harder to discover the truth. And these potential efforts are exactly the objects of discussion in the forthcoming parts.

[45] Balzer and Walther (2018, Rn 265).

during the judge's training programs. Yet, the handwriting inspection under German law may play a supplementary role for the fact-finding mechanism besides the system of expert identification, which is in fact suitable for the judicial practice in China.[46] Some judges may also point out the obvious flaws in the documents submitted by the parties, such as existing alteration tracks, difference in handwriting color, strength and trace, rewriting on the copy of the original to pretend to be an original, and so forth.

In legal practice, it is also common that, when signing a contract of great stake, one party to the contract will actively inquire about the signature of the legal representative of the other party filed with the registration authority to avoid the obvious risk of signing by others. In the transaction of negotiable instruments, the payer shall also bear the obligation of substantial examination on whether the negotiable instrument presented for payment is forged or altered, especially whether the seal on the instrument is consistent with the seal reserved by the bank.

Although the practicing lawyers and staff of financial institutions may not have the qualification and ability of professional expert identification institutions, they are still able to and have to verify the authenticity of documents. To be considered are, e.g. folding the instrument twice from different angles to check the integrity of the seal (which is even required for the bank's staff), or other methods meeting higher technical standards. For judges who often face the issue of authenticity, the corresponding examination duty and ability are also worthy of consideration. If training in the sense of handwriting comparison can be strengthened within the judiciary in the future, we can expect judges to be able to independently determine the authenticity of disputed documents without the assistance of third-party agencies and technical investigation methods.

5.3.3.3 Necessity and Limitation of Expert Identification of Documents

Second, unlike the less used judicial inspection, expert identification of documents designated by judges refers to the primary means in practice, while relying on it too much deserves our attention. Even in Germany, although the court is not bound by the parties' application for expert opinion and has the discretion to decide whether or not to appoint an expert, the judge in practice is generally considered to be in need of the assistance of expert opinion[47] due to the importance of expert opinion in discovering the truth in individual cases.[48] In China, a court may entrust a qualified expert to provide identification opinions upon the application of a party concerned or on the court's own initiative (Article 79 of the *CPL*, and Article 121 paragraphs 2 and 3 of the *ICPL*). Such entrustment is mainly based on the application of the party, while the active role of the court is merely in a supplementary position (Article

[46] For an opposite opinion, see Yuan (2012, p. 129).

[47] Rosenberg et al. (2018, § 120 Rn 17); Berger (2015, § 442 Rn 1, Vor § 402 Rn 26, 28 et seq.); Schreiber (2020, § 442 Rn 1); Reichold (2019, § 442 Rn 1); Ahrens (2014, § 442 Rn 3).

[48] Gottwald (2018a); Meller-Hannich (2016).

30 of the *2019 Evidence Provisions*).[49] The theoretical approach discussed in this chapter is also aimed at this, especially the allocation of disadvantageous consequences when no one applies for the expert identification.[50] It is also argued that it is necessary to clarify the elements for the court to decide an application for expert identification of documents, so as to avoid the abuse of identification procedures in practice when identification should not be carried out. A judge shall rely on the fundamental rule provided by Article 121 paragraph 1 of the *ICPL* to determine whether the documentary evidence in dispute is related to the facts to be proved (relevance of the evidence) and can produce (substantial) probative force regarding proving these facts. The judge shall also consider whether the facts to be proved corresponding to the matters to be identified are meaningful to the resolution of the dispute in individual cases. In contrast, whether the expert identification can be carried out due to the limitation of scientific and technological conditions cannot be taken as an additional element of examining the application in the first place. Instead, the expert identification procedure shall be started first, and then the judge can consider the aforementioned objective conditions. In terms of the proportionality of costs for expert identification, the goal of finding the truth in civil proceedings shall still be given priority in China. Hence, it is also possible to apply for the expert identification in cases where simplified proceedings and small claims proceedings apply.[51]

On the whole, we should be more vigilant about the improper influence of the manipulated expert identification on the judicial power of adjudication. Adopting the means of expert identification does not affect the degree of high probability that the conviction of facts ought to reach (Article 108 paragraph 2 of the *ICPL*). Whether the judge's evaluation of evidence in an individual case meets this ordinary standard of proof depends on the judge's substantial evaluation rather than the conclusion provided by the expert opinion. As in the case of German law, the standard of full proof (*vollen Beweis*) (Article 440 paragraph 1 of the *German Code of Civil Procedure*) shall apply,[52] i.e. the judge has established an internal conviction which satisfies the ordinary standard of proof. Even if an expert has been entrusted and the expert opinion has been obtained, the court still has the authority to make a different factual conviction.[53]

In China, it is noted that the facts ascertained in the traffic accident liability report, prepared by the traffic police, should not have substantial probative force on the course of the objective happening. Rather, the report can merely prove which facts were (subjectively) ascertained by the traffic police at that time (formal probative force). Similarly, the expert identification opinion only represents the expert's understanding of the objective facts. In no case may the judge transfer the statutory

[49] For a detailed discussion, see Cao (2021).

[50] For a detailed discussion, see Cao (2020a).

[51] For a detailed discussion, see Cao (2020b).

[52] BGH NJW 2001, 448, 449; NJW 1995, 1683; Geimer (2020, § 440 Rn 1).

[53] BayObLG FamRZ 2005, 1782, 1783–1784; OLG München NJW 1970, 1924, 1925 (conflict of expert opinions).

power of fact-finding and making judicial decisions to the expert witness. Otherwise, the system of expert identification, which is supposed to assist the judge in promoting civil proceedings, would become the decisive force to dominate the legal proceedings and their results on the merits.

5.3.3.4 Making Use of Other Procedural Tools

Third, we can consider using other procedural tools to solve the difficulty in proving the facts indirectly. Also coming to the German solution, the producer's confirmation of the authenticity of documents outside the proceedings is considered as an extra-judicial admission (similar to the rule of Article 3 of the *2019 Evidence Provisions*), which can be used as indirect evidence to influence the judge's evaluation of evidence. And German practice recognizes some exceptions, e.g. the court may directly confirm the authenticity of commercial accounts that are correct in form and content.[54] In this sense, the Chinese judiciary can also gradually acknowledge a series of cases of *prima facie* evidence on the authenticity of documents[55] and establish a highly probable link between the authenticity of the signature and the authenticity of the relevant document itself. It means that once the signature is deemed to be genuine, the party alleging forgery should be required to prove the fact of forgery to a great extent while the objective burden of proof does not shift to this party.[56] For example, this party has to prove that although the documentary evidence contains a real signature, this document submitted by the other party is actually the product of grafting (removing the substance of the original document and adding something new on top of the original signature) or creating (writing on the basis of a blank signed document).

Under both German and Chinese legal regimes, it is worth noting that, unlike the aforementioned allocation of burden of proof, the duty to produce documents and its consequences may also affect the judicial ascertainment of facts in judicial practice. It handles the rule of frustrating evidence (*Beweisvereitelung*) (Article 48 and 95 of the *2019 Evidence Provisions*, Article 112 of the *ICPL*, Article 75 of the *2001 Evidence Provisions*).[57] For instance, the plaintiff claims for the price under the sales contract, while its copy of the contract was lost. Currently, merely the defendant holds an original contract. Under such circumstances, if the court requests the defendant to produce the contract and the defendant refuses to do so, the court may, in its discretion, make an evaluation that the content of the contract is as described by the plaintiff.[58] Furthermore, where special circumstances are satisfied, the court may even find that

---

[54] Berger (2015, § 440 Rn 1 & Fn 2); Schreiber (2020, § 440 Rn 2).

[55] Cao (2019).

[56] The reason for this procedural arrangement is that the *prima facie* evidence differs from the legal presumption, such as the presumption of authenticity of public documents, which has the effect of shifting the objective burden of proof.

[57] Yuan (2015, pp. 129–132).

[58] Civil Judgment of the SPC (2013) Min Ti Zi No. 205. For a theoretical discussion, see Zhang (2017b).

the factual allegation of the other party's, which is to be supported by the documents concerned, is true (Article 48 paragraph 2 of the *2019 Evidence Provisions*). It is correct that making good use of the rule of frustrating evidence is also a good way for experienced judges to regulate the litigation conducts of the parties in practice. As a result, the parties can be deterred by the substantive, procedural and administrative rules imposed by the judge. Civil proceedings would be promoted by the parties together then in good faith as much as possible.[59]

5.3.3.5 Innovative Significance of New Technological Means

Finally, similar to the general situation discussed in Chap. 11, new technological means can, to a considerable extent, overcome the difficulties in determining the authenticity of documents. Just as registration of real property rights may solve the problem of changes in real rights, commercial registration for shareholders may simplify the determination of the timing of changes in equity, and the registration of receivables in factoring contracts may clarify the priority relationship among multiple factoring contracts (Article 768 of the *Civil Code of the P.R.C.*). The registration of contracts can also play a fundamental role in commercial society.

To some extent, the blockchain technology is of far-reaching significance in the development of technologies and industry, and the related technological change is affecting the process and results of legal communication from various aspects.[60] If electronic contracts or the electronic version of paper contracts concluded by the parties can embed a trusted timestamp, that is, a digital signature is attached to the document besides the handwriting signature of the producer, the problem of authenticity of documents would be solved. In the contract concluded electronically, an electronic signature with a HASH value and a special e-mail system with specific technical support should lead to the purely electronic and paperless civil proceedings in Germany, which was expected already years ago.[61] Moreover, it can be cited that the new dispute resolution mode, represented by the e-commerce-related Arbitration and Mediation Center (eBRAM Center), an online dispute resolution platform established with funding by the Hong Kong SAR government in 2018, is said to provide convenient evidence preservation solutions for the parties through the evidence preservation system that assists in the conclusion of contracts while specializing in *ex post* dispute resolution.[62]

At the same time, under the existing technical conditions, it is possible to consider other easier and more convenient methods of indirect evidence to strengthen the proof of the authenticity of documents, such as taking fingerprints, taking photos while holding ID cards and the contract, taking photos of the parties during their

---

[59] Fu (2017).

[60] Smart contracts, which are considered to be self-executing, are even more typical examples. For example, Xia (2020).

[61] Stürner (2022); Gottwald (2018b).

[62] eBRAM (2024).

meeting holding the contract, and videotaping the whole signing process (and using blockchain technology to prevent counterfeiting) and so forth. Although these means have gone beyond the core scope of civil procedure, through presentation and cross-examination during the court hearing, they may connect the procedural principles and lawyers' practical wisdom.

5.4 Formal Probative Force of Documents and Presumed Truthfulness of Public Documents

As discussed previously, the requirement of declaration, the application of norm theory and various practical means directly aimed at the truth discovery can provide the basic rules to determine the authenticity of documents. However, due to legislative and theoretical reasons, documentary evidence may further be presumed to be true to different extents and matters which may even get rid of the difficulty in proving by changing the object to be proved. Hence, it is necessary to pay further attention to the rules of presumption of probative force. The reason is that the rule of presumption of authenticity of public documents itself refers to a direct allocation of burden of proof. Then, different from the aforementioned norm theory which requires the classification of fundamental facts to be proved, the burden of proof should now be borne by the opposing party to the party submitting the public documents. It means that following the presumption rules, the opposing party has always to prove the disputed document is inauthentic and the disadvantageous consequences in case of *non-liquet* status stay in its side. Considering that the rules of probative force of documentary evidence under Chinese law do not simply transplant the counterparts of other jurisdictions, it is also advisable to discuss the succession and abandonment of the theoretical system of continental law systems in China.

5.4.1 Scientific Systems of the Probative Force of Documents

5.4.1.1 Threefold Mode in Germany

Under German law, the scientific system of probative force of documents is threefold, i.e. its authenticity, formal probative force and substantial probative force. Only authentic documentary evidence has probative force to the relevant facts to be proved, while false evidence has no probative force at all. Hence, the court shall first determine whether the document is authentic, and then move to the evaluation of formal and substantial probative force, respectively. The authenticity of a document refers to the situation where an instrument is indeed prepared by the person who creates the document as alleged by the party who may benefit from such documentary evidence, when the judge makes the decision from the current form and content of the document.

It does not make a difference whether the evidence is produced by one party or collected by the court *sua sponte*. Moreover, the formal probative force of a document refers to the making of the relevant declaration in the document, while the substantial probative force is on the correctness of its content, i.e. whether the document may reflect the objective truth.

Unlike Article 126 paragraph 1 of the *German Civil Code* which requires an original signature for legal transactions in written form, a document in procedural context may be signed by another person rather than the signer but following the will of the signer. The relevant document in this case is still an authentic document which should also have formal probative force.[63] As discussed previously, a German court is to determine whether a document is authentic through an independent declaratory claim for authenticity of documents or as a disputed issue within ordinary civil proceedings. Then, public documents are presumed to be authentic (Article 437 paragraph 1 of the *German Code of Civil Procedure*), while private documents are subject to the aforementioned two-stage examination procedure, i.e. declaring by the opposing party and then proving by the party taking the burden of proof according to the norm theory based on substantive laws.

5.4.1.2 Twofold Mode in Japan and China Taiwan

Different from the threefold mode of German law, systems of probative force of documents in Japan and China Taiwan adopt a twofold mode. It means both legal systems merely distinguish the formal and the substantial probative force of a document, while the authenticity of documents is not an independent component of the respective scientific system. Article 228 paragraph 1 of the *Civil Procedure Law of Japan* requires the party producing the evidence to prove that the establishment of the document is true. The Japanese leading opinion considers the authenticity of documentary evidence as a part of its formal probative force. For instance, it is held that "when the document is made on the basis of the specific person's thought claimed by the producer of the document, the establishment of the document can be said to be true from the perspective of procedural law"; "if the party intends to deny the authenticity of the establishment of the document, this party must explain the reasons"; "regarding whether the establishment of the document is true or not, the determination of the court also depends on the judge's free evaluation of evidence, while there are some presumption provisions as well".[64]

In other words, the confirmation of the authenticity of documents is considered as a prerequisite fact for the formal probative force which is also included in the term of formal probative force. It means that this term should be divided into two elements, i.e. the instrument was made authentically (different from forging the instrument) and can express the thoughts of the one who creates the document (different from

[63] Rosenberg et al. (2018, § 120 Rn 11).

[64] Shindo (2019, p. 653).

practicing calligraphy).[65] On the contrary, only a relatively small number of scholars, influenced by German law, insist on strictly distinguishing the formal probative force of documentary evidence from the authenticity of documentary evidence.[66]

The situation in China Taiwan is similar to that in Japan and the concepts of authenticity and formal probative force of documentary evidence are treated as one. Scholars generally hold the viewpoint that "the probative force of a document is its formal probative force, which refers to the situation where it is sufficient to prove that the author and signer indeed gave the statement or report recorded in the document",[67] or "a document is said to have formal probative force when it is truly established and not forged".[68] Some scholar also points out that "the formal probative force of a document refers to the situation where it can be proven that the document in fact represents the thoughts of the author, i.e. the effect that the document is authentic".[69]

5.4.1.3 Chinese Solution

Traditionally, the authenticity of evidence is regarded as a component of its probative force under Chinese law, and the neigbouring concept that is the admissibility of evidence refers to the issue whether some materials can be taken as the evidence in civil proceedings. The mainstream viewpoints in China are more inclined to the understanding of Japan and China Taiwan. There is merely a distinction between formal and substantial probative force,[70] or the authenticity of documentary evidence is considered covering both formal and substantial truth.[71] Although this contribution takes German counterpart as the primary object of comparison, it nevertheless does not advocate that Chinese law should trace back to the German threefold mode with strict distinction of three different terms. Comparing both twofold and threefold modes, the difference does not lie in whether the authenticity of documents is a part of the system of probative force of documents or whether it should constitute the object of evidential examination of the court.

Rather, whether to recognize the independent status of the concept of authenticity in the scientific system is the key issue. For the twofold mode, the authenticity issue is directly included in the understanding of the formal probative force, so that the

---

[65] Ito (2016, p. 414); see Takahashi (2007, p. 104); Kaneko and Takeshita (1995, pp. 125–126).

[66] Matsumoto and Ueno (2015, pp. 506–507).

[67] Yang (2013, p. 284).

[68] Jiang (2018, p. 198) (even equating the concepts of formal probative force and admissibility); Chen and Lin (2014, p. 152).

[69] Lv (2018, p. 567).

[70] Zhang (2017a, p. 30); Li (2016, p. 149); Wang (2015, p. 207); Shao (2009, p. 251). For this understanding in practice, see Civil Judgment of the High People's Court of Shanghai (2010) Hu Gao Min Er (Shang) Zai Ti Zi No. 4; Civil Judgment of the Intermediate People's Court of Xuzhou City of Jiangsu Province (2016) Su 03 Min Zhong No. 4817.

[71] Zhang (2015, pp. 17–18); Xiao (2010, p. 92). For a similar opinion that these two terms are in fact discussing the same concept of authenticity of documentary evidence from two different perspectives, see Shao (2009, p. 255).

concept of formal probative force itself should include both the true production of the document and the true expression of thoughts. The authenticity of documents means that the author and signer should be responsible for the document. The basis of the German threefold mode is that the authenticity of documentary evidence is clearly stipulated by the statute as the precondition of the rules of probative force, which highlights the independence of the concept of authenticity in Germany *de lege lata*.

However, similar to the rejection of the German approach of an independent declaratory claim for authenticity of documents, there is no need to be too complicated in the theoretical construction and system design, especially for China where no statutory limitation exists. The concept of authenticity ultimately serves the truth concept and the facts to be proved. As long as the probative force of documentary evidence, whether formal or substantial, must take the authenticity of documents as the precondition, the attempt of simplifying the scientific system is preferable. To some extent, making a mountain out of a molehill is less productive when there is no specific reason to do so. When there is no substantial difference in the content of the two conceptual modes, following German law due to the path dependence provides no strong argument at all. Moreover, there are no German-style delicate rules in China. Hence, it is more appropriate to adopt the more concise twofold mode *de lege ferenda*.

Of course, it can be observed from another perspective that German law focuses on the authenticity of documentary evidence, which is the most controversial part in practice, and then regards this issue as a separate one. This general legislative attitude is fit for the situation in China where the good-faith operation of civil proceedings is still expected and has a long way to go. Under the threefold mode of German law, only when the authenticity of documentary evidence is determined, can the formal and substantial probative force of documents become a genuine issue within any ongoing civil proceedings. In other words, unauthentic documents have no probative force at all. Hence, the authenticity of documentary evidence is not so much a part of its probative force but rather a precondition for its probative force.

Meanwhile, because the authenticity of documentary evidence can be taken as an independent fact to be proved and is subject to independent rule on the burden of proof, the threefold approach is also conducive to highlighting the special status of the authenticity issue. As this issue attracts much attention in Chinese practice, to promote its scientific status may contribute to solving the difficulty in this area. Hence, if we rely on the rule of Article 92 paragraph 1 of the *2019 Evidence Provisions* to gradually develop rules for determining the authenticity of documentary evidence in order to respond to the great demand in practice, the threefold mode may also be an option for Chinese scientific system of procedural law. Yet, it is to emphasize that a potential threefold mode will not be chosen simply because of the inheritance or transplantation of German law. Rather, it should be the solution to meet the judicial practice in China.

5.4.2 *Differences Between Public and Private Documents in Theory*

5.4.2.1 Formal Probative Force of Public Documents

Once again, this contribution continues learning from the theories of documentary evidence in civil law jurisdictions (especially Germany and Japan) and tries to understand the formal probative force of documents under German law in detail. As public documents that are presumed to be authentic also have the formal probative force which is also presumed to be true (dual presumption), public and private documents are discussed here respectively.

As far as the formal probative force of public documents is concerned, a distinction shall be made among records for the declaration given before the relevant competent bodies, orders or judicial decisions as well as other public documents. Specifically speaking, first of all, when the party concerned makes the declaration to engage in relevant legal transactions before the notaries, marriage registration authorities, land registration authorities and other competent bodies, the public documents recorded by the relevant authorities shall establish full proof of the process of the declaration given by the party concerned (Article 415 paragraph 1 of the *German Code of Civil Procedure*).[72] If the opposing party intends to raise an objection, it has no other choice but to produce the evidence as the side of party taking the burden of proof, i.e. the proof to the contrary(*Beweis des Gegenteils*)[73] and then to meet the standard of proof. Then, this party may be able to prove that the record has been altered or is incomplete and inaccurate. In this sense, Article 415 paragraph 2 of the *German Code of Civil Procedure* reads that evidence proving that the transaction has been improperly recorded is admissible.

Second, evidence such as administrative orders and court decisions themselves contains the written declaration of the public authority with direct external effects[74] and the German statute considers that these kinds of evidence cannot be forged or altered. Therefore, they cannot be objected to by any party (Article 417 of the *German Code of Civil Procedure*).[75]

The first and second types of evidence which show the declaration of either legal transactions or public authorities are also collectively referred to as constitutive documents (*konstitutive Urkunde*), also known as documents which are taking effect (*(be)wirkende Urkunde*), dispositional documents (*Dispositivurkunde*) or documents

---

[72] Rosenberg et al. (2018, § 120 Rn 21).

[73] Geimer (2019, § 415 Rn 6); Feskorn (2020, § 415 Rn 7); Huber (2021, § 415 Rn 12). On the contrary, for the position that the simple opposing evidence (*Gegenbeweis*) is sufficient: Schreiber (2020, § 415 Rn 30).

[74] BGH NJW-RR 2011, 953, 954, Tz 19.

[75] Schreiber (2020, § 417 Rn 7).

containing the elements of substantive rights (*Tatbestandsurkunde*), because these documents cover the process of facts to be proved.[76]

Finally, there are also facts which are proved by other public documents (Article 418 paragraph 1 of the *German Code of Civil Procedure*) such as transcripts of proceedings, documents of service, land registry records, birth and death certificates and so forth.[77] These documents belong to the category of testimonial documents (*bezeugende Urkunde*) and are conceptually separated from the constitutive documents as mentioned. As Article 418 paragraph 2 of the *German Code of Civil Procedure* says that evidence proving that the facts set out therein are wrong is admissible unless the laws of a German federal state rule out or limit such evidence, the opposing party may produce opposing evidence. If this party can meet the usual standards of proof in the manner of free evidence (*Freibeweis*), a full proof of these facts will be achieved.

For instance, in the case of whether the relevant time limit on the appeal has been satisfied, and the stamp affixed to the reasons for appeal in the court dossier proved that this time limit was overdue, the appellant shall prove that it has duly stamped before the expiration of the time limit (e.g. before midnight of the date of stamping).[78] Then the correctness of this document with stamping was considered as completely denied.[79] A special case is the part of alleged facts of the case within German judgments. As discussed previously, the objects of formal probative force of this part shall include, in addition to the judge's de facto decision as stated in the operative part of the judgment, the statements and allegations of the parties as stated in the part of alleged facts of the case. There is then an extraordinary probative force of alleged facts of the case which ought to be subject to special rules (Chap. 3).

5.4.2.2 Formal Probative Force of Private Documents

The formal probative force of private documents is usually related to the authenticity of the signature. And since there is no rule similar to the presumption of the formal probative force of public documents, the formal probative force shall be evaluated by a judge according to the principle of free evaluation of evidence. The German law provides that when a private document has a genuine signature or the abbreviation of the signature (*Handzeichen*) used has been notarized, the document is sufficient proof that the author and signer of the document made a declaration or statement (Article 416 of the *German Code of Civil Procedure*). Under this specialized statutory evidential rule, the judge's free evaluation of evidence is to be excluded.[80] Of

[76] Rosenberg et al. (2018, § 120 Rn 9); Musielak and Voit (2016, Rn 804); also Chen and Lin (2014, p. 151). The Japanese law classifies these documents as dispositive certificates and report instruments. Ito (2016, pp. 411–412).

[77] Rosenberg et al. (2018, § 120 Rn 25).

[78] BGH NJW 2017, 2285, 2286, Tz 19; NJW 2002, 3164.

[79] Rosenberg et al. (2018, § 120 Rn 26).

[80] BGHZ 198, 32 = NJW 2013, 3306, 3308, Tz 31.

course, the probative force under procedural law is different from considerations under substantive law.[81]

The formal probative force of private documents refers to the issuance of the declaration of the author and signer.[82] Since the formal probative force of private documents does not embrace the entire factual process which may be proved by public documents,[83] private documents normally have no formal probative force as to the content of the declaration which they contain. However, there is an exception in the practice of contract law, i.e. there is a factual presumption that the declaration of legal transactions is correct and complete. Hence, when an oral agreement is alleged by the opposing party, this party should produce evidence until the judge considers that the norm of burden of proof should apply. In other words, the opposing party has to go against the factual presumption based on the *prima facie* evidence.[84]

The *German Code of Civil Procedure* does not explicitly deny the right of the party against the document to provide opposing evidence. And this possibility of providing opposing evidence was confirmed by the precedents of the Federal Court of Justice (*Bundesgerichtshof*) of Germany.[85] In such circumstances, this party may not only be able to raise new factual allegations, which refer to the proof to the contrary, e.g. that this party has withdrawn the private document or that it was lost (then was subsequently issued on its behalf).[86] Moreover, subject to the same standard of proof to the contrary, this party may also challenge the legal presumption that the authenticity of the signature can lead to the authenticity of the document (Article 440 paragraph 2 of the *German Code of Civil Procedure*).[87]

5.4.3 Rule for Presumption of Public Documents Should Be Clarified

5.4.3.1 Interpreting the Presumption of the Formal Probative Force

The *CPL* does not stipulate that public documents meeting the requirements have formal probative force.[88] Article 114 sentence 1 of the *ICPL* only provides that, as introduced at the very beginning of this chapter, unless there is sufficient evidence to the contrary, the matters recorded in the documents prepared by state organs or other organizations with law-based social management functions within the scope

---

81 Schreiber (2020, § 416 Rn 4).

82 Rosenberg et al. (2018, § 120 Rn 28); Schreiber (2020, § 416 Rn 8).

83 BGH NJW-RR 2006, 847, 848, Tz 16.

84 Schreiber (2020, § 416 Rn 9–10).

85 BGH NJW-RR 2006, 847, 848, Tz 15 et seq. The dissenting view, see Schreiber (2020, § 416 Rn 11).

86 BGHZ 198, 32 = NJW 2013, 3306, 3308, Tz 31.

87 Rosenberg et al. (2018, § 120 Rn 17, 30).

88 Zhang (2015, pp. 18–21).

of their authority should be presumed to be true. This rule with the nature of legal interpretation is inherited from Article 77 paragraphs 1 and 2 of the *2001 Evidence Provisions*, which are related to the documents produced by bodies with public law nature according to their authorities.[89] Hence, it is the contents of the documentary evidence and the facts to be proved (substantial probative force) that are presumed to be true rather than the public document itself which is presumed to be authentic and to show the declaration of the author and signer (formal probative force).

Nevertheless, it is argued *de lege lata* in this chapter that the current law actually presumes the formal probative force of public documents simultaneously. On the one hand, the premise for matters recorded in documents to be presumed to be true is that the documents themselves are true. When the documentary evidence is false or its authenticity is *non-liquet*, the documentary evidence cannot prove the matters recorded therein at all. Furthermore, authentic public documents will also have the effect of proving the author's declaration to make the documents, while the two together are equal to the contents of the formal probative force of documentary evidence. According to the official elaboration of the *ICPL*, the SPC pays full attention to the formal and substantial probative force of documentary evidence in the process of preparing this rule, while the explicit rule merely provides the rule for the substantial probative force. It can be said that the drafters take the formal probative force of documents for granted. Hence, they do not think that it would be necessary to make special provisions for the formal one.[90] After all, if documentary evidence has no formal probative force, it naturally has no substantial probative force.[91]

Meanwhile, we can also interpret the limitation on admissibility of copies and duplicates of documents (Article 77 paragraph 3 of the *2001 Evidence Provisions*), a kind of derivative evidence, to mean that the authenticity[92] or formal probative force of documents is relatively low.[93] Hence, comprehensive examination is of necessity (Article 111 paragraph 2 of the *ICPL*), while the substantial probative force of these documents on the facts to be proved is reduced. From a *de lege ferenda* perspective and based on the theoretical system of the probative force of documentary evidence mentioned previously, both kinds of probative force of documents should be regulated respectively,[94] so as to emphasize that the formal probative force is indeed the precondition of the substantial probative force of documentary evidence. In other words, the presumption of substantial probative force of documentary evidence

[89] Shen (2015, p. 376).

[90] Shen (2015, pp. 375–376).

[91] Zhang (2017a, p. 30); Li (2016, p. 149); Zhang (2015, pp. 17–18); Xiao (2010, p. 92). For the same comparative view, see, for example, Takahashi (2007, pp. 105–106); Jiang (2018, p. 198); Chen and Lin (2014, p. 152).

[92] Zhang (2017a, p. 20); Chen (2018, pp. 148–149).

[93] For such understanding in practice, see, for example, Civil Judgment of the High People's Court of Guangdong Province (2017) Yue Min Zhong No. 223 (citing the reasoning of the first-instance judgment).

[94] Gao (2016, p. 585); Zhang (2015, pp. 28–29).

provided in the Article 114 sentence 1 of the *ICPL* should be extended to cover the presumption of the formal probative force explicitly.

On the other hand, the second sentence of Article 114 of the *ICPL* further provides that the court may require the organ or organization preparing the document to explain the authenticity of documents if necessary. In this regard, the SPC considers Article 355 paragraph 2 of the *Civil Procedure Law of China Taiwan*,[95] while the first sentence of this provision refers exactly the presumption rule for the formal probative force of documentary evidence. The *Civil Procedure Law of China Taiwan* in fact copies the provisions of Article 228 paragraph 3 of the *Civil Procedure Law of Japan*, and both provisions are also in line with the original provisions of Germany, i.e. Article 437 paragraph 2 of the *German Code of Civil Procedure*. Therefore, when it comes to the source in comparative law, it can be concluded that the same rule is implied under Chinese law inexplicitly.

In clear contrast to the aforementioned provisions, Article 115 of the *ICPL* explicitly provides the elements for taking evidentiary materials of organizations, which are by their nature private documents. It is also required that the relevant person has to be investigated and verified or appear in court as a witness if necessary, otherwise the documentary evidence will not be eligible to be used as the basis for determining the case. In practice, some courts directly interpret this requirement as the requirement for the formal probative force of the documentary evidence.[96] From the difference of the existing laws between the evidentiary materials of organizations and public documents, it can be observed that public documents indeed have a special status under Chinese law.

5.4.3.2 Questioning the Presumption of the Substantial Probative Force

Although the current law provides this rule of legal presumption for the substantial probative force of public documents explicitly, this contribution still deems that this issue is better to be handled by judges during their free evaluation of evidence.[97] It is true that both the aforementioned threefold and twofold modes treat the issue of substantial probative force as one of their components. Systematically speaking, this rule also has close relationship with the predetermined effect of effective final judgments (Chap. 7).

If the presumption is accepted, one of the most significant consequences is that the objective burden of proof regarding the relevant facts to be proved is to be overturned (*Umkehr der Beweislast*).[98] According to the official elaboration of the *ICPL*, the SPC says that the opposing party to the producer of the documentary evidence is supposed to take the burden of proof to prove that the contents of the public document are false

---

[95] Shen (2015, p. 375).

[96] Civil Judgment of the Intermediate People's Court of Nantong City of Jiangsu Province (2016) Su 06 Min Zhong No. 4693.

[97] Cao Z (2020c).

[98] Pan (2016, p. 7).

while in case of private documents, the producer ought to be one having the relevant burden of proof.[99] And regarding the traffic accident liability report, it is for instance considered by a provincial court that the challenging party should take the burden of proof and prove that the recorded happening of the traffic accident is incorrect. Even if the contents of the report lie in the status of *non liquet* due to the efforts of this party, the obligation of proving is still not satisfied. On such occasions, the People's court should acknowledge the probative force of the traffic accident liability report.[100]

However, such presumption does not exist in the civil law jurisdictions considered in this chapter. As mentioned, the presumption there refers to the formal probative force rather than the substantial one. It also means even for public documents, their substantial probative force and their connection with the objective truth to be proven are not presumed. In principle, the principle of free evaluation of evidence still governs.[101] There is no ground to limit the authority of decision-makers in the process of factual conviction. And the exception exists when the objects of the formal and substantial probative force overlap in case of the aforementioned dispositional document. For instance, when it comes to the registration of marriage, this registration as a kind of public documents can prove the process of making legal transactions between each side of the couple, i.e. the consensus between them of getting married. And such a process and consensus can be presumed to be true. Yet, it can still be interpreted as an example of the presumption of formal probative force.

On the other hand, testimonial documents should generally not be presumed to be true when it handles their substantial probative force. For instance, a traffic accident liability report can be presumed to prove the determination of the policeman, as its formal probative force, while it cannot prove the happening of the accident which refers to the substantial probative force. Still, exceptions should be acknowledged due to statutory rules regulating otherwise. One prominent illustration is Article 15 of the *Civil Code of the P.R.C.* which says in its first sentence that the time of birth and the time of death of a natural person shall be the ones recorded on his or her birth certificate or death certificate; or in the absence of a birth certificate or death certificate, the time shall be the one recorded in the household registration or any other valid identity registration. And the second sentence of the same provision continues that if there is any other evidence sufficient to overturn the aforementioned time, the time proved by such evidence shall prevail.

References

Ahrens HJ (2014) In: Wieczorek B, Schütze RA, ZPO, Band 6, 4. Aufl. De Gruyter, Berlin
Althammer C (2018) In: Stein F, Jonas M, ZPO, Band 4, 23. Aufl. Mohr Siebeck, Tübingen

[99] Shen (2015, p. 376).

[100] Civil Ruling of the High People's Court of Gansu Province (2018) Gan Min Shen No. 1446.

[101] Rosenberg et al. (2018, § 120 Rn 32).

Balzer C, Walther B (2018) Beweisaufnahme und Beweiswürdigung im Zivilprozess. Erich Schmidt Verlag GmbH & Co, Berlin
Berger C (2015) In: Stein F, Jonas M, ZPO, Band 5, 23. Aufl. Mohr Siebeck, Tübingen
Bork R (1988) Der Vergleich. Duncker & Humblot, Berlin
Cao Z (2018) Identifying affirmative civil claim in Chinese law. Law Science 11:45–60 (in Chinese)
Cao Z (2019) Two modes of applying the *prima facie* evidence: reconsidering the 'Pengyu' decision. The Jurist 5:31–44+192 (in Chinese)
Cao Z (2020a) Need for the identification of documentary evidence and the allocation of costs. China Law Review 3:187–196 (in Chinese)
Cao Z (2020b) Judicial review to the application for judicial identification of a party. Law Science 12:112–129 (in Chinese)
Cao Z (2020c) The restriction of the presumption rule of the substantial proving effects of public documents. Journal of National Prosecutors College 2:137–154 (in Chinese)
Cao Z (2021) Allocation of powers and rights in commencing judicial identification in civil cases. Contemporary Law Review 2:134–146 (in Chinese)
Chen G (2000) Research on the law of burden of proof. Renmin University of China Press, Beijing (in Chinese)
Chen R (2018) Criminal evidence law. Peking University Press, Beijing (in Chinese)
Chen J, Lin C (2014) Civil procedure law, Volume I. Sanmin Book Co., Taipei (in Chinese)
Chu F (2018) Three dimensions of authenticity of electronic evidence. Chinese Journal of Law 4:121–138 (in Chinese)
eBRAM (2024) https://ebram.org/. Accessed 2 May 2024
Feskorn C (2020) In: Zöller R, ZPO, 33. Aufl. Otto Schmidt, Köln
Fu Y (2017) On the duty of good faith of parties in civil proceedings. Law and Modernization 6:130–145 (in Chinese)
Gao X (2016) The research on the probative value of public documents in civil proceedings. Evidence Science 5:576–587 (in Chinese)
Geimer R (2019) In: Thomas H, Putzo H, ZPO, 40. Aufl. C. H. Beck, München
Geimer R (2020) In: Zöller R, ZPO, 33. Aufl. Otto Schmidt, Köln
Gottwald P (2018a) Die Stellung des Sachverständigen und seines Gutachtens im deutschen Zivilprozess. Ritsumeikan Law Review 36:121–133
Gottwald P (2018b) Electronic documents and electronic signatures in German civil proceedings (trans: Cao Z) In Jiang S (ed) Electronic documents and e-commerce related substantive and procedural issues. Taiwan New Sharing Press, Taipei, pp 407–452 (in Chinese)
Hu D (2017) The rule of 'who claims, who proves': its historical evolution and contemporary application. Chinese Journal of Law 3:107–124 (in Chinese)
Hu X (2017) Restatement of the normentheorie of burden of proof. The Jurist 1:63–76+177 (in Chinese)
Huber M (2021) In: Musielak HJ, Voit W, ZPO, 18. Aufl. Vahlen, München
Ito M (2016) Civil procedure law. Yuhikaku Publishing, Tokyo (in Japanese)
Jacobs M (2005) Der Gegenstand des Feststellungsverfahrens. Mohr Siebeck, Tübingen
Jiang S (2016) Civil procedure law, Volume I. Taiwan New Sharing Press, Taipei (in Chinese)
Jiang S (2018) Civil procedure law, Volume II. Taiwan New Sharing Press, Taipei (in Chinese)
Kaneko H, Takeshita M (1995) Civil procedure law (trans: Bai L). Law Press, Beijing (in Chinese)
Klass D (1998) Reformansätze im zivilrechtlichen Persönlichkeitsschutz unter besonderer Berücksichtigung der Persönlichkeitsrechtlichen Feststellungsklage. Peter Lang GmbH, Internationaler Verlag der Wissenschaften, Berlin
Li H (2016) Civil procedure law. Law Press, Beijing (in Chinese)
Li H (2017) Research on the classification of legal elements from the perspective of the norm theory. Journal of Law Application 15:2–9 (in Chinese)
Liu P (2017) Authentification of electronic evidence: reflections on the QVOD player case. Peking University Law Journal 1:89–103 (in Chinese)
Liu Z (2018) Limitation on the scope of the declaratory claim and its implementation method. Chinese Journal of Law 1:126–145 (in Chinese)
Lv T (2018) Civil procedure law. Taiwan Angle Publishing, Taipei (in Chinese)

Matsumoto H, Ueno Y (2015) Civil procedure law. Koubundou Publishers, Tokyo (in Japanese)
Meller-Hannich C (2016) Die Rolle des Sachverständigen im deutschen Zivilprozess. Zeitschrift für Zivilprozess 129:263–294
Musielak HJ, Voit W (2016) Grundkurs ZPO, 13. Aufl. C. H. Beck, München
Pan J (2016) On burden of proof in civil cases. Political Science and Law 11:2–12 (in Chinese)
Prütting H (2020) In: Krüger W, Rauscher T, Münchener Kommentar ZPO, Band 1, 6. Aufl. C. H. Beck, München
Reichold K (2019) In: Thomas H, Putzo H, ZPO, 40. Aufl. C. H. Beck, München
Ren Z (2017) Rethinking Rosenberg's theory of burden of proof. Journal of Law Application 15:18–28 (in Chinese)
Rosenberg L, Schwab KH, Gottwald P (2018) Zivilprozessrecht. C. H. Beck, München
Roth H (2016) In: Stein F, Jonas M, ZPO, Band 3, 23. Aufl. Mohr Siebeck, Tübingen
Saenger I (2019) In: Saenger I, ZPO, Handkommentar, 8. Aufl. Nomos, Baden-Baden
Schreiber K (2020) In: Krüger W, Rauscher T, Münchener Kommentar ZPO, Band 2, 6. Aufl. C. H. Beck, München
Seiler C (2019) In: Thomas H, Putzo H, ZPO, 40. Aufl. C. H. Beck, München
Shao M (2009) Realizing truth in due procedure. Law Press, Beijing (in Chinese)
Shen D (ed) (2015) Understanding and application of the judicial interpretation of the civil procedure law of the SPC. People's Court Press, Beijing (in Chinese)
Shindo K (2019) Civil procedure law. Koubundou Publishers, Tokyo (in Japanese)
Shyuu S (2003) Change, addition and clarification of the claims. National Taiwan University Law Journal 3:209–294 (in Chinese)
Stürner M (2022) Der digitale Zivilprozess. Zeitschrift für Zivilprozess 135:369–400
Takahashi H (2007) Key lecture notes on civil procedure law (trans: Zhang W, Xu K). Law Press, Beijing (in Chinese)
Thole C (2018) In: Stein F, Jonas M, ZPO, Band 4, 23. Aufl. Mohr Siebeck, Tübingen
Wang F (2015) Civil procedure law. Tsinghua University Press, Beijing (in Chinese)
Wu Z (2017) Burden of proof in private lending lawsuit. China Legal Science 5:258–278 (in Chinese)
Wu Z (2018) The obligation of the party not responsible for the burden of proof to clarify the case. Peking University Law Journal 5:1360–1379 (in Chinese)
Wu Y (2020) Procedural principles of burden of proof. Nanjing University Law Journal 2:57–72 (in Chinese)
Xia Q (2020) From the traditional contract to smart contract: the transformation from ex post court judgment to ex ante automatic performance. The Jurist 2:14–28+191 (in Chinese)
Xiao J (2010) Authenticity of documentary evidence and its burden of proof. China Trial 7:92–93 (in Chinese)
Yang C (2013) Essentials of civil procedure law (revised by Cheng J). Peking University Press, Beijing (in Chinese)
Yi Y (2017) Evidence law. Law Press, Beijing (in Chinese)
Yuan Z (2012) The issue of 'burden of proof' about the authenticity of documents in civil proceedings. The Jurist 6:126–136+177 (in Chinese)
Yuan Z (2014) Essential defects of the norm theory and their overcoming. Chinese Journal of Law 6:147–161 (in Chinese)
Yuan Z (2015) Practice and reflection on the obligation of producing documents. Contemporary Law Review 2:126–135 (in Chinese)
Zhang Z (2010) The presumption rules for the probative value of private documents. Science of Law 4:154–159 (in Chinese)
Zhang H (2015) The application of presumption in judging the authenticity of documentary evidence. Global Law Review 4:17–34 (in Chinese)
Zhang W (2017a) Civil evidence law. Law Press, Beijing (in Chinese)
Zhang W (2017b) Institutional construction of the party's duty of producing documents. The Jurist 3:31–44+176 (in Chinese)

Chapter 6
Burden of Proof: Chinese Approach to Resolving the Factual Issue of *Non-liquet*

6.1 Introduction

In civil cases, it is always necessary for the judge to consider what the judge could do when the facts of the case could not be ascertained at the end of court hearings. And one of the most crucial differences between the common law and continental law traditions is their different theories and practices on the status of *non liquet* and its process of legal application. In continental law, the *non-liquet* status of a factual allegation is considered as the natural consequence of the limitations of human cognition together with evidential production, which is a pre-condition of the objective burden of proof (*objektive Beweislast*) in civil judgments. On the contrary, the Anglo-American legal system does not shed much light on this status. The only issue that matters is the burden of persuasion. If a claimant cannot satisfy the requirement of burden of persuasion, a judge should take the factual proposition as non-existent.[1] This chapter summarizes this phenomenon as different modes of burden of proof.

In continental countries when it comes to the proof of a factual allegation, there are three classifications where a judgment should be made by applying the norm of burden of proof (threefold mode of burden of proof), namely it is existent, or it is non-existent, or *non-liquet*. The common law tradition, however, admits only the first two classifications and the fact might be directly regarded as not existing, when the relevant party cannot persuade the judge. In the Mainland of China, it seems easy to deem that the continental thinking is followed, at least according to academic circles and two judicial interpretations issued by the SPC, namely the *ICPL* which took effect in February 2015, and *2001 Evidence Provisions* in April 2002.

Nevertheless, when we look at civil judgments in reality, it is almost impossible to find any examples of the application of *non-liquet* status. If the party shouldering the burden of proof is not able to present sufficient evidence, judges seem to simply adopt the common law tradition and regard the factual allegation as non-existent,

[1] Liu (2010, p. 92).

Z. Cao, *Civil Judgments at First Instance*, Contemporary Chinese Civil and Commercial Law, https://doi.org/10.1007/978-981-97-8662-6_6

D 1

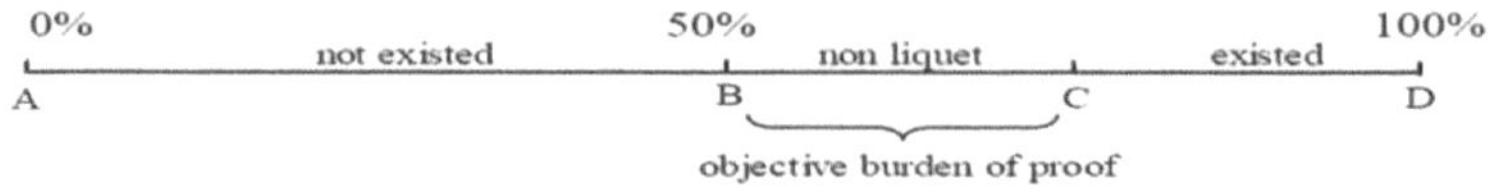

Fig. 6.1 Threefold mode of burden of proof in Germany and Japan .

rather than explicitly identify the status of *non liquet* and apply the norm of burden of proof afterward. Moreover, the regulations in the aforementioned SPC's judicial interpretations are also not without confusion on the selection of continental mode.

This deviation gives rise to the following questions: does the status of *non liquet* really exist in the judicial process in China? Does the mode of burden of proof in Chinese legislation belong to the threefold or the twofold mode? Why is the threefold classification, which reflects the common view in academic circles, hardly recognized by the judicial branch? At first, we may need to clarify these two modes.

6.2 Modes of Burden of Proof in Comparative Context

6.2.1 Threefold Mode in Germany and Japan

In the continental law tradition, the leading opinion is that according to the principle of judging on the basis of evidence, even if a party endeavors to provide evidence, at the end of a trial a judge may still fail to be sure about his results of evidential evaluation on disputed factual issues, and this is the existence of doubt on a factual issue (*non liquet*) (diagram 6.1,[2] between B and C, while the standard of proof is at C).[3] According to the explanation by academics, the conditions which constitute *non-liquet* status are: (1) the claimant supplies a factual allegation supporting a claim upon which relief can be granted; (2) the defendant renders a substantial factual allegation adverse to the plaintiff's case; (3) a disputed allegation is supposed to be proved; (4) the judge cannot take the facts as proved even with all procedurally possible means; (5) this situation lasts until the end of oral hearings.[4]

Generally speaking, the *non-liquet* status occurs when (1) the claimant cannot provide enough evidence, which could lead to the judicial evaluation of the existence or non-existence of the disputed factual allegation; or (2) although both parties supply evidence, which could prove the existence of their own factual allegation separately, the statements from the parties are so opposed that both could not be true at the same time.

---

[2] It is hardly possible to describe the sophisticated phenomenon in the judicial and human cognition with simple number or ratio. Therefore, the mentioned percent offers only reference and assistance in understanding diagrams. Comments, for instance, see Taruffo (2003, pp. 669–670).

[3] Laumen (2019, Kap. 9 Rn 1); Prütting (2019, Kap. 11 Rn 1); Prütting (1983, p. 112); Rosenberg (1965, pp. 9, 14); Takahashi (2003, p. 419).

[4] Prütting (1983, p. 14).

Then, due to the judicial obligation to give a judgment, there is the problem of judicial methodology. The leading opinion in the continental legal system is that when judging on factual issues, judges cannot only apply the laws[5] but shall use some specific norm of burden of proof,[6] when the factual allegation has the status of *non liquet*. This is on the ground that owing to the traditional syllogism, the application of law should be based on findings of facts. However, the status of *non liquet* does not give rise to any conclusions of fact and therefore no conclusions of law either. Under these circumstances, judges should confirm the status of *non liquet* and give their judgments on the basis of burden of proof, which means cases are decided in accordance with the rules of burden of proof.[7]

How the burden of proof is then allocated between both parties, is an issue of substantive law (Chap. 5, the so-called norm theory). While it shows the clear connection between the substantive law and procedural law, it means also the judge does not have any discretional power to allocate the burden of proof in individual cases.[8] It shows a great change from the *2001 Evidence Provisions* to *2019 Evidence Provisions*, since Article 7 of the former *2001 Evidence Provisions* which empowers the individual judge to allocate the burden of proof regarding certain factual allegations is deleted in the *2019 Evidence Provisions*. Concretely speaking, Article 7 says that where there are no explicit statutory provisions and it is not possible to decide who shall shoulder the burden of proof according to the *2001 Evidence Provisions* or other judicial interpretations, the People's court may determine the burden of proof according to the principle of fairness and the principle of good faith and taking such elements as the ability to produce evidence into consideration. While the *2019 Evidence Provisions* was effective in practice, the SPC then clarified that rather than changing the burden of proof in individual cases, if necessary, the judge should apply for a specific reply from the SPC. In other words, merely the SPC is eligible to change the rules of burden of proof, not judges in all cases.

Also, that there must be rules of burden of proof to be applied is attributed to the fact that there must be cases where the judge fails to discover the objective facts. Conversely, these rules are with no doubt also able to encourage the party shouldering the burden of proof regarding certain factual allegations to strive to collect the evidence and to avoid the application of these rules. Moreover, even if

[5] Rosenberg (1965, p. 12); Schwab (1978, pp. 505, 519). In China, some scholars are also in support of this theory of not applying the laws. For instance, Li Hao is one of the upholders. Li (2007, pp. 240–253).

[6] Rosenberg et al. (2018, § 116 Rn 7–8); Prütting (1983, pp. 145–151); Musielak (1975, pp. 19–32, 293); Leipold (1966, pp. 59–66); Shindo (2019, p. 604).

[7] For instance, AG Hamburg-Altona: Urteil vom 4.11.2008 – 316 C 153/08, BeckRS 2010, 00470. Moreover, this negative result of failure to bear burden of proof does not always lead to losing claim. If both parties cannot fulfill their own burden of proof on different factual allegations (For example, plaintiff should prove the existence of the alleged contract and defendant is to prove that he has no civil capability), judges are supposed to make their judgments on the merits in favor of defendant. Prütting (1983, p. 113). In this situation, although the defendant takes the negative result due to burden of proof, he can still win the case.

[8] Zheng et al. (2020, A6).

D 2

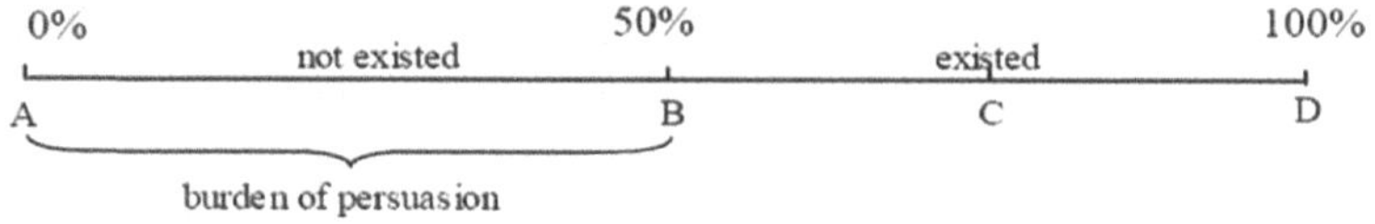

Fig. 6.2 Twofold mode of burden of persuasion in the U.S. (preponderance of evidence)

D 3

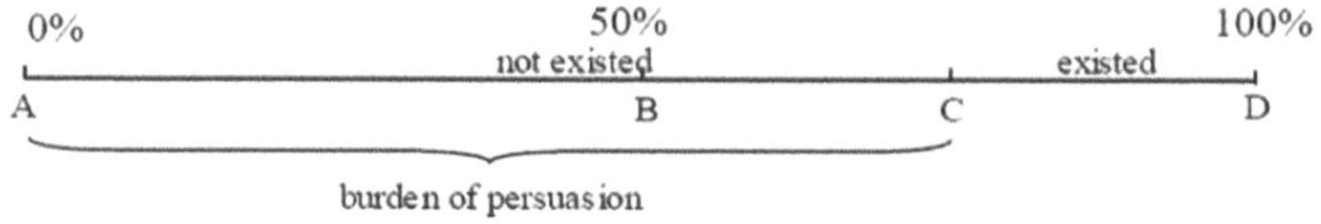

Fig. 6.3 Twofold mode of burden of persuasion in the U.S. (clear and convince evidence)

the Chinese judiciary is said to be following the principle of party presentation in principle nowadays, according to which the parties have to present facts in civil cases, the existence of these rules does not exempt judges from their duty to dig out the truth if possible. A possible last resort for the judges does not deny the possibility of doing their job better, i.e. resolving the disputes while finding the facts.

6.2.2 *Twofold Mode in the U.S.*

In the U.S., the burden of persuasion or risk of non-persuasion makes a great difference to a party's risk of not proving a factual allegation at issue (in diagram 6.2 between A and B or in diagram 6.3 between A and C). Similar to the continental mode, when a trial judge or jury throws doubt on or considers the existence or non-existence of a fact allegation as equally likely,[9]the burden of persuasion also focuses on the method of decision making or the rule of judging.[10] Generally speaking, the standard of preponderance of evidence (diagram 6.2 where the standard of proof is at B) fulfills the requirement and the standard of clear and convincing evidence (diagram 6.3 where the standard of proof is at C) only applies to cases referring to crucial private rights or interests.[11]

The U.S. approach takes the basic attitude of all-or-nothing while does not take the status of *non liquet* seriously. In most cases, in which the standard of proof is at B, the claimant should prove that the occurrence of the fact allegation is more

[9] The strictly equal situation of convincing force of proof from both parties exists hardly in the reality. As a result, according to the discussion in the U.S., a de facto requirement of 55% is more reasonable to define the border of factual deadlock. Kaplow (2012, p. 758 n. 34).

[10] Mueller et al. (2018, pp. 108, 113); James et al. (2001, §§ 7.12–7.13); Morgan (1956, p. 74); Thayer (1898, p. 355); Tapper (2007, pp. 130–132).

[11] Grogan v. Garner, 498 U.S. 279, 286 (1991); Technology Licensing Corp. v. Videotek, Inc., 545 F.3d 1316, 1326–1327 (Fed. Cir., 2008); James et al. (2001, § 7.14).

D 4

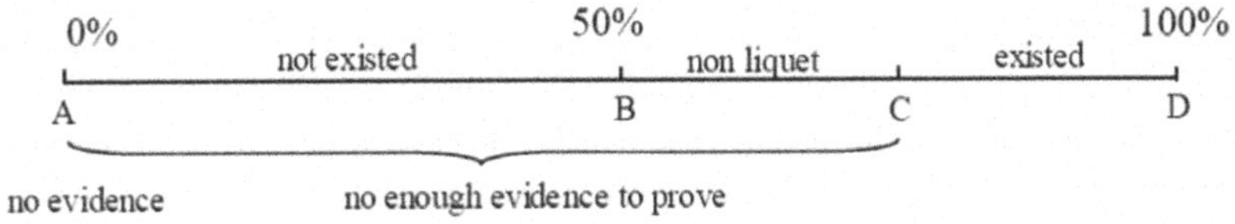

Fig. 6.4 Mode of burden of proof in China

likely than not. Otherwise, the fact-finder is supposed to regard this issue as non-existent and the respective claimant could lose the case accordingly. It relates to both the lower probability of occurring and the situation of *non liquet* (see also the expression and wording in the *ICPL* and *2001 Evidence Provisions* and diagram 6.4). Moreover, due to the lack of demand, there is also a scarcity of discussions on relevant methodological issues in common law systems.

6.2.3 *Consideration During Selecting Modes of Burden of Proof*

To answer the question as to why, within the common law systems, there is no independent theory of modes of burden of proof, which points to the application of law in cases of *non liquet*, four elements must be considered.

First, the different attitudes toward legal methodology provide insight into this issue. The common law tradition places less weight on methodological issues in evidential proceedings and does not care much about the nature and content of the norms which decide the rules of applying law in cases of *non liquet*.[12] The continental law tradition tends to discuss these philosophical issues with more patience. German scholars have published many articles and monographs on the interpretation of the burden of proof issue. Nevertheless, the fact that the allocation of burden of proof results from the substantive law brings the discussions little difference in practice. Actually, the academic disputes are only about various approaches to explanation which concerns the nature of norms of burden of proof and methodological significance of these norms.[13]

Second, the starting points of civil litigation are traceable in both law traditions. According to the contribution from Nakamura Muneo, continental law traditions belong to the norm-origin category, while common law traditions are of the fact-origin category. The norm-origin category focuses on the process of making decisions, which comprises the search for legal sources, the findings of facts and subsequently

[12] It is obviously not to say that common law courts do not respect the logical reasoning characterized by the syllogism. For instance, Posner RA (1990, pp. 38–42). This chapter intends merely to emphasize that generally speaking, they may incline not to cherish the rational structure very much. A recent research in this sense, see McGrath et al. (2014, pp. 727–736) (Also on the pragmatic understanding in continental law traditions).

[13] Prütting (2019, pp. 136–141); Prütting (1983, pp. 145–178); Heinrich (1996, pp. 37–42).

the subsumption itself.[14] The purpose of fact-finding work is the application of rules and as a result, it should shape and adapt the facts at issue to meet demands of these rules. If the facts or the parties' cases do not correspond with the elements of a specific legal norm, judges should choose a new norm to fit the requirements of laws (*Gesetzmäßigkeit*).[15] On the other hand, the fact-origin category of the common law systems means that the court makes its judicial decision in accordance with the facts or the actual dispute itself, in order to discover the proper natural law or justice rather than the application of written statutes, namely the recovery of so-called sovereignty of nomos from a German perspective.[16] Judges' primary duty is to ensure a reasonable allocation of interests and then resolve disputes. Correspondingly, investigating facts accurately ought to comply with these requests.[17] For this reason, there is no need to particularly articulate the judicial norm in cases of *non liquet*.

Third, the more pragmatic approach taken by common law countries supplies us with another possible elucidation. In both legal systems, if the standards of proof were identical, the application of substantive law would lead to the same result. The aim of an evidence provider is the confirmation of facts. If the efforts to prove do not meet the standard of proof, it implies only failure for the party having the objective burden of proof. It makes no difference whether the judges identify the non-existence or *non-liquet* status of facts. For the defendant, dragging the judges' evidential evaluation back to the standard of proof is the best weapon to defeat the opposing party. Whether we should make a finer conceptional classification after the dragging plays no role for the results on the merits. It is easy to understand why common law countries, which emphasize real effects rather than concepts, choose not to develop a relatively sophisticated mode of burden of proof.

Finally, the role of non-professional participants in the fact-finding process could give a possible answer as well.[18] In the U.S.,[19] the arbitrator of facts, the jury, is sometimes separate from a judge on legal issues. Generally speaking, only if a jury is unable to get rid of a deadlock, could a judge be authorized to intervene and ignore the verdict. The jury system, which earns much respect inside the American legal system

---

[14] Zippelius (2012, pp. 71–83).

[15] Engisch (2005, p. 68).

[16] Nakamura (2009, pp. 262–263).

[17] Damaska (1998, p. 304).

[18] In 2011, only 1.1% of all cases (in total: 302,922) entered the trial phrase in the federal court system in the U.S. Administrative Office of the U.S. Courts (2012, p. 149 table C-4). In 2018, it comes to 0.9% of all cases (in total: 275,879). Administrative Office of the U.S. Courts (2018). In 2023, the number of cases reduces to 0.7% of all cases (in total: 293,539). Administrative Office of the U.S. Courts (2023). However, although there are some negative remarks (see for example, Stürner (2005, p. 241)), both in theory and in practice, American always takes the jury trial as the fundamental procedural element in the civil justice system. It is also noticeable that the jury trial has its deep roots in the political background in the U.S. (see Carrington (2003)), and therefore, it can hardly be taken as a practicable option in China.

[19] The reason for ruling out England is that in contemporary England, there are only a few civil cases which deserve a jury trial (right now even not the defamation cases, *Defamation Act 2013*, Section 11), while a judge has the discretion to deny the right of jury trial (Senior Courts Act 1981, s 69).

together with its litigation culture, enjoys great authority on the factual judgment and the judicial branch regards every single verdict as legally unchallengeable. The twofold mode reflects just this institutional trust. Conversely, the continental law traditions do have some forms of layman participation, whereas professional judges almost always take control of dealing with factual and legal problems.[20] And the fact-finders, who are mostly professional judges, are not free from substantial and procedural controls such as the principle of free evaluation of proof, the laws of nature or human experience, and the review during appellate proceedings. These fact-finders should obey the tradition of preference for objective truth. Therefore, continental legal systems are prone to follow the threefold mode.[21]

6.3 Reviewing the Situation in China

6.3.1 Modes of Burden of Proof in Academic Circles

It is commonly agreed that the concept of burden of proof has undergone a long process of development, in which three theories, "single subjective burden of proof", "subjective together with objective burden of proof" and then "risk of losing claims", have dominated academia sequentially in different phases after the reconstruction of the rule *by* law (法制) in the 1980s. At present, the theory of "risk of losing claims" is the leading one which means "one party's risk of losing claims when disputed facts are *non-liquet*".[22] Hence, it is unanimous that the Mainland of China adheres to the continental legal family.

Some leading academics even follow the aforementioned German legal methodology explicitly. They adopt the norm theory of burden of proof (similar to the situation in Chap. 5), consider the status of *non liquet* as "true" or "false" and then apply the substantive norm to make decisions. Concretely speaking and according to their understanding, at the level of factual allegations, judges should first announce related fundamental facts as *non liquet* (step 1). Then, in the sense of methodology, judges ought to get rid of this status using legal fictions (step 2). Third, on the allocation of results, the assignment of risk depends on the rules of substantive law. If laws demand the claimant to shoulder burden of proof, *non liquet* is to be assumed as non-existent. If, conversely, the party denying the claim has to bear burden of proof, *non liquet* is hypothesized as existent (step 3).[23]

Other scholars start with different ideas like "position of parties' proof" and "position of judicial judgment" and call "clashing content and confusing logic" inside the

---

[20] For instance in Germany, the lay judges participate only in certain types of cases, such as commercial and agriculture litigation, which call for special knowledge in the eyes of legislators. Schilken (2007), Rn 523.

[21] Zhang (2019a, pp. 159–160, 165–166).

[22] Zhang (2019b, p. 246); Jiang et al. (2015, p. 202).

[23] Zhang (2005, p. 33); Chen (2000, pp. 141–143).

theoretical system of burden of proof into question, which arises out of a lack of research on the burden of proof as a judicial methodology.[24] Recently, some scholar still doubts the necessity of having *non-liquet* status and went back to the substantial argument against having it, although Article 108 paragraph 2 of the *ICPL* refers to the *non-liquet* status obviously.[25] Since the *CPL* is always untouched, the academic doubt on *non-liquet* status is with no doubt arguable. However, it is for this contribution of less practical relevance nowadays.

Therefore, this chapter has to return to the original question as to whether *non-liquet* status really exists or not. With the observation of the text of the legislation (judicial interpretations inclusive) and judicial practices, it is very hard to verify the leading theoretical interpretation. Instead, judges in practice seem to take a compromise approach that facts should be directly recognized as non-existent[26] and laws should be applied accordingly when the claimant does not provide enough evidence. For the practice, it seems that there is no need to identify the status of *non liquet* and apply the independent norm of burden of proof.[27]

6.3.2 Modes of Burden of Proof in Legislation

6.3.2.1 2001 Evidence Provisions

Because the *CPL* does not touch on this issue at all, the related legislation, the *ICPL* as well as the 2001 *Evidence Provisions*, should be carefully re-examined. In this regard, merely Article 67 of the *CPL* stipulates that it is the duty of a party to provide evidence in support of the allegations, which with no doubt has less to do with the burden of proof in the context of this chapter.

Article 2 paragraph 2 of the *2001 Evidence Provisions* provides that "the party bearing burden of proof should take the disadvantageous results, if no evidence or not enough evidence, which could prove the party's factual allegation, has been provided". According to the quasi-official published explanation of the *2001 Evidence Provisions*, its draftsmen hold that this paragraph means the burden of proof observed from the results and theoretically adopts the theory of objective burden of proof.[28] Nevertheless, although the losing results have been allocated, this chapter doubts the opinion held by those draftsmen on the ground that there is no single word relating to the status of *non liquet* and, in fact, this rule equates *non liquet* with factual non-existence. In other words, if the standard of proof has been overstepped,

[24] Xiao (2008, pp. 198–219).

[25] Ou (2016, pp. 26–31). The opposing comment, see Ren (2017, pp. 20–21).

[26] The non-existence here is used in the sense of the twofold mode in common law traditions.

[27] This conclusion is the same as the judgment of Huang Kuo-Chang on comparative law and the judicial practice in China Taiwan. Huang (2008, p. 139). The similar situation in Japan, see Duan (2012, p. 172).

[28] Li (2002, p. 33); Huang (2002, p. 15).

facts should be acknowledged. Otherwise, no fact could be declared and the party with burden of proof should tolerate the negative results (diagram 6.4, between A and C, similar to diagram 6.3). Although the drafters of this judicial interpretation may not be aware of their own internal attitude, the document plainly shows that they favor the common law approach and twofold mode, namely "no persuasion, no existence".

This observation could be queried in two ways. First, the "burden of proof" should mean the objective burden of proof and the draftsmen of the *2001 Evidence Provisions* just regulate both situations together, i.e. non-existent and *non liquet*, and did not adopt the common law approach intentionally. This chapter would say that this viewpoint with good will may go too far and ignore the key point. If the logical major premise inside the legal norm cannot cover the minor premise in the fact-finding process and accordingly the syllogistic reasoning cannot be achieved, judges are supposed to refuse to apply the norm and make the decision to dismiss the claim. As a result, the application of law in cases of non-existent facts is of certainty. However, the critical issue here is as to how the law can be applied when factual allegation lies in *non-liquet* status. In the text of this paragraph and the explanation from drafters and scholars, these two distinct circumstances (non-existent and *non-liquet*) are unable to be found and deserve further clarification in theory.

On the other hand, one may say that even if Article 2 paragraph 2 of the *2001 Evidence Provisions* does not answer clearly, Article 73 paragraph 2 there, which is on the standard of proof, could also act as a reference. This paragraph says that judges should adopt the rules allocating burden of proof, when the probative value of the evidence from one party is not able to overtake that from the other party. It implies the rule to judge on the basis of *non-liquet* facts.

However, the doubt stays. This point of view gives direction on the application of law in cases of *non-liquet* status and might represent the attitude of draftsmen of the *2001 Evidence Provisions* that they have taken the threefold mode of burden of proof. Nevertheless, this paragraph still conflicts with the aforementioned procedural theory.

First, draftsmen do acknowledge the existence of *non-liquet* status (step 1), whereas they in the meantime have extended the scope of application. Their idea can be part of the twofold mode. According to their writing, "the probative value of the evidence fails to be decided" includes both the situation that the probative value of the evidence from both parties is in equipoise and that the evidence presented by both parties cannot be taken as the ground for the factual conviction.[29] The former situation refers to the traditional status of *non liquet* but the second relates to admissibility of evidence on account of the failure to confirm the authentication of the evidence. As mentioned, assuming that there is no evidence to support the factual allegation, judges shall in terms of the threefold mode declare the non-existence of facts and dismiss the claim. Yet, this paragraph directs that judges should rather apply the rule on the allocation of burden of proof in this situation. It follows the path of "no persuasion, no existence".

[29] Huang (2002, p. 354).

Second, this paragraph fails to mention the theory of burden of proof in a legal methodological sense either (step 2). It is also said that the entire theory of burden of proof consists of the status of *non liquet* and the methodology of law application. Although as the practical guidance, rules within the judicial interpretation need scarcely to elaborate the concrete process of reasoning, the SPC should have taken this suitable opportunity to "prove" that the Chinese civil procedure belongs to the threefold family.

Lastly, it is to be noticed that Article 73 paragraph 2 of the *2001 Evidence Provisions* has less value than Article 2 paragraph 2 of the *2001 Evidence Provisions* regarding the burden of proof. The former paragraph mainly points at the standard of proof and refers to the judicial method incidentally. Consequently, the latter one, which regulates burden of proof directly, is more convincing and has been considered as the main source for the construction of the theory of burden of proof in the *2001 Evidence Provisions*, at least by the drafters of the judicial interpretation and most scholars. As discussed, Article 2 paragraph 2 of the *2001 Evidence Provisions* shows an example of the twofold family.

In conclusion, despite the existence of *non-liquet* status in the 2001 *Evidence Provisions*, without limiting the application of the burden of proof rule to the *non-liquet* status and constructing the relevant legal methodology, it is hard to be persuaded that we have followed the leading theory in continental law traditions. At the same time, the direct rule on burden of proof insists on the attitude of "no persuasion, no existence" in fact, which shows a strong proof of transplantation from common law traditions. This chapter even supposes that as a distinguishing feature, the *2001 Evidence Provisions* does applaud the twofold mode with the sole exception to admittance of the status of *non liquet*. Could it be a fresh endeavor which combines both modes of burden of proof? At least the "legislators" and most scholars in China do not agree with this speculation.

6.3.2.2 Development Through the 2015 ICPL

The *ICPL* in 2015 is generally considered as the termination of the previous debate regarding the burden of proof. While compared with Article 2 paragraph 2 of the *2001 Evidence Provisions*, the *ICPL* adds the limitation "before making a judgment" into its Article 90 paragraph 2, the substantial change is given in Article 108. It is said in the first paragraph that if the competent People's court, through examination of the evidence provided by a party bearing the burden of proof and in light of relevant facts, is convinced that it is highly likely that the facts to be proved by such evidence have occurred, the People's court shall find that such facts do exist. While discussing the standard of proof, this paragraph focuses on the perspective of the party who has to allege and then prove certain essential factual allegations in the sense of primary proof (*Hauptbeweis*).

Then, more crucially, its second paragraph stipulates that where one party concerned provides evidence to refute the facts alleged by the party bearing the burden of proof, the competent People's court shall find that the facts to be proven do not exist if, through examination of the evidence and in light of relevant facts, the People's court considers that the relevant facts lie in the *non-liquet* status. As it emphasizes that a *non-liquet* factual allegation should be considered a non-existent one, the issues discussed in the era of the *2001 Evidence Provisions* are clearly resolved. In other words, the separate status of *non liquet* and the related legal methodology are given hereby and the threefold approach is explicitly chosen by the SPC.[30] And compared to the first paragraph, the second paragraph looks at the perspective of the opposing party who may produce opposing evidence (*Gegenbeweis*) considering the allocation of burden of proof.

And its third paragraph provides that the provisions otherwise prescribed by law on the standard of proof which the facts to be proven should reach shall prevail.Currently, besides the general "highly likely" (Article 108 paragraph 1 of the *ICPL*) standard of proof, the factual allegations relating to fraud, coercion, malicious collusion, oral testament or gift are under the exceptional "no reasonable doubt" (Article 109 of the *ICPL*) standard of proof.

One left issue regarding Article 108 of the *ICPL* is the term of burden of proof used in China. The Chinese term "举证证明责任" (ju zheng zheng ming ze ren) contains both the subjective (producing evidence) and objective (proving, proven) perspectives of burden of proof. Yet, as the threefold approach is taken by the structure and content of this provision, the issue of terms is merely a minor academic one.

6.3.3 Modes of Burden of Proof in Judicial Practices

Furthermore, the aforementioned assumption regarding the mode of burden of proof has been preliminarily proved by Chinese judicial practices. When citing Article 2 paragraph 2 of the *2001 Evidence Provisions*, judges often apparently adopt the twofold mode of burden of proof. For example, in *Junxin Vanguard Co. v. Lvguweiye Co.*, (君信创业公司诉绿谷伟业公司等出资合同纠纷案),[31] a contribution agreement dispute, the High People's Court of Ningxia Province "failed to establish whether Lvguweiye Company contributes falsely" on the basis of the evidence rendered by the plaintiff Junxin Company. The court deemed that the plaintiff should carry the burden of proof and risk of losing the claim on this factual issue, which fits the objective theory of burden of proof. However, the SPC held that "both parties hand in opposing evidence on the same fact and each of them cannot overrule the evidence from the other side. Due to the limitation of the evidential probative value, we shall not establish the fact on the appellant's (here: plaintiff) side". Therefore, the claim was dismissed. Another illustration is *Chengdu branch of China Life Insurance (Group) Co. and Hualong Co.* (中国人寿保险公司成都分公司诉华隆公司等证券侵权纠纷案), a security tort dispute, where the High People's Court of Sichuan Province deemed that "because the third party could not prove that (the action) was taken

[30] Ren (2017, p. 20–21).

[31] Civil Judgment of the SPC (2004) Min Er Zhong Zi No. 260.

by the plaintiff with sufficient evidence, the third party must have done that".[32] In both cases, the burden of "non-persuasion" seems to have been adopted by courts.[33] Specifically, the expression in cases such as "failure to provide evidence on this aspect",[34] "unable to establish the fact because of the insufficient evidence",[35] "the evidence is of no probative value and cannot prove the fact (of producing damage)"[36] shows the inclination for the common law mode in judicial practice in China.

Because of the little possibility of reviewing the evidence collected by judges in every single case to strengthen the argument, it is rather probable that the factual issues in dispute are really supposed to be decided as non-existent rather than *non-liquet*. It might be unnecessary to apply the norm of burden of proof in the first place. However, the purpose of this contribution is only to present the challenge to the leading doctrine. Without more elaborate empirical research, there is no need to be concerned about my assumption. On one side, judges just cite the expression in the *2001 Evidence Provisions* (diagram 6.4) explicitly, which prefers the twofold (diagram 6.2) rather than threefold (diagram 6.1) mode. On the other side, there is no acknowledgment of *non-liquet* status and the finding of factual non-existence written in the judgment cannot support that the evidential evaluation of judges is below the line of *non liquet* (between A and B in diagram 6.4). Otherwise, we would have a vicious circle in the argument. For these reasons, this contribution insists on the previous conclusion, unless the opposite opinion fulfills the "burden of production" on this issue and reverses the *prima facie* argument offered by this contribution.

Recently, due to the stipulation of Article 108 paragraph 2 of the *ICPL*, which has been applied by Chinese courts at all levels every day, it is at present quite easier to discover that the status of *non-liquet* appears in the judicial practice more often. As of 1 April 2021, for instance, there are already more than 45,000 results in the official database of judicial decisions (http://wenshu.court.gov.cn). This chapter could not review all of them case by case, but it could be estimated that the positive finding of *non-liquet* in the reasoning part of judgments is already the common happening in China.[37]

It is true that compared to the annual amount of civil cases in China, the quantity of cases applying the rules of burden of proof is small. The burden of proof is even not a real issue since normally the facts of individual cases could be discovered.

---

32 Civil Judgment of the SPC (2004) Min Er Zhong Zi No. 137 (citing the judgment at first instance by the High People's Court of Sichuan Province: Civil Judgment of the High People's Court of Sichuan Province (2003) Chuan Min Chu Zi No. 22). In other words, the judge convicts in this case the existence of the opposing fact.

33 On the contrary, Li Hao deems that this expression shows the theory of not applying the laws (It can be inferred that Li Hao considers that the court has mentioned the status of *non liquet*) and judges use this way to "explain the reason of judgment directly". Li (2007, p. 248).

34 Civil Judgment of the High People's Court of Guangdong Province (2006) Yue Gao Fa Min San Zhong Zi No. 127.

35 Civil Judgment of the SPC (2004) Min Yi Zhong Zi No. 104.

36 Civil Judgment of the Intermediate People's Court of Hainan Province (2005) Hainan Min Er Zhong Zi No. 105.

37 Discussion in detail, see Cao (2021).

Hence, in principle, there is no room for judges to apply Article 108 paragraph 2 of the *ICPL*.[38] But still, we could try to locate the reasons for why there is an obvious gap between the legal theories and the judicial practice in the past, which might lead to some better understanding of the Chinese approach to the rule of law in civil cases.

6.4 Analysis of Causes of the Mode of Burden of Proof in China

6.4.1 Judicial Truth and Aim of Litigation

First, this situation relates to two factors: the understanding of the truth during judicial proceedings and the aim of litigation in China. As to the first factor, an objective understanding of truth, which occupied the mainstream years ago, believes that confirmation of facts by judges should be objective facts and to seek truth is for judges not only a possibility but also an obligation.[39] Nevertheless, the leading theory right now emphasizes that the fact-finding standard should be the degree that based on the evidence, proving of facts is enough to be legally regarded as truth. As a result, even if facts in the case may differ from the objective truth, they can still be assumed as true in the sense of legal truth. However, this leading theory fails to take into consideration the distinction between factual non-existence and legal status of *non liquet*. In responding to the common overcorrection in China, this chapter would infer that judges deem that the status of *non liquet* only takes place in the real world. From the perspective of the aforementioned legal truth, facts can only be of existence or non-existence, which leads to denial of the third nature of facts, *non liquet* in the sense of law.

At the same time, judges could close cases with many alternative methods rather than making judgment on the basis of burden of proof, such as declination to make decisions on the merits, dismissal of claims, refusal to issue a complaint, mediation, judgment according to the proportion of confirmation of facts, postponement of making decisions and reduction of the standard of proof.[40] In the extreme, even an apportionment between parties could be a solution. For instance, in *Jintan Construction & Installation Engineering Co. v. Daqing Qinglong Real Estate Development Co., Limited* (金坛市建筑安装工程公司与大庆市庆龙房地产开发有限公司建设工程结算纠纷案),[41] a construction project liquidation dispute, the parties stipulated that costs in 1999 were to be paid according to the contract. Nevertheless, the parties later agreed on the supplement of the all-in price when the liquidation problem of some installed cables arose. The SPC was of the opinion that 7 cables

[38] For instance, Pan (2016, p. 4).

[39] Li (1993, p. 233).

[40] Li (2005); Prütting (1983, pp. 120–152).

[41] Civil Judgment of the SPC (2004) Min Yi Zhong Zi No. 118.

aside, which were installed in 1999 and gave rise to no controversy, the disputed costs of 14 cables, CNY 1,708,497.48, shall be shared between parties. The reasoning was that both parties were not able to make an agreement, and both failed to provide evidence to prove their own factual allegation.

As to the second factor, in most countries, the resolution of disputes is considered as at least one of the aims of litigation.[42] In China also, apart from the cultural tradition of dropping lawsuits,[43] judges in practice take dispute resolution between parties very seriously. They focus on rectifying judicial errors, which is represented by the regime of judicial supervision (rather than the obvious errors in Chap. 9), and weigh the "mediation mode of civil justice"[44] which coexists with the idea that "when cases have been closed, disputes should be resolved at the same time". In addition, the judicial ideology of "satisfying citizens" or "serving the people" (为人民服务) coupled with the enhancement of social harmony should not be forgotten. In the real world, under the pressure of parties' petitions, appeals and even repeating frivolous litigation and petitions, the interests of judges and courts themselves closely relate to the resolution of disputes. For these reasons, judges need to resolve cases quickly and convincingly for the parties. And it will improve their performance within the whole judiciary.

Relying on this analysis, we should reconsider judges' way of thinking in practice. On matters of fact, to persuade parties and allow them to further accept the decision, it is more convenient as well as easier to say that a judgment is justified and in accordance with the objective truth, namely "digging out the truth of facts". However, a judgment relying on burden of proof is doomed to be the *ultima ratio* when facts cannot be determined,[45] which means this legal status of *non liquet* in their judgments is also destined to be sometimes inconsistent with objective truth. If judges specify the status of *non liquet*, they can merely rely on the hope that the parties might agree that the objective truth of facts cannot be acquired by any means. This approach departs severely not only from the common understanding of truth, but also from the judicial propaganda spread by the judicial branch itself, not to mention its difficulty (in proving some negative factual allegation that there is not any way to discover the truth). In many occasions, it is not possible to reach the aim of resolving disputes in this way.

Moreover, the allocation of burden of proof in China depends on the norm theory (*Normentheorie*) rather than the theory of probability. Therefore, this allocation has nothing to do with the possibility of happening, which means that the probability of making a right or wrong decision is the same. From a realistic perspective, judges would better establish certain facts in connection with the consideration of minor factual elements (such as the "entire content of the hearings", which is regarded as the exception to the principle of judging relying on evidence, or the effect of a merchant's

[42] Rosenberg et al. (2018, § 1 Rn 18); Shindo (2019, pp. 2–3); Damaska (1997, pp. 110–113, 120); Jolowicz (2000, p. 70). The Chinese discussion, see Zhang (2019b, pp. 9–10).

[43] You (2012).

[44] Wang (1994).

[45] Laumen (2019, Kap. 11 Rn 1).

reputation on the possibility of breaking a contract in a certain transaction). In this way, the obtained result of evidential evaluation may fit for the objective truth and substantial justice while the parties are more likely to be persuaded. Consequently, "among judges is more popular to artificially classify the alleged facts as true or false by manipulating the standard of proof".[46]

6.4.2 *Factual Standard at Second Instance*

Moreover, regarding the fact-finding process in the judicial hierarchy, the review standard at second instance exceeds the continental counterpart, the mode of "resumption of hearing", in the scope of review and matches the mode of "de novo review".[47] According to this mode, the supervision function in the judicial hierarchy is heavily amplified and results in a stronger capability of discovering the truth. However, the judicial system puts lower-level judges at a disadvantage when they try to establish facts. At the same time, it may make the threefold mode of burden of proof tougher to follow.

First, the unclear fact-finding standard, which says that the judgment should be reversed and altered by the court at higher instance, when a fact is not clear, creates more risk for judges of making wrong decisions and contributes to the avoidance of burden of proof judgment. On one hand, the *non liquet* status literally meets this standard of "unclear fundamental facts" (基本事实不清) (Article 177 paragraph 3 sub-paragraph 3 of the *CPL*)[48] or the well-recognized "unclear facts, insufficient evidence" (事实不清，证据不足) standard in criminal proceedings. *Non liquet* is just an alternative expression of these standards which conforms to remanding or alteration. In other words, these two standards leave no space for the status of *non liquet*. On the other hand, the de novo mode, which is represented by the unclear fact standard, does not limit its aim to the rectification of errors and enhances the focus on the fact-finding function. This standard fails to adopt the mode of "resumption of

[46] Duan (2007, p. 26).

[47] Fu (2002, pp. 94–95); Fu (2005, pp. 40–41).

[48] According to Article 333 of the *ICPL*, "fundamental facts" include those with substantial influence on the results of judgments, such as the facts relating to parties' procedural status, nature of dispute, substantive right and obligation.

hearing",[49] which values the determination by the trial judge, but encourages appellate judges to take the path of retrial without restriction. If we take the aforementioned approval of objective understanding of truth in practice into account, appellate judges could announce the existence or non-existence of facts in the delicate situation of *non liquet*. In particular, the condition of adopting burden of proof, that "judges fail to get the factual conviction when all possible procedural means are exhausted", is quite flexible. "Exhausted or not" is based on the result of the interaction between justice and efficiency. It relates to the invested amount of social and private costs and the judicial judgment in the specific litigation situation, which may result in divergences between judges in different occasions.

Second, due to this standard, trial judges must assume more burden of reasoning. Facts can only have existence or non-existence and the legal status of *non liquet* is obviously an exception. The general rule of proof which overtakes the proof in litigation is that the party in support of a special rule should bear the "responsibility to prove/reason". Therefore, if trial judges announce in the judgment that they have failed to establish certain facts, they should prepare sufficient arguments to persuade higher-level judges; otherwise, the general rule has to be applied. If trial judges make a positive or negative decision on facts, the situation is to be overturned. Based on the division and collaboration of labor and function among courts at different levels, if judges at second instance try to reverse a factual conviction, they should also arrange grounds for refusal. If not, they have to respect the decision of trial judges, who are closest to factual materials of individual cases. In other words, if trial judges consider facts as *non liquet*, they should bear the "burden of proof" to prove the existence of special grounds. If trial judges make the conviction of existence or non-existence, this "burden of proof" should be assumed by the reviewer and judges at second instance must prove the special grounds, in case that they intend to reverse the judgment of trial judges. Therefore, trial judges can reduce their probability of making wrong judgments and being rejected by higher-level judges due to laziness, if they have made a clear selection between existence and non-existence. So, why not?

Also, without a well-done precedent system, judges are deficient in reference and therefore more likely to fail to interpret the proper standard of proof in specific cases. Following the principle of judging on the basis of evidence, judges who investigate facts need to go through the evidential evaluation under the standard of proof.

---

[49] Shindo (2019, pp. 926–929); Fu (2005, p. 43). In Germany, although the statute regards the respect for factual determination by trial judges as a general rule and does not allow factual review unless specific indications show up (Article 529 paragraph 1 item 1 of the *German Code of Civil Procedure*), the leading theory still emphasizes the function of discovering truth in the appellate proceedings. BGHZ 162, 313 = NJW 2005, 1583, 1584; BGHZ 159, 254 = NJW 2004, 2828, 2829; Rosenberg et al. (2018, § 139 Rn 33 et seq.); Rimmelspacher (2020, § 529 Rn 8 et seq.); Reichold (2019, § 529 Rn 1 et seq.). The opposing viewpoint focuses on the meaning of the statute. Unberath (2007, pp. 342–345). In China, the current crucial task is the completion of factual adjudication at first instance and therefore right now, a factual review by the appellate court is still of necessity. The speed of reform aiming for a stricter mode of "resumption of hearing" (including the undiscussed issue in this contribution, i.e. the preclusion of new facts and evidence), should be decided after evaluating the reform's effects. On this point, the empirical research of Huang Kuo-Chang on the criminal appeals system in China Taiwan sets a good example. Huang (2009, pp. 447–495).

However, the standard of proof in both legal systems is quite abstract[50] and to secure the uniform justice, assistance is of necessity from the precedent system. Although the professional quality of judges in China has improved remarkably (Chap. 10), without an advanced system of guiding cases which is the Chinese version of precedent system, the understanding of standard of proof is prone to rest with the judge. As a result, different understandings of the unclear fact standard could exist not only among judges at the same level but also between judges at first and second instances.

Lastly, if a judge makes a wrong decision, he risks a lot. Within a regime of judicial administration (审判管理) in Chinese context,[51] a trial judge whose judgment is reversed may suffer from damage to economic condition and reputation. This negative effect extends to his peers as well. Under this Sword of Damocles, judges have to act with more prudence and endeavor to avoid judgments on the basis of *non liquet*.[52]

6.4.3 Separation of Theory and Practice During Legal Transplantation

Furthermore, among less developed countries that wish to build rule-of-law states, it is very common to transplant the system of law or legal theories from another developed jurisdiction. Due to the separation of legal system from the social environment during this process, this transplantation has to deal with the tension between foreign models and local customs as well as practices. For instance, this phenomenon happened in Japan in the Meiji era and after World War II. The Meiji government intended to learn from the German legal system, whereas scholars wanted to graft the French mode onto the old feudal ground. During the post-war period, the government had no strong will to amend the civil procedure law, while academia preferred the experience of the

---

[50] The standard of proof is a major controversial issue in the comparative civil procedure and relates to different aspects such as the regulation in texts and practice, the reference of other social sciences and making value judgments in various jurisdictions. Rosenberg et al. (2018, § 114 Rn 11 et seq.); Laumen (2019, Kap 5 Rn 4 et seq.); Prütting (1983, pp. 59–66); Clermont (2009); Clermont et al. (2002); Taruffo (2003). Due to the purpose of this contribution, no complete discussion is to be made. To meet our consistent demand on truth, "highly possible" still can be the general standard, which is identical with the leading theory in Germany. In individual cases, the standard of proof is supposed to be selected by judges according to the concrete situation. Based on the judicial experience, statutes, judicial interpretations or guiding cases can also reduce the standard of proof to equally likely in some types of cases.

[51] The comparative research on this Chinese concept and the case management in many jurisdictions, see Cadiet and Fu (2023).

[52] In the U.S., it is also possible to make factual judgments contrary to burden of proof. For example, a jury may ignore an instruction from a judge and the judge may "violate the law" intentionally while hoping that the appellate court does not rectify the fact-finding. Broun et al. (2006, § 336). It is argued in this contribution that the tension between practice and theory exists in different countries with different forms. But in China, the incomplete judicial system and the personal incentive of judges could give rise to more severe problems.

U.S.[53] In 1908, there was also the situation of "copying from Japan with intention of learning from Germany" in China.[54] Right now, our academics focusing on civil procedure law favor the basic framework of the continental legal system on account of the academic and institutional tradition.[55] Only the ideology in litigation and some specific institutions come from the common law system. However, the difference between objective burden of proof and burden of persuasion attracts less attention (the situation has improved recently).

The reasons for the aforementioned situation could be that English has become the major working language and that legal globalization, especially in the areas of international transactions, legal education, and legal writing, is moving closer to the American mode,[56] and some researchers do not mark the distinguishing trait of different modes of legal methodology/legal reasoning while placing great emphasis only on achieving the same results in litigation. Considering the reality in practice, one is liable to realize the complexity of the separation between theory and practice. For these reasons, the objective burden of proof may be mixed up with the terms and language of the common law system (non-persuasion) without being cautious about drawing a line between concepts. This happening is quite normal at present when the Chinese characters or elements in the legal system[57] have not been constructed finally.

Does the *non-liquet* status exist in the system of proving facts in civil cases in China? This question refers not only to some conceptional discussion but also to different modes of law application on the same status of proof in litigation. In the process of answer-searching, the operation of the objective burden of proof theory in practice has been at least partially uncovered. While academia appeals to the status of *non liquet*, the judicial interpretation and a large number of judicial judgments showed no respect for it previously. Conversely, they choose the more direct path in common law tradition: "no persuasion, no existence".

It may be said that the theory of burden of proof in the continental legal system and the legal methodology behind it are too complicated for the judicial practices in China, not to mention that the results on the merits cannot be affected at all. There is no need to copy everything from Germany or Japan. Indeed, the theory pulls no

[53] Nakamura (2009, p. 258).

[54] Deng (2009, p. 166).

[55] For instance, Zhang (2014, p. 9); Chen (2012). The opposite opinion, see Tang (2013, pp. 145, 150); Wu (2011, p. 188).

[56] Ho (2005, pp. 1–23). A recent research on the American advantages with the emphasis on the conception of law in its legal training, which works comparatively better than the civil law counterpart in current global context, see Reimann (2014).

[57] Comparison with the development of civil law science, see Wang (2011). It could be argued in this contribution that this legal system is still on his way from the rule *by* law to a particular form of thick rule of law (socialist). For a nice elaboration of the difference among the concepts, see Peerenboom (2004, pp. 2–10). Lastly, in this sense, the emphasized "ruling in line with the Constitution" (依宪执政，宪治) since the Fourth Plenary Session of the 18th CPC Central Committee from 20 to 23 October 2014 could also differ from the Western constitutionalism (宪政), which deserves more observation from a comparative aspect. Subject to the topic, this contribution is not to go into it.

weight in the results of cases. But is it truly too sophisticated? Definitely not. The burden of proof theory in the continental legal system is complicated because of its foundation, i.e. the highly developed law science. The complexity reflects only the thinking process and integrity of theoretical explanation. On the other side, judges are supposed to recognize the status of *non liquet*, transfer it into true or false status in accordance with the norm of burden of proof and then apply the law as usual. For judges, there is in fact only one more step in the fact-finding process which requires them to specify the *non-liquet* status. It means that judges have to explain the case and expound the process of decision-making in their judgment. In other words, the judgment ought to improve their reasoning skills. Nothing more.

The main purpose of this chapter is to explain the tension between theories as well as between theory and practice. Yet, it does not pay much attention to a suitable solution for China, due to the necessity to argue for the acknowledgment of difference first. Concisely speaking, this solution should be threefold. First, we must contemplate from a higher level what kind of theory of legal application we need, which inevitably requires the integration of research in civil procedure with the abstract reasoning of jurisprudence. Second, some fundamental issues, such as mode of appellate review, standard of proof and system of guiding cases, ought to be discussed through systematic comparison. Third, to discover the particularities relating to the mode of burden of proof in China, broader empirical research has to be conducted in the future, which is able to reveal the extent of acceptance among judges, lawyers and parties scientifically (not only with some unproved assumptions). In any event, the discussion on *non liquet* may just raise a series of problems. To solve them, every step needed in the construction of rule-of-law state is to be cherished.

References

Administrative Office of the U.S. Courts (2012) 2011 annual report of the director: judicial business of the U.S. Courts. Washington DC

Administrative Office of the U.S. Courts (2018) Table C-4. U.S. district courts–civil cases terminated, by Nature of suit and action taken, during the 12-month period ending September 30, 2018. https://www.uscourts.gov/sites/default/files/data_tables/jb_c4_0930.2018.pdf

Administrative Office of the U.S. Courts (2023) Table C-4. U.S. district courts–civil cases terminated, by Nature of suit and action taken, during the 12-month period ending September 30, 2023. https://www.uscourts.gov/sites/default/files/data_tables/jb_c4_0930.2023.pdf

Broun KS et al. (2006) McCormick on evidence. Thomas/West, St. Paul, MN

Cadiet L, Fu Y (eds) (2023) On judicial management from comparative perspective: international association of procedural law conference (8–10 November 2017, Tianjin, PRC). Springer, Singapore

Cao Z (2021) New practical development of judgments based on the burden of proof. Yenching Legal Studies 2:154–170 (in Chinese)

Carrington PD (2003) The civil jury and American democracy. Duke journal of comparative & international law (Special Issue) 13:79–94

Chen G (2000) Research on the law of burden of proof. Renmin University of China Press, Beijing (in Chinese)

Chen G (2012) The significance of awareness of legal family in the study of civil procedural law. Chinese Journal of Law 5:40–43 (in Chinese)
Clermont KM (2009) Standards of proof revisited. Vermont Law Review 33:469–487
Clermont KM, Sherwin E (2002) A comparative view of standards of proof. The American Journal of Comparative Law 50:243–275
Damaska MR (1997) Evidence law adrift. Yale University Press, New Haven
Damaska MR (1998) Truth in adjudication. Hastings Law Journal 49:289–308
Deng F (2009) Why China adopted the civil legal system: a political economic explanation of transitional justice in later Ch'ing's empire. Peking University Law Journal 2:165–186 (in Chinese)
Duan H (2007) The practical interaction and institutional coordination between burden of proof, standard of proof and evaluation of proof. Journal of Nanjing Normal University (Social Science Edition) 3:24–30 (in Chinese)
Duan W (2012) Reflection on the structure of norm-based civil judgments. Law Press, Beijing (in Chinese)
Engisch K (2005) Einführung in das juristische Denken, 10 Aufl. Kohlhammer, Stuttgart
Fu Y (2002) Constructive principles of judicial hierarchy. Social Sciences in China 4:84–99 (in Chinese)
Fu Y (2005) The function and structure of civil appellate procedure. Law Review 4:36–44 (in Chinese)
Heinrich C (1996) Die Beweislast bei Rechtsgeschäften. Heymann, Köln
Ho B (2005) Common law education in China. CUPL Press, Beijing (in Chinese)
Huang S (ed) (2002) The understanding and application of judicial interpretation on evidence in civil procedure. China Legal Publishing House, Beijing (in Chinese)
Huang K (2008) New perspective of civil procedure theory. Peking University Press, Beijing (in Chinese)
Huang K (2009) Evaluation of reform proposal for criminal appeals system: an empirical approach. In: Huang K (ed) Empirical studies of judicial systems 2008. Institutum Iurisprudentiae (Preparatory Office), Taipei, pp 447–495 (in Chinese)
James F, Hazard GC, Lubsdorf J (2001) Civil procedure. Foundation Press, New York
Jiang W, Fu Y (eds) (2015) Civil procedure law. Peking University Press, Beijing (in Chinese)
Jolowicz JA (2000) On civil procedure. Cambridge University Press, New York
Kaplow L (2012) Burden of proof. Yale Law Journal 121:738–859
Laumen H (2019) In: Baumgärtel G, Laumen H, Prütting H, Handbuch der Beweislast: Grundlagen. Heymann, Köln
Leipold D (1966) Beweislastregeln und Gesetzliche Vermutungen. Duncker & Humblot, Berlin
Li H (1993) On civil burden of proof. CUPL Press, Beijing (in Chinese)
Li G (ed) (2002) The understanding and application of 'some provisions of the SPC on evidence in civil procedures' by the SPC. China Legal Publishing House, Beijing (in Chinese)
Li H (2005) Comparison on the solution of factual *non liquet*. Studies in Law and Business 3:104–111 (in Chinese)
Li H (2007) On the frontier issues in the legislation of civil evidence law. Law Press, Beijing (in Chinese)
Liu Z (2010) Burden of proof in American law: from the perspective of judicial procedure. Contemporary Law Review 3:86–94 (in Chinese)
McGrath CP, Koziol H (2014) Is style of reasoning a fundamental difference between the common law and the civil law. The Rabel Journal of Comparative and International Private Law 78:709–749
Morgan EM (1956) Some problems of proof under the Anglo-American system of litigation. Columbia University Press, New York
Mueller CB, Kirkpatrick LC, Richter LL (2018) Evidence. Aspen Publishing, California
Musielak HJ (1975) Die Grundlagen der Beweislast im Zivilprozess. De Gruyter, Berlin

Nakamura H (2009) The research on civil procedure law and I. In: Nakamura M, Nakamura H (eds) The methodology of procedure law—the essence of Nakamura's theory of civil procedure (trans: Chen G, Duan W). China Legal Publishing House, Beijing (in Chinese)

Ou Y (2016) On abandonment of proposition of *non liquet* of fact. Political Science and Law 11:23–31 (in Chinese)

Pan J (2016) On burden of proof in civil cases. Political Science and Law 11:2–12 (in Chinese)

Peerenboom R (2004) Varieties of rule of law: an introduction and provisional conclusion. In: Peerenboom R (ed) Asian discourses of rule of law. Routledge, London

Posner RA (1990) The problems of jurisprudence. Harvard University Press, Cambridge, Mass

Prütting H (1983) Gegenwartsprobleme der Beweislast. C. H. Beck, München

Prütting H (2019) In: Baumgärtel G, Laumen H, Prütting H, Handbuch der Beweislast: Grundlagen. Heymann, Köln

Reichold K (2019) In: Thomas H, Putzo H, ZPO, 40. Aufl. C. H. Beck, München

Reimann M (2014) The American advantage in global lawyering. The Rabel Journal of Comparative and International Private Law 78:1–36

Ren Z (2017) Rethinking Rosenberg's theory of burden of proof. Journal of Law Application 15:18–28 (in Chinese)

Rimmelspacher B (2020) In: Krüger W, Rauscher T, Münchener Kommentar ZPO, Band 2, 6. Aufl. C. H. Beck, München

Rosenberg L (1965) Die Beweislast, 5. Aufl. C. H. Beck, München

Rosenberg L, Schwab KH, Gottwald P (2018) Zivilprozessrecht, 18. Aufl. C. H. Beck, München

Schilken E (2007) Gerichtsverfassungsrecht, 4.Aufl. Heymann, Köln

Schwab KH (1978) Zur Abkehr Moderner Beweislastlehren von der Normentheorie. In: Frisch W and Schmid W (eds) Festschrift für Hans-Jürgen Bruns zum 70. Geburtstag. Heymann, Köln

Shindo K (2019) Civil procedure law. Koubundou Publishers, Tokyo (in Japanese)

Stürner R (2005) The principles of transnational civil procedure: an introduction to their basic conceptions. The Rabel Journal of Comparative and International Private Law 69:201–254

Takahashi H (2003) Key points in civil procedure law (trans: Lin J). Law Press, Beijing (in Chinese)

Tang W (2013) The modernizing direction of China's science of civil procedure law. Tsinghua University Law Journal 5:143–154 (in Chinese)

Tapper C (2007) Cross and tapper on evidence. Oxford University Press, Oxford

Taruffo M (2003) Rethinking the standards of proof. The American Journal of Comparative Law 51:659–677

Thayer JB (1898) A preliminary treatise on evidence at the common law. Little, Brown and Company, Boston

Unberath H (2007) Der Zweck der Rechtsmittel nach der ZPO-Reform – Theorie und Praxis. Zeitschrift für Zivilprozess 120:323–346

Wang Y (1994) On the reformation of civil and economic trial mode. Social Sciences in China 1:3–22 (in Chinese)

Wang Y (2011) On Chinese elements in China's civil legislations. Law Science Magazine 4:27–32 (in Chinese)

Wu Y (2011) An analysis of the involution of China's litigation object theory. China Legal Science 2:177–190 (in Chinese)

Xiao J (ed) (2008) Discussion on civil procedure law in areas of legislation and theory. Law Press, Beijing (in Chinese)

You C (2012) A fact of litigiousness hidden beneath the illusion of litigation loathing? Peking University Law Journal 4:815–834 (in Chinese)

Zhang Y (2005) On the unableness to distinguish true from false in litigation and its solution. Law Review 2:26–35 (in Chinese)

Zhang W (2014) The poverty of civil procedural jurisprudence. Tsinghua University Law Journal 2:5–34 (in Chinese)

Zhang W (2019a) Comparative research methodology of civil procedure law. Journal of National Prosecutors College 6:157–174 (In Chinese)

Zhang W (2019b) Civil procedure law. Law Press, Beijing (in Chinese)
Zheng X, Liu M, Song C, Pan H (2020) Comprehension and application on some issues about the new stipulation on civil evidence. People's Court Daily, 26 March 2020 (in Chinese)
Zippelius R (2012) Juristische Methodenlehre, 11. Aufl. C. H. Beck, München

Chapter 7
Effects of Final Judgments (I): Predetermined Effect of Convicted Facts

7.1 Introduction

Just as judgments are supposed to resolve disputes according to the laws, final civil judgments enjoy multiple effects in legal sense. A system of *res judicata* or a principle of finality is widely accepted in general,[1] although there are many concrete differences in distinct jurisdictions. For instance, the concepts of formal and substantial *res judicata* (*formelle und materielle Rechtskraft*) are further discussed in continental legal systems.[2] And when it comes to a judgment for monetary or other kinds of performance, a special effect of forced enforcement is also recognized and the final judgment, as the most typical kind of enforcement title (*titres exécutoires*), is able to initiate civil enforcement proceedings.

Besides them, this contribution intends to discuss two less popular issues of judgment's effects which indicate the characteristics of Chinese civil procedure. Hence, in this chapter refers to the predetermined effect of the factual conviction of civil judgments which is somewhat comparable with the evidential value of court's judgments as public documents (Chap. 5). And Chap. 8 concerns the possible binding effect of the determined intermediate legal relationship of civil judgments which can be handled by the separate intermediate declaratory claim (*Zwischenfeststellungsklage*). What these procedural systems are and how to evaluate these systems on the basis of the continental legal tradition need to be addressed in this contribution.

Specifically speaking, Article 9 of the *2001 Evidence Provisions* stipulates that the facts confirmed by effective judgments and rulings have a so-called predetermined effect. Then, Article 93 of the *ICPL* and Article 10 of the *2019 Evidence Provisions* have inherited the institutional legacy of this rule. The currently binding norm, i.e. Article 10 of the *2019 Evidence Provisions*, says in its paragraph 1 that a party concerned is not required to produce any evidence to prove the following facts: …

---

[1] Van de Velden (2017); Yeazell and Schwartz (2019, pp. 703–773).

[2] For instance, Rosenberg et al. (2018, §§ 151–152).

Z. Cao, *Civil Judgments at First Instance*, Contemporary Chinese Civil and Commercial Law, https://doi.org/10.1007/978-981-97-8662-6_7

(6) Fundamental facts that have been ascertained by legally effective judgments or rulings rendered by People's courts … Moreover, Article 10 paragraph 2 of the *2019 Evidence Provisions* regulates that the facts prescribed by item 2 through to item 5 of the preceding paragraph shall be considered as proved unless the opposing party has sufficient evidence to the contrary to refute the relevant factual allegation. And according to the same paragraph 2, the facts prescribed by item 6 and item 7 of the preceding paragraph shall be considered as proved if the opposing party has sufficient evidence to the contrary to overturn the relevant factual allegation.

Theoretically speaking, it means that in any later lawsuit, the judge should apply the legal presumption of facts to the facts confirmed in the judgment of a former lawsuit. In other words, the allocation of burden of proof should be turned over (*Umkehr der Beweislast*). In judicial practice, these rules in judicial interpretations have also been widely recognized and applied. Nevertheless, after the promulgation of these rules, some scholars present severe criticism of them. For example, Li Hao considers that the basis of such provisions should not be *res judicata* effect but the theory of issue preclusion, and it goes too far away for China's practice.[3] From the perspective of procedure safeguard, litigation efficiency and party autonomy, Weng Xiaobin is even more clearly opposed to this predetermined effect while advocating instead that finally we need a theoretical solution of limiting the scope of *res judicata* effect to the operative part of judgments.[4] On the contrary, some scholars emphasize the Chinese characteristics of predetermined effect and its distinction from the theory of *res judicata* and other theories.[5] It can be argued that the elements for the effect of predetermined facts should be clarified[6] or at the very least, the system of predetermined effect is to be further enhanced by distinguishing between determined issues and convicted facts.[7]

Yet, this chapter argues that this predetermined effect of facts is better to be rejected *de lege ferenda*. This effect cannot be supported by the traditional theory of *res judicata* while different theories of expanding the scope of *res judicata* effect in comparative context are not suitable for current China. In addition, this predetermined effect is different from the preclusion of facts within the *res judicata* effect, and is also different from the rule of probative force of public documentary evidence. Unfortunately, from the very beginning, the predetermined effect of the factual conviction of civil judgments has never been clarified, which gives rise to difficulties in practice already for many years.

---

[3] Li (2011).

[4] Weng (2006).

[5] For instance, Jiang Wei and Chang Tingbin made a comparison among the concepts of predetermined effect of convicted facts and *res judicata* effect, effect of disputed issues, issue preclusion, and judicial notice. Jiang and Chang (2008). For similar comparison, see Zou (2010, pp. 100–101). The viewpoint clarifies that the predetermined effect refers to an issue of facts while the *res judicata* effect concerns an issue of law, see Lin (2006, pp. 19–20).

[6] Ji (2013).

[7] Fu (2008).

7.2 Predetermined Effect Cannot Be Supported by the Theory of *Res Judicata*

7.2.1 Theoretical Classification of Predetermined Effect

In line with the aforementioned analysis in Chinese literature, the first step of reconsidering the effect of predetermined facts should be the theories related to *res judicata*. Scholars who support the predetermined effect may argue that the effect of *res judicata* means that the same claim cannot be brought again, while the predetermined effect merely refers to a factual presumption. Hence, there is an obvious difference between both effects. With no doubt, this contribution also completely agrees with the difference in the degree of effects between both of them. Since there are always opportunities for the opposing party to produce evidence to the contrary, the predetermined effect does not reject hearing and making a decision once again. In other words, the predetermined effect technically stays at the level of facts, rather than the level of claims or more precisely the subject matter of claims (in detail: Fig. 5. 1). However, except for a few cases where the parties hold direct evidence with high probative value, reallocating the burden of proof will improperly increase the evidential difficulty of the opposing party and reduce its chance of winning the case on the merits. Now, technically speaking, this opposing party is converted actually to be the party who has the objective burden of proof. The evidence produced by this side is now the primary evidence (*Hauptbeweis*) in the form of proof to the contrary (*Beweis des Gegenteils*) rather than the easier opposing evidence (*Gegenbeweis*) (see also Chap. 5).

Meanwhile, when it comes to the framework of the procedural science in the continental legal system, the predetermined effect can be classified under the impact of the reasoning part within the civil judgment rendered in the former lawsuit on a latter lawsuit. On the contrary, if the subject matter of claims or the operative part of the judgment of the former lawsuit is concerned, the judge of the latter lawsuit will obviously be bound by the effect of *res judicata*. And the fact that there is a claim enjoying the effect of *res judicata* needs to be examined by the judge *sua sponte*.[8] Hence, for example under German law, where the ownership of an item or some obligation of contractual payment is determined in the operative part of the judgment of the preceding lawsuit, there must be no new claim repeating the same subject matter of claims. Also, the claim for restitution of the possession of the same item or compensation for breach of contract and liquidated damages thereafter must be based on the determination in the operative part of the preceding lawsuit's final judgment.[9]

[8] In the U.S., on the contrary, the issue of *res judicata* refers still to an issue which needs to be raised by the relevant party.

[9] BGH NJW 2008, 1227, 1228, Tz 9; NJW 2003, 3058, 3059; NJW 1993, 3204, 3205; Rosenberg et al. (2018, § 152 Rn 15); Gottwald (2020, § 322 Rn 52–53).

7.2.2 Traditional Viewpoints in German Law as the Starting Point

In order to make clear the object of discussion, a brief introduction to the general ideas in the traditional theories of the civil law system can be beneficial. Again, this contribution takes the German counterpart as the primary example. In Germany, the theory of a limited *res judicata* effect has been the leading opinion for a long period of time. If there is no intermediate declaratory claim and the related judgment (Article 256 paragraph 2 of the *German Code of Civil Procedure*), the preliminary issue or legal relationship determined incidentally by the judgment, i.e. not decided in the operative part of the judgment, does not enjoy *res judicata* effect. Hence, compared to the incidental determination in a former lawsuit, the judge in a latter lawsuit can still hear and decide the same issue differently.[10] For similar reasons, the legal qualification in the former lawsuit does not have *res judicata* effect in principle, e.g. the determination of fault in the former lawsuit.[11] It is with no doubt that the preliminary issue is also not the same as the grounds of the action which is significant while identifying the subject matter of claims.[12] Considering the fundamental historical choice and the literal meaning of the *German Code of Civil Procedure*, both the traditional substantive law theories and procedural law theories are in support of this understanding. Meanwhile, because both substantive rights or legal relationships involved and the claim for relief are different respectively, the subject matter of the independent intermediate declaratory claim for the relevant preliminary legal relationships (*präjudizielle Rechtsverhältnisse*) is different from that of claims for performance aiming at individual substantive rights.[13]

In contemporary times, German scholars usually adjust their attitudes toward the leading opinion of the procedural law theory with two branches (*zweigliedrig*) because of the spread of the key point theory (*Kernpunkttheorie*) of the subject matter of claims in European law. This so-called key point theory does not consider the claim for relief anymore, while it does merely take the factual situation in a broad sense into account. The direct result of this theoretical choice is to bring the preliminary issue of law into the scope of *res judicata* effect. In this vein, the European judiciary may avoid parallel and duplicate actions as far as possible, while it nevertheless makes the standard of identifying the same subject matter of claims vaguer. Although similar

---

[10] BGHZ 183, 77 = NJW 2010, 2210, 2211, Tz 9–10; Rosenberg et al. (2018, § 154 Rn 14 et seq.); Gottwald (2020, § 322 Rn 92 et seq., 174); Schwab (1969, pp. 324–325); Roth (2011, pp. 5–6); Hahn (1880, pp. 290 et seq.) (dissenting Savigny's claim for extended *res judicata* effect); Hahn (1880, pp. 607 et seq.) (minutes).

[11] BGHZ 183, 77 = NJW 2010, 2210, 2211–2212, Tz 14 et seq.; Althammer (2018, § 322 Rn 111 et seq.) (handled differently according to the types); Gottwald (2020, § 322 Rn 94 et seq.); Roth (2011, pp. 7 et seq.).

[12] Rosenberg (1929, pp. 252–253).

[13] The viewpoints of the traditional substantive theories, for example: Lent (1959, pp. 103, 178). Under the procedural theories, since the claim for relief is taken as one of the criterions for identifying the subject matter of claims, the two are obviously different.

viewpoints appeared already in Germany before the prevalence of the EU law,[14] this key point theory mainly represents the way of thinking in Anglo-American legal systems (concentrating on the disputed facts rather than substantive rights) under the special EU legal background.[15] As Rolf Stürner pointed out, under the impact of the European law, a new era of legal transplantation was about to start, and "the era when the theory of the subject matter of claims could remain pure in legal dogmatics and systematic during interpretation is also gone".[16]

However, scholars would not object to the idea of adopting the two-branch procedural theory regarding *res judicata* effect and distinguishing between the subject matter of claims and the preliminary legal relationship. For example, Herbert Roth, who advocates that different forms of right protection (*Schutzformen*), i.e. declaratory, performance or alteration, cannot lead to multiple subject matters of claims, also deems that the judgment on the subject matter of claims should not cover the preliminary legal relationship. It means that the declaratory claim for the non-existence of a contract is not precluded by a previous claim for performance out of the same contract.[17] Moreover, Peter Gottwald, who advocates that the key point theory should be promoted consistently in the German theory of subject matter of claims in his personal contributions, is also of the opinion that the traditional two-branch procedural theory should still be insisted when it comes to the *res judicata* effect.[18] In other words, it is the fundamental position of German law that the preliminary legal relationship should not have the effect of *res judicata.*

If we combine the leading opinion in practice and the outstanding viewpoints of proceduralists, it can be argued that this German position is also the product of long-term consideration of practice and related procedural values. In conclusion, the issue concerning Chinese predetermined facts can be classified into the preliminary issue and legal relationship in German doctrines, while this issue or relationship does not enjoy any effect of predetermination in Germany.

7.2.3 Circumvention with the Independent Intermediate Declaratory Claim

As mentioned previously, under the traditional theories, if the parties intend to incorporate the court's judgment on the disputed points into the scope of *res judicata*

---

[14] Baumgärtel (1974, pp. 73 et seq.); Baumgärtel (1968, p. 406).

[15] Roth (2016, pp. 46 et seq.); Gottwald (2000, pp. 85 et seq.); Rüßmann (1998, p. 399); Bork (1988, pp. 431 et seq.).

[16] Stürner (1997, p. 836). He says that "*Jedenfalls ist auch in der Streitgegenstandslehre die Zeit dogmatischer Unschuld und systematischer Konstruktion vorbei*".

[17] Roth (2016, Vor § 253 Rn 55, § 261 Rn 31). Same viewpoints: Rüßmann (1998, p. 407 Fn 43, 414 et seq.); Walker (1998, pp. 437 et seq., 454); Zeuner (1997, pp. 1017–1018).

[18] Gottwald (2000, pp 85 et seq., 94). It is noted that this viewpoint is distinct from the one in the prominent textbook (Rosenberg/Schwab/Gottwald) which is modified and developed by him.

effect, they need to file a special lawsuit for intermediate declaration. It means that an independent claim for declaration which is dependent on the pending lawsuit is to be additionally brought before the same court, whose purpose is to extend the *res judicata* effect of the prospective final judgment of the case to the preliminary legal relationships.[19] In China, some scholars also allege that the system for intermediate declaration claim should be introduced *de lege ferenda*.[20]

Specifically speaking, in Germany, a plaintiff can file a major claim (the action for payment, declaration and alteration) and a claim for intermediate declaration at the same time.[21] The plaintiff can also consolidate various claims subsequently via adding some new subject matters of claims during ongoing proceedings,[22] while a defendant can file a counterclaim for intermediate declaration as well. In either first-instance or second-instance proceedings, these claims for intermediate declaration from the side of the plaintiff or the defendant can be brought to the responsible court.[23] However, such claims are not allowed during the third instance because a subsequent consolidation of claims is hereby generally forbidden.[24] Subject to their respective conditions, the parties are free to file an action for intermediate declaration or an action for independent confirmation.[25]

Typically, the plaintiff can file a claim for payment of only a part of the total debt, while the defendant files a counterclaim for intermediate declaration as to the existence of a preliminary legal relationship. The purpose of this counterclaim is to avoid the *res judicata* effect being limited to the part of the claim which the plaintiff sued for while the plaintiff may sue for the remaining part of the entire claim in a subsequent but separate lawsuit at the plaintiff's discretion.[26]

A judgment of intermediate declaration can be incorporated into the judgment of the original claim. Yet, if the decision on the preliminary legal relationship is already ripe prior to the judgment of the original claim, the court can also make a partial judgment, which is by nature a final judgment (Article 301 of the *German Code of Civil Procedure*), to provide a preliminary determination before making the judgment on the merits in the sense of the subject matter of claims.[27]

Since the parties have the right to appeal independently against both the partial final judgment and the final judgment against the remaining part of the entire claim

---

[19] BGHZ 169, 153 = NJW 2007, 82, 83, Tz 12; BGH NJW 1992, 1897.

[20] For example, Ding (2012, pp. 139–143, 217–220); Zhang (2002).

[21] This actually goes beyond the literal meaning of the statutory provision since it allows an intermediate declaratory claim, which is against a predetermined legal relationship that has been disputed, to be filed even before the lawsuit is brought before the court formally.

[22] This can also take the form of consolidation in chief and the subordinate claim. BGH NJW 1992, 1897.

[23] BGHZ 169, 153 = NJW 2007, 82, 83, Tz 10.

[24] BGH NJW 1961, 777, 779.

[25] Roth (2016, § 256 Rn 9, 102).

[26] BGHZ 69, 37 = NJW 1977, 1637; Rosenberg et al. (2018, § 97 Rn 38); Roth (2016, § 256 Rn 9, 102).

[27] BGH NJW-RR 2012, 849, 850, Tz 13; NJW 2006, 915; NJW 1961, 75; Rosenberg et al. (2018, § 97 Rn 47); Roth (2016, § 256 Rn 119); Becker-Eberhard (2020, § 256 Rn 92).

(*Schlussurteil*),[28] an intermediate declaration judgment made independently should also apply the same rule. Moreover, a final judgment for the original claim, made before the effectiveness of the intermediate declaration judgment, will be extinguished (*auflösend bedingt*) if the intermediate declaration judgment is revoked (analogy to Article 304 paragraph 2 of the *German Code of Civil Procedure*).[29]

In theory, the system for intermediate declaration claim represents a prudent attitude to the pursuit of one-time dispute resolution.[30] Like other theories, the pursuit of one-time dispute resolution is always confronted with the issue of degree and boundary, while it also shows the eternal conflict between substantive justice and litigation economy. In Chinese context, where neither the jury system (Anglo-American) nor the unification of different national laws (EU) is involved, this pursuit should not be promoted too aggressively.[31] In such circumstances, the claim for intermediate declaration is eligible for being a safety fuse to balance the advantages and disadvantages of this pursuit. And this contribution is to revisit this system later in Chap. 8 as well.

Concretely speaking, in principle, the priority should be given to substantive justice to avoid procedural flaws impairing the parties' right to be heard before the state court, i.e., the legal system should preserve the parties' right to bring a separate lawsuit on relevant disputed issues as much as possible. Exceptionally, however, if at least one of the parties decides to pursue litigation economy,[32] the court may expand its scope of dispute resolution after providing sufficient procedural safeguards. It means that the judgment on the subject matter of claims should also finally determine the issue of preliminary legal relationships. It deserves to be considered that this balanced relationship of rule and exception (*Regel-Ausnahme-Verhältnis*) should be adopted in China. Yet, the current system of predetermined effects, although merely with reduced force rather than a strong preclusion effect of *res judicata*, takes a one-size-fits-all mode of rules. There is literally no possibility of having exceptions, while the party does not enjoy any right of participation e.g. raising the claim for intermediate declaration. Rather, it is highly possible that this system primarily, if not solely, considers the convenience of the judiciary itself. Yet, the judiciary should never be the purpose rather than the means in respect of the judiciary's users, i.e. the ordinary citizens searching for legal remedies.

[28] Rosenberg et al. (2018, § 59 Rn 25).

[29] Becker-Eberhard (2020, § 256 Rn 94).

[30] For a different understanding, see Wu (2011).

[31] For a detailed discussion of the application of this concept in Germany, see Stürner (2005, pp. 1068–1069).

[32] In order to guarantee the equality of the rights and obligations of the two parties (Article 8 sentence 1 and Article 54 sentence 2 the second half of the *CPL*), that one party exercises the right of disposition is enough, just as in the case of commencing the action.

7.2.4 *Predetermined Effect is Different from the So-Called Factual Preclusion Within the* **Res Judicata** *Effect*

In the theories of civil procedure in civil law systems, there is so-called factual preclusion within the *res judicata* effect or relative *res judicata* effect (*relative Rechtskraft*). Regarding the scientific classification, this concept of factual preclusion refers to the time scope of *res judicata* effect, i.e. the preclusion of any subsequently submitted factual allegations in a latter lawsuit that have been existing before the end of the last oral hearing in the preceding lawsuit and fall within the scope of the same "facts of ordinary life" (*Lebenssachverhalt*). These facts of ordinary life are taken as one of the branches of the procedural law theories in identifying the subject matter of claims under German law, while the other branch is the claim for relief. In terms of their nature, the facts of ordinary life should contain all the facts that "should belong to the factual factors (*Tatsachenkomplex*) stated by the parties for the purpose of judgment from the natural observation of the parties (*bei einer vom Standpunkt der Parteien ausgehenden natürlichen Betrachtungsweise*)", or should be "determined by the whole historical life process" (*durch den gesamten historischen Lebensvorgang bestimmt*). Whether or not these facts were actually stated by the parties and whether or not the parties could state them at the time do not affect the determination of these facts of ordinary life.[33] In particular, it is difficult to describe the criteria for identifying different facts of ordinary life in theory. The German law rather relies on the judicial precedents and classification of cases to secure the legal certainty (*Rechtsfrieden*).

On the contrary, only allegations that are irrelevant to the materials in the preceding lawsuit may be exempted from being precluded in this sense. The reason is that the litigation materials submitted by the parties, the facts found as well as the laws applied by the judge are the basis of making the judgment in individual cases. They are also the premises for the operative part of the preceding judgment to enjoy *res judicata* effect, and the correctness of these premises should not be challenged by the parties in any subsequent lawsuit.[34] Hence, it is of certainty that we shall distinguish between the reasoning part and the operative part of the same final judgment. However, if the factual basis of the prior lawsuit, which leads to the operative part of the final judgment would be overruled, the operative part and its *res judicata* effect will be

[33] BGHZ 194, 314 = GRUR 2013, 401, 402, Tz 18 et seq.; BGHZ 168, 179 = GRUR 2006, 960, 961, Tz 15; BGHZ 157, 47 = NJW 2004, 1252, 1253; BGHZ 117, 1 = NJW 1992, 1172, 1173; BGHZ 34, 337 = NJW 1961, 917; BGHZ NJW 2011, 2785, 2786, Tz 9; NJW 1983, 388, 389; Rosenberg et al. (2018, § 93 Rn 12); Roth (2016, vor § 253 Rn 11–12); Habscheid (1956, pp. 206 et seq., 221–222, 282 et seq.) (but distinguishing the preclusion based on *res judicata* corresponding to facts raised in the former lawsuit and the general preclusion corresponding to the entire scope of facts of ordinary life); Büscher (2012, pp. 23 et seq.).

[34] BGHZ 157, 47 = NJW 2004, 1252, 1253; BGHZ 131, 82 = NJW 1996, 57; Rosenberg et al. (2018, § 156 Rn 5 et seq.); Gottwald (2020, § 322 Rn 142 et seq.); Jacobs (2005, pp. 208 et seq.); Schwab (1969, pp. 322 et seq.); Schwab (1954, p. 146) (on the basis of the essence of the judgment which is separated from the *res judicata* effect).

baseless literally. In other words, predetermined facts do not have a universal effect, but they can be binding within the scope of *res judicata* effect of the current case.

In this regard, it should be noted that this factual preclusion takes effects merely within the scope of the subject matter of claims of the preceding lawsuit. Under the two-branch procedural law theories, it means that where the claim for relief in a latter lawsuit is the same as that in the previous one, specific factual elements, which fall into the scope of facts of ordinary life identified in the previous lawsuit, cannot be raised in the latter lawsuit. It makes no difference even if these factual elements are not raised in the previous lawsuit at all. Moreover, the second lawsuit cannot be forwarded for a substantial hearing because it fails to satisfy the requirements of the proceedings.[35] In other words, the court shall give a procedural ruling, which shows that no substantial dispute is resolved in this case, rather than a final judgment on the merits. In fact, this merely repeats the content of *res judicata* effect from the perspective of factual allegations[36] and cannot support the aforementioned generalized effect of preliminary determination on convicted facts in China.

7.3 Expansion of *Res Judicata* Effect and Comments

7.3.1 Glimpsing the German Academic Trajectory

In the long German academic history, some scholars have tried to challenge the conclusion that the effect of *res judicata* should be limited to the operative part of civil judgments.[37] Since the middle of the twentieth century, Albrecht Zeuner has advocated that the reasoning part of the civil judgment in a previous lawsuit may enjoy the effect of *res judicata* when the determination within this reasoning part involves "meaning connections" (*Sinnzusammenhänge*) or "exchange connections" (*Austauschzusammenhänge*) in substantive law.[38] And Wolfram Henckel and Bruno Rimmelspacher, who favor new substantive law theories of the subject matter of claims, have also spoken for the concepts like identical economic value (*wirtschaftliche Wert*)[39] or legal position (*Rechtsposition*)[40] to support similar conclusions.

At present, some scholars also hold the viewpoint that, in rare cases, a preliminary legal relationship may exceptionally be binding in the sense of *res judicata*. For instance, the prevailing opinion among many scholars deems that in the claim for correcting the land registration (Article 894 of the *German Civil Code*), the purpose of

[35] Gottwald (2020, § 322 Rn 147–148); Schwab (1954, p. 167).

[36] On the contrary, see Wu (2011).

[37] For an introduction to the German and Japanese related theories in Chinese literature, see Lin (2006, pp 83–91).

[38] Zeuner (1959, pp. 42 et seq., 72 et seq., 115–116).

[39] Henckel (1970, pp. 171 et seq.).

[40] Rimmelspacher (1970, pp. 202 et seq., 259 et seq.).

the action is obviously to confirm the ownership of the land. Hence, this kind of claim could even technically be regarded as a claim for the confirmation of ownership, while the claim for correction indicates merely legal decoration and formality. Therefore, although the operative part of the former judgment on the merits in favor of the plaintiff does not contain any confirmation of ownership, the relevant confirmation ought to nevertheless be embraced by its *res judicata* effect.[41]

However, leaving aside the fact that the most conservative and traditional viewpoints entirely reject the expansion of *res judicata* effect to preliminary legal relationships,[42] a majority of scholars also widely question any more aggressive opinions beyond the aforementioned rare cases. One of these aggressive opinions refers to the validity of a bilateral contractual relationship which is deemed as one of the preliminary issues which can enjoy *res judicata* effect. Similarly, the existence of opposing substantive claims, which appeared as a defense in the former lawsuit, is not finally determined by the final judgment of the former claim for performance.[43] Moreover, the ownership itself cannot be confirmed with prejudice by the claim for restitution against a possessor requested by the owner of a specific item (Article 985 of the *German Civil Code*).[44]

7.3.2 Comments Both in German and Chinese Contexts

Taking this German academic trajectory into account, this contribution yet does not intend to make a comprehensive analysis from the perspective of historical development. Rather, it mainly focuses on the difficulties which this relatively new theory may have to face both in German and Chinese contexts.

First of all, the aforementioned standards provided by scholars go beyond the literal meaning of German legal provisions. And because it is against the original intention of the legislators, the interpretation of teleological reduction (*teleologische Reduktion*) cannot be applied.[45] As for the "cases whose judgments, rulings and consent judgments have taken legal effect" stipulated in Article 127 item 5 of the

---

[41] Viewpoints prevailing to some extent: Picker (2019, § 894 Rn 166); Kohler (2020, § 894 Rn 45); Rosenberg et al. (2018, § 155 Rn 7); Althammer (2018, § 322 Rn 83, 209); Gottwald (2020, § 322 Rn 57, 103). On the contrary, the leading opinion claims that in this case, as in the case of restitution on the ground of ownership, deciding ownership is merely a preliminary issue and does not enjoy *res judicata* effect. BGH NJW 2019, 71, 72 et seq., Tz 15 et seq.; NJW-RR 2008, 1397, 1398–1399, Tz 19; NJW-RR 2002, 516, 517; Herrler (2020, § 894 Rn 12); Seiler (2019, § 322 Rn 10); Vollkommer (2020, Vor § 322 Rn 36). While the prevailing opinion means the popular idea among researchers, the leading opinion shows the (long-lasting) acceptance of the judiciary.

[42] Musielak (2021, § 322 Rn 27).

[43] Althammer (2018, § 322 Rn 86, 204–205); Gottwald (2020, § 322 Rn 58, 101); Seiler (2019, § 322 Rn 30); Vollkommer (2020, Vor § 322 Rn 28, 36). Minority Viewpoints, see Rosenberg and Schwab (1986, p. 986); Henckel (1970, pp. 198 et seq.); Zeuner (1959, p. 75).

[44] BGH NJW-RR 2008, 1397, 1398, Tz 19. Minority Viewpoints, see Zeuner (1959, p. 151).

[45] Different opinions: Foerste (1995, pp. 176 et seq.).

CPL, the "case" here should be understood as the claim or the subject matter of claims of the current dispute. Hence, there is no space for the interpretation to incorporate preliminary issues or legal relationships.

Second, the standards extending the scope of *res judicata* effect are too abstract to give reliable solutions to individual types of cases. It may also give rise to a surprise judgment (*Überraschungsentscheidung*) to some parties who are not aware of such extended preclusion of the relevant judgment. Moreover, in the context of current German law, the possible disadvantageous conclusion in case of contradictory allegations under the free evaluation of evidence as well as in extremely exceptional cases, the possibility of applying the rules on abuse of rights or the principle of good faith can achieve similar functions as the extended *res judicata* effect. On the contrary, too wide a scope of *res judicata* effect is not constructive for the maintenance of the finality of civil judgments and legal certainty.

In this aspect, the reasons are partially that insisting on the broad scope of *res judicata* effect may limit the pursuit of justice in individual cases, while frequently denying the *res judicata* effect in individual cases is not beneficial to judicial stability and judicial authority.[46] If the preclusion effect of the final judgment is extended, both parties and judges definitely have to prepare more for individual ongoing cases to make sure that all relevant preliminary issues are to be developed thoroughly. The substantial consideration in China can be similar. Merely it should be paid more attention that the justice in individual cases for individuals is taken very seriously at least from the institutional perspective. The overwhelming inclination for the individual justice can be the clarification for many concrete procedural systems, e.g. strong trial supervision proceedings and other extraordinary approaches to redress private grievance, which are quite reluctant to accept the finality or *res judicata* effect of civil judgments.

Third and finally, from the perspective of legal tradition and family, the German approach of *res judicata* effect and the Anglo-American counterpart consisting of issue preclusion (collateral estoppel) are "opposite" to some extent which may show distinct attitudes toward ancient Germanic law. Hence, the change to the theory of civil procedure by an extended *res judicata* effect would probably be overarching.[47] In short, the issue preclusion means that the essential facts or legal issues actually debated during hearings and finally decided by the relevant final judgment cannot be raised again in any subsequent lawsuit.[48]

Hence, other rules in comparative law can be embodied as intermediate ones between these two opposing modes. For instance, merely in terms of the content of the theory of *res judicata* effect, the French approach lies in somewhere between Germany and Anglo-American counterparts: on one hand, French law limits the

---

[46] BGH NJW 2003, 3058, 3059; Althammer (2018, § 322 Rn 202 et seq.); Gottwald (2020, § 322 Rn 54 et seq.); Musielak (2021, § 322 Rn 26–27); Peters (1963).

[47] Gottwald (2020, § 322 Rn 56).

[48] Yeazell and Schwartz (2019, pp. 735–757); Zuckerman (2013, para 25.86–25.90); Albrecht (2013, pp. 202 et seq.); Althammer (2012, pp. 110–111). For related discussions in China, see also Ji (2013); Guo (2010).

factual grounds involved in the *res judicata* effect to the part of facts which were alleged by the party concerned during the process of litigation; on the other hand, French civil procedural rules expand the scope of *res judicata* effect to the preliminary issues in the reasoning part of final judgments.[49] And the position of the ECJ, which creates and follows the key point theory of the subject matter of claims, is more for the French and Anglo-American legal systems.[50] In such circumstances, as mentioned before, civil law systems, especially the German tradition, are taken as the primary counterparts for comparative observation in the field of civil procedure in general. And China does not follow the pattern of federalism or has to handle complicated situations of legal sources in the EU. It is then acceptable to be more vigilant against the institutional impact which may be brought about by any rash change, e.g. issue preclusion, in the legal system.

7.3.3 Scientific Development in Japan

On the basis of the aforementioned approaches of two legal systems, Japanese scholars led by Shindo Koji tried to introduce a theory of issue preclusion into the Japanese law as well, which later becomes the prevailing one in Japan and China Taiwan.[51] According to Shindo's own clarification, his theory is mainly inspired by the Anglo-American theory of issue preclusion, while there are also other Japanese scholars at about the same time who developed similar theories concentrating on the disputed issues by introducing German relevant theories as mentioned previously. It is the focus of Shindo's academic research to connect his theory with the traditional theories of *res judicata* effect and to adapt to different theories of the subject matter of claims.[52]

Briefly speaking, the issue preclusion in the context of Shindo's theory refers to the situation that major disputed issues, e.g. the ownership of disputed items, the existence of the claim for damages out of torts, and the validity of the disputed contract, are fully debated by the parties and tried by the court in the former lawsuit and appear in the reasoning part of the final judgment. And later, these issues become preliminary issues in a second lawsuit, while the economic values of the interests in dispute involved both in the former and latter lawsuit are the same. Then, the determination of such disputed issues shall be binding on both the parties and the judge. This effect of issue preclusion is different from the effect of *res judicata* produced by the operative part of the final judgment as well as the effect of factual

[49] Zeuner (1981, pp. 608 et seq.).

[50] It is also argued that the German theory of narrow *res judicata* effect is more suitable for transnational legal disputes, whose justification can be found from the difficulty in understanding foreign judgments accurately due to various languages used. Stürner (1999, pp. 920 et seq., 926 et seq., 934 et seq.).

[51] On the situation in China Taiwan, see e.g. Shen et al. (2010).

[52] Shindo (2019, pp. 718–720); see Lin (2006, pp. 91–112).

preclusion within the *res judicata* effect. In essence, this theory of issue preclusion expands the coverage of *res judicata* effect following the spirit of procedural law theories of the subject matter of claims. Moreover, it also provides a systematic solution arguing the binding force of legal determination within the reasoning part of the final judgment.[53]

Evaluating this theory of issue preclusion can be twofold. While it enhances the pursuit of one-time and efficient dispute resolution in theory, the disadvantages of other theories extending the scope of *res judicata* effect, such as vague standards, lack of foreseeability, and possible waste of litigation resources, also exist hereby in this modified theory. In this regard, in Japan or China Taiwan, where the traditional theories and the related practice have been developed to a high extent, to create the system of issue preclusion may be fit for the academic circle together with the localized judiciary. Jurists there are able to search for the most suitable "leading opinions" for their own legal environment via the full interaction of scholars and judges using this new theory as a proper test. The preconditions for this positive future are, however, a good foundation to cultivate such interaction and an already established legal community, a developed system of legal knowledge and a widely recognized rule of law. Hence, in China, where there is at least much room for development in the traditional legal science, it is hard to be optimistic about the potential contribution of the advanced theory of issue preclusion.[54]

7.3.4 Overall Comparative Observations

From a perspective of comparative civil procedure, the main difference between Zeuner's theory extending the scope of *res judicata* effect together with Shindo's theory of issue preclusion and the German leading opinions lies in the effective scope of claim for intermediate declaration. For the former theories, the preliminary legal relationship automatically produces *res judicata* effect when the prior and subsequent lawsuits involve substantive connection. Hence, there is no need to resort to a separate claim for intermediate declaration. On the contrary, the German leading opinion imposes a mandatory requirement on the parties who seek a wider effect of *res judicata* to file the claim for intermediate declaration explicitly.[55] Besides the possible issue of functional jurisdiction[56] and the emphasis on the dispositional

[53] Shindo (2019, pp. 718, 720–729). Although the effect of such theory is partly the same as the key point theory of the subject matter of claims under the EU law, the two are entirely different. For the key point theory, see e.g. EuGH, Urt. v. 08. 12.1987, Rs.144/86, Slg. 1987, 4871, 4875–4876, Rn 12–17 (Gubisch/Palumbo).

[54] Theoretically speaking, some scholars also generally hold a positive attitude, e.g., see Zhang (2019, pp. 447–448); Guo (2010, pp. 239–253).

[55] Zeuner (1959, pp. 173–174).

[56] For example, the claim for relief in the former lawsuit is to stop infringement, while the latter lawsuit request for a huge amount of damages. Peters (1963, pp. 236–237). In China, the same situation may occur as well (Article 13 of the *Measures on the Payment of Litigation Costs*).

principle, this context delves deeper into the authors' anticipation of the ideal type for the involved parties. Specifically, it explores whether the majority of litigants prefer to resolve the issue of preliminary legal relationship ultimately in the current case or harbor hopes for the prospect of reassessing and refining their strategies and evidence collection directions in future.

Different answers to this question are decisive for the default choice regarding the understanding of *res judicata* effect. In China, at least considering the opinions expressed by many scholars, German solution of limiting *res judicata* effect to the operative part of the final judgment is still widely accepted.[57] And Japanese and Chinese Taiwanese leading opinions which reject the theory of issue preclusion provide another footnote. Hence, this contribution is against the negative evaluation of the adjudicative techniques of making the intermediate declaration claim that these techniques constitute a circular argument, or even become the so-called "dragon-slaying skills" which are supposed to be useless in reality.[58] Rather, as argued all through this contribution, adjudicative techniques should serve as means for better civil judgments in China.

In addition, we also need to be aware of the understanding of contradictory judgments in civil law systems. In fact, only when some contradiction can be found in the operative part of the judgment, the judgment should be considered truly as a contradictory one. The reason for this is that this kind of contradiction will directly affect the determination of the ownership of substantive rights and then hinder the enforcement of the judgment when it comes to a claim for performance. Instead, it is unnecessary to worry about the conflict of reasons for the judgment, because the decisions on the disputed issue could be different in two or even more cases since the requirements of fact-finding are varied or the relevant issue may not always be the focus of the current case. This kind of conflict will not give rise to the consequences at the level of the subject matter of claims. Rather, it can be redressed via appeals within the judicial hierarchy if necessary. Moreover, as the legal truth is gradually taken as the fact-finding standard (also Chap. 6) and the dispute resolution is normally given priority, conflicts mainly existing at the level of facts can be tolerated by the Chinese judiciary and the majority of ordinary citizens.

[57] For example, Li (2011); Lin (2006, pp. 58–66, 155–164) (analysing rules in civil law systems and the reasons why such rules should be adopted in China); Weng (2006).

[58] Wu (2011).

7.4 Presumption of Substantial Proof Value and Predetermined Effect

7.4.1 Predetermined Effect is Different from Rules Concerning Probative Force of Legal Documents

Finally, the rule of evidential presumption of public documents in civil law jurisdictions (e.g. Article 417 of the *German Code of Civil Procedure*) cannot be the basis for the rule on the predetermined effect either.[59] Indeed, this rule of proof value does not have some effect of complete preclusion, but merely the effect of proof which presumes the record written in public documents is true (Chap. 5). Hence, this effect is similar to the predetermined effect introduced in this chapter.[60]

In Chinese context, there are additionally two points to clarify. On one hand, German law has never recognized the proving effect (*Beweiswirkung*) of judgments in the sense of Anglo-American laws,[61] nor has it given some predetermined effect to judgments in criminal and public security cases when it comes to the content of these judgments, i.e. the facts found in the judgment. The reason for some Chinese scholars' misunderstanding is that the Chinese translation of the Rosenberg's textbook[62] does not take notice that the original paragraph only introduces the legislative recommendations of the *Justice Modernization Act of 2003 (Justizmodernisierungsgesetz)* (proposed Article 415a paragraph 1 of the *German Code of Civil Procedure*).[63]

However, such recommendations did not eventually become the statute after the 16th Edition of the textbook was published,[64] while the situation was already clear at the time when the Chinese translation was published. The newest 18th edition of this textbook completely removes the relevant recommendations.[65] Moreover, in essence, the aforementioned recommendation attempts to return to the legal status before the time of the *German Code of Civil Procedure*. It would overturn the existing system of proof in Germany, while ignoring the great differences in procedural principles and rules of proof between criminal and civil procedures. As a result, it may also bring difficulties in evidence law to criminal victims who seek civil remedies outside criminal proceedings.[66] Hence, even without considering the actual situation of German legislation, China may not be necessary to consider the aforementioned recommendation.

---

[59] For a different opinion, see Ji (2013).

[60] For a detailed discussion, see Cao (2020).

[61] Jacobs (2005, p. 206); Mendelssohn Bartholdy (1900, pp. 362 et seq.). For relevant discussion in China, see Qi and Ji (2011).

[62] Rosenberg et al. (2007, pp 886–887).

[63] BT-Drucks 15/1508, pp 20–21.

[64] BT-Drucks. 15/3482, p. 17; Ahrens (2014, Vor § 415 Rn 9 et seq.).

[65] However, it seems that the leading opinion of French law does recognize such effects. Shi (2014).

[66] Critical Opinions in Germany: Huber (2003, pp. 270–271); Vollkommer (2003, pp. 2061–2062).

On the other hand, as mentioned in Chap. 3, the probative force of the part of alleged facts in the case (*Tatbestand*) within effective judgments (Article 314 of the *German Code of Civil Procedure*) only refers to a written certification of statements of the parties, not to the findings of facts made by the relevant court. These alleged facts in a written judgment do not present the facts evaluated by the judge and they do not involve any legal issues. Instead, they are facts in the eyes of the parties. Then, it is to be presumed that all these alleged facts of this case were produced by the parties during the court hearings and the court did take the legal transactions as the judgment records. However, this part of alleged facts can just confirm the statements of the parties, rather than prove the historical facts themselves.

7.4.2 Restricting the Applicable Scope of Predetermined Effect During Interpretation

Since special importance is attached to public documents in China's practice, it is scientifically possible to endure some rules of predetermined effects of the factual conviction *de lege lata*. Following the original intention of the legislators in China, it can be argued that the factual conviction in civil judgments can exceptionally have strong substantial probative force which leads to the reallocation of objective burden of proof for the facts to be proved. In other words, final judgments represent a special group of public documents whose contents are also presumed to be true.

In particular, if the application scope of this rule is further limited to the parties to the previous case, i.e. the effective judgment would merely have the predetermined effect in subsequent lawsuits where the same two parties confront each other once again,[67] it should be possible to avoid the most controversial scenario in practice that both parties, walking hand in hand, intend to abuse the civil process. Since there would be no predetermined effect of convicted facts while initiating the false litigation, the relevant parties in bad faith cannot collude to create a presumption of facts unfavorable to any third party. In this regard, this interpretative approach would be able to facilitate the other means against false litigation, such as Article 307 paragraph 1 of the *Criminal Law of the P.R.C.* incriminating any civil claim relying on fabricated facts (false litigation in the broad sense), Article 115 paragraph 1 of the *CPL* punishing collusion of both parties (false litigation in the narrow sense) and especially Article 115 paragraph 2 of the *CPL* against fabricating facts by one party. Additionally, the judicial policies represented by the *Guiding Opinions of the SPC on the Prevention and Sanction of False Litigation* and numerous informal precedents released in this field need also to be taken into account. To a large extent, the efforts

[67] Fu (2018, pp. 1428–1429). The different viewpoint that the effect of predetermination should just function "when the parties in the previous and latter lawsuits are not identical", see Wang and Chen (2015, pp. 18–19). Regarding the typology analysis on the ground that the parties in both cases are the same, one side of the party is the same and the parties are different, see Duan (2015, pp. 110–111).

of the Chinese judiciary against the bad practice of abusing civil process are explicit and countless.

Yet, it ought to be stressed that it would be better if the issue of false litigation would be handled during the ongoing civil proceedings themselves. Hence, narrowing the predetermined effect is with no doubt among the most suitable tools which would reduce the incentive of planning false litigation in the first place. In contrast, the claim of third-party revocation, as a remedy afterward, is not a good solution. As Fu Yulin argues, the predetermined effect tears a crack in the rigorous net of the theory of judgments' effectiveness and related procedural safeguards. The third-party revocation claim is like a huge patch, which creates more new problems than it solves while patching the net.[68]

Instead, besides the hereby applauded suggestion of narrowing the predetermined effect, multiple approaches are considered and clarified by Chinese scholars: e.g. strengthening parties' obligation to ensure the truth and integrity of factual allegations, which is formally established in Article 63 of the *2019 Evidence Provisions*; directly dismissing the false litigation in case-filing or other stages of civil proceedings[69]; providing a new remedy *de lege ferenda* similar to the intervention claim to prevent deception in comparative experience[70]; introducing a new ground of false litigation in the *Tort Law of the R.P.C.* from a substantive law perspective[71]; or even considering the establishment of a special procedure[72] and specialized judges[73] for identifying false litigation (regardless of whether such suggestions are realistic within the current judicial system).

Moreover, leaving the aforementioned narrowing the subjective scope of predetermined effect aside, it is also arguable to preclude the mediation agreement from the scope of the relevant judgments producing a predetermined effect, while denying facts admitted by the parties having the predetermined effect.[74] Even the *2019 Evidence Provisions* tries to solve this problem as well. Regarding the scope of convicted facts, the new version of the judicial interpretation limits the "facts" recognized in effective court judgments and rulings, which was used in the previous *2001 Evidence Provisions*, to "fundamental facts". This reduction of literal wording does, to a certain extent, provide new room for possible interpretation in favor of narrowing the predetermined effect. Yet, this normative move seems overly cautious and circuitous, which must be less effective than the direct approaches suggested in this chapter.

---

68 Fu (2017, p. 136).

69 Liu (2019, pp. 145–147); Wu (2017, pp. 14–19).

70 For example, Wang (2014, p. 140); Xiao (2000).

71 Zhang (2016, pp. 158–160).

72 Ji (2017, p. 29).

73 Niu (2019, p. 103).

74 Ren (2014, p. 261).

7.4.3 Theoretical Basis for Denying the Predetermined Effect

From the perspective *de lege ferenda*, this contribution is still reluctant to agree on the predetermined effect of convicted facts within civil judgments and rulings. On one hand, although judgments are considered as dispositive public documents (Chap. 5), it is the judicial transaction rendered by the court that is dispositive, i.e. the judgment or ruling as described in the operative part of it is given in fact. Yet, the relationship between the content of the judgment or ruling and the objective truth is not included in the dispositive transaction. Therefore, as mentioned in Chap. 5, the substantial probative force of the judgment or ruling shall not be affirmed. In other words, the objective facts of the case convicted in civil judgments should not be presumed to be true.

Also under German law, the civil judgment itself is considered to contain the written expression of intention of the public authority.[75] Because the judgment cannot be forged or tampered with, the interpretation of Article 417 of the *German Code of Civil Procedure* would say that the parties cannot even object to the record of the civil judgment.[76] As argued in Chap. 3, this contribution suggests that there should be part of alleged facts in Chinese civil judgments, which has a special function of recording and proving just as in the German counterpart. Hence, reasoning how the facts of the case are convicted should be fully reflected in the reasoning part of the judgment.[77]

Of course, regardless of which approach is taken, i.e. whether the predetermined effect ought to be admitted in future, the judges' findings of undisputed facts and their determination of the issues in dispute with reasons will be shown in civil judgments (Article 97 of the *2019 Evidence Provisions* and Article 79 of the *2001 Evidence Provisions*). If the system of alleged facts would be established in China, civil judgments, as direct evidence, can prove the opinions of all parties raised during court hearings and the persons who raised them. And as indirect evidence, they can provide judges rather than the ones making the judgment with the factors and supporting materials that have been considered by judges making the judgment while establishing their own free evaluation. Hence, the other judges are able to establish their own free evaluation of the fundamental/major facts on this basis.[78]

With these structural changes and functional conversions of civil judgments, the SPC can at least get rid of its difficulty in ascertaining the fact whether the money borrowed shall be returned in a private lending dispute. On such occasions, the SPC admitted explicitly that it was not able to determine whether this fact of return, convicted in three related civil judgments, was "recognized by both parties or instead ascertained by the court of second instance". However, while the SPC also wondered how this fact was found in reality by the court at a lower level, the SPC still ascertained

---

[75] BGH NJW-RR 2011, 953, 954, Tz 19.

[76] Schreiber (2020, § 417 Rn 7).

[77] For a similar conclusion, see Ren (2016, p. 47).

[78] For a slightly different view, see Duan (2015, pp. 112–113).

this fact merely due to the predetermined effect.[79] The part of alleged facts, which must have a standard writing style, will have to list all factual allegations and the respective attitudes of the opposing party. Moreover, the China's judiciary may avoid the reduction of its credibility caused by the judges' simple assertion of predetermined effect. Rather, individual judges would have to discover the facts as to what needs to be done while they, as representatives of the sole enforcement organ in China, i.e. People's courts, have to dig out the assets of the enforcement debtors.[80]

Furthermore, Duan Wenbo may correctly trace back to the origin of the theory of predetermined effect of convicted facts. This theory can be found in the civil procedure theory of the Soviet Union and its inheritance at large by Chinese scholars. However, according to Duan's research, there are insurmountable theoretical barriers to the predetermined effect from the perspectives of judges' independent trial, procedural guarantee for parties of the latter lawsuit, the general understanding of *res judicata* effect as well as judges' free evaluation of evidence in the latter lawsuit.[81] As to whether in future, the predetermined effect of facts may find its theoretical basis in the principle of estoppel in common law legal systems, or whether it should be modified following the example of issue preclusion also in common law traditions, this contribution does not have a temporary answer while being open to further discussion. It could be at least one of the interesting scientific issues in comparative procedural law.

References

Ahrens HJ (2014) In: Wieczorek B, Schütze RA, ZPO, Band 6, 4. Aufl. De Gruyter, Berlin

Albrecht H (2013) Die Streitsache im deutschen und englischen Zivilverfahren. Mohr Siebeck, Tübingen

Althammer C (2012) Streitgegenstand und Interesse. Mohr Siebeck, Tübingen

Althammer C (2018) In: Stein F, Jonas M, ZPO, Band 4, 23. Aufl. Mohr Siebeck, Tübingen

Baumgärtel G (1968) Studien zum Einstweiligen Rechtsschutz. Archiv für die Civilistische Praxis 168:401–407

Baumgärtel G (1974) Zur Lehre vom Streitgegenstand. Juristische Schulung 14:69–75

Becker-Eberhard E (2020) In: Krüger W, Rauscher T, Münchener Kommentar ZPO, Band 1, 6. Aufl. C. H. Beck, München

Bork R (1988) Der Vergleich. Duncker & Humblot, Berlin

Büscher W (2012) Klagehäufung im Gewerblichen Rechtsschutz. Gewerblicher Rechtsschutz und Urheberrecht 114:17–25

Cao Z (2020) The restriction of the presumption rule of the substantial proving effects of public documents. Journal of National Procurators College 2:137–154 (in Chinese)

Cao Z (2022) Discovery of debtor's assets in the enforcement of monetary judgments in China. Ritsumeikan Law Review 40:69–87

Ding B (2012) Study on the *res judicata* of civil judgments. Law Press, Beijing (in Chinese)

[79] Civil Judgments by the SPC (2018) Zui Gao Fa Min Zhong No. 1163.

[80] For the latter one, see Cao (2022).

[81] Duan (2015, pp. 107–110).

Duan W (2015) The criticism of the effect of predetermination and the development of the effect of evidence regarding facts. Science of Law 5:106–114 (in Chinese)
Foerste U (1995) Zur Rechtskraft in Ausgleichszusammenhängen. Zeitschrift für Zivilprozess 108:167–191
Fu Y (2008) Preliminary issue and interlocutory adjudication. China Legal Science 6:155–169 (in Chinese)
Fu Y (2017) On the duty of good faith of parties in civil proceedings. Law and Modernization 6:130–145 (in Chinese)
Fu Y (2018) Studies on civil procedure law in China in the forty-year era of reform and opening up. Peking University Law Journal 6:1423–1448 (in Chinese)
Gottwald P (2000) Streitgegenstandslehre und Sinnzusammenhänge. In: Peter G, Reinhard G, Hanns P (eds) Dogmatische Grundfragen des Zivilprozesses im geeinten Europa: Akademisches Symposium zu Ehren von Karl Heinz Schwab aus Anlass seines 80. Geburtstages. Gieseking, Bielefeld
Gottwald P (2020) In: Krüger W, Rauscher T, Münchener Kommentar ZPO, Band 1, 6. Aufl. C. H. Beck, München
Guo X (2010) Study on the theory of issue preclusion in civil cases. Beijing Normal University Press, Beijing (in Chinese)
Habscheid WJ (1956) Der Streitgegenstand im Zivilprozess und im Streitverfahren der Freiwilligen Gerichtsbarkeit. Dt. Heimat-Verl, Bielefeld
Hahn C (1880) Die gesammten Materialien zur Civilprozessordnung. Decker, Berlin
Henckel W (1970) Prozessrecht und materielles Recht. Schwartz, Göttingen
Herrler S (2020) In: Palandt, Bürgerliches Gesetzbuch, 79. Aufl. C. H. Beck, München
Huber M (2003) Modernisierung der Justiz? Zeitschrift für Rechtspolitik 36:268–272
Jacobs M (2005) Der Gegenstand des Feststellungsverfahrens. Mohr Siebeck, Tübingen
Ji G (2013) The western sample of the legal effect of 'disputed issues' and China's path. China Legal Science 3:109–120 (in Chinese)
Ji G (2017) Rethinking the governance of false litigation in civil litigation. SJTU Law Review 2:21–30 (in Chinese)
Jiang W, Chang T (2008) On the predetermine force of confirmed facts. China Legal Science 3:102–109 (in Chinese)
Kohler J (2020) In: Säcker FJ, Rixecker R, Oetker H, Limperg B, Münchener Kommentar BGB, Band 8, 8. Aufl. C. H. Beck, München
Lent F (1959) Zivilprozessrecht, 9. Aufl. C. H. Beck, München
Li H (2011) Evidence provisions and amendments to rules of civil evidence. China Legal Science 3:31–40 (in Chinese)
Lin J (2006) Study on the objective scope of *res judicata* effect of civil judgments. Xiamen University Press, Xiamen (in Chinese)
Liu J (2019) On the normative nature and procedural framework of false litigation. Contemporary Law Review 4:140–149 (in Chinese)
Mendelssohn Bartholdy A (1900) Grenzen der Rechtskraft. Duncker & Humblot, Leipzig
Musielak HJ (2021) In: Musielak HJ, Voit W, ZPO, 18. Aufl. Vahlen, München
Niu Y (2019) Study on dual control model during identifying civil fraud litigations. Social Sciences of Beijing 1:99–107 (in Chinese)
Peters E (1963) Zur Rechtskraftlehre Zeuners. Zeitschrift für Zivilprozess 76:229–243
Picker C (2019) In: Staudinger, Kommentar zum Bürgerlichen Gesetzbuch. De Gruyter, Berlin
Qi S, Ji J (2011) Issues concerning the effect of previous judgments in English evidence law. Tsinghua University Law Journal 5:136–142 (in Chinese)
Ren Z (2014) On false litigation: comments on China's practice in third-party revocation claims. China Legal Science 6:241–262 (in Chinese)
Ren Z (2016) On the theoretical consensus of civil procedure in China. Contemporary Law Review 3:38–51 (in Chinese)

Rimmelspacher B (1970) Materiellrechtlicher Anspruch und Streitgegenstandsprobleme im Zivilprozess. Schwartz, Göttingen
Rosenberg L (1929) Lehrbuch des deutschen Zivilprozessrechts. O. Liebmann, Berlin
Rosenberg L, Schwab KH (1986) Zivilprozessrecht. C. H. Beck, München
Rosenberg L, Schwab KH, Gottwald P (2007) Zivilprozessrecht (trans: Li D) China Legal Publishing House, Beijing (in Chinese)
Rosenberg L, Schwab KH, Gottwald P (2018) Zivilprozessrecht. C. H. Beck, München
Roth H (2011) Materielle Rechtskraft und rechtliche Qualifikation. Zeitschrift für Zivilprozess 124:3–28
Roth H (2016) In: Stein F, Jonas M, ZPO, Band 3, 23. Aufl. Mohr Siebeck, Tübingen
Rüßmann H (1998) Die Streitgegenstandslehre und die Rechtsprechung des EuGH-nationales Recht unter gemeineuropäischem Einfluß? Zeitschrift für Zivilprozess 111:399–427
Schreiber K (2020) In: Krüger W, Rauscher T, Münchener Kommentar ZPO, Band 2, 6. Aufl. C. H. Beck, München
Schwab KH (1954) Der Streitgegenstand im Zivilprozess. C. H. Beck, München
Schwab KH (1969) Die Bedeutung der Entscheidungsgründe. In: Festschrift für Eduard Bötticher zum 70. Geburtstag. Duncker & Humblot, Berlin
Seiler C (2019) In: Thomas H, Putzo H, ZPO, 40. Aufl. C. H. Beck, München
Shen K et al. (2010) Objective scope of *res judicata* effect and issue preclusion of civil judgments. In: the Civil Procedure Law Research Foundation (ed) Discussion on civil procedure law (XVII). Sanmin Book Co., Taipei, pp 1–92 (in Chinese)
Shi P (2014) The theory of *res judicata* in criminal law and its application in China. Chinese Journal of Law 1:150–170
Shindo K (2019) Civil procedure law. Koubundou Publishers, Tokyo (in Japanese)
Stürner R (1997) Der deutsche Prozeßrechtslehrer am Ende des 20. Jahrhunderts. In: Festschrift für Gerhard Lüke zum 70. Geburtstag. C. H. Beck, München
Stürner R (1999) Rechtskraft in Europa. In: Festschrift für Rolf A. Schütze zum 65. Geburtstag, Wege zur Globalisierung des Rechts. C. H. Beck, München
Stürner R (2005) Parteidisposition über Anfang, Gegenstand und Umfang des Verfahrens in wichtigen europäischen Prozessordnungen. In: Festschrift für Andreas Heldrich zum 70. Geburtstag. C. H. Beck, München
Van de Velden JB (2017) Finality in Litigation. Kluwer Law International, Alphen aan den Rijn
Vollkommer G (2003) Bindungswirkung des rechtskräftigen Strafurteils im nachfolgenden Schadensersatzprozess des Geschädigten. Zeitschrift für Wirtschaftsrecht 25:2061–2063
Vollkommer G (2020) In: Zöller R, ZPO, 33. Aufl. Otto Schmidt, Köln
Walker W (1998) Die Streitgegenstandslehre und die Rechtsprechung des EuGH. Zeitschrift für Zivilprozess 111:429–454
Wang Y (2014) Re-examination on the plaintiff's standing in third-party revocation claims. Chinese Journal of Law 6:132–146 (in Chinese)
Wang Y, Chen X (2015) Impact of the judgment of a prior litigation on a subsequent litigation. ECUPL Journal 6:6–20 (in Chinese)
Weng X (2006) On the predetermined effect of decided facts. China Legal Science 4:180–189 (in Chinese)
Wu Y (2011) An analysis of the involution of China's litigation object theory. China Legal Science 2:177–190 (in Chinese)
Wu Z (2017) Regulation of false litigation under the background of civil procedure theories. SJTU Law Review 2:7–20 (in Chinese)
Xiao J (2000) The function of the major participation claim to prevent fraud. Law Science Magazine 5:30–31 (in Chinese)
Yeazell SC, Schwartz JC (2019) Civil procedure. Aspen Publishing, California
Zeuner A (1959) Die objektiven Grenzen der Rechtskraft im Rahmen rechtlicher Sinnzusammenhänge. Mohr Siebeck, Tübingen

Zeuner A (1981) Rechtsvergleichende Bemerkungen zur objektiven Begrenzung der Rechtskraft im Zivilprozeß. In: Festschrift für Konrad Zweigert zum 70. Geburtstag. Mohr Siebeck, Tübingen
Zeuner A (1997) Zum Verhältnis zwischen internationaler Rechtshängigkeit nach Art. 21 EuGVÜ und Rechtshängigkeit nach den Regeln der ZPO. In: Festschrift für Gerhard Lüke zum 70. Geburtstag. C. H. Beck, München
Zhang J (2002) A legislative thinking on the intermediate declaratory judgment. China Legal Science 5:109–117 (in Chinese)
Zhang Y (2016) The study of types of false litigation and the review of the current rules. Political Science and Law 7:151–160 (in Chinese)
Zhang W (2019) Civil procedure law. Law Press, Beijing (in Chinese)
Zou B (2010) Nine-step method on elements of the civil trial. Law Press, Beijing (in Chinese)
Zuckerman AAS (2013) Zuckerman on civil procedure: principles of practice. Sweet & Maxwell, London

Chapter 8
Effects of Final Judgments (II): Scope of *Res Judicata* Effect and Possible Issue Preclusion?

8.1 Introduction

Following the Chap. 7, this chapter focuses on a new kind of effect of final judgments in Chinese context. Among others, the term legal transactions (*Rechtsgeschäfte*) is understood as a decisive concept in civil and commercial legal relationships and their changes. Since the existence or non-existence of the legal transactions and their validity serve as fundamental premises for other subsequent substantive determinations, the substantial review of the validity of contracts conducted by a judge has a significant impact on various types of cases. China's judicial practice, which could be represented by the SPC, holds that regardless of whether there is any dispute between the parties, or whether the parties request the court to review the validity in writing or orally within the complaint or in the course of civil litigation,[1] "the validity of a legal activity involves the determination of the nature and validity of the legal relationship disputed by the parties, and is the content for the People's court to hear and determine *sua sponte*".[2] The judge's authority to review the validity of contracts *sua sponte* has nothing to do with whether the parties explicitly claim to confirm the validity of contracts. Rather, this authority is directly embedded in the judge's judicial power.

[1] Civil Judgment of the SPC (2019) Zui Gao Fa Min Zhong No. 120, Civil Judgment of the SPC (2018) Zui Gao Fa Min Zhong No. 1167 and Civil Judgment of the SPC (2018) Min Ti No. 232.

[2] The First Civil Division of the SPC (2020, p 498). This contribution narrows the scope of concern to the issue of the validity in contract cases. The main reason is that this is the most typical and core scenario when discussing the expansion of *res judicata* effect of final judgments to the precedential legal relationships. For example, for the determination of the ownership of property rights in the claim for restitution of such property, the adjudication techniques of review *sua sponte* can also be shared. However, in China's current practice, courts are not generally required to actively identify the ownership of property rights. However, it should be noted that the first sentence of Article 8 of *the Opinions of the SPC on the Coordinated of Case Docketing, Trial and Enforcement by People's Courts* requires that "the status of the ownership of the property to be confirmed shall be inquired". Therefore, the necessity of review *sua sponte* will not discuss this issue.

Z. Cao, *Civil Judgments at First Instance*, Contemporary Chinese Civil and Commercial Law, https://doi.org/10.1007/978-981-97-8662-6_8

From the perspective of civil substantive law, the judge has the power to actively review the validity of contracts as a civil law defense in the same litigation, which is also the classical understanding of "review of the validity of contracts *sua sponte*" in the civil law system. However, such power of judicial review should be based on the relevant factual allegations raised by the parties under the doctrine of party presentation (*Verhandlungsmaxime*). From the perspective of civil procedure law, this review rule can also reflect the coordination between the judge's authority, i.e. the power and duty of clarification (*Aufklärungspflicht*), and the parties' right of disposition regarding changing the subject matter of claims (*Streitgegenstand*). The judge's role extends beyond merely identifying the types of civil lawsuits, such as those seeking specific performance, a declaration, or a change in a specific legal relationship. Rather, the judge also has the authority to suggest the parties the possibility of consolidating overlapping claims, combining the claim in chief and the subordinate claim (in the sense of *eventuelle Klagehäufung*), or including counterclaims against the original claims. In this way, the scope of adjudication in the current lawsuit could be extended through the change of subject matters of claims, which is decided by the parties on their own initiative.[3]

At the same time, the aforementioned judicial review on the validity of contracts may also affect the court's determination regarding whether a latter lawsuit is to be identified as relitigation. In the traditional theory of civil procedure, such review authority is related to the *res judicata* effect of the reasoning part of a final judgment on a forthcoming lawsuit.[4] Concretely speaking, in what sense does the issue of contract's validity, which should be fully dealt with by the judge of the former lawsuit, bind and affect the judicial activities of the judge of the latter lawsuit? Is such determination of *res judicata* effect related to how the judge of the former lawsuit exercises the judicial clarification power according to Article 53 of the *2019 Evidence Provisions* in the former lawsuit? Compared with the intermediate declaratory claim, which is common in other jurisdictions (Chap. 7),[5] could China's legal and technical solutions to deal with a similar issue provide sufficient procedural protection for the parties concerned? And under the current legal rules preventing relitigation in the framework of Article 247 of the *ICPL*, what is the current situation of the Chinese law and is there any room for improvement?

Especially, the scholars of civil procedure have paid extensive attention to the similarities and differences of the identification theories of the subject matter of claims and have provided fruitful but sometimes opposing research contributions regarding the rules *de lege ferenda* and the possible interpretation *de lege lata*.[6] How to theoretically understand the *res judicata* effect following the *sua sponte* review of the validity of contracts in China, which seems to have been accepted implicitly by the practice, and how to ascertain the extent and limits of *sua sponte* review within the trial mode of civil procedure in general, have become core issues during

[3] Cao (2021b).

[4] For example, Wang (2021); Yan (2017, pp 548–554).

[5] For previous studies, for example, Zhang (2002).

[6] For example, Ren (2021b); Chen et al. (2020, pp 283–303).

the reflection of civil procedure in China. Considering that there is no *sua sponte* review of the validity of contracts in the sense of *res judicata* in comparative law, it is the scientific duty of this chapter to extract and perfect a feasible explanation from Chinese practice and shape the academic thinking and discourse regarding civil procedure research with Chinese characteristics through the systematization of various procedural norms. Then, we may properly deal with the precedential substantive issue of claims presented in the case from a functional perspective.[7]

This chapter recognizes that the disputed issue of the validity of contracts, as the premise of a judgment on performance, is typically included in the *res judicata* effect of relevant judgments in China. This perspective differs significantly from the counterparts in civil law jurisdictions, which insist that the reasoning part of final judgments has no *res judicata* effect. Under the two different modes regarding the scope of *res judicata* effect, namely the expansion and limitation modes, the validity of civil contracts cannot be disputed in the former mode and can rather be disputed again in the latter one respectively. This is related to the differences in understanding the relationship between disputed issues and the claim for performance in these two modes and is also subject to the attitudes of both parties on whether the reasoning part of a previous final judgment should be binding on the latter lawsuit.

Considering that China has paid greater attention to the adjudicative techniques regarding narrowing disputed issues in the process of civil proceedings, we should find the mutual basis for both modes of *res judicata* effect while focusing on the administration of court proceedings and the exercise of judicial clarification. In this way, we may promote the substantialization of *sua sponte* review of the validity of civil contracts and the extent of procedural safeguard during civil litigation. Furthermore, this chapter intends to construct the effect of *sua sponte* review of the validity of civil contracts by re-interpreting the rules against relitigation and the elements of Article 247 of the *ICPL*, namely "subject matter of claims", "identical claim for relief/procedural entitlement", and "substantial negation of the claim for relief" which means that the claim for relief in a latter process is negating substantially the one in a preceding lawsuit.

[7] For the fundamental systematic consideration, see Fu (2008).

8.2 Influence of *Sua Sponte* Review of Contract's Validity on Forthcoming Cases in China

8.2.1 Determination of Contract's Validity Has Res Judicata *Effect in General*

Whether the *res judicata* effect of a judgment on performance covers the confirmation of the validity of the relevant contract in the reasoning part of such judgment and whether it is binding on the subsequent civil lawsuits,[8] remains controversial in the practice and theory in China. In judicial practice, it is commonly understood that when the plaintiff files a lawsuit against the defendant for specific performance due to a civil contract between them, the defendant's counterclaim for declaring voidness of such contract is to be classified as "substantial negation of the claim for relief". As a result, it is regarded as a form of relitigation and is typically dismissed without deciding the merits of the case.[9] This understanding could be taken as the leading opinion in China.

On the contrary, when the court "determined that there is no legal relationship of designated investment with specific targets between the parties" in the reasoning part of a former judgment and rejected the relevant claim for performance on the merits, the defendant's "new claims, which aim to confirm the validity of the disputed 'Designated Investment Agreement with Specific Targets' and to the further performance, obviously constitute the confrontation or denial of the procedural results of the former lawsuit".[10] A similar situation happens when the plaintiff claims initiates a new lawsuit seeking the continuous performance of the contract, after a court has declared the termination of the contract.[11] In this scenario, the procedural consequence is not the substantive denial of the latter court's jurisdiction over the case, rather due to the *res judicata* effect, the direct procedural dismissal of the latter lawsuit by the court. In other words, the judgment made here should be a procedural decision, similar to the procedural judgment (*Prozessurteil*) under German law while leaving the requirement of having court hearings aside, rather than the judgment on the merits (*Sachurteil*).[12]

And when a previous final arbitral award required a person, who was the plaintiff in the latter lawsuit, to deliver land materials, surrender the relevant land, cooperate in the registration of change of rights, and pay liquidated damages, and in the latter lawsuit, such person claims for declaring the voidness of the relevant contract and for demanding his defendant to pay back the enforced performance in the earlier lawsuit

[8] Due to the topic, this contribution does not discuss the relationship between the civil judgment on performance and the criminal judgment regarding the determination of the validity of contracts respectively in a civil and criminal case.

[9] Shen (2015, p 635); Chen W (2020).

[10] Civil Ruling of the SPC (2017) Zui Gao Fa Min Zhong No. 1.

[11] Civil Ruling of the SPC (2016) Zui Gao Fa Min Zhong No. 189.

[12] Civil Ruling of the SPC (2016) Zui Gao Fa Min Li Zhong No. 35.

adversely, the SPC also holds that there is a case of relitigation.[13] Even before the promulgation of the *ICPL*, some courts already held that the claim for declaring the voidness of the relevant contract in the latter lawsuit is repetitive when the former lawsuit confirmed the validity of contracts and then decided to terminate the contract and demand the debtor to repay the principal and interest of the monetary loan.[14] This should represent the leading viewpoint in China's judicial practice.

Meanwhile, a series of cases that have undergone five rounds of litigation and were even discussed twice by the Adjudication Committee of the SPC also involve the adjudication of the contract's validity, the lawsuit to confirm the validity of such contract, and the rules against relitigation.[15] Company A entrusted Company B to hold the stock equity of Company C in the name of Company B. Later, a dispute arose between Company A and Company B over such shareholding under the incorrect name of the shareholder. Under certain influence of the factors beyond the case, Company A, Company B, and Company D entered into a joint agreement and transferred the share equity of Company C to Company D. In return, Company D paid Company A CNY 2.16 billion and Company B CNY 702 million.

In the first lawsuit, Company A claimed among others that Company B should return the CNY 702 million to it. The SPC, after internal discussion among its Adjudication Committee, held that the contract concluded by Company A and Company B constituted a contract for entrusted money management, and that the profit distribution agreement concluded by Company A, Company B and Company D together was valid. Therefore, the claim brought by Company A was dismissed on the merits.[16] Subsequently, Company A initiated a new lawsuit against Company B, Company D and others, to confirm the voidness of the disputed Transaction Price Payment Agreement between Company B and Company C and to pay tort damages of CNY 702 million and the interests thereon of CNY 28 million.

Hence, the SPC held that "the current lawsuit and the previous lawsuit are based on the same facts and are all filed against the Transaction Price Payment Agreement to obtain the equity transfer price of CNY 702 million. Therefore, it can be determined that the two lawsuits have the same subject matter of claims" and "the current lawsuit is a lawsuit for performance, while the claim for relief is to obtain CNY 702 million...... (the current lawsuit) claims to confirm that...... the Transaction Price Payment Agreement is void, and describe CNY 702 million now as compensation of loss, these particulars are merely grounds to obtain CNY 702 million".[17] After the Adjudication Committee discussed the case again, the SPC decided to dismiss the lawsuit without deciding the merits of the case. Although the final judgment of the current lawsuit did not separately answer the procedural law issue of whether a new claim for declaration can be filed in the latter litigation, the answer can be presumed

[13] Civil Ruling of the SPC (2020) Zui Gao Fa Min Shen No. 2951.

[14] For instance, Civil Ruling of Guangzhou Intermediate People's Court of Guangdong Province (2014) Sui Zhong Fa Li Min Zhong No. 3228.

[15] Civil Ruling of the SPC (2019) Zui Gao Fa Min Zhong No. 137.

[16] Civil Judgment of the SPC (2013) Zui Gao Fa Min Zhong No. 20.

[17] Civil Ruling of the SPC (2018) Zui Gao Fa Min Zhong No. 135.

to be a "no", i.e. no more claim for declaration in this regard, based on both the reasoning part and the overall results of the SPC's ruling in the second lawsuit.

8.2.2 Circumstances Where **Res Judicata** *Effect Does not Expand Exceptionally*

As a relatively rare circumstance, the SPC once pointed out that "the final judgment made by a People's court has *res judicata* effect, but such effect is merely limited to the operative part of the judgment. As for the ascertainment in the reasoning part of 'this court considers', if there is evidence to overturn it, a latter judgment shall not be affected by the earlier judgment".[18] In one of its retrial cases which aimed to challenge a final judgment in exceptional cases, the SPC also held explicitly that the original final judgment merely confirmed the validity of the patent transfer contract in the reasoning part of such judgment rather than in the operative part of the judgment. On such occasions, the scope of *res judicata* effect does not include such confirmation, and the final judgment does not exceed the claim of the plaintiff.[19]

Then, we could also further examine the relationship between the determination of issues, not limited to the validity of contracts, and *res judicata* effect. In a previous final judgment for repayment of the contractual debt, the determination of the ownership of the thermal power plant related to the relevant debt in the reasoning part of this judgment was held to have no *res judicata* effect. Nevertheless, such determination was able to have the effect of predetermination of the facts which should be presumed to be true in subsequent lawsuits (Chap. 7).[20] Concretely speaking, the latter lawsuit involved two legal relationships, i.e., the confirmation of the ownership of the thermal power plant and the return of the construction costs in the name of a money loan. In this case, considering the fairness of the overall results of the dispute settlement between the parties (one party shall not be left alone to pay the monetary debt without obtaining the disputed object), the SPC held that the court shall not, based on the former lawsuit, determine that the thermal power plant belongs to the seeming lender (in the sense that there is no real money borrowing relationship and

[18] Civil Judgment of the SPC (2019) Zui Gao Fa Min Zai No. 384. On the contrary, when the court confirmed the amount of construction work involved in the reasoning part of a final judgment which also confirmed creditor's ordinary bankruptcy rights in its operative part, the court of the latter claim held that it referred to "the primary facts confirmed by the effective judgment, and such main disputed facts … after the parties produced evidence, examined evidence and fully debated with each other, … the substantial judgment made for such disputed facts has the *res judicata* effect". Civil Judgment of the SPC (2019) Zui Gao Fa Min Zhong No. 302.

[19] Civil Judgment of the SPC (2013) Min Shen No. 2320. For the same viewpoint, see Civil Judgment of the SPC (2014) Min Shen No. 60. As to the understanding of the lower court that a claim for declaration and a claim for performance has different subject matters of claims and do not constitute relitigation, see Li and Yang (2013, p 73).

[20] Some scholars also hold a different view that the "basic essential facts" that "have been fully tried as disputed issues and have been clearly determined by an effective judgment" should have the positive effect of *res judicata*. Wang and Chen (2015, pp 16–17).

the loan is used for construction work), and demand the seeming borrower to return the loan that in fact does not exist. Therefore, the court needed to remand the case to the court of lower instance on the ground of errors of fundamental facts.[21]

In other words, the validity of contracts and other disputed issues identified in the reasoning part of a previous judgment, which are often considered unchallengeable through another lawsuit, do not belong to the objective scope of *res judicata* effect of the previous judgment. If the existence of *res judicata* effect of the first judgment is decisive for the determination whether a second lawsuit can be brought or not, then considering the general judicial practice regarding the aforementioned *sua sponte* review, there may be some additional standards of the determination, such as the theory of issue preclusion in both civil law and common law legal systems (Chap. 7). It is also necessary to reconsider whether the common understanding of *res judicata* effect in the civil law system is also applicable to China.[22]

Moreover, in one of its second-instance judgments, the SPC even asserted that although courts have the authority to review the validity of contracts *sua sponte* in civil proceedings, the findings of such review do not necessarily give rise to the *res judicata* effect. "The parties in the other case did not dispute over the validity of contracts, and the courts of first instance and second instance of the other case held that the contract was valid but did not render a judgment on the issue of the contract's validity. As a result, the final judgment of the other case does not produce *res judicata* effect on the determination of the validity of contracts. The parties' determination as to whether the contract is valid does not affect the People's court's determination of the validity of contracts according to the facts ascertained by the court and relevant legal provisions".[23]

Hence, besides that the court's review of the validity of contracts *sua sponte* is not limited by the parties' claims, the SPC held that a latter court is not limited by the review result of the court in a previous case, if the first court does not try the issue of the contract's validity as an independent item of the operative part of its final judgment, i.e. a separate subject matter of claims. In this sense, the positive/negative role of *res judicata* effect was in doubt in the reasoning part of this judgment. Instead, this viewpoint of the SPC is similar to the leading opinion in the civil law system. Although discovering such an opposing viewpoint may challenge the reliability of the arguments in this contribution, more crucially, it does reminds us that this contribution is concerned about a "real problem" of non-unified judicial precedents that do exist before Chinese courts at different levels. It is worth further observing the inherent requirements of civil law traditions and comparing it with the practical logic within the widely spreading judicial practice in China.

---

[21] Civil Ruling of the SPC (2011) Min Er Zhong No. 30. In addition, Article 75 item 4 of the *1992 Opinions Application CPL*, published in 1992, should not be cited for this case, while Article 9 paragraph 1 item 4 and paragraph 2 of the *2001 Evidence Provisions* should be applied.

[22] For example, Chen X (2020, pp 125–132); Yan (2017, pp 548–554).

[23] Civil Judgment of the SPC (2018) Zui Gao Fa Min Zhong No. 33.

8.3 Mode of Limiting the Objective Scope of *Res Judicata* Effect and Its Expansion in Germany and Japan

8.3.1 Res Judicata *Effect Does not Expand to Contract's Validity*

In general, according to the customary practice of reviewing the validity of contracts *sua sponte* in China, the disputed issue on the validity of contracts, as the premise of a judgment on performance, is typically considered within the scope of *res judicata* effect, or at least has the predetermined effect of the fact-finding of a previous final judgment which is similar to the substantive probative force of a public document (Chap. 7).[24] In contrast, in the civil procedural theory of some civil law systems, the so-called precedential legal relationships (*präjudizielle Rechtsverhältnisse*), i.e. the preconditions for the establishment of relevant substantive rights claimed in the pleadings, are distinguished from the substantive rights themselves decided in the judgment on performance. The typical situation concerning such a legal relationship is the judge's determination of the validity of contracts. Considering the coverage of the final judgment, the judgment on performance is not only related to the specific performance, e.g.a specific amount of monetary payment, but also confirms the corresponding claim for the performance itself. Nevertheless, such judgment does not necessarily embrace the determination of the precedential legal relationship.[25]

Similar to the exceptional understanding within Chinese practice, it is generally agreed in the civil law system that the content of the reasoning part of the final judgment does not possess *res judicata* effect (Article 322 of the *German Code of Civil Procedure*, Article 114 of the *Civil Procedure Law of Japan* and Article 400 of the *Civil Procedure Law of China Taiwan*).[26] It means that the determination of the validity of contracts in the reasoning part of the final judgment is not able to prohibit relitigation regarding the same issue of validity. Therefore, according to e.g. German law, when some disputed issues/precedential legal relationships of a previous lawsuit are brought in the latter lawsuit as the subject matters of claims, there is in the previous final judgment in principle no determination with prejudice regarding such legal relationships on which the subject matter of claims relies.[27] Because the same identification criteria of the subject matter of claims apply to the issue of *res judicata* and the issue of prohibiting dual pendency of the same claim (*lis pendens*), after the former lawsuit for performance is filed, the declaration interests (*Feststellungsinteresse*) in a latter declaratory claim will not be affected

[24] Cao (2020b, pp 144–147); also Yan (2017, p 552).

[25] Cao (2021a, pp 128–130).

[26] Gottwald (2020, § 322 Rn 87 et seq.); Matsumoto and Ueno (2015, pp 623–627); also Lv (2018, p 651); Zhang (2019, p 446).

[27] BGH NJW-RR 2010, 640, 641, Tz 15 (defense against litigation); Roth (2016, § 256 Rn 6).

by the subject matter of the former lawsuit for performance.[28] However, while it is expressly stated that the *res judicata* effect is limited to the operative part of the final judgment (Article 322 of the *German Code of Civil Procedure*), with the exception to the case of set-off, German law allows the parties to explicitly request the court to extend the *res judicata* effect of the previous final judgment to the precedential legal issues through submitting new claims for relief.[29] This special kind of civil claims is indicated as intermediate declaratory claim (*Zwischenfeststellungsklage*).

Due to the considerable scope for discussion regarding the system of intermediate declaratory claims in China, besides Chap. 7, this chapter mainly draws upon the leading understanding of this system in Germany and constructs relevant Chinese rules on such a basis. The purpose of this contribution is not to entirely replicate the relatively mature practice and theory in Germany, but to focus on the realization of the procedural safeguard to the same extent. In other words, considering the Chinese inquisitorial trial mode which emphasizes the judge's authority more intensively, it is now more reasonable to further legitimize the expansion of *res judicata* effect which is attributed to the rules of *sua sponte* review of the validity of contracts.

8.3.2 Res Judicata *Effect Could Be Expanded Exceptionally in Civil Law Jurisdictions*

8.3.2.1 Intermediate Declaratory Claim as the Basic Tool for Expansion

Because the determination of the validity of precedential legal relationships plays a crucial role in civil cases, the so-called intermediate declaratory claim/judgment is specially established in civil law jurisdictions (Article 256 paragraph 2 of the *German Code of Civil Procedure* and Article 145 of the *Civil Procedure Law of Japan*). The legal relationship, which has precedential function and is required by the intermediate declaratory claim, is the same as that in the independent claim for declaration. That is, the legal relationship between persons or between persons and property arising from concrete facts of ordinary life (*Lebenssachverhalt*). On the contrary, no plaintiff could bring an intermediate declaratory claim for the precedential issues or elements of the legal relationship.[30] Even if the legal relationship between a party of the lawsuit and a third party is concerned, which could become the object to be ascertained in

[28] BGH NJW-RR 2010, 640, 641, Tz 16; NJW-RR 2008, 1495, 1499, Tz 49 (regarding defense against legal pendency). The case would be different when the claim for performance is considered as covering the declaratory claim with respect to the subject matter of claims. Such a case appears when it comes to the declaratory claim for the existence of the civil obligation for performance itself rather than precedential legal relationships.

[29] Rosenberg et al. (2018, §§ 97 Rn 36, 154 Rn 14); Albrecht (2013, pp 206–207, 215–216); Hahn (1880, p 291).

[30] BGH NJW-RR 2018, 906, 913, Tz 65; NJW 2011, 2195, 2196, Tz 19; Becker-Eberhard (2020, § 256 Rn 84). For detailed introduction to the requirement of the legal relationship in an independent declaratory claim, see Cao (2018b, pp 47–49).

the case of an independent claim for declaration, the intermediate declaratory claim could also be initiated following the same rule.

The preconditions for it are twofold, namely the intermediate declaratory claim satisfies the to-be-discussed precedential requirements and the trial over it is still meaningful beyond the subject matter of claims in the current case.[31] For instance, when the entrusting party of a contract for renovation construction works sues the guarantor of the principal debtor, the entrusting party is entitled to confirm the validity of the guarantee contract between the principal debtor and the guarantor, since the guarantor may, according to Article 821 of the *German Civil Code*, exercise the debtor's right to a defense of profit pursuant to Article 768 paragraph 1 of the *German Civil Code*. On such occasions, the guarantee contract between the defendant and the third party constitutes the precedential legal relationship in the lawsuit for performance between the plaintiff and the defendant.[32]

The special requirement of an intermediate declaratory claim is that the legal relationship mentioned above should have the precedential function (*Vorgreiflichkeit*), which replaces the requirement of declaration interests and becomes a special requirement of the proceedings in this special type of claims for confirmation.[33] According to Article 256 paragraph 2 of the *German Code of Civil Procedure*, the precedential function means that "the judgment on the disputed case depends wholly or partly on the existence or non-existence of such legal relationship". Such a legal relationship is considered to be an essential part of the subsumption for making the relevant judgment.[34] In other words, the existence or non-existence of the disputed legal relationship will be determined by the current judgment in any case.[35] Regarding how to determine the relationship between the disputed legal relationship and the process of subsumption in the case, we need to go back to the grounds of substantive rights and the general methodology of law application (Chap. 4), which is undoubtedly closely related to the reasoning duty of judges.

Specifically speaking, the requirement of precedential function herein is satisfied with e.g. the confirmation of ownership of some objects in a claim for restitution of such objects, the confirmation of a contract's validity in a claim for performance, or the change of legal relationships, the confirmation of monetary principal in a claim for interest, the confirmation of the obligation for all damage in a claim for damages due to property or mental harm, and the confirmation of the effect of an assignment of creditor's substantive right.[36] If the plaintiff only claims for partial performance, the debtor may also file a counterclaim for interlocutory confirmation of the non-existence of the contract.[37]

---

[31] BGH NJW-RR 2018, 906, 912–913, Tz 65; NJW 2018, 703, 704, Tz 23.

[32] BGH NJW 2011, 2195, 2196, Tz 20.

[33] BGHZ 197, 162 = NJW-RR 2013, 873, 875, Tz 29; BGHZ 69, 37 = NJW 1977, 1637; Becker-Eberhard (2020, § 256 Rn 81). For similar opinions in Japanese law, see Ito (2019, pp. 423–425).

[34] Becker-Eberhard (2020, § 256 Rn 85).

[35] BGHZ 197, 162 = NJW-RR 2013, 873, 875, Tz 28.

[36] Roth (2016, § 256 Rn 104).

[37] BGHZ 69, 37 = NJW 1977, 1637.

It is noticed that the legal relationship of negotiable instruments does not necessarily consider the validity of its legal relationship, e.g. sales or loan relationship, which represents the cause of issuing such negotiable instruments, as its essential element. However, the validity of the relationship as the cause could become a defense against the relationship of negotiable instruments, which makes the relationship as the cause to be regarded as a precedential legal relationship.[38] And if, after the filing of an intermediate declaratory claim, the original lawsuit is withdrawn or dismissed without deciding the merits of the case, or the claims are dismissed with prejudice while there is no decision on the precedential relationship, such non-independent declaratory claim could merely be transformed into an independent claim for declaration if the elements of the independent claim for declaration are satisfied, as the non-independent claim lacks an actual affiliated relationship ("intermediate" requirement). Otherwise, if such transformation is not possible, the requirements of the proceedings (*Prozessvoraussetzung*) regarding the intermediate declaratory claim are not satisfied and the lawsuit can merely be dismissed without deciding the merits of the case.[39]

From the perspective of civil law systems, the main significance of the intermediate declaratory claim is to admit the parties' dispositional rights via bringing the lawsuit regarding the scope of *res judicata* effect.[40] As mentioned in Chap. 7, the intermediate declaratory claim represents a prudent attitude to the concept of one-time dispute resolution. In principle, the civil proceedings shall guarantee the parties' right to file a new lawsuit on the disputed issues. Only with the explicit intention of the parties and the purposed procedural safeguard of the court, could the court exceptionally resolve the precedential issues together with the subject matter of claims in the current action.[41] Besides the most ordinary approach of the intermediate declaratory claim, the party may also incorporate the precedential legal relationship into the (objective) scope of *res judicata* effect with other means. To be named are an independent declaratory claim (which needs to satisfy the independent requirement of declaration interests), which is brought up along with the claim for performance, and a title-supplementing declaratory claim (*titelergänzende Feststellungsklage*), which is brought after the claim for performance and is able to supplement the operative part of the final judgment.[42]

---

[38] BGHZ 125, 251 = NJW 1994, 1353, 1354.

[39] Roth (2016, § 256 Rn 105).

[40] In addition, the system of intermediate declaratory claim is also compatible with the parties' duty to enable a concentrated jurisdiction of the litigation *de lege ferenda*. Zhao (2017, p 115).

[41] Cao (2015a, p 133).

[42] BGHZ 183, 77 = NJW 2010, 2210, 2212, Tz 15, 18; BGH NJW 2019, 71, 73, Tz 20.

8.3.2.2 Multiple Possibilities of Reasoning Judgments

It is worth mentioning the case where the judge has multiple possibilities of reasoning their judgments. According to the German leading understanding, the aforementioned requirement of the necessity of the legal relationship in a judgment shall be interpreted loosely, and it is not necessary only to consider the legal reasoning adopted by a court. Rather, the legal relationship which is intermediately confirmed needs to be necessary and precedential for any possible reasoning approach that may be adopted by the court.[43]

For instance, the plaintiff contractor requested the defendant to pay the remuneration for the decoration project, but the defendant refused to accept the project and make the payment due to several defects in the project. After the first-instance court partially dismissed the claims of the plaintiff on the merits, the defendant, besides insisting on the dismissal of the plaintiff's claims on the merits, supplemented before the second-instance court an intermediate declaratory claim for the confirmation that the plaintiff was obliged to remedy various defects in the roof insulation works.

The Federal Court of Justice (*Bundesgerichtshof*) of Germany, enjoying the general jurisdiction and having the function of revision, held that such an intermediate declaratory claim fulfills the requirements of the proceedings. It is unnecessary to consider whether the court relied solely on a particular work defect or on the defects in the work as a whole when upholding the defendant's right to refuse the acceptance and accordingly deny the ripeness of the wage claim (Article 640 and Article 641 of the *German Civil Code*). The reason is that the judge has no obligation to choose a certain reasoning approach, and the parties could not anticipate the choice of the court. Therefore, as one of the requirements of the proceedings, the requirement of the necessity of the legal relationship should not depend on the specific reasoning choice of a specific judge.[44]

8.3.2.3 Procedural Interests Regarding Right Protection Still Needed

As mentioned above, during examining the procedural requirements of the intermediate declaratory claim, the precedential function of the legal relationship replaces the element of declaration interests regarding the ordinary declaratory claim. When having satisfied the requirement of the precedential function, the interests of claims or in other words, the necessity of protecting substantive rights should be recognized accordingly. However, even considering such declaration interests, there is still room for the procedural element of interests regarding right protection (*Rechtsschutzinteresse*) as a general requirement.[45] If the current lawsuit has fully covered

[43] BGH NJW-RR 2010, 640, 642, Tz 19; Becker-Eberhard (2020, § 256 Rn 85). On the contrary, the view that the legal relationship must be de facto an essential part of the reasoning part of the final judgment given by the court, see Foerste (2021, § 256 Rn 41).

[44] BGH NJW-RR 2008, 262, 263, Tz 11–12.

[45] Seiler (2019, § 256 Rn 28–29).

the legal relationships between the parties concerned and the object of interlocutory declaration still falls within the scope of the subject matter of claims as well as the *res judicata* effect of the original claim,[46] the court may still exceptionally deny the existence of interests regarding right protection at this moment. On the contrary, if the precedential relationship functions out of the scope of *res judicata* effect, the intermediate declaratory claim should be permitted by the court.[47] Under this circumstance, the most common situation in German judicial practice is that the parties concerned have disputes over other substantive rights within the precedential legal relationship.[48]

There is also a relatively more complicated case. Even if the multiple substantive rights raised in the plaintiff's claim and the defendant's counterclaim have covered all litigation possibilities under the legal relationships between the parties concerned (in other words, the dispute can be entirely resolved by the current lawsuit and there is no need for another lawsuit), the court may still recognize that the precedential legal relationship of these claims is eligible for an intermediate declaratory claim.[49] For instance, there was a construction contract between the plaintiff and the defendant as the construction contractor. The parties disagreed on whether the notice of rescission (*Kündigung*) sent by the plaintiff constituted a rescission for good cause (*Kündigung aus wichtigem Grund*) or free rescission (*freie Kündigung*). The plaintiff claimed a refund of overpaid moneys, additional expenses for continuing to complete the disputed works by a third party and damages for the delay of the works. The defendant filed a counterclaim for damages for the designated expert identification and photocopying fees, remaining construction price after settlement, and compensation for the unperformed part due to the rescission of this contract.

Hence, the Federal Court of Justice of Germany first held that different grounds for the notice of termination could lead to different subsequent legal consequences and thus could constitute the legal relationship which referred to the subject matter of the declaratory claim.[50] Then, the court pointed out that regarding the precedential legal relationship, it could enter a partial judgment, which was able to have a substantial *res judicata* effect on the subsequent partial judgments, if any, and the remaining judgment. The court also held that in this specific case, the causes for notice of termination constituted a precedential legal relationship with respect to the plaintiff's additional expenses after completion of the work and the defendant's compensation due to the notice of termination. A partial judgment on such causes could also avoid conflicting judgments with respect to the plaintiff's claim and the defendant's counterclaim in future. Therefore, such partial judgment satisfied the procedural requirements for the entry of a partial judgment by the court.[51]

---

[46] BGHZ 169, 153 = NJW 2007, 82, 83, Tz 12.

[47] BGHZ 125, 251 = NJW 1994, 1353, 1354; BGHZ 69, 37 = NJW 1977, 1637, 1638.

[48] Jauernig and Hess (2011, § 35 Rn 25).

[49] BGH NJW 2018, 549, 550, Tz 25.

[50] BGH NJW 2013, 1744, Tz 16–17.

[51] BGH NJW 2013, 1744, 1745, Tz 19–20. Although this German judgment does not mention that, following the court's partial judgment on the precedential legal relationship, the parties will enjoy a

8.4 Comparison of Principles of *Sua Sponte* Review and Limitation Mode

8.4.1 Internal Logic of the Limitation Mode of Res Judicata *Effect*

8.4.1.1 Different Solutions in the Limitation Mode and Expanding Mode

As mentioned, in regard to whether the determination of the validity of contracts should be incorporated into the scope of *res judicata* effect, the judicial review of the civil contracts' validity *sua sponte* in China and the civil law counterpart represented by Germany take different positions. Under the mode of expanding the *res judicata* effect in China, the court automatically expands the scope of *res judicata* effect of final judgments by exercising its authority to review the validity of contracts. It means in any subsequent lawsuit involving determining the validity of contracts, the court will no longer consider the specific litigation situation during the previous lawsuit to evaluate whether such determination of a disputed issue ought to enjoy *res judicata* effect. Thus, a relevant latter lawsuit directly confirming the validity of contracts as its subject matter of claims is supposed to be dismissed without deciding the merits of the case. Rather, in the latter lawsuit in which the validity of contracts is merely regarded as a disputed issue, the judge should take the confirmation of the contract's validity in the previous lawsuit as the basis for its further hearing and adjudication.

In contrast, under the German mode of limiting *res judicata* effect, the validity of contracts involved and confirmed in the former lawsuit could in principle be disputed again. At this time, the parties can present new evidence and arguments on the relevant issues for the first time or once again, and the case materials which were relied on by one party in the former lawsuit to obtain a favorable judgment could still be made use of. Only when one party explicitly raised an intermediate declaratory claim in the former lawsuit, the scope of *res judicata* effect of the previous final judgment could also cover the judge's determination of the validity of contracts. In other words, this intermediate declaratory claim expands the scope of *res judicata* effect.

8.4.1.2 Limitation Mode and Dismissal Judgments on the Merits

For the comparison of these two theoretical solutions, namely the *sua sponte* review in China and the limitation mode in Germany, we need to first understand the internal logic of the limitation mode of *res judicata* effect. In a claim for performance involving the validity of contracts, different approaches have their roots in the varied understanding of the relationship between the disputed issue within the entire

common starting point for further negotiations, this chapter considers that we could presume judges would agree with such observation.

claim and the claim for performance itself. For the same claim for performance, the required procedural materials may be different due to the relevant precedential legal relationships or disputed issues alleged by the parties. Different procedural materials will also lead to different directions in court hearings which indicate how the judge should manage the case. Rather than those substantive rights of legal defenses (*Einrede*) which should be actively exercised by the parties, the validity of contracts is to be regarded as a substantive ground of legal defense (*Einwendung*) which ought to be examined by the judge *sua sponte.* And from the perspective of procedural law, the party alleging the invalidity should nevertheless bear the burden of allegation and burden of proof in principle.[52]

For instance, in a contract-based claim for delivery of the subject matter of the sale or damages for breach of a contract, the judge should review all the elements of the relevant substantive rights regarding whether they arose previously and still exist currently. Only when the court considers that none of the elements can be falsified or doubtful, could it make a judgment on performance in accordance with the plaintiff's claim. However, this treatment in substantive law does not necessarily mean that the result of such review should be included in the objective scope of *res judicata* effect of final judgments.

In a dismissal judgment on the merits of the case, the validity of contracts is not necessarily the subject matter of the judge's judgment, because the judge may choose substantive matters other than the validity of contracts as grounds for denying the existence of the relevant substantive rights. When there is a precedential issue in the case, such as whether the contract has been established in the claim for monetary payment, there is no need to consider the existence of fraud as a ground for revoking an established contract if the contract has not been established in the first place.

However, when according to substantive law, some substantive matter which ought to be examined subsequently is clearly not established, examining such matter should have priority. As an illustration, when the statute of limitations for the claim has expired, there is no need to determine the defendant's liability for the disputed torts or whether there are other joint wrongdoers.[53] In other words, when the same ground of substantive rights may not be established based on multiple reasons, in principle merely the most definite and persuasive reason needs to be produced.[54] While the EU law nowadays adopts the key point theory (*Kernpunkttheorie*) which extends the understanding of the subject matter of claims, the mainstream within the German academic community remains confident in its domestic legal approach and refuses

---

[52] For example, Yuan (2021, pp 106–109).

[53] Huber (2003, Rn 397).

[54] The Federal Court of Justice of Germany has also affirmed this approach by implicitly agreeing with the attitude of the lower court in the case to set aside the issue of the validity of contracts. BGH NJW-RR 2010, 640. It is worth noting that if the traditional substantive law theory of the subject matter of claims was adopted, the number of parallel reasoning of the lawsuit that might be involved here would be significantly reduced, because where there is a concurrence of substantive rights, the different (grounds of) substantive rights would constitute independent subject matters of claims rather than reasoning of the lawsuit. For a discussion of this issue between the correlating substantive law and procedural law, for example, Zhang (2018); Zhao (2018).

to equate the precedential legal relationship with the claim for performance with respect to determining the subject matter of claims.[55] This approach adopted by the limitation mode in Germany tolerates the possibility of contradictory judgments, because if instead the scope of *res judicata* effect would be extended, it may lead to uncertainty of the judgment's effect as well as unforeseeable potential legal effects.[56]

8.4.1.3 Limitation Mode and Judgments on Performance Based on a Contract

Compared to the aforementioned dismissal judgments, the situation where the court renders a judgment on performance based on a contract is more complicated. It needs to be explained why the judge, who has the duty to examine the validity of contracts, nevertheless fails to fully discover the facts suggesting the invalidity of contracts. It should be noted that, in a contract case, although the judge has the general duty and function of conducting a comprehensive review and the specific duty and function of asking questions to the parties in this regard, the judge cannot complete such a task simply by imagining all kinds of hypothetical situations that may occur in reality. Instead, the judge has to make the legal evaluation on the basis of the facts of the case presented by the parties.

For the situation where the expression of the party's will is void due to false representation of both sides of the contract, i.e. the situation provided in Article 146 paragraph 1 of the *Civil Code of the P.R.C.*, the hidden true consensus is difficult to be identified from the false consensus itself. Rather, the true consensus could often merely be ascertained by further information provided by one party. For example, considering the case of an inter-bank discount agreement for which the bill has not been endorsed as provided in Article 102 of the *2019 Civil Conference Minutes of the SPC* (a *quasi* judicial interpretation for more detailed rules), in order to explore whether the parties hope to conclude the inter-bank discount contract or a loan contract, it is necessary to determine their true intention. Obviously, it is impossible to merely rely on the inter-bank discount contract for commercial acceptance bills of exchange. Rather, the judge must collect other facts and evidence. Alternatively, for the circumstance where the parties maliciously collude with each other to damage the interests of a third party (Article 154 of the *Civil Code of the P.R.C.*), although it is entirely possible for the judge to see through the fraud by virtue of the trial experience and previous knowledge, the review is still subject to the premise that the judge finds clues and implications of the fraud. Otherwise, it is difficult to identify whose interests are affected by the malicious contract between the parties. Even under the circumstance that a contract is null and void due to the violation of

---

[55] Althammer (2012, pp 472–473). The European approach is also rejected based on European law's special legislative purpose of harmonizing conflicts of multiple actions among member states, see also Musielak (2021, Einl. Rn 72a).

[56] BGH NJW 2003, 3058 (3059); Pohlmann (2018, Rn 701); Hahn (1880, pp 290 et seq.); against Savigny's claim for lenient *res judicata* effect, Hahn (1880, pp 607 et seq.) (Minutes).

law or public order or good customs (Article 153 of the *Civil Code of the P.R.C.*), the judge may indeed make a judgment by reviewing the factual allegations that are relevant to the conclusion and validity of contracts and have been stated by any party. Yet, further concrete facts and circumstantial evidence may be needed at this time, which still requires the assistance of the parties,[57] whether voluntarily or being forced to do as demanded.

And with respect to the legal capacity of a natural person (Article 143 paragraph 1, Article 144 and Article 145 of the *Civil Code of the P.R.C.*), which is an element for winning a lawsuit on the merits, we may at first set aside the exceptional situation where the review of the legal capacity could be completed incidentally by the review of litigation capacity of such person which theoretically belongs to the requirements of the proceedings and needs to be examined *sua sponte*.[58] When a judge is examining whether an adult has some serious mental illness, the judge should have seen the relevant factual allegations or have observed some abnormal actions during court hearings. It is difficult to imagine that a judge would require every party to submit an expert opinion or other evidence before the court, proving that all parties are not insane and capable of fully identifying their own conducts (Article 21 paragraph 1 and Article 22 of the *Civil Code of the P.R.C.*), simply because the judge must examine the validity of the relevant contract *sua sponte*.

Furthermore, for grounds of unreal expression of intent such as serious misunderstanding, fraud, coercion, and obvious unfairness (Article 147 to Article 151 of the *Civil Code of the P.R.C.*), the law directly stipulates the substantive right of revocation (*Anfechtungsrecht*) and the right of action regarding the alteration of legal rights or relationships (*Gestaltungsklagerecht*). Therefore, although the judge merely needs to determine that the contract has not been revoked while examining the existence of the relevant substantive rights, the judge does not have the authority to review the validity of legal transactions such as civil contracts on its own initiative. Conversely, the judge has the authority to review the validity only if the party exercises its substantive right of revocation by filing a claim for the alteration of legal rights or relationships on time. Similar logic applies when it comes to the rule on the contract's rescission (*Kündigung*). The judge needs to determine whether the contract is rescinded as well as whether the relevant substantive rights currently do not exist anymore and accordingly whether a liquidation relationship in the framework of obligations in a broader sense arises. Moreover, the substantive right of rescission itself still needs to be actively exercised by the parties.[59]

---

[57] In theory, whether indirect facts are the object of the principle of party presentation (Germany) or whether they are raised by the parties is not binding on the judge (Japan), the judge should exercise the power of clarification when hearing indirect facts in order to avoid the lack of procedural safeguards. Shindo (2019, pp 472–480, 587); Koichi, Kasai, Kakiuchi and Hishida (2018, pp 209–213); see Cao (2020a, pp 127–128).

[58] However, at this time, it should be insisted that the factual allegations held by the parties are binding upon the court. Yuan (2020, pp 190–192).

[59] For in-depth thinking about the invalidity, voidness and rescission of a contract, see Chen T (2020, pp. 118-140). Moreover, we should understand the claim for rescission of a contract as a declaratory claim from the perspective of procedural law, considering the rule regarding the effective date of

To sum up, although we need to acknowledge the general duty of examination of the validity of contracts, we must realize that this kind of examination is not "a tree without roots", and the judicial review must be based on clues collected from the submitted litigation materials during civil proceedings. What the judge could do is to "follow the vine to get the melon", but not to review comprehensively in each case. Going through everything is both unrealistic and unnecessary and is a waste of scarce judicial resources and may even be interpreted as unreasonable harassment to the parties concerned.

8.4.1.4 Considering Police Factors as a Special Illustration

When it comes to observing judicial reality in China, in many types of contract cases, the judges in China may also focus on the disputed issues between the parties themselves, and do not exercise their power to review the validity of contracts. In contrast, in other public order and good customs cases involving financial security, market order, national macro-policies, and so forth, the judges are likely to exercise the power to review more actively, partly out of their sensitivity regarding policy factors affecting civil procedure and their familiarity with the "mandatory provisions on validity" (Article 30 paragraph 2 of the *2019 Civil Conference Minutes of the SPC*). This not only often causes judges to reconsider whether there could be unequal treatment of the same case, but also may reflect the professional habits and styles of arbitrators with different backgrounds in commercial arbitration. We are encountering an issue of realistic choice which the adjudicators in a broad sense have always to face up to.

In fact, the aforementioned policy factors that attract special attention in specific dispute fields are accumulated by long-term trial experience. Especially, they belong to the clues that need special consideration in two types of cases, namely, cases involving pretended conducts and hidden conducts and cases involving malicious collusion to damage the interests of a third party. This can also be applied to private money lending cases, in which Article 18 and Article 19 of the *Private Lending Provisions*, which was amended for the second time in 2020, are applicable and the judge ought to examine false civil lawsuits and impose corresponding sanctions respectively. Considering that the principle of party presentation concerning factual allegations and evidence may lead to the failure of judges' examination of the contract's validity according to substantive legal rules *sua sponte*, we should also pay attention to such failure in practice and its reasons. Moreover, the hypothesis itself that the judge should have performed such an obligation of full-scaled examination on its own initiative is supposed to be reconsidered. Yet, these ideas may go across the boundary of the scientific discussion in this chapter.

---

the rescission of a contract via lawsuits according to Article 565 paragraph 2 of the *Civil Code of the P.R.C.*

8.4.2 *Scope of* Res Judicata *Effect and Parties' Dispositional Rights*

8.4.2.1 Overall Comparison

When one party explicitly intends to make a binding confirmation of the precedential relationship/the validity of civil contracts, both the Chinese rules of *sua sponte* review and the German mechanism of intermediate declaratory claims have the same effect, that is, relitigation on the validity of contracts is prohibited in principle. It does not matter whether the other party opposes it or not. In this regard, it is not appropriate to separately discuss whether the reasoning part of final judgments and the precedential legal relationship therein produce the *res judicata* effect.[60]

In China's practice, a considerable number of parties will also file an incidental claim for declaration of the validity of contracts in addition to their claim for performance, which is very similar to the intermediate declaratory claim. Under the Chinese current mode of *sua sponte* review, the judge should also specifically respond to the claim for declaration in the operative part of the judgment.[61] However, if the rule on *sua sponte* review is considered to have covered the determination of the contract's validity and have the effect of precluding another lawsuit, then the incidental claim for declaration will not enlarge the scope of *res judicata* effect. Conversely, when the party only files a lawsuit for performance, we cannot simply infer the party's intention as that such party refuses to enable the court's confirmation of the precedential legal relationship to enjoy *res judicata* effect through such party's disposition of the claims.

What determines the scope of *res judicata* effect is the parties' intention in the case, that is, the scope of the dispositional rights exercised by the parties. The difference between the German and Chinese modes is whether the parties' intention to enlarge the scope of *res judicata* effect is presumed (*sua sponte* review) or determined by filing the lawsuit by the parties explicitly (intermediate declaratory claim). Considering that the parties can determine the subject matter of claims through their respective claims/counterclaims, the German mode can expand the scope of *res judicata* effect as long as at least one of the parties expresses that the judicial determination of the contract's validity should be binding.

Hence, in cases that parties' dispositional rights are respected extremely, parties may have a veto right, that is, the scope of *res judicata* effect cannot be expanded to the validity of contracts as long as one of the parties disagrees. Neither China nor Germany adopts such an extreme solution. The reason for this is that, between the procedural justice and parties' dispositional rights, more attention is paid to the procedural justice for all parties, on which this contribution focuses on. Therefore, the right of disposition of one party is compromised to some extent.

---

[60] This tendency, for example, Yan (2017, pp 553–554).

[61] Cao (2021b, pp 209–211).

This contribution argues that the current solution where one party's right of disposition plays a decisive role in extending the scope of *res judicata* effect reflects the principle of party disposition (*Dispositionsprinzip*) in civil procedure. According to this principle, both the plaintiff and the defendant have the right to exercise their procedural right of disposition through filing a claim or counterclaim, and thus they could determine the object of the court's jurisdiction. In this sense, the attacking party is not limited to the plaintiff who files the lawsuit first, because the defendant of the case may also obtain the status of the attacking party by filing a counterclaim. Hence, both sides of civil proceedings could be regarded as equally treated during the ongoing procedure (but their rights are not exactly the same). In other words, the determination of the subject matter of claims and the scope of *res judicata* effect depend on the intention of the attacking party in civil cases, and it is unnecessary to consider the intention of the defending party.

8.4.2.2 Special Situation with Intermediate Declaratory Claims

When one party expresses the intention to extend the scope of *res judicata* effect, such scope under the German mode may even be broader than that the one under the Chinese mode. Under the German mode, after the relevant party exercises the right of disposition via an intermediate declaratory claim or a lawful counterclaim, the validity of the precedential legal relationship will be incorporated into the scope of *res judicata* effect and cannot be claimed in another lawsuit. Correspondingly, when the subject matter of a previous lawsuit constitutes a precedential issue in a latter lawsuit, the judge of the latter lawsuit will be bound by the *res judicata* effect of the final judgment in the former lawsuit.

For instance, when regarding the subject matter of claims the former lawsuit has determined the ownership of the disputed object or the obligation of performance under the contract, the claim for the restitution of the object or ordinary damages and liquidated damages for breach of contract must be based on the determination within the operative part of the former judgment.[62] Because the precedential legal relationship refers to the subject matter of the former lawsuit, both parties have already obtained the opportunity to be notified together with to be heard completely. And there will be no possibility of surprise judgments (*Überraschungsentscheidungen*). According to general principles of civil procedure, both the plaintiff and the defendant should have the opportunity to submit the substantive issues to the court for dispute settlement, or in other words, each party has a natural right of action which merely such party has the corresponding right to exhaust.[63] Whether such an opportunity exists makes a difference from the perspective of procedural law. It doesn't matter whether the relevant issues have been considered substantially and fully.

[62] BGHZ 157, 47 = NJW 2004, 1252, 1254; BGH NJW 2008, 1227, 1228, Tz 9; NJW 2003, 3058, 3059; NJW 1993, 3204, 3205 (*res judicata*); Rosenberg et al. (2018, § 152 Rn 15); Gottwald (2020, § 322 Rn 52–53).

[63] Wu (2015, p 128).

Under the Chinese mode, in comparison, the current law requires the judge to regard the contract's validity as a disputed issue and the focus of court hearings, regardless of whether the matter of the contract's validity has been clarified and suggested by the judge or how to identify the scope of prohibited relitigation. Different from the German mode where the substantive legal issues are precluded with prejudice as long as they are covered by the subject matter of claims, under the Chinese mode, these issues must in fact become the focus of court hearings and then would be precluded. If this requirement is understood as a duty of taking specific litigation conducts rather than a non-binding provision, as the consequence of this duty, failure to be the focus of court hearings should enable the relevant party to reserve the opportunity of bringing another lawsuit on such substantive legal issues.

Furthermore, from the perspective of comparative law, the scope of the German mode's claim preclusion in respect of the precedential legal relationship is wider than that of the theory of issue preclusion.[64] The reason is that the claim preclusion in the German mode does not require the relevant substantive legal issues to be heard substantially, whereas the theory of issue preclusion cannot be applied to the issue that is not heard. As a result, the requirement of the theory of issue preclusion is stricter than the aforementioned German theory of claim preclusion.

8.4.2.3 Two Procedural Scenarios Showing the Differences Between Modes

As for the determination of the contract's validity, there are still differences between the aforementioned modes. Not considering the influence of such a determination on the claim for performance while interpreting the current rules against relitigation, the differences between these two modes lie in the other two procedural scenarios, namely when the parties do not make a clear statement on the *res judicata* effect of the determination of the validity and both parties mutually oppose to bring such determination into the scope of *res judicata* effect.

On one hand, when the parties do not make a clear statement, the scope of *res judicata* effect of a judgment in China includes the determination of precedential legal relationship by default, whereas, under German law, the scope of *res judicata* effect does not include the precedential legal relationship because neither party expresses a clear intention to embrace the intermediate declaratory claim. On such occasions, we may need to consider how to justify the expansion of *res judicata* effect according to the Chinese rule. When the parties do not make a clear statement, as this contribution is to discuss in detail, the judge needs to clarify (*aufklären*) the situation and urge the parties to specify their attitude on the determination of precedential legal relationship and launch a corresponding attack or defense. In this way, we could enable the parties and their lawyers to avoid making a misjudgment if they are unclear about the procedural consequences due to the aforementioned examination *sua sponte*. This

---

64 For a detailed discussion, for example, Guo (2010); Lin (2006, pp 78–116). Comparative research, see Gottwald (2020, § 322 Rn 54 et seq.); Shindo (2019, pp 718–732); Lv (2018, pp 651–656).

kind of clarification should not only focus on understanding the parties' intentions,[65] but also correspond with the construction of *res judicata* effect under Chinese law.

On the other hand, when both parties make a unanimous statement against the expansion of *res judicata* effect (although it would be with no doubt rare in practice), it is necessary to examine whether the agreement on this objection/procedural contract is binding on the court. If such a procedural contract is not recognized, according to the general rule, the *res judicata* effect of the final judgment in China will cover the determination of the precedential legal relationship in the reasoning part of this judgment. Conversely, if such a procedural contract is recognized by the Chinese judiciary, the determination of the contract's validity in the reasoning part of the judgment will not produce *res judicata* effect. In the latter case, the scope of *res judicata* effect of civil judgments in China will be smaller, which is the same as the situation under German law when there is no intermediate declaratory claim brought before the court.

8.5 Substantial Reform of Rules of *Sua Sponte* Review of Contract's Validity

8.5.1 Issue of Contract's Validity Should Be the Focus of Court Hearings

In view of *res judicata* effect, the key to reforming the rules of *sua sponte* review in China lies in the understanding of the focus of court hearings in civil litigation. Under Chinese law, as mentioned, besides the court's independent authority to incorporate the validity of contracts into the scope of the trial, the court should also take such issue as the focus of court hearings of the case as a procedure requirement. Specifically speaking, there are three types of situations, namely where the disputed issues are considered by the parties themselves, where there is a difference between the court and the parties regarding such issues, and where a special notice should be given when the court and the parties are in agreement.

First, Article 226 of the *ICPL* provides that the People's courts shall sum up the focus of disputes based on the claim for relief of the plaintiff, defense opinions of the defendant, and the situation of evidence exchange, and collect the opinions of the parties on the focus of disputes summed up. Clarifying disputed issues is an important task for a judge during the trial.[66] In order to accelerate the procedure and to facilitate the settlement of disputes, the judge should narrow the disputed issues by sorting them out as much as possible at the pre-trial stage.[67] Such preparation for court hearings does not merely facilitate the subsequent ordinary hearings, but also

---

65 Zhang (2006, pp 137–138).

66 For example, Liu (2021); Huang (2021); Xiong (2007, pp 240–263); Qiu (2001).

67 For example, Meng (2020).

ought to be advantageous to the making of a correct and well-reasoned judgment at the end of the procedure. In cases where both parties have opposing views on the validity of contracts, whether the contract is valid or void ought to become the disputed issue of the case that needs to be thoroughly analyzed in detail by the court in the reasoning part of the judgment.[68]

Second, when there is no dispute between the parties, but the court and the parties hold different opinions, according to the first sentence of Article 53 paragraph 1 of the *2019 Evidence Provisions*, the court should also consider the validity of the civil contract as the focus of court hearings at the stage of adducing and exchanging evidence. Even prior to the *2019 Evidence Provisions*, the SPC may similarly suggest courts at all levels consider this issue as the focus of court hearings after conducting *sua sponte* review and clarifying the nature of the legal relationship (Article 36 paragraph 3 of the *2019 Civil Conference Minutes of the SPC*).[69] From the original intention of *sua sponte* review, although such focus of court hearings is attributed to the difference between the court and the parties, it could still be understood as a disputed issue of the case, and it should also be treated as a key issue in the reasoning part of forthcoming judgments.

It is worth noting that the second sentence of Article 53 paragraph 1 of the *2019 Evidence Provisions* also provides that if the court considers that the nature of the legal relationship[70] makes no difference both regarding the reasoning and the results of the judgment, "there is no need for the parties to debate this issue, and there is naturally no need for the People's court to hear this issue as the focus of court hearings".[71] Since hereby the issue of the contract's validity is not mentioned, it seems that such a rule is not applicable to the issue of the contract's validity. Therefore, as long as the judge's preliminary determination of the contract's validity differs from that of the parties, the issue of the validity must be taken as the focus of court hearings.

Furthermore, the exceptional rule that "the relevant issues have been fully debated by the parties" provided in the second sentence of Article 53 paragraph 1 of the *2019 Evidence Provisions* states that, regardless of whether the issue is raised and confronted by the parties on their own initiative or is taken as the focus of court hearings by the court itself, the parties should fully debate whether the relevant contract is valid. In other words, the focus of court hearings should secure the sufficiency of the court's debate and exhaust all possible disputes related to the validity of contracts. This could not only give the parties the opportunity to be heard and require the judge to sufficiently protect the parties' right to debate,[72] but also remind the parties that if they do not completely raise the substantive grounds that are favorable to them, they

[68] There is also a contrary practice in reality, for example, Civil Judgment of the SPC (2018) Zui Gao Fa Min Zhong No. 1345.

[69] For example, Civil Ruling of the SPC (2019) Zui Gao Fa Min Shen No. 5589.

[70] Discussing this issue in detail, see Yu (2021).

[71] The First Civil Division of the SPC (2020, p 502). The earlier viewpoint argues that, besides the inconsistent understanding between judges and parties, the necessity of changing the claims should also be considered. This idea also aims at this exceptional rule. Cao (2016, pp 116–121).

[72] Wang (2020).

may not have such opportunity to resort to them anymore in future. It means that, as long as a full debate has been completed, the court could make its judgment on the basis of its determination of the court's validity.[73] Therefore, if the parties express their opinions on the validity of contracts on their own initiative and confront each other, and the judge deems that the confrontation and debate are ripe and sufficient, the judge may directly incorporate its determination of the validity issue into the final judgment without disclosing such determination to the parties in the course of litigation.

Finally, in order to reconstruct the Chinese rules against relitigation, there could be further problems in the situation where no disputed issue has arisen either between the judge and the parties or between the parties. Under such circumstances, even if there are potential grounds hampering the validity of contracts or the case has infringed or will infringe upon the public interests or the interests of a third party, there is normally no clue for the court to conduct a further review as the parties do not disagree with each other in the proceedings. The parties and the court share the same understanding of the validity or invalidity of contracts, whereas they merely have different positions on the claim for performance based on the contract or not. Indeed, we could still recognize the judge's duty to examine the validity of contracts *sua sponte*, since "the validity of contracts, on which the legal relationship between the parties is based, is the basis of handling the dispute between the parties".[74] However, in the absence of specific doubts, there is no disputed issue for the judge to deal with. As a result, it seems that stating in the relevant final judgment that "the contract is valid since the expression of the parties' intention is true and its content does not violate the mandatory provisions of laws and administrative regulations"[75] is sufficient to satisfy the requirements of the judge's duty of examination. Nevertheless, this contribution is of the idea that, under the Chinese mode of reviewing the validity of contracts *sua sponte*, it is necessary to take such validity issue as the focus of court hearings so as to coordinate with the forthcoming procedural consequences due to the prohibition of relitigation regarding the same issue of the contract's validity.

8.5.2 Dual Significance of Becoming the Focus of Court Hearings

8.5.2.1 Understanding from the Negative Side

Taking the issue of the validity of contracts as the focus of court hearings has both negative and positive significance. On the negative side, this adjudicative technique

[73] The First Civil Division of the SPC (2020, p 503).

[74] Civil Judgment of the SPC (2015) Min Ti Zi No. 232.

[75] Civil Judgment of the SPC (2020) Zui Gao Fa Min Zhong No. 264 (a first-instance judgment).

could prevent the judge from making a surprise judgment when the parties are negligent and fail to pay attention to the legal issues of the validity of contracts.[76] By addressing this issue, the parties are given the opportunity to be heard on this issue, and their procedural rights are regarded as protected accordingly.[77] Nevertheless, in practice, it is possible that the court rather determines the contract to be invalid *sua sponte* without giving notice to the parties. In this regard, the SPC once held that "it is indeed inappropriate for the court to not clarify to the parties on the application of law regarding the validity of contracts and the relevant issue should have been debated between the parties before the court. Yet, the result of the judgment is not incorrect".[78] However, this opinion of the SPC may merely reflect the particularity of the Chinese supervision and retrial procedure as a special remedy which is rarely granted in practice. It does not represent any well-accepted judicial theory and is not appropriate to be generalized as binding precedents.

Alternatively from the perspective of literal meaning, the first sentence of Article 53 paragraph 1 of the *2019 Evidence Provisions* seems to have a certain logical inversion. That is, the court should first ascertain that it is of legal opinions different from those of the parties on a specific issue, then treat such disputed issue as the focus of court hearings. This may highlight the impropriety of "making determination before hearing the case", as if the court formally gave the parties an opportunity to be heard solely to avoid making a surprise judgment. This contribution deems that a more accurate interpretation of such provision should be as follows: if the court is to hold that e.g. a contract does not exist because the parties failed to reach an agreement (the contract is invalid in the broad sense), when the parties nevertheless alleged that the contract was valid, the court must clarify this concern to and give notice to the parties when there is doubt about the consensus of their intentions. Then the court should hear the parties' opinions, and in this way hear the issue as the focus of court hearings. In other words, the emphasis of the rule is on the necessity of hearing the relevant issue as the focus of court hearings, rather than on the chronological order of hearing the case. At this point, such a hearing with a specific focus should be regarded as the precondition for the determination of the relevant issue of the validity, which is by nature a binding norm of adjudication. In this sense, such a hearing with a specific focus should effectively become a procedural tool to facilitate the court to obtain the evaluation of evidence.

When the judge and the parties share the same understanding of the contract's validity, it is also of great significance to hear the validity issue as the focus of court hearings which is not yet established by existing legal rules. First of all, the current pre-trial preparation proceedings in China are different from the pre-trial proceedings within the continental law and common law traditions, and the ordinary

[76] Yang (2016); Duan (2011); Xiong (2008).

[77] The First Civil Division of the SPC (2020, p 502).

[78] Civil Ruling of the SPC (2015) Min Shen 1803.

trial hearings have to undertake the function of narrowing disputed issues.[79] In this regard, the court may also find that it does not accept the parties' determination of the validity of contracts during its hearings, and then determine that the validity issue should be the focus of court hearings. Especially when a collegial bench is trying the case, the presiding judge should announce an adjournment and generate the majority opinion among the judges of the panel. Then the presiding judge should conclude the validity of contracts as one of the disputed issues during the procedural stages of court investigation and court debate within the ordinary hearings.[80]

In other words, due to the dynamic nature of civil proceedings,[81] the consensus between the judge and the parties may change during the process of civil proceedings. Moreover, the judge may discover doubts about the validity of contracts through questioning and inquiring after having considered the validity of contracts as a disputed issue in the first place. On such occasions, the judge will overturn its previous preliminary determination through substantial hearings which confirm the doubts.

Second, we should pay attention to the connection between the defense strategy chosen by the parties and the trial logic decided by the judge in dismissing the case on the merits mentioned above. The defendant could merely raise the grounds which are considered to be justifiable obviously due to incorrect factual basis or legal viewpoints, such as the defense of statute of limitations, and for practical considerations such as "saving trouble", saving time or legal service costs. And the defendant does not attempt to argue from the perspective of the validity of contracts, which could cover e.g. that the contract is illegal or against good customs. However, although the court's understanding of the validity of contracts is the same as the parties, the court may have a different understanding of the defense raised by the defendant (for instance, the court believes that the statute of limitations has been interrupted). At the same time, the court does not detect any doubt about the validity of contracts, so it uphold the claims of the plaintiff on the merits. On such occasions, there could be worries about a surprise judgment. Although, in general, the defendant must raise all possible defenses, we could easily understand the reason why the defendant merely chooses several rather than all defenses. It is simply not possible to go through all possible legal grounds in all cases. Hence, if the judge could be suggested to give the parties further opportunities to supplement arguments and defenses when it thinks that e.g. the defense of statute of limitations is not established, the defendant normally will refer to further relevant legal grounds. Then, such solution would enable the court to evaluate more possible legal grounds in the same case. It should help facilitate the dispute resolution function of the current case since there would be no second lawsuit if all possible legal grounds would be discussed and determined in the first case.

---

[79] With respect to the argument for the establishment of the pretrial preparatory procedure following the *Termin*-type (rather than constituting independent proceedings) on the aforementioned basis, see Duan (2017).

[80] The First Civil Division of the SPC (2020, p 503).

[81] From the perspective of comparative law, the representative doctrine that considers civil proceedings as a series of legal statutes (*Rechtslage*) and adheres to a dynamic approach, see Goldschmidt (1925).

Finally, even if the judge of first instance shares with both parties the same understanding of the validity of contracts from beginning to end of first-instance proceedings, such a judge should also take into account the possible second-instance proceedings and other possible lawsuits and treat the validity of contracts as one of the focuses of court hearings. Although there is no surprise judgment by the judge of first instance, the court of second instance will also examine the validity of contracts comprehensively. Then it is possible that the proceedings are delayed due to remanding the case back to the first-instance court which is caused by unclear fact-finding results regarding fundamental facts of the case. To avoid such inefficient operation of proceedings, it is desirable to enhance the examination of the validity of contracts during the first-instance proceedings. In this regard, we must take seriously the scarcity of judicial resources in general as well as the human nature that a compulsory duty to reconsider the judge's preliminary judgment is hard to make a difference on the merits in the end (since a judge is now judging its own judgment). It is noted that such a judge's duty of examination is imposed by the current Chinese rules on the validity of contracts. The suggestion of this contribution is merely to highlight the necessity of the judge's "look before you leap" and the effectiveness of substantially transforming the existing rules in China, and finally to justify the expansion of *res judicata* effect which is aimed by the current Chinese rules.

8.5.2.2 Understanding from the Positive Side

In contrast to the aforementioned negative significance of treating the validity of contracts as the focus of court hearings, this treatment has positive significance as well. By being the focus of court hearings, the validity of the legal relationship can be thoroughly clarified during civil proceedings, or at least the parties should be given a full opportunity to be heard. As discussed previously, if there is a full-scale trial already in the current lawsuit, there is no need to look forward to a forthcoming lawsuit to resolve any remaining disputes.

Specifically speaking, comparing the possible defects of the validity of contracts in a specific case with the final adjudication results given by the judge, the following four procedural scenarios may emerge. First, the parties have already taken the initiative to fully prepare the issues related to the legal relationship, so that a full-scale trial could be achieved regardless of whether there are the aforementioned procedural provisions with respect to the focus of court hearings. Considering the one-time settlement of civil disputes in this case, there is no doubt that the current judgment should have the effect of excluding other lawsuits.

Second, even if the parties have not prepared for arguing or attacking the validity of contracts, when the court takes such validity issue as the focus of court hearings, the parties will be given notice.[82] As a result, the parties have improved their preparation during the proceedings, for example, one party mentions new grounds of voidness or raises new grounds for revoking the contract by means of supplementing new subject

[82] For the same viewpoint, see Ren (2020, p 134).

matters of claims. In this way, the same results in the first situation could be obtained in ordinary court hearings.

Third, even if the court has tried the case focusing on the validity of contracts or clarified the parties regarding the possibility of consolidating chief and subordinate claims under Article 36 of the *2019 Civil Conference Minutes of the SPC*, which makes the parties aware of a completely different litigation strategy based on a different determination of the validity issue, the parties may still decide to insist on their previous choice due to self-confidence or litigation strategies. They will refuse to further argue the doubtful points regarding the validity of contracts that may arise in the current case. On such occasions, hearing the case focusing on validity issue has just been superficially completed from the perspective of the court, and the substantial confrontation which is required for forming the focus of court hearings does not exist.

Fourth, although the parties have made supplementary arguments on the validity of contracts, due to their limited personal capacity or the limitations of the case, they have not discovered sufficient grounds for the non-existence, revocability, or invalidity of contracts which have been omitted in the current case. Then, whether deliberatedly or not, the parties have also not achieved substantial confrontation on the specific disputed issues of the contract's validity. Hence, the court is incapable of completing its own *sua sponte* review due to the lack of the necessary clues.

These four circumstances refer to the question of whether the court could accomplish the substantial trial of the case when there are indeed legal grounds affecting the validity of contracts according to the objective facts. From a civil procedure perspective, after losing the previous lawsuit, both parties may re-examine and review the previous lawsuit, then dig out some "reasonable" or "plausible" grounds to challenge the final judgment. This is because, prior to their own trial, the judge of the subsequent lawsuit does not have access to know the correct answer which is merely accessible after the discovery of the objective truth. This judge cannot rely on such a correct answer as the basis for its own decision.

Rather, the judge can only depend on the theory of the subject matter of claims to determine whether the claim raised in a second lawsuit regarding relevant matters is precluded by the *res judicata* effect or similar effects of the final judgment of the first lawsuit. When the determination of the validity of contracts does not become the subject matter of claims in the first lawsuit, the effect of claim preclusion may not be sufficiently supported. Especially we should consider that the parties may claim for performance and the confirmation of the contract's validity at the same time in practice, which gives a feasible example for the specification of the subject matter of claims and a clear coverage of the validity issue in the scope of *res judicata* effect of the final judgment. Accordingly, as this contribution is to develop, different rules on *res judicata* effect may be formulated respectively based on whether the validity of contracts clearly becomes the subject matter of claims.

8.5.3 Procedural Marks and Judges' Clarification Regarding Res Judicata *Effect*

8.5.3.1 Necessity of Introducing Procedural Marks

As mentioned previously, Article 53 of the *2019 Evidence Provisions* represents by its nature a substantial transformation of the rules of *sua sponte* review of the contract's validity, that is, the issue of the contract's validity should be tried as the focus of court hearings if this issue meets the preconditions stipulated in the Article 53. In this way, Chinese law could achieve the same adjudication effect in the current lawsuit whose claim for relief aims at the alleged performance as when one of the parties files an independent claim for confirming the contract's validity besides the claim for performance. Then, the procedural consequences of prohibiting relitigation could be normalized and rationalized. This solution is also in accordance with the pursued institutional aim of its comparative counterpart of intermediate declaratory claim, which is to resolve the relevant disputes once and for all in the original lawsuit. In other words, although the Chinese mode does not take the name of the intermediate declaratory claim, the adjudicative techniques of intermediate declaratory claims in other jurisdictions can be equally applied. On such foundation, this contribution further argues that even when the judge does agree with both parties, the determination of the contract's validity should be regarded as the focus of court hearings as well.

However, it should be noted that the intermediate declaratory claim under German law requires independent claims for relief and a separate place in the operative part of the final judgment, and the content of the independent subject matter of claims can be directly identified by the parties and the court, which is already adequately highlighted since the commencement of the proceedings. Comparatively speaking, the solution of trying the validity issue as the focus of court hearings under Chinese law is somehow dissimulated in the court's promotion of the proceedings, and is, to a large extent, subject to the working habits of individual judges. This practical solution still needs further efforts to be improved. If the court cannot properly inform the parties and accordingly record that the validity of contracts is the focus of court hearings, and the determination of such validity will have the *res judicata* effect, the parties may still not be able to substantially participate in the confrontation with respect to such validity issue.

Then, the appellate court in this case and the subsequent courts responsible for any relevant new lawsuits may not accurately discover the hearings and decisions which have been carried out and are likely to have been accomplished by the trial court in the previous lawsuit. Merely when the effects of their litigation activities are fully known by the parties, can they be responsible for the proceedings and results of the litigation involving them. On such occasions, a modern civil procedure system could be established.[83]

[83] Li (2010).

At the same time, the emphasis on attaching marks for such procedural steps will also have a positive impact on the performance of the judge's duty to examine the contract's validity. Judges who do not pay enough attention to such a duty will be reminded by such procedural requirements, and then think carefully about the necessity of determination the validity of contracts in their cases. In fact, both the results[84] and the process of narrowing disputed issues play a crucial role in such proceedings, on which the substantialization and refinement of civil litigation can be achieved.

8.5.3.2 Fulfillment of the Judges' Clarification

Considering that Chinese law does not explicitly stipulate the scope of *res judicata* effect of a final judgment, the judge should clearly clarify both parties that the objective scope of *res judicata* effect, which is usually limited to the operative part of the judgment, also includes the determination of the precedential legal relationship in the reasoning part of the judgment. This clarification caters to the aforementioned practice that the parties often file a claim for confirming the validity of contracts besides the claim for performance in China, and theoretically in terms of adjudicative techniques, such clarification has the substantially same function as its foreign counterparts of the intermediate declaratory claim.

In other words, treating the contract's validity as the focus of court hearings needs the cooperation of the court's clarification to the parties, whose content refers to the *res judicata* effect which the determination of the judge in this lawsuit on the relevant matters enjoys. From the perspective of litigation conducts, the judge's clarification on *res judicata* effect can suggest the parties fully produce factual allegations and evidence on the validity of the relevant contract (in the sense of conducts to be taken) and inform the parties that they are in principle not allowed to contest relevant disputes again (in the sense of the results of conducts). The situation that the parties "have not received the relevant warning of possible forfeiture in or before the previous lawsuit"[85] should be avoided, which is similar to the Japanese doctrine that "a proper exercise of the right of clarification could provide justification for expanding the effect of forfeiture".[86] Then, the Chinese solution of hearing the case with a focus on the validity issue will lay a more solid basis of procedural materials for the determination of the precedential legal relationship, and as a result, such determination is more likely to be correct. The parties will also be equipped with a procedural guarantee equivalent to the one provided by the solution of intermediate declaratory claims.

In this regard, although the first paragraph of Article 53 of the *2019 Evidence Provisions* omits the provision in its previous 2001 version that "the parties shall be

[84] For relevant discussion, see Shen (2021).

[85] Similarly, the emphasis on the argument that "EOS Company had obtained no relevant warning of losing procedural rights within or prior to the previous case" and on the existence of corresponding surprise judgments, see Yan (2013, p 106).

[86] Yamamoto (2019, p 9).

informed that they may change their claims", the way of writing the current provision should not be interpreted as an explicit prohibition of the court's clarification. Rather, the content of the court's clarification just falls into the scope of the general authority of clarification, which means the court "has the discretion to clarify".[87] This interpretation of the rule is in line with the systematic aim of one-time dispute resolution[88] in Chinese civil procedure which are discussed previously for the sake of procedural efficiency. Even from the perspective of law *de lege ferenda*, it is possible to further enhance the discretion of judges and even come back to the duty to clarify which was previously stipulated in 2001. Such potential modification of written rules could be based on the judge's authority/duty to examine the validity of contracts *sua sponte*.

Furthermore, the solution of hearing the case with a focus on the validity issue should also request recording the relevant judicial clarification within the final judgment.[89] The documentary recording of this important procedural matter not only indicates to the parties that their procedural rights have been protected, but it also indicates to the court of a latter lawsuit that the previous court has performed its duty to clarify, and that such court incorporates the determination of the precedential legal relationship into the scope of *res judicata* effect of the final judgment. In order to keep track of the judicial conducts of clarification during the litigation on time, the responsible judge may also make an oral clarification, then record it in transcripts of evidence exchange, transcripts of pre-trial meetings (Article 224 of the *ICPL*) or even transcripts of court hearings. Considering the formality and seriousness of the relevant judicial conducts, it is acceptable to issue an independent written legal instrument in the name of Clarification Order. Nevertheless, in case the court in fact completes the conducts of clarification but fails to record it accurately, the substantial interpretation shall prevail and it can refer to the issue of proving effects.[90] The court in forthcoming lawsuits shall make a substantial evaluation on whether the procedural safeguard, which the extension of the scope of *res judicata* effect to the determination of the precedential legal relationship requires, is sufficient in individual cases.

---

87 Xiong (2021, pp 172, 178–179).

88 Ren (2021a).

89 Ren (2018, pp 234–235); Cao (2015b, pp 238–239).

90 Similar issue of alleged facts in the case, see chapter 3.

8.6 Identification Rules and Nature of the Objective Scope of *Res Judicata* Effect

8.6.1 Procedural Effect of Rules of Sua Sponte *Review in China*

Under the rules of *sua sponte* review of the validity of civil contracts, whether another lawsuit for confirmation of the validity of contracts constitutes relitigation should be determined by the interpretation of the existing legal elements stipulated in Article 247 of the *ICPL*. Setting the impact of the party-related factor aside, the identification standards under Chinese law are embodied in the understanding of the three review elements: the "subject matter of claims", "claim for relief", and "substantial negation of the claim for relief". In this regard, there are various theories in the domestic academic circle and judicial practice, and the discussion of such standards is with no doubt one of the most popular and theoretically valuable issues in the field of civil procedure.

The fundamental attitude of the rules of *sua sponte* review in dealing with the issue of relitigation is that, besides the concrete claim for performance itself constituting one subject matter of claims, the subject matter of the former lawsuit also covers the existence of the entire contractual legal relationship, and any claim raised in a latter lawsuit contrary to the conclusion on the determination of the contract's validity in the previous lawsuit is to be constructed as a substantial negation of the claim for relief. In this context, when based on a valid contract, the former lawsuit demanded the defendant to continue performing its civil obligation or pay liquidated damages, both parties cannot independently file another lawsuit to confirm the invalidity of contracts, nor can they raise a new claim for performance based on the invalidity of contracts; when the former lawsuit dismisses the plaintiff's claim for performance on the merits due to non-existence of the contract, the parties cannot independently file another lawsuit to confirm the existence of the contractual legal relationship, nor can they raise a new claim for performance presuming that the contract is valid. Even if it is later found that the determination of the contract's validity is incorrect, the parties can merely redress their grievance through the supervision and retrial proceedings which is a special remedy for final judgments rather than by filing a new lawsuit.

Based on current Chinese law, what this chapter suggests previously is an additional procedural condition that the court should treat the validity of contracts as the focus of court hearings and should through its clarification make the parties aware that the scope of *res judicata* effect covers the judicial determination of such validity. Without such clarification, the scope of *res judicata* effect of the previous final judgment is still limited to the operative part of the judgment. On such occasions, the parties ought to have the right to file a separate lawsuit confirming the validity of contracts, or file a latter lawsuit based on a different determination of the contract's validity compared to the determination made by the former lawsuit. For instance, if the former lawsuit for delivery of the purchased goods according to a sales contract fails to satisfy the two aforementioned procedural preconditions, the judgment for performance of the former lawsuit will therefore not produce any *res judicata* effect regarding the determination of the validity of the sales contract in the reasoning part of the former final judgment. In a latter lawsuit where the seller claims restitution of unjust enrichment on the ground of the invalidity of contracts, the court may once again determine the validity of contracts and make a judgment demanding the defendant buyer to return the goods when the seller has delivered such goods after the former lawsuit. Hereby, the buyer still has the right to claim for refunding the price of the goods by means of a counterclaim or a new lawsuit.

It means that the existing rules of *sua sponte* review could, according to the viewpoints of this contribution, impose two procedural preconditions in addition to the requirements of Article 247 of the *ICPL*. In order to incorporate both the operative part and the reasoning part of the judgment into the scope of *res judicata* effect, China and some civil law jurisdictions have adopted different approaches. Corresponding to the aforementioned two procedural preconditions is the intermediate declaratory claim under German law which needs to be filed separately. Considering that both can determine the scope of the trial and remind the parties of such scope, supplementing these two restrictive elements to Article 247 of the *ICPL* can be upheld by the comparative legal experience.

As for the content of the aforementioned contractual legal relationship, besides the issue of the contract's validity, it also includes the circumstances where the contract is not concluded at all. For instance, when the debtor claimed for confirming the invalidity of contracts in the former lawsuit, the court dismissed the claim on the merits because the contract was not concluded. The court has a general obligation to examine the validity of contracts *sua sponte* in its hearings, and the content of the examination includes not merely the validity of the disputed contract, but also the determination of whether the relevant civil contract exists. On such occasions, rather than saying that the creditor must file a counterclaim to confirm the validity of contracts in individual cases, otherwise it will not be able to claim for the same confirmation via a new lawsuit due to the forbidden relitigation,[91] it is better to directly hold that in the former lawsuit, the issue of the contract's validity belongs to the scope of adjudication and of *res judicata* effect. While the creditor shall not file a separate lawsuit to confirm the validity of contracts, even if the creditor did claim for confirmation in the former lawsuit, neither the scope of the court's adjudication will be expanded, nor should it be held that there is insofar any compulsory obligation of bringing counterclaims under Chinese law. In the civil law systems, in principle, the subject matter of claims for declaration refers to the issue of whether the legal relationship exists or not. Such an issue could also cover the contract's validity and its establishment, which leads to the same results as the ones according to the Chinese mode.

Moreover, considering the potential complexity regarding the determination of the precedential legal relationship/the validity of contracts, it is crucial to address the situation where both parties object to extending the *res judicata* effect to the

[91] For this viewpoint, see Yan (2017, pp 554–555).

determination of the contract's validity. The arrangement for this situation could highlight the difference between the rules of *sua sponte* review in China and the system of intermediate declaratory claim in Germany. It could be argued that there should be an exceptional rule which enables the parties to file another lawsuit on the validity of contracts. Although such an exception can be fit for the Chinese practice that the court *sua sponte* requests the plaintiff to bring a new separate lawsuit to deal with some of subject matters of claims which have been brought to the current court,[92] it is more closely related to our understanding of litigation contracts and the theoretical solution of reserving the right of action based on such understanding. Furthermore, it involves the comparative methodological discourse on whether we could somehow transplant the system of express reservation by the court in the American case law,[93] even if in general, Chinese law is following the tradition of civil law systems regarding the issue of *res judicata*. Having these matters in mind, a full examination and construction deserves a place in forthcoming research out of this chapter.

8.6.2 Interpretation of Current Rules Against Relitigation

8.6.2.1 Requirement of the Subject Matter of Claims

Meanwhile, in order to establish clear rules against repeated litigations *de lege lata*, it remains essential to construct the relevant legal requirements under Article 247 of the *ICPL*, namely "subject matter of claims" and the alternative elements of "identical claim for relief" and "substantial negation of the claim for relief".

First, while interpreting the requirement of the "subject matter of claims", a claim for performance and the intermediate confirmation of the contractual legal relationship should be considered respectively. On one hand, as far as a claim for performance related to the validity of contracts is concerned, the identification standard of the subject matter of claims should be the individual grounds of substantive rights.[94] Thus, whether the former lawsuit is based on the right to claim for performance of the contract as stipulated or the right to claim damages for breach of contract, such a lawsuit is different from the lawsuit based on the right to claim restitution for unjust enrichment when the contract is alleged to be void. The reason is that in both cases, the grounds of substantive rights in civil law are different. Therefore, filing a latter lawsuit will not be hindered when it comes to the requirement of the subject matter of claims.

---

[92] For reform suggestions, see Ma (2021); for the dissenting view, see Cao (2017, pp 24–25).

[93] American Law Institute (1982, § 26(1)(b), cmt. b); Freer (2017, p 675).

[94] Shen (2015, p 635). Due to the limitation of space and subject, this contribution will not discuss the theoretical possibility of not directly using grounds of substantive rights as the identification standard, while still using some substantive law factors as the identification standard. For the long-term efforts of the German academic community in this sense, see Cao (2018a).

On the other hand, we have to consider the *res judicata* effect of the intermediate determination of the contract's validity, which is based on the rules of *sua sponte* review of the contract's validity. If the requirement of the "subject matter of claims" is hereby loosely constructed, not merely the contractual legal relationship itself, but also the relationship of restitution based on the invalidity of contracts (Article 157 of the *Civil Code of the P.R.C.*) also falls within the scope of *res judicata* effect of the previous final judgment.[95] It means that both relationships could then be covered by the same subject matter of claims. Therefore, assuming that the alternative requirement of the "identical claim for relief" or "substantial negation of the claim for relief" is satisfied, when liquidated damages based on a valid contract are upheld in the former lawsuit, the parties could neither file an independent subsequent claim to confirm the invalidity of contracts, nor bring a subsequent lawsuit for restitution of property or repayment of unjust enrichment based on the invalidity of contracts, since such a lawsuit constitutes a relitigation which is to be dismissed from the procedural perspective. In other words, this solution does not only, due to the requirements of the proceedings, preclude another lawsuit directly concerning the precedential legal relationship/validity of contracts. But it is also more likely to hold that a forthcoming claim for performance based on the determination of the validity of contracts, which differs from the determination made by the previous final judgment, will also be dismissed by the procedural law.

This, by contrast, is similar to the understanding of the transaction test under US law,[96] and nevertheless is distinct from the leading German procedure law theory on the subject matter of claims, which consists of two elements, namely the claim for relief and the factual grounds, and is generally considered to have provided a relatively looser test. According to the German leading doctrines, the substantive right to perform a contract (based on a valid contract) and the substantive right to claim restitution for unjust enrichment (based on a void contract) constitute different subject matters of claims.[97] And therefore, regardless of the comparison of the claims for relief in different cases, there is no room for applying the rules against relitigation. Exceptionally, when a party brings an intermediate declaratory claim in the previous lawsuit, the judge in a second lawsuit cannot make a determination contrary to the former decision in the intermediate claim, the operative part of which contains specific content of confirmation and is binding on any latter lawsuits. However, when the former judgment determined that the contract is valid, it is still technically allowed that a party subsequently brings a claim for performance based on the invalidity of contracts. The reason is that the claim for performance, whose preconditions include the contract's validity, is not precluded by the *res judicata* effect of a final judgment on the validity itself (the issue of the validity refers insofar to a precedential legal relationship for the latter claim for performance). On such occasions, since the contract

---

[95] Teng (2020).

[96] American Law Institute (1982, § 25 cmt. h & illus. 12–14) (modifying the attitude during the First Restatement).

[97] BGH NJW 1990, 1795, 1796 (unter I 2); Gottwald (2020, § 322 Rn 120); Musielak (2021, Einl. Rn 75).

was deemed to be valid in terms of substantive law, the judge of the latter lawsuit must dismiss the plaintiff's claim for performance on the merits rather than from the procedural perspective. Coming back to the Chinese law, if the understanding of the "subject matter of claims" is not extended to the relationship of restitution assuming the contract is valid (which this contribution also agrees), the parties could still bring a second claim for performance, which is the same as the solution provided by the German counterpart.

8.6.2.2 Requirement of the Identical Claim for Relief

Second, the requirement of "identical claim for relief" may appear in the comparison between the claims for relief of a latter lawsuit and the claim for specific performance and the claim for confirming the existence of contractual legal relationships in the previous lawsuit respectively. On one hand, when it comes to the claim for performance, as long as it refers to some substantive right for monetary performance, the requirement of "identical claim for relief" is then formally met. Even if the relevant claims in two lawsuits refer respectively to a claim for performance of the contract (based on a valid contract) and a claim for restitution of unjust enrichment (based on an invalid contract), as long as the claims aim at the performance of money, we could find the "identical claim for relief". For instance, leaving aside the aforementioned discussion on the requirement of the "subject matter of claims", we may consider that the plaintiff requested the defendant to pay a price based on a contract for the sale of specific goods in the first lawsuit. Then, it turned out that the specific goods have perished due to some reason after the first lawsuit. In the second lawsuit, the plaintiff requests the defendant to return the substituted pecuniary interests (assumed to be the same amount as the price) alleging that the sale contract is in fact void. On such occasions, it is to be interpreted that the identical claim for relief is raised in both lawsuits. Following the aforementioned limited interpretation of the subject matter of claims, even if the claims for relief in different lawsuits are the same, the latter lawsuit does not constitute the relitigation because there are different subject matters of claims in both lawsuits.

On the other hand, the claim for confirming the existence of contractual legal relationships is the target. If the operative part of the former final judgment contains the judicial answer to, in addition to the claim for performance, a determination of the contract's validity, then from the perspective of prohibiting any relitigation, the latter claim should not decide the issue of the validity once again. It makes no difference whether the operative part of the judgment itself includes a consolidation of claims or the claim for declaration is to be derived from the Chinese *sua sponte* review of the validity of contracts. However, it is noted that there is an exceptional rule specified in Article 248 of the *ICPL*. For example, if a party exercises its substantive right of changing legal relationship after the final judgment of the former lawsuit is rendered, in order to deal with the "new facts" because of such substantive rights, it is still necessary to hear the new lawsuit for confirmation on the premise that the requirement of declaratory interests is satisfied.

8.6.2.3 Requirement of the Substantial Negation of the Claim for Relief

Third, it also comes to the prospective objective of the "substantial negation of the claim for relief" rule which mainly applies to "circumstances where the latter lawsuit raises an opposite claim for relief". For instance, the SPC elaborates in its interpretation of Article 247 of the *ICPL* that "if Party A sues Party B for confirming the validity of the legal relationship, and Party B sues Party A for confirming the invalidity of the legal relationship, there then is a case of *ne bis in idem*".[98] Specifically speaking, if the plaintiff in the former lawsuit claims for the validity of contracts (in essence, for confirming the existence of the contractual legal relationship) separately or in parallel with the claim for performance, the latter lawsuit shall not claim for confirming the invalidity of contracts. As mentioned previously, the Chinese rule on *sua sponte* review of contract's validity changes the determination of contract's validity into an independent subject matter of claims. As a result, when the contractual legal relationship has been confirmed or denied in the reasoning part of the final judgment on the contract-related performance, the parties should respectively not bring any claim for positive or negative confirmation of the contractual legal relationship.

In theory, the current situation is similar to the declaratory claim which is directly opposed to the previous lawsuit (*unmittelbares Gegenteil*) under German law. That is, when the plaintiff in the former lawsuit confirms that the plaintiff is the owner of a specific object, the defendant in the former lawsuit should not file another lawsuit to confirm that this object rather belongs to the defendant; when the plaintiff in the former lawsuit confirms that the defendant has an obligation to compensate for any damage which will arise in future, the defendant should not file another lawsuit to confirm that it does not have such obligation. And it may even cover the following situation of incompatibility (*Unvereinbarkeit*): the court in the former lawsuit demands the seller in the sale contract to deliver the relevant object to the buyer, while the court in the latter lawsuit ought not to decide that the seller has the right to request the buyer to return the object on the ground of unjust enrichment based on the determination that the sale contract is rather invalid.[99]

Due to the considerable flexibility as well as unpredictability of the concept of "substantial negation of the claim for relief", Chinese judicial practice has further enriched its application after the promulgation of the *ICPL*. Its institutional innovation from the perspective of comparative law also leads to the fact that such a concept has also attracted considerable attention in the academic circle.[100] If the scope of the claim for relief having the effect of substantial negation could be broadly interpreted, then after the judgment on performance in the current lawsuit has confirmed the validity of contracts in its reasoning part, a latter claim directly for confirming validity of contracts will be excluded due to the *res judicata* effect. Moreover, a latter lawsuit for performance, which is based on the invalidity of contracts, will also be

[98] Shen (2015, p 635).

[99] Rosenberg et al. (2018, § 155 Rn 5 et seq.).

[100] For example, Zheng (2020); Yuan (2019); Fan (2019, pp 25–27).

constructed as "a substantial negation of the claim for relief", even if the claims for relief in both lawsuits are in fact different. Thus, if it is argued that other than the viewpoint of this contribution, the element of "subject matter of claims" also includes the claim for performance based on the invalidity of contracts, it is indeed possible to hold that the aforementioned latter lawsuit for either confirmation or performance constitutes relitigation, and the judge should dismiss the case without deciding the merits of the case.[101] Meanwhile, another case related to "substantial negation of the claim for relief" is that after the current court has dismissed the claim for confirming the existence of the contractual relationship, the claim for performance in accordance with the agreement of the contract in the subsequent lawsuit may also be deemed as a "substantive negation".[102]

In either case, considering the expanded *res judicata* effect under the rules of *sua sponte* review of the contract's validity (presuming that the preconditions suggested by this contribution are satisfied), the determination of the validity of contracts constitutes an independent subject matter of claims. Accordingly, such determination enjoys the *res judicata* effect which will not be excessively expanded to the claim for performance in the subsequent lawsuit. Therefore, a subsequent lawsuit directly confirming the validity of contracts shall be dismissed without deciding the merits of the case. For the claim for performance in the subsequent lawsuit which is based on the adverse determination of the contract's validity in the previous lawsuit, in accordance with the positive effect of *res judicata* effect, the court shall proceed with substantial hearings. The relevant adjudication should be given on the basis of the determination of the contract in the previous lawsuit. This means that the judge should dismiss the claim on the merits. In other words, the essential purpose of the solution advocated in this contribution is to narrow the over-generalized understanding and application of the rules against relitigation which rely on the rule of "substantial negation of the claim for relief" in China's current judicial practice.

8.6.3 Comparison of Expansion Mode of Res Judicata *Effect and Effect of Disputed Issues*

According to the revised rules of *sua sponte* review of the contract's validity, this contribution argues that the adjudicative technique of the intermediate declaratory claim under German law should be applied to the determination of the validity issue of civil contracts under Chinese law. The purpose of this revision is to preclude the review of such contract's validity in another lawsuit and accordingly, the determination of such validity is included in the objective scope of *res judicata* effect of a final judgment. For example, for a claim for performance based on a sale contract,

---

[101] However, considering the narrowing understanding of the elements of the "subject matter of claims", the latter lawsuit for performance based on the invalidity of contracts can be filed because it does not constitute the same "subject matter of claims".

[102] Xiao (2015, p 15).

regardless of whether the judge and the parties have the same understanding of the contractual relationship, the judge should regard the issue of the contract's validity as the focus of court hearings and clarify the parties regarding the expansion of *res judicata* effect in the written record.

It makes no difference whether the parties have substantially and fully confronted each other after being given the opportunity to express their opinions and being informed of the legal consequences in the hearings focusing on the validity issue. From the perspective of theoretical requirements, the German mode of intermediate declaratory claim is broader regarding the scope of prohibited relitigation than the Chinese mode and the mode of issue preclusion since the German mode does not require the relevant determination to be fully disputed or taken as the focus of court hearings. Then, regarding the interpretation *de lege lata* in China, when the opinions of the parties are contrary to those of the court, the court is not bound by the position of the parties and may examine the validity of contracts on its own initiative, or may ask questions and require the parties to ensure the completeness and truthfulness of the answers (Article 63 paragraph 1 of the *2019 Evidence Provisions*). When suspecting false litigation, the court also has the authority to collect evidence *sua sponte* (Article 96 paragraph 1 item 4 of the *ICPL*). However, the parties are the ones who know the particulars of the case best. The available hours that the judge can invest in individual cases are of scarcity, and the judge cannot dig into the truth of the case regardless of costs and deadlines. Therefore, as mentioned above, there is the possibility that the judge cannot find the right issue, cannot find specific grounds of non-existence, revocation, or invalidity of contracts and cannot conduct a comprehensive hearing.[103] Whether both the court and the parties consider that the relevant contract is valid or invalid, the judge will also face this difficulty and cannot find the clues which give rise to the necessity of having any further hearings.

The core and often controversial content of *res judicata* theory is that, in principle, its coverage depends on the scope of the subject matter of claims identified according to objective standards and is not affected by the factual allegations and evidence submitted by the parties. Both as the content of the objective and temporal scope of *res judicata* effect, the particulars that should have been raised but were not actually disputed also fall into the scope of the prohibition of relitigation.[104] As for the reason why it is necessary to enter the scope of the subject matter of claims to produce the preclusion of relitigation, the argument of this contribution is based on the unified theory of identification of the subject matter of claims, which can obtain the biggest consensus.[105] Such consideration results from the purpose of this contribution which

[103] Although a comprehensive hearing by the judge on the validity of a contract is different from a comprehensive search of different grounds of substantive rights or even different claims for performance, the two ways of handling the cases may face similar difficulties in reality. For the discussion on the necessity of fixed claims (for relief), see, for example, Zou (2010, pp 67–69).

[104] Rosenberg et al. (2018, § 156 Rn 5 et seq.). For related discussion, see Cao (2015a, pp 135–137).

[105] From the viewpoint of non-unified theory of the subject matter of claims, the suggested plan of this contribution can also be interpreted as expanding the scope of *res judicata* effect based on procedural safeguard without explicitly raising the subject matter of claims regarding the validity of contracts in the current case. For the discussion of non-unified theory, see Chen (2016).

aims to some "tiny repair and minor supplement" as far as possible within the existing civil procedure rules and theoretical framework.

As an exception to the *res judicata* rule, if the relevant grounds can constitute independent subject matters of claims, the protection of the parties' right of action in respect of their substantive rights should be prioritized. For instance, it ought to be permitted that the parties concerned, after the entry into force of the judgment on the performance of the relevant contract, exercise their substantive right to revoke the voidable contract and file a respective claim regarding the alteration of legal rights or relationships, or exercise their substantive right to rescind the contract and file a claim for the relevant performance (in the sense of repaying the economic interests paid previously).[106]

No matter which of the aforementioned situations regarding the positive significance of becoming the focus of court hearings arises after such hearings, for example, whether a substantial issue has been generated between the parties, which may then lead to the application of the doctrine of issue preclusion under Japanese law or Anglo-American law, as mentioned previously, the possible grounds for challenging the validity of contracts will be precluded. In addition to the effect of resolving more disputes at one time, as in the case of an intermediate declaratory claim, the advantage of the Chinese solution, with or without the additional elements suggested by this contribution, is that it is clear and foreseeable in the sense that it avoids the complicated situation of determining whether an issue has been adjudicated substantially.

This complexity can be illustrated as follows. Considering that the validity of contracts is related to many specific rules on the establishment and obstruction of substantive rights while the defense in civil law and the essential facts can be further subdivided in an individual case, there could be disputed issues at different levels of factual allegations. Even if we do not take the issue of law and its distinction with the issue of fact into account, it is still difficult to decide at what level the boundary of substantial hearings ought to be drawn. For instance, Buyer A, having paid the price, sues Seller B for performing the sale contract for some specific goods. In a former lawsuit, the judge completed the review that the sales contract may be invalid due to illegality but did not inquire about the legal capacity of the parties and upheld the claim of Party A for the delivery of the stipulated goods. The final judgment has been enforced by the court and the delivery has accordingly been completed. In the latter lawsuit, Seller B requested the return of the enforced goods on the ground of unjust enrichment relying on the invalidity of contracts, Seller B raised some prohibitive legal provisions which the judge had not noticed in the former lawsuit, and provided evidence of Buyer A's serious mental illness (however, in the former lawsuit, Buyer A was in the inactive stage of mental illness and the symptoms were suppressed by drugs, which was unknown to any third person).

Hence, if it would be necessary to determine the effect of issue preclusion, the court of the latter lawsuit shall determine whether the former proceedings have not

[106] For the viewpoint that the blocking effect of judgments, namely one extended effect within the system of *res judicata* effect, shall be admitted in principle, see Wang (2021).

completed substantial hearings regarding the validity of contracts. The judge needs to e.g. make a specific decision on whether the matters, which lead to the invalidity of contracts, have been substantially examined in the former lawsuit due to the review of some other provisions which could also be violated (presuming that the prohibitive provisions alleged in the latter lawsuit have not appeared in the former lawsuit). Or the judge even needs to determine whether all possible reviews of the validity of contracts should be deemed as having been completed simply because the previous lawsuit has examined some illegal matters which lead to the invalidity of contracts (presuming that the issue of legal capacity has not been considered in the former prosecution). In this respect, the effect of precluding any other repeated lawsuits under the doctrine of issue preclusion is smaller than that of the mode of intermediate declaratory claim, and it is practically difficult to determine whether there should be issue preclusion at all. Such difficulty may lead to further disputes in individual cases. Therefore, this contribution deems that the doctrine of issue preclusion shall be considered prudently in China if it was to be made use of at all.

To sum up, the goal of the theoretical solution provided in this chapter is to attempt and exemplify the symbiotic interaction between comparative legal methods and legal dogmatic methods. We should rely on the Chinese rules of *sua sponte* reviewing the contract's validity to handle the classical problem of prohibiting repeated litigations in comparative law. When it comes to the (expanded) *res judicata* effect of the determination of the precedential legal relationship, there are two substantial differences between the mode of expanding *res judicata* effect in China and the mode in Germany, namely, the explicit procedural mark and the judicial clarification of *res judicata* effect regarding the disputed issues, both of which are realized by the system of intermediate declaratory claim under German law. Because such a procedural mark and the judicial clarification have the obvious functions of procedural safeguards and could justify the *res judicata* effect of the precedential legal relationship, the Chinese mode of expanding *res judicata* effect by default should incorporate these two systems. By filling up this gap, the Chinese mode could finally allow itself to have an equal function to its foreign counterparts. Under such prospective expansion of the objective scope of *res judicata* effect, it is of necessity to reconstruct the rules of prohibiting repeated litigations under current Chinese law.

References

Albrecht H (2013) Die Streitsache im deutschen und englischen Zivilverfahren. Mohr Siebeck, Tübingen

Althammer C (2012) Streitgegenstand und Interesse. Mohr Siebeck, Tübingen

American Law Institute (1982) Restatement (second) of judgments. American Law Institute Publishers, St. Paul

Becker-Eberhard E (2020) In: Krüger W, Rauscher T, Münchener Kommentar ZPO, Band 1, 6. Aufl. C. H. Beck, München

Cao Z (2015a) Reflection on the pre-determinant force of facts. Modern Law Science 1:130–138 (in Chinese)

Cao Z (2015b) Remodeling the structure and reasoning of civil judgments. China Legal Science 4:226–246 (in Chinese)
Cao Y (2016) Essentials and effects of the exercise of the right to clarify. Contemporary Law Review 6:116–128 (in Chinese)
Cao Z (2017) On the correction of omitted judgments at first instance of civil proceedings. Law Science 7:22–38 (in Chinese)
Cao Z (2018a) Development of the German substantive law theory on the subject matter of claims: focusing on the procedural treatment of the concurrence of grounds of substantive rights. SJTU Law Review 1:33–44 (in Chinese)
Cao Z (2018b) Identifying affirmative civil claim in Chinese law. Law Science 11: 45–60 (in Chinese)
Cao Z (2020a) Models of proof of factual allegations in civil process. Journal of Soochow University (Law Edition):124–136 (in Chinese)
Cao Z (2020b) The restriction of the presumption rule of the substantial proving effects of public documents. Journal of National Prosecutors College 2:137–154 (in Chinese)
Cao Z (2021a) On the procedural principles and identification of the claim for performance: concentrating on the contents of performance. Nanjing University Law Journal 5:125–141 (in Chinese)
Cao Z (2021b) Reconsidering judicial power to examine validity of civil contracts *sua sponte* in civil process. Law and Social Development 3:205–224 (in Chinese)
Chen H (2016) New paradigm of the theory of the subject matter of claims. Chinese Journal of Law 4:170–189 (in Chinese)
Chen T (2020) Comparison of restitution effects of the invalidity of a contract and the rescission of a contract. Taiwan Law Review 12:118–140 (in Chinese)
Chen W (2020) Restructuring of the standards for defining repeated lawsuits. Peking University Law Journal 6:1596–1613 (in Chinese)
Chen X (2020) Research on systemization of effects of judgment in China with a perspective of comparative law. China Social Sciences Press (in Chinese)
Chen H, Lu P, Chao Z, Shi M (2020) The theory on the subject matter of the civil litigation under a new paradigm. China Legal Publishing House (in Chinese)
Duan W (2011) The countermeasures and implications of unexpected application of laws in Germany. Science of Law 6:190–199 (in Chinese)
Duan W (2017) On civil pretrial preparatory procedure from the perspective focusing on court hearings. China Legal Science 6:203–220 (in Chinese)
Fan W (2019) Theoretical interpretation and practice of “decision results” in repeated prosecution rules. Journal of Gansu Political Science and Law Institute 5:20–30 (in Chinese)
Foerste U (2021) In: Musielak HJ, Voit W, ZPO, 18. Aufl. Vahlen, München
Freer RD (2017) Civil procedure. Aspen Publishing, California
Fu Y (2008) Preliminary issue and interlocutory adjudication. China Legal Science 6:155–169 (in Chinese)
Goldschmidt J (1925) Prozess als Rechtslage: eine Kritik des Prozessualen Denkens. Springer, Berlin, Heidelberg
Gottwald P (2020) In: Krüger W, Rauscher T, Münchener Kommentar ZPO, Band 1, 6. Aufl. C. H. Beck, München
Guo X (2010) Study on the theory of issue preclusion in civil cases. Beijing Normal University Press, Beijing (in Chinese)
Hahn C (1880) Die gesammten Materialien zur Civilprozessordnung. Decker, Berlin
Huang Y (2021) Induction of disputed issues in civil trial: technical analysis and comprehensive application. Law Press, Beijing (in Chinese)
Huber M (2003) Das Zivilurteil. C. H. Beck, München
Ito M (2019) Civil procedure law (trans: Cao Y), 4th edn. Peking University Press, Beijing (in Chinese)
Jauernig O, Hess B (2011) Zivilprozessrecht. C. H. Beck, München

Koichi M, Kasai M, Kakiuchi S, Hishida Y (2018) Civil procedure law. Yuhikaku Publishing, Tokyo (in Japanese)
Li H (2010) Self-liability of party in civil procedure. Chinese Journal of Law 3:120–133 (in Chinese)
Li L, Yang J (2013) The nature and application of continued performance of contracts. Journal of Law Application 9:71–74 (in Chinese)
Lin J (2006) Study on the objective scope of *res judicata* effect of civil judgments. Xiamen University Press, Xiamen (in Chinese)
Liu Y (2021) The *status quo* and development of issue arrangement from the perspective of elaborate civil procedures—analysis of practices based on rules and judgments. The Jurist 2:131–146+195 (in Chinese)
Lv T (2018) Civil procedure law. Taiwan Angle Publishing, Taipei (in Chinese)
Ma J (2021) Reflection on the criteria and procedure to hear the case in another lawsuit. Peking University Law Journal 3:703–722 (in Chinese)
Matsumoto H, Ueno Y (2015) Civil procedure law. Koubundou Publishers, Tokyo (in Japanese)
Meng X (2020) Exploration and perfection of effective issue narrowing mode. Journal of Central South University (Social Science) 1:75–86 (in Chinese)
Musielak HJ (2021) In: Musielak HJ, Voit W, ZPO, 18. Aufl. Vahlen, München
Pohlmann P (2018), Zivilprozessrecht, C. H. Beck, München
Qiu L (2001) Methodology of arranging disputed issues. Sanmin Book Co., Taipei
Ren Z (2018) On the boundary of clarification in China's civil proceedings. China Legal Science 6:217–238 (in Chinese)
Ren Z (2020) Reflection and reconstruction of interpreting new litigation materials in China. Contemporary Law Review 5:122–135 (in Chinese)
Ren Z (2021a) On the boundary of the one-time settlement of civil disputes. Tribune of Political Science and Law 3:94–103 (in Chinese)
Ren Z (2021b) On the relationship between the subject matter of claims and the procedural entitlement of civil litigation. China Legal Science 2:245–263 (in Chinese)
Rosenberg L, Schwab KH, Gottwald P (2018) Zivilprozessrecht. C. H. Beck, München
Roth H (2016) In: Stein F, Jonas M, ZPO, Band 4, 23. Aufl. Mohr Siebeck, Tübingen
Seiler C (2019) In: Thomas H, Putzo H, ZPO, 40. Aufl. C. H. Beck, München
Shen D (ed) (2015) Understanding and application of the judicial interpretation of the civil procedure law of the SPC. People's Court Press (in Chinese)
Shen F (2021) Identification of the settlement result of the disputed issues and the simplified agreement for the disputed issues. In: the Civil Procedure Law Research Foundation (ed) Discussion on civil procedure (XXV). Sanmin Book Co., Taipei, pp 1–106 (in Chinese)
Shindo K (2019) Civil procedure law. Koubundou Publishers, Tokyo (in Japanese)
Teng J (2020) Application of restitution rules in the event of nullity of a contract. The Jurist 6:40–53 (in Chinese)
The First Civil Division of the SPC (2020) Understanding and application of the new provisions of the SPC on evidence in civil proceedings. People's Court Press, Beijing (in Chinese)
Wang F (2020) Review on remedy by right to debate. Law Science 10:93–106 (in Chinese)
Wang F (2021) On the blocking effect of the civil judgment. China Legal Science 3:265–286 (in Chinese)
Wang Y, Chen X (2015) The impact of the judgment of the former claim on the latter claim—analysis of article 93 and article 247 of the ICPL. ECUPL Journal 6:6–20 (in Chinese)
Wu Y (2015) The human rights nature of the right to sue—from the perspective of historical evolution. Social Sciences in China 6:112–130, 207–208 (in Chinese)
Xiao F (2015) The improvement of some problems in the ordinary procedure of first instance. Journal of Law Application 4:13–19 (in Chinese)
Xiong Y (2007) Research on pretrial preparatory procedure in civil proceedings. People's Publishing House, Beijing (in Chinese)
Xiong Y (2008) Court's obligation of pointing out its legal viewpoints in civil litigations. China Legal Science 4:119–127 (in Chinese)

Xiong Y (2021) From clarification regarding changing claims to clarification regarding legal viewpoints: analysis of article 53 of new rules of evidence in civil proceedings. Modern Law Science 3:171–182 (in Chinese)
Yamamoto K (2019) Debate on the subject matter of claims in civil procedure in Japan after World War II (trans: Shi M). Tsinghua University Law Journal 6:5–12 (in Chinese)
Yan R (2013) Localized approach on the subject matter of claims in civil procedure. Chinese Journal of Law 3:91–109 (in Chinese)
Yan R (2017) New developments on the objective range of *res judicata*. Peking University Law Journal 2:536–559 (in Chinese)
Yang Y (2016) The prevention of surprise judgments in civil actions: on orientation of modern trial theory application. China Legal Science 4:266–286 (in Chinese)
Yu C (2021) Form and substance of the determination of legal transactions. Law Science 7:97–112 (in Chinese)
Yuan L (2019) Approach to identifying repeated civil lawsuits. Law Science 9:155–167 (in Chinese)
Yuan Z (2020) On the power of investigation and evidence collection of judges in civil procedure. China Legal Science 5:184–201 (in Chinese)
Yuan Z (2021) Distributing burden of proof on disputes of liability for breach of contract—focusing on article 577 of the civil code. Law Science 5:103–114 (in Chinese)
Zhang J (2002) A legislative thinking on the intermediary declaratory judgment. China Legal Science 5:109–117 (in Chinese)
Zhang W (2006) The development of the concept of "clarification" in civil procedure. Peking University Law Journal 2:129–146 (in Chinese)
Zhang J (2018) Interpretation of the overlapping civil liability in Chinese law. SJTU Law Review 1:5–11 (in Chinese)
Zhang W (2019) Civil procedure law. Law Press, Beijing (in Chinese)
Zhao X (2017) On procedural values of declaratory claims. The Jurist 6:108–115+179 (in Chinese)
Zhao X (2018) Conflict and coordination between overlapped theories of grounds of substantive rights and of the subject matter of claims. SJTU Law Review 1:23–32 (in Chinese)
Zheng T (2020) On the structure and practice of repeated lawsuits of substantive negation type in civil procedure. Science of Law 6:165–178 (in Chinese)
Zou B (2010) Nine-step method on elements of the civil trial. Law Press, Beijing (in Chinese)

Chapter 9
Correction of Obvious Errors at First Instance

9.1 Introduction

Making complete and correct judgments is one of the most basic requirements of the judiciary. It is widely accepted that selecting disputes suitable for litigations through some case diversion mechanisms, strengthening the preparation of disputed issues and discovery of facts between the two parties during court hearings, and standardizing and improving the reasoning in judicial decisions are important issues of China's waves of judicial reforms since tens of years ago. They are also important approaches to facilitating the rule of law or the law-based governance with Chinese characteristics. However, judges may make mistakes in their judgments, and there must be follow-up issues as to how to provide remedies for the parties. Mistakes made by judges may take various forms, including substantial errors, such as unclear fact-finding conclusion and incorrect application of law, and formal errors such as wrong calculation and wrong writing (clerical errors), as well as even the omission of making judgments,[1] i.e. omission of claims raised by the claimants. Therefore, it is essential to establish different remedy approaches depending on different types and natures of these mistakes.[2]

While much attention has been paid to the procedural remedies which are aimed at substantial errors,[3] more still needs to be done to study the latter two types of errors, i.e. clerical errors and omitted claims. As far as obvious errors are concerned in this chapter, this basic procedural issue has not been given due importance. In practice, deficiencies can be often detected in judicial decisions. Specifically, although the

---

[1] [1]Discussion in detail, see Cao (2017).

[2] [1]Taking the aforementioned three systems as the same one without making any distinction, see Zhang and Zheng (2014, p. 104); Chen (2008, pp. 47–49); Cao (2006). For critical opinions, see Du (2007, pp. 78–79). For the view that different remedies should be established for civil rulings, see Hu (2014, pp. 94–156).

[3] If the court makes its judgment on some relevant claims, while one party is dissatisfied with such a judgment, it merely refers to appellate relieves rather than the omission of claims.

Z. Cao, *Civil Judgments at First Instance*, Contemporary Chinese Civil and Commercial Law, https://doi.org/10.1007/978-981-97-8662-6_9

system of correction rulings has long been created and recognized in PRC laws and practices, these rules are not stipulated by the *CPL* itself. Also, the *ICPL* merely sets forth basic rules for such rulings. In other words, Article 166 of the *1992 Opinions Application CPL* is re-promulgated in the *ICPL* after adjusting the serial number of legal provisions in the revised *CPL*. This choice preserves the consistency of the rules and practice in China while leaving the ambiguity of the original rules untouched. Hence, in order to clarify the application of correction rulings and avoid the abuse of the rules in practice, it is necessary to elaborate and perfect the system by more clearly interpreting the current rules. Therefore, we should discover the consideration behind current rules and emphasize that the object of correction rulings is the obvious errors in the judgment as detailed below.

Considering the comparative experience of common law system and civil law system as well as the judicial practice in China, this chapter deems that the current rules for correction of clerical errors shall be divided into two systems: those for correction of obvious errors and those for correction of errors in the alleged facts of judgments. The former is much more significant and should be the focus of the interpretative research. It is to be considered that under German law, the correction of formal errors aims at both obvious errors and errors in the alleged facts of judgments. As for the correction procedure, the former can be corrected *sua sponte* by the original court making the judgment or the appellate court at any time, while the latter can merely be corrected by the original court upon application of the party within a certain time limit. Taking the second type of formal errors into account is consistent with the general structure of civil judgments in Chap. 3. Similar to the German system, American and Japanese law also provide for the correction of judgment's errors.

In China, when correcting obvious errors, the court shall consider the interpretation of the judge's true intention, the standard of obviousness and the parties' needs for the correction. The applicable scope of the correction ruling can be clarified by the collected real cases in China's practice. For the sake of judicial practical need and efficiency, the scope of the judicial authority of making corrections should be expanded and correction may be initiated at any time by the court's own initiative, while the appellate judge may also rectify the errors within appellate proceedings. As for the errors in the alleged facts of judgments which is suggested by this chapter *de lege ferenda*, merely the original judges who made the original judgment can initiate the correction upon the application of the party according to the original situation, since such correction just refers to the correction of the record in the past.

9.2 Practice of Correcting Formal Errors in Civil Judgments in China

Under Chinese law, where there are clerical errors or miscalculations in civil judgments, omission or miscalculation of litigation costs, and other clerical errors, the court may correct such errors through non-appealable rulings (Article 157 paragraph

1 item 7 and paragraph 2 of the *CPL* and Article 245 of the *ICPL*).[4] If a judge finds any literal errors or faulty sentences after pronouncing or serving a judgment, the judge shall recall the judgment[5] and make corrections by means of supplementing the proofreading seal, remaking the judicial decisions or making a correction ruling (Article 54 of the *Code of Conduct for Judges*). The key issue here is clerical errors or literal errors, which are obviously different from substantial errors and omissions of claims to be rectified in the forthcoming appellate proceedings. Of course, the aforementioned correction mechanism is mainly in cases where errors must be corrected. In practice, it is also common that parties do not care about the formal errors at all, so there is no need to correct them. Furthermore, many courts hold that the aforementioned errors in the operative part of judgments cannot be rectified through any correction ruling. They deem that errors in the operative part are per se not clerical errors, and that the original judgment should be amended or revised through appeals or trial supervision proceedings.[6]

In this way, with respect to formal errors, the current law has established a system of correction rulings, which has formed a relatively stable practice since the relevant norm has remained unchanged for a long time. However, how to determine the connotation and denotation of clerical errors and arrange the concrete procedure of correction still requires further interpretation. As mentioned in detail below, the understanding of clerical errors by courts at all levels varies greatly in practice, and the appropriateness of these interpretations should depend on specific facts of individual cases. The so-called "miswriting, miscalculation and omission" are just forms of judgment errors, from which the common standard behind them should be further clarified.

In the literature, some Chinese scholars, similar to this chapter, hold that the object of correction rulings should be interpreted as obvious errors which could cover more situations.[7] Others (more extremely) criticize that the existence of correction rulings

[4] For the view that the *ICPL* expands the rules of the *CPL*, see Zhan (2017, p. 170).

[5] In practice, there has been an informal practice that the court neither recalls the judgment formally nor issues a correction ruling, but rectifies the error and puts the corrected one in the dossier of the case which is to be transferred to the appellate court. For example, Civil Ruling of the High People's Court of Jilin Province (2014) Ji Min Shen Zi No. 789.

[6] Civil Ruling of the First Intermediate People's Court of Hainan Province (2015) Hainan Yi Zhong Min Yi Zhong Zi No. 28. Li C (2015, pp. 73–75 and Fn.6) (however, the independent type of altering civil judgments advocated in this contribution deviates from Article 405 paragraph 2 of the *ICPL* literally). Such practice can also be seen, e.g., in Civil Judgment of the Intermediate People's Court of Nanjing City of Jiangsu Province (2015) Ning Shang Zhong Zi No. 571. The opposite practice can be seen, for example, in Civil Ruling of the High People's Court of Chongqing Municipality (2015) Yu Gao Fa Min Shen Zi No. 00652; Civil Ruling of the High People's Court of Shanxi Province (2014) Jin Min Shen Zi No. 224; Civil Judgment of the Beijing First Intermediate People's Court (2015) Yi Zhong Min Zhong Zi No. 3809 (recording a correction ruling on the amount of compensation after the first-instance judgment which demands the defendant to pay money. Hence, any adjustment to the compensation amount will lead to subsequent change of that amount in the operative part); Civil Judgment of the Primary People's Court of Siming District of Xiamen City of Fujian Province (2015) Si Min Chu Zi No. 460.

[7] Hu (2009, p. 72); Du (2005, p. 8).

shows in fact an institutional connivance to the judges' errors.[8] In this regard, the SPC has previously decided that "judicial decisions with inaccurate wording shall not be published" (Article 4 of the *Administrative Measures for the Proclamation of Judicial Decisions of the SPC* in 2000). Although this regulation may be reasonable and understandable due to practical situations, it can indeed be categorized as "institutional connivance" as criticized. However, the correction rulings should not be held accountable. Social common sense and general experience indicate that errors are inevitable in any kinds of work, e.g., considering "Murphy's Law" in the field of management. While errors should be prevented from occurring as much as possible, corresponding remedies should also be designed in advance so that the work affected by errors can return to the normal track as soon as possible. Hence, it is necessary to maintain and improve the system of correction rulings.[9]

Furthermore, there is also great disagreement among researchers on the procedure for making correction rulings. Some judges hold that the erroneous expression of the judgment should be corrected via a written ruling, and that the trial judge or the appellate judge shall make correction *sua sponte* or upon application of the parties, if appropriate in individual cases. Such correction is not subject to the time limit for application and the correction ruling shall have retrospective effect.[10] Another scholar argues that the right to correct the judgment should be vested exclusively in the judge who made the original judgment on the merits. The judge shall apply different time limits to different circumstances.[11]

Hence, this contribution would claim that the key to responding to the above divergences is to distinguish the types of clerical errors and clarify their respective objects of correction. Therefore, the German rules adopting this distinction are primarily to be discussed, which other comparative experience deserves attention as well, and the essence of different views is to be clarified.

9.3 Comparative Experience in Correcting Formal Errors in Civil Judgments

Using comparative methods ordinarily adopted in this contribution, the chapter would like to discuss the tradition of the civil procedure within civil law systems in Germany and Japan for the purpose of designing the above remedies. However, before going forward to the more fundamental and more experienced German law in this field,

[8] Wei (2012, p. 56).

[9] In the other direction, the analysis from judges points out that, whether or not a correction ruling is issued, the court will be accused of making mistakes, and "the court's motivation of self-correction" is to be reduced. Zhao and Chen (2015, p. 66). This could be one of the minor reasons why the judiciary is now reluctant to publish real judgments online and such issue attracted much attention in China's society at the end of 2023.

[10] Hu (2009).

[11] Du (2005).

this chapter will first give a brief introduction to the relevant system in the U.S. for the later comparison.

9.3.1 *Correction of Clerical Errors and Omissions in the U.S.*

In the U.S., clerical errors in court's decisions or other materials in the case dossier and other kind of errors resulting from omissions may be corrected by the court upon application or *sua sponte*. If the case goes to the appellate proceedings, the correction needs to be subject to the permission of the Court of Appeal (*U.S. Federal Rules of Civil Procedure*, Rule 60 (a)).[12] While clerical errors and errors of omission are hereby parallel, the latter ones leave more room for interpretation. For example, although further explanations and clarifications of the operative part of the judgment are clearly not clerical errors, courts often hold that by interpreting errors of omission, a correction can also include the case when the operative part of the judgment does not fully meet the judge's intentions.[13] Moreover, such clerical errors and omissions are not limited to mistakes of court personnel,[14] but may involve the supplement of missing materials in the court's dossier as well.[15]

Regarding the specific content, although the correction seeks the original intent of the court and the parties,[16] it should not be used to change the original judgments.[17] For example, after ordering the transfer of a certain amount of stocks, the trial court should not additionally require the debtor to pay the difference resulting from the decline of the stock price on the ground of justice in the specific case. Otherwise, the method of estimating damages chosen in the original judgment would be substantially changed.[18] The interest loss of principal creditor's rights accrued before the judgment that was not claimed by the parties or at least not upheld in the judgment cannot be

[12] If the appellate court has rendered a final judgment, the trial court does not need a leave from its superior court to make the correction. Of course, the relevant correction hereby cannot change the content of the appellate decision. Hartis *v.* Chicago Title Ins. Co., 694 F.3d 935, 950 (8th Cir. 2012).

[13] Sartin *v.* McNair Law Firm PA, 756 F.3d 259, 265–266 (4th Cir.2014); Tattersalls, Ltd. *v.* DeHaven, 745 F.3d 1294, 1297–1298 (9th Cir. 2014); Rivera *v.* PNS Stores, Inc., 647 F.3d 188, 195 (5th Cir. 2011).

[14] Pattiz *v.* Schwartz, 386 F.2d 300, 303 (8th Cir. 1968) (however, the court clerk failed to show the party's intent by failing to record an amended complaint); see 11 Wright & Miller, Fed. Prac. & Proc. Civ., § 2854 (westlaw).

[15] U.S. *v.* Stuart, 392 F.2d 60, 62–63 (3d Cir. 1968).

[16] 756 F.3d at 265–266; Niederland *v.* Chase, 425 Fed. Appx. 10, 14 (2d Cir. 2011) (emphasis the original meaning of the judgment); Agro Dutch Industries Ltd. *v.* U.S., 589 F.3d 1187, 1192 (Fed. Cir. 2009); Kocher *v.* Dow Chemical Co., 132 F.3d 1225, 1229 (8th Cir. 1997).

[17] Whitney Nat. Bank of New Orleans *v.* Smith, 613 So.2d 312, 316 (Miss. 1993) (State Supreme Court).

[18] Trahan *v.* First Nat. Bank of Ruston, 720 F.2d 832, 833 (5th Cir.1983).

corrected after giving the judgment.[19] In other words, the correction procedure for clerical errors should deal with errors that can be discovered in a formal sense. When correcting, the judge need not to consider the legal ground but the nature of the errors, the intention of the court, and the impact of the correction on the parties' substantive rights.[20] By contrast, those substantial errors should be corrected through other parallel mechanisms, such as the system for altering or amending judgments, which is required to be filed within 28 days after the judgment is given (*U.S. Federal Rules of Civil Procedure*, Rule 59 (e)) or the system of setting aside final judgments on substantial grounds (*U.S. Federal Rules of Civil Procedure*, Rule 60 (b)).

In practice, subjects of correction orders may be errors such as the standing of the party,[21] the wrong name or age of the parties, the wrong time recorded, the misplaced figures or calculation errors in the operative part, as well as other errors in the recording of expenses.[22] Regarding the relationship between the operative part of the judgment and findings of facts, if the court ruled for liquidated damages in the factual part but upheld only unpaid salaries and attorney's fees in the operative part of the judgment entered on the same day, it would be an error arising from oversight or omission that needs to be corrected.[23] On the contrary, if an allegation is not found in the factual part of the judgment, the court generally cannot simply add anything into the operative part through a correction order.[24] Instead, the court needs to seek other concrete evidence. For example, when citing the attorney's fee allocation agreement agreed upon by the parties in the factual part of the judgment, the court states that the contents of the agreement depend on the stipulation between the parties. Nevertheless, some payments were actually omitted.[25] Additionally, the object of the judgment[26] and *res judicata* effect of the judgment,[27] i.e. whether the judgment is with prejudice, are frequently in controversy.

---

[19] Osterneck *v.* Ernst & Whinney, 489 U.S. 169, 176 n.3 (1989) (dictum); Winslow *v.* F.E.R.C., 587 F.3d 1133, 1135–1136 (D.C. Cir. 2009); McCalla *v.* Royal MacCabees Life Ins. Co., 369 F.3d 1128, 1133–1134 (9th Cir. 2004). By contrast, where the trial court has in its judgment upheld a claim for interest but only leaves the concrete amount for future determination, this is then within the scope of the correction order. Pogor *v.* Makita U.S.A., Inc., 135 F.3d 384, 386–388 (6th Cir.1998).

[20] Rhodes *v.* Hartford Fire Ins. Co., 548 Fed.Appx. 857, 859–860 (4th Cir.2013) (per curiam); 647 F.3d at 193–194.

[21] Wallace *v.* Mulholland, 957 F.2d 333, 335 Fn 2 (7th Cir. 1992) (wrong defendant); Wisconsin Carpenters Pension Fund *v.* Jokipii Demolition LLC, 2007 WL 1,308,847, * 4 (E.D. Wis. 2007).

[22] 11 Wright & Miller, Fed. Prac. & Proc. Civ., § 2854 (westlaw); Note, A History and Interpretation of Rule 60 (a) of the Federal Rules of Civil Procedure, 42 Drake Law Review 461, p. 470 (1993). Calculation errors include the case where the amount of payment made by the jury is too much due to a calculation error while the judgment fully supports the plaintiff's claim: U.S. ex rel. Miss. Road Supply Co. *v.* H.R. Morgan, Inc., 542 F.2d 262, 269 (5th Cir. 1976).

[23] Chavez *v.* Balesh, 704 F.2d 774, 776 (5th Cir.1983).

[24] Rutherford *v.* Harris County, Tex., 197 F.3d 173, 190 (5th Cir.1999).

[25] Dura-Wood Treating Co. *v.* Century Forest Industries, Inc., 694 F.2d 112, 114 (5th Cir. 1982).

[26] Britt *v.* Whitmire, 956 F.2d 509, 515 (5th Cir. 1992).

[27] 548 Fed. Appx. at 860 (judgment not satisfying the requirement for the specification of facts at the case-filing stage); 647 F.3d at 194–195 (summary judgment).

There is no procedural limit on the time limit for making formal corrections. This conclusion could be drawn from the literal interpretation of the provision itself ("whenever one is found"), from the systematic interpretation which considers the explicit time limit for substantial corrections requiring a reasonable time or even within one year (*U.S. Federal Rules of Civil Procedure*, Rule 60 (c) (1)), or from ordinary judicial practice.[28] Even after a case has been appealed and even after an appellate judgment has been rendered, the trial court usually retains the power to correct clerical errors so long as the appellate court did not make its own judgment on the relevant issues.[29] By contrast, the appellate court would not correct such an obvious error on its own initiative, but might remind the party in its own judgment that the obvious errors can be subsequently corrected by an application to the trial court. Alternatively, the appellate court may also disregard the trial court's obvious error and assume that the first-instance judgment was correctly rendered (i.e., correct the error by itself) and subsequently reach its own judgment in appellate proceedings.[30]

The aforementioned authority of the judge is discretionary in nature and the judge may choose not to correct the errors. Hence, even if the statutory rule does not regulate the time limit for requesting correction, the judge can take into consideration the fact that a party is delayed in making the application, and therefore refuses to correct it.[31] Whether it is necessary to give notice to the parties also depends on the judge's exercise of discretion. However, if the correction procedure is based on the evidence that is not collected in the case dossier, the court is deemed to be obliged to give notice to all parties.[32]

9.3.2 System of Correction Order in Civil Law Jurisdictions

9.3.2.1 Overview

Comparatively speaking, the approaches in civil law jurisdictions are different. As a general rule, courts therein are bound by their own judgments and may not revoke,

---

[28] 756 F.3d at 268; 694 F.2d at 114; Scola *v.* Boat Frances, R., Inc., 618 F.2d 147, 152 (1st Cir.1980).

[29] Diaz *v.* Jiten Hotel Mgmt., Inc., 741 F.3d 170, 175 (1st Cir.2013); Klingman *v.* Levinson, 877 F.2d 1357, 1363 (7th Cir.1989); Panama Processes, S.A. *v.* Cities Serv. Co., 789 F.2d 991, 994 (2d Cir.1986); 694 F.2d at 114 & n. 2.

[30] 694 F.3d at 949–950; Prows *v.* Department of Justice, 1993 WL 118,235, * 1 (D.C. Cir. 1993); 957 F.2d at 335 Fn 2; Sarkar v. McCallin, 636 F.3d 572, 574–575 (10th Cir. 2011); In re U.S. Healthcare, Inc., 193 F.3d 151, 158 n.2 (3d Cir. 1999); Huey *v.* Teledyne, Inc., 608 F.2d 1234, 1237 (9th Cir. 1979); DeVilliers *v.* Atlas Corp., 360 F.2d 292, 295–296 (10th Cir. 1966); Brown *v.* Moore, 247 F.2d 711, 714 n.2 (3d Cir. 1957); see 11 Wright & Miller, Fed. Prac. & Proc. Civ., § 2856 (westlaw). These cases also involve, in part, the choice of remedies for both the omission of judgment and clerical errors.

[31] In re Wolverine, Proctor & Schwartz, LLC, 527 B.R. 809, 843–844 (D.Mass. 2015).

[32] Albion-Idaho Land Co *v.* Adams, 58 F. Supp. 579, 580 (D. Idaho 1945); 613 So.2d at 315; see 11 Wright & Miller, Fed. Prac. & Proc. Civ., § 2855 (westlaw).

modify, or supplement such judgments (on the negative side), and in content, other judgments at the same level within the judicial hierarchy may not deviate from this earlier judgment (on the positive side).[33] This intra-procedural binding effect targets the limitation on the capability of the same court to rescind or modify its own judgments. Rather, it has nothing to do with the nature of judgments enjoying formal *res judicata* effect which requires that these judgments cannot be challenged by a party once again.[34] Moreover, since the judgment will come into effect immediately from the declaration or service upon issuance of the judgment, this intra-procedural binding effect predates the time when the *res judicata* effect is to be recognized.[35] This general understanding undoubtedly applies to final judgments on the merits, the adjudicative techniques of which are the most typical ones among all kinds of judicial decisions.

As an exception, however, the authority of the first-instance court to correct formal errors or omissions in judgments is also recognized. On one hand, formal errors are the objects of the system of correcting judgments as discussed in this chapter. In order to accurately express the judgment expected by the court and avoid technical errors, the court which renders the judgment originally is exceptionally entitled to the limited authority to alter its own judgment. On the other hand, omissions of making judgments refer to the system of supplementing judgments (*Ergänzungsurteil*), the function of which is to cover the claims of the parties completely.

Although it may be theoretically clear, different systems of rectifying judgments could overlap during their application. Generally speaking, German law provides for two types of correction rulings, one for obvious errors (Article 319 of the *German Code of Civil Procedure*) and the other for errors in the part of alleged facts (*Tatbestand*) of civil judgments (Article 320 of the *German Code of Civil Procedure*) (Chap. 3) respectively. Under Japanese law, a ruling correcting obvious errors in a judgment can be made *sua sponte* or upon one party's application (Article 257 paragraph 1 of the *Civil Procedure Law of Japan*).[36] If the relevant legal issues affect the operative part of judgments together with the interests of the parties and a new trial is not yet necessary, the court that rendered the previous judgment may also amend the erroneous judgment *sua sponte* within one week of giving such a judgment (Article 256 of the *Civil Procedure Law of Japan*), in order to avoid the judgment being revoked by the appellate court in advance and reduce the caseload of this superior court.[37] In China Taiwan, the overall system for correcting obvious errors is similar to the German system, while, as in Japan, no particular emphasis has been placed on the errors in the part of alleged facts of civil judgments.[38]

---

[33] Rosenberg et al. (2018, § 61 Rn 1); Althammer (2018, § 318 Rn 9); Musielak (2020, § 318 Rn 3); Shindo (2019, p. 675); Ito (2016, pp. 509–510); Matsumoto and Ueno (2015, p. 601).

[34] Rosenberg et al. (2018, § 150 Rn 1).

[35] Althammer (2018, § 318 Rn 1); Musielak (2020, § 318 Rn 9).

[36] Ito (2016, p. 510).

[37] Shindo (2019, pp. 677–678).

[38] Fan (1996).

As in other chapters, the German solution is to be more considered in detail due to relevant supporting systems and the convenience of German materials, while the Japanese rules are merely briefly explained. Particularly with regard to the amendment of judgments in Japanese law is concerned, legal issues in China often involve "different understandings" between courts at different levels within the judicial hierarchy. It seems more appropriate to submit these issues directly to the relevant appellate court in order to avoid unnecessary damage to the public trust in the judiciary. If the parties do not appeal at all, it seems even less necessary to consider extraordinary remedies for correcting errors. Therefore, this chapter does not consider this procedural institution.

9.3.2.2 German Model as an Example

Obvious errors, ones of the formal errors, refer to the key to the whole system of correction rulings for judgments. The so-called obvious errors mean that hereby the intentions of the relevant courts are inconsistent with the expression in the written judgments, rather than the case where the intentions themselves suffer from certain defects. The obviousness of the errors mentioned above requires that an objective or external standard should be met. In other words, at least the party in possession of the litigation materials of the current case should be able to discover the errors by itself. Thus, the errors that can merely be detected by the adjudicating judge are not obvious enough.[39]

More specifically, correction of obvious errors requires the following. First, in terms of scope, the errors, whether caused by the party or the judge,[40] which appear in the introductory part, the operative part, the part of alleged facts or the part of reasoning, should all be corrected. However, as the errors discussed are limited to formal ones, in some borderline cases, a detailed discussion of practical cases is still necessary to avoid abusing the correction rulings.[41] Second, as for the basis for correction, other parts of the judgment, case dossiers and the *prima facie* evidence can be considered by the judge making the correction.[42] Third, since the correction procedure is merely to make more accurately disclosing the true intention of the court rather than overturning the merits of the judgment, the correction procedure can be initiated by the court that rendered the original judgment or the appellate court (depending on the factual location of the case dossier) after the judgment is published. If the case enters into the appellate stage, the appellate court may also rectify errors directly in the appellate judgment.[43] Especially in Japan, where a party issues a

---

[39] Rosenberg et al. (2018, § 61 Rn 11).

[40] Rosenberg et al. (2018, § 61 Rn 8); Shindo (2019, p. 676).

[41] Althammer (2018, § 319 Rn 16); Musielak (2020, § 319 Rn 8); Feskorn (2020, § 319 Rn 18). Japanese law also does not distinguish errors in the operative part and the reasoning part of civil judgments: Ito (2016, p. 510).

[42] Musielak (2020, § 319 Rn 7); Shindo (2019, p. 676).

[43] Althammer (2018, § 319 Rn 22, 30); Musielak (2020, § 319 Rn 15); Ito (2016, p. 511).

legitimate appeal upon merits of the case, an immediate complaint, i.e. a procedural appeal, is not admissible, as an appellate judgment would be sufficient to grant reliefs (Article 257 paragraph 2 latter sentence of the *Civil Procedure Law of Japan*). The correction is issued in the form of a ruling, i.e., a formal hearing is not required and whether the judge is to meet the parties is determined upon the circumstances of the relevant error. Lastly, in terms of the effect, the correction of a judgment can be made retroactively to the time when the judgment was originally issued.[44] An appeal against a correction ruling can also be brought in the form of immediate complaint (Article 319 paragraph 3 of the *German Code of Civil Procedure* and the first sentence of Article 257 paragraph 2 of the *Civil Procedure Law of Japan*), which requires the appellate judge to reconsider whether the conditions for granting a correction ruling are sufficient and whether an obvious error could be found. Nevertheless, the appellate judge ought not to review the merits of the ruling itself.[45] On the contrary, neither German law nor the Japanese leading opinion allows the parties to seek relief for an application for correction which has been rejected substantially (Article 319 paragraph 3 of the *German Code of Civil Procedure*).[46]

On the other hand, as far as the errors in the part of alleged facts within the judgment are concerned, only the court that has rendered the judgment has the authority to correct it upon the party's application. As introduced in Chap. 3, the part of alleged facts of German judgments corresponds to the part of "it is ascertained upon trial" or "the court ascertains that" within the judgments given in China. However, the Chinese system is aimed at the findings as the judge has investigated and convicted the facts of the case, while the German counterpart considers the facts alleged that have not been evaluated by the court.

When it comes to the procedure for correcting the errors in the part of alleged facts within the judgment, the application for correction of such errors has to be made within two fixed weeks after the service of the judgment. The judgment cannot be corrected at all after three months from its issuance, unless the revision court deems that the criteria for reviewing violations of the laws can be met (Article 320 paragraph 2 of the *German Code of Civil Procedure*). If the case proceeds to a substantial hearing, i.e., the application for correction has been admitted by the court, the judge will decide whether to hold a hearing. It is noteworthy that, due to legislative changes, the decision to hold a hearing before making the correction ruling no longer depends on the application of the parties (Article 320 paragraph 3 of the *German Code of Civil Procedure*, deleted since 2020).

In this procedure, the evidence does not have to be examined (Article 320 paragraph 3 sentence 1 of the *German Code of Civil Procedure*), which leaves no room for admissions by a party. Rather, the memory and notes of the original judges and the

---

[44] Rosenberg et al. (2018, § 61 Rn 17); Shindo (2019, p. 677).

[45] Althammer (2018, § 319 Rn 46).

[46] The Leading opinion in Germany, see BGH NJW-RR 2004, 1654, 1655; Musielak (2020, § 319 Rn 25); Feskorn (2020, § 319 Rn 41). The leading opinion in Japan, see Shindo (2019, p. 677). The dissenting minor opinion, see Ito (2016, p. 512). Unlike under the German law, both Japanese authors admit the possibility of an appeal against a procedural rejection (Article 328 paragraph 1 of the *Civil Procedure Law of Japan*).

court transcript are to be relied on (Article 314 paragraph 2 sentence 2 of the *German Code of Civil Procedure*).[47] A correction ruling must be made by the judges who rendered the original judgment (Article 320 paragraph 3 sentence 2 of the *German Code of Civil Procedure*). Once the original sole judge or the entire collegiate bench is unable to participate in the correction procedure, there is no other choice but to exceptionally deny the binding effect of the part of alleged facts in order to guarantee the parties' claim for judicial protection.[48] Such a correction can also be traced back to the time when the original judgment was given. However, before an appellate judgment or a correction is given, the correction of alleged facts of the case does not affect the rest part of the original judgment (Article 320 paragraph 4 of the *German Code of Civil Procedure*). Since the evidential evaluation and factual findings are major constitutional elements of the reasoning part within the judgment, the correction does not alter them as well, which were based on alleged facts of the case.[49] Finally, in principle, such a correction ruling is incontestable (Article 320 paragraph 3 sentence 4 of the *German Code of Civil Procedure*).

9.3.3 Chinese Observation Based on Comparison

The comparative law experience is helpful in responding the different thinking of by Chinese scholars on the procedure of correction ruling. Similar to the aforementioned distinction among formal errors, substantial errors and omissions of claims on the merits, the correction procedures for obvious errors and errors of alleged facts should also be distinguished in academic discussions.[50] They have distinct targets and functions, while they refer to different possibilities of parties' disposition. Considering the aforementioned experience of civil law systems, correcting obvious errors can be initiated *ex officio* by the court without any time limit, and these errors can also be examined by the appellate court and should be excluded as far as possible (however, such appellate review would not lead to remand or revocation of the original judgment). On the contrary, correcting errors in the part of alleged facts within the original judgment can be initiated merely upon application by the parties and with a time limit. Errors of this kind can only be corrected by the judge(s) giving the original judgment. Such corrections should base on the intention of the parties and need to take the principle of orality and immediacy into account. In conclusion, this split solution partly answers the controversy among Chinese scholars about the subjects making the correction and whether the time limit should be set. That is, different rules should be applied to these two procedures of correction.

---

47 Althammer (2018, § 320 Rn 19); Musielak (2020, § 320 Rn 10) (interpreting the old laws: Musielak (2016, § 320 Rn 9)).

48 BVerfG NJW 2005, 657, 658–659; Althammer (2018, § 320 Rn 22).

49 Althammer (2018, § 320 Rn 11); Musielak (2020, § 320 Rn 11).

50 On the contrary, for the view that there is no distinction between the two systems, see Hu (2009, p. 71); Du (2005, p. 10).

Meanwhile, the aforementioned comparative law systems can also remind us of the mutual points of correcting judgment's errors in continental and common law legal systems. To sum up, the correction systems in both legal systems are mainly aimed at formal obvious errors within judgments, while their function is mainly to make the judgment in line with the judge's original intention, rather than to substantially modify the content of existing judgments. There is no time limit for the correction ruling, and the errors usually can also be corrected during the appellate proceedings.

It is to be emphasized that the function of comparative law experience is to provide ideas for analysis and solution for reference. Intended to perfect China's correction ruling system, the existing practice in China should be considered as of more importance as well. The forthcoming discussion needs not merely to confirm the real practice in China, but also to provide alternative solutions in real cases to reduce the errors that arise in correction rulings. In this sense, although the chapter does not intend to transplant the foreign rules and practices into Chinese law, comparative law approach as introduced can also enrich the theoretical explanation of the existing rules in China.

9.4 Possibility of Improving System of Correction Rulings in China

9.4.1 Objects of Correction Rulings

9.4.1.1 Clear Cases in Judicial Practice

Following the aforementioned Chinese rules that have been clarified in the *CPL*, relevant judicial interpretations and other normative documents, the main issues to be discussed here are the definition of formal obvious errors and the convenience of the correction procedure. There would not be much controversy if the object of correction rulings under Chinese law is labeled as obvious errors. Hence, the next step is to discuss the scope of application of the correction ruling, while the purpose of the prospective reform is to reduce the judge's discretion and to perfect rules of the *CPL*.

In judicial practice in China, it is very common to correct formal obvious errors through correction rulings. Specifically speaking, these errors can be identified as follows: wrongly written Chinese characters; incorrect personal[51] or corporate

[51] For example, Civil Judgment of the Intermediate People's Court of Wenzhou City of Zhejiang Province (2014) Zhe Wen Zhi Min Zhong Zi No. 2.

name,[52] gender, date of birth,[53] identity[54] or address of the party; wrong cited number in the part of facts of the judgment; numbers,[55] titles or manners of legal citation in the part of law application of the judgment[56]; omissions in list of property in dispute[57] or other content of the operative part of the judgment[58]; wrong case docketing number of the current case in the procedural part of the judgment,[59] or wrong docketing number in the operative part indicating the revoked judgment,[60] the number of the judges[61] or the judge's signature.

Considering that the process of making judgments is all electronic, and a lot of structured judgments or fixed expressions are almost the same, it is almost inevitable that the computer cutting and pasting of the responsible judge would result in a careless mismatch of context. These errors, which are obviously abnormal in the context of individual cases, are, of course, obvious errors.[62]

---

[52] For example, Civil Judgment of the Intermediate People's Court of Guiyang City of Guizhou Province (2014) Zhu Min Yi Zhong Zi No. 219.

[53] For example, Civil Judgment of the Intermediate People's Court of Xingtai City of Hebei Province (2014) Xing Min Si Zhong Zi No. 603.

[54] For example, Civil Ruling of the Primary People's Court of Ganjingzi District of Dalian City of Liaoning Province (2015) Gan Min Chu Zi No. 637.

[55] Since the statutes in China may be revised frequently, considering that e.g. the *CPL* is revised almost every two years recently, it is extremely possible that during the transitional months after the revision takes effect, the judges may be busy with giving correction rulings to rectify the number of the frequently cited legal provisions within the *CPL*.

[56] The so-called wrong citation manner mainly refers to the non-standard reference to legal provisions, which may with no doubt occur in practice.

[57] For example, Civil Judgment of the Intermediate People's Court of Jiangmen City of Guangdong Province (2014) Jiang Zhong Fa Min Zai Zi No. 8. It is noteworthy that although after the judgment of first instance, the trial court has made a correction ruling by adding the missing items of the operative part, the court of retrial still revoked the original first-instance and second-instance judgments in full and made the correct operative part of the judgment instead. It means that the original judgment would have been correct after the correction afterward (and should be sustained). But the court at higher levels may rewrite the operative part of the judgment for the purpose of avoiding misunderstandings.

[58] For example, Civil Ruling of the SPC (2014) Min Shen Zi No. 646 ("Dismissing … claims on the merits" shall be corrected as "Dismissing … all other claims on the merits").

[59] For example, Civil Ruling of the Primary People's Court of Ganjingzi District of Dalian City of Liaoning Province (2014) Gan Min Chu Zi No. 5597. Furthermore, the judgments of two cases shared the case number of "(2015) Dan Min Chu Zi No. 651" on the Internet (the difference of the two cases is whether there are brackets or not; searched on 9 February 2016). If there is such similarity in the judgments formally served on the parties concerned, a ruling of correction needs to be given.

[60] For example, Civil Ruling of the SPC (2015) Min Shen Zi No. 826 (the case number of the first-instance case that was to be revoked was mistakenly taken as the case number of the second-instance case in the judgment).

[61] Civil Ruling of the Intermediate People's Court of Huaihua City of Hunan Province (2014) Huai Zhong Min Er Zhong Zi No. 315.

[62] For example, Civil Judgment of the Beijing High People's Court (2014) Gao Min (Shang) Shen Zi No. 4007 (the mistake hereby resulted from copying another ruling made by the same court a

As for litigation costs, "omission of litigation expenses" as stipulated in Article 245 of the *ICPL* means that the court has already made a judgment on the allocation of litigation costs but has failed to indicate such costs in the judgment. This kind of errors needs to be corrected by a correction ruling as well.[63]

However, in certain borderline cases, the true intention of the court and judge shall be ascertained depending on the specific circumstances of the case. For example, which of the brothers Zhang A or Zhang B is the successor of the a specific item in the operative part of the judgment in an inheritance case; whether the disputed object is the house No. 134 or No. 143 in a property right case[64]; the width of the real estate which is the subject matter in the case; that the credit which passed the limitation of statute in a contract case is wrongly indicated as another credit; whether the statutory provisions cited are primary rules or the exceptional rules (or two provisions with similar constitutional elements are cited); whether the provisions are incorrectly written when cited or provisions applied are incorrect rules at all.

9.4.1.2 Borderline Cases and Need for Interpretation

On these occasions, the judge may consider the theory of interpretation of declaration of intention (*Willenserklärung*) in the civil substantive law and may consider other parts of the judgment and the procedural supporting materials such as the court hearing transcripts. For example, the reasoning part of the second-instance judgment may indicate that there is a calculation error in its operative part. However, considering the specific composition of the damages awarded in the first-instance judgment comprehensively, it can still be ascertained that the court of second instance merely failed to explain the calculation composition of damages in the operative part. Hence, this second-instance case does not contain a miscalculation.[65] If a court's ruling directly cites the content of one or more legal provisions[66] that have no relationship to the specific case, a clerical error could be detected. For example, in the dispute over the allocation of compensation for expropriation of the contracted land,[67] the legal provision corresponding to the loan contracts was cited, or the rule on the withdrawal of appeal was cited in the second-instance judgment.[68] However, if the two legal provisions concerned are similar and only one of them can be applied in the disputed case, e.g., Articles 16 and 45 of the *Law of the P.R.C. on the Contracting*

few months ago. Also, the expression "to sum up" was used in the ruling of this case while there was actually no reasoning).

[63] The different interpretation, see Zhao (2008, p. 89). For a different theoretical view that litigation costs should not be the object of a supplementary judgment, see Hu (2011, pp. 173–174).

[64] Fan (1996, p. 458).

[65] Civil Judgment of the High People's Court of Shandong Province (2013) Lu Min Zai Zi No. 5.

[66] For example, Civil Ruling of the SPC (2015) Min Shen Zi No. 1 (Article 58 of the Old *Contract Law of the P.R.C.*).

[67] Civil Ruling of the High People's Court of Guizhou Province (2014) Qian Gao Min Shen Zi No. 634.

[68] Civil Ruling of the High People's Court of Hubei Province (2014) E Min Shen Zi No. 01128.

of Rural Land corresponding to different contracting methods, there may be legal application errors in substantive law and reasoning errors in procedural law. The errors should be corrected in the reasoning part of the judgment by the appellate or retrial court while upholding the judgment of the lower court as a whole (Article 405 paragraph 1 the second half of the *ICPL*). This error is not simply a clerical one. Hence, it cannot be corrected through a correction ruling merely on the ground that the operative part of the judgment is correct.[69]

Similarly, some courts hold that if it is not clear from the reasoning part of the judgment that the first-instance court considered the unpaid house loan as joint and several debts, evaluating the result of divorce property division is necessary. When the division can be regarded as having reflected the aforementioned loan, there should be no formal error or omission in judgment.[70] Of course, a better approach at this time may be to provide other materials to prove that the court of first instance has considered the aforementioned debt, such as the hearing transcript or other materials to which both parties have access. Yet, materials such as deliberation records of the collegial panel belong to trial secrets which need to be collected in the secretly preserved dossier, while such materials may not help determine the extent of the obviousness of the relevant errors. Therefore, if e.g. the hearing transcript proves that the court of first instance heard two amounts of payment in dispute (one was omitted in the judgment) but dismissed the claims on the merits in the end, it can be deemed that the first-instance court has respected the plaintiff's right of disposition,[71] and merely the reasoning in the judgment is insufficient. This interpreting approach may also help avoid wasting judicial resources in cases that the responsible judge has already tried the case substantially.[72] After all, if the judge's real intention can be ascertained, a correction ruling is more efficient and more convenient than a supplementary judgment on the omitted claims or another lawsuit.

Yet, such an approach has its limitations as well. It is mainly applicable to the situation where a sole judge makes a judgment instantly after the court hearing, and under such situation, since the court hearing is relatively coherent, it is presumed that the judge adheres to the judge's original opinion. On the contrary, if the judge chooses another date to make the judgment, it is hard to be sure that the judge has not changed the original opinions between hearing the case in the courtroom and writing the judgment in the office. When it comes to a collegial bench hearing, there

[69] An example of such improper practice, see Civil Ruling of the High People' Court of Guizhou Province (2014) Qian Gao Min Shen Zi No. 634.

[70] Civil Judgment of the Intermediate People's Court of Weifang City of Shandong Province (2014) Wei Min Zai Zhong Zi No. 8.

[71] Civil Judgment of the Intermediate People's Court of Jinan City of Shandong Province (2014) Ji Min Yi Zhong Zi No. 157 (the transcript of court hearings confirms that the case has been tried as normal). German law also admits the possibility of making correction based on sources as are available to the parties: Musielak (2020, § 319 Rn 7); Feskorn (2020, § 319 Rn 6).

[72] Similar position in the U.S.: 636 F.3d at 575. Japanese scholar Ito Makoto also points out that if such errors are not corrected by some simplified proceedings, the scope of *res judicata* effect may be unclear and the trust (of the parties and the general public) in court's decisions may be impaired. Ito (2016, p. 510).

may also be a time difference between the court hearing and the collegial panel's deliberations. The judges have the opportunity to consider further materials, argue their viewpoints and even debate with each other. As original ideas mentioned above are unlikely to be adhered to, there should be no *prima facie* evidence regarding the consistence of judge's thoughts. Hence, the standard of obvious errors could not be met. In particular, a case "tried" and "judged" cannot be regarded as equivalent. Since it is still possible for a case to be tried but not judged, the latter one does involve the omission of making judgments.

From a different perspective, some situations, which are regarded as clerical errors in judicial practice, may be worth further consideration because these errors are not obvious enough. Regarding procedural issues, when the second-instance judgment lists one of the appellants as the appellee and does not indicate the appellate grounds of that party, it appears from the judgment that the judge does merely consider an appellant as an appellee. If there are no other materials for further explanation, such error cannot be regarded as a clerical one to be corrected by a correction ruling.[73] Also, if the first-instance judgment applies the ordinary proceedings but is signed by merely one judge, it would be extremely difficult to prove from materials available to the parties that there was indeed a collegial panel for discussions and deliberations (after all, the hearing transcript can only prove that the collegial panel held a hearing together). Hence, there is no alternative but to remand the case as a serious procedural violation.[74]

With respect to the fact-finding issue, if the correction ruling deletes some factual statement, e.g. "it is also found out that Du Gang and Chen Shurong are husband and wife",[75] or replace "conclude and sign" with "sign to acknowledge the receipt",[76] it is necessary to reaffirm whether the finding in the original judgment is completely fictitious, or alternatively, the correction involves substantive law issues or factual and evidential issues. If the latter is the case, it will then not fall into the category of obvious errors.

There are even more circumstances which are more inappropriate to be considered as obvious errors. For instance, the court ruled that the defendant's tractor and trailer were covered by one compulsory auto liability insurance, but later the court changed

[73] For cases under such circumstances, see Civil Judgment of the Intermediate People's Court of Shenzhen City of Guangdong Province (2014) Shen Zhong Fa Fang Zai Zi No. 46.

[74] With respect to such correction by the appellate court in practice, see Civil Ruling of the Intermediate People's Court of Huaihua City of Hunan Province (2014) Huai Zhong Min Er Zhong Zi No. 315 (the court of first instance made a ruling to correct the errors within its own judgment, while the court of second instance revoked the judgment and remanded the case for retrial). On the other hand, the judgment of second instance upholding the correction ruling regarding the erroneous signature of the collegiate bench member, see Civil Judgment of the Intermediate People's Court of Shaoguan City of Guangdong Province (2014) Shao Zhong Fa Min Yi Zhong Zi No. 1021.

[75] Civil Ruling by the Primary People's Court of Ganjingzi District of Dalian City of Liaoning Province (2014) Gan Min Chu Zi No. 3830.

[76] Civil Judgment of the SPC (2013) Min Ti Zi No. 128.

one to two through a correction ruling. And due to the increased coverage of property damages by the compulsory auto liability insurance, the corresponding indemnity amount of the third-party liability insurance would be reduced accordingly.[77] Although car owners are obliged to buy the compulsory auto liability insurance, it does not mean that they must have actually purchased the insurance. If there are no other materials supporting that the court does find two copies of such insurance in the first place, this kind of error should not be regarded as a clerical error.

Furthermore, after making a judgment based on the parties' settlement agreement, the court of first instance then changed the identified nature of the disputed contract (from "de facto affiliation relationship" to "de facto labor subcontracting relationship") through a correction ruling and additionally decided that the contract was terminated. While the court of second instance denied the legality of this correction ruling, this superior court also affirmed the original judgment on the ground that the appellant raised no objection to the operative part of the judgment.[78] From a substantive law perspective, the relevant "de facto affiliation relationship" and the "de facto labor subcontracting relationship" have different legal consequences and the legal identification of the disputed contract indicates the major disputed issue between the parties. The termination of this contract is also a substantive law issue. Hence, even in the part of facts of the judgment, these errors in the eyes of the first-instance court are not suitable to be changed via a correction ruling.

And the same incorrect situation happens with regard to the relationship between the judgment and the claims. If the plaintiff changes the amount of interest loss for five months to that for four months and the court still determines the compensation for five months, the judgment already exceeds the claim of the plaintiff and therefore should be regarded as a wrongful judgment on the merits. Although it merely concerns one-month loss of interest, it shall not be corrected simply by a ruling.[79] Finally, as for the case where the bus emergency braking causes damage to the plaintiff who claimed for relevant damages, the "failure to reduce the amount of CNY 22,140.4 paid" obviously constitutes an error on the merits. Again, the trial court should not rely on a correction ruling to rectify the substantive error in its judgment.[80]

---

[77] Civil Judgment of the Primary People's Court of Luozhuang District of Linyi City of Shandong Province (2014) Lin Luo Min Yi Chu Zi No. 1244.

[78] Civil Judgment of the Intermediate People's Court of Shenzhen City of Guangdong Province (2014) Shen Zhong Fa Fang Zhong Zi No. 1307.

[79] Regarding such improper practice, see Civil Ruling of the High People's Court of Zhejiang Province (2013) Zhe Min Shen Zi No. 1359.

[80] Civil Ruling of the High People's Court of Shanxi Province (2014) Jin Min Shen Zi No. 698.

9.4.2 Convenience for Correction and Judicial Efficiency

When the error concerned is obvious, the convenience for court to correct the error and the corresponding judicial efficiency shall also be taken into account. The "obviousness" of formal errors means that they should be objective existing and verifiable without going forward to a court hearing. Considering the court which detects the error and where the case dossier is located, it should not be emphasized that merely the first-instance courts or even the judges making first-instance judgments have the authority to make corrections. For example, if a party is not satisfied with clerical errors and applies for retrial on the ground of these errors, the court of retrial can directly issue a correction ruling to correct the errors, even if the errors do not meet the existing statutory grounds of opening retrial proceedings.[81] In addition, the fact that Chinese law does not allow a party to appeal merely against a correction ruling (Article 157 paragraph 1 item 7 and paragraph 2 of the *CPL*), shows that the current law takes into consideration the nature of the possible appellate reliefs, institutional functions of the correction ruling, and the characteristics of the correction procedure.[82] Hence, the dissatisfying party may merely appeal against the first-instance final judgment during the appeal period, while within the ongoing appellate proceedings, this party can attach additionally the appeal against the correction ruling.[83] After all, correcting obvious errors shows the judicial system's effort to clarify the intents of individual judges in individual cases. Such obvious errors should not be made at all. Once made, they should also be corrected as quickly and conveniently as possible. Moreover, the comparative experience of both common law and continental legal systems suggests that it would be better to correct obvious errors directly through the appellate proceedings.

As for the controversial question of whether the operative part of a judgment can be corrected, according to this contribution, it is necessarily to elaborate the standard of "obviousness". There is not simple answer regarding whether the operative part, which refers directly to the judicial decision made on the merits, is suitable to be rectified without going forward to appellate proceedings. In fact, unless the claim is dismissed entirely, a miscalculation will usually lead to changes to the amount determined in the operative part. If the amount of the operative part is not allowed to be changed via a correction ruling, the possibility of using this ruling to rectify a miscalculation is in principle denied. Such a negative answer would be contrary to the original purpose of establishing the system of correction rulings.

Hence, considering the specific circumstances of individual cases, if a simple calculation error can be found from the pleadings, hearing transcripts and other parts of the judgment, the amount determined in the operative part can certainly be corrected through a correction ruling. We may have these cases in practice as well.

---

[81] For example, Civil Ruling of the High People's Court of Jiangsu Province (2014) Su Shen San Min Shen Zi No. 0411.

[82] For a detailed discussion on the basic principles of the civil relief mechanism, see Pan (2015).

[83] For example, Civil Ruling of the Intermediate People's Court of Zhoukou City of Henan Province (2015) Zhou Min Zhong Zi No. 286.

For example, there is a miscalculation when "CNY 2,000,000" is wrongly written as "CNY 20,000,000,000"[84] or the court determines that the appellee has served for 15 years, but the compensation is calculated based on service time of 12 years.[85] Since the court has already cited the rule that liquidated damages for breach of contract shall not exceed 30% of the loss caused, it is obviously wrong to calculate the liquidated damages based on 130%, different from 30% of the loss as cited.[86] Furthermore, if the real estate certificate number of a house has been already indicated in the operative part of the judgment and a court then gave a correction ruling to add its determination of ownership of this house, such correction is rightful.[87]

For the same reason, the necessity for making any correction should be affected by the parties' willingness of correcting errors. In order to maintain the seriousness of civil judgments and satisfy the party's request, the court ought to rectify the errors concerned and even issue the correction ruling when any of the parties desires the correction. However, if the parties do not care about the errors, correcting them *sua sponte* could be hardly significant in practice, since the correction makes no difference for all relevant persons and to realizing the correction may consume the precious judicial resources. The correction may be inefficient when it comes to the cost–benefit-analysis.[88] Hence, it would be better for the judge to decide on the discretion whether to correct the relevant formal errors. From another perspective, the correction *sua sponte* means that the initiation of the correction procedure is not subject to the application of the parties. However, the party's intention still has to be considered when deciding whether corrections should be made. If the parties have already settled the dispute between them, and they do not care about the specific wording of the judgment, there is no strong reason for the court to make a correction ruling and arrange for service for this ruling just to correct e.g. the name or address of the parties. For example, if the plaintiff expressly waives the claims within second-instance proceedings,[89] there is no need to correct following the intention of the parties. After all, it is common in practice for judgments to be flawed in one way or another,[90] while the Chinese civil justice has to constantly face up to the conflict between the scarcity of judicial resources and the rising demand for protecting private rights. What the court should strive for is not merely the justice in all individual cases, but also the optimal allocation of limited resources.[91] As the old saying goes:

[84] Civil Judgment of the SPC (2014) Min Yi Zhong Zi No. 108.

[85] Civil Judgment of the Intermediate People's Court of Xuzhou City of Jiangsu Province (2014) Xu Min Zhong Zi No. 00547.

[86] Civil Ruling of the SPC (2015) Min Shen Zi No. 493.

[87] Civil Judgment of the Intermediate People's Court of Jiangmen City of Guangdong Province (2014) Jiangzhong Fa Min Zai Zi No. 8.

[88] Methodological insights, see Wagner (2009); Shavell (1995).

[89] Civil Judgment of the Intermediate People's Court of Wuxi City of Jiangsu Province (2014) Xi Min Zhong Zi No. 2263 (considered as an omitted claim).

[90] The situation found based on the evaluation of real judgments shows that obvious errors exist generally in practice. Of a sample of 560 judgments published online, more than 90% were found to have major or minor problems. Li X (2015).

[91] Similar developments in the United Kingdom, see Sorabji (2014).

"Good steel should be used in the knife's edge". Similarly, the American rule as introduced regards the power to correct judgment as a judicial discretion which reserves flexibility for the judge.

Yet, in aforementioned cases such as the correction ruling against errors in the operative part of the judgment, the fundamental requirement of the service system and the procedural justice of the judgment should still be upheld. Even, it is arguable in such an exceptional circumstance that the time limit for bringing appeals needs to be renewed after the service of a correction ruling (according to the viewpoint in this contribution, there is a legislative leak which needs to be filled). Otherwise, for the party who suffers a disadvantageous change through a correction ruling, the judgment will lack legitimacy and acceptability, while it is highly likely to intensify the conflicts between the parties and even between the parties and the court. How would the plaintiff who had previously won the case feel and respond, if, suddenly half a month after service of the judgment, the plaintiff received a correction ruling pointing out that the real judgment between him and the defendant was to dismiss all the claims brought? Maybe the judge is just careless and makes a clerical error, but this error is enough to create a very bad social perception.

9.4.3 Correcting Errors in Part of Alleged Facts Within Civil Judgments

Finally, this contribution argues that, although most jurisdictions do not establish any special proceedings to correct the errors in the part of facts within civil judgments, we can still take account of the aforementioned German experience in China. No matter whether the function of judicial decisions in China would change from determining and confirming to recording and proving in future, as discussed in Chap. 3, the part of alleged facts within judgments will have a probative force to the relevant facts due to either the probative force of written judgment as public documents (Chap. 5) or the preliminary effect of effective judgments (Chap. 7). Yet, these relevant facts here may be the facts "ascertained" by judges in the current proceedings, or the facts "alleged" by the parties. Under the doctrine of legal truth as the fact-finding standard, the facts found by the judge are not necessarily the same as the objective truth. Rather, the judge may also take undisputed factual allegations of the parties as the basis for the discovery of the facts.[92] Therefore, the parties' attitudes toward the part of facts within judgments should be taken into consideration, and the judge does not need to correct error there *sua sponte*. According to this leading understanding in China, the Chinese system can also learn from the means of correcting facts within judgments adopted by its German counterpart. On the contrary, under the doctrine

[92] Advocating pursuing the objective truth in civil proceedings, see Zhang (2012); Jiang and Wu (2002, pp. 25–28). Under the theory of objective truth, the obligation of the judiciary to discover the truth is much stronger than the situation when merely the legal truth is the procedural aim. Hence, perhaps correction of errors *sua sponte* is a more theoretically consistent solution hereby.

of objective truth as the fact-finding standard, judicial authorities are more obliged to find the historical truth. Hence, correcting errors on the court's initiative may be a more theoretically consistent choice.

However, after all, the part of alleged facts of the written judgment is supposed to be a restatement of original trial proceedings, which cannot be supplemented or corrected even by the consensus between the parties afterward. Also, the materials for any potential correction is limited to persons involved in the original proceedings and records of these proceedings. Meanwhile, since the part of alleged facts may affect the appellate proceedings of this case or the proof of relevant factual allegations in another lawsuit, the correction of such errors cannot be made at any time but shall be limited to a certain deadline. There should be a period of time for the parties to discover the errors in the first place and then to apply for correction, while it should be not hard for parties to discover errors since they must be very familiar with the case and the entire civil proceedings before the court. Therefore, it is argued in this contribution that, according to the usual practice of setting a time limit in China and the aforementioned comparative law experience, a deadline of 15 days after the judgment is served would be appropriate.

In addition, due to the nature of formal errors, there is no need to establish an extra appeal system for the correction ruling as discussed. It makes no difference whether the clerical errors or errors of alleged facts are concerned. Finally, in terms of the relationship between such correction and the supplementary judgment system for omissions of making judgments, since the supplementary judgment is based on the complete record of claims of the parties in the part of alleged facts of judgments, errors in the part of alleged facts shall be rectified first. And merely then, the supplementary judgment can be considered and adopted.[93] On many occasions, it is precisely because the part of alleged facts within the judgment fails to record a certain claim that the omitted judgment occurs.[94]

References

Althammer C (2018) In: Stein F, Jonas M, ZPO, Band 4, 23. Aufl. Mohr Siebeck, Tübingen

Cao S (2006) On the procedure for correcting defects in civil judgments. People's Judicature 6:58–61 (in Chinese)

Cao Z (2017) On the correction of omitted judgments at first instance of civil proceedings. Law Science 7:22–38 (in Chinese)

Chen X (2008) Remedy of defects and supplementary remedies of rights: procedure for correcting defects in civil judgments. Journal of Law Application 9:46–49 (in Chinese)

Du R (2005) On correcting judgments. Journal of Southwest University of Political Science and Law 2:7–11 (in Chinese)

Du R (2007) On the legal meaning and issues of supplementary judgment system. People's Judicature·11:78–82 (in Chinese)

[93] BGH NJW-RR 2005, 790, 791; Musielak (2020, § 321 Rn 7).

[94] Situation in Germany, see Jauernig and Hess (2011, § 58 Rn 38).

Fan K (1996) Correction of judgments. In: Discussion on civil procedure law (I), Sanmin Book Co., Taipei, pp 439–477 (in Chinese)
Feskorn C (2020) In: Zöller R, ZPO, 33. Aufl. Otto Schmidt, Köln
Hu X (2009) Errors in statements within judicial decisions and their correction. Journal of Law Application 10:70–73 (in Chinese)
Hu X (2011) Omission within civil judgments and its relief. In: Zhang W (ed) On civil procedure, Volume 6. Xiamen University Press, Xiamen (in Chinese)
Hu S (2014) Research on civil adjudication. Social Science Academic Press, Beijing (in Chinese)
Ito M (2016) Civil procedure law. Yuhikaku Publishing, Tokyo (in Japanese)
Jauernig O, Hess B (2011) Zivilprozessrecht. C. H. Beck, München
Jiang W, Wu Z (2002) A legal philosophical analysis of some basic problems of the law of evidence. China Legal Science 1:24–38 (in Chinese)
Li C (2015) Value recognition and practice ideas on 'altering' civil judgments at the second instance. Journal of Law Application 2:71–75 (in Chinese)
Li X (2015) The status, problems and countermeasures regarding civil judgments published online. Science of Law 4:191–201 (in Chinese)
Matsumoto H, Ueno Y (2015) Civil procedure law. Koubundou Publishers, Tokyo (in Japanese)
Musielak HJ (2016) In: Krüger W, Rauscher T, Münchener Kommentar ZPO, 5. Aufl. C. H. Beck, München
Musielak HJ (2020) In: Krüger W, Rauscher T, Münchener Kommentar ZPO, Band 1, 6. Aufl. C. H. Beck, München
Pan J (2015) On the basic principles of establishment of civil procedural rights relief mechanism. China Legal Science 2:29–42 (in Chinese)
Rosenberg L, Schwab KH, Gottwald P (2018) Zivilprozessrecht. C. H. Beck, München
Shavell S (1995) The appeals process as a means of error correction. The Journal of Legal Studies 24:379–426
Shindo K (2019) Civil procedure law. Koubundou Publishers, Tokyo (in Japanese)
Sorabji J (2014) English civil justice after the Woolf and Jackson reforms. Cambridge University Press, Cambridge
Wagner G (2009) Ökonomische Analyse der Rechtsmittel. In: Bork R, Eger T, Schäfer HB (eds) Ökonomische Analyse des Verfahrensrechts: Beiträge zum XI. Travemünder Symposium zur ökonomischen Analyse des Rechts. Mohr Siebeck, Tübingen. pp 157–193
Wei S (2012) Face-to-face reasoning, strengthening rhetoric and focusing on major issues: some thoughts over how to improve court decisions in China. Science of Law 5:48–60 (in Chinese)
Zhan S (2017) Errors of expressions in civil judgments and their correction. Law Science 8:164–173 (in Chinese)
Zhang Y (2012) Objective truth values are the soul of the evidence system. Law Review 1:38–44 (in Chinese)
Zhang J, Zheng L (2014) Reorganization and optimization of the remedy procedure for omissions in civil judgments. People's Judicature 9:102–106 (in Chinese)
Zhao Z (2008) Supplementary judgment system of omission in civil judgments. Tribune of Political Science and Law 5:84–93 (in Chinese)
Zhao R, Chen B (2015) Rational responses to the 'post-judgment effect' under the background of judicial decision going online. Journal of Law Application 8:65–70 (in Chinese)

Chapter 10
Context of Civil Judgments and Procedural Arrangement

10.1 Introduction

Besides civil adjudicative techniques which refer to civil judgments themselves directly, the supporting factors of making a proper civil judgment are also able to play an important role. They mainly include two aspects: judicial system and litigation mechanism. Regarding the judicial system, court organization, judicial openness and non-legal factors represented by lawsuit-related petitions via letters and visits are worthy of further attention. And when it comes to the litigation mechanisms, judicial mediation and the interaction between the different stages of a civil process and their corresponding adjudicative techniques present the targets of this chapter. Moreover, the overarching aim of the ongoing judicial reform in China which is to separate the complicated cases from the simple ones and to classify civil proceedings accordingly, may affect the application of adjudicative techniques as well. The purpose of this chapter is to pursue other factors related to adjudicative techniques from an external perspective, and to find out the possible impact of these factors on obtaining civil judgments with good quality.

10.2 Judgment-Related Judicial System

10.2.1 Court and Judges

10.2.1.1 Quality of Judges

The persons who are making judicial decisions and applying the related adjudicative techniques are the courts in general and individual judges. Hence, the specific situation of the court organization will affect the system of civil judgments in practice. To

Z. Cao, *Civil Judgments at First Instance*, Contemporary Chinese Civil and Commercial Law, https://doi.org/10.1007/978-981-97-8662-6_10

begin with, the quality of judges will make a great difference. The level of adjudicative techniques applied is directly related to the judge's professional knowledge and general knowledge. How judges in individual cases understand the world and social life, will be reflected in the judgments on the merits they made. The premises of a better civil judgment would be that the judge should not merely master the procedural theories represented by the theory of civil claims, including e.g. the subject matter of claims, preconditions of a claim which is legally brought into the court. But the judge has also to correctly apply the principles and rules in the field of substantive law, and then sufficiently and effectively develop the judicial arguments for reaching the desired conclusions.[1] The relationship between adjudicative techniques in China, which are mainly related to continental law systems which are seen as models for China to follow, and the real situation in China's transitional era (especially the *status quo* of Chinese judges), has become a relatively explicit problem in China. Although the ability of judges in China has been on the rise for a long period of time, theoretical misunderstandings and arbitrary behaviors in practice are still widespreading. Such situations hinder the further improvement of making good judgments in general.

Of course, this is not to ask the judge to be responsible for judgments of poor quality. Rather, the deficiency in legal research, legal education and judicial training could all act as the major impetus for having inadequate judgments. When the academic community has not yet developed mature adjudicative techniques, and when the scholars have not predicted the possible occurrence of dispute and provided the preliminary analysis in advance, and even when the existing research results have not been widely and timely disseminated within the judiciary, the practical judges' efforts alone cannot turn the tide. Yet, since the judges are the ones who are hearing the cases and adjudicating the disputes, the group of judges is the most direct element which affects the quality of civil judgments.

Generally speaking, the more theoretical and abstract adjudicative techniques for better judgments are more acceptable to the new generation of judges (with formal legal training, higher education, and relatively limited time immerged in practice). On the contrary, it is less attractive to senior judges who have long relied on their social experience to handle cases. Some senior judges are even subject to path dependence on their old-day habits before the gradual construction of rule-based state, and hence, have doubts and go against developing more adjudicative techniques. In fact, this kind of generational difference is widely reflected in various kinds of issues, such as judges' views on using judicial mediation, professionalism within civil justice and so forth. Even without considering the natural generational replacement within the group of judges in the following period of time, it is still believed that formal adjudicative techniques are general tools and methods while making judicial decisions, which should be universally applied to all judges. With no doubt, the adjudicative techniques for better judgments proposed in this contribution do not

[1] Comparatively speaking, China requires judges to achieve good results at the levels of law, society and politics at the same time, which undoubtedly puts forward higher requirements for judges than merely applying adjudicative techniques. For example, Zhu Suli believes that, facing China's complex judicial issues, judges should have more wisdom, enthusiasm and creativity, even if from a pragmatic point of view rather than an ideological point of view. Zhu (2010, p. 188).

mean to deny senior judges' judicial intuition based on long-term trial experience, nor to challenge the balance of interests in civil justice which takes the sophisticated human nature and attitudes of various interest groups into account. Nevertheless, to be considered is merely that judges can follow a unified way of thinking and rules of reasoning based on laws, i.e. substantive and procedural ones.

Another issue could be, for various historical or personnel reasons, the proportion of judges who in fact give judgments in all qualified judges was not very high not long ago. Many qualified judges turned to engage in administrative work for various reasons. Many excellent judges were promoted to be leaders at different levels and the number of cases they handled decreased or even they ceased to take cases. Some passive judges even chose to skip their job through long-term sick leave. Even the judges who were active in adjudicating cases would have to face up to a series of practical problems such as a lack of assistants, many social activities other than hearing cases and political study, and complex judicial management and so forth.[2] Although other assignments could be beneficial for judges or the general public, it is hard to deny that what a judge could do best is hearing and adjudicating cases.

When it is difficult to optimally allocate judges as a kind of scarce resources, the direct result is that judges who were actually engaged in trial job may not have enough time and energy to polish their decisions delicately. Hence, not to mention that the possibility of making judgment's mistakes greatly increases, the opportunities to develop adjudicative techniques which are beneficial for better judgments in future would be even less. After the reform of judicial accountability and the judge quota system, the situation in reality has been improved to a certain extent, but new phenomena, e.g. whether there is a large group of judges leaving the judiciary,[3] and other problems[4] may occur. In any case, the allocation of judicial powers and the judge system are crucial for promoting good judgments.

10.2.1.2 Judicial Credibility

The authority of the court in the civil society and the confidence of the ordinary citizen in the judiciary will also affect the application of adjudicative techniques for better judgments in practice. The level of judicial credibility directly affects the acceptance of the parties and the general public of civil judgments, and also determines the demand for adjudicative techniques of the judiciary. Under the ideal situation, where judicial decisions were fully trusted by all parties concerned, there would be no need to develop a delicate set of adjudicative techniques. It would be fine as long as some competent authority could decide right and wrong and relevant responsibilities. In this sense, the jury system in Anglo-American law systems could provide a living example since a jury is allowed merely to make a judgment without giving any reason. On the contrary, when the court users doubt or even mistrust the judiciary,

[2] For relevant analysis, see He (2013, p. 5) (Judge He spoke for a new judge quota system).

[3] For example, Zhang (2018); Li (2018); Liu (2015).

[4] For example, Wu (2019); Chen (2018); Fu (2015).

only decisions that conform to the adjudicative techniques could (at least partially) dispel their doubts and win their trust back. The reason is that the procedural and substantive principles behind the adjudicative techniques represent rules of the laws applying to everyone, while the requirement of reasoning ensures that the judgment's results are rational and justified.[5]

Under the principle of hearing according to the laws, judges should not merely apply the laws following the aforementioned adjudicative techniques, but also need to rely on adjudicative techniques to find facts in dispute. In this way, we may avoid errors of judgments caused by inherent cognitive limitations of human beings. When it comes to the objective truth in the real world, although with the help of life experience, judges may in the end find the objective facts in most cases, the occurrence of errors is still only a matter of time and probability based on the so-called Murphy's Law in management science.

Hence, other external mechanisms must be introduced to remind the decision-makers and even reduce the possibility of making errors. Specifically in the field of civil procedure, these mechanisms could be the requirement of fact-finding based on the evidence, free evaluation of evidence and related systems of proofing. Even the judge's professional conscience, which is extended from the general ethics, as well as the system of limited judicial accountability,[6] may become a feasible means to solve some difficult cases.

In addition, some adjudicative techniques can also help clarify the boundaries of the judge's judicial power, such as reshaping the powers and responsibilities between the case-filing judge and the trial judge, or the competent scope of the judge which is to be restricted both by any related judgment prior to the current lawsuit and the parties' disposition in the current lawsuit. This function shows the necessity of taking the adjudicative techniques seriously.

Of course, just like the aforementioned discussion of judges' ability, the lack of public trust in courts in the transitional period of China's society cannot be entirely blamed on the courts themselves. Rather, we have to take notice of the limited role that courts play in the dispute resolution mechanisms in China, since there are other public organs (including the internal mechanisms of the CPC) that share the power and responsibility of the judiciary. And the controversies before the courts are indeed diversified and intensified. Under the generally accepted *status quo* of "Too many cases but too few judges" within the Chinese judiciary, whether to develop the potential from the internal or to divert the pressure out of the judiciary, may nevertheless give rise to new difficulties. The process of trying to deal with such difficulties, in other words normalizing the current judicial practice, will even generate new challenges.[7]

---

[5] Wang (2018, p. 2).

[6] Lu (2020).

[7] Yu (2019).

10.2.1.3 Judicial Professionalism?

Meanwhile, the allocation of judicial power which is against professionalism and following partially the logic of administrative power will have a negative impact on the application of adjudicative techniques in reality. What is concerned here is not merely the usual adjudication tasks, but also applying adjudicative techniques to specialized trial work.

As far as the former is concerned, the fundamental problem is how to understand and implement the principle of judicial independence with Chinese characteristics. In China, the judiciary as a whole rather than individual judges is considered independent.[8] Hence, in some cases, the "judges" in the sense of decision-makers are not the members of the collegial panel who hear the case in person. Rather, they are e.g. members of the judicial committee (审判委员会) of the relevant court.

From the procedural principle of orality and immediateness, these formal "judges" are obviously limited considering their contacts with litigation materials and the court hearings themselves. And the possibility of making correct judgments is bound to be greatly reduced. And for the members of the collegial panel, as the adjudicators signing the effective judgments, it would be hard for them to improve the quality of related judgments, whether in terms of their enthusiasm for reasoning or their inability to disclose the real reasons for making such judgments. These problems may be more obvious in cases in which the opinion of the collegial panel is different from that of the court's president, the prevailing conclusion of the judicial committee, or the one of the specialized judges' conference.[9] For these cases, it is probably a natural outcome that the development of adjudicative techniques is seriously affected in general.

As for the latter, this contribution only takes commercial litigation as an example, which will face increasingly specialized requirements in future. From the experience of comparative law, the design of specialized commercial trial organizations has been widely recognized for the need to introduce specialized knowledge and speed up litigation proceedings.[10] In recent years, dozens of countries and regions have

---

[8] For example, Chen (2013). The analytical framework of judicial independence in China focusing on the diversified solutions based on types of cases, see Fu and Peerenboom (2012).

[9] The SPC released *Guiding Opinions on Improving the Mechanism for Professional Judges' Meetings of the People's Courts* in January 2021. The Guiding Opinions stipulates systems for specialized judges meetings of different scales, and replaces *the Guiding Opinions on Improving the Working Mechanism for Presiding Judges' Meetings of People's Courts* (For Trial Implementation) issued by the SPC. In the meantime, Articles 18 and 19 of *Implementation Measures for the Pilot Program of the Reform of Improving the Trial Levels and Functional Orientations of Courts Structured in a Four-Tier System* issued in September 2021 also propose further reform requirements on the improvement of the judicial power operating mechanism of the SPC, the constitution of collegial panels across different judicial organs and specialized judges sessions. Although this reform plan was terminated without any normative changes later in September 2023, this part of the reform plan may not be the problem at all.

[10] For example, Baum (2011) (He Fan and Fang Siyuan provide a Chinese translation which is published by Peking University Press in 2019); Cao (2015). To further reflect on the localization and emphasis on the judicial law in the construction of specialized courts in China, see Wu (2021).

set up specialized commercial courts or tribunals to varying degrees.[11] China also established an international commercial division within the SPC and a supporting "one-stop" international commercial dispute resolution mechanism in 2018,[12] while e.g. Beijing Financial Court was established in March 2021.

Since long ago, many Chinese courts have assigned their commercial cases, under the name of "civil and commercial cases", to a specific civil division. In practice, the Second Civil Division is considered mainly responsible for commercial cases, while in different courts, there could be several civil divisions which are competent for commercial cases. However, even if regarding the courts' organization, independent commercial trial divisions are common in China, it may not necessarily meet the practical needs of commercial litigations. The main considerations of the court's allocation of cases among its divisions are the average caseload and the convenience of court management. Hence, the commercial division within courts may also be responsible for hearing land contracting disputes, labor disputes, applications for revoking domestic arbitration awards, applications for reconsideration and so forth, which in fact have nothing to do with commercial cases. Such practice can be understood as a negative example of judicial specialization. Even worse, when courts having heavy caseload intend to do a rush job to close cases at the end of a year,[13] judges from criminal divisions or the administrative division are often borrowed to hear commercial cases.

Indeed, there is no empirical research on the issue of whether judges who are normally handling with criminal or administrative cases but then rushed into plenty of commercial cases are competent.[14] Yet, judging from the concern of substantive law scholars that the non-specialized judges may lack "commercial ideology"[15] or misunderstand the difference between civil contracts and commercial contracts,[16] the doubt on the borrowed judges' ability to handle commercial cases is not entirely unfounded. The reason is simple: even judges with extensive experience of hearing civil cases may not get themselves totally prepared for the special nature of commercial cases. Unlike especially the American counterpart, Chinese judges are normally not generalist judges. On most occasions, the specialized training and experience is

[11] Blair (2019, p. 212); Isidro (2019, p. 4); Applebaum (2011, p. 74).

[12] *Provisions on International Commercial Courts* in 2018. For discussion, see for example, He (2017).

[13] It was found in a court in the central region of China more than ten years ago that if the president of the court considered that certain divisions might not be able to clear their cases in a timely manner due to the overwhelming number of cases this year, e.g. after the implementation of the *Labor Contract Law*, the president of the court may change the case allocation rules in the middle of the year for the purpose of performance evaluation within the judiciary. Then, the president allowed other divisions to hear cases while the cases still had their case numbers under the commercial division.

[14] Considering the turnover within the court, the borrowed judges may include judges with previous experience in commercial cases who are transferred to other positions within the judiciary. However, generally speaking, the specialized trial experience of the borrowed judges still needs to be questioned.

[15] Ye (2007).

[16] Cui (2022).

highly emphasized. For instance, these judges may misapply civil law principles in determining business losses, evaluating commercial registration, protecting business operation rights and so forth.[17] A fortiori, what about judges who are temporarily transferred from criminal divisions and the administrative division? Therefore, the aforementioned deficiency in the allocation of judges may directly affect the application and development of adjudicative techniques in commercial cases. The quality of civil judgments is accordingly jeopardized.

10.2.2 Judicial Openness

Judicial openness may have broader meanings, including the "four platforms" consisting of judicial process disclosure, court hearing disclosure, judicial decisions disclosure as well as enforcement information disclosure (Chap. 11). The disclosure of judicial decisions discussed in this contribution is merely an important part of this broad landscape of openness. In this regard, on 21 November 2013, the SPC issued the *Provisions on the Publication of Judgments on the Internet*. While replacing the previous judicial document under the same name issued in 2010, the SPC has strengthened the requirement that the original judicial decisions must be published on the internet and accessible through a unified platform (Articles 4, 9 and 12 of the *Provisions on the Publication of Judgments on the Internet*). The *Provisions on the Publication of Judgments on the Internet* responded to the calls of various interest groups, especially the law professions for judicial information disclosure[18] and judicial decisions disclosure.[19]

It is also a continuation of the long-term efforts in the field of judicial openness made by the SPC and courts at all levels.[20] Although there were various technical difficulties and obstacles during the implementation process, it seems that the SPC's determination to implement the system remains the same. Moreover, the combination of online disclosure and the introduction and deepening of the electronic litigation system[21] represents to some extent a prominent feature of the judicial reform in China. Such rapid development may even enable the Chinese judiciary to surpass Western developed countries based on the rule of law. The breadth of the collection and dissemination of judicial decisions have been guaranteed to a greater extent, although there are considerable differences in different locations.[22]

---

[17] Fan (2010, p. 146); Wang J (2010, p. 146).

[18] Li and Huang (2013); Tan (2012).

[19] For example, Jiang and Long (2013, p. 43); Jiang (2011, pp. 46–47), Research Group of the Beijing First Intermediate People's Court (2009, pp. 45, 47).

[20] For example, in 2009, Henan High People's Court promulgated and implemented the Implementation Opinions on the Publication of Judgments Online, requiring in principle all judgments in its jurisdiction to be published online.

[21] For example, Zheng and Yang (2020); Zhou (2018); Wang (2016).

[22] For example, Tang (2018a).

And the platform of judicial decisions disclosure has been improved at a visible speed, when it comes to the user-friendly search function and the stability of the database access. The *5th Five-Year Outline of the Program for Reform of People's Courts* released in 2019 also continues emphasizing: "upgrading the website of China Judgments Online, improving the automatic and intelligent level of technical processing online judicial decisions, and focusing on improving user experience. Strengthening the research and utilization of judicial decisions data resources..." In response to the aforementioned requirement of searching in a unified platform and the idea of further utilizing data resources, Article 3 of the *Guiding Opinions of the SPC on Unifying the Application of Laws to Strengthen the Search of Similar Cases (for Trial Implementation)* also proposes a guiding provision in July 2020 that "the responsible judge shall search similar cases based on the China Judgments Online, the trial case database and so forth, and be responsible for the authenticity and accuracy of the search".

Although it was seriously considered by the SPC in the second half of 2023 whether to limit the access to the website China Judgments Online which attracted attention nationwide, it turned clear months later that "China's determination and efforts to promote judicial openness will not be weakened, and its approach to ensuring transparency will become more diverse".[23] Besides the China Judgments Online which is for everyone accessible, including foreigners with personal accounts after registration, there is currently a China Judgments Database Intranet (全国法院裁判文书库) which is merely accessible within the judiciary, as well as a Digest of Cases of People's Courts (人民法院案例库).[24] Until 4 May 2024, there are all together 3,886 published cases in this database. In comparison, there are 146,351,038 cases collected in the China Judgments Online. These two numbers speak for themselves and one database can never replace the other.

After all, disclosing judicial decisions to the general public can affect the development of adjudicative techniques and improve the quality of civil judgments in two ways. For one thing, the appearance of the aforementioned duty of disclosure will significantly expand the scope and quantity of judgments available to the observers outside the judiciary. In this way, it reduces the difficulty of obtaining practice materials. The publication of more than 146 million judicial decisions of all types of cases can with no doubt provide researchers with materials for case studies, studies according to various categories and even quantitative studies following scientific methods. It means that researchers may respond rapidly to new problems arising in practice and they could enhance lawyers' understanding of relevant legal issues through further argument or criticism. Moreover, the necessary nourishment for the growth of lawyers' community could be found. A large number of cases on the internet can even stimulate the spontaneous growth of the Chinese system of judicial precedents, which is different from the guiding cases with Chinese characteristics.[25]

---

[23] Cao (2023).

[24] SPC (2024).

[25] For example, Gu (2018). Hou Meng points out that "citing judgments in written...is also a process of making the adjudication more institutionalized and standardized...Without citing them

For another, the duty of publication will also be a booster for judges to improve their own adjudicative techniques, because the responsible judge should prepare the related judicial decisions for the internet-based release within seven days after they become effective (Article 8 of the *Provisions on the Publication of Judgments on the Internet*) and in principle, the decisions may not be withdrawn or modified (Article 11 of the *Provisions on the Publication of Judgments on the Internet*). In other words, once the judicial decisions are uploaded on the internet, they will face the professional scrutiny of other lawyers and the non-professional evaluation of the public. Even if public trust has no impact on judicial openness according to the empirical research, while merely authority and the level of marketization have a positive relationship with judicial openness,[26] public supervision should make a difference in the future. Thus, besides that this judicial policy may improve the motivation of practicing judges, in such situations, judges have to improve their ability to use adjudicative techniques as much as possible in order to reduce the possibility of being found wrong after their judgments take effect and are published. Judges must want to avoid negative consequences in the system of judicial management, e.g. lower evaluation score in the personal ranking.

Therefore, the aforementioned promotion of judicial openness means good news from any point of view, and of course, it will urge and contribute to the evolution of adjudicative techniques in all aspects. Hence, we may look forward to better judgments under the eyes of the people. Otherwise, it is really hard to justify a judicial system which tries to keep the overwhelming majority of judicial decisions secret while emphasizing all the time that its judicial logic is a people-oriented one. The China Judgments Online can merely be optimized and improved, e.g. to protect the personality rights of the relevant persons and rightful business secrets better.

10.2.3 Petitions via Letters and Visits

Finally, the system of lawsuit-related petitions via letters and visits (涉诉信访) can also be classified into a broad understanding of the judicial system. Different from the western understanding that the court is considered as the final relief of dispute resolution, China currently assigns the power of dispute resolution to public organs other than the judiciary as well. Besides the relevant CPC's organs, varied kinds of governmental organs may share some procedural power. Among them, many these kinds of organs are responsible for taking petitions from the ordinary citizens and providing non-legal remedies. The petition system has a long history in P.R.C. Either by letters or personal visits, the ordinary citizen could approach the government

directly in written judgments, it may give rise to more management costs and cause more judgments bypassed". Hou (2021, p. 128). On the comparative advantages of citing judgments over applying judicial interpretations, ibid., pp. 102–108.

[26] Tang (2018b).

departments with different jurisdictions and functions and ask them to redress their grievance on the merits.

It is noted that the dispute resolution provided by the petition system is not controlled by any kind of judicial review, and may become a possible relief even when final judicial decisions are given. In terms of institutional effect, the relationship between authorities for petition and the judiciary is sensitive. In fact, an "effective" petition in the eyes of the parties concerned can indeed achieve some extra-judicial relief, and in some cases, such facilitated results may be closer to the objective situation of rights and the justice between the parties. Nevertheless, some "effective" lawsuit-related petitions further dilute the authority, credibility and independence of the judiciary as well as (if any) the *res judicata* effect of the relevant final judgments. To handle petitions occupies a number of judicial resources that could be used on the main judicial work, namely hearing and deciding cases. And often, the rare success in a limited number of cases conceals the cruel fact that most petitions could bring no remedy at all.[27]

Under this background, lawsuit-related petitions may be able to achieve the same objective effect in a small number of cases as the plan of strengthening adjudicative techniques, which are advocated in this contribution, while it is still incompatible with the idea of adjudicative techniques in terms of pursued goals and long-term effects in general. Yet, from another point of view, the widespread existence of lawsuit-related petitions just shows that the public confidence in the judiciary is not high, and one of the reasons for this situation could be the low development of adjudicative techniques. The aim of advocating adjudicative techniques is just to provide satisfactory judicial service, i.e. judicial dispute resolution approaches, for the general public, and to enhance the public confidence in the judiciary to reduce the dissatisfaction of the parties with the trial and judgment results. With improved quality of judicial service, the extraordinary and non-legal system of petitions will gradually step back from the stage of history.

Due to the theme, this contribution has no intention of in-depth discussion of the substantial issues related to the system of petitions. Rather, it merely concerns the possible interaction between the system of petitions and adjudicative techniques. At present, we need to think about how the theory of adjudicative techniques should respond to this judicial reality with lawsuit-related petitions. In this sense, whether to integrate or even expand the power of petition[28] or implement the accountability mechanism of petitions,[29] whether to regard the system of petitions as a special administrative remedy under the modern rule of law, which is to filter, supplement and solve difficult problems,[30] whether to normalize the operation of the petition power,[31] or whether to abolish the system of petitions after gradual reforms,[32] would not make a

[27] For example, Zhang and Dai (2009, p. 72).

[28] Ji (2005, pp. 83–84).

[29] Lin (2007).

[30] For example, Ying (2004, pp. 70–71). For a critical view, see Xiao and Hu (2008, pp. 63–65).

[31] For example, Ren (2011, p. 41); Lu (2006, pp. 42–43).

[32] For example, Zhao (2005, pp. 89–90); Yu (2005, pp. 73–74); Chen (2004, p. 238).

difference. The most outstanding problem here is the relationship between effective judgments and lawsuit-related petitions. Under the existing judicial framework, it would be reasonable to bring the petitions into the track of the current trial supervision procedure and clear procedural norms should be provided for them.[33] In other words, the enhanced judicial hierarchy of Chinese courts ought to be the best solution.

10.3 Judgment-Related Procedural Arrangement

10.3.1 Judicial Mediation

As a non-adjudicative dispute resolution approach, judicial mediation has the most direct and profound impact on making civil judgments. Successful judicial mediation can instantly eliminate the necessity of making civil judgments. Responsible judges would be exempted from their obligation to apply procedural rules and doctrines as well as get rid of their duty to provide reasons in civil judgments. Moreover, there would be no need to rely on the adversary system in the modern judicial structure at all.[34] Hence, the importance of judicial mediation is sound and clear. In particular, China has long attached special importance to various kinds of conciliation and mediation mechanisms including judicial mediation in practice, and from time to time introduces new possibilities into this field,[35] which obviously does not need to be written too much in this contribution. Rather, this contribution will not discuss the specific ideas and techniques related to judicial mediation.

It is worth noting that each specific method of dispute resolution shall seek to resolve disputes that are appropriate to it.[36] Adopting one of the methods too much would restrict the possibility of maximizing the functions of civil justice system.[37] The previous "priority of mediation" policy should be restricted by "combination

---

[33] For example, Hu (2013, p. 1); Wang (2005, p. 11).

[34] However, in Chinese context, the attention ought to also be attached to the similarities between judicial mediation and civil trial. For instance, Li (2011). It can be argued that in some occasions, the civil trial may share the same principle as during judicial mediation and the court may not obey strictly the laws but provide a compromise on the merits in the form of civil judgments. There are also some views that attempt to achieve the procedural classification of judicial mediation based on the pluralism of mediation standards of "Ascertaining the Facts" and "Discerning between Right and Wrong". Lu (2019).

[35] Here we only take the *Rules for the Online Mediation by People's Courts* implemented on 1 January 2022, as well as the *2020 Pilot Program* (whose Part II refers to the judicial confirmation procedure) and *Guiding Opinions of the SPC on Further Improving the Mechanism of Designated Mediation*, both promulgated in January 2020, as examples.

[36] Pan (2000).

[37] Throughout the changes of the relationship between the adjudication and mediation since the founding of the P.R.C., the most common thing is that one of them is unduly emphasized, which leads to the consequence that the courts are somewhat missing between the general logic of dispute resolution and the concrete guidance indicated by the judicial policy. Pan and Liu (2010).

of mediation and adjudication",[38] and can merely make a difference on the premise of the consent of the parties.[39] Otherwise, it is rather difficult to achieve the goal of substantially resolving civil disputes. As to whether this policy partially overthrows the concept of "adversary system and adjudication", which is a western-style of civil justice, and introduces "a new mechanism of generating legal order", or just restates that "in the process of resolving a large number of daily disputes before grass-roots courts, it is still necessary as far as possible to maintain the characteristics or advantages of China's traditional trial mode",[40] more observation and empirical data are needed.[41] It shows also the Chinese ancient philosophy of avoiding any extreme solution to real problems.

In western developed countries, the emphasis on mediation and other alternative dispute resolution mechanisms is built on the basis that ordinary procedures have been completed to a great extent. Even these formal procedures are more and more considered as excessively cumbersome, time-consuming and expensive. Such emphasis can also be shown by the more professional and specialized mediation as well as the enrichment of choices of alternative dispute resolution mechanisms.[42] In this regard, the development of People's mediation together with combining litigation and mediation in China are different from the western counterparts since they have different motives, traditions and institutional aims.[43] The Chinese mediation system cannot be justified simply by either the popular trend in western world or the function of enhancing the legitimacy of justice.[44]

At least in general, China's civil justice system still needs to strengthen the control of its performance both relying on the concrete conditions and the law-based process with more detailed rules. Overemphasizing the mediation's function of replacing civil judgments goes against the improvement of the rule of law in China.[45] And if mediation is compulsorily proposed, it is more likely to harm the already inadequate judicial remedies in current laws (e.g. Article 125 of the *CPL*).[46] In recent practice, attempts of pre-action mediation are widely enforced before courts at all levels, while the one-stop dispute resolution mechanism (Chap. 11) is dominating as well. In this sense, judicial mediation and even other systems under the name of conciliation and

---

[38] Li (2013).

[39] Wu (2013, p. 555); Fan (2011, p. 51); Li (2012a, pp. 120–121); Zhang and Xiao (2012).

[40] Wang Y (2010, Preface, pp. 6–8).

[41] For an in-depth analysis of the aforementioned relationship between mediation and adjudication in Chinese context, see Wu (2013, pp. 544–554).

[42] Stipanowich and Fraser (2017, p. 839).

[43] For a detailed discussion on the local foundation and operation of the cooperative mechanism between litigation and mediation, see Pan (2013).

[44] Chen (2011, p. 65). In addition, the mediation-oriented research theme has intensified the separation between researchers and practitioners, and triggered scholars to reflect on the academic autonomy of the discipline. Wang (2011, pp. 5–6); Zhang (2011, pp. 42–43).

[45] For example, Ye (2015).

[46] Li (2012b, p. 7); Cao (2012). For opposing views, see Tang and Qi (2012, pp. 86–88); Tang (2012, p. 94).

mediation system should be taken as a reference system when it comes to the research of civil judgments in China.[47]

10.3.2 *Impact of Different Stages of Civil Proceedings*

10.3.2.1 Case-Filing and Answer Stage (Pleading Stage)

The first-instance procedure may be roughly divided into three stages, namely the pleadings stage, the pre-trial stage and the court hearing stage. First, the pleadings procedure refers both to the case-filing procedure which is triggered by the plaintiff via the claim form and the answer to the claim form which is submitted by the defendant. Responding to the defendant's answer, the plaintiff may submit the re-answer (*Replik*) in due time while the defendant may reply to it (*Duplik*) as well.

Generally speaking, it is in China necessary to evaluate the formal and substantive requirements of the proceedings (*Prozessvoraussetzung*), which are also essential preconditions for making proper final judgments, so the related adjudicative techniques deserve more attention. Meanwhile, the structure and functions of the pleadings procedure may affect the adjudicative techniques in return. For example, from the perspective of the principle of proportionality, the examination of the plaintiff's factual allegations at the pleadings stage appears too much. Rather, the academic circle in China generally considers that the problems caused by the existing substantial case-filing examination shall be resolved.[48]

Especially, the Chinese law ought to separate the procedural elements at the case-filing stage (*Ordnungsmäßigkeit der Klageerhebung*) and the elements at the later stages of the civil process and clarify the judicial functions of judges who are responsible for registrating the filed civil cases. Also, when it comes to the participation of the parties concerned, the provision on the defendant's obligation of producing written defense (Article 128 paragraph 1 of the *CPL* and Article 49 of the *2019 Evidence Provisions*) could not make a difference in practice, because there is no consequence if the defendant fails to perform such obligation (Article 128 paragraph 2 of the *CPL*).[49] Such practice makes the summary of disputed issues sometimes impossible since the court has no idea what is in dispute between both parties. Then it also increases the possibility of making wrong judgments at the end of court hearings.

Hence, to rectify the structural deficiency, we should consider endowing the judge with the power of extending the period of producing pleadings from the defendant's

---

[47] Looking at the research of other social sciences, it can be seen that the operation of judicial system is inseparable from the evaluation of extrajudicial systems. For example, the analysis of the factual standard for filing a lawsuit in the U.S. and the related case-selection effect, see Gelbach (2012, p. 2270); also Huang (2009).

[48] For example, Zhang (2009, pp. 66–68); Fu (2011a).

[49] The First Civil Division of the SPC (2020, pp. 466–472).

side, prescribing the shortest period from the expiration of the period of answer to the start of the forthcoming court hearings. And a relatively systematic rule of precluding defendant's pleadings is desirable when the defendant fails to produce the answer within the prescribed period, so as to strengthen the role of defendant's answer in civil proceedings.[50]

In this case, there is an interactive relationship between the pleadings procedure and adjudicative techniques. The existing case-filing procedure restricts the development of related adjudicative techniques, while the defects of this procedure call for the emergence of more advanced adjudicative techniques. These procedural shortcomings not only reduce the efficiency of the civil litigation, but also impede the alternative dispute resolutions, as only full information exchange between pleadings of both sides could facilitate early identification of issues and possible attempts of settlement. Thus, the existing pleadings procedure makes some cases that do not need to be adjudicated have to be determined by applying adjudicative techniques, resulting in the inability to achieve effective distribution of cases. Accordingly, the current pleadings procedure will harm the judicial resources necessary for the application and development of adjudicative techniques. In addition, within the pleading procedure, the judge may also face issues concerning the subject matter of claims[51] or various disputed issues of the case, besides that decisions may be given regarding procedural requirements of civil proceedings. If this function of the pleading procedures cannot be fully exerted, the application of adjudicative techniques in the final judgment will also be affected.

10.3.2.2 Pre-Trial Stage

The impact of the pre-trial stage of civil proceedings on adjudicative techniques is mainly reflected in two areas: summarizing disputed issues and collecting the evidence. In the area of summarizing disputed issues, in order to achieve the goals of accelerating proceedings and settling the disputes, the judge should narrow the scope of disputed issues as much as possible at the pre-trial stage.[52] This will not merely facilitate the follow-up formal court hearings, but also be beneficial for rendering accurate and well-reasoned judgments after the whole civil procedure.

Yet, the existing pre-trial procedures in China are quite different from the ones in the continental and Anglo-American legal systems. The function of summarizing disputed issues would be fulfilled even within the court hearings, which in other words, include the functions of pre-trial procedures in western jurisdictions. In the pre-trial proceedings, the judge does not have the power to determine the appropriate preparatory procedures, nor can the judge set the time limit for the submission of preparation pleadings. Except for the reimbursement of expenses as provided in

[50] Cao (2014).

[51] However, it is argued by this chapter that the clarification of the subject matter of claims itself is not a requirement in the case-filing procedure in China. Cao (2020b).

[52] For example, Meng (2020).

Article 102 paragraph 3 of the *ICPL*, there is in principle no procedural regulation that reflects the cooperation of the parties in the allocation of legal expenses (see Article 40 of *Measures on the Payment of Litigation Costs*).[53]

And in the area of evidence collection, the evidence application (*Beweisantrag*) and its review are not yet systematically regulated in China.[54] Rather, Article 95 of the *ICPL* is the primary rule which says that if the evidence which a party applies for investigation and collection is irrelevant or meaningless to the facts to be proven or is otherwise unnecessary to be investigated and collected, the court shall not approve the application. There is still much room for development in interpreting and applying this norm.[55] Moreover, with the promulgation of the *2019 Evidence Provisions*, and especially the further improvement of the system of documents submission order, the existing system which the judge relies on to collect evidence *ex officio* or upon parties' application has greatly improved the ability of the parties to collect evidence. It is necessary for China to further control the judicial discretion allowed in current laws (Article 47 paragraph 1 items 1 5 of the *2019 Evidence Provisions*), after the categories of documentary evidence to be collected have been clarified (Article 47 paragraph 1 items 1 4 of the *2019 Evidence Provisions*). Moreover, the rules on obstructing evidential collection (*Beweisvereitelung*) in general (Article 95 of the *2019 Evidence Provisions* and Article 75 of the *2001 Evidence Provisions*) and specifically for documentary evidence (Article 48 of the *2019 Evidence Provisions* and Article 112 paragraph 2 of the *ICPL* in 2015) needs to be enhanced.[56]

And in terms of the time limit for producing evidence (Article 68 paragraph 2 of the *CPL*), the court should give priority to evidence preclusion, and an exceptional rule, which concentrates on the delay in litigation caused by overdue evidential submissions, should be added to bridge the seemingly unlimited discretion of the rules of the *2019 Evidence Provisions*.[57] In this regard, Article 102 paragraph 1 of the *ICPL* provides that "evidence provided by a party beyond the time limit deliberately or due to gross negligence shall be deemed inadmissible by the court. However, the evidence which is related to the basic facts of the case shall be deemed admissible by the court which shall impose an admonition or a fine…" While filling in the aforementioned discretionary space, this provision has in fact eliminated the preclusion effect of the time limit for adducing evidence to a large extent.

In both the aforementioned fields of summarizing disputed issues and collecting evidence, a part of the reasons for the defects of the current pre-trial procedures

---

[53] Generally speaking, the rule of cost-shifting does not apply to civil proceedings in China, while the sharing of litigation fees is roughly in proportion to the proportion of winning the case on the merits. Considering the aforementioned special nature of commercial litigations, appropriate adjustment to the rules on the sharing of costs may be conducive to the achievement of the overall goal of civil proceedings by taking the experience of common law systems into account. Some scholar argued that costs sanction may be adopted for more situations such as the case where new evidence was produced after the deadline of evidence production. Li (2009, pp. 166–168).

[54] Cao (2020a).

[55] For example, Ma (2019).

[56] For an earlier discussion, see Cao (2011).

[57] Similar considerations, see Fu (2012, p. 93); Zhang (2012, p. 111).

lies in the insufficiency of procedural adjudicative techniques, which cannot prompt the parties to put forward all means of attack or defense (*Angriffs- und Verteidigungsmittel*) in a designated period of time, and the lack of a more mature method for determining the factual and legal issues. While the system of evidence collection is making progress, there is still much room for continued improvement.[58]

Meanwhile, the underdeveloped situation of the pre-trial procedures also restricts the progress of the adjudicative techniques of making adequate judgments. The ambiguity of the disputed issues at an early stage of civil proceedings and the lack of evidence will undoubtedly affect the quality and efficiency of the judge's reasoning. In some difficult cases, some judges even have to rush into the jungle of burden of proof and admit that the facts to be discovered lie in the *non-liquet* situation. Although as mentioned in Chap. 6, in the *non-liquet* situation the judges could still make their decisions, these decisions could merely be taken as the last resort of individual cases. Instead, discovering the facts and knowing the truth must be the primary aim of civil judges in most cases.

10.3.2.3 Structure of Court Hearings

To discuss the impact of the structure of court hearings on the adjudicative techniques, it is necessary to first analyze the characteristics of the existing court hearings. The ordinary court hearing organized in Chinese practice includes a phase of court investigation first and a forthcoming phase of court debate (Articles 141 and 144 of the *CPL*). According to the former provision, the court investigation consists of the following steps sequentially: statements by the parties; informing the witnesses of their rights and obligations, collecting witness testimony or written statements of absent witnesses; presentation of documentary evidence, material evidence, audio-visual material and electronic data; reading of expert identification opinions; and reading of records of inspection. With respect to the court debate, Article 144 paragraph 1 of the *CPL* stipulates its order as follows: oral statements by the plaintiff and the litigation representatives; defense by the defendant and the litigation representatives; oral statement or defense by the third party and the litigation representatives; and debate between/among different sides. Additionally, Article 144 paragraph 2 of the *CPL* says that at the end of the court debate, the presiding judge shall ask each side, first the plaintiff, then the defendant, and then the third party, for their final conclusion respectively.

From a comparative point of view, such structure has obvious shortcomings and correspondingly affects the adjudicative techniques. Proceedings emphasizing the division of various internal phases will lead to artificial separation of factual issues and legal issues. Then, the objects to be proven within the phase of court's investigation will be inaccurate while the phase of court debate will be in lack of necessary

[58] Among them, the judicial identification (expert witness) system, which is directly stipulated in *2019 Evidence Provisions* and is additionally covered by legal documents of both the SPC and the Ministry of Justice in 2020, is outstanding.

fact-finding results. In the end, the correctness of fact-finding in the case and the efficiency of the whole proceedings are to be affected.[59] Moreover, from the perspective of adjudicative techniques, accuracy of factual ascertainment and law application will be affected under the current procedural structure, and a procedural ruling on procedural issues on time is less accessible under such conditions. Within the current two-stage structure, the court hearings are unable to provide sufficient information for making the final judgment.

And in China, the precondition for the parties to debate with each other is that the facts of the case have been found out. Hence, even though both parties concerned expressed their respective viewpoints at the pleading stage as well as the preparation stage via their statements, the determination of disputed issues of facts is still to a large extent controlled by the judge, since there is no substantial confrontation between the parties. In this way, a strong inquisitorial character is visible in Chinese civil justice. This is not to say that the judge arbitrarily decides the issues without considering the parties' position when deciding the issues in dispute. With no doubt, the issues arise from the summarization of the parties' claim and defense, while the judge will often give the parties an opportunity to be heard. As provided in Article 226 of the *ICPL*, the court shall, in accordance with the claims and arguments of the parties as well as the circumstances on evidence exchange, summarize the disputed issues and consult the parties' opinions on such issues.

However, since the parties submit their opinions independently, and sometimes the defendant fails to submit the opinions in a timely manner, the judge has often to face litigation materials without previous confrontation when summing up the disputed points. As the saying goes, "A clever housewife cannot cook bricks without straw", the judge has no choice but to bite the bullet and sum up the disputed points merely in the formal sense. Later, it would turn out during the hearings that these issues would not be the proper ones in the current case.

Of course, this problem does not exist when evidence exchange has been organized before the hearings and the presiding judge has already summed up the disputed points after seeking the parties' opinions.[60] However, at least for most cases where it is not necessary to organize the exchange of evidence, this kind of disputed issues

59 Zhang (2019, p. 312); Duan (2015); Zhang (2015); Fu (2011b, p. 7). In this regard, some judge also holds that the court should not organize its investigation and debate by distinguishing different stages of the court hearing anymore but should try the case based on the disputed issues of law item by item. Huang (2013, p. 30).

60 For example, in the contract dispute case between Beijing Zhuangsheng Real Estate Development Co., Ltd. and Beijing Cinda Investment Co., Ltd. and Beijing Cinda Real Estate Co., Ltd., a pretrial conference was held on 18 August 2020, and the collegial panel summarized the disputed points of this case in the live broadcast of the open court hearing. For an earlier typical case, see the records of live broadcasting court hearing of an appeallate case, Beijing Qihoo 360 Technology Co., Ltd. v. Tencent (Shenzhen) Co., Ltd. and Shenzhen Tencent Computer System Co., Ltd., which is over the abuse of market dominance and heard by the SPC in a partially open trial. At the beginning of the court hearing, presiding judge Wang Chuang read out 22 specific disputed issues in five categories summed up in the pre-trail stage. Appeal Case of Civil Dispute of Qihoo v. Tencent by Abuse of Market Dominance dated 26 November 2013 at 9:00 AM (http://www.chinacourt.org/chat/fulltext/listId/34059/template/courtts20131126.shtml, 26 November 2013).

agreed by the parties may not be a feasible choice. Either the judge, in a responsible manner, prepares the outline of organizing the hearings before the trial,[61] or the judge may just adapt to the situation during the trial, putting off the unclear issues to the next court hearing, or even being unable to summarize the disputed issues at all. In the last situation, the judge would probably discover, as late as at the end of the court hearings and when the judgment would be drafted, that indispensable factual issues to make the judgment would be omitted. Then, the judge would have to reopen a new trial, or ask the parties to supplement written opinions afterward. In addition, before filing a motion to dismiss on the merits, the defendant can still raise procedural objections with respect to the jurisdictional issue. Although this may be included in the parties' statements in form, it is obviously a matter of court debate rather than an investigation.

Partly due to the aforementioned reasons, there was also an attempt in China's practice to consolidate the above two stages of the court hearing, namely the stages of court's investigation and court's debate (Article 230 of the *ICPL*). In the pilot reform of the year 2020, claims and other elements of the case have been considered as the keywords in replacing the aforementioned procedural trial structure (Article 8 paragraph 2 and Article 13 item 3 of the *2020 Pilot Program*),[62] and summarizing disputed issues during court hearings is also regarded as an important step of a better adjudicative methodology.[63]

10.3.3 Impact of Mechanism of Separating Complicated and Simple Procedures

If "combining mediation with making the judgment, resolving the disputes while concluding the case" (调判结合，案结事了) is the major working method of the China's judiciary, "separating complicated and simple cases to suit the individual needs" (繁简分流，各取所需) is the consensus on reforming the civil procedure in China. Widely recognized from the comparative perspective are to make ordinary proceedings more formal and substantial in order to strengthen the authority of the proceedings themselves, to make simplified proceedings more rapid and convenient in order to achieve the efficiency of proceedings themselves, and to make the conditions for transition between different types of proceedings clearer in order to facilitate the feasibility of the proceedings. Yet, under the influence of the judicial tradition, practical resources and the allocation of power in China, these procedural aims are doomed to be difficult to be brought into reality. The course of the waves of judicial reforms shows clearly: few voices are against doing things using discretionary rights

[61] Zou (2010, pp. 119–122, 128–129).

[62] Earlier reports, e.g., see Li and Hu (2012). (in response to the elements (to be tried) table submitted by the parties concerned, the judge presides over the element-centered court hearings and gives element-centered judgments). For the relevant discussion, see Teng and Liu (2016).

[63] Zou (2010, pp. 117–129).

and giving priority to efficiency, but there is obvious resistance to strengthening the formality of civil proceedings and the authority of adjudicative power.[64]

Hence, besides taking the impact of judicial mediation on adjudicative techniques discussed above into account, the focus of the separation of complicated and simple procedures in China may still fall on the simplification of proceedings themselves. The recent judicial reform is attempting to enhance the efficiency of simplified cases within the overall framework of the judicial dispute resolution, e.g. by introducing small claims proceedings and the referral of undisputed cases to the special procedure of debt collection by the case-filing division of the court (Articles 165 and 136 paragraph 1 of the *CPL*). Meanwhile, we should also pay attention to the significance of the diversion effect of simplified proceedings, in order to select the appropriate types and number of cases for the increasingly formal ordinary proceedings, and to secure the high-standard operation of civil cases before the judiciary. Through constructing a rational system for procedural classification and conversion, as mentioned above, different judicial needs can find their own suitable judicial services and products.[65] Facing the polarized needs of a developed society, being paranoid about either end of the spectrum is unacceptable.

In recent years, the Chinese judiciary has been operated under high pressure which could be summarized as the situation of "Too many cases but too few judges". The focus of China's judicial reform has shifted to the separation of complicated and simple cases, the connection of litigation and mediation, the management of lawsuit sources (诉源), and small claims proceedings, all of which are located in the opposite to the formal judicial process (although this contribution does not object to their practical and theoretical significance). The core reform object concentrates on the construction and improvement of one-stop diversified dispute resolution mechanism and one-stop litigation service center (Chap. 11).[66] Hence, the SPC announced in its 2021 Work Report that "while the number of litigation cases docketed by courts nationwide broke the threshold of 20 million cases in 2016 and 30 million cases in 2019, this number dropped in 2020 for the first time since 2004, and in particular, the number of civil litigation cases dropped for the first time after 15 years of continuous growth at an average annual growth rate of 10%".[67]

Furthermore, the new reform of separating complicated and simple cases is expected to provide an opportunity to further streamline the system of civil litigation and reflect the recent technological development. The new reform is especially represented by the latest "Pilot Program of the Reform of Separation of Cases into Simple Cases and Complicated Ones under Civil Procedure". The SPC launched this pilot

---

[64] Wang Yaxin also believes that the theoretical circle and the practice circle have reached a consensus e.g. on the justice for the people and the diversified approaches of dispute resolution, while there are obvious differences of opinion on issues of mediation, the active justice, the Ma Xiwu (马锡五) trial method and so forth which may circulate formal litigation proceedings in fact. Wang (2011, p. 5).

[65] Fu (2011c, pp. 51–55), Pan (2000).

[66] *Opinions of the SPC on Building One-stop Diversified Dispute Resolution Mechanisms and One-stop Litigant Service Centers* in 2019.

[67] Xinhua (2021).

project for two years on 15 January 2020.[68] The first four items of this project, namely optimizing the judicial confirmation procedure, improving small claims proceedings, improving rules on simplified proceedings and expanding the application scope of the sole-judge trial, are more of attempts to amend and supplement the current litigation systems. It can be said that they show a quite significant institutional factor affecting the workload of judges in practice. The fifth item, i.e. improving rules of electronic litigation, is more of a summary of the reform efforts in recent years and the completion of further institutional construction (Chap. 11). Especially in light of the COVID-19 epidemic situation that broke out merely one week after the launch of the pilot project, these rules are just in time. Most of these items within the pilot project were incorporated by the national legislators in the *CPL* Amendment Act at the end of 2021.

The adjudicative techniques for making civil judgments must also reflect the aforementioned procedural arrangement. Not merely the structure of civil judgments ought to be different according to the complexity of the disputed issues, but also the application of adjudicative techniques can be different. In the context of this contribution, adjudicative techniques are mainly aimed at cases applying ordinary proceedings, enjoying high-level procedural protection, and requiring self-responsibility of the parties themselves. In contrast, their application in simplified cases is to be limited. For example, when it comes to simplified cases, it is not necessary to make use of strict procedural rules such as the ones referring to the preclusion of the defendant's answer. The preclusion rules, which require the parties to be legally equipped with professional knowledge and skills, are merely applicable to ordinary proceedings.[69] Also, it is unnecessary to make an interlocutory judgment on any disputed issue or procedural matter which may make the whole procedure more complicated.

In fact, well-developed adjudicative techniques are also of great benefits to realizing the accelerating function of simplified proceedings. Although adjudicative techniques may be fully stimulated and developed in complicated cases and formal proceedings, the essence of adjudicative techniques is the ability or skill, based on a logical legal thinking, to classify and evaluate the claims and factual materials presented by the parties within a certain legal framework. In China's practice, simplified proceedings can be primarily summarized as a more informal procedure which does not require formal legal service, a well-prepared pre-trial preparation stage, and a distinction between court's investigation and debate within court hearings. If using well-developed adjudicative techniques can solve complex cases in an acceptable manner, it could be presumed that adopting some of the techniques in simplified cases should be much easier.

---

[68] *Decision of the Standing Committee of the NPC on Authorizing the SPC to Carry out the Pilot Program of the Reform of Separation of Cases into Simple Cases and Complicated Ones under Civil Proceedings* in 2019; *Plan of the SPC for the Pilot Program of the Reform of Separation between Complicated Cases and Simple Ones in Civil Proceedings* in 2020.

[69] For a detailed discussion, see Cao (2014).

References

Applebaum L (2011) The steady growth of business courts. In: Flango CR, McDowell AM, Campbell CF, Kauder NB (eds) Future trends in state courts. National Center for State Courts, Williamsburg

Baum L (2011) Specializing the courts. University of Chicago Press, Chicago

Blair W (2019) The new litigation landscape: international commercial courts and procedural innovations. International Journal of Procedural Law 9:212–234

Cao Z (2011) Ruling on application for documentary evidence collection: a comparison of modes. Modern Law Science 5:151–160 (in Chinese)

Cao Z (2012) On revising the case-filing procedure: judicial reality and theoretical design. China Social Sciences Today, 9 May 2012, A–07 (in Chinese)

Cao Z (2014) The preclusion of the defendant's answer in ordinary proceedings. Peking University Law Journal 2:483–508 (in Chinese)

Cao Z (2015) The specialization and models of commercial trial organs in China. Journal of National Prosecutors College 1:121–130 (in Chinese)

Cao Z (2020a) Judicial review to the application for judicial identification of a party. Law Science 12:112–129 (in Chinese)

Cao Z (2020b) Reflection on the examination of the subject matter of claims in the civil case-filing proceedings. China Legal Science 1:283–303 (in Chinese)

Cao Y (2023) Top court reaffirms dedication to improving judicial transparency. https://enapp.chinadaily.com.cn/a/202312/27/AP658b7ee4a3103582ac04ef18.html. Accessed 2 May 2024

Chen B (2004) Contentious lawsuits, petitions and the new Chinese legal tradition—contentious issues in the period of legal transformation. Peking University Law Journal 2:226–238 (in Chinese)

Chen H (2011) On 'one system' of Chinese courts: the history, practice and theory. Law and Social Development 6:57–68 (in Chinese)

Chen G (2013) Principles of judicial independence with Chinese characteristics from the perspective of comparative law. Journal of Comparative Law 2:1–12 (in Chinese)

Chen R (2018) Theoretical reflection on the reform of the judge quota system. The Jurist 3:1–14+191 (in Chinese)

Cui J (2022) On the differentiation between civil contracts and commercial contracts. Tribune of Political Science and Law 1:56–73 (in Chinese)

Duan W (2015) Recognition on the structure of sessions of civil court's hearings in China. China Legal Science 2:81–107 (in Chinese)

Fan T (2010) Reflection and reconstruction of Chinese commercial trial system. Hebei Law Science 2:145–150 (in Chinese)

Fan Y (2011) Judgment combination to mediation: an analysis based on the practice. Law and Social Development 6:49–56 (in Chinese)

Fu Y (2011a) Function and structure of the case-filing procedure in Chinese civil litigation. The Jurist 1:99–113 (in Chinese)

Fu Y (2011b) The logic and corresponding skills of trial and judgment. People's Court Daily, 19 January 2011 (in Chinese)

Fu Y (2011c) Small claims and classification of proceedings. Tsinghua University Law Journal 3:46–55 (in Chinese)

Fu Y (2012) Review on the value orientation of the revision of the civil procedure law. Journal of the East China University of Political Science and Law 4:79–93 (in Chinese)

Fu Y (2015) The focus of judicial accountability is the boundary of duties. China Law Review 4:169–174 (in Chinese)

Fu Y, Peerenboom R (2012) A new analytic framework for understanding and promoting judicial independence in China. In: Peerenboom R (ed) Judicial independence in China: lessons for global rule of law promotion. Cambridge University Press, Cambridge, pp 95–133

Gelbach JB (2012) Locking the doors to discovery? Assessing the effects of Twombly and Iqbal on access to discovery. Yale Law Journal 121:2270–2345
Gu P (2018) Causes and effects of spontaneous application of precedents. Chinese Journal of Law 2:76–96 (in Chinese)
He F (2013) How many judges are enough? People's Court Daily, 7 June 2013 (in Chinese)
He Q (2017) The idea of justice in a large country and the development of international civil procedure in China. Social Sciences in China 5:123–146+208 (in Chinese)
Hou M (2021) The operative process of justice: based on the observation of the SPC. China Legal Publishing House, Beijing (in Chinese)
Hu X (2013) Rule of law represents the basic direction of the reform of law-related or litigation-related petitions system. People's Court Daily, 23 November 2013 (in Chinese)
Huang K (2009) Evaluation of reform proposal for criminal appeals system: an empirical approach. In: Huang K (ed) Empirical studies of judicial systems 2008. Institutum Iurisprudentiae (Preparatory Office), Taipei, pp 447–495 (in Chinese)
Huang Y (2013) Problems in the summary of the disputed points in civil court trial and countermeasures. People's Judicature 5:26–30 (in Chinese)
Isidro MR (2019) International commercial courts in the litigation market. International Journal of Procedural Law 9:4–49
Ji W (2005) The tide of petitions and the solutions for the complaint system. Twenty-First Century 3:79–84 (in Chinese)
Jiang D (2011) 'What the judge says': problem awareness, special knowledge and interpretive skills. Chinese Journal of Law 6:43–47 (in Chinese)
Jiang H, Long F (2013) The disclosure of justice in Hong Kong and Macao and its enlightenment. Journal of Law Application 4:39–43 (in Chinese)
Li H (2009) 'New evidence' after the revision of civil procedure law: possible contribution of defining the 'new evidence' in the judicial interpretation on judicial supervision. China Legal Science 3:156–168 (in Chinese)
Li H (2011) Restatement of the principle of 'ascertaining the facts and discerning between right and wrong.' Chinese Journal of Law 4:120–135 (in Chinese)
Li H (2012a) Treating mediation first rationally—an analysis based on court mediation. Journal of National Prosecutors College 1:117–125 (in Chinese)
Li H (2012b) Understanding and cognition of the nature of antecedent mediation. People's Court Daily, 17 October 2012 (in Chinese)
Li H (2013) On separating mediation from adjudication in the civil justice. China Legal Science 3:5–18 (in Chinese)
Li H (2018) An investigation into judges' resignation from the bench. Law and Modernization 3:1–13 (in Chinese)
Li R, Hu Q (2012) Shenzhen: breaking through the bottleneck of civil and commercial judgments writing. People's Court Daily, 27 November 2012 (in Chinese)
Li R, Huang Y (2013) Preliminary research on openness of judicial information of courts. Law Science Magazine 4:105–114 (in Chinese)
Lin Y (2007) Thoughts on some problems of the accountability of the petition work. Law Science 2:26–32 (in Chinese)
Liu B (2015) On the institutional logic of the reform of the judge quota system based on the phenomenon of judges' resignation. Law Science 10:47–56 (in Chinese)
Lu X (2006) Going forward and backward of the petition system: thoughts on functions of the organs for petitions. Contemporary Law Review 3:42–46 (in Chinese)
Lu X (2019) A perspective study of the phenomenon of 'mediation with judgment factors'—also a study of the pluralistic positioning of 'clear facts and clarified responsibilities' in the judicial mediation. The Jurist 1:101–111+193–194 (in Chinese)
Lu Y (2020) The conscience of judges under the background of judicial accountability system. Modern Law Science 3:14–28 (in Chinese)

Ma J (2019) Prevention and limitation of evidence prediction in civil proceedings. Science of Law 3:180–190 (in Chinese)
Meng X (2020) Exploration and perfection of effective issue narrowing mode. Journal of Central South University (Social Sciences) 1:75–86 (in Chinese)
Pan J (2000) On the coherency between civil disputes and its solving methods. Modern Law Science 6:59–62 (in Chinese)
Pan J (2013) Reflections on the 'cooperative mechanism between litigation and mediation' under the background of revising civil procedure law. Contemporary Law Review 3:102–111 (in Chinese)
Pan J, Liu Z (2010) On the relationship between court mediation and dispute resolution—from the perspective of building a harmonious society. Journal of Comparative Law 4:70–81 (in Chinese)
Ren X (2011) The right of petition as a 'new' right. Studies in Law and Business 4:37–41 (in Chinese)
Research Group of the Beijing First Intermediate People's Court (2009) Research report on strengthening the construction of judicial disclosure. People's Judicature 5:44–48 (in Chinese)
SPC (2024) Digest of cases of people's courts. https://rmfyalk.court.gov.cn. Accessed 2 May 2024 (in Chinese)
Stipanowich T, Fraser V (2017) The international task force on mixed mode dispute resolution: exploring the interplay between mediation, evaluation and arbitration in commercial cases. Fordham International Law Journal 40:839–886
Tan S (2012) On judicial information disclosure. Northern Legal Science 3:76–84 (in Chinese)
Tang L (2012) Between 'compulsion' and 'consensus': dilemma and future of the judicial mediation in civil litigation. Modern Law Science 3:86–96 (in Chinese)
Tang Y (2018a) Leader's will, institution's capacity and judicial openness: a preliminary study on online access of judicial decisions in Beijing, Shanghai and Guangdong. China Law Review 6:90–102 (in Chinese)
Tang Y (2018b) The decisive factors in promoting judicial openness: the data statistics regarding China judgments online. Tsinghua University Law Journal 4:35–47 (in Chinese)
Tang W, Qi T (2012) The drifting civil mediation system in China. Journal of Comparative Law 5:78–90 (in Chinese)
Teng W, Liu L (eds) (2016) Element-centered trial methods: innovation of court hearing manners and judicial decisions. People's Court Press, Beijing (in Chinese)
The First Civil Division of the SPC (2020) Understanding and application of the new provisions of the SPC on evidence in civil proceedings. People's Court Press, Beijing (in Chinese)
Wang Y (2005) Interplay between the alternative dispute resolution mechanism and civil trials: centering on the treatment of 'law-related petitions'. Journal of Law Application 2:9–11 (in Chinese)
Wang J (2010) Application of law in China's commercial judicial practice: difficulties and solutions. Modern Law Science 5:141–149 (in Chinese)
Wang Y (2010) Adversary and adjudication: basic structures of civil procedure in Japan. Tsinghua University Press, Beijing (in Chinese)
Wang Y (2011) Twenty years of civil procedure law. Contemporary Law Review 1:3–7 (in Chinese)
Wang F (2016) Legal basis of construction of the electronic litigation system. Chinese Journal of Law 6:88–106 (in Chinese)
Wang Y (2018) Interpreting and reasoning in judgments and enhancing judicial credibility, People's Court Daily, 16 June 2018 (in Chinese)
Wu Y (2013) 'Mediation first': reform paradigm and legal interpretation: taking the reform in the court of O city as an example. Peking University Law Journal 3:536–555 (in Chinese)
Wu H (2019) Judicial reform and change of motivation circumstance of legal profession. China Legal Science 4:165–185 (in Chinese)
Wu Y (2021) The construction of special courts from the perspective of the modernization of governance capacity. Law and Modernization 3:47–60 (in Chinese)
Xiao P, Hu R (2008) Analysis about the nature of petitions. Law Science Magazine 4:63–66 (in Chinese)

Xinhua (2021) Working report of the SPC. https://www.court.gov.cn/zixun/xiangqing/290831.html. Accessed 2 May 2024 (in Chinese)
Ye L (2007) Commercial law concept and commercial adjudication. Journal of Law Application 9:17–20 (in Chinese)
Ye X (2015) Rethinking the phenomenon of 'zero judgment.' Tribune of Political Science and Law 3:155–163 (in Chinese)
Ying X (2004) The remedy of 'letter and visit': a special administrative remedy. Chinese Journal of Law 3:58–71 (in Chinese)
Yu J (2005) Reform of the petition system and constitutional construction. Twenty-First Century 3:71–78 (in Chinese)
Yu L (2019) The strategy to resolve case-filing pressure within people's court and its reform. Modern Law Science 5:23–35 (in Chinese)
Zhang W (2009) Difficulty in filing a lawsuit: thinking on a 'Chinese issue.' Chinese Journal of Law 6:65–76 (in Chinese)
Zhang W (2011) Civil procedure law: delay and progress. Chinese Journal of Law 6:40–43 (in Chinese)
Zhang W (2012) Analysis on countermeasures to delayed evidential submission in civil procedures. The Jurist 5: 104–114+178–179 (in Chinese)
Zhang W (2015) Review on the procedures and manners of civil court hearings in China and its rebuilding. China Legal Science 2:66–80 (in Chinese)
Zhang Q (2018) The prospect and explanation for local-level judges' resignation: a case study from Y-province. Tsinghua University Law Journal 4:48–67 (in Chinese)
Zhang W (2019) Civil procedure law. Law Press, Beijing (in Chinese)
Zhang M, Dai J (2009) Difficulties and solutions: a rational exploration of the court's litigation-related petition system in the transitional period. Journal of Law Application 6:71–74 (in Chinese)
Zhang W, Xiao G (2012) The relationship between court mediation and making judgments. Tribune of Political Science and Law 6:168–174 (in Chinese)
Zhao X (2005) Institutional logic of petitions. Twenty-First Century 3:85–90 (in Chinese)
Zheng F, Yang M (2020) The challenge and influence of internet court trials on traditional civil evidence system. Evidence Science 1:59–71 (in Chinese)
Zhou C (2018) The construction and prospect of internet courts. Journal of Law Application 3:38–43 (in Chinese)
Zhu S (2010) Judicial management and social management: how can the court effectively respond to "too many cases but too few judges"? China Legal Science 6:176–189 (in Chinese)
Zou B (2010) Nine-step method on elements of the civil trial. Law Press, Beijing (in Chinese)

Chapter 11
Challenges of Online Dispute Resolution: New Possibilities and Boundaries

11.1 Introduction

Discussing how to make civil judgments in China cannot ignore the major event in recent years, i.e., the outbreak of the COVID-19 pandemic, which shows another contextual element of civil judgments. The impact of this element can even be developing after the termination of the pandemic. In the time of the global pandemic, the scientifically inevitable strategy of lockdown and the epidemiological necessity of keeping social distance put a huge barrier between the justice services and its users.[1] Civil judgments are the results of these services and show the possible interaction between the judiciary and the parties. And there are various practical issues relating to how to prevent the spread of a disease-causing virus and manage court proceedings efficiently and appropriately.[2] These issues are definitely challenging different civil justice systems. However, since humankind today is better equipped with scientific and technological tools than at the time of the 1918 influenza, it has not so far been necessary to postpone dispute resolution or hold hearings merely outdoors in open spaces like parks.[3]

In such circumstances, it is hardly possible to insist on regular judicial activities in most cases. Rather, in pursuit of procedural and substantive justice, many jurisdictions have had to adjust to the usage of ODR, which is not a new concept in comparative context.[4] This adjustment may start with the choice of using software such as Skype, Zoom, CISCO Webex or other national systems operated by the authorities.[5] When business travelers are forbidden from traveling, or at least severely restricted

[1] Krans and Nylund (2021).

[2] E.g. the discussion in Germany, see Heiden (2020, p. 1023).

[3] Scholz-Berger and Schumann (2020, p. 469).

[4] United Nations Commission on International Trade Law (1966).

[5] A comparatively full-scaled lists of these software systems, see Sanders (2021, pp. 68–69).

Z. Cao, *Civil Judgments at First Instance*, Contemporary Chinese Civil and Commercial Law, https://doi.org/10.1007/978-981-97-8662-6_11

from doing so, having virtual hearings instead must be the most reasonable choice.[6] The current discussion on ODR, which nowadays[7] uses more advanced electronic technologies, represents a further global development since the 2010 IAPL conference which primarily focuses on the relationship between electronic technologies and the civil procedure.[8] In addition to the well-accepted ADR mechanism, ODR is one of the "two global movements" that can dramatically affect the "complexion of justice".[9] The "convergence of ODR and ADR within the courts is transforming the nature of access to justice",[10] although some scholar argues for emphasizing the distinction between online ADR and online courts.[11] ADR mechanisms, whether competing with or supplementing the state judiciary, show the citizens the alternatives when they have to face up to civil disputes. Hence, these alternatives are also crucial for civil judgments which also present the citizens resolution of civil disputes.

Since China has taken the experience of Germany in the area of civil justice seriously, which is shown widely through this contribution, the situation of ODR in Germany ought to attract the attention of any related Chinese study, even though it may be the case that the U.S. has taken the global lead in this area.[12] It should be noted for the case of Germany that although the respective legal norms in Article 128a of the *German Code of Civil Procedure* were introduced 20 years ago, their activation has been primarily attributed to the outbreak of the COVID-19 pandemic.[13] At present, online hearings are conducted far more frequently than before the pandemic.[14] Yet, although the need for video-conferences was relatively strong following the outbreak of the COVID-19, the technical preparation for this fundamental change to how hearings are held was to a large extent inadequate.[15] As an illustration, the courts under the direction of the *Oberlandesgericht Köln* took weeks to purchase their cameras after the initiation of the pilot project on videoconferencing in the autumn 2020.[16] However, it is not just courts and judges that have faced challenges in the legal and technical sense, but also practicing lawyers.[17] And even when the pandemic is over, it will be highly necessary to discuss whether ODR could be a better option

[6] E.g., in the area of international commercial arbitration, Queen Mary University of London and White & Case LLP (2021).

[7] The situation for example more than 10 years ago, see Poblet (2011); also Pappas (2008).

[8] Kengyel and Nemessányi (2012).

[9] Quek Anderson (2019, p. 126).

[10] Quek Anderson (2019, pp. 132–143).

[11] Legg (2016, p. 227).

[12] ABA Center for Innovation (2020).

[13] Windau (2020, p. 2753); Schmidt and Saam (2020, pp. 216–217). The similar situation in Austria, see Scholz-Berger and Schumann (2020, p. 469).

[14] This finding is based on the results of an online survey which 663 German judges have taken part in. Rebehn (2021a, p. 90).

[15] Rebehn (2020, p. 164).

[16] Lamsfuß and Werner (2021, p. 50).

[17] Schmidt and Saam (2020, p. 216).

for civil justice in future. ODR can indeed be the future of justice[18] or at least the future for some types of civil cases.[19] Similar to the case of other professions, even home offices for judges should not be ruled out entirely.[20]

Moreover, both the national judiciary and ADR mechanisms have been heavily affected. For instance, in the area of international commercial arbitration,[21] the relatively new empirical international arbitration survey of the Queen Mary University of London shows that compared with the survey findings from three years prior, comprehensive virtual hearings are much more frequently held. Even in this case, however, the practice of videoconferencing has not changed dramatically.[22] Although the question of whether the already well-established arbitration belongs to ADR depends on the definition of ADR in national or international context, it is clear that arbitration and other ADR mechanisms need to be adjusted as well. Lawyers and other professionals now try to ensure that they can continue their work with the solution of ODR which does differ from traditional dispute resolution.

The adoption of ODR in the judiciary is not merely a case of combining new technologies with the traditional judicial business. All steps of the judicial proceedings and various judicial activities are covered by online technologies. In China, even all dispute resolution mechanisms (civil courts, commercial arbitration, facilitated mediation, and e-commerce) have introduced ODR into their operations. All four mechanisms face the same online conditions and thus face similar problems. This situation makes the Chinese legal approach to addressing the issues a good example for observation. And since Chinese courts[23] were already prepared to embrace ODR, the emergency situation due to the global pandemic did not shake their determination to improve their online judicial service. It is also less important to distinguish temporary measures from the "new normal" after the pandemic.[24] While the justice system should be evolving and adapt itself to the new e-system, there may be some additional challenges. Besides the insistence on the principle of due process,[25] there are other special elements of ODR to be considered as well. Hence, to introduce how ODR was brought into the Chinese context and how various mechanisms perform, to report the challenges especially to civil justice while insisting on the requirement of due process, and to evaluate the impacts of new technologies, are the purposes of this chapter.

---

[18] A loud and clear voice in this direction, see Susskind (2019).

[19] Sanders (2021, p. 71).

[20] Köbler (2021, p. 52). However, at least Article 128a of the *German Code of Civil Procedure* does not provide any exceptional rules for judges to do their jobs outside the courtroom. Schupp (2021, pp. 66–67) (supporting hearings outside the courtroom); Windau (2020, p. 2753).

[21] Gu (2018a, pp. 165–169).

[22] The School of International Arbitration Queen Mary University of London and White & Case LLP (2021).

[23] On the background of Chinese courts and their recent evolvement, see Gu (2021, pp. 20–50).

[24] Fu (2021, p. 42).

[25] E.g. Ghoshray (2006, pp. 317, 334–348).

11.2 Widely Accepted Online Dispute Resolution in China

11.2.1 Commercial Arbitration

In the area of commercial arbitration, online operations are generally accepted. In practice, because of the convenience of arbitral proceedings, the commercial arbitration is popular in the whole business world. If the parties could mutually choose for online proceedings in specific cases, the responsible arbitration institutions should respect the needs of parties and prepare the necessary framework to improve their own arbitral service. Prior to the global pandemic, the online service had already been adopted by Chinese arbitration institutions. For instance, the SCIA released its *Online Arbitration Rules of the SCIA* in 2019. Among others, Article 3 of *Online Arbitration Rules of the SCIA* provides that for disputes arising from online transactions or other commercial disputes, where the parties agree to submit their dispute to the SCIA for online arbitration, it is understood that the parties have agreed to that arbitration. Article 6 of *Online Arbitration Rules of the SCIA* makes clear that online arbitration cases will be heard online, and related follow-ups, such as case acceptance, payment of fees and costs, service, exchange of evidence, hearing, mediation, rendering of awards, and other procedures, will be generally conducted online.

It is also noted that the CIETAC, a leading institution of commercial arbitration, has also been the pioneer in ODR in China. In addition to having established an online arbitration platform in 2009,[26] the CIETAC registered "ODR" as part of the domain name at one of its websites, namely the Online Dispute Resolution Center.[27] This agency resolves, in fact, disputes over.CN domain names and generic top-level domain names.[28] Moreover, the CIETAC announced its *CIETAC COVID-19 Guidelines*[29] in summer 2020. Among others, according to Article 2.1 of the *CIETAC COVID-19 Guidelines*, the parties and their representatives are encouraged to file their arbitration applications with CIETAC's online case filing system or to use the postal service or other noncontact means to submit their arbitration applications. To promote the efficient service of documents, parties are always encouraged to agree to submit and receive arbitration documents via emails at all phases of the arbitration process. Where the CIETAC personnel asks in the Notice of Arbitration for the parties' opinions on the submission, receipt, and service of arbitration documents by email, the parties are urged to consider approving submission by email (Article 2.2 of the *CIETAC COVID-19 Guidelines*).

In the *CIETAC COVID-19 Guidelines*, a virtual oral hearing is specifically held in accordance with the Arbitration Rules of the CIETAC. During the pandemic, Article 2.6 of the *CIETAC COVID-19 Guidelines* requests that arbitral tribunals for cases to be examined with oral hearings consider holding virtual hearings. Concretely

---

[26] CIETAC (2022a).

[27] CIETAC (2022b).

[28] Id.

[29] CIETAC (2020).

speaking, the tribunal is requested to comprehensively consider factors such as the parties' opinions, the complexity of the case, the volume of evidence, any witness to be present, any arguments against holding a virtual hearing, and the convenience and equality of participants' access to the virtual hearing facilities. Article 2.6 of the *CIETAC COVID-19 Guidelines* also states that during any virtual hearings, the arbitral tribunal shall fully protect the parties' procedural rights to present their cases reasonably and to enforce the arbitral award equally under the applicable procedural law.

Furthermore, Article 2.6 of the *CIETAC COVID-19 Guidelines* stipulates that after consulting with the parties, an arbitral tribunal can adopt one of the available means for virtual hearings based on the case circumstances. First, if arbitrators, parties to a case, their representatives, and other participants are located in different parts of the Mainland of China, the tribunal can hold a virtual hearing on the CIETAC smart oral hearing platform.[30] Second, if arbitrators, parties, their representatives, and other participants are located in different jurisdictions, or if the hearing will not be held in Chinese, a virtual hearing is possible on a video conferencing platform, rather than the CIETAC's platform, that the parties agree to and the CIETAC approves. Third, once the CIETAC facilities are reopen to the public, all case participants can participate in virtual hearings at their nearest CIETAC facilities. Lastly, if case participants are located in different jurisdictions, virtual hearings can be held on joint platforms between the CIETAC and other foreign arbitration institutions.

Under these rules, we may figure out the importance of the agreement between parties, the flexibility of arbitral proceedings and the power of the arbitral tribunals. The special consideration is given to the pandemic, while the aforementioned concrete rules could be of utility for the normal operation of proceedings when the pandemic is over. For successful arbitral proceedings, the convenience of dispute resolution and the parties' intention are two crucial elements. Especially, arbitration is the result of private autonomy and parties' choice. There is less doubt about the admissibility of having online steps of the proceedings when the parties have agreed to adopt such proceedings. Nevertheless, when it comes to the state's court and its statutory civil proceedings, the lawyers may consider whether procedural agreements, in any form, could regulate the parties to outline the current or future civil proceedings in the public court.[31]

11.2.2 Facilitated Mediation

ODR is also popular in mediation. Mediation is a way for a third party to facilitate the settlement between the parties, while arbitration targets at making an adjudicative

[30] CIETAC (2021).

[31] Cabral (2019, pp. 364–365).

decision to the case at issue.[32] Mediation is also considered as a traditional working method in China to make the society more harmonious and conflicting human relationship restored again. Recently, a so-called Fengqiao Model (枫桥经验),[33] which among others incorporates mediation and other mechanisms other than going to the court, is promoted vigorously as one of the CPC's leading policy in the field of social government and management.

Since both arbitration and mediation have been acknowledged as major approaches to resolving disputes, an outsider may presume that just like the situation in commercial arbitration, the same online transformation happens in the area of facilitated mediation. Besides the commercial mediation or other forms of mediation out of the judicial process, there is so-called judicial mediation in China as well. It represents that the mediation organized by the trial judges themselves is already an ordinary part of the civil process in China.[34] In this respect, online judicial mediation is possible just as online litigation. Despite that there are already countless online mediation cases previously, the *Rules for the Online Mediation by People's Courts* was issued on 30 December 2021. This judicial interpretation says basically that the judges and other mediators could mediate the cases before the commencement of or during civil proceedings. Designated Internet Courts may even have conference rooms reserved for online mediation. Moreover, the out-of-court mediation can also use means of ODR.

Among various mediation possibilities, a Chinese integrated mechanism deserves some discussion in this contribution which is indicated as the system of "one-stop diversified dispute resolution" (一站式多元解纷平台). In October 2016, according to a special report released by the SPC in 2019, the SPC launched a unified online mediation platform to cover mediation processes from acceptance to classification, resolution, and feedback. The platform has multiple functions, such as court-annexed mediation before and after filing an application for court approval.[35] By 31 October 2019, it is said that the SPC online mediation platform had served 2,679 courts, 21,379 professional mediation organizations, and 79,271 mediators and resolved a total of 1,369,134 cases via mediation.[36]

As one example of this ongoing ODR plan, the First Intermediate People's Court in Hainan Province established the first online platform for mediation[37] in December 2019. It has connections with the mediation facilities in Hong Kong SAR and Macao SAR as well as various governmental branches, arbitration centers, and local Women's Federation. The Women's Federation, a government-affiliated organization whose main responsibilities are to represent and safeguard women's rights and interests, has been able to use this online platform to help with settling family

[32] For details on the framework of dispute resolution mechanisms, see Menkel-Meadow, Porter-Love, Kupfer-Schneider and Moffitt (2019, pp. 425–474); Stipanowich and Fraser (2017, p. 839).

[33] Peng (2023).

[34] For a comprehensive observation, see Gu (2021, pp. 157–187).

[35] SPC (2019a, pp. 66–67).

[36] Id. p 67.

[37] First Intermediate People's Court in Hainan Province and Hainan High People's Court (2020).

disputes more effectively.[38] It is reported that as of October 2021, there were in total 328 cases handled on this platform, 135 cases among which were international commercial cases.[39]

To establish a platform for resolving international commercial disputes[40] with the organic connection of litigation, mediation, and arbitration,[41] the General Office of the Central Committee of the CPC and the General Office of the Chinese State Council set a target of forming a "one-stop" diversified mechanism for resolving international commercial disputes in June 2018.[42] Both General Offices then published their *Opinion of the CPC Central Leading Group for Comprehensively Deepening Reform Concerning the Establishment of the Belt and Road International Commercial Dispute Resolution Mechanism and Institutions*[43] which settled the framework of transnational dispute resolution.

Half a year later, the SPC published a judicial document called the *Notice of the General Office of the SPC on Determining the First Group of International Commercial Arbitration and Mediation Institutions Included in the "One-Stop" Diversified Mechanisms for Resolving International Commercial Disputes.* Hence, it selected the CIETAC, the Shanghai International Economic and Trade Arbitration Commission, the SCIA, the Beijing Arbitration Commission, the China Maritime Arbitration Commission, and the Mediation Center of the China Council for the Promotion of International Trade and the SCMC as the first group of arbitration and mediation institutions involved in this program. In this judicial document, there are also provisions regarding the overall layout of "smart courts", stipulating that the SPC should continue strengthening the information-based construction of the "one-stop" diversified settlement mechanism for international commercial disputes; optimizing the functionality of online dispute settlement platforms; and effectively promoting the organic connection of mediation, arbitration, and litigation. Such efforts aim to resolve international commercial disputes in a fair, efficient, and convenient manner. A senior SPC judge saw the aforementioned measures as "vigorously promoting the development of the CICC's information infrastructure … and striving to achieve the goal of the 'smart trial.'".[44]

It is also stipulated that ODR providers can be private entities rather than governmental branches. In addition to the court system (pure public) and leading arbitration institutions (public and private) that already facilitate mediation, there are private mediation entities as well. The aforementioned SCMC, established in 2011, has staked a claim as the first institution in China to specialize in commercial dispute

[38] Xiao and Ma (2019).

[39] Jin (2021).

[40] For details on this platform, see Holloway (2020, pp. 51–80).

[41] On the legal harmonization in the context of commercial arbitration under the Belt and Road Initiative, see Gu (2018b).

[42] Long (2020, p 1305).

[43] Xinhuanet (2018).

[44] Sun X (2020, pp. 49–50).

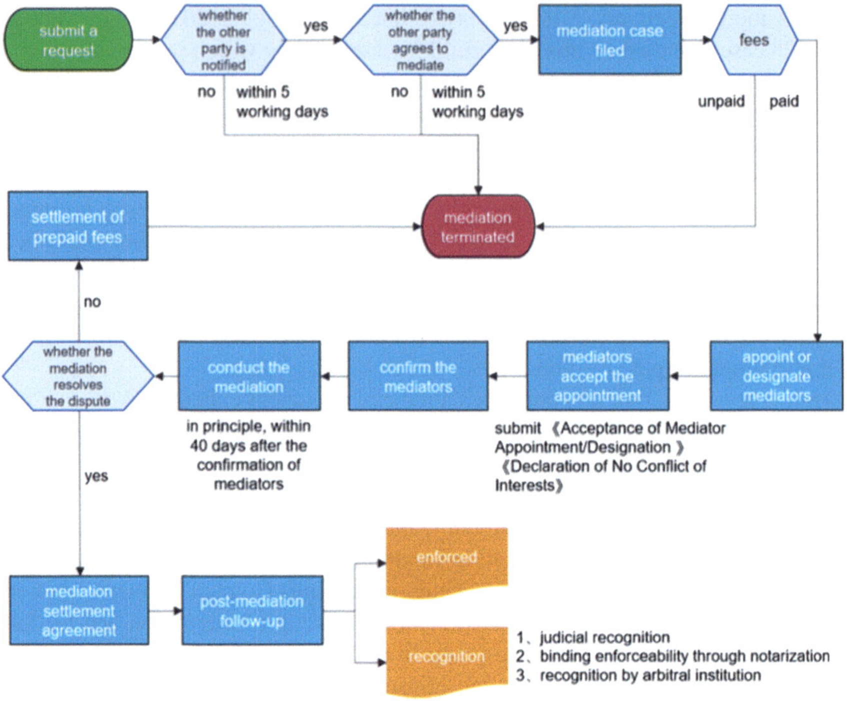

Fig. 11.1 The BCI & BIMC service procedure[47]

mediation,[45] which provides services both online and offline. Moreover, there is a private player in the city of Shenzhen called BCI & BIMC. On 26 October 2019, BCI & BIMC added mediation to its services offering based on its platform for foreign law ascertainment. The agency has also actively invited Chinese and international leading mediators with abundant experience across the country to join. The services of BCI & BIMC can connect to civil litigation in certain courts. For example, the Shenzhen Intermediate People's Court can use those services for online or offline mediation.[46] The BCI & BIMC business mode can be summarized in the following Fig. 11.1.

One might wonder if public resources are used to financially support these private providers. The answer is 'no.' Even if promoting ODR is one of China's policies, ODR itself is not eligible for any government subsidies. Instead, the parties to any online mediation normally pay the fees in advance, with actually allocated amounts agreed to by the parties. For instance, BCI & BIMC charges three kinds of fees for its mediation services, i.e. registration, administration, and mediation itself. Fees are calculated in consultations between the parties and mediators and can be hourly,

[45] SCMC (2015).

[46] BCI & BIMC (2019a).

[47] BCI & BIMC (2019b).

weekly, or in proportion to the dollar amount being contested. Parties agree on hourly or weekly rates when it is difficult to calculate the contested amount.[48] Meanwhile, the CIETAC and other online arbitral proceedings are governed by a special fee chart with slightly lower than the standard charges.[49] However, this special arrangement does not waive the fees for the parties to pay.

11.2.3 E-commerce Systems

E-commerce could, by nature, call for the internet-based ADR.[50] On one hand, it is noted that the commercial arbitration concentrates mainly on the enforcement of commercial contracts. If there are some contractual disputes in the field of e-commerce, the parties could rely on the commercial arbitration to determine the controversial issues when they previously have concluded a valid arbitral agreement. Regarding the e-commerce, there should be many materials or evidence generated online. An internet-based arbitration may at least be of advantages during evidential exchange and evaluation. On the other hand, some internet platforms are even responsible for resolving e-commerce disputes. Specifically, Article 63 of the *E-Commerce Law of the P.R.C.* states that an e-commerce platform business should establish an online dispute settlement mechanism; develop and publish dispute settlement rules; and equitably and impartially settle disputes based on voluntary mutual agreement. Article 61 of the *E-Commerce Law of the P.R.C.* emphasizes that when a consumer buys commodities or receives services on an e-commerce platform and is involved in a dispute with the in-platform business, the e-commerce platform business must protect the consumer's lawful rights and interests. Actually, ODR could protect consumers' rights just as it could protect other rights.[51]

In particular, online platforms such as JD (Chinese version of Amazon)[52] and Taobao (Chinese version of eBay)[53] provide multiple ODR modes to facilitate dispute resolution, as other internet platforms do. For instance, Taobao's dispute resolution service is a nonbinding, third-party evaluation system. The platform's special commissioners, who are ordinary employees of Taobao company, perform the dispute resolution functions. There are requirements for the burden of evidential production and the standard of proof. Under this public jury system established in 2012, even a voluntarily registered jury could participate in arbitration of some types of disputes. Today, Taobao reports more than 4 million jurors registered and 16 million cases

---

[48] Id.

[49] CIETAC (2015).

[50] Perritt (2000, p. 675).

[51] General observation, see Rule and Schmidtz (2017).

[52] JD (2020).

[53] Taobao (2019). Under these general rules, there are concrete rules for different types of goods such as cellphone, clothes, shoes, and so forth.

concluded.[54] In addition to ordinary e-commerce between consumers and service providers, Taobao governs intellectual property disputes under a separate intellectual property dispute resolution mechanism.[55] Weibo (Chinese version of Twitter) has a similarly comprehensive set of community rules.[56]

11.3 Internet Justice System and Its Various Stages

11.3.1 Development of Online Courts in China

When the aforementioned ADR mechanisms fail, the state judiciary will play a key role as the last resort in dispute resolution. After all, the existing disputes need to be resolved in a civilized society. Here come civil judgments as well. On such occasions, standard court proceedings govern the resolution of disputes and provide the default rules. Chinese courts take ODR into account very seriously and have been attempting to lead the trend in ODR in the whole world. E-courts take one of two forms, internal or external. An internal e-court takes place in a physical courtroom with communications technologies, whereas an external e-court could be entirely virtual.[57] As Susskind points out, there is a certain question of whether courts represent a service of the state for dispute resolution or places for people to congregate.[58]

Not only were three special Internet Courts[59] established between 2017 and 2018, but numerous cases were also filed, prepared, heard and finally decided in an electronic environment. In this sense, the outbreak of the COVID-19 gave more incentive to the development of ODR as well. For instance, Fu Yulin promptly observed that Chinese courts received 16.51 million new cases and resolved 13.08 million cases during the worst months of the pandemic from January to July 2020 and that the ratio of closed cases remained stable year-on-year.[60] Enduring restrictive measures during these months, without ODR there is no way to achieve this performance.

Moreover, the adoption of ODR in the Chinese court system is a product of the longstanding judicial reform (Chap. 10), which has distinct key aims for various periods of time.[61] Following the clarification of the SPC, Chinese courts are said to take judicial openness as the point of departure for the application of internet technologies in the judiciary. Since 2013, Chinese courts have been striving for and

[54] Alibaba (2024a).

[55] Alibaba (2024b).

[56] Sina Weibo (2021).

[57] Wang (2021, p. 196).

[58] Susskind (2019, pp. 95–176).

[59] Suggestion for centralised Internet Courts in Germany, see Dickert (2020, pp. 296, 298).

[60] Fu (2021, p. 41).

[61] Fu and Cao (2012, pp. 495–519); Minzner (2011, p. 935).

have accomplished the creation of four official websites—i.e. China Judicial Process Information Online,[62] China Judgment Online,[63] China Trial Live Broadcast (then changed to China Court Trial Online),[64] and China Executive Information Online[65]—to promote judicial openness and transparency. To satisfy the diverse needs for justice, Chinese courts continually experiment with online judicial practice.[66]

As of April 2021, according to the daily updated number on the aforementioned websites, there were nearly 120 million judicial decisions published online and more than 12 million trials streamed openly online where everyone could register and log in to watch the live trials. On 20 December 2022, there are nearly 140 million judicial decisions published online and more than 20 million trials streamed openly online, while on 13 October 2023, the number of published decisions reached 142 million while 22 million trials were streamed. And on 27 May 2024, we could find 146 million decisions published and almost 23 million trials streamed.

The three special Internet Courts deserve more attention for the purpose of this chapter. Article 1 of the *Provisions on Internet Courts* sets the general principle that an Internet Court shall try cases online, and the acceptance, service, mediation, evidence exchange, pre-trial preparation, court trial, judgment pronouncement and other procedural steps concerning a case shall generally be completed online. On the application of a party or depending on the need for the trial, an Internet Court may decide to complete certain parts of the procedural steps offline. It means that the parties actually have no right to reject the adoption of e-justice. It means that merely the court has the discretionary power to determine the form of proceedings adopted. Since their establishment (until 31 October 2021), three Internet Courts were said to have taken more than 350,000 cases and concluded more than 330,000 cases. The rate of online hearing is more than 93% and the average duration of an individual hearing is about 25–38 min. Also, the average period of the case is about 37–70 days. The rate of serving judgments electronically is 82.4%–92.4%, while the rate of automatic performance is up to 93.6%.[67]

Specifically, it is said that the Hangzhou Internet Court conducts all its procedures online, from case filing to the enforcement of judgments. Its special jurisdiction shows the cases which are suitable for ODR, which will be introduced later. Both civil and administrative disputes could be subject to the jurisdiction of Internet Courts. And the Hangzhou Internet Court has delivered more than 4,600 civil judgments in the first three years since its establishment.[68] Besides the Hangzhou Internet Court, the Beijing Internet Court and the Guangzhou Internet Court operate in a similar manner. The plan is that, in the near future, all courts in China should function as Internet

[62] SPC (2024a).

[63] SPC (2024b).

[64] SPC (2024c).

[65] SPC (2024d).

[66] SPC (2019a, pp. 60–61).

[67] Jing (2022, pp. 49, 53–54).

[68] Wang (2021, p. 197).

Courts, which will enable the use of ODR methods completely. The three now-independent Internet Courts should then be competent for internet-based cases that require professional knowledge of technology and experience in the field.

Besides the well-known Internet Courts, there are other courts with high-quality online environment. In 2018, the SPC established two international commercial courts as standing judicial organs that covered major international commercial cases, and both courts incorporated ODR mechanisms. In this context, these two courts are not independent courts but divisions under the framework of the SPC.[69] Article 10 of the *Provisions on International Commercial Courts* stipulates that an international commercial court may collect evidence and conduct cross-examination using audiovisual transmission technology or through other information networks. Article 18 of the *Provisions on International Commercial Courts* adds that an international commercial court may provide electronic litigation, trial process information disclosure, and other litigation services, as well as support case filing, payment of court fees, inspections of case dossiers, exchange of evidence, service of litigation documents, and online hearings.

In addition, two specialized Financial Courts, one established in Shanghai in April 2018 and the other in Beijing in March 2021, have also taken up many possible e-technologies. The Beijing Financial Court adopted advanced online case management in early 2021. All steps in cases were taken online, and e-dossiers were used instead of paper during the entire proceedings. Both parties took part in the online hearings, in which e-dossiers and any additional evidence were uploaded before presentation to the trial panels. These e-dossiers were subsequently stored for record retention. The panel members examined and evaluated the evidence, and the judges' opinions were collected in an automatic interpretation system that then produced transcripts. After proceedings, judges' assistants sent out decisions by electronic service. For instance, as reported, the whole process for some individual civil cases took only nine days. These cases, by their nature, required setting aside arbitral awards, which demands a great extent of the formal review and is thus easier to determine than cases being judged on their merits. Nevertheless, the performance of this newborn Beijing Financial Court could still represent the possibility of promoting electronic proceedings more generally in China.[70] The fact that Beijing Financial Court took seriously the official news reports about these new electronic processes reflects the practical stress on electronic proceedings.

---

[69] Furthermore, both in December 2020 and December 2021, two more international commercial courts were established within the separate intermediate People's courts in individual cities, namely Suzhou and Beijing.

[70] Xinhuanet (2021).

11.3.2 Reform Initiative in 2020

The major example of the movement of Chinese dispute resolution procedures online can be found in the operation of judicial processes. It means that not only the filing process but also the service of documents, the preparatory phase and the successive hearings could take place online. It should be noted that, in accordance with the *2020 Pilot Program* published in January 2020, China is running an ongoing reform experiment in order to separate complicated cases from simple ones in civil proceedings. This two-year-long experiment was started on 15 January 2020 and was carried out in some areas of 15 provinces (municipalities) out of a total of 34.

The prospective result of this experiment, which passed its mid-term evaluation in February 2021,[71] was planned to provide some guidance for the modification of the *CPL* statute later. A year into the experiment, it is reported that among the selected courts, the percentage of online cases on the docket is 54.5%, 17% higher than before this pilot program, and the percentage of electronic service is 56.1%, 34% higher than before this pilot program. Moreover, nearly 30% of all hearings take place online and the average length of hearings is 46 min, which is 60% shorter than the offline hearings.

For the purpose of this chapter, the separate part of this reform experiment that concerns improving electronic litigation is of importance. Specifically, Article 21 paragraph 1 of the *2020 Pilot Program* provides that the People's courts, the parties and other litigation participants may conduct litigation activities online through some information technology-based litigation platform. The online litigation activities of litigation participants shall have the same effect as offline litigation activities. Meanwhile, Article 21 paragraph 2 lays down that a People's court may decide whether or not to complete the relevant litigation proceedings online based on the technical conditions, the circumstances of the case, the wishes of the parties and other factors. Then, the *Online Litigation Rules*, which came into force on 1 August 2021, elaborates various rules to promote online proceedings.

Since the *2020 Pilot Program* contains the experiment for the forthcoming revision of the *CPL* statute, Chinese lawyers looked forward to a new Civil Procedure Law in the latter half of 2021. In October 2021, the NPC released a draft for revising this statute which mainly followed this experiment and then immediately gave rise to fierce debate among professionals and practitioners. The crucial concern is the insistence on following the principle of due process in different areas of civil justice, not just limited to internet justice. With several changes, the revised statute came into force on 1 January 2022.

In this regard, the related rules of the *2020 Pilot Program* have been generally adopted by the latest revision of the *CPL*.[72] The newly added Article 16 of the *CPL* statute confirms Article 21 of the *2020 Pilot Program*, whereas it incorporates the

[71] Zhou (2021).

[72] Decision of the Standing Committee of the NPC to Amend the Civil Procedure Law of the P.R.C., adopted at the 32nd Session of the Standing Committee of the Thirteenth NPC on 24 December 2021. (in Chinese).

consent of the parties as the precondition to have online civil proceedings. This precondition shows the efforts of the academics in China who endeavor to stand for the ordinary citizens during the legislative process. Since the procedural rights of the parties to civil processes, who are the primary justice users, will be affected by the new reform equipped with rules for online proceedings, we have to be prudent and cautious to require for the agreement of the parties on having online proceedings. It could be another issue whether in the end, the online proceedings should be the default proceedings for civil cases or even other types of cases in China.

11.3.3 Filing Civil Lawsuits Online

To commence a civil action, the first step is to file a lawsuit. At the end of 2019, the SPC declared that it would be possible from then on to register a case in any court other than the registration court. In this way, some cross-regional filing services have been built up. In January 2015, Quanzhou Intermediate People's Court of Fujian Province took the lead in introducing the cross-regional mode for filing cases. This approach was gradually taken up nationwide. In 2018, it was reported that more than 120,000 cases were successfully filed cross-regionally all over the country. From January to June 2019, online filing and cross-regional filing services were fully implemented within Zhejiang province, with 100% of the courts providing such services. A total of 253,000 civil cases were filed online, accounting for 59.7% of the total.[73] In short, the court visited by the plaintiff in person will assist the registration court to check the necessary materials for filing a lawsuit. If the visited court finds out that the legally regulated case docket criteria have been met, it will inform the registration court to register the case in its own docketing system. Then, the registration court will inform the plaintiff directly that its claim form has already been accepted by the registration court.

For comparison, the SPC announced in its annual report to the NPC of 2021[74] that all Chinese courts are now able to register cases using online registration systems. There is then no need for the plaintiff to visit any court, whereas some physical visits are still required by the aforementioned cross-regional filing service. Instead, the plaintiff can make use of the relevant system online or use the official smartphone app operated by the judiciary. Then, their cases are to be reviewed and docketed directly by the registration court. Yet, this is merely the general description regarding the expectation of real judicial practices. It is true that many parties can now file their cases online, while many other parties still have to visit the court at all levels personally for many practical reasons, e.g. because oral explanation for the current case is necessary or the evidence submitted at the pre-action stage needs to be examined physically.[75]

[73] SPC (2019a, p. 69).

[74] Xinhua (2021).

[75] Cao (2024).

In this respect, Chinese courts are said to be promoting the "Mobile Court" litigation service platform based on WeChat's softwares. Using facial recognition, remote audio and video systems, e-signature and other technologies, parties and judges can easily use mobile phones to conduct online litigation activities, such as filing, service, hearings, evidence exchange, mediation, and so forth. Looking back to the beginning of this reform, Ningbo Yuyao Primary People's Court of Zhejiang province initiated the "Mobile Court" platform in October 2017. After the gradual extension from the court at the local level to the provincial level, the SPC then decided to expand the "Mobile Court" pilot scheme to 12 provinces in March 2019.[76]

Meanwhile, the e-dossier system, which allows the parties to check on their case at any time, is widely accepted. Article 21 of the *Provisions on Internet Courts* establishes that Internet Courts shall generate electronic dossiers in synchrony with the cases through some litigation platform and then form electronic archives. Where all paper case archives have been converted into electronic archives, electronic archives may replace paper archives for the purposes of transfer of appeal cases and the storage of files. Article 20 of the *Provisions on Internet Courts* also states that, as for cases tried by Internet Courts online, electronic transcripts may be generated synchronously through speech recognition technology during mediation, evidence exchange, the court trial, the collegiate bench meeting and other procedural steps. Electronic transcripts shall, after being verified and confirmed online, have the same legal validity as written transcripts.

11.3.4 Ordinary Proceedings of Hearings

If we consider the internet streaming of physical trial hearings on the website China Court Trial Online since September 2016 as a type of ODR, then the online system has already been established for many years. This streaming system enables the general public to observe and replay the whole process of a court hearing. By 11 February 2018, all Chinese courts had been put online on this website, and most of them had begun to broadcast their hearings. However, courts can perform quite differently. For instance, according to a well-acknowledged third-party evaluation report for the open trials of People's courts provided by the Institute of Law of the Chinese Academy of Social Sciences, many courts in Jiangsu province were leading in the area of judicial transparency in 2018, while some courts in Xinjiang province got comparatively very low scores in this field. Some courts performed better in 2018 than in 2017, and vice versa.[77] By 4 December 2020, more than 10 million hearings had been broadcast live at China Court Trial Online.[78] This record made by the Chinese judiciary is worth celebrating. And as indicated previously, on 27 May 2024 there are almost 23 million trials streamed.

---

[76] SPC (2019a, p. 70).

[77] Zhi and Ye (2019, p. 103).

[78] Sun H (2020, p. 1).

By its nature, the streaming of a court hearing still relies on the physical hearing taking place in a courtroom, which certainly differs from the mode of virtual hearings. Instead, Article 10 of the *Opinions on Optimizing the Allocation of Judicial Resources* of 2016 provides that for civil and administrative cases to which the simplified proceedings apply in the final hearing, with the consent of the parties, the court hearing may use the technology of videoconferencing. The witness, expert identifier or victim in a criminal case may use audio-visual transmission technology or a synchronous video witness room to present their evidence. Since videoconferencing and related technologies have been in use for several years, when the pandemic came, there was for many participants to civil proceedings no strong reluctance to try or be tried online. Comparatively speaking, there may have been strong resistance in this respect, for example, in Germany.[79] Yet, at least according to a relatively new survey of around 400 practicing judges, the number of video-conferences[80] in 2020 was five times than in 2019.[81]

Relying on this mode of remote trial, the advanced version of an online hearing is a hearing carried out solely online. The major example of this mode in China is hearing cases before Internet Courts. Accordingly, Article 12 of the *Provisions on Internet Courts* requires that an Internet Court shall hold a court hearing via videoconferencing. Where it is truly necessary to ascertain identities, verify originals or inspect physical objects in court, or under any other special circumstance, the Internet Court may decide to hold a court hearing offline, but other procedural steps shall still be completed online.

Moreover, Article 13 of the *Provisions on Internet Courts* establishes the possibility of deviating from the procedural requirements of any ordinary hearing. An Internet Court may, in light of actual circumstances, decide to simplify the proceedings of court hearings. Respectively, the following methods could be adopted. First, if the verification of the identities of the parties, the notification of procedural rights and obligations, and the taking of oaths to observe the discipline for a court hearing have been completed online before a court hearing is held, it is not required to conduct them again in a court hearing. Second, if the parties have completed the evidence exchange online, the undisputed evidence may no longer be produced or cross-examined after the judge has made statements in the court hearing. Third, with the consent of the parties, the statement of the parties, court investigation, court debate and other steps of court hearings may be integrated. For a simple civil case, the court hearing may be conducted directly around the claims of the parties or the elements of the case in accordance with substantive legal provisions.

---

[79] Vierkötter (2021, p. 263).

[80] Heil (2020, pp. 14–15).

[81] Rebehn (2021b, pp. 130, 131).

11.3.5 Online Service of Legal Documents

Moreover, serving or notifying legal documents to the parties and competent entities during any proceeding shows one key element of due process which exists in every legal jurisdiction. It is clear that proceedings should not go forward unless all parties have been properly noticed.[82] In fact, this requirement for service and notice in civil proceedings is rather a well-acknowledged principle of civil procedure. To prove it, we could among others turn to the new Model European Rules of Civil Procedure,[83] which has a subtitle of "Service, Due Notice and the Right to be Heard". Forms of notice are generally stipulated by fixed legal rules that might be "beyond the constitutional requirements" for "mechanics of notice and service".[84] However, it is noticeable that the electronic means of service follows different processes and the same set of rules should apply to these means. Beyond ADR, Chinese courts have developed detailed procedures for service that can extend to other areas of dispute resolution. The rules for civil proceedings could introduce serving litigation documents as an example of potential internet-based arbitration and mediation.

Generally speaking, Chinese civil procedure is a court-driven one. Once a court registers a new civil case, it has the judicial responsibility to serve the litigation documents to the defendant, which holds for online proceedings as well. Article 87 paragraph 1 of the *CPL* (2012) stated that with the consent of the person to be served, a court could serve litigation documents by fax, email, or any other means that allows a sender to confirm receipt by the person being served except for judgments, rulings, and consent judgments. If the court adopts one of the above means, according to Article 87 paragraph 2 of the *CPL* (2012), the time when the fax, email, or other means reaches the intended recipient is considered the date of service. Following this revolutionary new rule, Article 135 of the *ICPL* (2015) adds that, in its first paragraph, litigation documents can electronically be served via fax, email, mobile communications, and other specific systems. Hence, based on Article 135 paragraph 2 of the *ICPL* (2015), the date the document reaches the recipient within the specific systems is the date of service recorded in the relevant system. However, according to the same second paragraph, when a recipient can confirm that he or she received the document on a different date from what was indicated in the court's system, the former prevails. Article 136 of the *ICPL* (2015) also says that a person who agrees to be served electronically must confirm this.

At the end of 2016, the SPC released *Opinions on Optimizing the Allocation of Judicial Resources*. Among others, Article 3 of the *Opinions on Optimizing the Allocation of Judicial Resources* is a comprehensive one which covers different perspectives of serving legal documents and therefore could be used as a suitable illustration for the Chinese approach of online notification during civil proceedings. Hence, it stipulates that if parties agree on a service address before any dispute arises, the court can use it as the confirmed address for serving litigation documents.

---

[82] Andrews (2019, pp. 735–736); also Chase et al. (2017, pp. 234–251).

[83] ELI/UNIDROIT (2021).

[84] Yeazell and Schwartz (2019, pp. 172–176).

A party that brings an action or submits a defense must confirm the service address in written form. Moreover, if parties have agreed to electronic service of documents, they must provide and confirm such electronic service addresses as fax number, email address, and WeChat ID. Still within Article 3, the *Opinions on Optimizing the Allocation of Judicial Resources* call for taking full advantage of China Judicial Process Information Online and establishing a uniform electronic service platform for courts across the country, such as improving how the national postal institution serves litigation documents by offering the exclusive delivery service for courts.

In February 2017, following the promise made in the SPC's annual report,[85] a National Unified Electronic Service Platform for Courts (全国统一电子送达平台)[86] began trial after the establishment of smart courts. Four individual courts, namely, Fengman District People's Court in Jilin Province, Huadian City People's Court in Jilin Province, Hangzhou Railway Transport Court, and Yuhuan People's Court in Zhejiang Province, were selected as the pilot sites. Litigation documents in these courts were available through Sina Weibo, Sina Email, Alipay, and other platforms, whose channels are particularly efficient because of popular social media in China.[87]

Article 24 paragraph 1 of the *2020 Pilot Program* provides that with the consent of the person being served, the courts can deliver litigation documents and evidential materials by electronic means such as the China Judicial Process Information Online, the National Court Unified Service Platform, fax, email, and instant messaging. In this regard, Article 24 paragraph 2 of the *2020 Pilot Program* lists specifically that any of the four circumstances constitutes consent to electronic service under court rules.[88] Article 25 of the *2020 Pilot Program* regulates that after receiving the express consent of the person being served, the People's court may electronically serve judicial decisions such as judgments, rulings, and consent judgments. However, if a party requests printed versions of these instruments, the court must provide them. Before Articles 24 and 25 of the *2020 Pilot Program*, meanwhile, Article 15 of the *Provisions on Internet Courts* established substantially similar rules. Combining Article 87 paragraph 1 of the *CPL* (2012) and Article 25 of the *2020 Pilot Program*, Article 90 paragraph 1 of the current *CPL* makes it clear that with the consent of the person to be served, the court could serve litigation documents using electronic means that allows a sender to confirm receipt by the person being served. While serving judgments, rulings, and consent judgments, if a party requests printed versions of these

[85] Zhou (2016).

[86] SPC (2024e).

[87] Wang (2021, p. 196).

[88] These circumstances are provided as followed. First, the person being served must give express consent. Second, the person being served must agree that electronic service applies to the litigation. Third, the person being served must voluntarily provide an electronic address for service in its complaint or answer filed. Fourth, the person being served accepts the completed electronic service by returning a receipt, participating in the litigation, and other means and by not expressly disagreeing with electronic service. Article 29 of the *Online Litigation Rules* accepts the substantially same rules, as well.

instruments, the courts must provide them. Such new rules refer to a significant breakthrough since the Chinese legislators are hereby considering the service of documents for tens of millions of cases. In any case, civil proceedings are to be terminated by some form(s) of judicial decisions of the competent court. Nevertheless, in theory, it is of equal importance to notice that the consent of either party is still essential for the adoption of electronic service. How far procedural contracts could stipulate is a genuine issue of due process.[89] The new statute shows the unavoidable emphasis in China on the contractualization of civil litigation which has also been grasped in the aforementioned relationship between arbitration and litigation.[90]

Even though the parties agree to e-service, its effectiveness comes into question. Article 26 paragraph 1 of the *2020 Pilot Program* clarifies that if a People's court uses an electronic address voluntarily provided or confirmed by a person being served, service actually takes place when the information served reaches the system where the electronic address is located. Article 26 paragraph 2 of the *2020 Pilot Program* then stipulates that if the person being served consents to electronic service but fails to voluntarily provide or confirm an electronic address, and the People's court uses an available electronic address of the person being served for service, whether service is completed is determined according to the different circumstances.[91] Lastly, according to Article 26 paragraph 3 of the *2020 Pilot Program*, if the service is completed effectively, the court must prepare for an acknowledgment of electronic service as the effective receipt. Prior to Article 26 of the *2020 Pilot Program*, Article 17 of the *Provisions Internet Courts 2018* had already established substantially similar rules. The suggested rules themselves are provided in a complicated way. However, they intend to meet the needs of various courts and practitioners by incorporating varied situations in one single provision.[92]

Compared to these previous rules, Article 90 paragraph 2 of the current *CPL* chooses to be straightforward and alters Article 87 paragraph 2 of the *CPL* (2012) only slightly. The current rule orders that when the court serves litigation documents using electronic means, service actually takes place when the information served reaches the specific system of the person being served. It means that the new statute refuses the efforts of the SPC to distinguish between the situation where the party has been formally served and the situation where the party has been notified substantially. However, Article 31 of the *Online Litigation Rules* has already incorporated Article

[89] General discussion, see Nylund and Cabral (2023).

[90] Fu (2012, p. 55); Zhang (2004, p. 73).

[91] Article 26, paragraph 2 of the *2020 Pilot Program* clarifies the circumstance as followed. On one hand, if the person being served acknowledges having received the served materials or performs a corresponding litigant act according to the served content, the service is considered to have been completed effectively. On the other hand, if the email platform of the person being served indicates that a message was read or there is other evidence of notice by the person being served, service is presumed to be completed effectively. However, such presumption could be rebutted, if the person being served could prove that this person did not receive the served content. For instance, the person being served could prove that a system error exists, that this person does not use the address for service, or that another person rather than the person being served read the message and so forth.

[92] Zhou (2022, p. 149).

26 of the *2020 Pilot Program*, and this *Online Litigation Rules* ought to be applied in spite of the new *CPL* statute. In other words, it may be concluded that Article 26 of the *2020 Pilot Program* fails to cut a way through the whole legislation process and find a proper place in the new statute, while the same rule is still effective before courts. For other dispute resolution mechanisms, the aforementioned distinction between presumed service and de facto notification could show the correct way to inform the party to be served. In any case, the issue of service is always sensitive and is an essential ingredient for the due process and the fair play. In China, the issue of service shows especially a long-lasting problem in civil justice.[93]

11.4 Securing the General Principle of Due Process

11.4.1 Identifying Suitable Cases for Internet Justice

Although internet justice in China has proved itself to be a very effective system which is still developing rapidly, it definitely encounters some difficulties and challenges too. First of all, based on the comparative research on ODR, there may be specific fields in which ODR has been proven especially effective at resolving disputes. For instance, it could be argued that in Japan sharing economy disputes, some financial disputes, such as those relating to young consumers and Financial Technology, and disputes around small and medium-sized enterprises are more suitable for ODR. In addition, traffic accident disputes, small claims, family cases such as divorce, e-commerce disputes, and neighbor disputes are said to be well solved using ODR in Japan.[94] Since even the same kind of dispute may have quite distinct legal framework and social conditions, the relevant comparative analysis may not be accurate in other jurisdictions. Rather, it shows a possible scientific approach to pick up the most suitable cases for ODR. However, it is even hard to list the types of cases in China which are relatively more suitable for ODR. Rather, since the Chinese judiciary, as mentioned, promotes the usage of ODR generally, it could be said that there are only a few kinds of cases which are not suitable for resolving online.

At least those cases which the Internet Courts are competent to adjudicate are presumed to be appropriate cases for ODR. Article 2 of the *Provisions on Internet Courts* lists these types of cases clearly. The Internet Courts in Beijing, Guangzhou and Hangzhou shall have centralized jurisdiction over a variety of cases at first instance within the jurisdictions of the cities where they are located, and this jurisdiction should be respected by other local People's courts.[95] Moreover, the parties

---

[93] Chen (2016, p. 40).

[94] The questionnaire prepared by Deguchi Masahisa and Miyashita Maiko for the IAPL conference 2021.

[95] In order to provide the foreign audience with specific illustrations of the business of Internet Courts, these cases are listed fully: (1) disputes arising from the signing or performance of online shopping contracts through e-commerce platforms; (2) disputes over network service contracts

can agree that the Internet Courts have jurisdiction over their dispute. Article 3 of the *Provisions on Internet Courts* says that the parties may, within the scope of the disputes over contracts and other property rights and interests determined in the aforementioned Article 2, legally agree upon the jurisdiction of an Internet Court at the place which is actually connected with the dispute. The jurisdiction of multiple Internet Courts could also be established on the agreement of parties, because where a jurisdiction agreement provides that two or more courts at places with a substantial connection to a dispute shall have jurisdiction over the dispute, according to Article 30 paragraph 2 of the *ICPL*, the plaintiff may initiate a lawsuit in one of these courts. However, where an e-commerce operator or network service provider, among others, concludes a jurisdiction agreement with a user in the form of standard clauses, it must comply with the provisions of laws and judicial interpretations regarding standard clauses. It means that the legal norms in the area of substantive civil law should apply.

Nevertheless, there could be types of cases that are not suitable for being tried online. Article 23 paragraph 1 of the *2020 Pilot Program* provides a negative list. It states that a People's court may try any case in court by means of internet streaming, but an online trial is not permitted under any of the following circumstances: (1) where the two parties expressly disagree, or a party disagrees with good reasons; (2) where neither party has the technical conditions and capability to participate in an online trial; (3) where the ascertaining of identity, verifying originals, and inspecting physical things on the spot are required; and (4) in circumstances the People's court otherwise considers unsuitable for an online trial. Article 23 paragraph 3 of the *2020 Pilot Program* says that in a case tried online, if any of the aforementioned circumstances occurs during the trial, the People's court shall switch the case to an in-person trial which is then offline. The online trial activities that have been completed shall have legal effects.

which are both signed and performed on the internet; (3) disputes over financial loan contracts or small loan contracts which are both signed and performed on the internet; (4) disputes over the ownership of copyrights or neighboring rights of works published on the internet for the first time; (5) disputes arising from infringements upon copyrights or neighboring rights of works published or disseminated online through the internet; (6) disputes over internet domain name ownership, infringements and contracts; (7) disputes arising from infringements upon others' personal rights, property rights and other civil rights and interests on the internet; (8) product liability disputes arising from infringements upon others' personal and property rights and interests by products purchased through e-commerce platforms due to product defects; (9) internet public interest litigation cases filed by procuratorial organs; (10) administrative disputes arising from the administrative acts taken by administrative organs in respect of internet information service management, internet commodity trading, and related service management; (11) other internet civil and administrative cases the jurisdiction over which is designated by the People's courts at higher levels.

11.4.2 Absence of Physical Trials and Consequences

11.4.2.1 Legal Right to a Physical Trial?

Just as in all civil proceedings, the principle of due process requires the internet-based judiciary to provide a suitable dispute resolution mechanism that could secure the parties' substantive and procedural rights and enable the parties to take part in court proceedings substantially. Otherwise, civil judgments made would be void due to serious procedural errors. Among others, physical trials are at least, if not the most obvious one, one of major characteristics of the due process and fair proceedings. Hence, one may wonder whether both parties have the legal right to a physical trial rather than a virtual one and whether, without a day before the physical court, the final judgment given after a virtual hearing ought to have the same legal effect as well as persuasive force to the parties concerned and other ordinary citizens.

In Chinese context, both Article 21 of the *2020 Pilot Program* and Article 1 of the *Provisions on Internet Courts* adopt the same attitude that the parties to proceedings have no dispositional right to opt for or refuse the use of electronic proceedings. Global experiences show that the responses to this issue can be different.[96] For instance, in Germany, parties have the right to enter the courtroom physically at any time during civil proceedings.[97]

Additionally, when it then comes to the principle of publicity in civil proceedings, it is also worth considering whether there should be a legal right for the general public to have access to any hearings that are broadcasted live, since the capacity of the virtual courtroom is almost unlimited. To answer this question, a delicate analysis of the balance of interests should be carried out. In some sense, a democratic process like legislating represents only part of the solution because the conflict of distinct fundamental rights—for example the protection of dignity, the preservation of privacy and the procedural principle of openness and so forth—requires a judicial review of constitutionality.[98] Accordingly, there should also be criteria for instead having in-camera proceedings. Due to the topic, this contribution is not to go forward to the details.

11.4.2.2 Possibility of an Asynchronous Trial?

As electronic proceedings allow the parties to be present while they are physically located in different places, it is easy to ask what would happen when the parties are not involved in court hearings at the same time. In this vein, Article 23 paragraph 2 of the *2020 Pilot Program* confirms that if only one party opts for an online trial, the People's court may be in session in such a manner that this initiating party is

---

[96] Sanders (2021, p. 70).

[97] Musielak/Voit/Stadler (2021, § 128a Rn 4); Schupp (2021, p. 66).

[98] Alan Uzelac and C.H. van Rhee are to be thanked for their insights during the Fifteenth Public and Private Justice Course and Conference, which was organised virtually in May 2021 in Dubrovnik.

present online, while the other party is present physically before the court, based on the circumstances of the case.[99] This is not something new. The Hangzhou Internet Court, considering litigants for whom it is not convenient to participate in the hearing at the same time, for example because they are at work, on a business trip or living in other countries, explored the approach of an "asynchronous trial" (异步开庭)[100] in practice. In other words, the court allowed the parties to log in for the different stages of electronic proceedings at different times and places. It is reported that as of the end of 2019, a total of 2,495 cases were successfully concluded through this system, saving six hours in traveling for litigants in each case on average.[101] Article 20 of the *Beijing Regulation on Electronic Litigation* confirms the principle of attending the hearing simultaneously, but it does exceptionally allow an asynchronous trial if one party has submitted a written application and then both parties have agreed, and the court approves it later.

In this situation, in order to have a proper hearing promoted, it should also be inquired whether the court could hear the defendants online even if they are unwilling to attend their trial on the internet.[102] The answer to this question should come back to the aforementioned Article 23 paragraph 1 of the *2020 Pilot Program* regarding the types of cases which are not suitable for being tried online. Concretely speaking, besides some objective grounds which have nothing to do with the will of any parties, it depends on whether the party disagreeing with the online trial has a good reason for doing so. Also, there may be some issues which need the physical appearance of the parties (see the aforementioned Article 12 of the *Provisions on Internet Courts*).

11.4.2.3 Examination of Factual Witnesses

The examination of factual witnesses can be special and rather difficult in internet-based proceedings.[103] Generally speaking, where the examination of the witness and the parties themselves is less technically secured with sufficient hardware/software surroundings, practitioners do worry about the impact of online trials. There could be a poor internet connection which could lower the quality of the witness examination. However, if the local infrastructure can generally ensure an affordable 5G connection, which is able to transmit accurate facial expressions or even micro-expressions of all participants, these worries may be reduced gradually. If not, it is true that examination in ODR will be less effective. In that case, one suggestion is for the judiciary to make some well-equipped witness rooms available for the witnesses to use if they so choose.[104]

---

[99] Lamsfuß and Werner (2021, pp. 50–51); Köbler (2021, pp. 52–53).

[100] SIFoCC (2021).

[101] SPC (2019a, pp. 73–74).

[102] Sung (2020, pp. 11–12).

[103] Considerations regarding physically face-to-face evidence and arguments, see also SIFoCC (2021).

[104] Schmidt and Saam (2020, pp. 216, 218).

More substantially, the witness is generally allowed to be examined online when related statutory requirements have been met. Article 76 of the *CPL* stipulates that upon notice by a People's court, a witness shall testify in court. There are yet some statutory circumstances[105] in which a witness may testify by written testimony, audio-visual transmission technology, audio-visual recordings or any other means permitted by a People's court. Accordingly, Article 76 of the *2019 Evidence Provisions* states that where a witness has compelling difficulty in testifying before court and moves to testify by written testimony, audio-visual transmission technology, audio-visual recordings or otherwise, he or she shall submit an application to the People's court. The application shall state the specific reasons for not appearing in court. If the circumstances as specified in Article 76 of the *CPL* are met, the People's court shall grant the motion. Article 77 of the *2019 Evidence Provisions* adds that a witness shall sign a written undertaking if he or she testifies by means of written testimony with the approval of the People's court, or sign and read aloud a written undertaking if he or she testifies by means of audio-visual transmission technology or audio-visual recordings.

Furthermore, the regulation on the participation of factual witnesses can be a hardship. Article 72 paragraph 2 of the *2019 Evidence Provisions* states that a witness shall neither attend the court trial before testifying nor present their testimony by means of reading aloud written materials prepared in advance. However, when it comes to the witness examination during ODR, it is rather difficult to supervise the behaviors of the witness. During an internet-based trial, it is hardly possible to lock the witness in a waiting room before their appearance in the courtroom. One cause for concern is that since only a limited number of persons can be shown simultaneously on the computer monitor of the court,[106] misbehavior such as coaching a factual witness is hard to prevent if there is no pragmatic method to keep an eye on every witness during the proceedings. In this respect, the *Beijing Regulation on Electronic Litigation* proposes some possible solutions. Its Article 16 requires that the location where the witness will appear for the online hearing should be approved by the court and should not be the same location as where the parties or other litigation participants will take part in the online hearing. The court could ask the witness to visit the court physically to attend the hearing. According to Article 17 of the *Beijing Regulation on Electronic Litigation*, the court shall take the necessary measures to ensure that the witness is not capable of observing the online hearing before and after giving testimony. And Article 18 of the *Beijing Regulation on Electronic Litigation* declares that the hearing shall not be streamed on the internet if any witness will be participating in the online hearing. However, the video of the hearing shall be released promptly after the hearing. Whether these means are able to deter the misuse of online proceedings needs more observation in practice.

---

[105] These are that the witness is unable to appear in court: (1) for health reasons; (2) because they live far from the court and experience travel difficulties; (3) because of force majeure, such as a natural disaster; and (4) for any other justifiable reason.

[106] For a suggestion that there should be another court which oversees the activities of witnesses, see Schupp (2021, pp. 66–67).

11.4.2.4 Verifying Parties' Identification

Then, there is the issue of verifying the parties' identification in an electronic environment. Unlike for parties who physically appear before judges and whose identity can be checked instantly, there could be doubt in online proceedings as to whether the alleged parties are the right ones. If not, there is no way to provide the misrepresented party with any due process. In this aspect, Article 6 paragraph 1 of the *Provisions on Internet Courts* stipulates that where the parties and other litigation participants carry out litigation activities through litigation platform, they shall complete their identity authentication by online means, such as certificate and license comparison, biometric identification or certification on the state unified identity authentication platform, and set up specific accounts for logging into the litigation platform.

The next question is whether the alleged parties could be held accountable for any legal transactions taken during the proceedings. Article 5 paragraph 1 of the *Provisions on Internet Courts* requires that an Internet Court shall establish an internet litigation platform as the special platform for the court to handle cases and for the parties and other litigation participants to carry out litigation activities. Any litigation activity carried out through a litigation platform has legal force. Following this rule, Article 6 paragraph 2 of the *Provisions on Internet Courts* stipulates that the transactions conducted on the litigation platform, which is logged into with special accounts, shall be deemed to be transactions conducted by the authenticated persons themselves, unless errors of the relevant system arise for technical reasons on the litigation platform, or the authenticated persons can prove that their accounts for the litigation platform have been stolen. Article 8 of the *Provisions on Internet Courts* makes clear that after docketing a case, an Internet Court may, through the mobile phone numbers, fax numbers, e-mail addresses, and instant messaging accounts, among others, provided by the plaintiff, notify the defendant and any third party that the case association and identity authentication is being conducted through the litigation platform. The defendant and the third party shall be given information about the case, receive and submit litigation materials, and carry out litigation activities through the litigation platform.

11.4.2.5 Improper Behaviors in Electronic Proceedings

Next, improper behaviors during online hearings also need to be addressed. In practice, bad internet connections and intentionally interrupting the connection are the most frequently challenged issues. That one party is able to jump out of an ongoing civil process is unfair to the opposing party. Hence, Article 14 of the *Provisions on Internet Courts* stipulates that an Internet Court shall, according to the characteristics of online court trials, apply the relevant provisions of the *Court Rules of the People's Courts of the P.R.C.* Parties shall be deemed to have "refused to appear in court" if they fail to participate in an online court hearing on time, or be deemed to have "retreated during a court hearing" if they leave the virtual courtroom during a court hearing without permission, unless the court finds that the party truly did so for such reasons as network failure, equipment damage, power interruption or force majeure.

Thanks to the e-justice system, the parties and other participants do not need to set aside time to go to the courtroom physically, which by its nature asks its visitors to act seriously. Adding to this impression are the special security forces inside the court, which implies that the direct pressure on outsiders is also very clear. It may be assumed that if visitors nevertheless take wrongful actions within a court, they would be stopped instantly or at least quickly. However, rather than going to the courtroom being the only option, the parties in an online hearing may decide where they would like to attend the hearing virtually. In this respect, during the first stage of the global pandemic, in February 2020, the Beijing Internet Court published its trial regulation, namely the *Beijing Regulation on Electronic Litigation.*[107] Among others, it stipulates that the parties have to be well dressed during the hearing (Article 8), for instance no pajamas, and be in a suitable environment for the hearing, for instance not in a shopping mall (Article 9). Appearing in an online hearing while driving a car or being drunk is prohibited (Article 10). The parties have to make sure that during the online hearing, their heads should be completely visible in their cameras (Article 12). Moreover, the parties are supposed to put their mobile phone on silent and follow the judge's orders. In particular, they are not allowed to stand up or move around casually, eat, intentionally leave the camera's view, record the hearing, broadcast the hearing in any form, compromise others' reputation, consult with others or enable others to witness the hearing without permission of the trial bench (Article 13). Although, frankly speaking, some of these provisions relate to strange behaviors which may not be understood by foreign observers, such actions have been taken by some parties in reality and therefore need to be explicitly declared illegal. In this sense, the *Beijing Regulation on Electronic Litigation* is in fact responsive.

11.4.3 Pros and Cons of the One-Stop Dispute Resolution Mechanism

The aforementioned one-stop dispute resolution mechanism, which represents a more combined mode of mediation, is believed to have different advantages and thus needs to be promoted all over China. It could provide convenience to the parties not just because the one-stop mechanism could help the justice users resolve their disputes with different procedural options, but the clients to civil justice could visit and utilize multiple facilities while sitting at home all the time. This mechanism, which could be regarded as an advanced counterpart of the Sanders' "multi-door courthouse" design,[108] can be served for the ordinary citizens more easily.

Within this integrated mechanism, there could be fewer disputes on the connection or transfer of the case from one form of dispute resolution to another form. In this way,

[107] Beijing Internet Court (2020).

[108] Sander (1976, p. 111).

the combination of different forms of dispute resolution, such as Med-Arb, Arb-Med, Med-Arb-Med or pre-action mandatory mediation,[109] could be streamlined accordingly.[110] Conversely, all alternative forms of dispute resolution are undoubtedly in the shadow of court proceedings.[111] Furthermore, some collected evidential materials such as the judicial expert identification (equivalent: factual expert witness or *Sachverständigung*) in the pre-action phase could also be acknowledged as the statutory evidence which could be submitted and evaluated during the court's hearings. Otherwise, these materials would be rejected to be admissible evidence as they do not meet the statutory requirement that evidence ought to be collected during the judicial process.

In the meantime, the practitioners at local level may worry about the impact of this one-stop policy in practice. The possibility of pre-action mediation or some kinds of consultation might jeopardize the parties' fundamental right of action before courts. The reason is that other than having their day in court instantly after filing lawsuits, the parties would normally be transferred to the mediation facilities at first. In some regions, although there is a written form for plaintiffs to agree on the mediation, no option is even listed in the form for them to reject. Then, the parties have to wait for the mediation facilities which would send the case back to the competent court in case of the failure of mediation attempts. The whole process may take months in reality. If there is indeed no chance to reach any settlement between parties, these pre-action proceedings make no difference and are therefore a waste of time. Theoretically, we may have to accept a "mediatory continuum" between the court proceedings and mediation[112] as the Weber's ideal type. However, the delay of civil proceedings should never be attributed to the chance of mediation. In this sense, the new online form of dispute resolution outside the court may change the specific methods to do justice, but the procedural safeguard of civil justice is still supposed to be maintained. Justice delayed is justice denied, and ODR cannot be an excuse to postpone the proceedings.

Concretely speaking, the crucial concern refers to the insistence on the due process principle in different areas of civil justice which is not limited to the internet justice. Previously, it is recognized that the one-stop mechanism could contribute to the convenience of dispute resolution which may relate to more flexible and then simplified proceedings. Indeed, there are too many cases before Chinese courts and too few qualified judges who could resolve the relevant disputes. As a result, the one-stop mechanism is not merely for the ordinary citizens, but also for the court system itself. Yet, it should be kept in mind that the court is to deliver justice to the justice users. The court should decide which party has rights and which party is truly a wrongdoer who is accountable for his behaviors. In other words, the civil justice cannot flee

---

[109] Shipman (2011, p. 163).

[110] For details on the impact of mediation's results on the civil justice, see de Roo and Jagtenberg (2018).

[111] Mnookin and Kornhauser (1979, p. 950).

[112] Shapiro (1986, pp. 8–17).

away from its duty to make such decisions. The other dispute resolution facilities could neither do such job instead nor provide ordinary due process for the parties.

One of the right approaches to handling the overburdened caseload is, besides designating more competent judges, to reduce the cases which could flow into the judiciary or to slow down the pace of courts while managing the cases in dispute. Justice delayed could to some extent still be justice, whereas justice with serious errors, which are caused by accelerated proceedings, would be even more troublesome. If we only emphasize the necessity of having some speedy, cheap, polite judicial services which are nevertheless not supported with sufficient resources, the chance of having defective judiciary is much higher. It is not desirable for the public trust in the judiciary and is also toxic for the individual judges who are already working very hard to finish their professional assignments. It is not fair for these hard-working judges, especially the judges at grass-root level who form the targeted group of any judicial reform, but have less influence on the policy-making process and will have to endure or undertake the anger of individual parties.

Moreover, the legal techniques should be enhanced. For instance, there ought to be advanced procedural institutions which allow the resolution of multiple and complex disputes in one single litigation. This chapter would like to draw attention to the usage of consolidation of claims/parties, compulsory aggregation of claims and the deepened understanding of *res judicata* effect of final civil judgments. Not merely the claims of the plaintiff should be adjudicated in the current case, but the counterclaims of the defendant and even related disputes ought to be encouraged to be incorporated into the scope of adjudication of the original case. In other words, besides other alternative dispute resolution mechanisms, it is exactly the judiciary that should manage the sources of disputes and reduce the potential claims in any other civil proceedings. To satisfy this function of management does not mean that the court should do as the other private entities or public organs do. Rather, functioning as active decision-makers in individual cases shows the correct solution for the courts at all levels. Yet, being active does not require judges to decide what the parties have not claimed or alleged, but it indicates primarily the possibility of embracing more disputes (in the formal sense) or conflicts of economic/social interests (in the substantial sense) in their ongoing cases with appropriate steps of case management and final judgments. It is advisable that the same group of judges make judicial decisions for more disputes in one single case.

11.4.4 Internet-Based Advance Arbitral Awards?

Following the general coverage of Chinese ODR mechanisms, observers may wonder what the limitations of internet-based dispute resolution should be. Hence, the principle of due process should be stressed for securing parties' substantive and procedural rights in the process of ODR. There is no need to emphasize the importance of due process for Chinese and foreign audiences, but disputes can be existing on whether due process has been sufficiently protected. Particularly, in the context of

ODR, which, by its nature, represents creative measures, there could be even more room for practitioners to tell their stories.

Here, it is worth introducing a well-known example of advance arbitral awards (先予仲裁裁决) in Chinese practice, which literally means arbitral awards which have already been given even before the related disputes arise. In recent discussion in the field of commercial arbitration in China, the story of these awards is taken as an illustration of when the principle of due process was violated and then restored. Also, arbitral awards during arbitral proceedings indicate in fact the counterpart of civil judgments in civil proceedings and may give some lessons to our observation of civil judgments as well.

Because ODR has at least partly been developed because of lawyers' efforts to think and practice creatively, there can always be new attempts to use ODR methods, but some attempts can go too far and jeopardize procedural justice materially. The following case refers to an arbitration institution addressing advance arbitral awards which were ruled in favor of money lending companies. To respond to the practice of these awards and the business of the related institution, in June 2018, the SPC released a special judicial interpretation called the *Reply on Advance Arbitral Awards or Mediations*, which aimed to target the misuse and manipulation of arbitral proceedings, especially online proceedings.

Internet-based arbitration is time-saving and efficient because it eliminates the physical limitations on conducting arbitral proceedings, making it appealing to money lending companies, among other entities. Money lending contracts contain a clause stating that the companies can enforce contracts as final arbitral awards, although, to date, there have been no lending disputes. For marketing purposes, some arbitration institutions will facilitate these agreements if they do not initiate them in the first place, and they will make final arbitral awards according to the contracts. For practical purposes, the borrowers have no access to substantial arbitral proceedings. These standardized lending arrangements deprive debtors of their constitutional right to be heard before the court.[113] What they have are merely pretended arbitral proceedings in the formal sense.

When the online arbitration process began and disputes came to arise in lower courts, the SPC tried to set rules for this disputed case category. The *Reply on Advance Arbitral Awards or Mediations* stipulates that, under Article 2 of the *Arbitration Law*, an institution will arbitrate existing contract disputes and other property rights and interest disputes. For cases in which money lending companies apply to enforce an arbitral award or mediation ruling rendered before a genuine dispute occurs, courts must not accept the applications, and if an application is accepted, it should be rejected. The reason for this rule is that the judiciary does not take the aforementioned advance arbitral awards or mediations as valid enforcement titles (*titres exécutoires*). Therefore, these awards or mediations are not capable of initiating enforcement proceedings under Chinese law.[114]

---

[113] For details, see Guo (2020, p. 146).

[114] On the requirements before the commencement of enforcement proceedings in China, see Cao (2021a, pp. 30–32).

Additionally, also in the *Reply on Advance Arbitral Awards or Mediations*, the SPC recognizes the following two circumstances as indicating that the "composition of the arbitration tribunal or the arbitration procedure has violated the statutory proceedings" set out in Article 237 paragraph 2 item 3 of the *CPL (2017)* (currently: Article 248 paragraph 2 item 3 of the *CPL*). On one hand, an arbitration institution neither hears a dispute, nor presides over a mediation under the procedures of the *Arbitration Law*. Instead, it renders a decision according to the settlement or mediation agreement signed by the parties to a P2P lending contract before the dispute occurs. On the other hand, an arbitration institution does not protect the parties' fundamental procedural rights prescribed in the *Arbitration Law*, such as applying for disqualification of arbitrators, providing evidence, and defending themselves during the prospective arbitral proceedings. Furthermore, where a party to a P2P lending contract claims that the arbitral proceedings do not violate the legal proceedings based on the agreed waiver clause, the People's court shall not grant support thereto. Lastly, this *Reply on Advance Arbitral Awards or Mediations* applies to enforcing arbitral awards or mediations on contract and property rights and interest disputes.

Hence, these advance arbitral awards or mediations of some arbitration institutions were declared void by the Chinese judiciary. This rapid response from the judicial branch is of great importance in practice, because a great number of potential enforcement cases are then prevented from going into the enforcement organ, namely the People's courts themselves.[115] For the relevant parties in arbitral proceedings, the *Reply on Advance Arbitral Awards or Mediations* also means that their due days in arbitral hearings could be safeguarded. Then, it comes to a further question: to what extent the internet-based arbitral proceedings could be simplified without prejudice to the requirement of due process? With our example of advance arbitral awards or mediations we could merely determine the bottom line of procedural justice from the perspective of the SPC. It is rather up to the commercial and judicial practitioners to develop feasible paths for the online arbitration.

11.5 New Technologies for ODR

11.5.1 Technologies and Neutrality of the Court

Electronic technologies, whether in service to courts or in other uses, raise concerns about data protection, security protocols, and necessary software and equipment[116] with respect to protecting proceedings after successful cyberattacks. As both practicing lawyers and even judges do not yet have substantial experience with such

[115] General discussion, see Cao (2021b).

[116] Yet, it is reported that in international arbitration proceedings, the consideration given to cybersecurity could be different depending on the nature of the dispute and the interests and identity of the parties. The School of International Arbitration Queen Mary University of London and White & Case LLP (2021).

problems, they must rely on technological developments by, for example, the creative efforts of big internet service providers. The principle of due process in electronic court proceedings calls for incorporating practical IT expert advice to make judicial business more customer-friendly and efficient. Lawyers themselves are not good at antivirus software for cybersecurity needs, which is, of course, insufficient protection. Specialized IT engineers are required to keep the electronic environment clean and healthy.

Ironically, however, in regard to the interactions between lawyers and IT experts, there could be some challenges to the neutrality of the court. Since the IT experts have electronic technologies, they may be taking control of many legal and judicial activities. In this case, lawyers are losing their professional territory. Also, if the engineers are not only assisting the judges but getting involved in disputes themselves, the relationships become complicated. A noticeable example of such complications is the correlation between the Hangzhou Internet Court and the e-commerce giant Alibaba, which is located just within this court's jurisdiction.[117] Concerns will arise if the court takes a case relating to Alibaba while at the same time using Alibaba's customized internet services. Because local protectionism has frequently been disputed in Chinese context,[118] even if local courts no longer rely on local governments financially, which actively support large local companies to demonstrate their progress in governance, outside observers continue to question the connection between courts and giant companies. Based on *prima facie* evidence in the judicial statistics, many citizens and even lawyers believe that some large internet-based companies in southeastern China can hardly lose a case if the local court has competence with territorial jurisdiction over the companies. Despite the lack of in-depth empirical data, we could still keep eyes on the development of this observation in future.

11.5.2 Electronic Evidence and Special Legal Regimes

Relating to the substantive adjudication of civil cases, evidentiary submissions play a crucial role in civil proceedings and also need to be accomplished electronically. Hence, new technologies have given rise to the new types and forms of evidence because intangible evidence, such as electronic evidence, could be a factual basis for any kind of adjudication under the framework of ODR. This kind of evidence requires new policies to address concerns. For instance, electronic contracts do not leave a trail of written documentation. Rather, they are merely electronically stored data which consist of the consensus between business partners. If such data are verified, the function of written contracts could still be fulfilled entirely. And Article 9 of the *Provisions on Internet Courts* stipulates, as procedural requirements, that where an Internet Court organizes an online evidence exchange, the parties shall upload

[117] Guo (2021, pp. 8–9).

[118] He (2012, pp. 397–399); also Clarke (1996, pp. 41–49).

and import the online electronic data into the litigation platform, or electronically process the offline evidence via scanning, copying, duplicating or other means, and then upload it to the litigation platform so as to prove the facts, and may also support their factual allegations by using the electronic data that has been imported into the litigation platform.

To address this matter, Article 63 paragraph 1 item 5 of the *CPL (2012)* began recognizing electronic data as a type of civil evidence, and Article 66 paragraph 1 item 5 of the current *CPL* keeps it untouched. Also, Article 14 of the *2019 Evidence Provisions* designates the following as admissible electronic data: information released online such as by webpages or blogs; communication through network application services such as short text messages, emails, instant messaging, and chat groups; user registration or identity authentication data, electronic transaction records, communication records, login logs, and other information; and electronic documents, pictures, audio recordings, video recordings, digital certificates, and computer programs. Then, in a broader sense, Article 14 of the *2019 Evidence Provisions* states in its fifth and last item that the scope of admissible electronic data extends to cover information stored, processed, and transmitted in digital form which can prove the facts of the case. It is then up to the judicial practice to develop which kinds of electronic data could be taken as evidence before courts. This extension facilitates ODR proceedings since the proceedings of arbitration or mediation could regard these rules as model rules. Following these rules, special evidential examination and evaluation requirements were further introduced by the *2019 Evidence Provisions.*[119]

Compared with the traditional approach to evidential production, furthermore, the essential evidence of a case being heard online has to be submitted differently. It means that electronic evidence could be an alternative form of other kinds of evidence such as documentary evidence or expert opinions. Since electronically submitted materials are generally not in its original form, there can be doubts about their admissibility.[120] Article 22 of the *2020 Pilot Program* stipulates that electronically submitted litigation and evidential materials submitted by the parties can be used directly in the litigation. In this case, paper originals are not required. However, if courts require original documents for any reason, such as requested by either party or needed by the case itself, these must be provided. Article 10 of the *Provisions on Internet Courts* states that documents related to personal identification or duplicate business licenses, authorization letters, identification of legal representatives and other litigation materials, documentary evidence, judicial expert opinions, inspection

---

[119] Article 93 and Article 94 of the *Provisions Evidence 2019*. For details on the comparative framework for electronic evidence in Germany, see Brand and Skowronek (2021, p. 178); Gottwald (2018); Preuß (2016, p. 421); Wagner (2016); Bacher (2015); Rüßmann (2012, pp. 233–260).

[120] It is the situation in Germany in accordance with Article 128a paragraph 2 and Article 420 of the *German Code of Civil Procedure*, which decline the examination of documentary evidence in a video-conference and request their physical presentation in principle. Musielak/Voit/Stadler (2021, § 128a Rn 5); Schupp (2021, p. 66); Schmidt and Saam (2020, p. 216). Only with the additional consent of the opposing party according to Article 284 sentence 2 of the *German Code of Civil Procedure*, can the court collect documentary evidence differently. Fritsche (2020, § 128a Rn 13).

records, and other evidentiary materials that are submitted and processed electronically are deemed to meet the formal requirements for originals after the courts have examined the materials. If an opposing party raises any objection to the authenticity of any such materials and has reasonable grounds, the Internet Court will, according to Article 10 of the *Provisions on Internet Courts*, require the party submitting the related evidence to provide the originals.[121] These provisions allow electronically submitted evidence to be interpreted and regulated in accordance with the general theory of evidence law, which has been traditionally prepared for physical evidence. Yet, it attracts our attention that there could be some cases where it is not suitable to substitute physical evidence with electronic evidence. For instance, it happens when there is numerous physical evidence or evidence which is highly disputed. Such occasions also show the boundary of electronic proceedings and e-justice.

And according to the SPC's special report, the Chinese judiciary aims at innovating the online preservation and authentication of e-evidence. Blockchain technology in combination with big data and cloud storage is used in the judicial process. As of 31 October 2019, courts in 22 provinces (municipalities) had interconnected with national e-evidence platforms underpinned by blockchain, which is widely linked to 27 sites, including the National Time Service Center. It has finally diversified dispute resolution platforms, notary offices, and forensic sciences centers. About 194 million pieces of e-evidence have been preserved on the platform, supporting evidence authentication and examination in future hearings. In this aspect, all three Internet Courts have mapped out their own exploratory plan in detail.[122] It can be argued that not only the regulated types of electronic data but also the rules on electronic submission of evidence could be comparable in both the area of commercial arbitration and different forms of mediation.

11.5.3 Impact of AI Systems on Civil Proceedings

Lastly, the potential use of AI systems in China, as opposed to other jurisdictions,[123] is a very popular research topic.[124] Under the SPC's current reform plan for 2019–2023, the courts are to develop intelligent case assistant systems and improve the functionality of similar case references, outcome comparisons, data analyses, and

[121] Article 12 sentence 2 of the *Online Litigation Rules* supplements the circumstances where the court shall require the party submitting evidence to provide the original documents or original items. Also, Article 13 of the *Online Litigation Rules* lists the situation where the court may determine those electronic materials meet the requirements for the forms of original documents or original items.

[122] SPC (2019a, pp. 75–76). For details on the scheme of using blockchain technology in civil justice, see Beijing Internet Court (2019a); Beijing Internet Court (2019b, pp. 20–21); Sung (2020, pp. 4–6, 12–13).

[123] For details on the discussions in Germany, see Neubert (2021, p. 108); Heil (2020, pp. 14–15). More general discussion, see Zuckerman (2020); Susskind (2019, pp. 263–292).

[124] Chen and Li (2020, p. 1).

warnings against adjudication defects.[125] This process will call for deploying AI systems in adjudication. Current AI applications in courtrooms, virtual or offline, include synchronous, real-time voice transcription, and intelligent voice cloud platforms. However, these general examples do not fully reflect usages of specialized legal AI technology that most lawyers are looking for in civil proceedings.

In practice, computer programs and websites can provide preliminary answers to legal questions. Beyond private service providers, Shanghai courts responded to nearly 10,000 frequently asked procedural questions that had accumulated over the years by producing FabaoZhicha (法宝智查), a Q&A database that contains 2,300 prepared answers.[126] The site provides multiple resources and links such as official websites, litigation service bots, and WeChat official accounts to satisfy parties' diverse needs in civil proceedings.[127] Other courts could provide these services as well. For instance, the Online Diversified Dispute Resolution Platform operated by the High People's Court of Zhejiang Province is also accessible on the internet at no cost.[128] Also, different courts have litigation risk assessment systems and terminals in their Litigation Service Centers.[129] Following Article 21 of the *Opinions of the SPC on Building One-stop Diversified Dispute Resolution Mechanisms and One-stop Litigant Service Centers*, the SPC intends to place intelligent equipment such as all-in-one computers, like automats, for facilitative services in courts' litigation service halls. Also, the SPC plans to improve the 12,368 litigation service telephone hotline with improved intelligent answering.

However, it is considered that the current e-technologies are too elementary to be regarded as AI technologies that will radically change the understandings and behaviors of the legal community.[130] AI is not a webpage of fixed answers to specific legal questions. In addition, even AI-facilitated judgments are still to a great extent made by human judges as usual, AI-generated solutions have no substantial impact on judges' decisions, but they are merely references. Even if judges obtain suggestions from their colleagues, the opinions of attorneys, or textbooks, AI is not substituting human decision-makers.[131]

Although big data can provide insights over traditional legal methods, this chapter would suggest that two major preconditions are required for successful deep learning to predict judgments: (1) the data should be collected and coded properly[132]; and (2) the real elements that determine case results can be disclosed in most final judgments.

---

[125] SPC (2019b, p. 72).

[126] SPC (2019a, p. 68).

[127] Id.

[128] Zhejiang High People's Court (2021).

[129] Chen and Li (2020, pp. 10–12).

[130] A more developed example for AI judging, see Medvedeva (2020, pp. 277–280).

[131] For details on similar scepticism in the area of international commercial arbitration, see The School of International Arbitration Queen Mary University of London and White & Case LLP (2021).

[132] For details on similar consideration in German discussion, see Neubert (2021, p. 111).

It is difficult to say that China's judiciary today is meeting these two preconditions. Accordingly, invoking AI systems in the court remains in future.

While these two preconditions would be met later, we may encounter the well-known saying of John von Neumann while trying to solve the problem of complexity: "with four parameters I can fit an elephant, and with five I can make him wiggle his trunk".[133] A complex model may fit the collected data with abundant parameters, whereas using this model to predict the future is another thing.

AI systems and the relevant research are popular in China, but until now they do not fully represent specialized legal AI technologies. It means the Chinese lawyers are still looking forward to advanced AI systems for forthcoming dispute resolution attempts. For instance, there are already legal products which are adjusted to multiple Large Language Models, ChatGPT inclusive, and are able to assist the moot courts preparing, smart searching together with contract producing.[134]

11.6 Limitation of Adopting ODR

By their nature, ODR methods are internet-based and as a result, they could be cheaper, more expeditious, more flexible and more customizable compared to traditional dispute resolution mechanisms. For disputes relating to consumers' rights, for instance, ODR is able to provide effective platforms.[135] As one of the pioneers of online justice, Richard Susskind has argued for the use of online courts in order to enhance access to justice worldwide.[136]

Indeed, ODR is a globally attractive option. However, it does not self-evidently mean an advanced stage in the trajectory of dispute resolution. ODR is not only one of the different forms for resolving disputes, but it should contain substantial legal rules and institutions. On one hand, ODR strongly connects to other dispute resolution mechanisms. If traditional dispute resolution output is of low quality in one jurisdiction, the respective online output is unlikely to be high. To a great extent, ODR could be a mirror for the performance of traditional dispute resolution mechanisms like court service within a physical courtroom or other mediation, arbitration or mixed choices. The internet-based characteristic of ODR means merely a different environment for dispute resolution. Whether ODR is managed successfully or not, depends on the general understanding and operation of dispute resolution. On the other hand, the notion of ODR itself consists of various forms or models. The pandemic gives rise to the very strong need for online alternatives, while China is among the leading jurisdictions which are in support of internet-based experiments. While online civil justice goes for these years, especially during the pandemic, it is hard to tell that the judgments given during these years are relatively of poor quality compared to the

[133] Mayer, Khairy, and Howard (2010, p. 648).

[134] PKULAW (2024).

[135] Schmitz and Rule (2017).

[136] Susskind (2019). (updating information https://remotecourts.org).

previous ones. The Chinese experience could show both a localized possibility of having ODR and a prospective future for the whole world.

Even, the development of ODR is dependent on the level of technological evolution and the improvement of local infrastructure, which differs dramatically from nation to nation. Speaking not of the future but of the present, there are a variety of practical difficulties which even developed countries have not yet solved entirely. If we accept that judicial resources are scarce, putting them into establishing an online platform may suggest that the traditional approaches to resolving disputes have to be left with fewer resources in the meantime. And under the pressure of global competition, national ODR needs to be set up as soon as possible and this kind of work can be very expensive. For developing jurisdictions in particular, a great deal of financial investment to be made in a short period of time may in fact present an invitation for bribery, corruption and misuse of public power.

It is also obvious that the adoption of ODR gives rise to significant challenges to traditional jurisprudence and to long-lasting legal traditions and doctrines. Some jurisdictions may understandably be reluctant to step forward to the era of ODR. Especially in Chinese context, it should be noted that the convenience of ODR could lead to more attempts by the claimant and the defendant to conspire to violate the substantive rights of certain third parties. Without a face-to-face examination of the parties and factual witnesses, while emphasizing the importance of efficiency, the accuracy of judicial decisions based on online hearings could be called into doubt. And this doubt is for good reason. Since conspiracy, i.e. a malevolent agreement between bad-faith parties to misuse access to civil justice, is not rare in Chinese civil cases,[137] being prudent with regard to ODR is merely the pragmatic choice, especially for current China. It also shows that the cultural background of a specific state should be taken seriously. It is ODR which must fit for circumstances in national context, and not the other way around. And these conclusions could be limited to developing countries such as China that are approaching a steady implementation of the rule of law. Nevertheless, the conclusions could also be an overarching one that can be generalized more broadly for various jurisdictions.

References

ABA Center for Innovation (2020) Online dispute resolution in the United States. https://www.americanbar.org/content/dam/aba/administrative/center-for-innovation/odrvisualizationreport.pdf. Accessed 2 May 2024 (updating information: https://datawrapper.dwcdn.net/q0u4d/1)

Alibaba (2024a) Alibaba public jury. http://pan.taobao.com. Accessed 2 May 2024 (in Chinese)

Alibaba (2024b) Platform for intellectual property protection. https://qinquan.taobao.com. Accessed 2 May 2024 (in Chinese)

Andrews N (2019) Andrews on civil processes. Intersentia, Cambridge

Bacher K (2015) Der elektronische Rechtsverkehr im Zivilprozess. Neue Juristische Wochenschrift 38:2753–2759

[137] For a similar situation within enforcement proceedings in China, see Cao (2021b, pp. 106, 120–121).

Beijing Internet Court (2019a) Tianping blockchain of the Beijing Internet Court. https://tpl.bjinternetcourt.gov.cn/tpl. Accessed 2 May 2024 (in Chinese)
Beijing Internet Court (2019b) White paper on trials of the Beijing Internet Court (14 October 2019). https://regional.chinadaily.com.cn/pdf/WhitepaperontrialsofBeijingInternetCourt.pdf. Accessed 2 May 2024 (in Chinese)
Beijing Internet Court (2020) Beijing Internet Court published its regulation on the trial of electronic litigation. https://www1.bjinternetcourt.gov.cn/cac/zw/1582274924940.html. Accessed 2 May 2024 (in Chinese)
BCI & BIMC (2019a) Introduction to our mediation business. http://www.bcisz.org/html/tjywjs. Accessed 2 May 2024 (in Chinese)
BCI & BIMC (2019b) Introduction. http://www.bcisz.org/html/ywtj. Accessed 2 May 2024
Brand T, Skowronek Y (2021) Die Herausforderungen der Digitalisierung für das zivilprozessuale Beweisverfahren. Recht Digital 4:178–186
Cabral A (2019) Designing procedure by contract: litigation agreements in contemporary civil procedure. International Journal of Procedural Law 2:363–380
Cao Z (2021a) Civil enforcement rules and mechanism in China: the past, present and the future. Peking University Law Journal 9:23–44
Cao Z (2021b) On the civil enforcement organ in China. China Legal Science 4:106–129
Cao Z (2024) Reflection on the requirement of evidence for case docketing in civil proceedings. Law Science 1:141–157 (in Chinese)
Chase O et al. (2017) Civil litigation in comparative context. West Academic Publishing, St. Paul
Chen H (2016) "Vulgar delivery": a sample of penetrating into the defects of Chinese civil judicature. Law and Social Development 6:40–51 (in Chinese)
Chen BM, Li Z (2020) How will technology change the face of Chinese justice? Columbia Journal of Asian Law 34:1–58
CIETAC (2015) Fee schedule. http://www.cietac.org/index.php?m=Article&a=show&id=2747. Accessed 2 May 2024 (in Chinese)
CIETAC (2020) China international economic and trade arbitration commission guidelines on proceeding with arbitration actively and properly during the COVID-19 pandemic (trial). http://www.cietac.org.cn/index.php?m=Article&a=show&id=16910. Accessed 2 May 2024 (in Chinese)
CIETAC (2021) Intelligent hearing platform of China international economic and trade arbitration commission. https://kt.cietac.org/portal/main/domain/index.htm. Accessed 2 May 2024
CIETAC (2022a) CIETAC online arbitration. http://www.cietacodr.org. Accessed 2 May 2024 (in Chinese)
CIETAC (2022b) Online dispute resolution center. http://odr.org.cn. Accessed 2 May 2024 (in Chinese)
Clarke DC (1996) Power and politics in the Chinese court system: the enforcement of civil judgments. Columbia Journal of Asian Law 10:1–92
de Roo A, Jagtenberg R (2018) 'Shadow of the law' or 'shadow of the settlement': experiences with the dutch act on collective settlement of mass damage (WCAM). In: Uzelac A, van Rhee CH (eds) Transformation of civil justice. Springer, Cham, pp 249–263
Dickert T (2020) Thesen zur Modernisierung des Zivilprozesses. Deutsche Richterzeitung 9:296–299
ELI/UNIDROIT (2021) ELI/UNIDROIT model European rules of civil procedure. Oxford University Press, Oxford
First Intermediate People's Court in Hainan Province and Hainan High People's Court (2020) Foreign-related civil and commercial cases online dispute resolution platform. https://hnodr.odrcloud.cn (now unaccessible) (in Chinese)
Fritsche J (2020) In: Krüger W, Rauscher T, Münchener Kommentar ZPO, Band 1, 6. Aufl. C. H. Beck, München
Fu Y (2012) Autonomous options of procedural issues upon the litigants' consent in the new civil procedure law. Journal of Comparative Law 5:55–66 (in Chinese)

Fu Y (2021) Civil justice in China in the COVID-19 period. In: Krans B, Nylund A (eds) Civil courts coping with COVID-19. Eleven International Publishing, The Hague
Fu Y, Cao Z (2012) The position of judges in civil litigation in transitional China: judicial mediation and case management. In: Chen L, van Rhee CH (eds) Towards a Chinese civil code: comparative and historical perspectives. Martinus Nijhoff Publishers, Leiden, pp 495–519
Ghoshray S (2006) Charting the future of online dispute resolution: an analysis of the constitutional and jurisdictional quandary. University of Toledo Law Review 38:317–350
Gottwald P (2018) Electronic documents and electronic signatures in German civil proceedings (trans: Cao Z) In: Jiang S (ed) Electronic documents and e-commerce related substantive and procedural issues. Taiwan New Sharing Press, Taipei, pp 407–452 (in Chinese)
Gu W (2018a) Looking at arbitration through a comparative lens: general principles and specific issues. Journal of Comparative Law 2:164–188
Gu W (2018b) China's belt and road development and a new international commercial arbitration initiative in Asia. Vanderbilt Journal of Transnational Law 51:1305–1352
Gu W (2021) Dispute resolution in China: litigation, arbitration, mediation, and their interactions. Routledge, London
Guo Q (2020) On the "advance arbitration" in internet-based lending disputes. Fudan University Law Review 1:146–157 (in Chinese)
Guo M (2021) Internet court's challenges and future in China. Computer Law & Security Review 40:1–13
He X (2012) A tale of two Chinese courts: economic development and contract enforcement. Journal of Law and Society 39:384–409
Heiden C (2020) Prozessrecht in Zeiten der Corona-Pandemie. Neue Juristische Wochenschrift 15:1023–1028
Heil B (2020) IT-Anwendung im Zivilprozess. Mohr Siebeck, Tübingen
Holloway D (2020) The new Chinese international commercial court and the future of dispute resolution in the belt and road initiative. In: Chen L, Janssen A (eds) Dispute resolution in China, Europe and World. Springer, Cham, pp 51–80
JD (2020) Disputes out of third-party transactions. https://help.jd.com/user/issue/list-450.html. Accessed 2 May 2024 (in Chinese)
Jin C (2021) The "trinity" diversified dispute resolution mechanism for international commercial disputes in Hainan Province. https://www.hainan.gov.cn/hainan/5309/202110/c7e9e25a92e9424baf1a156448891bc2.shtml. Accessed 2 May 2024 (in Chinese)
Jing H (2022) Era innovation of internet courts and China's contribution. China Legal Science 4:49–73 (in Chinese)
Kengyel M, Nemessányi Z (eds) (2012) Electronic technology and civil procedure: new paths to justice from around the world. Springer, Berlin
Köbler R (2021) Homeoffice hat bei den Gerichten Grenzen. Deutsche Richterzeitung 2:52–53
Krans B, Nylund A (eds) (2021) Civil courts coping with COVID-19. Eleven International Publishing, The Hague
Lamsfuß M, Werner I (2021) Pandemie und Video—Verhandlungen in der Praxis. Deutsche Richterzeitung 2:50–51
Legg M (2016) The future of dispute resolution: online ADR and online courts. Australasian Dispute Resolution Journal 27:227–235
Long F (2020) Innovation and development of the China international commercial court. The Chinese Journal of Comparative Law 8:40–44
Mayer J, Khairy K, Howard J (2010) Drawing an elephant with four complex parameters. American Journal of Physics 6:648–649
Medvedeva M et al. (2020) JURI SAYS: an automatic judgment prediction system for the European Court of Human Rights. In: Villata S, Harašta J, Křemen P (eds) Legal knowledge and information systems. IOS Press, Amsterdam
Menkel-Meadow CJ, Porter-Love L, Kupfer-Schneider A, Moffitt M (2019) Dispute resolution: beyond the adversarial model. Aspen Publishing, California

Minzner CF (2011) China's turn against law. The American Journal of Comparative Law 59:935–984

Mnookin RH, Kornhauser L (1979) Bargaining in the shadow of the law: the case of divorce. Yale Law Journal 88:950–997

Neubert K (2021) Der Einsatz von Künstlicher Intelligenz in der deutschen Justiz. Deutsche Richterzeitung 3:108–111

Nylund A, Cabral A (2023) Contractualisation of civil litigation. Intersentia, Cambridge

Pappas BA (2008) Online court: online dispute resolution and the future of small claims. UCLA Journal of Law and Technology 12:[i]–25

Peng X (2023) Fengqiao model and the structural changes of dispute resolution mechanisms in contemporary China. China Legal Science 6:23–44 (in Chinese)

Perritt HH (2000) Dispute resolution in cyberspace. Ohio State Journal on Dispute Resolution 15:675–704

PKULAW (2024) FabaoGPT. https://ai.pkulaw.com/shop. Accessed 2 May 2024 (in Chinese)

Poblet M (ed) (2011) Mobile technologies for conflict management: online dispute resolution, governance, participation. Springer, Berlin

Preuß N (2016) Der elektronische Zivilprozess—Nutzen oder Schaden. Zeitschrift Für Zivilprozess 119:421–456

Quek Anderson D (2019) The convergence of ADR and ODR within the courts: the impact on access to justice. Civil Justice Quarterly 1:126–143

Rebehn S (2020) Mehr Online-Verfahren vor Arbeits- und Sozialgerichten. Deutsche Richterzeitung 5:164–165

Rebehn S (2021a) Umfrage zeigt: Akzeptanz für Online-Verfahren wächst. Deutsche Richterzeitung 3:90–91

Rebehn S (2021b) Ein Jahr Krisenmodul. Deutsche Richterzeitung 4:130–131

Rüßmann H (2012) Electronic documents, security and authenticity. In: Kengyel M, Nemessányi Z (eds) Electronic technology and civil procedure: new paths to justice from around the world. Springer, Berlin, pp 233–260

Sander FEA (1976) Varieties of dispute resolution. 70 Federal Rules Decisions 79:111–134

Sanders A (2021) Videoverhandlungen in Europa und die COVID-19-Pandemie. Deutsche Richterzeitung 2:68–71

Schmitz AJ, Rule C (2017) The new handshake: online dispute resolution and the future of consumer protection. ABA Book Publishing, Chicago

Schmidt J, Saam D (2020) Videokonferenzen Im Zivilprozess. Deutsche Richterzeitung 6:216–219

Scholz-Berger F, Schumann J (2020) Die Videokonferenz als Krisenlösung für das Zivilverfahren. Ecolex 6:469–473

Schupp C (2021) Praktische Erwägungen zu Verhandlungen nach § 128a ZPO. Deutsche Richterzeitung 2:66–67

SCMC (2015) Overview of the SCMC. http://www.scmc.org.cn/page67?article_id=196&_l=en&menu_id=86. Accessed 2 May 2024

Shapiro M (1986) Courts: a comparative and political analysis. University of Chicago Press, Chicago

Shipman S (2011) Compulsory mediation: the elephant in the room. Civil Justice Quarterly 2:163–191

SIFoCC (2021) Second SIFoCC COVID-19 memorandum. https://cloud-platform-e218f50a4812967ba1215eaecede923f.s3.amazonaws.com/uploads/sites/25/2024/03/6.7119_JO_Second_SIFoCC_COVID-19_memorandum_WEB.pdf. Accessed 2 May 2024

Sina Weibo (2021) Weibo community agreement. https://service.account.weibo.com/roles/gongyue. Accessed 2 May 2024 (in Chinese)

SPC (2019a) Chinese courts and internet judiciary. People's Courts Press, Beijing (in Chinese)

SPC (2019b) Guidelines of the SPC on deepen the judicial system reform with comprehensive integrated reforms of people's courts—framework of the fifth Five-Year judicial reform for people's courts (2019–2023) (in Chinese)

SPC (2024a) China judicial process information online. https://splcgk.court.gov.cn/gzfwww. Accessed 2 May 2024 (in Chinese)

SPC (2024b) China judgment online. https://wenshu.court.gov.cn. Accessed 2 May 2024 (in Chinese)

SPC (2024c) China court trial online. http://tingshen.court.gov.cn. Accessed 2 May 2024 (in Chinese)

SPC (2024d) China executive information online. http://zxgk.court.gov.cn. Accessed 2 May 2024 (in Chinese)

SPC (2024e) Service platform for people's courts. http://songda.court.gov.cn. Accessed 2 May 2024 (in Chinese)

Stadler A (2021) In: Musielak HJ, Voit W, ZPO, 18. Aufl. Vahlen, München

Stipanowich T, Fraser V (2017) The international task force on mixed mode dispute resolution: exploring the interplay between mediation, evaluation and arbitration in commercial cases. Fordham International Law Journal 40:839–886

Sun H (2020) Over 10 million cases broadcasted at the China court trial online. People's Court Daily, 18 December 2022 (in Chinese)

Sun X (2020) A Chinese approach to international commercial dispute resolution: the China international commercial court. The Chinese Journal of Comparative Law 8:45–54

Sung HC (2020) Can online courts promote access to justice? A case study of the internet courts in China. Computer Law & Security Review 39:1–15

Susskind R (2019) Online courts and the future of justice. Oxford University Press, Oxford

Taobao (2019) General rules on the dispute resolution in Taobao platform. https://rule.taobao.com/detail-99.htm?tag=self#524. Accessed 2 May 2024 (in Chinese)

The School of International Arbitration Queen Mary University of London and White & Case LLP (2021) International arbitration survey: adapting arbitration to a changing world. http://www.arbitration.qmul.ac.uk/media/arbitration/docs/2021-International-Arbitration-Survey-Adapting-arbitration-to-a-changing-world.pdf. Accessed 2 May 2024

United Nations Commission on International Trade Law (1966) Online dispute resolution: on-line resources. https://uncitral.un.org/en/library/online_resources/online_dispute_resolution. Accessed 2 May 2024

Vierkötter G (2021) Einsatz von Videokonferenztechnik—Status quo ein Jahr nach "Corona"? Zeitschrift Für Die Anwaltspraxis 6:263–264

Wagner PP (2016) Das elektronische Dokument im Zivilprozess. Juristische Schulung 1:29–33

Wang F (2021) A brief note on the application of information and communication technology in civil judicial case management. In: Chan PCH, van Rhee CH (eds) Civil case management in the twenty-first century: court structures still matter. Springer, Berlin

Windau B (2020) Die Verhandlung im Wege der Bild- und Tonübertragung. Neue Juristische Wochenschrift 38:2753–2757

Xiao H, Ma R (2019) The diversified dispute resolution platform for foreign-related civil and commercial matters in Hainan Province, the first one nationwide, starts now. http://www.hnzhengfa.gov.cn/news/fayuandongtai/show-869.html. Accessed 2 May 2024 (in Chinese)

Xinhua (2021) Working report of the SPC. https://www.court.gov.cn/zixun/xiangqing/290831.html. Accessed 2 May 2024 (in Chinese)

Xinhuanet (2018) General Office of the Central Committee of the CPC and the General Office of the Chinese State Council have printed and distributed the opinion concerning the establishment of the belt and road international commercial dispute resolution mechanism and institutions. http://www.gov.cn/zhengce/2018-06/27/content_5301657.htm. Accessed 2 May 2024 (in Chinese)

Xinhuanet (2021) Beijing Financial Court accomplished its first patch of judicial review cases in the area of financial arbitration while having entirely paperless proceedings. https://www.chinacourt.org/article/detail/2021/04/id/5956800.shtml. Accessed 2 May 2024 (in Chinese)

Yeazell SC, Schwartz JC (2019) Civil procedure. Aspen Publishing, California

Zhang W (2004) On contractualisation of civil litigation: improving the fundamental framework of Chinese civil procedure law. China Legal Science 3:75–87 (in Chinese)

Zhejiang High People's Court (2021) QR code for dispute resolution of Zhejiang. https://yundr.gov.cn. Accessed 2 May 2024 (in Chinese)

Zhi Z, Ye Z (2019) A third-party evaluation report for the open trials of people's courts. Journal of Law Application 23:103–114 (in Chinese)

Zhou Q (2016) Annual working report of the SPC of 2016. SPC. http://gongbao.court.gov.cn/details/6ce239a82c31348f8856a986e9eb45.html?sw%3D. Accessed 2 May 2024 (in Chinese)

Zhou Q (2021) Mid-term report of the SPC to the standing Committee of the NPC on the performance of pilot program of the reform of separation between complicated cases and simple ones in civil procedure. NPC of P.R.C. http://www.npc.gov.cn/npc/c2/c30834/202102/t20210228_310186.html. Accessed 2 May 2024 (in Chinese)

Zhou H (2022) Innovation and analysis of the electronic service system under the background of "internet +." Journal of Henan University of Economics and Law 1:149–156 (in Chinese)

Zuckerman AAS (2020) Artificial intelligence—implications for the legal profession, adversarial process and rule of law. Law Quarterly Review 136:427–453

Cited Normative Documents in China

Z. Cao, *Civil Judgments at First Instance*, Contemporary Chinese Civil and Commercial Law, https://doi.org/10.1007/978-981-97-8662-6

The normative documents cited in this contribution are listed hereby both in Chinese and English, while the time when they turn into effectiveness and their official numbers are specified. The documents, which appear more than once in this contribution, are also referred to using their names in short.	
2024/2022/2017/2012/1991 Civil Procedure Law of the P.R.C. (CPL)	《中华人民共和国民事诉讼法》（中华人民共和国主席令第106号/中华人民共和国主席令第71号/中华人民共和国主席令第59号/中华人民共和国主席令第44号）
2023 Legislation Law of the P.R.C.	《中华人民共和国立法法》（中华人民共和国主席令第3号）
2022 Rules for the Online Mediation by People's Courts	《人民法院在线调解规则》（法释〔2021〕23号）
2021 Civil Code of the P.R.C.	《中华人民共和国民法典》（中华人民共和国主席令第45号）
2021 Guiding Opinions of the SPC on Improving the Mechanism for Professional Judges' Meetings of the People's Courts	《关于完善人民法院专业法官会议工作机制的指导意见》（法发〔2021〕2号）
2021 Guiding Opinions of the SPC on In-Depth Promotion of Integration of the Socialist Core Values into Interpretation of Law and Reasoning in Judicial Decisions (Opinions on Core Values)	《最高人民法院关于深入推进社会主义核心价值观融入裁判文书释法说理的指导意见》（法〔2021〕21号）
2021 Implementation Measures of the SPC for the Pilot Program of the Reform of Improving the Trial Levels and Functional Orientations of Courts Structured in a Four-Tier System	《关于完善四级法院审级职能定位改革试点的实施办法》（法〔2021〕242号）
2021 Interpretations of the SPC on the Application of the CPL of the P.R.C. (ICPL) (now revised)	《最高人民法院关于适用〈中华人民共和国民事诉讼法〉的解释》（法释〔2020〕20号）
2020 Plan of the SPC for the Pilot Program of the Reform of Separation between Complicated Cases and Simple Ones in Civil Proceedings	《民事诉讼程序繁简分流改革试点方案》（法〔2020〕10号）
2021 Rules of Online Litigation of People's Courts (Online Litigation Rules)	《人民法院在线诉讼规则》（法释〔2021〕12号）

(continued)

(continued)

2021 Several Opinions on Promoting the High-quality Development of Case Guidance	《关于推进案例指导工作高质量发展的若干意见》（法〔2021〕294号）
2021/1997 Several Provisions of the SPC on the Judicial Interpretation Work (modified via the Notice by the SPC of Issuing the Decision to Amend the Provisions of the Supreme People's Court on the Judicial Interpretation Work)	《最高人民法院关于司法解释工作的若干规定》（法发〔1997〕15号）；最高人民法院印发《关于修改〈最高人民法院关于司法解释工作的规定〉的决定》的通知（法发〔2021〕20号）
2020 Guiding Opinions of the SPC on Further Improving the Mechanism of Designated Mediation	《最高人民法院关于进一步完善委派调解机制的指导意见》（法发〔2020〕1号）
2020 Guidelines on Proceeding with Arbitration Actively and Properly during the COVID-19 Pandemic of the CIETAC (Trial) (CIETAC COVID-19 Guidelines)	《关于新冠肺炎疫情期间积极稳妥推进仲裁程序指引（试行）》
2020 Guiding Opinions of the SPC on Unifying the Application of Laws to Strengthen the Search of Similar Cases (for Trial Implementation)	《最高人民法院关于统一法律适用加强类案检索的指导意见（试行）》（法发〔2020〕24号）
2020 Measures of the SPC for the Implementation of the Pilot Program of the Reform of Separation between Complicated Cases and Simple Ones in Civil Procedure (2020 Pilot Program)	《民事诉讼程序繁简分流改革试点实施办法》（法〔2020〕11号）
2020 Provisions of the SPC on Several Issues concerning the Application of Law in the Trial of Private Lending Cases (Private Lending Provisions)	《最高人民法院关于审理民间借贷案件适用法律若干问题的规定》（法释〔2020〕17号）
2020 Regulation of the Beijing Internet Court on Court Hearings during Electronic Litigation (Beijing Regulation on Electronic Litigation)	《北京互联网法院电子诉讼庭审规范（试行）》
2020 Some Provisions of the SPC on Evidence in Civil Procedures (2019 Evidence Provisions)	《最高人民法院关于民事诉讼证据的若干规定》（法释〔2019〕19号）

(continued)

(continued)

2019 Decision of the Standing Committee of the NPC on Authorizing the SPC to Carry out the Pilot Program of the Reform of Separation of Cases into Simple Cases and Complicated Ones under Civil Proceedings	《全国人民代表大会常务委员会关于授权最高人民法院在部分地区开展民事诉讼程序繁简分流改革试点工作的决定》
2019 E-Commerce Law of the P.R.C.	《中华人民共和国电子商务法》（中华人民共和国主席令第7号）
2019 Law of the P.R.C. on the Contracting of Rural Land	《中华人民共和国农村土地承包法》（中华人民共和国主席令第17号）
2019 Minutes of the National Courts' Civil and Commercial Trial Work Conference in 2019 (2019 Civil Conference Minutes of the SPC)	《全国法院民商事审判工作会议纪要》（法〔2019〕254号）
2019 Online Arbitration Rules of the SCIA (now revised)	《深圳国际仲裁院网络仲裁规则》
2019 Opinions of the SPC on Building One-stop Diversified Dispute Resolution Mechanisms and One-stop Litigant Service Centers	《最高人民法院关于建设一站式多元解纷机制 一站式诉讼服务中心的意见》（法发〔2019〕19号）
2019 5th Five-Year Outline of the Program for Reform of People's Courts	《最高人民法院关于深化人民法院司法体制综合配套改革的意见——人民法院第五个五年改革纲要》（法发〔2019〕8号）
2018 Arbitration Law of the P.R.C.	《中华人民共和国仲裁法》（中华人民共和国主席令第76号）
2018 Guiding Opinions of the SPC on Improving the Working Mechanism for Presiding Judges' Meetings of People's Courts (For Trial Implementation) (now expired)	《关于健全完善人民法院主审法官会议工作机制的指导意见（试行）》（法发〔2018〕21号）
2018 Guiding Opinions of the SPC on Strengthening and Standardizing the Analysis and Reasoning in Judicial Decisions (Opinions Reasoning Judicial Decisions)	《关于加强和规范裁判文书释法说理的指导意见》（法发〔2018〕10号）
2018 Official Reply of the SPC on the Application of Law on Placing "Advance Arbitral" Awards or Mediations of Arbitration Institutions on File for Enforcement (Reply on Advance Arbitral Awards or Mediations)	《最高人民法院关于仲裁机构"先予仲裁"裁决或者调解书立案、执行等法律适用问题的批复》（法释〔2018〕10号）
2018 Opinion of the CPC Central Leading Group for Comprehensively Deepening	中央全面深化改革领导小组《关于建立"一带一路"国际商事争端解决机制和机

(continued)

(continued)

Reform Concerning the Establishment of the Belt and Road International Commercial Dispute Resolution Mechanism and Institutions	构的意见》
2018 Opinions of the SPC on the Coordinated of Case Docketing, Trial and Enforcement by People's Courts	《最高人民法院关于人民法院立案、审判与执行工作协调运行的意见》（法发〔2018〕9号）
2018 Provisions of the SPC on Several Issues Concerning the Establishment of International Commercial Courts (Provisions on International Commercial Courts)	《最高人民法院关于设立国际商事法庭若干问题的规定》（法释〔2018〕11号）
2018 Provisions of the SPC on Several Issues Concerning the Trial of Cases by Internet Courts (Provisions on Internet Courts)	《最高人民法院关于互联网法院审理案件若干问题的规定》（法释〔2018〕16号）
2018 Notice of the General Office of the SPC on Determining the First Group of International Commercial Arbitration and Mediation Institutions Included in the "One-Stop" Diversified Mechanisms for Resolving International Commercial Disputes	《最高人民法院办公厅关于确定首批纳入"一站式"国际商事纠纷多元化解决机制的国际商事仲裁及调解机构的通知》（法办〔2018〕212号）
2016 Court Rules of the People's Courts of the P.R.C.	《中华人民共和国人民法院法庭规则》（法释〔2016〕7号）
2016 Guiding Opinions of the SPC on the Prevention and Sanction of False Litigation	《关于防范和制裁虚假诉讼的指导意见》（法发〔2016〕13号）
2016 Several Opinions of the SPC on Further Promoting the Efficient Distribution of Complex and Simple Cases and Optimising the Allocation of Judicial Resources (Opinions on Optimising the Allocation of Judicial Resources)	《最高人民法院关于进一步推进案件繁简分流优化司法资源配置的若干意见》（法发〔2016〕21号）
2016 Specifications for Preparing Civil Judicial Decisions by the People's Courts (Specifications for Decisions)	《人民法院民事裁判文书制作规范》（法〔2016〕221号）
2016 Style of Civil Litigation Documents (Style Litigation Documents)	《民事诉讼文书样式》（法〔2016〕221号）
2015 4th Five-Year Outline of the Program for Reform of People's Courts	《最高人民法院关于全面深化人民法院改革的意见——人民法院第四个五年改革纲要》（法发〔2015〕3号）
2015 Criminal Law of the P.R.C. (now revised)	《中华人民共和国刑法》（中华人民共和

(continued)

(continued)

	国主席令第30号）
2015 Detailed Rules for the Implementation of the Provisions of the SPC on Case Guidance (Detailed Rules on Case Guidance)	《最高人民法院〈关于案例指导工作的规定〉实施细则》（法〔2015〕130号）
2015 Specifications for Preparing Judicial Decisions in Foreign-related Commercial and Maritime Cases	《涉外商事海事裁判文书写作规范》（法〔2015〕67号）
2014 Law on the Protection of Consumer Rights and Interests	《中华人民共和国消费者权益保护法》（中华人民共和国主席令第7号）
2014 Provisions of the SPC on the Publication of Judicial Decisions on the Internet by the People's Courts (Provisions on the Publication of Judgments on the Internet) (now revised)	《关于人民法院在互联网公布裁判文书的规定》（法释〔2013〕26号）
2013 Labor Contract Law of the P.R.C.	《中华人民共和国劳动合同法》（中华人民共和国主席令第73号）
2013 Style of Litigation Documents for Civil Petition for Retrial	《民事申请再审案件诉讼文书样式》（法办发〔2012〕17号）
2012 Interpretation of the SPC on Issues Concerning the Application of Law for the Trial of Cases of Disputes over Sales Contracts (now revised)	《最高人民法院关于审理买卖合同纠纷案件适用法律问题的解释》（法释〔2012〕8号）
2011 Model Legal Instruments of People's Courts for Bankruptcy Procedure (for Trial Implementation)	《人民法院破产程序法律文书样式（试行）》（法办发〔2011〕12号）
2010 Code of the SPC of Conduct for Judges	《法官行为规范》（法发〔2010〕54号）
2010 Copyright Law of the P.R.C. (now revised)	《中华人民共和国著作权法》（中华人民共和国主席令第26号）
2010 Provisions of the SPC on Case Guidance	《关于案例指导工作的规定》（法发〔2010〕51号）
2010 Several Opinions of the SPC on Regulating the Trial Work Relations between the People's Courts at Different Levels	《关于规范上下级人民法院审判业务关系的若干意见》（法发〔2010〕61号）
2010 Tort Law of the P.R.C. (now expired)	《中华人民共和国侵权责任法》（中华人民共和国主席令第21号）
2009 Interpretation of the SPC on the Application of the Contract Law of the P.R.C. (Interpretation of the Contract Law II) (now	《最高人民法院关于适用〈中华人民共和国合同法〉若干问题的解释（二）》（法释〔2009〕5号）

(continued)

(continued)

expired)	
2009 Provisions of the SPC on Citation of Normative Legal Documents such as Laws and Regulations in Judicial Decisions (Provisions on Citation in Judicial Decisions)	《最高人民法院关于裁判文书引用法律、法规等规范性法律文件的规定》（法释〔2009〕14号）
2009 3rd Five-Year Outline of the Program for Reform of People's Courts	《人民法院第三个五年改革纲要》（法发〔2009〕14号）
2008 Format and Explanation of the Beijing High People's Court for the Judgment of First Instance of Commercial Cases Applying Ordinary Procedure	《北京市高级人民法院<关于国内普通程序商事案件一审判决书制作样式>及说明》（京高法发〔2008〕238号）
2007 Measures on the Payment of Litigation Costs	《诉讼费用交纳办法》（中华人民共和国国务院令第481号）
2006 Notice of the SPC on Improving the Making of Civil Decisions (Notice Improving Civil Decisions)	《最高人民法院关于加强民事裁判文书制作工作的通知》（法〔2006〕145号）
2005 2nd Five-Year Outline of the Program for Reform of People's Courts	《人民法院第二个五年改革纲要》（法发〔2005〕18号）
2003 Interpretation of the SPC on Some Issues Concerning the Application of Law in the Trial of Cases on Compensation for Personal Injury (now revised)	《最高人民法院关于审理人身损害赔偿案件适用法律若干问题的解释》（法释〔2003〕20号）
2003 Several Provisions of the SPC on the Application of Simplified Procedures in the Trial of Civil Cases (Provisions on Simplified Proceedings) (now revised)	《最高人民法院关于适用简易程序审理民事案件的若干规定》（法释〔2003〕15号）
2003 Style of Litigation Documents for Civil Simplified Proceedings (for Trial Implementation)	《民事简易程序诉讼文书样式（试行）》（法发〔2003〕21号）
2002 Some Provisions of the SPC on Evidence in Civil Procedures (2001 Evidence Provisions) (now revised)	《最高人民法院关于民事诉讼证据的若干规定》（法释〔2001〕33号）
2000 Administrative Measures of the SPC for the Proclamation of Judicial Decisions	《最高人民法院裁判文书公布管理办法》（法办发〔2000〕4号）
2000 Judicial Interpretation of the SPC on Some Issues Regarding the Application of the Guarantee Law of the P.R.C. (now expired)	《最高人民法院关于适用〈中华人民共和国担保法〉若干问题的解释》（法释〔2000〕44号）
1999 Contract Law of the P.R.C. (now expired)	《中华人民共和国合同法》（中华人民共

(continued)

Cao Z (2024) Reflection on the requirement of evidence for case docketing in civil proceedings. Law Science 1:141–157 (in Chinese)
Carrington PD (2003) The civil jury and American democracy. Duke journal of comparative & international law (Special Issue) 13:79–94
Chase O et al. (2017) Civil litigation in comparative context. West Academic Publishing, St. Paul
Chen G (2000) Research on the law of burden of proof. Renmin University of China Press, Beijing (in Chinese)
Chen B (2004) Contentious lawsuits, petitions and the new Chinese legal tradition—contentious issues in the period of legal transformation. Peking University Law Journal 2:226–238 (in Chinese)
Chen X (2008) Remedy of defects and supplementary remedies of rights: procedure for correcting defects in civil judgments. Journal of Law Application 9:46–49 (in Chinese)
Chen H (2011) On 'one system' of Chinese courts: the history, practice and theory. Law and Social Development 6:57–68 (in Chinese)
Chen G (2012) The significance of awareness of legal family in the study of civil procedural law. Chinese Journal of Law 5:40–43 (in Chinese)
Chen G (2013) Principles of judicial independence with Chinese characteristics from the perspective of comparative law. Journal of Comparative Law 2:1–12 (in Chinese)
Chen H (2016a) "Vulgar delivery": a sample of penetrating into the defects of Chinese civil judicature. Law and Social Development 6:40–51 (in Chinese)
Chen H (2016b) New paradigm of the theory of the subject matter of claims. Chinese Journal of Law 4:170–189 (in Chinese)
Chen R (2018a) Criminal evidence law. Peking University Press, Beijing (in Chinese)
Chen R (2018b) Theoretical reflection on the reform of the judge quota system. The Jurist 3:1–14+191 (in Chinese)
Chen T (2020) Comparison of restitution effects of the invalidity of a contract and the rescission of a contract. Taiwan Law Review 12:118–140 (in Chinese)
Chen W (2020) Restructuring of the standards for defining repeated lawsuits. Peking University Law Journal 6:1596–1613 (in Chinese)
Chen X (2020) Research on systemization of effects of judgment in China with a perspective of comparative law. China Social Science Press (in Chinese)
Chen BM, Li Z (2020) How will technology change the face of Chinese justice? Columbia Journal of Asian Law 34:1–58
Chen J, Lin C (2014) Civil procedure law, Volume I. Sanmin Book Co., Taipei (in Chinese)
Chen H, Lu P, Chao Z, Shi M (2020) The theory on the subject matter of the civil litigation under a new paradigm. China Legal Publishing House (in Chinese)
Christensen R, Sokolowski M (2005) Die Krise der Kommunikation und die Möglichkeit juristischen Argumentierens. In: Lerch KD (ed) Die Sprache des Rechts, Band 2: Recht verhandeln: Argumentieren, Begründen und Entscheiden im Diskurs des Rechts. De Gruyter, Berlin
Chu F (2018) Three dimensions of authenticity of electronic evidence. Chinese Journal of Law 4:121–138 (in Chinese)
CIETAC (2015) Fee schedule. http://www.cietac.org/index.php?m=Article&a=show&id=2747. Accessed 2 May 2024 (in Chinese)
CIETAC (2020) China international economic and trade arbitration commission guidelines on proceeding with arbitration actively and properly during the COVID-19 pandemic (trial). http://www.cietac.org.cn/index.php?m=Article&a=show&id=16910. Accessed 2 May 2024 (in Chinese)
CIETAC (2021) Intelligent hearing platform of China international economic and trade arbitration commission. https://kt.cietac.org/portal/main/domain/index.htm. Accessed 2 May 2024
CIETAC (2022a) CIETAC online arbitration. http://www.cietacodr.org. Accessed 2 May 2024 (in Chinese)
CIETAC (2022b) Online dispute resolution center. http://odr.org.cn. Accessed 2 May 2024 (in Chinese)

Clarke DC (1996) Power and politics in the Chinese court system: the enforcement of civil judgments. Columbia Journal of Asian Law 10:1–92
Clermont KM (2009) Standards of proof revisited. Vermont Law Review 33:469–487
Clermont KM, Sherwin E (2002) A comparative view of standards of proof. The American Journal of Comparative Law 50:243–275
Cui J (2007) Comments on choice and its foundation of the patterns of remedy for right in rem. Journal of Tsinghua University (Philosophy and Social Sciences) 3:111–116 (in Chinese)
Cui J (2022) On the differentiation between civil contracts and commercial contracts. Tribune of Political Science and Law 1:56–73 (in Chinese)
Damaska MR (1997) Evidence law adrift. Yale University Press, New Haven
Damaska MR (1998) Truth in adjudication. Hastings Law Journal 49:289–308
Deng F (2009) Why china adopted the civil legal system: a political economic explanation of transitional justice in later Ch'ing's empire. Peking University Law Journal 2:165–186 (in Chinese)
Dickert T (2020) Thesen zur Modernisierung des Zivilprozesses. Deutsche Richterzeitung 9:296–299
Ding B (2012) Study on the *res judicata* of civil judgments. Law Press, Beijing (in Chinese)
Du R (2005) On correcting judgments. Journal of Southwest University of Political Science and Law 2:7–11 (in Chinese)
Du R (2007) On the legal meaning and issues of supplementary judgment system. People's Judicature 11:78–82 (in Chinese)
Duan H (2007) The practical interaction and institutional coordination between burden of proof, standard of proof and evaluation of proof. Journal of Nanjing Normal University (Social Science Edition) 3:24–30 (in Chinese)
Duan W (2011) The countermeasures and implications of unexpected application of laws in Germany. Science of Law 6:190–199 (in Chinese)
Duan W (2012) Reflection on the structure of norm-based civil judgments. Law Press, Beijing (in Chinese)
Duan W (2015a) The criticism of the effect of predetermination and the development of the effect of evidence regarding facts. Science of Law 5:106–114 (in Chinese)
Duan W (2015b) Recognition on the structure of sessions of civil court's hearings in China. China Legal Science 2:81–107 (in Chinese)
Duan W (2017) On civil pretrial preparatory procedure from the perspective focusing on court hearings. China Legal Science 6:203–220 (in Chinese)
Duan W (2020) Non-binding nature of Chinese civil admission system and its revision. Chinese Journal of Law 1:100–116 (in Chinese)
eBRAM (2024) https://ebram.org/. Accessed 2 May 2024
ELI, UNIDROIT, (2021) ELI/UNIDROIT model European rules of civil procedure. Oxford University Press, Oxford
Engisch K (1963) Logische Studien zur Gesetzesanwendung, 3. Aufl. C. Winter, Heidelburg
Engisch K (2005) Einführung in das juristische Denken, 10. Aufl. Kohlhammer, Stuttgart
Fan K (1996) Correction of judgments. In: Discussion on civil procedure law (I), Sanmin Book Co., Taipei, pp 439–477 (in Chinese)
Fan T (2010) Reflection and reconstruction of Chinese commercial trial system. Hebei Law Science 2:145–150 (in Chinese)
Fan Y (2011) Judgment combination to mediation: an analysis based on the practice. Law and Social Development 6:49–56 (in Chinese)
Fan W (2019) Theoretical interpretation and practice of "decision results" in repeated prosecution rules. Journal of Gansu Political Science and Law Institute 5:20–30 (in Chinese)
Fang L (2007) A cultural note on judicial behaviors and its selection. Science of Law 5:17–31 (in Chinese)
Feskorn C (2020) In: Zöller R, ZPO, 33. Aufl. Otto Schmidt, Köln

First Intermediate People's Court in Hainan Province and Hainan High People's Court (2020) Foreign-related civil and commercial cases online dispute resolution platform. https://hnodr.odrcloud.cn (now unaccessible) (in Chinese)

Fischer F (2005) Der Tatbestand im Zivilurteil unter besonderer Berücksichtigung der Bezugnahmen. Juristische Schulung 45:904–908

Fischer C (2007) Topoi verdeckter Rechtsfortbildungen im Zivilrecht. Mohr Siebeck, Tübingen

Foerste U (1995) Zur Rechtskraft in Ausgleichszusammenhängen. Zeitschrift für Zivilprozess 108:167–191

Foerste U (2021) In: Musielak HJ, Voit W, ZPO, 18. Aufl. Vahlen GmbH, München

Freer RD (2017) Civil procedure. Aspen Publishing, California

Fritsche J (2020) In: Krüger W, Rauscher T, Münchener Kommentar ZPO, Band 1, 6. Aufl. C. H. Beck, München

Fu Y (2000) The functions and styles of civil judicial decisions. Social Sciences in China 4:123–133 (in Chinese)

Fu Y (2002) Constructive principles of judicial hierarchy. Social Sciences in China 4:84–99 (in Chinese)

Fu Y (2003) The diversion of complicated and simple cases and the procedural safeguards. Chinese Journal of Law 1:50–63 (in Chinese)

Fu Y (2005) The function and structure of civil appellate procedure. Law Review 4:36–44 (in Chinese)

Fu Y (2008) Preliminary issue and interlocutory adjudication. China Legal Science 6:155–169 (in Chinese)

Fu Y (2011a) Small claims and classification of proceedings. Tsinghua University Law Journal 3:46–55 (in Chinese)

Fu Y (2011b) The logic and corresponding skills of trial and judgment. People's Court Daily, 19 January 2011 (in Chinese)

Fu Y (2011c) Function and structure of the case-filing procedure in Chinese civil litigation. The Jurist 1:99–113 (in Chinese)

Fu Y (2012a) Autonomous options of procedural issues upon the litigants' consent in the new civil procedure law. Journal of Comparative Law 5:55–66 (in Chinese)

Fu Y (2012b) Review on the value orientation of the revision of the civil procedure law. Journal of the East China University of Political Science of Law 4:79–93 (in Chinese)

Fu Y (2015) The focus of judicial accountability is the boundary of duties. China Law Review 4:169–174 (in Chinese)

Fu Y (2017) On the duty of good faith of parties in civil proceedings. Law and Modernization 6:130–145 (in Chinese)

Fu Y (2018) Studies on civil procedure law in China in the forty-year era of reform and opening up. Peking University Law Journal 6:1423–1448 (in Chinese)

Fu Y (2021) Civil justice in China in the COVID-19 period. In: Krans B, Nylund A (eds) Civil courts coping with COVID-19. Eleven International Publishing, The Hague

Fu Y, Cao Z (2012) The position of judges in civil litigation in transitional China: judicial mediation and case management. In: Chen L, van Rhee CH (eds) Towards a Chinese civil code: comparative and historical perspectives. Martinus Nijhoff Publishers, Leiden, pp 495–519

Fu Y, Peerenboom R (2012) A new analytic framework for understanding and promoting judicial independence in China. In: Peerenboom R (ed) Judicial Independence in China: lessons for Global Rule of Law Promotion. Cambridge University Press, Cambridge, pp 95–133

Gao X (2016) The research on the probative value of public documents in civil proceedings. Evidence Science 5:576–587 (in Chinese)

Gast W (2006) Juristische Rhetorik. C. F. Müller, Heidelberg

Ge Y (2014) The ideal of legal education. Peking University Law Journal 2:285–318 (in Chinese)

Ge Y (2015) A case report based on the method of Anspruchsgrundlage: application of law on a car accident case. Peking University Law Review 2:272–311 (in Chinese)

Geimer R (2019) In: Thomas H, Putzo H, ZPO, 40. Aufl. C. H. Beck, München

Geimer R (2020) In: Zöller R, ZPO, 33. Aufl. Otto Schmidt, Köln
Gelbach JB (2012) Locking the doors to discovery? Assessing the effects of Twombly and Iqbal on access to discovery. Yale Law Journal 121:2270–2345
Ghoshray S (2006) Charting the future of online dispute resolution: an analysis of the constitutional and jurisdictional quandary. University of Toledo Law Review 38:317–350
Goldschmidt J (1925) Prozess als Rechtslage: eine Kritik des Prozessualen Denkens. Springer, Berlin, Heidelberg
Gong C (2000) Thoughts on the reform of the mode of making civil judgments. Journal of Law Application 2:17–20 (in Chinese)
Gottwald P (2000) Streitgegenstandslehre und Sinnzusammenhänge. In: Peter G, Reinhard G, Hanns P (eds) Dogmatische Grundfragen des Zivilprozesses im geeinten Europa: Akademisches Symposium zu Ehren von Karl Heinz Schwab aus Anlass seines 80. Geburtstages. Gieseking, Bielefeld
Gottwald P (2011) Die Begründung von Gerichtsentscheidungen in Deutschland: aus Sicht der Praxis und der Wissenschaft. In: Tichý L, Holländer P, Bruns A (eds) Centrum právní komparatistiky, Právnická fakulta Univerzity Karlovy, Praha.
Gottwald P (2015) Reasoning in German judicial judgments: practice and doctrine (trans: Cao Z). Journal of Soochow University (Law Edition) 4:83–92 (in Chinese)
Gottwald P (2018a) Die Stellung des Sachverständigen und seines Gutachtens im deutschen Zivilprozess. Ritsumeikan Law Review 36:121–133
Gottwald P (2018b) Electronic documents and electronic signatures in German civil proceedings (trans: Cao Z) In: Jiang S (ed) Electronic documents and e-commerce related substantive and procedural issues. Taiwan New Sharing Press, Taipei, pp 407–452 (in Chinese)
Gottwald P (2020) In: Krüger W, Rauscher T, Münchener Kommentar ZPO, Band 1, 6. Aufl. C. H. Beck, München
Goutal JL (1976) Characteristics of judicial style in France, Britain and the U.S.A. The American Journal of Comparative Law 24:43–72
Gu P (2018) Causes and effects of spontaneous application of precedents. Chinese Journal of Law 2:76–96 (in Chinese)
Gu W (2018a) China's belt and road development and a new international commercial arbitration initiative in Asia. Vanderbilt Journal of Transnational Law 51:1305–1352
Gu W (2018b) Looking at arbitration through a comparative lens: general principles and specific issues. Journal of Comparative Law 2:164–188
Gu W (2021) Dispute resolution in China: litigation, arbitration, mediation, and their interactions. Routledge, London
Guo X (2010) Study on the theory of issue preclusion in civil cases. Beijing Normal University Press, Beijing (in Chinese)
Guo C (2012) Research on the citation of legal provisions in court's judgments. Law Science Magazine 7:136–140 (in Chinese)
Guo Q (2020) On the "advance arbitration" in internet-based lending disputes. Fudan University Law Review 1:146–157 (in Chinese)
Guo M (2021) Internet court's challenges and future in China. Computer Law & Security Review 40:1–13
Habscheid WJ (1956) Der Streitgegenstand im Zivilprozess und im Streitverfahren der Freiwilligen Gerichtsbarkeit. Dt. Heimat-Verl, Bielefeld
Hahn C (1880) Die gesammten Materialien zur Civilprozessordnung. Decker, Berlin
Hartmann P (2019) In: Baumbach A, Lauterbach W, Albers J, Hartmann P, ZPO. C. H. Beck, München
He X (2004) The standardization of civil judgments and the direction of reform. People's Court Daily, 7 January 2004 (in Chinese)
He B (2009) The Making and reasoning of civil and commercial judicial decisions. People's Judicature 3:37–43 (in Chinese)

He F (2009) Is it superfluous to add footnotes to judgments? Southern Weekend, 4 June 2009 (in Chinese)
He X (2012) A tale of two Chinese courts: economic development and contract enforcement. Journal of Law and Society 39:384–409
He F (2013) How many judges are enough? People's Court Daily, 7 June 2013 (in Chinese)
He Q (2017) The idea of justice in a large country and the development of international civil procedure in China. Social Sciences in China 5:123–146+208 (in Chinese)
He X, Wang S (2005) Analysis of several issues concerning making civil judgments. People's Judicature 12:4–7 (in Chinese)
He L, Zhong H (2006) On publicity in application of law in judgments. Journal of Law Application 3:17–20 (in Chinese)
Heiden C (2020) Prozessrecht in Zeiten der Corona-Pandemie. Neue Juristische Wochenschrift 15:1023–1028
Heil B (2020) IT-Anwendung im Zivilprozess. Mohr Siebeck, Tübingen
Heinrich C (1996) Die Beweislast bei Rechtsgeschäften. Heymann, Köln
Henckel W (1970) Prozessrecht und materielles Recht. Schwartz, Göttingen
Herrler S (2020) In: Palandt, Bürgerliches Gesetzbuch, 79. Aufl. C. H. Beck, München
Ho HL (2000) The judicial duty to give reasons. Legal Studies 20:42–65
Ho B (2005) Common law education in China. CUPL Press, Beijing (in Chinese)
Höhne N (2005) Vom Sandwichdiagramm zur Struktur einer selektiven Dokumentation—Die Tatbestandsfassung im Zivilurteil. Juristische Arbeitsblätter 37:290–294
Holloway D (2020) The new Chinese international commercial court and the future of dispute resolution in the belt and road initiative. In: Chen L, Janssen A (eds) Dispute resolution in China, Europe and World. Springer, Cham, pp 51–80
Hou M (2021) The operative process of justice: based on the observation of the SPC. China Legal Publishing House, Beijing (in Chinese)
Hu X (2009) Errors in statements within judicial decisions and their correction. Journal of Law Application 10:70–73 (in Chinese)
Hu Y (2009) On the reasoning of judicial decisions. Journal of Law Application 3:48–52 (in Chinese)
Hu X (2011) Omission within civil judgments and its relief. In: Zhang W (ed) On civil procedure, Volume 6. Xiamen University Press, Xiamen (in Chinese)
Hu X (2013) Rule of law represents the basic direction of the reform of law-related or litigation-related petitions system. People's Court Daily, 23 November 2013 (in Chinese)
Hu S (2014) Research on civil adjudication. Social Science Academic Press, Beijing (in Chinese)
Hu J (2016) Rules of grounds of substantive rights and codification of civil law. Journal of the East China University of Political Science & Law 6:38–48 (in Chinese)
Hu X (2017) Restatement of the normentheorie of burden of proof. The Jurist 1:63–76+177 (in Chinese)
Hu D (2017) The rule of 'who Claims, who Proves': its historical evolution and contemporary application. Chinese Journal of Law 3:107–124 (in Chinese)
Hu S, Liu S (2018a) Construction of the system and normative interpretation of the reasoning within judicial decisions in the new era (I): understanding and application of the guiding opinions on strengthening and standardizing the interpretation and reasoning of judicial decisions. Journal of Law Application (Judicial Case) 16:3–20 (in Chinese)
Hu S, Liu S (2018b) Construction of the system and normative interpretation of the reasoning within judicial decisions in the new Era (II): understanding and application of the guiding opinions on strengthening and standardizing the interpretation and reasoning of judicial decisions. Journal of Law Application (Judicial Case) 18:3–19 (in Chinese)
Huang S (ed) (2002) The understanding and application of judicial interpretation on evidence in civil procedure. China Legal Publishing House, Beijing (in Chinese)
Huang M (2007) Legal methods and modern civil law. Law Press, Beijing (in Chinese)
Huang K (2008) New perspective of civil procedure theory. Peking University Press, Beijing (in Chinese)

Huang K (2009) Evaluation of reform proposal for criminal appeals system: an empirical approach. In: Huang K (ed) Empirical studies of judicial systems 2008. Institutum Iurisprudentiae (Preparatory Office), Taipei, pp 447–495, (in Chinese)
Huang Y (2013) Problems in the summary of the disputed points in civil court trial and countermeasures. People's Judicature 5:26–30 (in Chinese)
Huang Y (2021) Induction of disputed issues in civil trial: technical analysis and comprehensive application. Law Press, Beijing (in Chinese)
Huang Z, Zhang J (2013) Legal reasoning and its rules under the case guidance system. Chinese Journal of Law 2:38–59 (in Chinese)
Huber M (2003a) Das Zivilurteil. C. H. Beck, München
Huber M (2003b) Modernisierung der Justiz? Zeitschrift für Rechtspolitik 36:268–272
Huber M (2004) Das Strafurteil. C. H. Beck, München
Huber M (2021) In: Musielak HJ, Voit W, ZPO, 18. Aufl. Vahlen, München
Hunke M (2020) In: Baumbach A, Lauterbach W, Hartmann P, Anders M, Gehle B, ZPO. C. H. Beck, München
Isidro MR (2019) International commercial courts in the litigation market. International Journal of Procedural Law 9:4–49
Ito M (2016) Civil procedure law. Yuhikaku Publishing, Tokyo (in Japanese)
Ito M (2019) Civil procedure law (trans: Cao Y), 4th edn. Peking University Press, Beijing (in Chinese)
Jacobs M (2005) Der Gegenstand des Feststellungsverfahrens. Mohr Siebeck, Tübingen
James F, Hazard GC, Lubsdorf J (2001) Civil procedure. Foundation Press, New York
Jauernig O, Hess B (2011) Zivilprozessrecht. C. H. Beck, München
JD (2020) Disputes out of third-party transactions. https://help.jd.com/user/issue/list-450.html. Accessed 2 May 2024 (in Chinese)
Ji W (2005) The tide of petitions and the solutions for the complaint system. Twenty-First Century 3:79–84 (in Chinese)
Ji G (2012) Does direct evidence really exist? Peking University Law Journal 3:594–606 (in Chinese)
Ji G (2013) The western sample of the legal effect of 'disputed issues' and China's path. China Legal Science 3:109–120 (in Chinese)
Ji G (2017) Rethinking the governance of false litigation in civil litigation. SJTU Law Review 2:21–30 (in Chinese)
Jiang D (2011) 'What the judge says': problem awareness, special knowledge and interpretive skills. Chinese Journal of Law 6:43–47 (in Chinese)
Jiang S (2016) Civil procedure law, Volume I. Taiwan New Sharing Press, Taipei (in Chinese)
Jiang S (2018) Civil procedure law, Volume II. Taiwan New Sharing Press, Taipei (in Chinese)
Jiang W, Chang T (2008) On the predetermine force of confirmed facts. China Legal Science 3:102–109 (in Chinese)
Jiang W, Fu Y (eds) (2015) Civil procedure law. Peking University Press, Beijing (in Chinese)
Jiang H, Long F (2013) The disclosure of justice in Hong Kong and Macao and its enlightenment. Journal of Law Application 4:39–43 (in Chinese)
Jiang W, Wu Z (2002) A legal philosophical analysis of some basic problems of the law of evidence. China Legal Science 1:24–38 (in Chinese)
Jin C (2021) The "trinity" diversified dispute resolution mechanism for international commercial disputes in Hainan Province. https://www.hainan.gov.cn/hainan/5309/202110/c7e9e25a92e9424baf1a156448891bc2.shtml. Accessed 2 May 2024 (in Chinese)
Jin J (2021) Thinking based on grounds of substantive rights: the "engine" of legal dogmatics of case study. Politic Science of Law 3:88–103 (in Chinese)
Jing H (2022) Era innovation of internet courts and China's contribution. China Legal Science 4:49–73 (in Chinese)
Jolowicz JA (2000) On civil procedure. Cambridge University Press, New York
Kaiser T, Kaiser H, Kaiser J (2018) Materielles Zivilrecht im Assessorexamen, 9. Aufl. Vahlen, München

Kaneko H, Takeshita M (1995) Civil procedure law (trans: Bai L). Law Press, Beijing (in Chinese)
Kaplow L (2012) Burden of proof. Yale Law Journal 121:738–859
Kaufmann A (1999) Das Verfahren der Rechtsgewinnung. C. H. Beck, München
Kaufmann A (2011) Problemgeschichte der Rechtsphilosophie. In: Kaufmann A, Hassemer W, Neumann U, Einführung in Rechtsphilosophie und Rechtstheorie der Gegenwart, 8. Aufl. C. F. Müller, Heidelberg
Kengyel M, Nemessányi Z (eds) (2012) Electronic technology and civil procedure: new paths to justice from around the world. Springer, Berlin
Klass D (1998) Reformansätze im zivilrechtlichen Persönlichkeitsschutz unter besonderer Berücksichtigung der Persönlichkeitsrechtlichen Feststellungsklage. Peter Lang GmbH, Internationaler Verlag der Wissenschaften, Berlin
Klug U (1982) Juristische Logik, 4. Aufl. Springer, Berlin, Heidelberg
Knöringer D (2014) Die Assessorklausur im Zivilprozess. C. H. Beck, München
Knöringer D (2018) Die Assessorklausur im Zivilprozess. C. H. Beck, München
Köbler R (2021) Homeoffice hat bei den Gerichten Grenzen. Deutsche Richterzeitung 2:52–53
Koch HJ, Rüßmann H (1982) Juristische Begründungslehre. C. H. Beck, München
Kohler J (2020) In: Säcker FJ, Rixecker R, Oetker H, Limperg B (eds) Münchener Kommentar BGB, Band 8, 8. Aufl. C. H. Beck, München
Koichi M, Kasai M, Kakiuchi S, Hishida Y (2018) Civil Procedure Law. Yuhikaku Publishing, Tokyo (in Japanese)
Kramer EA (2010) Juristische Methodenlehre, 3. Aufl. C. H. Beck, München
Krans B, Nylund A (eds) (2021) Civil courts coping with COVID-19. Eleven International Publishing, The Hague
Lamsfuß M, Werner I (2021) Pandemie und Video—Verhandlungen in der Praxis. Deutsche Richterzeitung 2:50–51
Larenz K (1991) Methodenlehre der Rechtswissenschaft, 6. Aufl. Springer, Berlin, Heidelberg
Laumen H (2019) In: Baumgärtel G, Laumen H, Prütting H, Handbuch der Beweislast: Grundlagen. Heymann, Köln
Legg M (2016) The future of dispute resolution: online ADR and online courts. Australasian Dispute Resolution Journal 27:227–235
Lei X, Huang W (2009) Analysis of current problems in courts' judgments and their reasons. Journal of Law Application 12:95–98 (in Chinese)
Leipold D (1966) Beweislastregeln und Gesetzliche Vermutungen. Duncker & Humblot, Berlin
Lent F (1959) Zivilprozessrecht, 9. Aufl. C. H. Beck, München
Li H (1993) On civil burden of proof. CUPL Press, Beijing (in Chinese)
Li C (2002) On the writing technique of civil judgments. Journal of Law Application 4:75–77 (in Chinese)
Li G (ed) (2002) The understanding and application of 'some provisions of the SPC on evidence in civil procedures' by the SPC. China Legal Publishing House, Beijing (in Chinese)
Li H (2005) Comparison on the solution of factual *non liquet*. Studies in Law and Business 3:104–111 (in Chinese)
Li H (2007) On the frontier issues in the legislation of civil evidence law. Law Press, Beijing (in Chinese)
Li H (2009) 'New evidence' after the revision of civil procedure law: possible contribution of defining the 'new evidence' in the judicial interpretation on judicial supervision. China Legal Science 3:156–168 (in Chinese)
Li H (2010) Self-liability of party in civil procedure. Chinese Journal of Law 3:120–133 (in Chinese)
Li Y (2010) Why guiding cases are not binding. Law and Social Development 4:86–96 (in Chinese)
Li H (2011a) Restatement of the principle of 'ascertaining the facts and discerning between right and wrong.' Chinese Journal of Law 4:120–135 (in Chinese)
Li H (2011b) Evidence provisions and amendments to rules of civil evidence. China Legal Science 3:31–40 (in Chinese)

Li H (2012a) Understanding and cognition of the nature of antecedent mediation. People's Court Daily, 17 October 2012 (in Chinese)
Li H (2012b) Treating mediation first rationally—an analysis based on court mediation. Journal of National Prosecutors College 1:117–125 (in Chinese)
Li H (2013) On separating mediation from adjudication in the civil justice. China Legal Science 3:5–18 (in Chinese)
Li C (2015) Value recognition and practice ideas on 'altering' civil judgments at the second instance. Journal of Law Application 2:71–75 (in Chinese)
Li X (2015) The status, problems and countermeasures regarding civil judgments published online. Science of Law 4:191–201 (in Chinese)
Li H (2016) Civil procedure law. Law Press, Beijing (in Chinese)
Li H (2017) Research on the classification of legal elements from the perspective of the norm theory. Journal of Law Application 15:2–9 (in Chinese)
Li H (2018) An investigation into judges' resignation from the bench. Law and Modernization 3:1–13 (in Chinese)
Li M (2018) Legal theory and theories as the source of civil law. Law Science 6:99–115 (in Chinese)
Li D, Fan H (2015) A new exploration of the reasoning model of judicial decisions in China under the division of rigid and weak needs. Law and Social Development 3:93–108 (in Chinese)
Li R, Hu Q (2012) Shenzhen: breaking through the bottleneck of civil and commercial judgments writing. People's Court Daily, 27 November 2012 (in Chinese)
Li R, Huang Y (2013) Preliminary research on openness of judicial information of courts. Law Science Magazine 4:105–114 (in Chinese)
Li L, Yang J (2013) The nature and application of continued performance of contracts. Journal of Law Application 9:71–74 (in Chinese)
Li W, Yin J (2009) The way of adjudication with disputed facts: a brief introduction to German court report method. Journal of Law Application 4:88–91 (in Chinese)
Liao Y (2003) Several mistakes should be avoided in the reform of civil judicial decisions. People's Court Daily, 16 September 2003 (in Chinese)
Lin J (2006) Study on the objective scope of *res judicata* effect of civil judgments. Xiamen University Press, Xiamen (in Chinese)
Lin Y (2007) Thoughts on some problems of the accountability of the petition work. Law Science 2:26–32 (in Chinese)
Lin X (2015) Empirical study on citation to constitutional norms in China's judgments. Science of Law 4:181–190 (in Chinese)
Liu R (1999) Defects in civil procedural legal transactions and its solution. China Legal Science 3:111–118 (in Chinese)
Liu X (2005) The reform and making of civil judicial decisions. People's Judicature 12:8–11 (in Chinese)
Liu Z (2010) Burden of proof in American law: from the perspective of judicial procedure. Contemporary Law Review 3:86–94 (in Chinese)
Liu B (2015) On the institutional logic of the reform of the judge quota system based on the phenomenon of judges' resignation. Law Science 10:47–56 (in Chinese)
Liu P (2017) Authentification of electronic evidence: reflections on the QVOD player case. Peking University Law Journal 1:89–103 (in Chinese)
Liu Z (2018) Limitation on the scope of the declaratory claim and its implementation method. Chinese Journal of Law 1:126–145 (in Chinese)
Liu J (2019) On the normative nature and procedural framework of false litigation. Contemporary Law Review 4:140–149 (in Chinese)
Liu L (2020) Reflection on the adjudication approaches in civil and commercial cases. Oriental Law 1:83–96 (in Chinese)
Liu S (2020a) No reasoning is not 'book': 23 lectures on the reasoning of judicial decisions. China Procuratorate Press, Beijing (in Chinese)

Liu S (2020b) A jurisprudential differentiation between "judgment basis" and "judgment reasoning" and their practical forms: observation centering on the judgment's effect. Law and Modernization 3:123–138 (in Chinese)

Liu Y (2021) The *status quo* and development of issue arrangement from the perspective of elaborate civil procedures—analysis of practices based on rules and judgments. The Jurist 2:131–146+195 (in Chinese)

Liu L, Sun J (2002) Comparison and reference of the reasoning of the judgments within two legal systems. Journal of Law Application 3:18–19 (in Chinese)

Long F (2020) Innovation and development of the China international commercial court. The Chinese Journal of Comparative Law 8:40–44

Lu X (2006) Going forward and backward of the petition system: thoughts on functions of the organs for petitions. Contemporary Law Review 3:42–46 (in Chinese)

Lu X (2019) A perspective study of the phenomenon of 'mediation with judgment factors'–also a study of the pluralistic positioning of 'clear facts and clarified responsibilities' in the judicial mediation. The Jurist 1:101–111+193–194 (in Chinese)

Lu Y (2020) The conscience of judges under the background of judicial accountability system. Modern Law Science 3:14–28 (in Chinese)

Luo X (2006) Research on civil judgments: basis and countermeasures. People's Court Press, Beijing (in Chinese)

Luo C (2015) Five misunderstandings to be avoided in promoting the reasoning reform of judicial decisions. People's Court Daily, 6 February 2015 (in Chinese)

Lv T (2018) Civil procedure law. Taiwan Angle Publishing, Taipei (in Chinese)

Lücke J (1987) Begründungszwang und Verfassung. Mohr Siebeck, Tübingen

Ma J (2019) Prevention and limitation of evidence prediction in civil proceedings. Science of Law 3:180–190 (in Chinese)

Ma J (2021) Reflection on the criteria and procedure to hear the case in another lawsuit. Peking University Law Journal 3:703–722 (in Chinese)

Matsumoto H, Ueno Y (2015) Civil procedure law. Koubundou Publishers, Tokyo (in Japanese)

Mayer J, Khairy K, Howard J (2010) Drawing an elephant with four complex parameters. American Journal of Physics 6:648–649

McGrath CP, Koziol H (2014) Is style of reasoning a fundamental difference between the common law and the civil law. The Rabel Journal of Comparative and International Private Law 78:709–749

Medicus D, Peterson J (2019) Bürgerliches Recht, 27. Aufl. Vahlen, München

Medicus D (2012) Grundwissen zum Bürgerlichen Recht: ein Basisbuch zu den Anspruchsgrundlagen (trans: Chen W, Tian S, Wang H and Zhang S). Law Press, Beijing (in Chinese)

Medvedeva M et al. (2020) JURI SAYS: an automatic judgment prediction system for the European Court of Human Rights. In: Villata S, Harašta J, Křemen P (eds) Legal knowledge and information systems. IOS Press, Amsterdam

Meller-Hannich C (2016) Die Rolle des Sachverständigen im deutschen Zivilprozess. Zeitschrift für Zivilprozess 129:263–294

Mendelssohn Bartholdy A (1900) Grenzen der Rechtskraft. Duncker & Humblot, Leipzig

Meng X (2020) Exploration and perfection of effective issue narrowing mode. Journal of Central South University (Social Science) 1:75–86 (in Chinese)

Menkel-Meadow CJ, Porter-Love L, Kupfer-Schneider A, Moffitt M (2019) Dispute resolution: beyond the adversarial model. Aspen Publishing, California

Minzner CF (2011) China's turn against law. The American Journal of Comparative Law 59:935–984

Mnookin RH, Kornhauser L (1979) Bargaining in the shadow of the law: the case of divorce. Yale Law Journal 88:950–997

Morgan EM (1956) Some problems of proof under the Anglo-American system of litigation. Columbia University Press, New York

Mueller CB, Kirkpatrick LC, Richter LL (2018) Evidence. Aspen Publishing, California

Musielak HJ (1975) Die Grundlagen der Beweislast im Zivilprozess. De Gruyter, Berlin

Musielak HJ (2016) In: Krüger W, Rauscher T, Münchener Kommentar ZPO, 5. Aufl. C. H. Beck, München
Musielak HJ (2020) In: Krüger W, Rauscher T, Münchener Kommentar ZPO, Band 1, 6. Aufl. C. H. Beck, München
Musielak HJ (2021) In: Musielak HJ, Voit W, ZPO, 18. Aufl. Vahlen, München
Musielak HJ, Voit W (2016) Grundkurs ZPO, 13. Aufl. C. H. Beck, München
Nakamura H (2009) The research on civil procedure law and I. In: Nakamura M and Nakamura H (eds) The methodology of procedure law—the essence of Nakamura's theory of civil procedure (trans: Chen G, Duan W). China Legal Publishing House, Beijing (in Chinese)
National Judges College and German Agency for International Cooperation (2014) Methods of application of law and methods of case analysis of contract law. China Legal Publishing House, Beijing (in Chinese)
Neubert K (2021) Der Einsatz von Künstlicher Intelligenz in der deutschen Justiz. Deutsche Richterzeitung 3:108–111
Neumann U (2011a) Juristische Logik. In: Kaufmann A, Hassemer W, Neumann U, Einführung in Rechtsphilosophie und Rechtstheorie der Gegenwart, 8. Aufl. C. F. Müller, Heidelberg
Neumann U (2011b) Theorie der juristischen Argumentation. In: Kaufmann A, Hassemer W, Neumann U, Einführung in Rechtsphilosophie und Rechtstheorie der Gegenwart, 8. Aufl. C. F. Müller, Heidelberg
Niu Y (2019) Study on dual control model during identifying civil fraud litigations. Social Sciences of Beijing 1:99–107 (in Chinese)
Nylund A, Cabral A (2023) Contractualisation of civil litigation. Intersentia, Cambridge
Ou Y (2016) On abandonment of proposition of *non liquet* of fact. Political Science and Law 11:23–31 (in Chinese)
PKULAW (2024) FabaoGPT. https://ai.pkulaw.com/shop. Accessed 2 May 2024 (in Chinese)
Pan J (2000) On the coherency between civil disputes and its solving methods. Modern Law Science 6:59–62 (in Chinese)
Pan J (2013) Reflections on the 'cooperative mechanism between litigation and mediation' under the background of revising civil procedure law. Contemporary Law Review 3:102–111 (in Chinese)
Pan J (2015) On the basic principles of establishment of civil procedural rights relief mechanism. China Legal Science 2:29–42 (in Chinese)
Pan J (2016) On burden of proof in civil cases. Political Science and Law 11:2–12 (in Chinese)
Pan J, Liu Z (2010) On the relationship between court mediation and dispute resolution–from the perspective of building a harmonious society. Journal of Comparative Law 4:70–81 (in Chinese)
Pappas BA (2008) Online court: online dispute resolution and the future of small claims. UCLA Journal of Law and Technology 12:[i]–25
Peerenboom R (2004) Varieties of rule of law: an introduction and provisional conclusion. In Peerenboom R (ed) Asian discourses of rule of law. Routledge, London
Peng Z (2020) On the judicial application of legal theory. Social Sciences in China 4:90–113+206 (in Chinese)
Peng X (2023) Fengqiao model and the structural changes of dispute resolution mechanisms in contemporary China. China Legal Science 6:23–44 (in Chinese)
Perritt HH (2000) Dispute resolution in cyberspace. Ohio State Journal on Dispute Resolution 15:675–704
Peters E (1963) Zur Rechtskraftlehre Zeuners. Zeitschrift für Zivilprozess 76:229–243
Picker C (2019) In: Staudinger, Kommentar zum Bürgerlichen Gesetzbuch. De Gruyter, Berlin
Pielke W (2006) Verweisungen im Tatbestand eines zivilgerichtlichen Urteils. Juristische Arbeitsblätter 38:202–205
Poblet M (ed) (2011) Mobile technologies for conflict management: online dispute resolution, governance, participation. Springer, Berlin
Pohlmann P (2018) Zivilprozessrecht, C. H. Beck, München
Posner RA (1990) The problems of jurisprudence. Harvard University Press, Cambridge, Mass

Shao M (2018) Jurisprudence of modern civil litigation and dispute procedure. Renmin University of China Press, Beijing (in Chinese)
Shapiro M (1986) Courts: a comparative and political analysis. University of Chicago Press, Chicago
Shavell S (1995) The appeals process as a means of error correction. The Journal of Legal Studies 24:379–426
Shen D (ed) (2015) Understanding and application of the judicial interpretation of the civil procedure law of the SPC. People's Court Press, Beijing (in Chinese)
Shen D (ed) (2016) The style of civil litigation documents. People's Court Press, Beijing (in Chinese)
Shen F (2021) Identification of the settlement result of the disputed issues and the simplified agreement for the disputed issues. In: the Civil Procedure Law Research Foundation (ed) Discussion on civil procedure (XXV). Sanmin Book Co., Taipei. pp 1–106 (in Chinese)
Shen K et al. (2010) Objective scope of *res judicata* effect and issue preclusion of civil judgments. In: Foundation TCPLR (ed) Discussion on civil procedure law (XVII). Sanmin Book Co., Taipei, pp 1–92 (in Chinese)
Shi P (2014) The theory of *res judicata* in criminal law and its application in China. Chinese Journal of Law 1:150–170
Shindo K (2008) New civil procedure law (trans: Lin J). Law Press, Beijing (in Chinese)
Shindo K (2019) Civil procedure law. Koubundou Publishers, Tokyo (in Japanese)
Shipman S (2011) Compulsory mediation: the elephant in the room. Civil Justice Quarterly 2:163–191
Shyuu S (2003) Change, addition and clarification of the claims. National Taiwan University Law Journal 3:209–294 (in Chinese)
Siegburg P (2002) Zum Tatbestand des erstinstanzlichen Urteils im Bauprozess. Zeitschrift für Deutsches und Internationales Bau- und Vergaberecht 25:635–640
Sina Weibo (2021) Weibo community agreement. https://service.account.weibo.com/roles/gongyue. Accessed 2 May 2024 (in Chinese)
Sorabji J (2014) English civil justice after the Woolf and Jackson reforms. Cambridge University Press, Cambridge
Stadler A (2021) In: Musielak HJ, Voit W, ZPO, 18. Aufl. Vahlen, München
Steiner E (2010) French law: a comparative approach. Oxford University Press, Oxford
Stipanowich T, Fraser V (2017) The international task force on mixed mode dispute resolution: exploring the interplay between mediation, evaluation and arbitration in commercial cases. Fordham International Law Journal 40:839–886
Stürner R (1997) Der deutsche Prozeßrechtslehrer am Ende des 20. Jahrhunderts. In: Festschrift für Gerhard Lüke zum 70. Geburtstag. C. H. Beck, München
Stürner R (1999) Rechtskraft in Europa. In: Festschrift für Rolf A. Schütze zum 65. Geburtstag, Wege zur Globalisierung des Rechts. C. H. Beck, München
Stürner R (2005a) Parteidisposition über Anfang, Gegenstand und Umfang des Verfahrens in wichtigen europäischen Prozessordnungen. In: Festschrift für Andreas Heldrich zum 70. Geburtstag. C. H. Beck, München
Stürner R (2005b) The principles of transnational civil procedure: an introduction to their basic conceptions. The Rabel Journal of Comparative and International Private Law 69:201–254
Stürner M (2022) Der digitale Zivilprozess. Zeitschrift für Zivilprozess 135:369–400
Su L (2001) Behind the judgments. Chinese Journal of Law 3:3–18 (in Chinese)
Su Q, Wu X (2015) Pros: to enhance reasoning can scholars' opinions be directly cited. Procuratorate Daily, 1 April 2015 (in Chinese)
Sun H (2020) Over 10 million cases broadcasted at the China court trial online. People's Court Daily, 18 December 2022 (in Chinese)
Sun X (2020) A Chinese approach to international commercial dispute resolution: the China international commercial court. The Chinese Journal of Comparative Law 8:45–54
Sung HC (2020) Can online courts promote access to justice? a case study of the internet courts in China. Computer Law & Security Review 39:1–15
Susskind R (2019) Online courts and the future of justice. Oxford University Press, Oxford

Takahashi H (2003) Key points in civil procedure law. (trans: Lin J). Law Press, Beijing (in Chinese)
Takahashi H (2007) Key lecture notes on civil procedure law (trans: Zhang W, Xu K). Law Press, Beijing (in Chinese)
Tan S (2012) On judicial information disclosure. Northern Legal Science 3:76–84 (in Chinese)
Tang W (2000) How judges reason cases: research and application of reasoning in judicial decisions. People's Court Press, Beijing (in Chinese)
Tang X (2000) Writing 'reasonable' judgment documents. Law Review 4:123–126 (in Chinese)
Tang L (2012) Between 'compulsion' and 'consensus': dilemma and future of the judicial mediation in civil litigation. Modern Law Science 3:86–96 (in Chinese)
Tang W (2013a) Text editing of the guiding cases. Law and Social Development 2:47–56 (in Chinese)
Tang W (2013b) The modernizing direction of China's science of civil procedure law. Tsinghua University Law Journal 5:143– 154 (in Chinese)
Tang Y (2018a) Leader's will, institution's capacity and judicial openness: a preliminary study on online access of judicial decisions in Beijing, Shanghai and Guangdong. China Law Review 6:90–102 (in Chinese)
Tang Y (2018b) The decisive factors in promoting judicial openness: the data statistics regarding China judgments online. Tsinghua University Law Journal 4:35–47 (in Chinese)
Tang W, Qi T (2012) The drifting civil mediation system in China. Journal of Comparative Law 5:78–90 (in Chinese)
Taobao (2019) General rules on the dispute resolution in Taobao platform. https://rule.taobao.com/detail-99.htm?tag=self#524. Accessed 2 May 2024 (in Chinese)
Tapper C (2007) Cross and tapper on evidence. Oxford University Press, Oxford
Taruffo M (2003) Rethinking the standards of proof. The American Journal of Comparative Law 51:659–677
Teng J (2020) Application of restitution rules in the event of nullity of a contract. The Jurist 6:40–53 (in Chinese)
Teng W, Liu L (eds) (2016) Element-centered trial methods: innovation of court hearing manners and judicial decisions. People's Court Press, Beijing (in Chinese)
Thayer JB (1898) A preliminary treatise on evidence at the common law. Little, Brown and Company, Boston
The First Civil Division of the SPC (2020) Understanding and application of the new provisions of the SPC on evidence in civil proceedings. People's Court Press, Beijing (in Chinese)
The School of International Arbitration Queen Mary University of London and White & Case LLP (2021) International arbitration survey: adapting arbitration to a changing world. http://www.arbitration.qmul.ac.uk/media/arbitration/docs/2021-International-Arbitration-Survey-Adapting-arbitration-to-a-changing-world.pdf. Accessed 2 May 2024
Thole C (2018) In: Stein F, Jonas M, ZPO, Band 4, 23. Aufl. Mohr Siebeck, Tübingen
Tong Z, Zhang H (2002) On the reform of reasoning of judgments. Journal of Zhejiang University (Humanities and Social Sciences) 2:26–33 (in Chinese)
Unberath H (2007) Der Zweck der Rechtsmittel nach der ZPO-Reform—Theorie und Praxis. Zeitschrift für Zivilprozess 120:323–346
United Nations Commission on International Trade Law (1966) Online dispute resolution: on-line resources. https://uncitral.un.org/en/library/online_resources/online_dispute_resolution. Accessed 2 May 2024
Van de Velden JB (2017) Finality in litigation. Kluwer Law International, Alphen aan den Rijn
Vierkötter G (2021) Einsatz von Videokonferenztechnik—Status quo ein Jahr nach "Corona"? Zeitschrift für die Anwaltspraxis 6:263–264
Vollkommer G (2003) Bindungswirkung des rechtskräftigen Strafurteils im nachfolgenden Schadensersatzprozess des Geschädigten. Zeitschrift für Wirtschaftsrecht 25:2061–2063
Vollkommer G (2020) In: Zöller R, ZPO, 33. Aufl. Otto Schmidt, Köln
Wach A (1896) Vorträge über die Reichs-Civilprocessordnung, 2. Aufl. De Gruyter, Berlin

Wagner G (2009), Ökonomische Analyse der Rechtsmittel. In: Bork R, Eger T, Schäfer HB (eds) Ökonomische Analyse des Verfahrensrechts: Beiträge zum XI. Travemünder Symposium zur ökonomischen Analyse des Rechts. Mohr Siebeck, Tübingen. pp 157–193
Wagner PP (2016) Das elektronische Dokument im Zivilprozess. Juristische Schulung 1:29–33
Walker W (1998) Die Streitgegenstandslehre und die Rechtsprechung des EuGH. Zeitschrift für Zivilprozess 111:429–454
Wang Y (1994) On the reformation of civil and economic trial mode. Social Sciences in China 1:3–22 (in Chinese)
Wang Y (2005) Interplay between the alternative dispute resolution mechanism and civil trials: centering on the treatment of 'law-related petitions'. Journal of Law Application 2:9–11 (in Chinese)
Wang Z (2005) Research on the reasoning of judicial decisions. Shandong Social Sciences 8:84–86+156 (in Chinese)
Wang S (2006) Complicated civil judgments should be different from the simple ones. Journal of Law Application 12:58–60 (in Chinese)
Wang Y (2009) On methods of bearing tort liability. Journal of the Renmin University of China 3:15–21 (in Chinese)
Wang J (2010) Application of law in China's commercial judicial practice: difficulties and solutions. Modern Law Science 5:141–149 (in Chinese)
Wang Y (2010) Adversary and adjudication: basic structures of civil procedure in Japan. Tsinghua University Press, Beijing (in Chinese)
Wang S (2011) Judge's rationality and reasoned judgments. Political Science and Law 12:86–96 (in Chinese)
Wang Y (2011a) On Chinese elements in China's civil legislations. Law Science Magazine 4:27–32 (in Chinese)
Wang Y (2011b) Twenty years of civil procedure law. Contemporary Law Review 1:3–7 (in Chinese)
Wang H (2014) Claim for return of original object: claim on property rights or form of tort liability. The Jurist 1:91–101+177 (in Chinese)
Wang Y (2014) Re-examination on the plaintiff's standing in third-Party revocation claims. Chinese Journal of Law 6:132–146 (in Chinese)
Wang F (2015) Civil procedure law. Tsinghua University Press, Beijing (in Chinese)
Wang F (2016) Legal basis of construction of the electronic litigation system. Chinese Journal of Law 6:88–106 (in Chinese)
Wang Y (2018) Interpreting and reasoning in judgments and enhancing judicial credibility. People's Court Daily, 16 June 2018 (in Chinese)
Wang T (2019) Legal thinking and case study: the system of grounds of substantive rights, China Taiwan (in Chinese)
Wang F (2020) Review on remedy by right to debate. Law Science 10:93–106 (in Chinese)
Wang L (2020) Reconsidering the direct citations of scholars' opinions in judicial decisions. Legal Forum 4:93–100 (in Chinese)
Wang Y (2020) An analysis and reconstruction of private rights. Peking University Press, Beijing (in Chinese)
Wang F (2021a) A brief note on the application of information and communication technology in civil judicial case management. In: Chan PCH, van Rhee CH (eds) Civil case management in the twenty-first century: court structures still matter. Springer, Berlin
Wang F (2021b) On the blocking effect of the civil judgment. China Legal Science 3:265–286 (in Chinese)
Wang Y, Chen X (2015) The impact of the judgment of the former claim on the latter claim—analysis of article 93 and article 247 of the ICPL. ECUPL Journal 6:6–20 (in Chinese)
Wei Z (2011) On the claim for restitution. Peking University Law Journal 6:1171–1193 (in Chinese)
Wei S (2012) Face-to-face reasoning, strengthening rhetoric and focusing on major issues: some thoughts over how to improve court decisions in China. Science of Law 5:48–60 (in Chinese)

Weng X (2006) On the predetermined effect of decided facts. China Legal Science 4:180–189 (in Chinese)
Windau B (2020) Die Verhandlung im Wege der Bild- und Tonübertragung. Neue Juristische Wochenschrift 38:2753–2757
Wu Q (2002) On the reform of judicial decisions and the exercise of judges' discretion. People's Judicature 12:54–57 (in Chinese)
Wu Y (2011) An analysis of the involution of China's litigation object theory. China Legal Science 2:177–190 (in Chinese)
Wu Y (2013) 'Mediation first': reform paradigm and legal interpretation: taking the reform in the court of O city as an example. Peking University Law Journal 3:536–555 (in Chinese)
Wu Y (2015) The human rights nature of the right to sue—from the perspective of historical evolution. Social Sciences in China 6(112–130):207–208 (in Chinese)
Wu Z (2017a) Burden of proof in private lending lawsuit. China Legal Science 5:258–278 (in Chinese)
Wu Z (2017b) Regulation of false litigation under the background of civil procedure theories. SJTU Law Review 2:7–20 (in Chinese)
Wu Z (2018) The obligation of the party not responsible for the burden of proof to clarify the case. Peking University Law Journal 5:1360–1379 (in Chinese)
Wu H (2019) Judicial reform and change of motivation circumstance of legal profession. China Legal Science 4:165–185 (in Chinese)
Wu X (2019) Systemization of grounds of substantive rights in the civil code codification. Social Sciences in Yunnan 5:95– 105+187 (in Chinese)
Wu X (2020) Claim basis thinking and its opponents. Nanjing University (Philosophy, Human Sciences and Social Sciences) 2:90–106+159 (in Chinese)
Wu Y (2020) Procedural principles of burden of proof. Nanjing University Law Journal 2:57–72 (in Chinese)
Wu Y (2021) The construction of special courts from the perspective of the modernization of governance capacity. Law and Modernization 3:47–60 (in Chinese)
Wu Z, Liu Y, Ma J (eds) (2013) Civil trial skills. China democratic legal publishing house, Beijing (in Chinese)
Xi X (ed) (2012) Understanding and application of amendments to the civil procedure law of the P.R.C. People's Court Press, Beijing (in Chinese)
Xi X, Nan Y, Ying Y, Liu X (eds) (2013) Courses on the writing of judgments by the people's courts. China Legal Publishing House, Beijing (in Chinese)
Xia Q (2020) From the traditional contract to smart contract: the transformation from *ex post* court judgment to ex ante automatic performance. The Jurist 2:14–28+191 (in Chinese)
Xia J, Xu Y (2012) The causes for the lack of explicit legal basis in civil judgments. Law Science 10:127–135 (in Chinese)
Xiao J (2000) The function of the major participation claim to prevent fraud. Law Science Magazine 5:30–31 (in Chinese)
Xiao H (2008) Tradition and modern transformation of reasoning in Chinese judgments. Law Press, Beijing (in Chinese)
Xiao J (ed) (2008) Discussion on civil procedure law in areas of legislation and theory. Law Press, Beijing (in Chinese)
Xiao J (2010) Authenticity of documentary evidence and its burden of proof. China Trial 7:92–93 (in Chinese)
Xiao F (2015) The improvement of some problems in the ordinary procedure of first instance. Journal of Law Application 4:13–19 (in Chinese)
Xiao P, Hu R (2008) Analysis about the nature of petitions. Law Science Magazine 4:63–66 (in Chinese)
Xiao H, Ma R (2019) The diversified dispute resolution platform for foreign-related civil and commercial matters in Hainan Province, the first one nationwide, starts now. http://www.hnzhengfa.gov.cn/news/fayuandongtai/show-869.html. Accessed 2 May 2024 (in Chinese)

Xing B (2015) How the court cites the constitution—centering on the judicial practice after the nullification of the judicial reply in Qiyuling case. China Law Review 1:127–157 (in Chinese)
Xinhua (2021) Working report of the SPC. https://www.court.gov.cn/zixun/xiangqing/290831.html. Accessed 2 May 2024 (in Chinese)
Xinhuanet (2018) General Office of the Central Committee of the CPC and the General Office of the Chinese State Council have printed and distributed the opinion concerning the establishment of the belt and road international commercial dispute resolution mechanism and institutions. http://www.gov.cn/zhengce/2018-06/27/content_5301657.htm Accessed 2 May 2024 (in Chinese)
Xinhuanet (2021) Beijing Financial Court accomplished its first patch of judicial review cases in the area of financial arbitration while having entirely paperless proceedings. https://www.chinacourt.org/article/detail/2021/04/id/5956800.shtml. Accessed 2 May 2024 (in Chinese)
Xiong Y (2007) Research on pretrial preparatory procedure in civil proceedings. People's Publishing House, Beijing (in Chinese)
Xiong Y (2008) Court's obligation of pointing out its legal viewpoints in civil litigations. China Legal Science 4:119–127 (in Chinese)
Xiong Y (2021) From clarification regarding changing claims to clarification regarding legal viewpoints: analysis of article 53 of new rules of evidence in civil proceedings. Modern Law Science 3:171–182 (in Chinese)
Xu R (2003) Some issues in the reform of civil and commercial judgments. Journal of Law Application1–2:30–33 (in Chinese)
Xu K (2009) Civil trial methods: introduction to essential facts. Law Press, Beijing (in Chinese)
Xu D (2013) The application of doctrinal approach in legal reasoning. Peking University Law Journal 5:937–973 (in Chinese)
Yamamoto K (2019) Debate on the subject matter of claims in civil procedure in Japan after World War II (trans: Shi M). Tsinghua University Law Journal 6:5–12 (in Chinese)
Yan R (2013) Localized approach on the subject matter of claims in civil procedure. Chinese Journal of Law 3:91–109 (in Chinese)
Yan R (2017) New developments on the objective range of *res judicata*. Peking University Law Journal 2:536–559 (in Chinese)
Yang J (2010) Change of civil cases reported in the "SPC Gazette." Modern Law Science 4:182–193 (in Chinese)
Yang C (2013) Essentials of civil procedure law (revised by Cheng J). Peking University Press, Beijing (in Chinese)
Yang L (2014) Nanjing court's judgment cites scholars' viewpoints, experts say that it is the first one countrywide and can enhance the degree of reasoning. http://www.thepaper.cn/newsDetail_forward_1287931. Accessed 2 May 2024 (in Chinese)
Yang Y (2016) The prevention of surprise judgments in civil actions: on orientation of modern trial theory application. China Legal Science 4:266–286 (in Chinese)
Yang H (2018) On procedural legal transactions of the parties. Law Press, Beijing, pp 235–276 (in Chinese)
Yang H, Shao X (2020) Empirical analysis and regulation refining of evidential reasoning in judgment. Journal of Law Application 6:16–32 (in Chinese)
Yao M (2020) Norms governing the liability for breach of contract in the civil code and grounds of substantive rights. Law and Modernization 5:39–45 (in Chinese)
Ye L (2007) Commercial law concept and commercial adjudication. Journal of Law Application 9:17–20 (in Chinese)
Ye X (2015) Rethinking the phenomenon of 'zero judgment.' Tribune of Political Science and Law 3:155–163 (in Chinese)
Yeazell SC, Schwartz JC (2019) Civil procedure. Aspen Publishing, California
Yi Y (2017) Evidence law. Law Press, Beijing (in Chinese)
Ying X (2004) The remedy of 'letter and visit': a special administrative remedy. Chinese Journal of Law 3:58–71 (in Chinese)

Ying X (2013) How judges identify the evidence during civil trials. Journal of Law Application 6:81–86 (in Chinese)
You C (2012) A fact of litigiousness hidden beneath the illusion of litigation loathing? Peking University Law Journal 4:815–834 (in Chinese)
Yu J (2005) Reform of the petition system and constitutional construction. Twenty-First Century 3:71–78 (in Chinese)
Yu L (2019) The strategy to resolve case-filing pressure within people's court and its reform. Modern Law Science 5:23–35 (in Chinese)
Yu C (2021) Form and substance of the determination of legal transactions. Law Science 7:97–112 (in Chinese)
Yuan Z (2012) The issue of 'burden of proof' about the authenticity of documents in civil proceedings. The Jurist 6:126–136+177 (in Chinese)
Yuan Z (2014) Essential defects of the norm theory and their overcoming. Chinese Journal of Law 6:147–161 (in Chinese)
Yuan Z (2015) Practice and reflection on the obligation of producing documents. Contemporary Law Review 2:126–135 (in Chinese)
Yuan L (2019) Approach to identifying repeated civil lawsuits. Law Science 9:155–167 (in Chinese)
Yuan Z (2020) On the power of investigation and evidence collection of judges in civil procedure. China Legal Science 5:184–201 (in Chinese)
Yuan Z (2021) Distributing burden of proof on disputes of liability for breach of contract—focusing on article 577 of the civil code. Law Science 5:103–114 (in Chinese)
Yuan L, Shao X (2017) An analysis of the relevance of the structure and reasoning of civil judgments in Germany. Journal of Law Application 1:113–120 (in Chinese)
Yun L (2012) How to strengthen the reasoning of judgments. China Trial 2:61–63 (in Chinese)
Zeuner A (1959) Die objektiven Grenzen der Rechtskraft im Rahmen rechtlicher Sinnzusammenhänge. Mohr Siebeck, Tübingen
Zeuner A (1981) Rechtsvergleichende Bemerkungen zur objektiven Begrenzung der Rechtskraft im Zivilprozeß. In: Festschrift für Konrad Zweigert zum 70. Geburtstag. Mohr Siebeck, Tübingen
Zeuner A (1997) Zum Verhältnis zwischen internationaler Rechtshängigkeit nach Art. 21 EuGVÜ und Rechtshängigkeit nach den Regeln der ZPO. In: Festschrift für Gerhard Lüke zum 70. Geburtstag. C. H. Beck, München
Zhan S (2017) Errors of expressions in civil judgments and their correction. Law Science 8:164–173 (in Chinese)
Zhang Z (1998) The structure and style of judicial judgments. Law Science 10:26–32 (in Chinese)
Zhang G (2000) Improvement of the basic structure of civil judgments. Law Science Magazine 5:49–51 (in Chinese)
Zhang W (2001) Investigation of facts: absoluteness tendency and its resolution. Chinese Journal of Law 4:70–79 (in Chinese)
Zhang J (2002a) A legislative thinking on the intermediary declaratory judgment. China Legal Science 5:109–117 (in Chinese)
Zhang J (2002b) The rational construction of legal reasoning mode. Studies in Law and Business 4:122–129 (in Chinese)
Zhang W (2004a) Conditions of case registration and elements of judgments on the merits. Chinese Journal of Law 6:58–68 (in Chinese)
Zhang W (2004b) On contractualisation of civil litigation: improving the fundamental framework of Chinese civil procedure law. China Legal Science 3:75–87 (in Chinese)
Zhang X (2005) Some jurisprudential considerations on the reform of judicial decisions. Journal of Law Application 2:70–73 (in Chinese)
Zhang Y (2005) On the unableness to distinguish true from false in litigation and its solution. Law Review 2:26–35 (in Chinese)
Zhang W (2006) The development of the concept of "clarification" in civil procedure. Peking University Law Journal 2:129–146 (in Chinese)

Zhang J (2008) A small case, a great impact: a legal logical analysis of Nanjing's "Pengyu" first-instance judgment. Journal of CUPL 2:103–116+160 (in Chinese)
Zhang W (2009) Difficulty in filing a lawsuit: thinking on a 'Chinese issue.' Chinese Journal of Law 6:65–76 (in Chinese)
Zhang Y (2009) Replacing 'it is ascertained upon trial' with 'the judgments are given as followed'. In: Wang L (ed) New exploration on making judgments. Shanghai Academy of Social Sciences Press, Shanghai (in Chinese)
Zhang Z (2009) Misunderstandings in making judicial decisions. Journal of the National Prosecutors College 2:77–84 (in Chinese)
Zhang Z (2010) The presumption rules for the probative value of private documents. Science of Law 4:154–159 (in Chinese)
Zhang S (2011) Tort liability for damage by animals (Tierhaftung). In: Zhu Q, Wang H, Zhang S, Tian S (eds) Sino-German private law studies, Volume 7. Peking University Press, Beijing (in Chinese)
Zhang W (2011) Civil procedure law: delay and progress. Chinese Journal of Law 6:40–43 (in Chinese)
Zhang W (2012) Analysis on countermeasures to delayed evidential submission in civil procedures. The Jurist 5: 104–114+178–179 (in Chinese)
Zhang Y (2012) Objective truth values are the soul of the evidence system. Law Review 1:38–44 (in Chinese)
Zhang W (2014) The poverty of civil procedural jurisprudence. Tsinghua University Law Journal 2:5–34 (in Chinese)
Zhang H (2015) The application of presumption in judging the authenticity of documentary evidence. Global Law Review 4:17–34 (in Chinese)
Zhang W (2015a) Reflection and reconstruction on system of registrating civil cases. Studies in Law and Business 3:3–15 (in Chinese)
Zhang W (2015b) A study of repeated suits regulation with a discussion on non bis in idem. China Legal Science 2:43–65 (in Chinese)
Zhang W (2015c) Review on the procedures and manners of civil court hearings in China and its rebuilding. China Legal Science 2:66–80 (in Chinese)
Zhang W (2015d) The principle of privity of *res judicata*: grounds, exceptions and institutionalization. Chinese Journal of Law 1:68–86 (in Chinese)
Zhang Y (2016) The study of types of false litigation and the review of the current rules. Political Science and Law 7:151–160 (in Chinese)
Zhang W (2017a) Civil evidence law. Law Press, Beijing (in Chinese)
Zhang W (2017b) Institutional construction of the party's duty of producing documents. The Jurist 3:31–44+176 (in Chinese)
Zhang J (2018) Interpretation of the overlapping civil liability in Chinese law. SJTU Law Review 1:5–11 (in Chinese)
Zhang Q (2018) The prospect and explanation for local-level judges' resignation: a case study from Y-province. Tsinghua University Law Journal 4:48–67 (in Chinese)
Zhang W (2019a) Civil procedural law. Law Press, Beijing (in Chinese)
Zhang W (2019b) Comparative research methodology of civil procedure law. Journal of National Prosecutors College 6:157–174 (in Chinese)
Zhang Z (2021) Cans and can-nots of judgments in citing the constitution—Jurisprudential interpretation of the dichotomy between "judgment reasoning" and "judgment basis." Law Science 6:57–75 (in Chinese)
Zhang M, Dai J (2009) Difficulties and solutions: a rational exploration of the court's litigation-related petition system in the transitional period. Journal of Law Application 6:71–74 (in Chinese)
Zhang W, Xiao G (2012) The relationship between court mediation and making judgments. Tribune of Political Science and Law 6:168–174 (in Chinese)

Zhang J, Zheng L (2014) Reorganization and optimization of the remedy procedure for omissions in civil judgments. People's Judicature 9:102–106 (in Chinese)
Zhang T et al. (2006) The third discussion on how to write a civil judgment. In: The Civil procedure law research foundation (ed) Discussion on civil procedure law (XIII). Sanmin Book Co., Taipei (in Chinese)
Zhao X (2005) Institutional logic of petitions. Twenty-First Century 3:85–90 (in Chinese)
Zhao Z (2008) Supplementary judgment system of omission in civil judgments. Tribune of Political Science and Law 5:84–93 (in Chinese)
Zhao C (2010) The realistic expression of judicial adjudication. Law Press, Beijing (in Chinese)
Zhao X (2017) On procedural values of declaratory claims. The Jurist 6:108–115+179 (in Chinese)
Zhao X (2018) Conflict and coordination between overlapped theories of grounds of substantive rights and of the subject matter of claims. SJTU Law Review 1:23–32 (in Chinese)
Zhao R, Chen B (2015) Rational responses to the 'post-judgment effect' under the background of judicial decision going online. Journal of Law Application 8:65–70 (in Chinese)
Zhejiang High People's Court (2021) QR code for dispute resolution of Zhejiang. https://yundr.gov.cn. Accessed 2 May 2024 (in Chinese)
Zheng T (2020) On the structure and practice of repeated lawsuits of substantive negation type in civil procedure. Science of Law 6:165–178 (in Chinese)
Zheng F, Yang M (2020) The challenge and influence of internet court trials on traditional civil evidence system. Evidence Science 1:59–71 (in Chinese)
Zheng X, Liu M, Song C, Pan H (2020) Comprehension and application on some issues about the new stipulation on civil evidence. People's Court Daily, 26 March 2020 (in Chinese)
Zhi Z, Ye Z (2019) A third-party evaluation report for the open trials of people's courts. Journal of Law Application 23:103–114 (in Chinese)
Zhong M, Fan Y (2002) Civil and commercial judgments need to be improved. People's Court Daily, 18 June 2002 (in Chinese)
Zhou X (2014) Research on reasoning of civil judgments. Law Press, Beijing (in Chinese)
Zhou Q (2016) Annual working report of the SPC of 2016. SPC. http://gongbao.court.gov.cn/details/6ce239a82c31348f8856a986e9eb45.html?sw%3D. Accessed 2 May 2024 (in Chinese)
Zhou C (2018) The construction and prospect of internet courts. Journal of Law Application 3:38–43 (in Chinese)
Zhou Q (2021) Mid-term report of the SPC to the standing Committee of the NPC on the performance of pilot program of the reform of separation between complicated cases and simple ones in civil procedure. NPC of P.R.C. http://www.npc.gov.cn/npc/c2/c30834/202102/t20210228_310186.html. Accessed 2 May 2024 (in Chinese)
Zhou H (2022) Innovation and analysis of the electronic service system under the background of "internet +." Journal of Henan University of Economics and Law 1:149–156 (in Chinese)
Zhou Z, Wei Z (2015) Cons: direct citation violates the requirement of taking the laws as the criterion. Procuratorate Daily, 1 April 2015 (in Chinese)
Zhu S (2010) Judicial management and social management: how can the court effectively respond to "too many cases but too few judges"? China Legal Science 6:176–189 (in Chinese)
Zhuang X (2015) The realistic context and institutional rationality of judicial decisions. Journal of Law Application 11:83–92 (in Chinese)
Zimmermann W (2019) Klage, Gutachten und Urteil. C. F. Müller, Heidelberg
Zippelius R (2012) Juristische Methodenlehre 11. Aufl. C. H. Beck, München
Zou B (2010) Nine-step method on elements of the civil trial. Law Press, Beijing (in Chinese)
Zuckerman AAS (2013) Zuckerman on civil procedure: principles of practice. Sweet & Maxwell, London
Zuckerman AAS (2020) Artificial intelligence—implications for the legal profession, adversarial process and rule of law. Law Quarterly Review 136:427–453

The manufacturer's authorised representative in the EU is Springer Nature Customer Service Centre GmbH, Europaplatz 3, 69115 Heidelberg, Germany. If you have any concerns regarding our products, please contact ProductSafety@springernature.com

Printed and bound by CPI Group (UK) Ltd, Croydon, CR0 4YY
01/10/2026
02225932-0012